Images of Man

The Classic Tradition
in Sociological Thinking

Images of Man

THE CLASSIC TRADITION
IN SOCIOLOGICAL THINKING

Selected and edited
with an introduction by

C. Wright Mills

George Braziller, Inc.

NEW YORK

First Printing, July, 1960
Second Printing, May, 1961

Library of Congress Catalog Card Number: 60-8989

Printed in the United States of America

Contents

INTRODUCTION: The Classic Tradition *by C. Wright Mills*   1

I: Obstacles and Orientations   19

    1. WALTER LIPPMANN: The World Outside and the Pictures in our Heads   21

    2. HERBERT SPENCER: The Class Bias   48

    3. KARL MANNHEIM: The Prospects of Scientific Politics   65

II: Types and Trends of Society   99

    4. KARL MARX & FRIEDRICH ENGELS: On Class   101

    5. MAX WEBER: Class, Status, Party   121

    6. THORSTEIN VEBLEN: Status and Discontent   136

    7. MAX WEBER: Bureaucracy   149

    8. GAETANO MOSCA: The Ruling Class   192

    9. ROBERT MICHELS: The Iron Law of Oligarchy   233

    10. ALFREDO PARETO: Elites, Force and Governments   262

    11. HERBERT SPENCER: Militant and Industrial Societies   292

    12. THORSTEIN VEBLEN: The Main Drift   336

    13. JOSEPH SCHUMPETER: On Capitalism   370

III: The Crisis of Individuality   403

    14. WILLIAM I. THOMAS & FLORIAN ZNANIECKI: Three Types of Personality   405

    15. GEORG SIMMEL: The Metropolis and Mental Life   437

    16. EMILE DURKHEIM: On Anomie   449

    17. KARL MARX & FRIEDRICH ENGELS: On Alienation   486

    18. KARL MANNHEIM: Types of Rationality and Organized Insecurity   508

Images of Man

The Classic Tradition
in Sociological Thinking

C. Wright Mills

Introduction
The Classic Tradition

THE STUDY of man contains a greater variety of intellectual styles than any other area of cultural endeavor. How different social scientists go about their work, and what they aim to accomplish by it, often do not seem to have any real common denominator. Some consider themselves to be working in close parallel with chemists and physicists; others believe they share the aims, if not the methods, of novelists and even of poets. These of course are the extreme limits of "social science" practice and proclamation. Between these extremes there are many ways of thinking, many conceptions and methods, ideas and just plain notions. Let us admit the case of our critics from the humanities and from the experimental sciences: social science as a whole is both intellectually and morally confused. And what is called sociology is very much in the middle of this confusion.

It will not quite do to excuse this condition by saying that the social sciences are after all very young. In the first place, they are not so very young, or rather they are young only if one restricts—rather arbitrarily, I believe—"social science" to some one or another more recent phase of work. In the second place, to say that they are young implies, or even assumes, that such studies may be understood to be going through some sort of biographical cycle, like an individual, to be growing in a more or less straight line towards maturity. But of course, the question is: if they were "mature," what then would they be? No one has answered this question in a way that is altogether convincing to those who are working in the social sciences.

There is an amusing little game played nowadays—especially in England—by literary people, a few physical scientists, and by historians. It consists of criticizing what they take to be sociology as a pretentious discipline having no firm conceptions and agreed-upon propositions. Behind this criticism there is the standard or the model of the physical sciences. The practitioners of sociology, they are saying, only ape these in an often ridiculous way, and accordingly: there is nothing much to sociology.

Such criticism is quite well taken—and quite irrelevant. It is true that many sociologists are ridiculous in their attempts to ape what they take to be physical science. But the point of irrelevance in this criticism is the standard chosen. The standards that ought to be used by critics of current social study and reflection are those that have slowly accumulated in the classic tradition. I know the idea is hard to grasp for those not acquainted with this tradition—and especially in the face of the current pretensions of many social scientists—but it is the only way in which criticism might be useful to the working student of man and society.

The classic tradition is difficult to characterize in a brief and coherent way. Like any intellectual tradition, it can be grasped only by exposure to the variety of books that compose it. Any brief statement defining the tradition can only be a single interpretation—in fact, a distinguishing mark of the "classic" is probably that it is subject to a variety of interpretations! For what it may be worth, my own interpretation rests mainly upon the kinds of questions that its practitioners ask and the manner in which they go about answering them. It is also, of course, illustrated by the selections presented in this book.

Every thinker tries to select his own intellectual past, and is in turn shaped by it. Many of the thinkers presented in this volume have, as it were, selected one another. They are leading representatives of the classic tradition of sociology. In every generation and in every domain of study, there comes about a general agreement that a small set of works are "classic" in the sense of being somehow indispensable. For by "classic" writers, we do not mean merely those who have been consistently read; we mean also those who, whether read directly or not, have continued to be a point of orientation for the work of others.

In some part, I think, one's intellectual heritage is rather arbitrary, and must be. The order in which one comes upon various books, and the phase in one's development at which the exposure occurs—these are not entirely controllable. And, of course, not everyone is especially concerned with the origins of the conceptions he comes to use. Nonetheless, the conceptions of some men do continue to inform social inquiry and reflection.

Such is the case, I believe with each of the thinkers presented here. To put it directly: they are worth reading, and re-reading. Their work represents the best that has been done by later 19th- and earlier 20th-century sociologists, and remains directly relevant to the best work that is being done today. Within its necessary limits of space, this collection of writings is intended to help us stand upon their shoulders.

1

Most of the ideas of the classic sociologists are not of the sort that can readily be shaped for precise testing. They are interpretive ideas, orienting us to various ways of looking at social realities. They are attempts to state the general historical trend, the main drift, of modern society, or, to use Dr. Ruth Glass' phrase, the "state and the fate" of societies in our time. They are attempts to make sense of what is happening in the world and to gauge what may be going to happen in the near future.

The classic sociologists are not inhibited by what are now the boundary lines of academic disciplines or specialties. In their work what are now called political science, social psychology, economics, anthropology and sociology are all used—and integrated so as to form a master view of the structure of society in all its realms, the mechanics of history in all their ramifications, and the roles of individuals in a great variety of their psychological nuances.

But the important thing about the classic sociologists is that even when they have turned out to be quite wrong and inadequate—as for example Spencer was in his notion of the trend from military to industrial society— even then, by their work and by the way in which they did it they reveal much about the nature of society, and their ideas remain directly relevant to our work today.

But how, it may be asked, can these men be so often wrong and yet remain so great? The answer lies, I think, in a signal characteristic of their work: their "great ideas" consist of what might be called "models," in contrast to specific theories or detailed hypotheses. In these working models are contained statements of (1) the elements to which attention must be paid if we are to understand some particular feature of society or a society as a whole, and (2) the range of possible relations among these elements. The elements are not left merely to interact in some vague way. Rightly or wrongly, they are constructed in close and specific interconnection with one another, and causal weights are assigned to each. These imputed connections and weights of course are specific theories.

In short, the classic sociologists construct models of society and use them to develop a number of theories. What is important is the fact that neither the correctness nor the inaccuracy of any of these specific theories necessarily confirms or upsets the usefulness or the adequacy of the models. The models can be used for the construction of many theories. They can be used for correcting errors in theories made with their aid. And they are readily open: they can themselves be modified in ways to make them more useful as analytic tools and empirically closer to the run of fact.

It is these models that are great—not only as contributions to the history of social reflection and inquiry, but also as influences on subsequent sociological thinking. They, I believe, are what is alive in the classic tradition of sociology. And I think, too, that they are the reason why so persistently there have been, under quite varied circumstances, so many "revivals" of the thinkers presented in these pages; in short, why their works are "classic."

The classic tradition, then, may not be defined by any one specific method, certainly not by the acceptance of any one theory of society, history, or human nature. Once that is acknowledged, a usable definition is simple enough—although its application in selecting a book of illustrative readings is by no means automatic. The classic tradition is most readily defined by the character of the questions that have guided and do now guide those who are part of it. These questions are generally of wide scope: they concern total societies, their transformations, and the varieties of individual men and women that inhabit them. The answers given by classic sociologists provide conceptions about society, about history and about biography, and in their work these three are usually linked closely together. The structure of society and the mechanics of history are seen within the same perspective, and within this perspective changes in human nature are also defined.

But it is not only the scope and the interrelations of their questions and the fact that they are "soaked in history" that define the classical workmen. It is also the fact that their intellectual problems are relevant to the public issues of their times, and to the private troubles of individual men and women. More than that—they have helped to define more clearly the issues and the troubles and the intimate relations between the two. People have read Spencer and Marx and Weber and Michaels not only to become informed. They have read in a search for orientation and out of their reading they have gotten orientation.

Other characteristics of the classic sociologists will no doubt become evident to the reader of these selections. But there is a final point about them I would mention here: In general, our immediate generation of social scientists is still living off their ideas.

2

Most of the sociological ideas that have become current—and in the United States even popular—after World War Two were quite well stated before our generation began its work. Many pivotal conceptions were well defined between the Enlightenment and the middle of the 19th century. But in the form in which we have received them, they emerged during the several decades prior to World War I. Certainly since the thirties, one can think of very few social-science productions that have the mark of the classic.

To be sure, many ideas have been more attractively stated; they have been further explained; some have been related to others in a scholarly way. Yet no one, I believe, has stated better, or more clearly, than did the company of thinkers presented in this volume the basic conceptions or theories of such matters as social stratification and political authority, of the nature of bureaucracy and of capitalism, of the scale and drift of modern life, of the ambiguity of rationality, of the malaise individual men so often feel. If to their company, we add Freud and his immediate disciples, certainly then we would have at hand the circle of ideas about man, society and history off which we are still living. The only exception I can readily think of is the work of such social psychologists as George H. Mead.

The general fact—that insofar as social ideas are concerned, our generation is living off the past—is often hidden, even from its leading members. In sociology particularly, a great busy-ness has diverted students from a history of their own discipline; often it is not a very central part of their present-day training. In fact, only in the last twenty years have many of the classic works of sociology become available in English, and some of them are not yet available. Then, too, conceptions in academic circles do have a way of taking on new guises, and much that appears new is merely a new terminology.

We must also realize that a very great deal of the classic sociological tradition came out of a debate with the ideas of Karl Marx. Not only is this fact often hidden or unknown, but the present generation of social scientists in the United States cannot be supposed to be altogether close students of Marx.

The political continuity—and the recent economic prosperity of the U.S.A.—also have something to do with the dearth of larger social and political ideas here. It is not true that upheaval and disaster inevitably result in great ideas; but it is generally true that complacency seldom gives rise to them. What it has given rise to politically is a diluted liberalism which is the political common denominator of most current social study.

I do not wish to give the impression that nothing of worth has been done or is being done since the work of the "greats." Of course there has been; of course there is. I want only to characterize our situation as it concerns the more basic conceptions and the larger theories that still guide our work, and to explain it. The explanation lies in part with the character of the classic tradition itself—which I have already indicated—and in part with certain characteristics of our present political and intellectual condition.

3

In considerable part our immediate situation in social study is characterized by plain and fancy retreats from the tasks which classic sociologists confronted so boldly. After all, it is easier and safer to restrict oneself to smaller problems as part of a tacit conspiracy of the mediocre, a tendency that in due course is reinforced by the selection and training of academic personnel.

But our condition cannot be entirely explained by this minor law of academic life. It is also due to the fact that historical change has been so very rapid in the past two decades that all one can hope to do is keep up with it descriptively. The journalistic report-in-depth, the documentary study, the statistical survey—these, after all, are leading features of our intellectual age, in which the sheer accumulation of fact from every side often overwhelms us.

The demand for facts increases, along with the invention of newer techniques for supplying them. This demand, it should be noted, is a commercial and political feature of society as well as an intellectual matter. Both the demand for facts and the ways of supplying them have now become part of well-established administrative routines—of business and government, of associations of all sorts, and also of the universities themselves. The facts are useful, necessary, and well paid for; accordingly they are supplied.

But in the meantime they are useful and used for the administrative purposes for which they are selected, rather than for answering the kinds of questions raised in the classic sociological tradition.

The general results of this are worth noting.

First, the most precise and best-tested facts of social inquiry today often have to do with a quite narrow sphere of society: with such affairs as the circulation of magazines, the buying habits of suburban wives, the possible effects of advertisements in the several media of mass communication.

Second, facts of such precision as these appear to be are usually expensive to come by. Moreover, a considerable number of people equipped to discover and present facts are used in these narrowed inquiries. Accordingly, a great deal of the money and the personnel for social inquiry as a whole are used up in this way.

Third, perhaps more importantly, the precision thus achieved, the methods of fact-finding, and even a kind of fact-fetishism, tend to become the standard for all social inquiry. "Nothing is so poor and melancholy," Santayana somewhere remarks, "as an art that is interested in itself and not in its subject."

Fourth, the use of this standard discourages many academic investigators and speculators from taking up the tasks inheritable from the classic tradition. In fact, often their situation makes it impossible for many individual scholars to do so. They are further discouraged because non-commercial sources of research funds, the foundations, also tend very strongly to support projects designed to meet the same sort of standard, to use the same sort of narrow models of inquiry. They seem most reluctant to support work in the classic manner. It is, accordingly, quite difficult today for social scientists—for a young man especially—to follow the classic styles of reflection and inquiry. Those who nevertheless do so must often work without much financial aid for their work and without much encouragement from their social science colleagues.

Fifth, one immediate result of all this is that work in the classic manner and with it, the confrontation of urgent public issues, the analysis of the trend of western societies, often either goes by default or is carried on in an unsatisfactory manner by writers who are not very well equipped for the task. However, some of the best work available is performed by journalists and commentators, by historians and literary critics, rather than by sociologists. The gap between our generation and the classic tradition of sociology is evident in all the more advanced nations of the world, but on all points mentioned it is most obvious in the U.S.A., where today the social studies are most deeply entrenched and their volume of output most overwhelming.

4

These matters are not merely of "professional" concern. They are part of what—all alarmism aside—must be called The Crisis of Social Reflection, and this crisis is very much a proper matter for public interest and debate. The crisis in social science today has two main features: one is the retreat into the supposed neutrality of sheer fact—which I have just discussed; the other pertains to the classic tradition itself.

In the more political essays of Max Weber, I am inclined to believe, the classic tradition in sociological thinking comes to a moral climax, a crisis of orientation, which we have by no means overcome. In fact, we have not even confronted it squarely. Weber presents the social world as a chaos of values, a hopeless plurality of gods; his is the pessimistic world of a classic liberal of supreme intelligence and enormous knowledge, thinking at the end of the liberal era and finding no basis for decision, no criterion other than his own personal will and integrity. But his condition is not merely a reflection of the crisis of classic liberalism; it also reflects the crisis of classic Marxism. These two legacies have very much in common, and the values common to them have closely informed the classic tradition of sociology. Certainly in the case of Weber—the most profound "revisionist" of Marx—his trouble is the issue of the secular and humanist tradition of Western civilization, of which liberalism and Marxism have been the leading political carriers.

The moral crisis of this humanist tradition, reflected in sociology, coincides with the retreat of our generation of social scientists into "mere fact." These are the two defining characteristics of the crisis of social reflection and inquiry today.

That this condition is important in connection with the state of our culture in general hardly needs to be stressed. It is also important in political ways that may not be obvious at a casual glance. We can confront this two-fold crisis only by taking up again the classic tradition, including the moral problems within it inherited from Marx and Marxism. In doing this cultural work, we would also be attempting to accomplish two political tasks, both of which very badly need doing.

Within our own societies, we would be doing our proper job of making relevant to the issues the best knowledge possible. If we do not do this, the best knowledge possible will not be available. It will not exist. Our possible colleagues in the Soviet bloc are not now able to take up such tasks, at least not politically, without running serious personal and professional risks. But we are free to do it.

Moreover, such is the most fruitful way for us to aid them in any possible cultural liberation that may become possible in Soviet-type societies. It is the way to get in touch with them and to make such intellectual relations as we may come to have with them the most fruitful, culturally and politically.*

* Communist and capitalist societies are now in cultural, as well as in military, industrial, and political, competition. In many areas of physical science, the Soviet establishment is now equal to or better than those of the leading capitalist nations. This is now obvious to everyone; a mere decade ago the suggestion that it might be so would have been taken as a joke.

In matters of social science, it is reasonable to suppose that Soviet scholars have not as yet gone much beyond the body of Marxist works generally available before the revolution. In particular, sociology as an academic discipline was eliminated in the twenties by Soviet authorities, and in due course in the nations that now form the Soviet bloc. Recently, some of them have begun to "rehabilitate" sociology, and in the Soviet Union itself there are signs of at least small new beginnings. I do not know whether they will become more than that, but if they do there are two courses sociological work may generally take.

It may become—like one of the dominant trends in the United States—mainly a fact-finding endeavor, without firm relation to more general ideas about the nature and trend of society. As such, it would undoubtedly be of great use to the authorities of a planned society, and accordingly it would possibly be somewhat broader in its focus than it is in the United States. Such sociology is quite compatible, I believe, with bureaucratic tyranny; indeed it may become a leading instrument of tyranny.

But sociological work may be allowed to develop in an intellectually, and hence politically, freer way. In this case, I should think it might well become a continuation of the classic tradition. My reason for believing so is that the ideas of Marx, and of later Marxists as well, are very much a part—and a great part—of this style of reflection.

Which course sociology may take depends mainly, of course, upon political factors, as these affect the extent of cultural freedom that is allowed by political authorities, and the extent to which freely developed ideas are allowed to be relevant to the making of public opinion and of policy. I am inclined to think the possibilities of such a development rather small in the more immediate future. But on two points I am rather convinced: if sociological work does develop freely in the Soviet Union, it might very well become central to a general cultural liberation; and from it there might issue considerable advances in sociological understanding.

I am not suggesting that competition with Soviet scholars is a useful reason for cultivating the social sciences in the United States. Neither politically nor culturally do I think such reasoning sound. My point is simpler and more direct: in taking up the classic tradition, we would be attempting to accomplish the cultural and political tasks indicated in the text.

The classic sociological tradition is a central part of the cultural tradition of Western civilization. The crisis of one is the crisis of the other; and of all the spheres of Western culture, the classic tradition of sociology is the most directly relevant to those areas where culture and politics come now to such a terrifying point of intersection.

That is why, under tyranny, "sociology" is among the very first of cultural disciplines to be either abolished or turned into the uses of an unfree ideology. In the well-known communist phrase, this "is no accident." Perhaps it is also no accident that in the United States today, the classic tradition of this discipline is drying up. Such a tradition may be suppressed by political authority; it may also be diverted by those institutional and academic trends that form the climate of cultural work. It may be suppressed by the default of those who ought to be practicing it.

5

Underneath the kinds of statement I have just been making, there are of course notions about how ideas develop, or about the processes of intellectual change. Some awareness of these increases our chance to understand the ways of the classic tradition and the relation to it of contemporary social study.

I do not know of any one theory of the history of social thought that is altogether convincing, but there are some three ways of conceiving it, each of which when taken alone is much too simple.

(1) The history of social reflection might be thought of as an accumulation of social facts, from which generalizations are made. As new facts are found out, and as old ones are proved mistaken, the generalizations are corrected and improved.

The objection to this view is that often it is by extending ideas in a purely deductive way, or by elaborating them logically without primary reference to any facts, new or old, that ideas come about and are worked out. It would generally seem to be the case that thought is only disciplined by facts; but it is advanced by ideas.* Very many social theories seem to be, at least immediately, the rather direct result of combining ideas which no one has previously thought of combining. For example: the basic doctrine of Marx comes about by his combining into one model features of British economics, German philosophy, French utopian socialism—and a great deal of historical knowledge, especially French and British. It is not reasonable to deny that this combining of ideas, rather than any new set of facts Marx or his contemporaries discovered, was the prime occasion for his work. Again, as I have already remarked, it is obviously as a kind of "conversation" with Marx that much of Max Weber's (as well as

---

* Cf. *The Sociological Imagination* by C. Wright Mills (New York: Oxford, 1959).

Veblen's) work occurs—not only with the idea of the Protestant ethic as one of the conditions for the development of capitalist economy, but also the historical function of bureaucracy (as against class struggle) and the elaboration of the categories of social stratification (as against simply economic classes). So too—as in the selections presented here—Mosca debates Spencer; Michels leans on Mosca.

Books of fact would seem to be most useful intellectually when they have direct relevance to some general idea of importance, upsetting it or confirming it. Facts about the accumulation of great fortunes, for ex-ample, satisfy this condition better than do the fluctuations of advertising revenues. Facts are most useful politically when they are about some topic that is being minimized in respectable discussions, and yet is very much within the concern of some public. Then the fact finder can succeed in letting the facts "speak for themselves." Gustavus Meyers' *History of Great American Fortunes* was beautifully timed in this way, linking as it did the indignation of the muckrakers and their public with the diligence of scholarship and general ideas about American capitalism.

(2) May social thought, then, be imagined as simply a great conversa-tion that goes on among great social thinkers? One man raises a question, another man answers it. In time, this answer is challenged, and a better one provided, which the company of thinkers comes to accept.

The objection to this view is that very many questions raised and dis-cussed by one generation, or by one circle within it, are neither answered nor even discussed by other circles or later generations. They are simply forgotten, overlooked, ignored, or shoved into the dark corners of the house of intellect. The notion of the history of social thought as a conver-sation does not tell us why some conversations are, and some are not, taken up by other circles and by later generations. The theory that ideas evolve from one another in some kind of inherent continuity is often called the "immanent" model of intellectual change. Its refutation—I believe its definitive refutation—as an adequate conception of intellectual history is perhaps the major burden of Karl Mannheim's work.

(3) The history of social thought might be supposed to consist of men addressing themselves to social problems and solving them. These solu-tions are knowledge. Then new problems arise and in due course they are solved. In this way, knowledge accumulates.

The objections to this view include some of those to the first and second notions. In addition, it must be recognized that many questions that have occupied social thinkers have very little obvious relevance to "social problems." Moreover, social problems are necessarily somebody's prob-lems; they occur when someone's values seem to be imperilled. Accord-ingly, it has to be asked why some people's problems are taken up by social thinkers and those of others are not. Still we should recall that Marx attempted and succeeded in defining what was called "The Social

Problem" for generations of Europeans, and for many men in other areas of the world as well. Durkheim, addressing himself to the problem of suicide, was able to develop his most interesting conceptions (although he did not solve the problem of suicide); and one of the first of Max Weber's economic studies, undertaken at the request of a reform society, dealt with agrarian problems in Eastern Germany.*

It is possible of course, to construct a history of sociology, or of social science generally, more or less along each of these suggested lines. There is little doubt that what is indicated in each of them has occurred and does occur in intellectual history; and there is little doubt that if used alone, each would result in rather arbitrary impositions. It seems obvious that were we writing a history of classic sociology, what we would need to do is combine these three lines of interpretation in such a way as to provide a flexible but, nonetheless, definite set of guidelines. We should need, in short, to organize the three into a model of intellectual change, and then to use it.

All I have wished to do here is to indicate that the accumulation-of-fact notion is only one rather narrow conception—as a matter of intellectual history, it accounts for very little of the development of classic sociology— and to suggest that the ideas this tradition contains are not inevitably going to be connected in any way with such facts as are now being accumulated. Much that is now lying about, in rather technical fragments, can be put together only by a renewal of the kind of thinking represented in the classic tradition.

6

The selections in the present book have not been made in any effort to "cover" any particular range of topical problems, although they do fall, I think, into three more or less coherent units.

The first part concerns the difficulties of thinking clearly and well about man and society, and suggests ways of overcoming them. Each selection, however, does more than this. Despite the truly enormous amount of study in the last quarter of a century devoted to the subject of public opinion, Walter Lippmann's work still remains, in terms of conception and theory, the definitive statement. Spencer's *Study of Society* is a real precursor of Mannheim's sociology of ideas—and also quite valuable in its own right. In these essays Spencer and Mannheim discuss the relations of ideas to the man who holds them and to his society, to the angle of view his position affords him.

Part II suggests a variety of conceptions about the elements that go to

* Cf. *From Max Weber: Essays in Sociology*, edited and translated by H. H. Gerth and C. Wright Mills. (New York: Oxford, 1946.)

make up a society, how these elements are related, and their roles in the main drift of modern society. We begin with Marx's and Engels' conception on all these matters, but particularly on class structure and the mechanics of history. Weber's essay and Veblen's are critical elaborations of Marx's; Weber goes somewhat further than Veblen, for he allows an even greater role to bureaucracy than to class struggle or revolution as the locomotive of history. Mosca, Michels, and Pareto, in their several ways, trace out various meanings of bureaucracy and introduce ideas of "the ruling class" or the "elite." Ideas about the main drift of capitalist society, and the mechanics that underpin it, form the burden of the essays by Spencer, Veblen and Schumpeter included in Part II.

Part III contains several of the original—also, one might say, originating—statements of the crisis of individuality. W. I. Thomas and Florian Znaniecki, in the selections made here, provide a framework of the general sociological view of "personality"—a view which I take to be the foremost contribution of American sociology. They also make a statement of three types of personality that is still of use; in fact, it informs several later and well-known formulations. Georg Simmel sees the individual in a mass-like society, overburdened and outpaced by a flood of sensations, and so becoming, in self-defense, blasé. This brilliant essay is a characterization of the big city from a humanist as well as a sociological point of view. It concerns the status panic and the heightened consciousness of self, as well as much else that now forms the theme of contemporary reflection about the individual in a mass society.

Emile Durkheim connects the individual malaise with the disintegration of social norms themselves: his conception of *anomie*, I think it will be generally agreed, is the most stimulating in his work. Marx's essay "On Alienation" is difficult, but it is fundamental and it has only recently become available in English. I have tried to help the reader with it by also printing simpler passages from "The German Ideology."

Karl Mannheim's essay on rationality contains the seeds of the most profound criticism of the secular rationalism of Western civilization. He did not work it out in just this way, but the passage given here is among the best writings of a man who is, I believe, one of the two or three most vital and important sociologists of the inter-war period.

I do not believe that all the men presented in this book are on the same level. Two of them, I think, stand up above the rest: Karl Marx and Max Weber. Were it necessary to limit ourselves to the works of two sociologists, these two would be my choice. Each of them is a rather difficult intellectual figure; they do not fit within any one academic boundary. Each of them held certain moral values rather passionately, although with different degrees of openness. Neither of them ever wrote anything like a textbook or what the book-trade calls a primer—a book that is easily understandable without previous reading on its topic. Each of them had a central preoccupation, but this preoccupation is not all that we now find of value in their work.

To Marx's class as an economic category both Weber and Veblen add status or prestige, and both realize that it is often prestige that is the readier clue to understanding the psychology of classes. Weber also sophisticated the idea of class itself. I think it not unreasonable to say that in this respect Weber completed the uncompleted work of Marx. His essay on class, status and party remains the definitive work on stratification; nothing since has added anything of basic significance to our conceptions of stratification.

While Veblen keeps the struggle of classes at the center of contemporary history—and behind it, of course, technology and industry versus the institutions of business—Weber does not. He uses this distinction, of course, but he shifts to the center of history, bureaucracy or, put more generally, the fact of rationalization and with it the still more generalized notion of a secular disenchantment of the world. The master clue to Veblen's work as a whole is undoubtedly the distinction between pecuniary and industrial employment, business and industry, institutions and technology. This distinction is in many ways a parallel and an extension of Marx's proletariat and bourgeoisie. But it is camouflaged, or if you like adapted, for an American academic audience, and it does tend to be more convincingly applicable to the American case. Veblen, I think, is the best social scientist America has produced.

One reason—in addition to those I have already given—why Marx and Weber are greater than, for example, Mosca or Durkheim is that every line they write is soaked in knowledge of history. They have truly assimilated it; others tend more to use it, at times rather externally, as illustrations of this or that theory. But in Marx and Weber, history, having been so thoroughly assimilated, pervades the whole. Of course they are both historians—or at least they both wrote history. But both go further.

In their work, sharp analytic conceptions are blended with an encyclopedic knowledge of history. They go to specific periods and events with definite questions firmly in mind. For them history provides that which is to be explained, and the materials used in their explanations. Unfortunately, due to limitations of space, I am unable to print in this volume anything of their more concrete historical work. Could I have done so, Marx's THE EIGHTEENTH BRUMAIRE and Weber's HISTORY OF AGRARIAN INSTITUTIONS would have been included.

Some thinkers, Spencer for example, have a central theme—Evolution —that we do not now find at all valuable; in fact, it has been said, with scholarly authority, that "Spencer is dead." If that were so, it would indeed be a great pity. This ill-founded rumor is based upon a consideration of his master formula; that *is* dead. But I think he still lives, for two simple reasons: very few sociologists, then or now, are his equal in building up a conception of a social *structure*. And he knows how to connect this structure with the character of the individuals that prevail within it. I am hopeful that my selections from Spencer will make both points obvious.

Spencer's idea that the transition from military to industrial society is the master clue to the drift of his epoch is, of course, an idea held by others: Saint-Simon, for example; and it is also very much available in Veblen, who "turned it on its side." Veblen saw not a sequence—from military to industrial—but two co-existing classes: the upper consisting of militaristic, and other feudal "survivals"; the lower, of industrial workmen.

Spencer's expected sequence, of course, turned out to be mistaken; in fact, misleading. Other thinkers of the time made better judgments. Jacob Burckhardt, as well as Karl Marx took quite a contrary view of the relations of industrial and military institutions to human freedom. At one point in his wonderfully varied speculations, Marx foresaw "industrial armies" and Burckhardt, a "militarized industry."*

Back in the American thirties, there was quite a craze for Pareto (nowadays it is very difficult, at least in New York City, to buy a copy of his four-volume *The Mind and Society*). I have never understood why, unless it was some kind of attempted antidote to Marxism which was so fashionable at the time. Pareto's is one of the tougher, even cynical, styles of thought; he seems to relish this posture for its own sake, although he disguises it, I imagine, by supposing it to be an essential part of Science. Of course it is nothing of the sort. As a whole, I find his work pretentious, dull and disorderly. Yet if one digs hard, one does find useful reflections. In particular his analytical definitions seem to me often suggestive, and that is why I have reprinted here several passages on problems of power.

Robert Michels I think first-rate: much of the value that is often found in Pareto has been better incorporated by Michels—and by Pareto's

---

* Burckhardt, who prophesied that military authority and industrial power would in due course merge, wrote in 1871 to a friend: "I have a premonition, which sounds like utter folly and yet which positively will not leave me: the military state must become one great factory. Those hordes of men in the great industrial centers will not be left indefinitely to their greed and want. What must logically come is a fixed and supervised stint of misery, glorified by promotions and uniforms, daily begun and ended to the sound of drums . . . Long voluntary subjection under individual Führers and usurpers is in prospect. People no longer believe in principles but will, periodically, probably believe in saviours . . . For this reason authority will again raise its head in the pleasant 20th century, and a terrible head."—Karl Löwith, *Meaning in History* (Chicago: Univ. of Chicago, 1949) Page 24.

academic rival, Gaetano Mosca. Michels' point I think relevant not only against socialist unions and parties (although, of course, that is what he wrote about and that is how his point is usually taken); I think it holds generally against liberalism! At least, that interpretation does lead to a very fruitful reading of his *Political Parties*. But I find Mosca weak in his defense of liberal principles in terms of the theory of balance. He gives us a theory of The Ruling Class, and then, by qualifications, he takes it away.*

It may be asked, finally, why I do not reprint Auguste Comte. The answer is, first, that I share Marx's judgment of his work, which consisted largely in ignoring him—as a kind of Philistine adapter of Saint-Simon; second, that I have recently tried once more to read him with attention and failed to do so. He is rather dull to read about and altogether dull to read. He seems to me pedantic and irrelevant. Of course he is, I suppose, important historically as a unit in some sequence, but my concern here is not with historical sequences as such. He is interesting today only in a mild way and on a small scale. But I have never had occasion to think in his way.

Perhaps I am just not up to the French! At any rate, compared with the Germans, classic French sociologists seem to me less clear and less profound. Much that they have done is done better elsewhere, by the British for example. Bagehot I find superior to Tarde on imitation and related matters, Spencer's "industrial society" more illuminating than Durkheim's "organic solidarity." Durkheim, however, remains the best of the French sociologists. Technically, the brilliant element in his work is the way in which he tries to link together empirical materials and conceptions, best displayed in his study of suicide. For the present volume I have selected from this book, and from his *Division of Labor*, passages dealing with his conception of *anomie*. This conception is at the center of Durkheim's concern; it points to the disintegration of modern society, to its normlessness, and it is developed in close connection with the effects of this disintegration upon the individual.

The necessary limits of a book have, of course, limited my choice of selections. Were it possible, I should have reprinted from the following: N. Lenin and Selig Perlman (on labor), Alfred Weber (on historical sociology), John Adams (on fame), A. de Tocqueville and James Bryce and Ortega y Gasset (on mass democracy), W. E. H. Lecky (on the heroic virtues), Walter Bagehot (on imitation), Jacob Burckhardt (on the idea

* A recent book of excellent scholarship on Mosca and affiliated thinkers: James H. Meisel, *The Myth Of The Ruling Class* (Ann Arbor: Univ. of Michigan, 1958.)

of individuality), Wilhelm Dilthey (on sympathy), John Hobson (on forms of capitalism), Franz Neumann (on Nazi Germany), Gunnar Myrdal (on the underdeveloped world), Leon Trotsky (on the law of combined stages), R. H. Tawney (on equality), Pitirim Sorokin (on philosophies of history), Harold D. Lasswell (on the psychology of politics), E. H. Carr (on international relations), Isaac Deuthcher (on Soviet Russia), John Dewey and George H. Mead (on human nature), George Lukàc (no the sociology of literature). And many others.

Yet we gain a great deal by limiting the number of thinkers chosen. Thus, I have not felt the need to cut up pieces and paste them together; I have not presented snippets from various longer works. In the main, the selections used are entire essays or chapters. In this way, I have also been able to avoid the strong temptation of any anthologist to favor those writers who are apt at the briefer essay. Nor have I cut essays in order to "speed them up." I have re-titled several essays—the original titles are of course given in a footnote on the first page of each reading.

7

When all is said and done, the editor of any Reader should answer this question: why should anyone read the selections he is offering? Two simple answers to this question have prompted me to make up the present book. To read the company of thinkers presented here helps one to understand what is happening in the world. It also helps one to understand what is happening in and to one's self.

One result of reading sociology ought to be to learn how to read a newspaper. To make sense of a newspaper—which is a very complicated thing—one must learn how to connect the events reported, how to understand them by relating them to more general conceptions of the societies of which they are tokens, and the trends of which they are a part.

To take a single example which I have little fear will become dated: much newspaper coverage has to do with "white-collar crime," with crime syndicates operated on business lines, tax evasion through expense accounts, rigged TV shows, and many other forms of fraud and deceit. It is not enough to read about each such item as it occurs. One must come to see these items as a whole, and one must try to grasp what they mean. When one keeps in mind how often this sort of thing is reported, and how much goes unreported, do they not immediately suggest a crowd of themes? Do they not reveal (1) the extent of manipulation as a form of exercising power, (2) the extent of a semi-organized irresponsibility, (3) the extent to which both these trends readily find individuals to service them, (4) who in turn, by their services, are further corrupted? And what is back of that? Does it not reveal (5) the supremacy of cash and kudos as the all-American values? Well, if it does not, what then are the supreme values? But go a little further: (6) is not one revealing image of contemporary American society a network of rackets? And should we not try to embrace in such a view the big rackets as well as the little ones?

Of course I am not trying to argue any given line of reflection. My point is: sociology, for one thing, is a way of going behind what we read in the newspaper. It provides a set of conceptions and questions which help us to do this. If it does not, then it has failed as part of liberal education.

It has also failed if it does not increase our awareness of what we are personally, and of what we might become as individuals. Reading sociology should increase our awareness of the imperial reach of social worlds into the intimacies of our very self. Such awareness, of course, is the cultural goal of all learning as well as of much art. For all humanistic disciplines, if properly cultivated, help us to transcend the moral sloth and the intellectual rigidities that constitute most of everyday life in every society of which we know.

Sociological reflection is only one way of carrying on this cultural struggle, but surely today it is among the most direct of ways. Through such reflection, we become aware of our own "common sense" as being itself a social phenomenon to be examined and understood. One cuts beneath it, locating it within a particular nation or class or race at a particular period of history. Important to the developing of such an attitude, by the way, is the acquisition of a vocabulary that is adequate for clear social reflection. Such a vocabulary need not be very extensive. In fact, I should say that only some twenty or so pivotal terms are essential. Most of them are used in these selections.

Classic sociology contains an enormous variety of conception, value, and method, and its relevance to the life-ways of the individual and to the ways of history-making in our epoch is obvious and immediate. This is why it is central to contemporary cultural work, and among the most valuable legacies of Western civilization.

I

Obstacles & Orientations

1. Walter Lippmann

The World Outside and
the Pictures in Our Heads

I.

There is an island in the ocean where in 1914 a few Englishmen, French-men, and Germans lived. No cable reaches that island, and the British mail steamer comes but once in sixty days. In September it had not yet come, and the islanders were still talking about the latest newspaper which told about the approaching trial of Madame Caillaux for the shoot-ing of Gaston Calmette. It was, therefore, with more than usual eagerness that the whole colony assembled at the quay on a day in mid-September to hear from the captain what the verdict had been. They learned that for over six weeks now those of them who were English and those of them who were French had been fighting in behalf of the sanctity of treaties against those of them who were Germans. For six strange weeks they had acted as if they were friends, when in fact they were enemies.

But their plight was not so different from that of most of the population of Europe. They had been mistaken for six weeks, on the continent the interval may have been only six days or six hours. There was an interval. There was a moment when the picture of Europe on which men were conducting their business as usual, did not in any way correspond to the Europe which was about to make a jumble of their lives. There was a time for each man when he was still adjusted to an environment that no longer existed. All over the world as late as July 25th men were making goods that they would not be able to ship, buying goods they would not be able to import, careers were being planned, enterprises contemplated, hopes and expectations entertained, all in the belief that the world as known was the world as it was. Men were writing books describing that world. They trusted the picture in their heads. And then over four years later, on a Thursday morning, came the news of an armistice, and people

From Lippmann, *Public Opinion* (New York: The Macmillan Company, 1922). Sections I-VII, pp. 3-32; sections VIII-XIV, pp. 79-100.

N. B. All footnotes in this volume, except those to the chapter titles, are by the author or the editor of the original books from which the selections are taken.

gave vent to their unutterable relief that the slaughter was over. Yet in the five days before the real armistice came, though the end of the war had been celebrated, several thousand young men died on the battlefields.

Looking back we can see how indirectly we know the environment in which nevertheless we live. We can see that the news of it comes to us now fast, now slowly; but that whatever we believe to be a true picture, we treat as if it were the environment itself. It is harder to remember that about the beliefs upon which we are now acting, but in respect to other peoples and other ages we flatter ourselves that it is easy to see when they were in deadly earnest about ludicrous pictures of the world. We insist, because of our superior hindsight, that the world as they needed to know it, and the world as they did know it, were often two quite contradictory things. We can see, too, that while they governed and fought, traded and reformed in the world as they imagined it to be, they produced results, or failed to produce any, in the world as it was. They started for the Indies and found America. They diagnosed evil and hanged old women. They thought they could grow rich by always selling and never buying. A caliph, obeying what he conceived to be the Will of Allah, burned the library at Alexandria.

Writing about the year 389, St. Ambrose stated the case for the prisoner in Plato's cave who resolutely declines to turn his head. "To discuss the nature and position of the earth does not help us in our hope of the life to come. It is enough to know what Scripture states. 'That He hung up the earth upon nothing' (Job xxvi 7). Why then argue whether He hung it up in air or upon the water, and raise a controversy as to how the thin air could sustain the earth; or why, if upon the waters, the earth does not go crashing down to the bottom? . . . Not because the earth is in the middle, as if suspended on even balance, but because the majesty of God constrains it by the law of His will, does it endure stable upon the unstable and the void."[1]

It does not help us in our hope of the life to come. It is enough to know what Scripture states. Why then argue? But a century and a half after St. Ambrose, opinion was still troubled, on this occasion by the problem of the antipodes. A monk named Cosmas, famous for his scientific attainments, was therefore deputed to write a Christian Topography, or "Christian Opinion concerning the World."[2] It is clear that he knew exactly what was expected of him, for he based all his conclusions on the Scriptures as he read them. It appears, then, that the world is a flat parallelogram, twice as broad from east to west as it is long from north to south. In the center is the earth surrounded by ocean, which is in turn surrounded by another earth, where men lived before the deluge. This

---

[1] Hexaëmeron, i. cap 6, quoted in The Mediaeval Mind, by Henry Osborn Taylor, Vol. I, p. 73.
[2] Lecky, Rationalism in Europe, Vol. I, pp. 276-8.

other earth was Noah's port of embarkation. In the north is a high conical mountain around which revolve the sun and moon. When the sun is behind the mountain it is night. The sky is glued to the edges of the outer earth. It consists of four high walls which meet in a concave roof, so that the earth is the floor of the universe. There is an ocean on the other side of the sky, constituting the "waters that are above the firmament." The space between the celestial ocean and the ultimate roof of the universe belongs to the blest. The space between the earth and sky is inhabited by the angels. Finally, since St. Paul said that all men are made to live upon the "face of the earth" how could they live on the back where the Antipodes are supposed to be? "With such a passage before his eyes, a Christian, we are told, should not 'even speak of the Antipodes.'"[1]

Far less should he go to the Antipodes; nor should any Christian prince give him a ship to try; nor would any pious mariner wish to try. For Cosmas there was nothing in the least absurd about his map. Only by remembering his absolute conviction that this was the map of the universe can we begin to understand how he would have dreaded Magellan or Peary or the aviator who risked a collision with the angels and the vault of heaven by flying seven miles up in the air. In the same way we can best understand the furies of war and politics by remembering that almost the whole of each party believes absolutely in its picture of the opposition, that it takes as fact, not what is, but what it supposes to be the fact. And therefore, like Hamlet, it will stab Polonius behind the rustling curtain, thinking him the king, and perhaps like Hamlet add:

> "Thou wretched, rash, intruding fool, farewell!
> I took thee for thy better; take thy fortune."

II.

Great men, even during their lifetime, are usually known to the public only through a fictitious personality. Hence the modicum of truth in the old saying that no man is a hero to his valet. There is only a modicum of truth, for the valet, and the private secretary, are often immersed in the fiction themselves. Royal personages are, of course, constructed personalities. Whether they themselves believe in their public character, or whether they merely permit the chamberlain to stage-manage it, there are at least two distinct selves, the public and regal self, the private and human. The biographies of great people fall more or less readily into the histories of these two selves. The official biographer reproduces the public life, the revealing memoir the other. The Charnwood Lincoln, for example, is a noble portrait, not of an actual human being, but of an epic figure, replete with significance, who moves on much the same level of

[1] Lecky, *op. cit.*

reality as Aeneas or St. George. Oliver's Hamilton is a majestic abstraction, the sculpture of an idea, "an essay" as Mr. Oliver himself calls it, "on American union." It is a formal monument to the statecraft of federalism, hardly the biography of a person. Sometimes people create their own façade when they think they are revealing the interior scene. The Repington diaries and Margot Asquith's are a species of self-portraiture in which the intimate detail is most revealing as an index of how the authors like to think about themselves.

But the most interesting kind of portraiture is that which arises spontaneously in people's minds. When Victoria came to the throne, says Mr. Strachey,[1] "among the outside public there was a great wave of enthusiasm. Sentiment and romance were coming into fashion; and the spectacle of the little girl-queen, innocent, modest, with fair hair and pink cheeks, driving through her capital, filled the hearts of the beholders with raptures of affectionate loyalty. What, above all, struck everybody with overwhelming force was the contrast between Queen Victoria and her uncles. The nasty old men, debauched and selfish, pigheaded and ridiculous, with their perpetual burden of debts, confusions, and disreputabilities— they had vanished like the snow of winter and here at last, crowned and radiant, was the spring."

M. Jean de Pierrefeu[2] saw hero-worship at first hand, for he was an officer on Joffre's staff at the moment of that soldier's greatest fame:

"For two years, the entire world paid an almost divine homage to the victor of the Marne. The baggage-master literally bent under the weight of the boxes, of the packages and letters which unknown people sent him with a frantic testimonial of their admiration. I think that outside of General Joffre, no commander in the war has been able to realize a comparable idea of what glory is. They sent him boxes of candy from all the great confectioners of the world, boxes of champagne, fine wines of every vintage, fruits, game, ornaments and utensils, clothes, smoking materials, ink-stands, paperweights. Every territory sent its speciality. The painter sent his picture, the sculptor his statuette, the dear old lady a comforter or socks, the shepherd in his hut carved a pipe for his sake. All the manufacturers of the world who were hostile to Germany shipped their products, Havana its cigars, Portugal its port wine. I have known a hairdresser who had nothing better to do than to make a portrait of the General out of hair belonging to persons who were dear to him; a professional penman had the same idea, but the features were composed of thousands of little phrases in tiny characters which sang the praise of the General. As to letters, he had them in all scripts, from all countries, written in every dialect, affectionate letters, grateful, overflowing with love, filled with adoration. They called him Savior of the World, Father of his Country, Agent of God, Benefactor of Humanity, etc. . . . And not only Frenchmen, but Americans, Argentinians, Australians, etc. etc. . . . Thousands of little children, without their parents' knowledge, took pen in hand and wrote to tell him their love: most of them called him Our Father. And there was poignancy about their effusions,

---

[1] Lytton Strachey, *Queen Victoria*, p. 72.
[2] Jean de Pierrefeu, *G. Q. G. Trois ans au Grand Quartier Général*, pp. 94-95.

their adoration, these sighs of deliverance that escaped from thousands of hearts at the defeat of barbarism. To all these naif little souls, Joffre seemed like St. George crushing the dragon. Certainly he incarnated for the conscience of mankind the victory of good over evil, of light over darkness.

Lunatics, simpletons, the half-crazy and the crazy turned their darkened brains toward him as toward reason itself. I have read the letter of a person living in Sydney, who begged the General to save him from his enemies; another, a New Zealander, requested him to send some soldiers to the house of a gentleman who owed him ten pounds and would not pay.

Finally, some hundreds of young girls, overcoming the timidity of their sex, asked for engagements, their families not to know about it; others wished only to serve him."

This ideal Joffre was compounded out of the victory won by him, his staff and his troops, the despair of the war, the personal sorrows, and the hope of future victory. But beside hero-worship there is the exorcism of devils. By the same mechanism through which heroes are incarnated, devils are made. If everything good was to come from Joffre, Foch, Wilson, or Roosevelt, everything evil originated in the Kaiser Wilhelm, Lenin and Trotsky. They were as omnipotent for evil as the heroes were omnipotent for good. To many simple and frightened minds there was no political reverse, no strike, no obstruction, no mysterious death or mysterious conflagration anywhere in the world of which the causes did not wind back to these personal sources of evil.

III.

Worldwide concentration of this kind on a symbolic personality is rare enough to be clearly remarkable, and every author has a weakness for the striking and irrefutable example. The vivisection of war reveals such examples, but it does not make them out of nothing. In a more normal public life, symbolic pictures are no less governant of behavior, but each symbol is far less inclusive because there are so many competing ones. Not only is each symbol charged with less feeling because at most it represents only a part of the population, but even within that part there is infinitely less suppression of individual difference. The symbols of public opinion, in times of moderate security, are subject to check and comparison and argument. They come and go, coalesce and are forgotten, never organizing perfectly the emotion of the whole group. There is, after all, just one human activity left in which whole populations accomplish the union sacrée. It occurs in those middle phases of a war when fear, pugnacity, and hatred have secured complete dominion of the spirit, either to crush every other instinct or to enlist it, and before weariness is felt.

At almost all other times, and even in war when it is deadlocked, a sufficiently greater range of feelings is aroused to establish conflict, choice, hesitation, and compromise. The symbolism of public opinion usually bears, as we shall see,[1] the marks of this balancing of interest. Think, for example, of how rapidly, after the armistice, the precarious and by no means successfully established symbol of Allied Unity disappeared, how it was followed almost immediately by the breakdown of each nation's symbolic picture of the other: Britain the Defender of Public Law, France watching at the Frontier of Freedom, America the Crusader. And think then of how within each nation the symbolic picture of itself frayed out, as party and class conflict and personal ambition began to stir postponed issues. And then of how the symbolic pictures of the leaders gave way, as one by one, Wilson, Clemenceau, Lloyd George, ceased to be the incarnation of human hope, and became merely the negotiators and administrators for a disillusioned world.

Whether we regret this as one of the soft evils of peace or applaud it as a return to sanity is obviously no matter here. Our first concern with fictions and symbols is to forget their value to the existing social order, and to think of them simply as an important part of the machinery of human communication. Now in any society that is not completely self-contained in its interests and so small that everyone can know all about everything that happens, ideas deal with events that are out of sight and hard to grasp. Miss Sherwin of Gopher Prairie,[2] is aware that a war is raging in France and tries to conceive it. She has never been to France, and certainly she has never been along what is now the battlefront. Pictures of French and German soldiers she has seen, but it is impossible for her to imagine three million men. No one, in fact, can imagine them, and the professionals do not try. They think of them as, say, two hundred divisions. But Miss Sherwin has no access to the order of battle maps, and so if she is to think about the war, she fastens upon Joffre and the Kaiser as if they were engaged in a personal duel. Perhaps if you could see what she sees with her mind's eye, the image in its composition might be not unlike an Eighteenth Century engraving of a great soldier. He stands there boldly unruffled and more than life size, with a shadowy army of tiny little figures winding off into the landscape behind. Nor it seems are great men oblivious to these expectations. M. de Pierrefeu tells of a photographer's visit to Joffre. The General was in his "middle class office, before the worktable without papers, where he sat down to write his signature. Suddenly it was noticed that there were no maps on the walls. But since according to popular ideas it is not possible to think of a general without maps, a few were placed in position for the picture, and removed soon afterwards."[3]

The only feeling that anyone can have about an event he does not

<hr>

[1] Part V.
[2] See Sinclair Lewis, *Main Street*.
[3] *Op. cit.*, p. 99.

experience is the feeling aroused by his mental image of that event. That is why until we know what others think they know, we cannot truly understand their acts. I have seen a young girl, brought up in a Pennsylvania mining town, plunged suddenly from entire cheerfulness into a paroxysm of grief when a gust of wind cracked the kitchen window-pane. For hours she was inconsolable, and to me incomprehensible. But when she was able to talk, it transpired that if a window-pane broke it meant that a close relative had died. She was, therefore, mourning for her father, who had frightened her into running away from home. The father was, of course, quite thoroughly alive as a telegraphic inquiry soon proved. But until the telegram came, the cracked glass was an authentic message to that girl. Why it was authentic only a prolonged investigation by a skilled psychiatrist could show. But even the most casual observer could see that the girl, enormously upset by her family troubles, had hallucinated a complete fiction out of one external fact, a remembered superstition, and a turmoil of remorse, and fear and love for her father.

Abnormality in these instances is only a matter of degree. When an Attorney-General, who has been frightened by a bomb exploded on his doorstep, convinces himself by the reading of revolutionary literature that a revolution is to happen on the first of May 1920, we recognize that much the same mechanism is at work. The war, of course, furnished many examples of this pattern: the casual fact, the creative imagination, the will to believe, and out of these three elements, a counterfeit of reality to which there was a violent instinctive response. For it is clear enough that under certain conditions men respond as powerfully to fictions as they do to realities, and that in many cases they help to create the very fictions to which they respond. Let him cast the first stone who did not believe in the Russian army that passed through England in August, 1914, did not accept any tale of atrocities without direct proof, and never saw a plot, a traitor, or a spy where there was none. Let him cast a stone who never passed on as the real inside truth what he had heard someone say who knew no more than he did.

In all these instances we must note particularly one common factor. It is the insertion between man and his environment of a pseudo-environment. To that pseudo-environment his behavior is a response. But because it *is* behavior, the consequences, if they are acts, operate not in the pseudo-environment where the behavior is stimulated, but in the real environment where action eventuates. If the behavior is not a practical act, but what we call roughly thought and emotion, it may be a long time before there is any noticeable break in the texture of the fictitious world. But when the stimulus of the pseudo-fact results in action on things or other people, contradiction soon develops. Then comes the sensation of butting one's head against a stone wall, of learning by experience, and witnessing Herbert Spencer's tragedy of the murder of a Beautiful Theory by a

Gang of Brutal Facts, the discomfort in short of a maladjustment. For certainly, at the level of social life, what is called the adjustment of man to his environment takes place through the medium of fictions.

By fictions I do not mean lies. I mean a representation of the environment which is in lesser or greater degree made by man himself. The range of fiction extends all the way from complete hallucination to the scientist's perfectly self-conscious use of a schematic model, or his decision that for his particular problem accuracy beyond a certain number of decimal places is not important. A work of fiction may have almost any degree of fidelity, and so long as the degree of fidelity can be taken into account, fiction is not misleading. In fact, human culture is very largely the selection, the rearrangement, the tracing of patterns upon, and the stylizing of, what William James called "the random irradiations and resettlements of our ideas."[1] The alternative to the use of fictions is direct exposure to the ebb and flow of sensation. That is not a real alternative, for however refreshing it is to see at times with a perfectly innocent eye, innocence itself is not wisdom, though a source and corrective of wisdom.

For the real environment is altogether too big, too complex, and too fleeting for direct acquaintance. We are not equipped to deal with so much subtlety, so much variety, so many permutations and combinations. And although we have to act in that environment, we have to reconstruct it on a simpler model before we can manage with it. To traverse the world men must have maps of the world. Their persistent difficulty is to secure maps on which their own need, or someone else's need, has not sketched in the coast of Bohemia.

IV.

The analyst of public opinion must begin then, by recognizing the triangular relationship between the scene of action, the human picture of that scene, and the human response to that picture working itself out upon the scene of action. It is like a play suggested to the actors by their own experience, in which the plot is transacted in the real lives of the actors, and not merely in their stage parts. The moving picture often emphasizes with great skill this double drama of interior motive and external behavior. Two men are quarreling, ostensibly about some money, but their passion is inexplicable. Then the picture fades out and what one or the other of the two men sees with his mind's eye is reënacted. Across the table they were quarreling about money. In memory they are back in their youth when the girl jilted him for the other man. The exterior drama is explained: the hero is not greedy: the hero is in love.

A scene not so different was played in the United States Senate. At breakfast on the morning of September 29, 1919, some of the Senators

[1] James, *Principles of Psychology*, Vol. II, p. 638.

read a news dispatch in the *Washington Post* about the landing of American marines on the Dalmatian coast. The newspaper said:

FACTS NOW ESTABLISHED

"The following important facts appear already *established*. The orders to Rear Admiral Andrews commanding the American naval forces in the Adriatic, came from the British Admiralty via the War Council and Rear Admiral Knapps in London. The approval or disapproval of the American Navy Department was not asked. . . .

WITHOUT DANIELS' KNOWLEDGE

"Mr. Daniels was admittedly placed in a peculiar position when cables reached here stating that the forces over which he is presumed to have exclusive control were carrying on what amounted to naval warfare without his knowledge. It was fully realized that the *British Admiralty might desire to issue orders to Rear Admiral Andrews* to act on behalf of Great Britain and her Allies, because the situation required sacrifice on the part of some nation if D'Annunzio's followers were to be held in check.

"It was further realized that *under the new league of nations plan foreigners would be in a position to direct American Naval forces in emergencies* with or without the consent of the American Navy Department. . . ." etc. (Italics mine.)

The first Senator to comment is Mr. Knox of Pennsylvania. Indignantly he demands an investigation. In Mr. Brandegee of Connecticut, who spoke next, indignation has already stimulated credulity. Where Mr. Knox indignantly wishes to know if the report is true, Mr. Brandegee, a half a minute later, would like to know what would have happened if marines had been killed. Mr. Knox, interested in the question, forgets that he asked for an inquiry, and replies. If American marines had been killed, it would be war. The mood of the debate is still conditional. Debate proceeds. Mr. McCormick of Illinois reminds the Senate that the Wilson administration is prone to the waging of small unauthorized wars. He repeats Theodore Roosevelt's quip about "waging peace." More debate. Mr. Brandegee notes that the marines acted "under orders of a Supreme Council sitting somewhere," but he cannot recall who represents the United States on that body. The Supreme Council is unknown to the Constitution of the United States. Therefore Mr. New of Indiana submits a resolution calling for the facts.

So far the Senators still recognize vaguely that they are discussing a rumor. Being lawyers they still remember some of the forms of evidence. But as red-blooded men they already experience all the indignation which is appropriate to the fact that American marines have been ordered into war by a foreign government and without the consent of Congress. Emotionally they want to believe it, because they are Republicans, fighting the League of Nations. This arouses the Democratic leader, Mr. Hitchcock of Nebraska. He defends the Supreme Council: it was acting under the war powers. Peace has not yet been concluded because the Republicans are delaying it. Therefore the action was necessary and legal. Both sides now assume that the report is true, and the conclusions they draw are the conclusions of their partisanship. Yet this extraordinary assumption is in a debate over a resolution to investigate the truth of the assumption. It reveals how difficult it is, even for trained lawyers, to suspend response until the returns are in. The response is instantaneous. The fiction is taken for truth because the fiction is badly needed.

A few days later an official report showed that the marines were not landed by order of the British Government or of the Supreme Council. They had not been fighting the Italians. They had been landed at the request of the Italian Government to protect Italians, and the American commander had been officially thanked by the Italian authorities. The marines were not at war with Italy. They had acted according to an established international practice which had nothing to do with the League of Nations.

The scene of action was the Adriatic. The picture of that scene in the Senators' heads at Washington was furnished, in this case probably with intent to deceive, by a man who cared nothing about the Adriatic, but much about defeating the League. To this picture the Senate responded by a strengthening of its partisan differences over the League.

V.

Whether in this particular case the Senate was above or below its normal standard, it is not necessary to decide. Nor whether the Senate compares favorably with the House, or with other parliaments. At the moment, I should like to think only about the world-wide spectacle of men acting upon their environment, moved by stimuli from their pseudo-environments. For when full allowance has been made for deliberate fraud, political science has still to account for such facts as two nations attacking one another, each convinced that it is acting in self-defense, or two classes at war each certain that it speaks for the common interest. They live, we are likely to say, in different worlds. More accurately, they live in the same world, but they think and feel in different ones.

It is to these special worlds, it is to these private or group, or class, or provincial, or occupational, or national, or sectarian artifacts, that the political adjustment of mankind in the Great Society takes place. Their variety and complication are impossible to describe. Yet these fictions determine a very great part of men's political behavior. We must think of perhaps fifty sovereign parliaments consisting of at least a hundred legislative bodies. With them belong at least fifty hierarchies of provincial and municipal assemblies, which with their executive, administrative and legislative organs, constitute formal authority on earth. But that does not begin to reveal the complexity of political life. For in each of these innumerable centers of authority there are parties, and these parties are themselves hierarchies with their roots in classes, sections, cliques and clans; and within these are the individual politicians, each the personal center of a web of connection and memory and fear and hope.

Somehow or other, for reasons often necessarily obscure, as the result of domination or compromise or a logroll, there emerge from these political bodies commands, which set armies in motion or make peace, conscript life, tax, exile, imprison, protect property or confiscate it, encourage one kind of enterprise and discourage another, facilitate immigration or obstruct it, improve communication or censor it, establish schools, build navies, proclaim "policies," and "destiny," raise economic barriers, make property or unmake it, bring one people under the rule of another, or favor one class as against another. For each of these decisions some view of the facts is taken to be conclusive, some view of the circumstances is accepted as the basis of inference and as the stimulus of feeling. What view of the facts, and why that one?

And yet even this does not begin to exhaust the real complexity. The formal political structure exists in a social environment, where there are innumerable large and small corporations and institutions, voluntary and semi-voluntary associations, national, provincial, urban and neighborhood groupings, which often as not make the decision that the political body registers. On what are these decisions based?

"Modern society," says Mr. Chesterton, "is intrinsically insecure because it is based on the notion that all men will do the same thing for different reasons. . . . And as within the head of any convict may be the hell of a quite solitary crime, so in the house or under the hat of any suburban clerk may be the limbo of a quite separate philosophy. The first man may be a complete Materialist and feel his own body as a horrible machine manufacturing his own mind. He may listen to his thoughts as to the dull ticking of a clock. The man next door may be a Christian Scientist and regard his own body as somehow rather less substantial than his own shadow. He may come almost to regard his own arms and legs as delusions like moving serpents in the dream of delirium tremens. The third man in the street may not be a Christian Scientist but, on the contrary, Christian. He may live in a fairy tale as his neighbors would say; a secret but solid fairy tale full of the faces and presences of unearthly friends. The fourth man many be a theosophist, and only too probably a vegetarian; and I do not see why I should not gratify myself with the fancy that the fifth man is a devil worshiper. . . . Now whether or not this sort of variety is valuable, this sort of unity is shaky. To expect that all men for all time will go on thinking different things, and yet doing the same things, is a doubtful speculation. It is not founding society on a communion, or even on a convention, but rather on a coincidence. Four men may meet under the same lamp post; one to paint it pea green as part of a great municipal reform; one to read his breviary in the light of it; one to embrace it with accidental ardour in a fit of alcoholic enthusiasm; and the last merely because the pea green post is a conspicuous point of rendezvous with his young lady. But to expect this to happen night after night is unwise. . . ."[1]

For the four men at the lamp post substitute the governments, the parties, the corporations, the societies, the social sets, the trades and professions, universities, sects, and nationalities of the world. Think of the legislator voting a statute that will affect distant peoples, a statesman coming to a decision. Think of the Peace Conference reconstituting the frontiers of Europe, an ambassador in a foreign country trying to discern the intentions of his own government and of the foreign government, a promoter working a concession in a backward country, an editor demanding a war, a clergyman calling on the police to regulate amusement, a club lounging-room making up its mind about a strike, a sewing circle preparing to regulate the schools, nine judges deciding whether a legislature in Oregon may fix the working hours of women, a cabinet meeting to decide on the recognition of a government, a party convention choosing a candidate and writing a platform, twenty-seven million voters casting their ballots, an Irishman in Cork thinking about an Irishman in Belfast, a Third International planning to reconstruct the whole of human society, a board of directors confronted with a set of their employees' demands, a boy choosing a career, a merchant estimating supply and demand for the coming season, a speculator predicting the course of the market, a banker deciding whether to put credit behind a new enterprise, the advertiser, the reader of advertisements. . . . Think of the different sorts of Americans thinking about their notions of "The British Empire" or "France" or "Russia" or "Mexico." It is not so different from Mr. Chesterton's four men at the pea green lamp post.

VI.

And so before we involve ourselves in the jungle of obscurities about the innate differences of men, we shall do well to fix our attention upon the extraordinary differences in what men know of the world.[2] I do not doubt that there are important biological differences. Since man is an animal it would be strange if there were not. But as rational beings it is worse than shallow to generalize at all about comparative behavior until there is a measurable similarity between the environments to which behavior is a response.

[1] G. K. Chesterton, "The Mad Hatter and the Sane Householder," *Vanity Fair*, January, 1921, p. 54.
[2] *Cf.* Wallas, *Our Social Heritage*, pp. 77 *et seq.*

The pragmatic value of this idea is that it introduces a much needed refinement into the ancient controversy about nature and nurture, innate quality and environment. For the pseudo-environment is a hybrid compounded of "human nature" and "conditions." To my mind it shows the uselessness of pontificating about what man is and always will be from what we observe man to be doing, or about what are the necessary conditions of society. For we do not know how men would behave in response to the facts of the Great Society. All that we really know is how they behave in response to what can fairly be called a most inadequate picture of the Great Society. No conclusion about man or the Great Society can honestly be made on evidence like that.

This, then, will be the clue to our inquiry. We shall assume that what each man does is based not on direct and certain knowledge, but on pictures made by himself or given to him. If his atlas tells him that the world is flat he will not sail near what he believes to be the edge of our planet for fear of falling off. If his maps include a fountain of eternal youth, a Ponce de Leon will go in quest of it. If someone digs up yellow dirt that looks like gold, he will for a time act exactly as if he had found gold. The way in which the world is imagined determines at any particular moment what men will do. It does not determine what they will achieve. It determines their effort, their feelings, their hopes, not their accomplishments and results. The very men who most loudly proclaim their "materialism" and their contempt for "ideologues," the Marxian communists, place their entire hope on what? On the formation by propaganda of a class-conscious group. But what is propaganda, if not the effort to alter the picture to which men respond, to substitute one social pattern for another? What is class consciousness but a way of realizing the world? National consciousness but another way? And Professor Giddings' consciousness of kind, but a process of believing that we recognize among the multitude certain ones marked as our kind?

Try to explain social life as the pursuit of pleasure and the avoidance of pain. You will soon be saying that the hedonist begs the question, for even supposing that man does pursue these ends, the crucial problem of why he thinks one course rather than another likely to produce pleasure, is untouched. Does the guidance of man's conscience explain? How then does he happen to have the particular conscience which he has? The theory of economic self-interest? But how do men come to conceive their interest in one way rather than another? The desire for security, or prestige, or domination, or what is vaguely called self-realization? How do men conceive their security, what do they consider prestige, how do they figure out the means of domination, or what is the notion of self which they wish to realize? Pleasure, pain, conscience, acquisition, protection, enhancement, mastery, are undoubtedly names for some of the ways people act. There may be instinctive dispositions which work toward such ends. But no statement of the end, or any description of the tendencies to seek it, can explain the behavior which results. The very fact that men theorize at all is proof that their pseudo-environments, their interior representations of the world, are a determining element in thought, feeling, and action. For if the connection between reality and human response were direct and immediate, rather than indirect and inferred, indecision and failure would be unknown, and (if each of us fitted as snugly into the world, as the child in the womb), Mr. Bernard Shaw would not have been able to say that except for the first nine months of its existence no human being manages its affairs as well as a plant.

The chief difficulty in adapting the psychoanalytic scheme to political thought arises in this connection. The Freudians are concerned with the maladjustment of distinct individuals to other individuals and to concrete circumstances. They have assumed that if internal derangements could be straightened out, there would be little or no confusion about what is the obviously normal relationship. But public opinion deals with indirect, unseen, and puzzling facts, and there is nothing obvious about them. The situations to which public opinions refer are known only as opinions. The psychoanalyst, on the other hand, almost always assumes that the environment is knowable, and if not knowable then at least bearable, to any unclouded intelligence. This assumption of his is the problem of public opinion. Instead of taking for granted an environment that is readily known, the social analyst is most concerned in studying how the larger political environment is conceived, and how it can be conceived more successfully. The psychoanalyst examines the adjustment to an X, called by him the environment; the social analyst examines the X, called by him the pseudo-environment.

He is, of course, permanently and constantly in debt to the new psychology, not only because when rightly applied it so greatly helps people to stand on their own feet, come what may, but because the study of dreams, fantasy and rationalization has thrown light on how the pseudo-environment is put together. But he cannot assume as his criterion either what is called a "normal biological career"[1] within the existing social order, or a career "freed from religious suppression and dogmatic conventions" outside.[2] What for a sociologist is a normal social career? Or one freed from suppressions and conventions? Conservative critics do, to be sure, assume the first, and romantic ones the second. But in assuming them they are taking the whole world for granted. They are saying in effect either that society is the sort of thing which corresponds to their idea of what is normal, or the sort of thing which corresponds to their idea of what is free. Both ideas are merely public opinions, and while the psychoanalyst as physician may perhaps assume them, the sociologist may not

[1] Edward J. Kempf, *Psychopathology*, p. 116.
[2] *Id.*, p. 151.

take the products of existing public opinion as criteria by which to study public opinion.

VII.,

The world that we have to deal with politically is out of reach, out of sight, out of mind. It has to be explored, reported, and imagined. Man is no Aristotelian god contemplating all existence at one glance. He is the creature of an evolution who can just about span a sufficient portion of reality to manage his survival, and snatch what on the scale of time are but a few moments of insight and happiness. Yet this same creature has invented ways of seeing what no naked eye could see, of hearing what no ear could hear, of weighing immense masses and infinitesimal ones, of counting and separating more items that he can individually remember. He is learning to see with his mind vast portions of the world that he could never see, touch, smell, hear, or remember. Gradually he makes for himself a trustworthy picture inside his head of the world beyond his reach.

Those features of the world outside which have to do with the behavior of other human beings, in so far as that behavior crosses ours, is dependent upon us, or is interesting to us, we call roughly public affairs. The pictures inside the heads of these human beings, the pictures of themselves, of others, of their needs, purposes, and relationship, are their public opinions. Those pictures which are acted upon by groups of people, or by individuals acting in the name of groups, are Public Opinion with capital letters. And so in the chapters which follow we shall inquire first into some of the reasons why the picture inside so often misleads men in their dealings with the world outside. Under this heading we shall consider first the chief factors which limit their access to the facts. They are the artificial censorships, the limitations of social contact, the comparatively meager time available in each day for paying attention to public affairs, the distortion arising because events have to be compressed into very short messages, the difficulty of making a small vocabulary express a complicated world, and finally the fear of facing those facts which would seem to threaten the established routine of men's lives.

The analysis then turns from these more or less external limitations to the question of how this trickle of messages from the outside is affected by the stored up images, the preconceptions, and prejudices which interpret, fill them out, and in their turn powerfully direct the play of our attention, and our vision itself. From this it proceeds to examine how in the individual person the limited messages from outside, formed into a pattern of stereotypes, are identified with his own interests as he feels and conceives them. In the succeeding sections it examines how opinions are crystallized into what is called Public Opinion, how a National Will, a Group Mind, a Social Purpose, or whatever you choose to call it, is formed.

The first five parts constitute the descriptive section of the book. There follows an analysis of the traditional democratic theory of public opinion. The substance of the argument is that democracy in its original form never seriously faced the problem which arises because the pictures inside people's heads do not automatically correspond with the world outside. And then, because the democratic theory is under criticism by socialist thinkers, there follows an examination of the most advanced and coherent of these criticisms, as made by the English Guild Socialists. My purpose here is to find out whether these reformers take into account the main difficulties of public opinion. My conclusion is that they ignore the difficulties, as completely as did the original democrats, because they, too, assume, and in a much more complicated civilization, that somehow mysteriously there exists in the hearts of men a knowledge of the world beyond their reach.

I argue that representative government, either in what is ordinarily called politics, or in industry, cannot be worked successfully, no matter what the basis of election, unless there is an independent, expert organization for making the unseen facts intelligible to those who have to make the decisions. I attempt, therefore, to argue that the serious acceptance of the principle that personal representation must be supplemented by representation of the unseen facts would alone permit a satisfactory decentralization, and allow us to escape from the intolerable and unworkable fiction that each of us must acquire a competent opinion about all public affairs. It is argued that the problem of the press is confused because the critics and the apologists expect the press to realize this fiction, expect it to make up for all that was not foreseen in the theory of democracy, and that the readers expect this miracle to be performed at no cost or trouble to themselves. The newspapers are regarded by democrats as a panacea for their own defects, whereas analysis of the nature of news and of the economic basis of journalism seems to show that the newspapers necessarily and inevitably reflect, and therefore, in greater or lesser measure, intensify, the defective organization of public opinion. My conclusion is that public opinions must be organized for the press if they are to be sound, not by the press as is the case today. This organization I conceive to be in the first instance the task of a political science that has won its proper place as formulator, in advance of real decision, instead of apologist, critic, or reporter after the decision has been made. I try to indicate that the perplexities of government and industry are conspiring to give political science this enormous opportunity to enrich itself and to serve the public. And, of course, I hope that these pages will help a few people to realize that opportunity more vividly, and therefore to pursue it more consciously.

VIII.

Each of us lives and works on a small part of the earth's surface, moves in a small circle, and of these acquaintances knows only a few intimately. Of any public event that has wide effects we see at best only a phase and an aspect. This is as true of the eminent insiders who draft treaties, make laws, and issue orders, as it is of those who have treaties framed for them, laws promulgated to them, orders given at them. Inevitably our opinions cover a bigger space, a longer reach of time, a greater number of things, than we can directly observe. They have, therefore, to be pieced together out of what others have reported and what we can imagine.

Yet even the eyewitness does not bring back a naïve picture of the scene.[1] For experience seems to show that he himself brings something to the scene which later he takes away from it, that oftener than not what he imagines to be the account of an event is really a transfiguration of it. Few facts in consciousness seem to be merely given. Most facts in consciousness seem to be partly made. A report is the joint product of the knower and known, in which the rôle of the observer is always selective and usually creative. The facts we see depend on where we are placed, and the habits of our eyes.

An unfamiliar scene is like the baby's world, "one great, blooming, buzzing confusion."[2] This is the way, says Mr. John Dewey,[3] that any new thing strikes an adult, so far as the thing is really new and strange. "Foreign languages that we do not understand always seem jibberings, babblings, in which it is impossible to fix a definite, clear-cut, individualized group of sounds. The countryman in the crowded street, the landlubber at sea, the ignoramus in sport at a contest between experts in

---

[1] E. g. cf. Edmond Locard, *L'Enquête Criminelle et les Méthodes Scientifiques.* A great deal of interesting material has been gathered in late years on the credibility of the witness, which shows, as an able reviewer of Dr. Locard's book says in *The Times* (London) Literary Supplement (August 18, 1921), that credibility varies as to classes of witnesses and classes of events, and also as to type of perception. Thus, perceptions of touch, odor, and taste have low evidential value. Our hearing is defective and arbitrary when it judges the sources and direction of sound, and in listening to the talk of other people "words which are not heard will be supplied by the witness in all good faith. He will have a theory of the purport of the conversation, and will arrange the sounds he heard to fit it." Even visual perceptions are liable to great error, as in identification, recognition, judgment of distance, estimates of numbers, for example, the size of a crowd. In the untrained observer the sense of time is highly variable. All these original weaknesses are complicated by tricks of memory, and the incessant creative quality of the imagination. Cf. also Sherrington, *The Integrative Action of the Nervous System,* pp. 318-327.

The late Professor Hugo Münsterberg wrote a popular book on this subject called *On the Witness Stand.*

[2] Wm. James, *Principles of Psychology,* Vol. I, p. 488.

[3] John Dewey, *How We Think,* p. 121.

a complicated game, are further instances. Put an inexperienced man in a factory, and at first the work seems to him a meaningless medley. All strangers of another race proverbially look alike to the visiting stranger. Only gross differences of size or color are perceived by an outsider in a flock of sheep, each of which is perfectly individualized to the shepherd. A diffusive blur and an indiscriminately shifting suction characterize what we do not understand. The problem of the acquisition of meaning by things, or (stated in another way) of forming habits of simple apprehension, is thus the problem of introducing (1) *definiteness* and *dictinction* and (2) *consistency* or *stability* of meaning into what is otherwise vague and wavering."

But the kind of definiteness and consistency introduced depends upon who introduces them. In a later passage[1] Dewey gives an example of how differently an experienced layman and a chemist might define the word metal. "Smoothness, hardness, glossiness, and brilliancy, heavy weight for its size . . . the serviceable properties of capacity for being hammered and pulled without breaking, of being softened by heat and hardened by cold, of retaining the shape and form given, of resistance to pressure and decay, would probably be included" in the layman's definition. But the chemist would likely as not ignore these esthetic and utilitarian qualities, and define a metal as "any chemical element that enters into combination with oxygen so as to form a base."

For the most part we do not first see, and then define, we define first and then see. In the great blooming, buzzing confusion of the outer world we pick out what our culture has already defined for us, and we tend to perceive that which we have picked out in the form stereotyped for us by our culture. Of the great men who assembled at Paris to settle the affairs of mankind, how many were there who were able to see much of the Europe about them, rather than their commitments about Europe? Could anyone have penetrated the mind of M. Clemenceau, would he have found there images of the Europe of 1919, or a great sediment of stereotyped ideas accumulated and hardened in a long and pugnacious existence? Did he see the Germans of 1919, or the German type as he had learned to see it since 1871? He saw the type, and among the reports that came to him from Germany, he took to heart those reports, and, it seems, those only, which fitted the type that was in his mind. If a junker blustered, that was an authentic German; if a labor leader confessed the guilt of the empire, he was not an authentic German.

At a Congress of Psychology in Göttingen an interesting experiment was made with a crowd of presumably trained observers.[2]

"Not far from the hall in which the Congress was sitting there was a public fête with a masked ball. Suddenly the door of the hall was thrown open and a

[1] Dewey, *op. cit.*, p. 133.
[2] A. von Gennep, *La formation des légendes*, pp. 158-159. Cited F. van Langenhove, *The Growth of a Legend*, pp. 120-122.

clown rushed in madly pursued by a negro, revolver in hand. They stopped in
the middle of the room fighting; the clown fell, the negro leapt upon him,
fired, and then both rushed out of the hall. The whole incident hardly lasted
twenty seconds.

"The President asked those present to write immediately a report since there
was sure to be a judicial inquiry. Forty reports were sent in. Only one had less
than 20% of mistakes in regard to the principal facts; fourteen had 20% to 40%
of mistakes; twelve from 40% to 50%; thirteen more than 50%. Moreover in
twenty-four accounts 10% of the details were pure inventions and this proportion was exceeded in ten accounts and diminished in six. Briefly a quarter of the
accounts were false.

"It goes without saying that the whole scene had been arranged and even
photographed in advance. The ten false reports may then be relegated to the
category of tales and legends; twenty-four accounts are half legendary, and six
have a value approximating to exact evidence."

Thus out of forty trained observers writing a responsible account of a
scene that had just happened before their eyes, more than a majority saw
a scene that had not taken place. What then did they see? One would
suppose it was easier to tell what had occurred, than to invent something
which had not occurred. They saw their stereotype of such a brawl. All
of them had in the course of their lives acquired a series of images of
brawls, and these images flickered before their eyes. In one man these
images displaced less than 20% of the actual scene, in thirteen men more
than half. In thirty-four out of the forty observers the stereotypes pre-
ëmpted at least one-tenth of the scene.

A distinguished art critic said[1] that "what with the almost numberless
shapes assumed by an object. . . . What with our insensitiveness and in-
attention, things scarcely would have for us features and outlines so
determined and clear that we could recall them at will, but for the
stereotyped shapes art has lent them." The truth is even broader than that,
for the stereotyped shapes lent to the world come not merely from art, in
the sense of painting and sculpture and literature, but from our moral
codes and our social philosophies and our political agitations as well.
Substitute in the following passage of Mr. Berenson's the words 'politics,'
'business,' and 'society,' for the word 'art' and the sentences will be no
less true: ". . . unless years devoted to the study of all schools of art have
taught us also to see with our own eyes, we soon fall into the habit of
moulding whatever we look at into the forms borrowed from the one art
with which we are acquainted. There is our standard of artistic reality.
Let anyone give us shapes and colors which we cannot instantly match in
our paltry stock of hackneyed forms and tints, and we shake our heads at
his failure to reproduce things as we know they certainly are, or we
accuse him of insincerity."

Mr. Berenson speaks of our displeasure when a painter "does not
visualize objects exactly as we do," and of the difficulty of appreciating the
art of the Middle Ages because since then "our manner of visualizing

[1] Bernard Berenson, *The Central Italian Painters of the Renaissance*, pp. 60, *et seq.*

forms has changed in a thousand ways."[1] He goes on to show how in regard to the human figure we have been taught to see what we do see. "Created by Donatello and Masaccio, and sanctioned by the Humanists, the new canon of the human figure, the new cast of features . . . presented to the ruling classes of that time the type of human being most likely to win the day in the combat of human forces. . . . Who had the power to break through this new standard of vision and, out of the chaos of things, to select shapes more definitely expressive of reality than those fixed by men of genius? No one had such power. People had perforce to see things in that way and in no other, and to see only the shapes depicted, to love only the ideals presented. . . ."[2]

IX

If we cannot fully understand the acts of other people, until we know what they think they know, then in order to do justice we have to appraise not only the information which has been at their disposal, but the minds through which they have filtered it. For the accepted types, the current patterns, the standard versions, intercept information on its way to consciousness. Americanization, for example, is superficially at least the substitution of American for European stereotypes. Thus the peasant who might see his landlord as if he were the lord of the manor, his employer as he saw the local magnate, is taught by Americanization to see the landlord and employer according to American standards. This constitutes a change of mind, which is, in effect, when the inoculation succeeds, a change of vision. His eyes see differently. One kindly gentlewoman has confessed that the stereotypes are of such overwhelming importance, that when hers are not indulged, she at least is unable to accept the brotherhood of man and the fatherhood of God: "we are strangely affected by the clothes we wear. Garments create a mental and social atmosphere. What can be hoped for the Americanism of a man who insists on employing a London tailor? One's very food affects his Americanism. What kind of American consciousness can grow in the atmosphere of sauerkraut and Limburger cheese? Or what can you expect of the Americanism of the man whose breath always reeks of garlic?"[3]

This lady might well have been the patron of a pageant which a friend

---

[1] Cf. also his comment on *Dante's Visual Images, and his Early Illustrators* in *The Study and Criticism of Italian Art* (First Series), p. 13. "We cannot help dressing Virgil as a Roman, and giving him a 'Classical profile' and 'statuesque carriage,' but Dante's visual image of Virgil was probably no less mediaeval, no more based on a critical reconstruction of antiquity, than his entire conception of the Roman poet. Fourteenth Century illustrators make Virgil look like a mediaeval scholar, dressed in cap and gown, and there is no reason why Dante's visual image of him should have been other than this."

[2] *The Central Italian Painters*, pp. 66-67.

[3] Cited by Mr. Edward Hale Bierstadt, *New Republic*, June 1, 1921, p. 21.

of mine once attended. It was called the Melting Pot, and it was given on the Fourth of July in an automobile town where many foreign-born workers are employed. In the center of the baseball park at second base stood a huge wooden and canvas pot. There were flights of steps up to the rim on two sides. After the audience had settled itself, and the band had played, a procession came through an opening at one side of the field. It was made up of men of all the foreign nationalities employed in the factories. They wore their native costumes, they were singing their national songs; they danced their folk dances, and carried the banners of all Europe. The master of ceremonies was the principal of the grade school dressed as Uncle Sam. He led them to the pot. He directed them up the steps to the rim, and inside. He called them out again on the other side. They came, dressed in derby hats, coats, pants, vest, stiff collar and polka-dot tie, undoubtedly, said my friend, each with an Eversharp pencil in his pocket, and all singing the Star-Spangled Banner.

To the promoters of this pageant, and probably to most of the actors, it seemed as if they had managed to express the most intimate difficulty to friendly association between the older peoples of America and the newer. The contradiction of their stereotypes interfered with the full recognition of their common humanity. The people who change their names know this. They mean to change themselves, and the attitude of strangers toward them.

There is, of course, some connection between the scene outside and the mind through which we watch it, just as there are some long-haired men and short-haired women in radical gatherings. But to the hurried observer a slight connection is enough. If there are two bobbed heads and four beards in the audience, it will be a bobbed and bearded audience to the reporter who knows beforehand that such gatherings are composed of people with these tastes in the management of their hair. There is a connection between our vision and the facts, but it is often a strange connection. A man has rarely looked at a landscape, let us say, except to examine its possibilities for division into building lots, but he has seen a number of landscapes hanging in the parlor. And from them he has learned to think of a landscape as a rosy sunset, or as a country road with a church steeple and a silver moon. One day he goes to the country, and for hours he does not see a single landscape. Then the sun goes down looking rosy. At once he recognizes a landscape and exclaims that it is beautiful. But two days later, when he tries to recall what he saw, the odds are that he will remember chiefly some landscape in a parlor.

Unless he has been drunk or dreaming or insane he did see a sunset, but he saw in it, and above all remembers from it, more of what the oil painting taught him to observe, than what an impressionist painter, for example, or a cultivated Japanese would have seen and taken away with him. And the Japanese and the painter in turn will have seen and remembered more of the form they had learned, unless they happen to be the very rare people who find fresh sight for mankind. In untrained observation we pick recognizable signs out of the environment. The signs stand for ideas, and these ideas we fill out with our stock of images. We do not so much see this man and that subject; rather we notice that the thing is man or sunset, and then see chiefly what our mind is already full of on those subjects.

X.

There is economy in this. For the attempt to see all things freshly and in detail, rather than as types and generalities, is exhausting, and among busy affairs practically out of the question. In a circle of friends, and in relation to close associates or competitors, there is no shortcut through, and no substitute for, an individualized understanding. Those whom we love and admire most are the men and women whose consciousness is peopled thickly with persons rather than with types, who know us rather than the classification into which we might fit. For even without phrasing it to ourselves, we feel intuitively that all classification is in relation to some purpose not necessarily our own; that between two human beings no association has final dignity in which each does not take the other as an end in himself. There is a taint on any contact between two people which does not affirm as an axiom the personal inviolability of both.

But modern life is hurried and multifarious, above all physical distance separates men who are often in vital contact with each other, such as employer and employee, official and voter. There is neither time nor opportunity for intimate acquaintance. Instead we notice a trait which marks a well known type, and fill in the rest of the picture by means of the stereotypes we carry about in our heads. He is an agitator. That much we notice, or are told. Well, an agitator is this sort of person, and so *he* is this sort of person. He is an intellectual. He is a plutocrat. He is a foreigner. He is a "South European." He is from Back Bay. He is a Harvard Man. How different from the statement: he is a Yale Man. He is a regular fellow. He is a West Pointer. He is an old army sergeant. He is a Greenwich Villager: what don't we know about him then, and about her? He is an international banker. He is from Main Street.

The subtlest and most pervasive of all influences are those which create and maintain the repertory of stereotypes. We are told about the world before we see it. We imagine most things before we experience them. And those preconceptions, unless education has made us acutely aware, govern deeply the whole process of perception. They mark out certain objects as familiar or strange, emphasizing the difference, so that the slightly familiar is seen as very familiar, and the somewhat strange as sharply alien. They are aroused by small signs, which may vary from a true index to a vague analogy. Aroused, they flood fresh vision with older images, and project into the world what has been resurrected in memory. Were there no practical uniformities in the environment, there would be no economy and only error in the human habit of accepting foresight for sight. But there are uniformities sufficiently accurate, and the need of economizing attention is so inevitable, that the abandonment of all stereotypes for a whole innocent approach to experience would impoverish human life.

What matters is the character of the stereotypes, and the gullibility with which we employ them. And these in the end depend upon those inclusive patterns which constitute our philosophy of life. If in that philosophy we assume that the world is codified according to a code which we possess, we are likely to make our reports of what is going on describe a world run by our code. But if our philosophy tells us that each man is only a small part of the world, that his intelligence catches at best only phases and aspects in a coarse net of ideas, then, when we use our stereotypes, we tend to know that they are only stereotypes, to hold them lightly, to modify them gladly. We tend, also, to realize more and more clearly when our ideas started, where they started, how they came to us, why we accepted them. All useful history is antiseptic in this fashion. It enables us to know what fairy tale, what school book, what tradition, what novel, play, picture, phrase, planted one preconception in this mind, another in that mind.

XI.

Those who wish to censor art do not at least underestimate this influence. They generally misunderstand it, and almost always they are absurdly bent on preventing other people from discovering anything not sanctioned by them. But at any rate, like Plato in his argument about the poets, they feel vaguely that the types acquired through fiction tend to be imposed on reality. Thus there can be little doubt that the moving picture is steadily building up imagery which is then evoked by the words people read in their newspapers. In the whole experience of the race there has been no aid to visualization comparable to the cinema. If a Florentine wished to visualize the saints, he could go to the frescoes in his church, where he might see a vision of saints standardized for his time by Giotto. If an Athenian wished to visualize the gods he went to the temples. But the number of objects which were pictured was not great. And in the East, where the spirit of the second commandment was widely accepted, the portraiture of concrete things was even more meager, and for that reason perhaps the faculty of practical decision was by so much reduced. In the western world, however, during the last few centuries there has been an enormous increase in the volume and scope of secular description, the word picture, the narrative, the illustrated narrative, and finally the moving picture and, perhaps, the talking picture.

Photographs have the kind of authority over imagination to-day, which the printed word had yesterday, and the spoken word before that. They seem utterly real. They come, we imagine, directly to us without human meddling, and they are the most effortless food for the mind conceivable. Any description in words, or even any inert picture, requires an effort of memory before a picture exists in the mind. But on the screen the whole process of observing, describing, reporting, and then imagining, has been accomplished for you. Without more trouble than is needed to stay awake the result which your imagination is always aiming at is reeled off on the screen. The shadowy idea becomes vivid; your hazy notion, let us say, of the Ku Klux Klan, thanks to Mr. Griffiths, takes vivid shape when you see the Birth of a Nation. Historically it may be the wrong shape, morally it may be a pernicious shape, but it is a shape, and I doubt whether any- one who has seen the film and does not know more about the Ku Klux Klan than Mr. Griffiths, will ever hear the name again without seeing those white horsemen.

XII.

And so when we speak of the mind of a group of people, of the French mind, the militarist mind, the bolshevik mind, we are liable to serious confusion unless we agree to separate the instinctive equipment from the stereotypes, and the formulae which play so decisive a part in building up the mental world to which the native character is adapted and re- sponds. Failure to make this distinction accounts for oceans of loose talk about collective minds, national souls, and race psychology. To be sure a stereotype may be so consistently and authoritatively transmitted in each generation from parent to child that it seems almost like a bio- logical fact. In some respects, we may indeed have become, as Mr. Wallas says,[1] biologically parasitic upon our social heritage. But certainly there is not the least scientific evidence which would enable anyone to argue that men are born with the political habits of the country in which they are born. In so far as political habits are alike in a nation, the first places to look for an explanation are the nursery, the school, the church, not in that limbo inhabited by Group Minds and National Souls. Until you have thoroughly failed to see tradition being handed on from parents, teachers, priests, and uncles, it is a solecism of the worst order to ascribe political differences to the germ plasm.

It is possible to generalize tentatively and with a decent humility about comparative differences within the same category of education and ex- perience. Yet even this is a tricky enterprise. For almost no two experiences

[1] Graham Wallas, *Our Social Heritage*, p. 17.

are exactly alike, not even of two children in the same household. The older son never does have the experience of being the younger. And therefore, until we are able to discount the difference in nurture, we must withhold judgment about differences of nature. As well judge the productivity of two soils by comparing their yield before you know which is in Labrador and which is in Iowa, whether they have been cultivated and enriched, exhausted, or allowed to run wild.

XIII.

There is another reason, besides economy of effort, why we so often hold to our stereotypes when we might pursue a more disinterested vision. The systems of stereotypes may be the core of our personal tradition, the defenses of our position in society.

They are an ordered, more or less consistent picture of the world, to which our habits, our tastes, our capacities, our comforts and our hopes have adjusted themselves. They may not be a complete picture of the world, but they are a picture of a possible world to which we are adapted. In that world people and things have their well-known places, and do certain expected things. We feel at home there. We fit in. We are members. We know the way around. There we find the charm of the familiar, the normal, the dependable; its grooves and shapes are where we are accustomed to find them. And though we have abandoned much that might have tempted us before we creased ourselves into that mould, once we are firmly in, it fits as snugly as an old shoe.

No wonder, then, that any disturbance of the stereotypes seems like an attack upon the foundation of the universe. It is an attack upon the foundations of *our* universe, and, where big things are at stake, we do not readily admit that there is any distinction between our universe and the universe. A world which turns out to be one in which those we honor are unworthy, and those we despise are noble, is nerve-racking. There is anarchy if our order of precedence is not the only possible one. For if the meek should indeed inherit the earth, if the first should be last, if those who are without sin alone may cast a stone, if to Caesar you render only the things that are Caesar's, then the foundations of self-respect would be shaken for those who have arranged their lives as if these maxims were not true.

A pattern of stereotypes is no neutral. It is not merely a way of substituting order for the great blooming, buzzing confusion of reality. It is not merely a short cut. It is all these things and something more. It is the guarantee of our self-respect; it is the projection upon the world of our own sense of our own value, our own position and our own rights. The stereotypes are, therefore, highly charged with the feelings that are attached to them. They are the fortress of our tradition, and behind its defenses we can continue to feel ourselves safe in the position we occupy.

XIV.

When, for example, in the fourth century B. C., Aristotle wrote his
defense of slavery in the face of increasing skepticism,[1] the Athenian slaves
were in great part indistinguishable from free citizens. Mr. Zimmern
quotes an amusing passage from the Old Oligarch explaining the good
treatment of the slaves. "Suppose it were legal for a slave to be beaten by
a citizen, it would frequently happen that an Athenian might be mistaken
for a slave or an alien and receive a beating;—since the Athenian people
is not better clothed than the slave or alien, nor in personal appearance
is there any superiority." This absence of distinction would naturally tend
to dissolve the institution. If free men and slaves looked alike, what basis
was there for treating them so differently? It was this confusion which
Aristotle set himself to clear away in the first book of his Politics. With
unerring instinct he understood that to justify slavery he must teach the
Greeks a way of *seeing* their slaves that comported with the continuance
of slavery.

So, said Aristotle, there are beings who are slaves by nature.[2] "He then
is by nature formed a slave, who is fitted to become the chattel of another
person, *and on that account is so*." All this really says is that whoever
happens to be a slave is by nature intended to be one. Logically the statement is worthless, but in fact it is not a proposition at all, and logic has
nothing to do with it. It is a stereotype, or rather it is part of a stereotype.
The rest follows almost immediatetly. After asserting that slaves perceive
reason, but are not endowed with the use of it, Aristotle insists that "it is
the intention of nature to make the bodies of slaves and free men different
from each other, that the one should be robust for their necessary purposes, but the other erect; useless indeed for such servile labours, but fit
for civil life. . . . It is clear then that some men are free by nature, and
other are slaves. . . ."

If we ask ourselves what is the matter with Aristotle's argument, we find
that he has begun by erecting a great barrier between himself and the
facts. When he had said that those who are slaves are by nature intended
to be slaves, he at one stroke excluded the fatal question whether those
particular men who happened to be slaves were the particular men intended by nature to be slaves. For that question would have tainted each
case of slavery with doubt. And since the fact of being a slave was not
evidence that a man was destined to be one, no certain test would have
remained. Aristotle, therefore, excluded entirely that destructive doubt.
Those who are slaves are intended to be slaves. Each slave holder was
to look upon his chattels as natural slaves. When his eye had been trained

[1] Zimmern: *Greek Commonwealth*. See his footnote, p. 383.
[2] *Politics*, Bk. 1, Ch. 5.

to see them that way, he was to note as confirmation of their servile character the fact that they performed servile work, that they were competent to do servile work, and that they had the muscles to do servile work.

This is the perfect stereotype. Its hallmark is that it precedes the use of reason; is a form of perception, imposes a certain character on the data of our senses before the data reach the intelligence. The stereotype is like the lavender window-panes on Beacon Street, like the doorkeeper at a costume ball who judges whether the guest has an appropriate masquerade. There is nothing so obdurate to education or to criticism as the stereotype. It stamps itself upon the evidence in the very act of securing the evidence. That is why the accounts of returning travellers are often an interesting tale of what the traveller carried abroad with him on his trip. If he carried chiefly his appetite, a zeal for tiled bathrooms, a conviction that the Pullman car is the acme of human comfort, and a belief that it is proper to tip waiters, taxicab drivers, and barbers, but under no circumstances station agents and ushers, then his Odyssey will be replete with good meals and bad meals, bathing adventures, compartment-train escapades, and voracious demands for money. Or if he is a more serious soul he may while on tour have found himself at celebrated spots. Having touched base, and cast one furtive glance at the monument, he buried his head in Baedeker, read every word through, and moved on to the next celebrated spot; and thus returned with a compact and orderly impression of Europe, rated one star, or two.

In some measure, stimuli from the outside, especially when they are printed or spoken words, evoke some part of a system of stereotypes, so that the actual sensation and the preconception occupy consciousness at the same time. The two are blended, much as if we looked at red through blue glasses and saw green. If what we are looking at corresponds successfully with what we anticipated, the stereotype is reinforced for the future, as it is in a man who knows in advance that the Japanese are cunning and has the bad luck to run across two dishonest Japanese.

If the experience contradicts the stereotype, one of two things happens. If the man is no longer plastic, or if some powerful interest makes it highly inconvenient to rearrange his stereotypes, he pooh-poohs the contradiction as an exception that proves the rule, discredits the witness, finds a flaw somewhere, and manages to forget it. But if he is still curious and open-minded, the novelty is taken into the picture, and allowed to modify it. Sometimes, if the incident is striking enough, and if he has felt a general discomfort with his established scheme, he may be shaken to such an extent as to distrust all accepted ways of looking at life, and to expect that normally a thing will not be what it is generally supposed to be. In the extreme case, especially if he is literary, he may develop a passion for inverting the moral canon by making Judas, Benedict Arnold, or Caesar Borgia the hero of his tale.

2. Herbert Spencer

The Class Bias

From the intrinsic natures of its facts, from our own natures as observers of its facts, and from the peculiar relation in which we stand towards the facts to be observed, there arise impediments in the way of Sociology greater than those in the way of any other science.

The phenomena to be generalized are not of a directly-perceptible kind—cannot be noted by telescope and clock, like those of Astronomy; cannot be measured by dynamometer and thermometer, like those of Physics; cannot be elucidated by scales and test-papers, like those of Chemistry; are not to be got at by scalpel and microscope, like the less obvious biological phenomena; nor are to be recognized by introspection, like the phenomena Psychology deals with. They have severally to be established by putting together many details, no one of which is simple, and which are dispersed, both in Space and Time, in ways that make them difficult of access. Hence the reason why even cardinal truths in Sociology, such as the division of labour, remain long unrecognized. That in advanced societies men follow different occupations, was indeed a generalization easy to make; but that this form of social arrangement had neither been specially created, nor enacted by a king, but had grown up without forethought of any one, was a conclusion which could be reached only after many transactions of many kinds between men had been noted, remembered, and accounted for, and only after comparisons had been made between these transactions and those taking place between men in simpler societies and in earlier times. And when it is remembered that the data for the inference that labour becomes specialized, are far more accessible than the data for most other sociological inferences, it will be seen how greatly the advance of Sociology is hindered by the nature of its subject-matter.

The characters of men as observers, add to this first difficulty a second that is perhaps equally great. Necessarily men take with them into sociological inquiries, the modes of observation and reasoning which they have been accustomed to in other inquiries—those of them, at least, who

From Spencer, *The Study of Sociology* (New York: D. Appleton & Co., 1874), pp. 72-74, 241-262.

make any inquiries worthy to be so called. Passing over the great majority of the educated, and limiting ourselves to the very few who consciously collect data, compare them, and deliberately draw conclusions; we may see that even these have to struggle with the difficulty that the habits of thought generated by converse with relatively-simple phenomena, partially unfit them for converse with these highly-complex phenomena. Faculty of every kind tends always to adjust itself to its work. Special adjustment to one kind of work involves more or less non-adjustment to other kinds. And hence, intellects disciplined in dealing with less-involved classes of facts, cannot successfully deal with this most-involved class of facts without partially unlearning the methods they have learnt. From the emotional nature, too, there arise great obstacles. Scarcely any one can contemplate social arrangements and actions with the unconcern felt when contemplating arrangements and actions of other kinds. For correct observation and correct drawing of inferences, there needs the calmness that is ready to recognize or to infer one truth as readily as another. But it is next to impossible thus to deal with the truths of Sociology. In the search for them, each is moved by feelings, more or less strong, which make him eager to find this evidence, oblivious of that which is at variance with it, reluctant to draw any conclusion but that already drawn. And though perhaps one in ten among those who think, is conscious that his judgment is being warped by prejudice, yet even in him the warp is not adequately allowed for. Doubtless in nearly every field of inquiry emotion is a perturbing intruder: mostly there is some preconception, and some *amour propre* that resist disproof of it. But a peculiarity of Sociology is, that the emotions with which its facts and conclusions are regarded, have unusual strength. The personal interests are directly affected; or there is gratification or offence to sentiments that have grown out of them; or else other sentiments which have relation to the existing form of society, are excited, agreeably or disagreeably.

And here we are introduced to the third kind of difficulty—that caused by the position occupied, in respect to the phenomena to be generalized. In no other case has the inquirer to investigate the properties of an aggregate in which he is himself included. His relation towards the facts he here studies, we may figure to ourselves by comparing it to the relation between a single cell forming part of a living body, and the facts which that living body presents as a whole. Speaking generally, the citizen's life is made possible only by due performance of his function in the place he fills; and he cannot wholly free himself from the beliefs and sentiments generated by the vital connexions hence arising between himself and his society. Here, then, is a difficulty to which no other science presents anything analogous. To cut himself off in thought from all his relationships of race, and country, and citizenship—to get rid of all those interests, prejudices, likings, superstitions, generated in him by the life of his own society and his own time—to look on all the changes societies have undergone and are undergoing, without reference to nationality, or creed, or personal welfare; is what the average man cannot do at all, and what the exceptional man can do very imperfectly.

The difficulties of the Social Science, thus indicated in vague outline, have now to be described and illustrated in detail.

Many years ago a solicitor sitting by me at dinner, complained bitterly of the injury which the then lately-established County Courts, were doing his profession. He enlarged on the topic in a way implying that he expected me to agree with him in therefore condemning them. So incapable was he of going beyond the professional point of view, that what he regarded as a grievance he thought I also ought to regard as a grievance: oblivious of the fact that the more economical administration of justice of which his lamentation gave me proof, was to me, not being a lawyer, matter for rejoicing.

The bias thus exemplified is a bias by which nearly all have their opinions warped. Naval officers disclose their unhesitating belief that we are in imminent danger because the cry for more fighting ships and more sailors has not been met to their satisfaction. The debates on the purchase-system proved how strong was the conviction of military men that our national safety depended on the maintenance of an army-organization like that in which they were brought up, and had attained their respective ranks. Clerical opposition to the Corn-Laws showed how completely that view which Christian ministers might have been expected to take, was shut out by a view more congruous with their interests and alliances. In all classes and sub-classes it is the same. Hear the murmurs uttered when, because of the Queen's absence, there is less expenditure in entertainments and the so-called gaieties of the season, and you perceive that London traders think the nation suffers if the consumption of superfluities is checked. Study the pending controversy about co-operative stores *versus* retail shops, and you find the shop-keeping mind possessed by the idea that Society commits a wrong if it deserts shops and goes to stores—is quite unconscious that the present distributing system rightly exists only as a means of economically and conveniently supplying consumers, and must yield to another system if that should prove more economical and convenient. Similarly with other trading bodies, general and special—similarly with the merchants who opposed the repeal of the Navigation Laws; similarly with the Coventry-weavers, who like free-trade in all things save ribbons.

The class-bias, like the bias of patriotism, is a reflex egoism; and like it has its uses and abuses. As the strong attachments citizens feel for their nation cause that enthusiastic cooperation by which its integrity is main-

tained in presence of other nations, severally tending to spread and subjugate their neighbours; so the *esprit de corps* more or less manifest in
each specialized part of the body politic, prompts measures to preserve the integrity of that part in opposition to other parts, all somewhat
antagonistic. The egoism of individuals leads to an egoism of the class
they form; and besides the separate efforts, generates a joint effort to get
an undue share of the aggregate proceeds of social activity. The aggressive
tendency of each class, thus produced, has to be balanced by like aggressive tendencies of other classes. The implied feelings do, in short, develop
one another; and the respective organizations in which they embody themselves develop one another. Large classes of the community marked-off
by rank, and sub-classes marked-off by special occupations, severally combine, and severally set up organs advocating their interests: the reason
assigned being in all cases the same—the need for self-defence.

Along with the good which a society derives from this self-asserting and
self-preserving action, by which each division and sub-division keeps itself
strong enough for its functions, there goes, among other evils, this which
we are considering—the aptness to contemplate all social arrangements in
their bearings on class-interests, and the resulting inability to estimate
rightly their effects on Society as a whole. The habit of thought produced
perverts not merely the judgments on questions which directly touch class-
welfare; but it perverts the judgments on questions which touch class-
welfare very indirectly, if at all. It fosters an adapted theory of social
relations of every kind, with sentiments to fit the theory; and a characteristic stamp is given to the beliefs on public matters in general. Take an
instance.

Whatever its technical ownership may be, Hyde Park is open for the
public benefit: no title to special benefit is producible by those who ride
and drive. It happens, however, that those who ride and drive make large
use of it daily; and extensive tracts of it have been laid out for their convenience: the tracts for equestrians having been from time to time increased. Of people without carriages and horses, a few, mostly of the kinds
who lead easy lives, use Hyde Park frequently as a promenade. Meanwhile, by the great mass of Londoners, too busy to go so far, it is scarcely
ever visited: their share of the general benefit is scarcely appreciable.
And now what do the few who have a constant and almost exclusive use of
it, think about the occasional use of it by the many? They are angry when,
at long intervals, even a small portion of it, quite distant from their
haunts, is occupied for a few hours in ways disagreeable to them—nay,
even when such temporary occupation is on a day during which Rotten
Row is nearly vacant and the drives not one-third filled. In this, anyone
unconcerned may see the influence of the class-bias. But he will have an
inadequate conception of its distorting power unless he turns to some
letters from members of the ruling class published in the *Times* in Novem-

ber last, when the question of the Park-Rules was being agitated. One writer, signing himself "A Liberal M.P.," expressing his disgust at certain addresses he heard, proposed, if others would join him, to give the offensive speakers punishment by force of fists; and then, on a subsequent day, another legislator, similarly moved, writes:—

"If 'M.P.' is in earnest in his desire to get some honest men together to take the law into their own hands, I can promise him a pretty good backing from those who are not afraid to take all the consequences.
                    "I am, Sir, your obedient servant,
                                                    "AN EX-M.P."

And thus we find class-feeling extinguishing rational political thinking so completely that, wonderful to relate, two law-makers propose to support the law by breaking the law!

In larger ways we have of late seen the class-bias doing the same thing—causing contempt for those principles of constitutional government slowly and laboriously established, and prompting a return to barbaric principles of government. Read the debate about the payment of Governor Eyre's expenses, and study the division-lists, and you see that acts which, according to the Lord Chief Justice, "have brought reproach not only on those who were parties to them, but on the very name of England," can nevertheless find numerous defenders among men whose class-positions, military, naval, official, &c., make them love power and detest resistance. Nay more, by raising an Eyre-Testimonial Fund and in other ways, there was shown a deliberate approval of acts which needlessly suspended orderly government and substituted unrestrained despotism. There was shown a deliberate ignoring of the essential question raised, which was—whether an executive head might, at will, set aside all those forms of administration by which men's lives and liberties are guarded against tyranny.

More recently, this same class-bias has been shown by the protest made when Mr. Cowan was dismissed for executing the Kooka rioters who had surrendered. The Indian Government, having inquired into the particulars, found that this killing of many men without form of law and contrary to orders, could not be defended on the plea of pressing danger; and finding this, it ceased to employ the officer who had committed so astounding a deed, and removed to another province the superior officer who had approved of the deed. Not excessive punishment, one would say. Some might contend that extreme mildness was shown in thus inflicting no greater evil than is inflicted on a labourer when he does not execute his work properly. But now mark what is thought by one who displays in words the bias of the governing classes, intensified by life in India. In a letter published in the *Times* of May 15, 1872, the late Sir Donald M'Leod writes concerning this dismissal and removal:—

"All the information that reaches me tends to prove that a severe blow has been given to all chance of vigorous or independent action in future, when emergencies may arise. The whole service appears to have been astonished and appalled by the mode in which the officers have been dealt with."

That we may see clearly what amazing perversions of sentiment and idea are caused by contemplating actions from class points of view, let us turn from this feeling of sympathy with Mr. Cowan, to the feeling of detestation shown by members of the same class in England towards a man who kills a fox that destroys his poultry. Here is a paragraph from a recent paper:—

"Five poisoned foxes have been found in the neighbourhood of Penzance, and there is consequently great indignation among the western sportsmen. A reward of 20l. has been offered for information that shall lead to the conviction of the poisoner."

So that wholesale homicide, condemned alike by religion, by equity, by law, is approved, and the mildest punishment of it blamed; while vulpicide, committed in defence of property, and condemned neither by religion, nor by equity, nor by any law save that of sportsmen, excites an anger that cries aloud for positive penalties!

I need not further illustrate the more special distortions of sociological belief which result from the class-bias. They may be detected in the conversations over every table, and in the articles appearing in every party-journal or professional publication. The effects here most worthy of our attention are the general effects—the effects produced on the minds of the upper and lower classes. Let us observe how greatly the prejudices generated by their respective social positions, pervert the conceptions of employers and employed. We will deal with the employed first.

As before shown, mere associations of ideas, especially when joined with emotions, affect our beliefs, not simply without reason but in spite of reason—causing us, for instance, to think there is something intrinsically repugnant in a place where many painful experiences have been received, and something intrinsically charming in a scene connected with many past delights. The liability to such perversions of judgment is greatest where *persons* are the objects with which pleasures and pains are habitually associated. One who has often been, even unintentionally, a cause of gratification, is favourably judged; and an unfavourable judgment is formed of one who, even involuntarily, has often inflicted sufferings. Hence, when there are social antagonisms, arises the universal tendency to blame the *individuals,* and to hold them responsible for the *system.*

It is thus with the conceptions the working-classes frame of those by whom they are immediately employed, and of those who fill the higher social positions. Feeling keenly what they have to bear, and tracing sundry real grievances to men who buy their labour and men who are most influential in making the laws, artizans and rustics conclude that, considered

individually and in combination, those above them are personally bad
—selfish, or tyrannical, in special degrees. It never occurs to them that
the evils they complain of result from the average human nature of our
age. And yet were it not for the class-bias, they would see in their dealings
with one another, plenty of proofs that the injustices they suffer are
certainly not greater, and possibly less, than they would be were the
higher social functions discharged by individuals taken from among themselves. The simple fact, notorious enough, that working-men who save
money and become masters, are not more considerate than usual towards
those they employ, but often the contrary, might alone convince them
of this. On all sides there is ample evidence having kindred meaning. Let
them inquire about the life in every kitchen where there are several
servants, and they will find quarrels about supremacy, tyrannies over
juniors who are made to do more than their proper work, throwings of
blame from one to another, and the many forms of misconduct caused by
want of right feeling; and very often the evils growing up in one of these
small groups exceed in intensity the evils pervading society at large. The
doings in workshops, too, illustrate in various ways the ill-treatment
of artizans by one another. Hiding the tools and spoiling the work of
those who do not conform to their unreasonable customs, prove how little
individual freedom is respected among them. And still more conspicuously
is this proved by the internal governments of their trade-combinations. Not
to dwell on the occasional killing of men among them who assert their
rights to sell their labour as they please, or on the frequent acts of violence
and intimidation committed by those on strike against those who undertake the work they have refused, it suffices to cite the despotism exercised
by trades-union officers. The daily acts of these make it manifest that the
ruling powers set up by working-men, inflict on them grievances as great
as, if not greater than, those inflicted by the ruling powers, political and
social, which they decry. When the heads of an association he has joined
forbid a collier to work more than three days in the week—when he is
limited to a certain "get" in that space of time—when he dares not accept
from his employer an increasing bonus for every extra day he works—
when, as a reason for declining, he says that he should be made miserable
by his comrades, and that even his wife would not be spoken to; it becomes clear that he and the rest have made for themselves a tyranny worse
than the tyrannies complained of. Did he look at the facts apart from
class-bias, the skilful artizan, who in a given time can do more than his
fellows, but who dares not do it because he would be "sent to Coventry"
by them, and who consequently cannot reap the benefit of his superior
powers, would see that he is thus aggressed upon by his fellows more
seriously than by Acts of Parliament or combinations of capitalists. And
he would further see that the sentiment of justice in his own class is
certainly not greater than in the classes he thinks so unjust.

The feeling which thus warps working-men's conceptions, at the same time prevents them from seeing that each of their unions is selfishly aiming to benefit at the expense of the industrial population at large. When an association of carpenters or of engineers makes rules limiting the number of apprentices admitted, with the view of maintaining the rate of wages paid to its members—when it thus tacitly says to every applicant beyond the number allowed, "Go and apprentice yourself else-where;" it is indirectly saying to all other bodies of artizans, "You may have your wages lowered by increasing your numbers, but we will not." And when the other bodies of artizans severally do the like, the general result is that the incorporated workers of all orders, say to the surplus sons of workers who want to find occupations, "We will none of us let our masters employ you." Thus each trade, in its eagerness for self-protection, is regardless of other trades, and sacrifices numbers among the rising generation of the artizan-class. Nor is it thus only that the interest of each class of artizans is pursued to the detriment of the artizan-class in general. I do not refer to the way in which when bricklayers strike they throw out of employment the labourers who attend them, or to the way in which the colliers now on strike have forced idleness on the ironworkers; but I refer to the way in which the course taken by any one set of opera-tives to get higher wages, is taken regardless of the fact that an eventual rise in the price of the commodity produced, is a disadvantage to all other operatives. The class-bias, fostering the belief that the question in each case is entirely one between employer and employed, between capital and labour, shuts out the truth that the interests of all consumers are involved, and that the immense majority of consumers belong to the working-classes themselves. If the consumers are named, such of them only are remem-bered as belong to the wealthier classes, who, it is thought, can well afford to pay higher prices. Listen to a passage from Mr. George Potter's paper read at the late Leeds Congress:—

"The consumer, in fact, in so high a civilization, so arrogant a luxuriousness, and so impatient an expectancy as characterize him in our land and age, is ever ready to take the alarm and to pour out the vials of his wrath upon those whom he merely suspects of taking a course which may keep a feather out of his bed, a spice out of his dish, or a coal out of his fire; and, unfortunately for the chances of fairness, the weight of his anger seldom falls upon the capitalists, but is most certain to come crushing down upon the lowly labourer, who has dared to stand upon his own right and independence."

From which it might be supposed that all skilled and unskilled artizans, all farm-labourers, all other workers, with all their wives and children, live upon air—need no food, no clothing, no furniture, no houses, and are therefore unaffected by enhanced prices of commodities. However fully prepared for the distorting effects of class-bias, one would hardly have expected effects so great. One would have thought it manifest even to an extreme partizan of trades-unions, that a strike which makes coals as dear again, affects in a relatively-small degree the thousands of rich consumers above described, and is very keenly felt by the millions of poor consumers, to whom in winter the outlay for coal is a serious item of expenditure. One would have thought that a truth so obvious in this case, would be recognized throughout—the truth that with nearly all products of industry, the evil caused by a rise of price falls more heavily on the vast numbers who work for wages than on the small numbers who have moderate incomes or large incomes.

Were not their judgments warped by the class-bias, workingmen might be more pervious to the truth that better forms of industrial organization would grow up and exinguish the forms which they regard as oppressive, were such better forms practicable. And they might see that the impracticability of better forms results from the imperfections of existing human nature, moral and intellectual. If the workers in any business could so combine and govern themselves that the share of profit coming to them as workers was greater than now, while the interest on the capital employed was less than now; and if they could at the same time sell the articles produced at lower rates than like articles produced in businesses managed as at present; then, manifestly, businesses managed as at present would go to the wall. That they do not go to the wall—that such better industrial organizations do not replace them, implies that the natures of working-men themselves are not good enough; or, at least, that there are not many of them good enough. Happily, to some extent organizations of a superior type are becoming possible: here and there they have achieved encouraging successes. But, speaking generally, the masses are neither sufficiently provident, nor sufficiently conscientious, nor sufficiently intelligent. Consider the evidence.

That they are not provident enough they show both by wasting their higher wages when they get them, and by neglecting such opportunities as occur of entering into modified forms of co-operative industry. When the Gloucester Waggon Company was formed, it was decided to reserve a thousand of its shares, of £10 each, for the workmen employed; and to suit them, it was arranged that the calls of a pound each should be at intervals of three months. As many of the men earned £2 10s. per week, in a locality where living is not costly, it was considered that the taking-up of shares in this manner would be quite practicable. All the circumstances were at the outset such as to promise that prosperity which the company has since achieved. The chairman is no less remarkable for his skill in the conduct of large undertakings than for that sympathy with the working-classes which led him to adopt this course. The manager had been a working-man; and possessed the confidence of working-men in so high a degree, that many migrated with him from the Midland counties when the company was formed. Further, the manager entered heartily into the plan—telling me himself, that he had rejoiced over the founding of a concern in which those employed would have an interest. His hopes, however, and those of the chairman, were disappointed. After the lapse of a year not one of the thousand shares was taken up; and they were then distributed among the proprietors. Doubtless, there have been in other cases more encouraging results. But this case is one added to others which show that the proportion of working-men adequately provident, is not great enough to permit an extensive growth of better industrial organizations.

Again, the success of industrial organizations higher in type, requires in the members a nicer sense of justice than is at present general. Closer co-operation implies greater mutual trust; and greater mutual trust is not possible without more respect for one another's claims. When we find that in sick-clubs it is not uncommon for members to continue receiving aid when they are able to work, so that spies have to be set to check them; while, on the other hand, those who administer the funds often cause insolvency by embezzling them; we cannot avoid the inference that want of conscientiousness prevents the effective union of workers under no regulation but their own. When, among skilled labourers, we find a certain rate per hour demanded, because less "did not suffice for their natural wants," though the unskilled labourers working under them were receiving little more than half the rate per hour, and were kept out of the skilled class by stringent rules, we do not discover a moral sense so much above that shown by employers as to promise success for industrial combinations superior to our present ones. While workmen think themselves justified in combining to sell their labour only on certain terms, but think masters not justified in combining to buy it only on certain terms, they show a conception of equity not high enough to make practicable a form of co-operation requiring that each shall recognize the claims of others as fully as his own. One pervading misconception of justice betrayed by them would alone suffice to cause failure—the misconception, namely, that justice requires an equal sharing of benefits among producers, instead of requiring, as it does, equal freedom to make the best of their faculties. The general policy of trades-unionism, tending everywhere to restrain the superior from profiting by his superiority lest the inferior should be disadvantaged, is a policy which, acted out in any industrial combinations, must make them incapable of competing with combinations based on the principle that benefit gained shall be portioned to faculty put forth.

Thus, as acting on the employed in general, the class-bias obscures the truth, otherwise not easy to see, that the existing type of industrial organization, like the existing type of political organization, is about as good as existing human nature allows. The evils there are in it are nothing but the evils brought round on men by their own imperfections. The relation of master and workman has to be tolerated, because, for the time being, no other will answer as well. Looked at apart from special interests, this organization of industry we now see around us, must be considered as one in which the cost of regulation, though not so great as it once was, is still excessive. In any industrial combination there must be a regulating agency. That regulating agency, whatever its nature, must be paid for— must involve a deduction from the total proceeds of the labour regulated. The present system is one under which the share of the total proceeds that goes to pay for regulation, is considerable; and under better systems to be expected hereafter, there will doubtless be a decrease in the cost of regulation. But, for the present, our comparatively-costly system has the justification that it alone succeeds. Regulation is costly because the men to be regulated are defective. With decrease of their defects will come economy of regulation, and consequently greater shares of profit to themselves.

Let me not be misunderstood. The foregoing criticism does not imply that operatives have no grievances to complain of; nor does it imply that trade-combinations and strikes are without adequate justifications. It is quite possible to hold that when, instead of devouring their captured enemies, men made slaves of them, the change was a step in advance; and to hold that this slavery, though absolutely bad, was relatively good— was the best thing practicable for the time being. It is quite possible also to hold that when slavery gave place to a serfdom under which certain personal rights were recognized, the new arrangement, though in the abstract an inequitable one, was more equitable than the old, and constituted as great an amelioration as men's natures then permitted. It is quite possible to hold that when, instead of serfs, there came free men working for wages, but held as a class in extreme subordination, this modified relation of employers and employed, though bad, was as good a one as could then be established. And so it may be held that at the present time, though the form of industrial government entails serious evils, those evils, much less than the evils of past times, are as small as the average human nature allows—are not due to any special injustice of the employing class, and can be remedied only as fast as men in general advance. On the other hand, while contending that the policy of trades-unions and the actions of men on strike, manifest an injustice as great as that shown by the employing classes, it is quite consistent to admit, and even to assert, that the evil acts of trade-combinations are the unavoidable accompaniments of a needful self-defence. Selfishness on the one side resisting selfishness on the other, inevitably commits sins akin to those it complains of—cannot effectually check harsh dealings without itself using harsh measures. Further, it may be fully admitted that the evils of working-class combinations, great as they are, go along with certain benefits, and will hereafter be followed by greater benefits—are evils involved by the transition to better arrangements.

Here my purpose is neither to condemn nor to applaud the ideas and actions of the employed in their dealings with employers; but simply to point out how the class-bias warps working-men's judgments of social relations—makes it difficult for working-men to see that our existing industrial system is a product of existing human nature, and can be improved only as fast as human nature improves.

The ruling and employing classes display an equally-strong bias of the opposite kind. From their point of view, the behaviour of their poorer fellow-citizens throughout these struggles appears uniformly blamable. That they experience from a strike inconvenience more or less considerable, sufficiently proves to them that the strike must be wrong. They think there is something intolerable in this independence which leads to refusals to work except at higher wages or for shorter times. That the many should be so reckless of the welfare of the few, seems to the few a grievance not to be endured. Though Mr. George Potter, as shown above, wrongly speaks of the consumer as though he were always rich, instead of being, in nine cases out of ten, poor; yet he rightly describes the rich consumer as indignant when operatives dare to take a course which threatens to raise the prices of necessaries and make luxuries more costly. This feeling, often betrayed in private, exhibited itself in public on the occasion of the late strike among the gas-stokers; when there were uttered proposals that acts entailing so much annoyance should be put down with a strong hand. And the same spirit was shown in that straining of the law which brought on the men the punishment for conspiracy, instead of the punishment for breach of contract; which was well deserved, and would have been quite sufficient.

This mental attitude of the employing classes is daily shown by the criticisms passed on servants. Read *The Greatest Plague in Life,* or listen to the complaints of every housewife, and you see that the minds of masters and mistresses are so much occupied with their own interests as to leave little room for the interests of the men and maids in their service. The very title, *The Greatest Plague in Life,* implies that the only life worthy of notice is the life to which servants minister; and there is an entire unconsciousness that a book with the same title, written by a servants about masters and mistresses, might be filled with equally-severe criticisms and grievances far more serious. The increasing independence of servants is enlarged upon as a change greatly to be lamented. There is no recognition of the fact that this increasing independence implies an increasing prosperity of the classes from which servants come; and that this amelioration in the condition of the many is a good far greater than the evil entailed on the few. It is not perceived that if servants, being in great demand and easily able to get places, will no longer submit to restrictions, say about dress, like those of past times, the change is part of the progress towards a social state which, if apparently not so convenient for the small regulating classes, implies an elevation of the large regulated classes.

The feeling shown by the rich in their thoughts about, and dealings with, the poor, is, in truth, but a mitigated form of the feeling which owners of serfs and owners of slaves displayed. In early times bondsmen were treated as though they existed simply for the benefit of their owners; and down to the present time the belief pervading the select ranks (not indeed expressed but clearly enough implied) is, that the convenience of the select is the first consideration, and the welfare of the masses a secondary consideration. Just as an Old English thane would have been astonished if told that the only justification for his existence as an owner of thralls, was that the lives of his thralls were on the whole better preserved and more comfortable than they would be did he not own them; so, now, it will astonish the dominant classes to assert that their only legitimate *raison d'être* is that by their instrumentality as regulators, the lives of the people are, on the average, made more satisfactory than they would otherwise be. And yet, looked at apart from class-bias, this is surely an undeniable truth. Ethically considered, there has never been any warrant for the subjection of the many to the few, except that it has furthered the welfare of the many; and at the present time, furtherance of the welfare of the many is the only warrant for that degree of class-subordination which continues. The existing conception must be, in the end, entirely changed. Just as the old theory of political government has been so transformed that the ruling agent, instead of being owner of the nation, has come to be regarded as servant of the nation; so the old theory of industrial and social government has to undergo a transformation which will make the regulating classes feel, while duly pursuing their own interests, that their interests are secondary to the interests of the masses whose labours they direct.

While the bias of rulers and masters makes it difficult for them to conceive this, it also makes it difficult for them to conceive that a decline of class-power and a decrease of class-distinction may be accompanied by improvement not only in the lives of the regulated classes, but in the lives of the regulating classes. The sentiments and ideas proper to the existing social organization, prevent the rich from seeing that worry and weariness and disappointment result to them indirectly from this social system apparently so conducive to their welfare. Yet, would they contemplate the past, they might find strong reasons for suspecting as much. The baron of feudal days never imagined the possibility of social arrangements that would serve him far better than the arrangements he so strenuously upheld; nor did he see in the arrangements he upheld the causes of his many sufferings and discomforts. Had he been told that a noble might be much happier without a moated castle, having its keep and secret passages and dungeons for prisoners—that he might be more secure without drawbridge and portcullis, men-at-arms and sentinels—that he might be in less danger having no vassals or hired mercenaries—that he might be wealthier without possessing a single serf; he would have thought the statements absurd even to the extent of insanity. It would have been useless to argue that the *régime* seeming so advantageous to him, entailed hardships of many kinds—perpetual feuds with his neighbours, open attacks, surprises, betrayals, revenges by equals, treacheries by inferiors; the continual carrying of arms and wearing of armour: the perpetual quarrellings of servants and disputes among vassals; the coarse and unvaried food supplied by an unprosperous agriculture; a domestic discomfort such as no modern servant would tolerate; resulting in a wear and tear that brought life to a comparatively-early close, if it was not violently cut short in battle or by murder. Yet what the class-bias of that time made it impossible for him to see, has become to his modern representative conspicuous enough. The peer of our day knows that he is better off without defensive appliances and retainers and serfs than his predecessor was with them. His country-house is more secure than was an embattled tower; he is safer among his unarmed domestics than a feudal lord was when surrounded by armed guards; he is in less danger going about weaponless than was the mail-clad knight with lance and sword. Though he has no vassals to fight at his command, there is no suzerain who can call on him to sacrifice his life in a quarrel not his own; though he can compel no one to labour, the labours of freemen make him immensely more wealthy than was the ancient holder of bondsmen; and along with the loss of direct control over workers, there has grown up an industrial system which supplies him with multitudinous conveniences and luxuries undreamt of by him who had workers at his mercy.

May we not, then, infer that just as the dominant classes of ancient days were prevented by the feelings and ideas appropriate to the then-existing social state, from seeing how much evil it brought on them, and how much better for them might be a social state in which their power was much less; so the dominant classes of the present day are prevented from seeing how the existing forms of class-subordination redound to their own injury, and how much happier may be their future representatives having social positions less prominent? Occasionally recognizing, though they do, certain indirect evils attending their supremacy, they do not see that by accumulation these indirect evils constitute a penalty which supremacy brings on them. Though they repeat the trite reflection that riches fail to purchase content, they do not draw the inference that there must be something wrong in a system which thus deludes them. You hear it from time to time admitted that great wealth is a heavy burden: the life of a rich peer being described as made like the life of an attorney by the extent of his affairs. You observe among those whose large means and various estates enable them to multiply their appliances to gratification, that every new appliance becomes an additional something to be looked after, and adds to the possibilities of vexation. Further, if you put together the open confessions and the tacit admissions, you find that, apart from these anxieties and annoyances, the kind of life which riches and honours bring is not a satisfactory life—its inside differs immensely from its outside. In candid moments the "social treadmill" is complained of by those who nevertheless think themselves compelled to keep up its monotonous round. As everyone may see, fashionable life is passed, not in being happy, but in playing at being happy. And yet the manifest corollary is not drawn by those engaged in this life.

To an outsider it is obvious that the benefits obtained by the regulative classes of our day, through the existing form of social organization, are full of disguised evils; and that this undue wealth which makes possible the passing of idle lives brings dissatisfactions in place of the satisfactions expected. Just as in feudal times the appliances for safety were the accompaniments to a social state that brought a more than equivalent danger; so, now, the excess of aids to pleasure among the rich is the accompaniment of a social state that brings a counterbalancing displeasure. The gratifications reached by those who make the pursuit of gratifications a business, dwindle to a minimum; while the trouble, and weariness, and vexation, and jealousy, and disappointment, rise to a maximum. That this is an inevitable result any one may see who studies the psychology of the matter. The pleasure-hunting life fails for the reason that it leaves large parts of the nature unexercised: it neglects the satisfactions gained by successful activity, and there is missing from it the serene consciousness of services rendered to others. Egoistic enjoyments continuously pursued, pall because the appetites for them are satiated in times much shorter than our waking lives give us: leaving times that are either empty or spent in efforts to get enjoyment after desire has ceased. They pall also from the want of that broad contrast which arises when a moiety of life is actively occupied. These negative causes of dissatisfaction are joined with the positive cause indicated—the absence of that content gained by successful achievement. One of the most massive and enduring gratifications is the sense of personal worth, ever afresh demonstrating itself to consciousness by effectual action; and an idle life is balked of its hopes partly because it lacks this. Lastly, the implied neglect of altruistic activities, or of activities felt to be in some way serviceable to others, brings kindred evils —a deficiency of certain positive pleasures of a high order, not easily exhausted, and a further falling-back on egoistic pleasures, again tending towards satiety. And all this, with its resulting weariness and discontent, we may trace to a social organization under which there comes to the regulating classes a share of produce great enough to make possible large accumulations that support useless descendants.

The bias of the wealthy in favour of arrangements apparently so conducive to their comforts and pleasures, while it shuts out the perception of these indirect penalties brought round on them by their seeming advantages, also shuts out the perception that there is anything mean in being a useless consumer of things which others produce. Contrariwise, there still survives, though much weakened, the belief that it is honourable to do nothing but seek enjoyment, and relatively dishonourable to pass life in supplying others with the means to enjoyment. In this, as in other things, our temporary state brings a temporary standard of honour appropriate to it; and the accompanying sentiments and ideas exclude the conception of a state in which what is now thought admirable will be thought disgraceful. Yet it needs only, as before, to aid imagination by studying other times and other societies, remote in nature from our own, to see at least the possibility of this. When we contrast the feeling of the Fijians, among whom a man has a restless ambition to be acknowledged as a murderer, with the feeling among civilized races, who shrink with horror from a murderer, we get undeniable proof that men in one social state pride themselves in characters and deeds elsewhere held in the greatest detestation. Seeing which, we may infer that just as the Fijians, believing in the honourableness of murder, are regarded by us with astonishment; so those of our own day who pride themselves in consuming much and producing nothing, and who care little for the well-being of their society so long as it supplies them good dinners, soft beds, and pleasant lounging-places, may be regarded with astonishment by men of times to come, living under higher social forms. Nay, we may see not merely the possibility of such a change in sentiment, but the probability. Observe, first, the feeling still extant in China, where the honourableness of doing nothing, more strongly held than here, makes the wealthy wear their nails so long that they have to be tied back out of the way, and makes the ladies submit to prolonged tortures that their crushed feet may show their incapacity for work. Next, remember that in generations gone by, both here and on the Continent, the disgracefulness of trade was an article of faith among the upper classes, maintained very strenuously. Now mark how members of the landed class are going into business, and even sons of peers becoming professional men and merchants; and observe among the wealthy the feeling that men of their order have public duties to perform, and that the absolutely-idle among them are blameworthy. Clearly, then, we have grounds for inferring that, along with the progress to a regulative organization higher than the present, there will be a change of the kind indicated in the conception of honour. It will become a matter of wonder that there should ever have existed those who thought it admirable to enjoy without working, at the expense of others who worked without enjoying.

But the temporarily-adapted mental state of the ruling and employing classes, keeps out, more or less effectually, thoughts and feelings of these kinds. Habituated from childhood to the forms of subordination at present existing—regarding these as parts of a natural and permanent order—finding satisfaction in supremacy, and conveniences in the possession of authority; the regulators of all kinds remain unconscious that this system, made necessary as it is by the defects of existing human nature, brings round penalties on themselves as well as on those subordinate to them, and that its pervading theory of life is as mistaken as it is ignoble.

Enough has been said to show that from the class-bias arise further obstacles to right thinking in Sociology. As a part of some general division of his community, and again as a part of some special subdivision, the citizen acquires adapted feelings and ideas which inevitably influence his conclusions about public affairs. They affect alike his conceptions of the past, his interpretations of the present, his anticipations of the future.

Members of the regulated classes, kept in relations more or less antagonistic with the classes regulating them, are thereby hindered from seeing the need for, and the benefits of, this organization which seems the cause of their grievances; they are at the same time hindered from seeing the need for, and the benefits of, those harsher forms of industrial regulation that existed during past times; and they are also hindered from seeing that the improved industrial organizations of the future, can come only through improvements in their own natures. On the other hand, members of the regulating classes, while partially blinded to the facts that the defects of the working-classes are the defects of natures like their own placed under different conditions, and that the existing system is defensible, not for its convenience to themselves, but as being the best now practicable for the community at large; are also partially blinded to the vices of past social arrangements, and to the badness of those who in past social systems used class-power less mercifully than it is used now; while they have difficulty in seeing that the present social order, like past social orders, is but transitory, and that the regulating classes of the future may have, with diminished power, increased happiness.

Unfortunately for the Social Science, the class-bias, like the bias of patriotism, is, in a degree, needful for social preservation. It is like in this, too, that escape from its influence is often only effected by an effort that carries belief to an opposite extreme—changing approval into a disapproval that is entire instead of partial. Hence in the one case, as in the other, we must infer that the resulting obstacle to well-balanced conclusions, can become less only as social evolution becomes greater.

3. Karl Mannheim

The Prospects of Scientific Politics

I. Why is There no Science of Politics?

The emergence and disappearance of problems on our intellectual horizon are governed by a principle of which we are not yet fully aware. Even the rise and disappearance of whole systems of knowledge may ultimately be reduced to certain factors and thus become explicable. There have already been attempts in the history of art to discover why and in what periods such plastic arts as sculpture, relief-modelling or other arts arise and become the dominant art-form of a period. In the same manner the sociology of knowledge should seek to investigate the conditions under which problems and disciplines come into being and pass away. The sociologist in the long run must be able to do better than to attribute the emergence and solution of problems to the mere existence of certain talented individuals. The existence of and the complex inter-relationship between the problems of a given time and place must be viewed and understood against the background of the structure of the society in which they occur, although this may not always give us an understanding of every detail. The isolated thinker may have the impression that his crucial ideas occurred to him personally, independent of his social setting. It is easy for one living in a provincial and circumscribed social world to think that the events which touch him are isolated facts for which fate alone is responsible. Sociology, however, cannot be content with understanding immediate problems and events emerging from this myopic perspective which obscures every significant relationship. These seemingly isolated and discrete facts must be comprehended in the ever-present but constantly changing configurations of experience in which they actually are lived. Only in such a context do they acquire meaning. If the sociology of knowledge should have any measure of success in this type of analysis, many problems which hitherto, as regards their origins at least, have been unsolved, would be cleared up. Such a development

From Mannheim, *Ideology and Utopia: An Introduction to the Sociology of Knowledge* (New York: Harcourt, Brace and Co., 1936), pp. 97-136. Translated by Louis Wirth and Edward Shils. Reprinted by permission of Harcourt, Brace and Company, Inc.

would also enable us to see why sociology and economics are of such recent birth and why they advanced in one country and were retarded and beset by so many obstacles in others. Likewise it will be possible to solve a problem which has always gone unanswered: namely why we have not yet witnessed the development of a science of politics. In a world which is as permeated by a rationalistic ethos, as is our own, this fact represents a striking anomaly.

There is scarcely a sphere of life about which we do not have some scientific knowledge as well as recognized methods of communicating this knowledge. Is it conceivable then, that the sphere of human activity on the mastery of which our fate rests, is so unyielding that scientific research cannot force it to give up its secrets? The disquieting and puzzling features of this problem cannot be disregarded. The question must have already occurred to many whether this is merely a temporary condition, to be overcome at a later date, or whether we have reached, in this sphere, the outermost limit of knowledge which can never be transcended?

It may be said in favour of the former possibility that the social sciences are still in their infancy. It would be possible to conclude that the immaturity of the more fundamental social sciences explains the retardation of this "applied" science. If this were so, it would be only a question of time until this backwardness were overcome, and further research might be expected to yield a control over society comparable to that which we now have over the physical world.

The opposite point of view finds support in the vague feeling that political behaviour is qualitatively different from any other type of human experience, and that the obstacles in the way of its rational understanding are much more insurmountable than is the case in other realms of knowledge. Hence, it is assumed that all attempts to subject these phenomena to scientific analysis are foredoomed to failure because of the peculiar nature of the phenomena to be analysed.

Even a correct statement of the problem would be an achievement of value. To become aware of our ignorance would bring considerable relief since we would then know why actual knowledge and communication are not possible in this case. Hence the first task is a precise definition of the problem which is—What do we mean when we ask: Is a science of politics possible?

There are certain aspects of politics which are immediately intelligible and communicable. An experienced and trained political leader should know the history of his own country, as well as the history of the countries immediately connected with his own and constituting the surrounding political world. Consequently, at the least, a knowledge of history and the relevant statistical data are useful for his own political conduct. Furthermore, the political leader should know something about the political institutions of the countries with which he is concerned. It is essential that his training be not only juristic but also include a knowledge of the social relations which underlie the institutional structure and through which it functions. He must likewise be abreast of the political ideas which mould the tradition in which he lives. Similarly he cannot afford to be ignorant of the political ideas of his opponents. There are still further though less immediate questions, which in our own times have undergone continual elaboration, namely the technique for manipulating crowds without which it is impossible to get on in mass-democracies. History, statistics, political theory, sociology, history of ideas, and social psychology, among many other disciplines, represent fields of knowledge important to the political leader. Were we interested in setting up a curriculum for the education of the political leader, the above studies would no doubt have to be included. The disciplines mentioned above, however, offer no more than practical knowledge which, if one happens to be a political leader, might be of use. But even all of these disciplines added together do not produce a science of politics. At best they may serve as auxiliary disciplines to such a science. If we understood by politics merely the sum of all those bits of practical knowledge which are useful for political conduct, then there would be no question about the fact that a science of politics in this sense existed, and that this science could be taught. The only pedagogical problem would consist, then, in selecting from the infinite store of existing facts those most relevant for the purposes of political conduct.

However, it is probably evident from this somewhat exaggerated statement that the questions "Under what conditions is a science of politics possible and how may it be taught?" do not refer to the above-mentioned body of practical information. In what then does the problem consist?

The disciplines which were listed above are structurally related only in so far as they deal with society and the state as if they were the final products of past history. Political conduct, however, is concerned with the state and society in so far as they are still in the process of becoming. Political conduct is confronted with a process in which every moment creates a unique situation and seeks to disentangle out of this ever-flowing stream of forces something of enduring character. The question then is: "Is there a science of this becoming, a science of creative activity?"

The first stage in the delineation of the problem is thus attained. What (in the realm of the social) is the significance of this contrast between what has already become and what is in the process of becoming?

The Austrian sociologist and statesman, Albert Schäffle,[1] pointed out that at any moment of socio-political life two aspects are discernible—first, a series of social events which have acquired a set pattern and recur regularly; and, second, those events which are still in the process of becoming, in which, in individual cases, decisions have to be made that

[1] Cf. Schäffle, A., "Über den wissenschaftlichen Begriff der Politik," *Zeitschrift für die gesamte Staatswissenschaften*, vol. 53 (1897).

give rise to new and unique situations. The first he called the "routine affairs of state", *laufendes Staatsleben;* the second "politics". The meaning of this distinction will be clarified by a few illustrations. When, in the accustomed life of an official, current business is disposed of in accordance with existing rules and regulations, we are, according to Schäffle, in the realm of "administration" rather than of "politics". Administration is the domain where we can see exemplified what Schäffle means by "routine affairs of state". Wherever each new case may be taken care of in a prescribed manner, we are faced not with politics but with the settled and recurrent side of social life. Schäffle uses an illuminating expression from the field of administration itself to give point to his distinction. For such cases as can be settled by merely consulting an established rule, i.e. according to precedent, the German word *Schimmel*,[1] which is derived from the Latin *simile* is used, signifying that the case in hand is to be disposed of in a manner *similar* to precedents that already exist. We are in the realm of politics when envoys to foreign countries conclude treaties which were never made before; when parliamentary representatives carry through new measures of taxation; when an election campaign is waged; when certain opposition groups prepare a revolt or organize strikes—or when these are suppressed.

It must be admitted that the boundary between these two classes is in reality rather flexible. For instance, the cumulative effect of a gradual shift of administrative procedure in a long series of concrete cases may actually give rise to a new principle. Or, to take a reverse instance, something as unique as a new social movement may be deeply permeated with "stereotyped" and routinizing elements. Nevertheless the contrast between the "routine affairs of state" and "politics" offers a certain polarity which may serve as a fruitful point of departure. If the dichotomy is conceived more theoretically, we may say: Every social process may be divided into a rationalized sphere consisting of settled and routinized procedures in dealing with situations that recur in an orderly fashion, and the "irrational" by which it is surrounded.[2] We are, therefore, distinguishing between the

---

[1] The German word *Schimmel* means "mould". [Translator's note.]

[2] For the sake of precision, the following remark should be added: The expression "settled routinized elements" is to be regarded figuratively. Even the most formalized and ossified features of society are not to be regarded as things held in store in an attic, to be taken out when needed for use. Laws, regulations, and established customs only have an existence in that living experiences constantly call them into being. This settledness signifies merely that social life, while consantly renewing itself, conforms to rules and formal processes already inherent in it and this constantly generates itself anew in a recurrent manner. Similarly, the use of the expression "rationalized sphere" must be taken in the broader sense. It may mean either a theoretical, rational approach, as in the case of a technique which is rationally calculated and determined; or it may be used in the sense of "rationalization" in which a sequence of events follows a regular, expected (probable) course, as is the case with convention, usage, or custom, where the sequence of events is not fully understood, but in its structure seems to have a certain settled character. Max Weber's

"rationalized" structure of society and the "irrational" matrix. A further observation presents itself at this point. The chief characteristic of modern culture is the tendency to include as much as possible in the realm of the rational and to bring it under administrative control—and, on the other hand, to reduce the "irrational" element to the vanishing point.

A simple illustration will clarify the meaning of this assertion. The traveller of 150 years ago was exposed to a thousand accidents. To-day everything proceeds according to schedule. Fare is exactly calculated and a whole series of administrative measures have made travel into a rationally controlled enterprise. The perception of the distinction between the rationalized scheme and the irrational setting in which it operates provides the possibility for a definition of the concept "conduct".

The action of a petty official who disposes of a file of documents in the prescribed manner, or of a judge who finds that a case falls under the provisions of a certain paragraph in the law and disposes of it accordingly, or finally of a factory worker who produces a screw by following the prescribed technique, would not fall under our definition of "conduct". Nor for that matter would the action of a technican who, in achieving a given end, combined certain general laws of nature. All these modes of behaviour would be considered as merely "reproductive" because they are executed in a rational framework, according to a definite prescription entailing no personal decision whatsoever. Conduct, in the sense in which we use it, does not begin until we reach the area where rationalization has not yet penetrated, and where we are forced to make decisions in situations which have as yet not been subjected to regulation. It is in such situations that the whole problem of the relations between theory and practice arises. (Concerning this problem, on the basis of the analyses thus far made, we may even at this stage venture a few further remarks.

There is no question that we do have some knowledge concerning that part of social life in which everything and life itself has already been rationalized and ordered. Here the conflict between theory and practice does not become an issue because, as a matter of fact, the mere treatment of an individual case by subjecting it to a generally existing law can hardly be designated as political practice. Rationalized as our life may seem to have become, all the rationalizations that have taken place so far are merely partial since the most important realms of our social life are even now anchored in the irrational. Our economic life, although extensively rationalized on the technical side, and in some limited connections calculable, does not, as a whole, constitute a planned economy.

---

use of the term "stereotype" as the broader class might be used here, and two subclasses of the stereotyping tendency then distinguished, (a) traditionalism, (b) rationalism. Inasmuch as this distinction is not relevant for our present purpose, we will use the concept "rationalized structure" in the more comprehensive sense in which Max Weber uses the general notion of stereotyping.

In spite of all tendencies towards trustification and organization, free competition still plays a decisive role. Our social structure is built along class lines, which means that not objective tests but irrational forces of social competition and struggle decide the place and function of the individual in society. Dominance in national and international life is achieved through struggle, in itself irrational, in which chance plays an important part. These irrational forces in society form that sphere of social life which is unorganized and unrationalized, and in which conduct and politics become necessary. The two main sources of irrationalism in the social structure (uncontrolled competition and domination by force) constitute the realm of social life which is still unorganized and where politics becomes necessary. Around these two centres there accumulate those other more profound irrational elements, which we usually call emotions. Viewed from the sociological standpoint there is a connection between the extent of the unorganized realm of society where uncontrolled competition and domination by force prevail, and the social integration of emotional reactions.

The problem then must be stated: What knowledge do we have or is possible concerning this realm of social life and of the type of conduct which occurs in it?[1] But now our original problem has been stated in the most highly developed form in which it seems to lend itself to clarification. Having determined where the realm of the political truly begins, and where conduct in a true sense is possible, we can indicate the difficulties existing in the relationship between theory and practice.

The great difficulties which confront scientific knowledge in this realm arise from the fact that we are not dealing here with rigid, objective entities but with tendencies and strivings in a constant state of flux. A further difficulty is that the constellation of the interacting forces changes continuously. Wherever the same forces, each unchanging in character, interact, and their interaction, too, follows a regular course, it is possible to formulate general laws. This is not quite so easy where new forces are incessantly entering the system and forming unforeseen combinations. Still another difficulty is that the observer himself does not stand outside the realm of the irrational, but is a participant in the conflict of forces. This participation inevitably binds him to a partisan view through his evaluations and interests. Furthermore, and most important, is the fact that not only is the political theorist a participant in the conflict because of his values, and interests, but the particular manner in which the problem presents itself to him, his most general mode of thought including

---

[1] It is necessary here to repeat that the concept of the "political" as used in conjunction with the correlative concepts, rationalized structure, and irrational field, represents only one of many possible concepts of the "political." While particularly suited for the comprehension of certain relationships, it must not be regarded as absolutely the only one. For an opposite notion of the "political" cf. C. Schmitt, "Der Begriff des Politischen," *Archiv für Sozialwissenschaft und Sozialpolitik*, vol. 58 (1928).

even his categories, are bound up with general political and social under-currents. So true is this that, in the realm of political and social thinking, we must, in my judgment, recognize actual differences in styles of thought —differences that extend even into the realm of logic itself.

In this, doubtless, lies the greatest obstacle to a science of politics. For according to ordinary expectations a science of conduct would be possible only when the fundamental structure of thought is independent of the different forms of conduct being studied. Even though the observer be a participant in the struggle, the basis of his thinking, i.e. his ob-servational apparatus and his method of settling intellectual differences, must be above the conflict. A problem cannot be solved by obscuring its difficulties, but only by stating them as sharply and as pronouncedly as possible. Hence it is our task definitely to establish the thesis that in politics the statement of a problem and the logical techniques involved vary with the political position of the observer.

II. The Political and Social Determinants of Knowledge

We shall now make an effort to show by means of a concrete example that political-historical thinking assumes various forms, in accordance with different political currents. In order not to go too far afield, we shall con-centrate primarily on the relationship between theory and practice. We shall see that even this most general and fundamental problem of a science of political conduct is differently conceived by the different his-torical-political parties.

This may be easily seen by a survey of the various political and social currents of the nineteenth and twentieth centuries. As the most im-portant representative ideal-types, we cite the following:—

> 1. Bureaucratic conservatism.
> 2. Conservative historicism.
> 3. Liberal-democratic bourgeois thought.
> 4. The socialist-communist conception.
> 5. Fascism.

The mode of thought of bureaucratic conservatism will be considered first. The fundamental tendency of all bureaucratic thought is to turn all problems of politics into problems of administration. As a result, the majority of books on politics in the history of German political science are *de facto* treatises on administration. If we consider the role that bureaucracy has always played, especially in the Prussian state, and to what extent the intelligentsia was largely an intelligentsia drawn from the bureaucracy, this onesidedness of the history of political science in Germany becomes easily intelligible.

The attempt to hide all problems of politics under the cover of administration may be explained by the fact that the sphere of activity of the official exists only within the limits of laws already formulated. Hence the genesis or the development of law falls outside the scope of his activity. As a result of his socially limited horizon, the functionary fails to see that behind every law that has been made there lie the socially fashioned interests and the *Weltanschauungen* of a specific social group. He takes it for granted that the specific order prescribed by the concrete law is equivalent to order in general. He does not understand that every rationalized order is only one of many forms in which socially conflicting irrational forces are reconciled.

The administrative, legalistic mind has its own peculiar type of rationality. When faced with the play of hitherto unharnessed forces, as, for example, the eruption of collective energies in a revolution, it can conceive of them only as momentary disturbances. It is, therefore, no wonder that in every revolution the bureaucracy tries to find a remedy by means of arbitrary decrees rather than to meet the political situation on its own grounds. It regards revolution as an untoward event within an otherwise ordered system and not as the living expression of fundamental social forces on which the existence, the preservation, and the development of society depends. The juristic administrative mentality constructs only closed static systems of thought, and is always faced with the paradoxical task of having to incorporate into its system new laws, which arise out of the unsystematized interaction of living forces as if they were only a further elaboration of the original system.

A typical example of the military-bureaucratic mentality is every type of the "stab in the back" legend, *Dolchstosslegende* which interprets a revolutionary outbreak as nothing but a serious interference with its own neatly planned strategy. The exclusive concern of the military bureaucrat is military action and, if that proceeds according to plan, then all the rest of life is in order too. This mentality is reminiscent of the joke about the specialist in the medical world, who is reputed to have said: "The operation was a splendid success. Unfortunately, the patient died."

Every bureaucracy, therefore, in accord with the peculiar emphasis on its own position, tends to generalize its own experience and to overlook the fact that the realm of administration and of smoothly functioning order represents only a part of the total political reality. Bureaucratic thought does not deny the possibility of a science of politics, but regards it as identical with the science of administration. Thus irrational factors are overlooked, and when these nevertheless force themselves to the fore, they are treated as "routine matters of state". A classic expression of this standpoint is contained in a saying which originated in these circles: "A good administration is better than the best constitution."[1]

---

[1] Obituary of Böhlau by the jurist Bekker. *Zeitschrift der Savigny-Stiftung.* Germanist Abtlg., vol. viii, p. vi ff.

In addition to bureaucratic conservatism, which ruled Germany and especially Prussia to a very great extent, there was a second type of conservatism which developed parallel to it and which may be called historical conservatism. It was peculiar to the social group of the nobility and the bourgeois strata among the intellectuals who were the intellectual and actual rulers of the country, but between whom and the bureaucratic conservatives there always existed a certain amount of tension. This mode of thought bore the stamp of the German universities, and especially of the dominant group of historians. Even to-day, this mentality still finds its support largely in these circles.

Historical conservatism is characterized by the fact that it is aware of that irrational realm in the life of the state which cannot be managed by administration. It recognizes that there is an unorganized and incalculable realm which is the proper sphere of politics. Indeed it focuses its attention almost exclusively on the impulsive, irrational factors which furnish the real basis for the further development of state and society. It regards these forces as entirely beyond comprehension and infers that, as such, human reason is impotent to understand or to control them. Here only a traditionally inherited instinct, "silently working" spiritual forces, the "folk spirit", *Volksgeist,* drawing their strength out of the depths of the unconscious, can be of aid in moulding the future.

This attitude was already stated at the end of the eighteenth century by Burke, who served as the model for most of the German conservatives, in the following impressive words: "The science of constructing a commonwealth or renovating it or reforming it, is like every other experimental science, not to be taught *a priori*. Nor is it a short experience that can instruct us in that practical science."[1] The sociological roots of this thesis are immediately evident. It "expressed" the ideology of the dominant nobility in England and in Germany, and it served to legitimatize their claims to leadership in the state. The *je ne sais quoi* element in politics, which can be acquired only through long experience, and which reveals itself as a rule only to those who for many generations have shared in political leadership, is intended to justify government by an aristocratic class. This makes clear the manner in which the social interests of a given group make the members of that group sensitive to certain aspects of social life to which those in another position do not respond. Whereas the bureaucracy is blinded to the political aspect of a situation by reason of its administrative preconceptions, from the very beginning the nobility is perfectly at home in this sphere. Right from the start, the latter have their eyes on the arena where intra- and inter-state spheres of power collide with one another. In this sphere, petty textbook wisdom deserts us and solutions to problems cannot be mechanically deduced from prem-

[1] Burke's *Reflections on the Revolution in France*, edited by F. G. Selby (London: Macmillan and Co., 1890), p. 67.

ises. Hence it is not individual intelligence which decides issues. Rather is every event the resultant of actual political forces.

The historical conservative theory, which is essentially the expression of a feudal tradition[1] become self-conscious, is primarily concerned with problems which transcend the sphere of administration. The sphere is regarded as a completely irrational one which cannot be fabricated by mechanical methods but which grows of its own accord. This outlook relates everything to the decisive dichotomy between "construction according to calculated plan" and "allowing things to grow".[2] For the political leader it is not sufficient to possess merely the correct knowledge and the mastery of certain laws and norms. In addition to these he must possess that inborn instinct, sharpened through long experience, which leads him to the right answer.

Two types of irrationalism have joined to produce this irrational way of thinking: on the one hand, precapitalistic, traditionalistic irrationalism (which regards legal thinking, for instance, as a way of sensing something and not as mechanical calculation), and, on the other hand, romantic irrationalism. A mode of thought is thus created which conceives of history as the reign of pre- and super-rational forces. Even Ranke, the most eminent representative of the historical school, spoke from this intellectual outlook when he defined the relations of theory and practice.[3] Politics is not, according to him, an independent science that can be taught. The statesman may indeed study history profitably, but not in order to derive from it rules of conduct, but rather because it serves to sharpen his political instinct. This mode of thought may be designated as the ideology of political groups which have traditionally occupied a dominant position but which have rarely participated in the administrative bureaucracy.

If the two solutions thus far presented are contrasted, it will become clear that the bureaucrat tends to conceal the political sphere while the historicist sees it all the more sharply and exclusively as irrational even though he singles out for emphasis the traditional factors in historical events and in the acting subjects. At this stage we come to the chief adversary of this theory which, as has been pointed out, arose originally out of aristocratic feudal mentality, namely, the liberal-democratic bourgeoisie and its theories.[4] The rise of the bourgeoisie was attended by an extreme intellectualism. Intellectualism, as it is used in this connection,

---

[1] Cf. "Das konservative Denken," loc. cit., pp. 89, 105, 133 ff.

[2] Ibid., p. 472, n. 129.

[3] Cf. Ranke, *Das politische Gespräch* (1836), ed. by Rothacker (Halle a.d., Saale, 1925), p. 21 ff. Also other essays on the same theme: "Reflexionen" (1832), "Vom Einfluss der Theorie," "Über die Verwandtschaft und den Unterschied der Historie und der Politik."

[4] For the sake of simplicity we do not distinguish liberalism from democracy, although historically and socially they are quite different.

refers to a mode of thought which either does not see the elements in life and in thought which are based on will, interest, emotion, and *Weltanschauung*—or, if it does recognize their existence, treats them as though they were equivalent to the intellect and believes that they may be mastered by and subordinated to reason. This bourgeois intellectualism expressly demanded a scientific politics, and actually proceeded to found such a discipline. Just as the bourgeoisie found the first institutions into which the political struggle could be canalized (first parliament and the electoral system, and later the League of Nations), so it also created a systematic place for the new discipline of politics. The organizational anomaly of bourgeois society appears also in its social theory. The bourgeois attempt at a thorough-going rationalization of the world is forced nevertheless to halt when it reaches certain phenomena. By sanctioning free competition and the class struggle, it even creates a new irrational sphere. Likewise in this type of thought, the irrational residue in reality remains undissolved. Furthermore, just as parliament is a formal organization, a formal rationalization of the political conflict but not a solution of it, so bourgeois theory attains merely an apparent, formal intellectualization of the inherently irrational elements.

The bourgeois mind is, of course, aware of this new irrational realm, but it is intellectualistic in so far as it attempts solely through thought, discussion, and organization to master, as if they were already rationalized, the power and other irrational relationships that dominate here. Thus, *inter alia,* it was believed that political action could without difficulty be scientifically defined. The science in question was assumed to fall into three parts:—

First—the theory of ends, i.e. the theory of the ideal State.
Second—the theory of the positive State.
Third—"politics," i.e. the description of the manner in which the existing State is transformed into a perfect State.

As an illustration of this type of thought we may refer to the structure of Fichte's "Closed Commercial State" which in this sense has recently been very acutely analysed by Heinrich Rickert[1] who himself, however, completely accepts this position. There is then a science of ends and a science of means. The most striking fact about it is the complete separation between theory and practice, of the intellectual sphere from the emotional sphere. Modern intellectualism is characterized by its tendency not to tolerate emotionally determined and evaluative thinking. When, nevertheless, this type of thought is encountered (and all political thought is set essentially in an irrational context) the attempt is made so to construe the phenomena that the evaluative elements will appear separable,

[1] Cf. Rickert, Heinrich, "Über idealistische Politik als Wissenschaft. Ein Beitrag zur Problemgeschichte der Staatsphilosophie," *Die Akademie*, Heft 4, Erlangen.

and that there will remain at least a residue of pure theory. In this the question is not even raised whether the emotional element may not under certain circumstances be so intertwined with the rational as to involve even the categorical structure itself and to make the required isolation of the evaluative elements *de facto* unrealizable. Bourgeois intellectualism, however, does not worry over these difficulties. With undaunted optimism, it strives to conquer a sphere completely purged of irrationalism.

As regards ends, this theory teaches that there is one right set of ends of political conduct which, in so far as it has not already been found, may be arrived at by discussion. Thus the original conception of parliamentarism was, as Carl Schmitt has so clearly shown, that of a debating society in which truth is sought by theoretical methods.[1] We know all too well and can understand sociologically wherein the self-deception in this mode of thought lay. To-day we recognize that behind every theory there are collective forces expressive of group-purposes, -power, and -interests. Parliamentary discussions are thus far from being theoretical in the sense that they may ultimately arrive at the objective truth: they are concerned with very real issues to be decided in the clash of interests. It was left for the socialist movement which arose subsequently as the opponent of the bourgeoisie to elaborate specifically this aspect of the debate about real issues.

In our treatment of socialist theory we are not for the time being differentiating between socialism and communism, for we are here concerned not so much with the plethora of historical phenomena as with the tendencies which cluster around the opposite poles that essentially determine modern thought. In the struggle with its bourgeois opponent, Marxism discovered anew that in historical and political matters there can be no "pure theory". It sees that behind every theory there lie collective points of view. The phenomenon of collective thinking, which proceeds according to interests and social and existential situations, Marx spoke of as ideology.

In this case, as so often in political struggles, an important discovery was made, which, once it became known, had to be followed up to its final conclusion. This was the more so since this discovery contained the heart of the problem of political thought in general. The concept ideology serves to point out the problem, but the problem is thereby by no means solved or cleared up.[2] A thoroughgoing clarification is attainable only by

---

[1] Cf. Carl Schmitt, *Die geistesgeschichtliche Lage des heutigen Parlamentarismus*, 2nd edit. (Leipzig, 1926).

[2] For what follows Part II should be referred to for further discussion of the problem, of which only the essentials will be repeated here. The concept of total, general, and non-evaluative ideology, as described earlier, is the one used in the present context (cf. p. 71 ff.). Part IV will deal with the evaluative conceptions of ideology and utopia. Henceforth the concept to be used will be determined by the immediate purposes of the investigation.

getting rid of the one-sidedness inherent in the original conception. First of all, therefore, it will be necessary for our purpose to make two corrections. To begin with, it could easily be shown that those who think in socialist and communist terms discern the ideological element only in the thinking of their opponents while regarding their own thought as entirely free from any taint of ideology. As sociologists there is no reason why we should not apply to Marxism the perceptions which it itself has produced, and point out from case to case its ideological character. Moreover, it should be explained that the concept "ideology" is being used here not as a negative value-judgment, in the sense of insinuating a conscious political lie, but is intended to designate the outlook inevitably associated with a given historical and social situation, and the *Weltanschauung* and style of thought bound up with it. This meaning of the term, which bears more closely on the history of thought, must be sharply differentiated from the other meaning. Of course, we do not deny that in other connections it may also serve to reveal conscious political lies.

Through this procedure nothing that has a positive value for scientific research in the notion of ideology has been discarded. The great revelation it affords is that every form of historical and political thought is essentially conditioned by the life situation of the thinker and his groups. It is our task to disentangle this insight from its one-sided political encrustation, and to elaborate in a systematic manner the thesis that how one looks at history and how one construes a total situation from given facts, depends on the position one occupies within society. In every historical and political contribution it is possible to determine from what vantage point the objects were observed. However, the fact that our thinking is determined by our social position is not necessarily a source of error. On the contrary, it is often the path to political insight. The significant element in the conception of ideology, in our opinion, is the discovery that political thought is integrally bound up with social life. This is the essential meaning of the oft-quoted sentence, "It is not the consciousness of men that determines their existence but, on the contrary, their social existence which determines their consciousness."[1]

But closely related to this is another important feature of Marxist thought, namely a new conception of the relationship between theory and practice. Whereas the bourgeois theorist devoted a special chapter to setting forth his ends, and whereas this always proceeded from a normative conception of society, one of the most significant steps Marx took was to attack the utopian element in socialism. From the beginning he refused to lay down an exhaustive set of objectives. There is no norm to be achieved that is detachable from the process itself: "Communism for us is not a condition that is to be established nor an ideal to which reality

[1] Marx, Karl, *A Contribution to the Critique of Political Economy*, tr. by N. I. Stone (Chicago, 1913), pp. 11-12.

must adjust itself. We call communism the actual movement which abolishes present conditions. The conditions under which this movement proceeds result from those now existing."[1]

If to-day we ask a communist, with a Leninist training, what the future society will actually be like, he will answer that the question is an undialectical one, since the future itself will be decided in the practical dialectical process of becoming. But what is this practical dialectical process?

It signifies that we cannot calculate *a priori* what a thing should be like and what it will be like. We can influence only the general trend of the process of becoming. The ever-present concrete problem for us can only be the next step ahead. It is not the task of political thought to set up an absolute scheme of what should be. Theory, even including communist theory, is a function of the process of becoming. The dialectical relationship between theory and practice consists in the fact that, first of all, theory arising out of a definitely social impulse clarifies the situation. And in the process of clarification reality undergoes a change. We thereby enter a new situation out of which a new theory emerges. The process is, then, as follows: (1) Theory is a function of reality; (2) This theory leads to a certain kind of action; (3) Action changes the reality, or in case of failure, forces us to a revision of the previous theory. The change in the actual situation brought about by the act gives rise to a new theory.[2]

This view of the relationship between theory and practice bears the imprint of an advanced stage in the discussion of the problem. One notes that it was preceded by the one-sidedness of an extreme intellectualism and a complete irrationalism, and that it had to circumvent all the dangers which were already revealed in bourgeois and conservative thought and experience. The advantages of this solution lie in the fact that it has assimilated the previous formulation of the problem, and in its awareness of the fact that in the realm of politics the usual run of thought is unable to accomplish anything. On the other hand, this outlook is too thoroughly motivated by the desire for knowledge to fall into a complete irrationalism like conservatism. The result of the conflict between the two currents of thought is a very flexible conception of theory. A basic lesson derived from political experience which was most impressively formulated by

---

[1] Cf. *Marx-Engels Archiv*, ed. by D. Ryazanov (Frankfurt, a.M.), vol. i, p. 252.

[2] "When the proletariat by means of the class struggle changes its position in society and thereby the whole social structure, in taking cognizance of the changed social situation, i.e. of itself, it finds itself face to face not merely with a new object of understanding, but also changes its position as a knowing subject. The theory serves to bring the proletariat to a consciousness of its social position, i.e. it enables it to envisage itself—simultaneously both as an object and a subject in the social process." (Lukács, Georg, *Geschichte und Klassenbewusstsein*, Berlin, 1923.)

"This consciousness in turn becomes the motive force of new activity, since theory becomes a material force once it seizes the masses." (Marx-Engels, *Nachlass*, i, p. 392.)

Napoleon in the maxim, *"On s'engage, puis on voit,"*[1] here finds its methodological sanction.[2] Indeed, political thought cannot be carried on by speculating about it from the outside. Rather thought becomes illuminated when a concrete situation is penetrated, not merely through acting and doing, but also through the thinking which must go with them.

Socialist-communist theory is then a synthesis of intuitionism and a determined desire to comprehend phenomena in an extremely rational way. Intuitionism is present in this theory because it denies the possibility of exact calculations of events in advance of their happening. The rationalist tendency enters because it aims to fit into a rational scheme whatever novelty comes to view at any moment. At no time is it permissible to act without theory, but the theory that arises in the course of action will be on a different level from the theory that went before.[3] It is especially revolutions that create a more valuable type of knowledge. This constitutes the synthesis which men are likely to make when they live in the midst of irrationality and recognize it as such, but do not despair of the attempt to interpret it rationally. Marxist thought is akin to conservative thought in that it does not deny the existence of an irrational sphere and does not try to conceal it as the bureaucratic mentality does, or treat it in a purely intellectual fashion as if it were rational, as liberal-democratic thinkers do. It is distinguished from conservative thought, however, in that it conceives of this relative irrationality as potentially comprehensible through new methods of rationalization.[4] For

[1] Indeed both Lenin and Lukács, as representatives of the dialectical approach, find justification in this Napoleonic maxim.

[2] "Revolutionary theory is the generalization of the experiences of the labour movement in all countries. It naturally loses its very essence if it is not connected with revolutionary practice, just as practice gropes in the dark if its path is not illumined by revolutionary theory. But theory can become the greatest force in the labour movement if it is indissolubly bound up with revolutionary practice, for it alone can give to the movement confidence, guidance, strength, and understanding of the inner relations between events and it alone can help practice to clarify the process and direction of class movements in the present and near future." (Joseph Stalin, *Foundations of Leninism*, rev. ed. New York and London, 1932, pp. 26-7.)

[3] Revolution, particularly, creates the situation propitious to significant knowledge: "History in general, the history of revolutions in particular, has always been richer, more varied, and variform, more vital and 'cunning' than is conceived of by the best parties, by the most conscious vanguards of the most advanced classes. This is natural, for the best vanguards express the consciousness, will, passions, and fancies of but tens of thousands, whereas the revolution is effected at the moment of the exceptional exaltation and exertion of all the human faculties—consciousness, will, passion, phantasy, of tens of millions, spurred on by the bitterest class war." (N. Lenin, *"Left" Communism: an Infantile Disorder*, published by the Toiler, n.d. pp. 76-7, also New York and London, 1934.)

It is interesting to observe that from this point of view revolution appears not as an intensification of the passions resident in men nor as mere irrationality. This passion is valuable only because it makes possible the fusion of the accumulated rationality tested out experimentally in the individual experiences of millions.

[4] Thus, fate, chance, everything sudden and unexpected, and the religious view which arises therefrom, are conceived of as functions of the degree in which our

even in this type of thought, the sphere of the irrational is not entirely irrational, arbitrary, or incomprehensible. It is true that there are no statically fixed and definite laws to which this creative process conforms, nor are there any exactly recurring sequences of events, but at the same time only a limited number of situations can occur even here. And this after all is the decisive consideration. Even when new elements in historical development emerge they do not constitute merely a chain of unexpected events; the political sphere itself is permeated by tendencies which, even though they are subject to change, through their very presence do nevertheless determine to a large extent the various possibilities.

Therefore, the first task of Marxism is the analysis and rationalization of all those tendencies which influence the character of the situation. Marxist theory has elaborated these structural tendencies in a threefold direction. First, it points out that the political sphere in a given society is based on and is always characterized by the state of productive relations prevailing at the time.[1] The productive relations are not regarded statically as a continually recurring economic cycle, but, dynamically, as a structural interrelationship which is itself constantly changing through time.

Secondly, it sees that changes in this economic factor are most closely connected with transformations in class relations, which involves at the same time a shift in the kinds of power and an ever-varying distribution of power.

But, thirdly, it recognizes that it is possible to understand the inner structure of the system of ideas dominating men at any period and to determine theoretically the direction of any change or modification in this structure.

Still more important is the fact that these three structural patterns are not considered independently of one another. It is precisely their reciprocal relations which are made to constitute a single group of problems. The ideological structure does not change independently of the class structure, and the class structure does not change independently of

---

understanding of history has not yet reached the stage of rationality.

"Fear of the blind forces of capitalism, blind because they cannot be foreseen by the masses of the people, forces which at every step in the lives of the proletariat and the small traders threaten to bring and do bring 'sudden', 'unexpected', 'accidental' disaster and ruin, converting them into beggars, paupers, or prostitutes, and condemn them to starvation; these are the roots of modern religion, which the materialist, if he desires to remain a materialist, must recognize. No educational books will obliterate religion from the minds of those condemned to the hard labour of capitalism, until they themselves learn to fight in a united, organized, systematic, conscious manner the roots of religion, the domination of capital in all its forms." (*Selections from Lenin—The Bolshevik Party in Action, 1904-1914*, ii. From the essay, "The Workers' Party and Religion," New York, pp. 274-5.)

[1] "The mode of production in material life determines the general character of the social, political, and spiritual processes of life." Marx, *Contribution to the Critique of Political Economy*, tr. by N. I. Stone (Chicago, 1913), p. 11.

the economic structure. And it is precisely the interconnection and inter-twining of this threefold formulation of the problem, the economic, the social, and the ideological, that gives to Marxist ideas their singularly penetrating quality. Only this synthetic power enables it to formulate ever anew the problem of the structural totality of society, not only for the past but also for the future. The paradox lies in the fact that Marxism recognizes relative irrationality and never loses sight of it. But unlike the historical school it does not content itself with a mere acceptance of the irrational. Instead it tries to eliminate as much of it as possible by a new effort at rationalization.

Here again the sociologist is confronted with the question of the general historical-social form of existence and the particular situation from which the mode of thought peculiar to Marxism arose. How can we explain its singular character which consists in combining an extreme irrationalism with an extreme rationalism in such a manner that out of this fusion there arises a new kind of "dialectical" rationality?

Considered sociologically, this is the theory of an ascendent class which is not concerned with momentary successes, and which therefore will not resort to a "putsch" as a means for seizing power, but which, because of its inherent revolutionary tendencies, must always be sensitive and alert to unpredictable constellations in the situation. Every theory which arises out of a class position and is based not on unstable masses but on organized historical groups must of necessity have a long range view. Consequently, it requires a thoroughly rationalized view of history on the basis of which it will be possible at any moment to ask ourselves where we are now and at what stage of development does our movement find itself.[1]

Groups of pre-capitalistic origin, in which the communal element prevails, may be held together by traditions or by common sentiments alone. In such a group, theoretical reflection is of entirely secondary importance. On the other hand, in groups which are not welded together primarily by such organic bonds of community life, but which merely occupy similar positions in the social-economic system, rigorous theorizing is a prerequisite of cohesion. Viewed sociologically this extreme need for theory is the expression of a class society in which persons must be held together not by local proximity but by similar circumstances of life in an extensive social sphere. Sentimental ties are effective only within a limited spatial area, while a theoretical *Weltanschauung* has a unifying power over great distances. Hence a rationalized conception of history serves as a socially unifying factor for groups dispersed in space, and at the same time furnishes continuity to generations which continuously grow up into similar social conditions. In the formation of classes, a similar position in

---

[1] "Without a revolutionary theory there can be no revolutionary movement." Lenin, *What Is To Be Done?* New York and London, 1931.

the social order and a unifying theory are of primary importance. Emotional ties which subsequently spring up are only a reflection of the already existing situation and are always more or less regulated by theory. Despite this extreme rationalizing tendency, which is implicit in the proletarian class position, the limits of the rationality of this class are defined by its oppositional, and particularly, by its allotted revolutionary position.

Revolutionary purpose prevents rationality from becoming absolute. Even though in modern times the tendency toward rationalization proceeds on such an extensive scale that revolts,[1] which originally were only irrational outbursts, are organized on this plane after a bureaucratic fashion, still there must remain somewhere in our conception of history and our scheme of life a place for the essential irrationality which goes with revolution.

Revolution means that somewhere there is an anticipation of and an intent to provoke a breach in the rationalized structure of society. It necessitates, therefore, a watchfulness for the favourable moment in which the attack must be risked. If the whole social and political sphere were conceived of as thoroughly rationalized, it would imply that we would no longer have to be on the lookout for such a breach. The moment, however, is nothing more than that irrational element in the "here and now," which every theory, by virtue of its generalizing tendency, obscures. But since, so long as one needs and wants revolution, one cannot allow this favourable moment, during which the breach occurs, to pass, there develops a gap in the theoretical picture which indicates that the irrational element is valued for what it really is—is valued essentially in its irrationality.

All this dialectical thinking begins by rationalizing what seemed to the historical-conservative groups totally irrational; it does not, however, go so far in its rationalizing tendency as to yield a totally static picture of what is in process of becoming.

This element of the irrational is embodied in the concept of dialectical transformation. The dominant tendencies in the political sphere are not here construed as mathematically calculable combinations of forces, but rather as capable, at a certain point, of sudden transformation when thrown out of the orbit of their original tendencies. Naturally, this transformation is never subject to prediction; on the contrary, it always depends on the revolutionary act of the proletariat. Thus intellectualism is by no means deemed legitimate in all situations. Quite on the contrary, there appear to be two occasions in which the intuition necessary to comprehend the situation is aroused. First, it always remains incalculable

---

[1] "The armed uprising is a special form of the political struggle. It has developmental laws of its own and these must be learned. Karl Marx expressed this with extraordinary vividness when he wrote that 'the revolt is just as much an art as war'." (Lenin, *Ausgewählte Werke*, Wien, 1925, p. 448.)

and is left for political intuition to ascertain when the situation is ripe for revolutionary transformation and, second, historical events are never so exactly determinable in advance that it is superfluous to invoke action to change them.

Marxist thought appears as the attempt to rationalize the irrational. The correctness of this analysis is vouched for by the fact that to the extent that Marxian proletarian groups rise to power, they shake off the dialectical elements of their theory and begin to think in the generalizing methods of liberalism and democracy, which seek to arrive at universal laws, whilst those who, because of their position, still have to resort to revolution, cling to the dialectical element (Leninism).

Dialectical thinking is in fact rationalistic but it culminates in irrationalism. It is constantly striving to answer two questions:—first, what is our position in the social process at the moment? second, what is the demand of the moment? Action is never guided simply by impulse but by a sociological understanding of history. Nevertheless it is not to be assumed that irrational impulses can be entirely eliminated by a logical analysis of the situation and of momentary occurrences. Only through acting in the situation do we address questions to it, and the answer we derive is always in the form of the success or failure of the action. Theory is not torn from its essential connection with action, and action is the clarifying medium in which all theory is tested and develops.

The positive contribution of this theory is that out of its own concrete social experience it shows more and more convincingly that political thought is essentially different from other forms of theorizing. This dialectical mode of thought is further significant in that it has incorporated within itself the problems of both bourgeois rationalism and the irrationalism of historicism.

From irrationalism it has derived the insight that the historical-political sphere is not composed of a number of lifeless objects and that therefore a method which merely seeks laws must fail. Furthermore this method is fully cognizant of the completely dynamic character of the tendencies that dominate the political realm and since it is conscious of the connection between political thinking and living experience, it will not tolerate an artificial separation of theory and practice. From rationalism, on the other hand, it has taken over the inclination to view rationally even situations which have previously defied rational interpretation.

As a fifth claimant to a place among modern currents of thought we should mention fascism, which first emerged in our own epoch. Fascism has its own conception of the relations of theory and practice. It is, on the whole, activistic and irrational. It couples itself, by preference, with the irrationalist philosophies and political theories of the most modern period. It is especially Bergson, Sorel, and Pareto who, after suitable modification of course, have been incorporated into its *Weltanschauung*.

At the very heart of its theory and its practice lies the apotheosis of direct action, the belief in the decisive *deed,* and in the significance attributed to the initiative of a leading *élite.* The essence of politics is to recognize and to grapple with the demands of the hour. Not programmes are important, but unconditional subordination to a leader.[1] History is made neither by the masses, nor by ideas, nor by "silently working" forces, but by the *élites* who from time to time assert themselves.[2] This is a complete irrationalism but characteristically enough not the kind of irrationalism known to the conservatives, not the irrational which is at the same time the super-rational, not the folk spirit (*Volksgeist*), not silently working forces, not the mystical belief in the creativeness of long stretches of time, but the irrationalism of the deed which negates even interpretation of history. "To be youthful means being able to forget. We Italians are, of course, proud of our history, but we do not need to make it the conscious guide of our actions—it lives in us as part of our biological make-up."[3]

A special study would be necessary to ascertain the different meanings of the various conceptions of history. It would be easy to show that the diverse intellectual and social currents have different conceptions of

[1] Mussolini: "Our programme is quite simple; we wish to rule over Italy. People are always asking us about our programme. There are too many already. Italy's salvation does not depend on programmes but on men and strong wills. (Mussolini, *Reden.* ed. by H. Meyer (Leipzig, 1928), p. 105. Cf. also pp. 134 ff.)

[2] Mussolini (loc. cit., p. 13): "You know that I am no worshipper of the new god, the masses. At any rate, history proves that social changes have always been first brought about by minorities, by a mere handful of men."

[3] From a statement by Brodrero at the Fourth International Congress for Intellectual Co-operation, Heidelburg, October, 1927.

It is rather difficult to organize fascist ideas into a coherent doctrine. Apart from the fact that it is still undeveloped, fascism itself lays no particular weight upon an integrally knit theory. Its programme changes constantly, depending on the class to which it addresses itself. In this case, more than in most others, it is essential to separate mere propaganda from the real attitude, in order to gain an understanding of its essential character. This seems to lie in its absolute irrationalism and its activism, which explain also the vacillating and volatile theoretical character of fascist theory. Such institutional ideas as the corporative state, professional organizations, etc., are deliberately omitted from our presentation. Our task is to analyse the attitude towards the problem of theory and practice and the view of history which results therefrom. For this reason, we will find it necessary from time to time to give some attention to the theoretical forerunners of this conception, namely Bergson, Sorel, and Pareto. In the history of fascism, two periods may be distinguished, each of which has had distinct ideological repercussions. The first phase, about two years in length, during which fascism was a mere movement, was marked by the infiltration of activistic-intuitive elements into its intellectual-spiritual outlook. This was the period during which syndicalist theories found entrance to fascism. The first "fasci" were syndicalist and Mussolini at that time was said to be a disciple of Sorel. In the second phase, beginning in November, 1921, fascism becomes stabilized and takes a decisive turn towards the right. In this period nationalistic ideas come to the fore. For a discussion of the manner in which its theory became transformed, in accordance with the changing class basis, and especially the transformations since high finance and large-scale industry allied themselves to it, cf. Beckerath, E. v., *Wesen und Werden des fascistischen Staates* (Berlin, 1927).

history. The conception of history contained in Brodrero's statement is not comparable either to the conservative, the liberal-democratic, or the socialistic conceptions. All these theories, otherwise so antagonistic, share the assumption that there is a definite and ascertainable structure in history within which, so to speak, each event has its proper position. Not everything is possible in every situation.[1] This framework which is constantly changing and revolving must be capable of comprehension. Certain experiences, actions, modes of thought, etc., are possible only in certain places and in certain epochs. Reference to history and the study of history or of society are valuable because orientation to them can and must become a determining factor in conduct and in political activity.

However different the picture which conservatives, liberals, and socialists have derived from history, they all agree that history is made up of a set of intelligible interrelations. At first it was believed that it revealed the plan of divine providence, later that it showed the higher purpose of a dynamically and pantheistically conceived spirit. These were only metaphysical gropings towards an extremely fruitful hypothesis for which history was not merely a heterogeneous succession of events in time, but a coherent interaction of the most significant factors. The understanding of the inner structure of history was sought in order to derive therefrom a measuring-rod for one's own conduct.

While the liberals and socialists continued to believe that the historical structure was completely capable of rationalization, the former insisting that its development was progressively unilinear, and the latter viewing it as a dialectical movement, the conservatives sought to understand the structure of the totality of historical development intuitively by a morphological approach. Different as these points of view were in method and content, they all understood political activity as proceeding on an historical background, and they all agreed that in our own epoch, it becomes necessary to orient oneself to the total situation in which one happens to be placed, if political aims are to be realized. This idea of history as an intelligible scheme disappears in the face of the irrationality of the fascist apotheosis of the deed. To a certain degree this was already the case with its syndicalist forerunner, Sorel,[2] who had already denied the idea of evolution in a similar sense. The conservatives, the liberals, the

[1] In contrast to this, Mussolini said: "For my own part I have no great confidence in these ideals [i.e. pacifism]. Nonetheless, I do not exclude them. I never exclude anything. Anything is possible, even the most impossible and most senseless" (loc. cit., p. 74).

[2] As regards Mussolini's relations with Sorel: Sorel knew him before 1914 and, indeed in 1912, is reported to have said the following concerning him: "Mussolini is no ordinary Socialist. Take my word, some day you will see him at the head of a sacred battalion, saluting the Italian flag. He is an Italian in the style of the fifteenth century—a veritable condottiere. One does not know him yet, but he is the only man active enough to be capable of curing the weakness of the government." Quoted from Pirou, Gaëtan, Georges Sorel (1847-1922), Paris (Marcel Rivière), 1927, p. 53. Cf. also the review by Ernst Posse in Archiv für die Geschichte des Sozialismus und der Arbeiterbewegung, vol. 13, pp. 431 ff.

socialists were one in assuming that in history it can be shown that there
is an interrelationship between events and configurations through which
everything, by virtue of its position, acquires significance. Not every event
could possibly happen in every situation. Fascism regards every interpretation of history as a mere fictive construction destined to disappear
before the deed of the moment as it breaks through the temporal pattern
of history.[1]

That we are dealing here with a theory which holds that history is
meaningless is not changed by the fact that in fascist ideology, especially
since its turn to the right, there are found the ideas of the "national
war" and the ideology of the "Roman Empire". Apart from the fact that
these ideas were, from the very first, consciously experienced as myths,
i.e. as fictions, it should be understood that historically oriented thought
and activity do not mean the romantic idealization of some past epoch or
event, but consist rather in the awareness of one's place in the historical
process which has a clearly articulated structure. It is this clear articulation of the structure which makes one's own participation in the process
intelligible.

The intellectual value of all political and historical knowledge *qua*
knowledge, disappears in the face of this purely intuitional approach,
which appreciates only its ideological and mythological aspect. Thought
is significant here only in so far as it exposes the illusory character of
these fruitless theories of history and unmasks them as self-deceptions.
For this activistic intuitionism, thought only clears the way for the pure
deed free from illusions. The superior person, the leader, knows that all
political and historical ideas are myths. He himself is entirely emanci-
pated from them, but he values them—and this is the obverse side of his
attitude—because they are "derivations" (in Pareto's sense) which stimulate enthusiastic feelings and set in motion irrational "residues" in men,
and are the only forces that lead to political activity.[2] This is a translation
into practice of what Sorel and Pareto[3] formulated in their theories of
the myth and which resulted in their theory of the role of the *élites* and
advance guards.

The profound scepticism towards science and especially cultural sci-

[1] Cf. the essay by Ziegler, H. O., "Ideologienlehre" in *Archiv für Sozialwissenschaft
und Sozialpolitik*, 1927, vol. 57, pp. 657 ff. This author undertakes from the point of
view of Pareto, Sorel, etc., to demolish the "myth of history". He denies that history
contains any ascertainable coherence and points out various contemporary currents
of thought which also affirm this unhistorical approach. Mussolini expressed the same
thought in political-rhetorical form: "We are not hysterical women fearfully awaiting
what the future will bring. We are not waiting for the destiny and revelation of
history" (loc. cit., p. 129) and further—"We do not believe that history repeats
itself, that it follows a prescribed route."

[2] Cf. Sorel, G, *Réflexions sur la violence* (Paris, 1921), chap. 4, pp. 167 ff.

[3] A concise statement of Pareto's sociological views may be found in Bousquet's
Précis de sociologie d'après Vilfredo Pareto (Paris, 1925).

ences which arises from the intuitional approach is not difficult to understand. Whereas Marxism placed an almost religious faith in science, Pareto saw in it only a formal social mechanics. In fascism we see the sober scepticism of this representative of the late bourgeois epoch combined with the self-confidence of a movement still in its youth. Pareto's scepticism toward the knowable is maintained intact, but is supplemented by a faith in the deed as such and in its own vitality.[1]

When everything which is peculiarly historical is treated as inaccessible to science, all that remains for scientific research is the exploration of that most general stratum of regularities which are the same for all men and for all times. Apart from social mechanics, social psychology alone is recognized. The knowledge of social psychology is of value to the leaders purely as a technique for manipulating the masses. This primitive deep-lying stratum of man's psyche is alike in all men whether we deal with the men of to-day, or of ancient Rome, or of the Renaissance.

We find here that this intuitionism has suddenly fused with the quest of the contemporary bourgeoisie for general laws. The result was the gradual elimination from positivism, as represented by Comte for instance, of all traces of a philosophy of history in order to build a generalizing sociology. On the other hand, the beginnings of the conception of ideology which marks the theory of useful myths may be traced largely to Marxism. There are, nevertheless, upon closer examination essential differences.

Marxism, too, raises the issue of ideology in the sense of the "tissue of lies", the "mystifications", the "fictions" which it seeks to expose. It does not, however, bring every attempt at an interpretation of history into this category but only those to which it is in opposition. Not every type of thought is labelled "ideology". Only social strata who have need for disguises and who, from their historical and social situation will not and cannot perceive the true interrelations as they actually exist, necessarily fall victims to these deceptive experiences. But every idea, even a correct one, through the very fact that it can be conceived, appears to be related to a certain historical-social situation. The fact that all thought is related to a certain historical-social situation does not, however, rob it of all possibility of attaining the truth. The intuitional approach on the other hand, which so repeatedly asserts itself in fascist theory, conceives of knowledge and rationalizability as somewhat uncertain and of ideas as of altogether secondary significance.[2] Only a limited knowledge about history or politics is possible—namely that which is contained in the social mechanics and social psychology referred to above.

[1] Mussolini, in one of his speeches, said: "We have created a myth. This myth is a faith, a noble enthusiasm. It does not have to be a reality [!], it is an impulse and a hope, belief, and courage. Our myth is the nation, the great nation which we wish to make into a concrete reality." (Quoted from Carl Schmitt, *Die geistesgeschichtliche Lage des heutigen Parlamentarismus*, p. 89.)

[2] "Temperaments divide men more than ideas." Mussolini, op. cit., p. 55.

For fascism, the Marxian idea of history as a structural integration of economic and social forces in the final analysis is also merely a myth. Just as the character of the historical process is, in the course of time, disintegrated, so the class conception of society is rejected too. There is no proletariat—there are only proletariats.[1] It is characteristic of this type of thought and this mode of life that history dissolves itself into a number of transitory situations in which two factors are decisive; on the one hand, the *élan* of the great leader and of the vanguard or *élites* and on the other the mastery of the only type of knowledge which it is believed possible to obtain concerning the psychology of the masses and the technique of their manipulation. Politics is then possible as a science only in a limited sense—in so far, namely, as it clears the way for action.

It does this in a twofold manner: first, by destroying all the illusions which make us see history as a process; and, secondly, by reckoning with and observing the mass-mind, especially its power-impulses and their functioning. Now to a great extent this mass psyche does, in fact, follow timeless laws because it itself stands outside the course of historical development. By way of contrast, the historical character of the social psyche is perceptible only to groups and persons occupying a definite position in the historical social structure.

In the final analysis, this theory of politics has its roots in Machiavelli, who already laid down its fundamental tenets. The idea of *virtù* anticipates the *élan* of the great leader. A disillusioning realism which destroys all idols, and constant recourse to a technique for the psyche manipulation of the deeply despised masses, are also to be found in his writings, even though they may differ in detail from the fascist conceptions. Finally, the tendency to deny that there is a plan in history and the espousal of the theory of direct intervention of the deed are likewise anticipated. Even the bourgeoisie has often made room in its theory for this doctrine concerning political technique and placed it, as Stahl quite rightly saw, alongside the idea of natural law, which served a normative function,[2] without, however, connecting the two. The more bourgeois ideals and the corresponding view of history were in part realized and in part disintegrated by disillusionment through the accession to power of the bourgeoisie, the more this rational calculation, without any consideration for the historical setting of facts, was recognized as the only form of political knowledge. In the most recent period, this totally detached political technique became associated with activism and intuitionism which denied the intelligibility of history. It became the ideology of those groups who prefer a direct, explosive collision with history to a gradual evolutionary change. This attitude takes many forms—appearing first in the anarchism

[1] Cf. Beckerath, E. v., op. cit., p. 142. Also Mussolini, op. cit., p. 96.
[2] Cf. Stahl, F. J., *Die Philosophie des Rechts*, vol. i, 4th ed., book 4, chap. 1, "Die neuere Politik."

of Bakunin and Proudhon, then in the Sorelien syndicalism, and finally in the fascism of Mussolini.[1]

From a sociological point of view this is the ideology of "putschist" groups led by intellectuals who are outsiders to the liberal bourgeois and socialist stratum of leaders, and who hope to seize power by exploiting the crises which constantly beset modern society in its period of transformation. This period of transformation, whether it leads to socialism or to a capitalistically planned economy, is characterized by the fact that it offers intermittent opportunities for the use of putschist tactics. In the degree that it contains within itself the irrational factors of modern social and economic life, it attracts the explosive irrational elements in the modern mind.

The correctness of the interpretation of this ideology as the expression of a certain social stratum is proved by the fact that historical interpretations made from this point of view are oriented towards the irrational sphere referred to above. Being psychologically and socially situated at a point from which they can discern only the unordered and unrationalized in the development of society, the structural development and the integrated framework of society remain completely hidden from their view.

It is almost possible to establish a sociological correlation between the type of thinking that appeals to organic or organized groups and a consistently systematic interpretation of history. On the other hand, a deep affinity exists between socially uprooted and loosely integrated groups and an a-historical intuitionism. The more organized and organic groups are exposed to disintegration, the more they tend to lose the sense for the consistently ordered conception of history, and the more sensitive they become to the imponderable and the fortuitous. As spontaneously organized putschist groups become more stable they also become more hospitable to long range views of history and to an ordered view of society. Although historical complications often enter into the process, this scheme should be kept in mind because it delineates tendencies and offers fruitful hypotheses. A class or similar organic group never sees history as made up of transitory disconnected incidents; this is possible only for spontaneous groups which arise within them. Even the unhistorical moment of which activism conceives and which it hopes to seize upon is actually torn out of its wider historical context. The concept of practice in this mode of thought is likewise an integral part of the putschist technique, while socially more integrated groups, even when in opposition to the existing order, conceive of action as a continuous movement toward the realization of their ends.[2]

---

[1] Cf. Schmitt, *Parlamentarismus*, ch. 4.

[2] Mussolini himself speaks convincingly concerning the change which the putschist undergoes after attaining power. "It is incredible how a roving, free-lance soldier can change when he becomes a deputy or a town official. He acquires another face. He begins to appreciate that municipal budgets must be studied, and cannot be stormed." (Op. cit., p. 166.)

The contrast between the *élan* of great leaders and *élites* on the one hand and the blind herd on the other reveals the marks of an ideology characteristic of intellectuals who are more intent on providing justifications for themselves than on winning support from the outside. It is a counter-ideology to the pretensions of a leadership which conceives itself to be an organ expressing the interests of broad social strata. This is exemplified by the stratum of conservative leaders who regarded themselves as the organ of the "people",[1] by the liberals who conceived of themselves as the embodiment of the spirit of the age (*Zeitgeist*), and by the socialists and communists who think of themselves as the agents of a class-conscious proletariat.

From this difference in methods of self-justification, it is possible to see that groups operating with the leader-mass dichotomy are ascendant *élites* which are still socially unattached, so to speak, and have yet to create a social position for themselves. They are not primarily interested in overthrowing, reforming, or preserving the social structure—their chief concern is to supplant the existing dominant *élites* by others. It is no accident that the one group regards history as a circulation of *élites*, while for the others, it is a transformation of the historical-social structure. Each gets to see primarily only that aspect of the social and historical totality towards which it is oriented by its purpose.

In the process of transformation of modern society, there are, as has already been mentioned, periods during which the mechanisms which have been devised by the bourgeoisie for carrying on the class struggle (e.g. parliamentarianism) prove insufficient. There are periods when the evolutionary course fails for the time being and crises become acute. Class relations and class stratification become strained and distorted. The class-consciousness of the conflicting groups becomes confused. In such periods it is easy for transitory formations to emerge, and the mass comes into existence, individuals having lost or forgotten their class orientations. At such moments a dictatorship becomes possible. The fascist view of history and its intuitional approach which serves as a preparation for immediate action have changed what is no more than a partial situation into a total view of society.

With the restoration of equilibrium following the crisis, the organized, historical-social forces again become effective. Even if the *élite* which has come to the top in the crisis is able to adjust itself well to the new situation, the dynamic forces of social life nevertheless reassert themselves in the old way. It is not that the social structure has changed, but rather that there has been a reshuffling—a shift in personnel among the various social classes within the frame of the social process which continues to

---

[1] Savigny in this sense created the fiction for evolutionary conservatism that the jurists occupied a special status as the representatives of the folk spirit. (*Vom Beruf unserer Zeit zur Gesetzgebung und Rechtswissenschaft*, Freiburg, 1892, p. 7.)

evolve. An example of such a dictatorship has, with certain modifications, already been witnessed in modern history in the case of Napoleon. Historically this signified nothing more than the rise of certain *élites*. Sociologically it was an indication of the triumph of the ascendant bourgeoisie which knew how to exploit Napoleonic imperialism for its own purposes.

It may be that those elements of the mind which have not as yet been rationalized become crystallized ever anew in a more stable social structure. It may be, too, that the position which underlies this irrationalistic philosophy is inadequate to comprehend the broad trends of historical and social development. None the less the existence of these short-lived explosions directs attention to the irrational depths which have not as yet been comprehended and which are incomprehensible by ordinary historical methods. That which has not yet been rationalized here joins with the non-historical and with those elements in life which cannot be reduced to historical categories. We are given a glimpse of a realm which up to the present appears to have remained unchanging. It includes the blind biological instincts which in their eternal sameness underlie every historical event. These forces can be mastered externally by a technique, but can never reach the level of meaning and can never be internally understood. Besides this sub-historical biological element a spiritual, transcendental element is also to be found in this sphere. It is of this element which is not fully embodied in history, and which, as something unhistorical and alien to our thought, eludes understanding, that the mystics spoke. Although the fascists do not mention it, it must nevertheless rank as the other great challenge to the historical rationalism.

All that has become intelligible, understandable, rationalized, organized, structuralized, artistically, and otherwise formed, and consequently everything historical seems in fact to lie between these two extreme poles. If we attempt to view the interrelations of phenomena from this middle ground, we never get to see what lies above and below history. If, on the other hand, we stand at either of these irrational, extreme poles, we completely lose sight of historical reality in its concreteness.

The attractions of the fascist treatment of the problem of the relations between theory and practice lie in its designation of all thought as illusion. Political thought may be of value in arousing enthusiasm for action, but as a means for scientific comprehension of the field of "politics" which involves the prognostication of the future it is useless. It seems nothing less than remarkable that man, living in the blinding glare of the irrational, is still able to command from instance to instance the empirical knowledge necessary to carry on his everyday life. Sorel once remarked apropos of this: "We know that the social myths do not prevent men from being able to take advantage of all the observations made in the course of everyday life, nor do they interfere with their execution of their regular tasks." In a footnote he added: "It has often been noted that

American and English sectarians, whose religious exaltation is sustained by apocalyptic myths, are none the less in many cases very practical people."[1] Thus man can act despite the fact that he thinks.

It has often been insisted that even Leninism contains a tinge of fascism. But it would be misleading to overlook the differences in emphasizing the similarities. The common element in the two views is confined merely to the activity of aggressive minorities. Only because Leninism was originally the theory of a minority uncompromisingly determined to seize power by revolutionary means did the theory of the significance of leading groups and of their decisive energy come to the fore. But this theory never took flight into a complete irrationalism. The Bolshevist group was only an active minority within a class movement of an increasingly self-conscious proletariat so that the irrational activistic aspects of its doctrines were constantly supported by the assumption of the rational intelligibility of the historical process.

The a-historical spirit of fascism can be derived in part from the spirit of a bourgeoisie already in power. A class which has already risen in the social scale tends to conceive of history in terms of unrelated, isolated events. Historical events appear as a process only as long as the class which views these events still expects something from it. Only such expectations can give rise to utopias on the one hand, and concepts of process on the other. Success in the class struggle, however, does away with the utopian element, and forces long range views into the background the better to devote its powers to its immediate tasks. The consequence is that in place of a view of the whole which formerly took account of tendencies and total structures, there appears a picture of the world composed of mere immediate events and discrete facts. The idea of a "process" and of the structural intelligibility of history becomes a mere myth.

Fascism finds itself serenely able to take over this bourgeois repudiation of history as a structure and process without any inconvenience, since fascism itself is the exponent of bourgeois groups. It accordingly has no intention of replacing the present social order by another, but only of substituting one ruling group for another within the existing class arrangements.[2] The chances for a fascist victory as well as for the justification of its historical theory depend upon the arrival of junctures in which a crisis so profoundly disorganizes the capitalist-bourgeois order, that the more evolutionary means of carrying on the conflict of interests no longer suffice. At moments like these, the chances for power are with him who knows how to utilize the moment with the necessary energy by stimulating active minorities to attack, thus seizing power.

[1] Sorel, op. cit., p. 177.

[2] As regards Mussolini's attitude toward capitalism: ". . . the real history of capitalism will now begin. Capitalism is not just a system of oppression—on the contrary it represents the choice of the fittest, equal opportunities for the most gifted, a more developed sense of individual responsibility," op. cit., p. 96.

III. Synthesis of the Various Perspectives as a Problem of Political Sociology

In the preceding pages we attempted to show concretely how one and the same problem, namely the relation between theory and practice, took a different form in accordance with the differing political positions from which it was approached. What holds true for this basic question of any scientific politics is valid also for all other specific problems. It could be shown in all cases that not only do fundamental orientations, evaluations, and the content of ideas differ but that the manner of stating a problem, the sort of approach made, and even the categories in which experiences are subsumed, collected, and ordered vary according to the social position of the observer.

If the course of political struggles thus far has decisively shown that there is an intimate relationship between the nature of political decisions and intellectual perspective, then it would seem to follow that a science of politics is impossible. But it is precisely at this point, where the difficulties become most pronounced, that we reach a turning point.

It is at this juncture that two new possibilities emerge and at this stage in the formulation of the problem we see two paths which may be followed. On the one hand it is possible to say: Since in the realm of politics the only knowledge that we have is a knowledge which is limited by the position which we occupy, and since the formation of parties is structurally an ineradicable element in politics, it follows that politics can be studied only from a party viewpoint and taught only in a party school. I believe, in fact, that this will prove one road from which immediate developments will follow.

But it has become evident and promises to become more so that, owing to the complicated character of contemporary society, the traditional methods of training the next generation of political leaders, which have had hitherto a largely accidental character, are not adequate to supply the present-day politician with the requisite knowledge. The political parties will therefore find it necessary to develop their party schools with increasing care and elaborateness. Not only will they provide the factual knowledge which will enable prospective political leaders to formulate factual judgments concerning concrete problems, but they will also inculcate the respective points of view from which experience may be organized and mastered.

Every political point of view implies at the same time more than the mere affirmation or rejection of an indisputable set of facts. It implies as well a rather comprehensive *Weltanschauung*. The significance that political leaders attach to the latter is shown by the efforts of all parties to mould the thinking of the masses, not only from a party standpoint, but also from the point of view of a *Weltanschauung*. Political pedagogy signifies the transmission of a particular attitude towards the world which will permeate all aspects of life. Political education to-day signifies further a definite conception of history, a certain mode of interpreting events, and a tendency to seek a philosophical orientation in a definite manner.

This cleavage in modes of thought and *Weltanschauungen* and this increasing differentiation according to political positions has been going on with an increasing intensity since the beginning of the nineteenth century. The formation of party schools will accentuate this tendency, and carry it to its logical conclusion.

But the formation of party schools and the development of party theories is only one of the inevitable consequences of the present situation. It is one which will appeal to those who, because they occupy an extreme position in the social order, must cling to their partisanship, must conceive of antagonisms as absolutes, and suppress any conception of the whole.

The present situation provides still another possibility. It rests, so to speak, on the reverse side of the fundamentally partisan character of political orientation. This alternative, which is at least as important as the other, consists in the following: not only the necessary partisan character of every form of political knowledge is recognized, but also the peculiar character of each variety. It has become incontrovertibly clear to-day that all knowledge which is either political or which involves a world-view, is inevitably partisan. The fragmentary character of all knowledge is clearly recognizable. But this implies the possibility of an integration of many mutually complementary points of view into a comprehensive whole.

Just because to-day we are in a position to see with increasing clarity that mutually opposing views and theories are not infinite in number and are not products of arbitrary will but are mutually complementary and derive from specific social situations, politics as a science is for the first time possible. The present structure of society makes possible a political science which will not be merely a party science, but a science of the whole. Political sociology, as the science which comprehends the whole political sphere, thus attains the stage of realization.

With this there comes the demand for an institution with a broader base than a party school where this science of the political totality may be pursued. Before going into the possibility and structure of this type of investigation, it is necessary to establish more firmly the thesis that each particular point of view needs to be complemented by all the others. Let us recall the instance which we used to illustrate the partisan setting of every problem.

We found that only certain limited aspects and areas of historical and political reality reveal themselves to each of the various parties. The bureaucrat restricted his range of vision to the stabilized part of the life of the state, historical conservatism could see only the regions in which the silently working *Volksgeist* was still operating, in which as in the realm of custom and usage, in religious and cultural association organic and not organized forces were at work. Historical conservatism also was aware that there was a place for a peculiar type of rationality in this sphere of organic forces: it had to decipher the inherent tendencies of growth. Even though the one-sidedness of historical conservatism consisted in the exaggeration of the significance of the irrational elements in the mind and of the irrational social forces corresponding to it in social-historical reality it did nevertheless bring out an important point which could not have been perceived from another standpoint. The same is true of the remaining points of view. Bourgeois-democratic thought both discovered and developed the possibility of a rational means of carrying on the conflict of interests in society which will retain its reality and function in modern life as long as peaceful methods of class conflict are possible.

The development of this approach to political problems was an historical and lasting achievement of the bourgeoisie, and its value may be appreciated even though the one-sidedness of its intellectualism has been completely laid bare. The bourgeois mind had a vital social interest in concealing from itself, by means of this intellectualism, the limits of its own rationalization. Hence it acted as if real conflicts could be fully settled by discussion. It did not realize, however, that closely connected with the realm of politics there arose a new kind of thinking in which theory could not be separated from practice nor thought from intent.

Nowhere is the mutually complementary character of socially-politically determined partial views more clearly visible than here. For here it becomes once more apparent that socialist thought begins at that point where bourgeois-democratic thought reaches its limits, and that it threw new light on just those phenomena which its predecessors, because of the intimate connection with their own interests, had left in the dark. To Marxism belongs the credit for discovering that politics does not consist merely in parliamentary parties and the discussions they carry on, and that these, in whatever concrete form they appear, are only surface expression of deeper-lying economic and social situations which can be made intelligible to a large extent through a new mode of thought. These discoveries signalize the raising of the discussion to a higher level from which a more extensive and more inclusive view of history and a clearer conception of what actually constitutes the domain of politics can be obtained. The discovery of the phenomenon of ideology is structurally closely bound up with this discovery. Although quite one-sided, it represents the first attempt to define the position of socially bound thought as over against "pure theory".

Finally, to return to the last antithesis, whereas Marxism focussed its attention too sharply on and overemphasized the purely structural foundation of the political and historical realm, fascism turned its attention to the amorphous aspects of life, to those "moments" in critical situations which are still present and still have significance, in which class forces become disjointed and confused, when the actions of men, acting as members of transitory masses, assume significance, and when the outcome entirely depends on the vanguards and their leaders who are dominating the situation at the moment. But here, too, it would be overemphasis of a single phase of historical reality to regard these eventualities, even though they are of frequent occurrence, as the essence of historical reality. The divergence of political theories is accounted for mainly by the fact that the different positions and social vantage points as they emerge in the stream of social life enable each one from its particular point in the stream to recognize the stream itself. Thus, at different times, different elementary social interests emerge and accordingly different objects of attention in the total structure are illuminated and viewed as if they were the only ones that existed.

All points of view in politics are but partial points of view because historical totality is always too comprehensive to be grasped by any one of the individual points of view which emerge out of it. Since, however, all these points of view emerge out of the same social and historical current, and since their partiality exists in the matrix of an emerging whole, it is possible to see them in juxtaposition, and their synthesis becomes a problem which must continually be reformulated and resolved. The continuously revised and renewed synthesis of the existing particular viewpoints becomes all the more possible because the attempts at synthesis have no less a tradition than has the knowledge founded upon partisanship. Did not Hegel, coming at the end of a relatively closed epoch, attempt to synthesize in his own work the tendencies which hitherto had developed independently? Even though these syntheses time and again turned out to be partial syntheses, and disintegrated in the course of subsequent development, producing, e.g., left and right Hegelianism, though they were, nevertheless, not absolute but relative syntheses, as such they pointed in a very promising direction.

A demand for an absolute, permanent synthesis would, as far as we are concerned, mean a relapse into the static world view of intellectualism. In a realm in which everything is in the process of becoming, the only adequate synthesis would be a dynamic one, which is reformulated from time to time. There is still the necessity, however, to solve one of the most important problems that can be posited, namely, that of furnishing the most comprehensive view of the whole which is attainable at a given time.

Attempts at synthesis do not come into being unrelated to one another, because each synthesis prepares the road for the next by summarizing the forces and views of its time. A certain progress towards an absolute synthesis in the utopian sense may be noted in that each synthesis attempts to arrive at a wider perspective than the previous one, and that the later ones incorporate the results of those that have gone before.

At this stage of the discussion two difficulties arise even in connection with the relative synthesis.

The first comes from the fact that we can no longer conceive of the partiality of a point of view as merely being a matter of degree. If the cleavage in political and philosophical perceptions consisted merely in the fact that each was concerned with another side or section of the whole, that each illuminated only a particular segment of historical events, an additive synthesis would be possible without further ado. All that would be necessary would be to add up these partial truths and to join them into a whole.

But this simplified conception is no longer tenable when we have seen that the determination of particular viewpoints by their situations is based not only on the selection of subject-matter, but also on the divergence in aspects and in ways of setting the problem, and finally in the divergence of categorical apparatus and principles of organization. The question then is this: is it possible for different styles of thought (by which we mean the differences in modes of thinking just described) to be fused with one another and to undergo synthesis? The course of historical development shows that such a synthesis is possible. Every concrete analysis of thinking which proceeds sociologically and seeks to reveal the historical succession of thought-styles indicates that styles of thought undergo uninterrupted fusion and interpenetration.

Moreover, syntheses in thought-styles are not made only by those who are primarily synthesists, and who more or less consciously attempt to comprehend a whole epoch in their thinking (as e.g. Hegel). They are achieved also by contending groups in so far as they try to unify and reconcile at least all those conflicting currents which they encounter in their own limited sphere. Thus Stahl essayed to bring together in conservatism all the hitherto existing contributory tendencies of thought, as, for example, connecting historicism with theism. Marx devoted himself to the fusion of the liberal-bourgeois generalizing tendency in thinking with Hegelian historicism, which itself was of conservative origin. It is clear then that not merely the contents of thought but also the basis of thought itself is subject to synthesis. This synthesis of hitherto separately developing thought-styles seems to be all the more necessary, since thinking must constantly aim to broaden the capacity of its categorical formal scope if it is to master the problems which daily grow in number and difficulty. If even those whose standpoints are party-bound are finding it necessary to have a broader perspective, this tendency should be all the more pronounced among those, who from the beginning have sought the most inclusive possible understanding of the totality.

II

Types & Trends of Society

4. Karl Marx and Friedrich Engels

On Class

I.

In the social production which men carry on they enter into definite relations that are indispensable and independent of their will; these relations of production correspond to a definite stage of development of their material forces of production. The sum total of these relations of production constitutes the economic structure of society—the real foundation, on which rises a legal and political superstructure and to which correspond definite forms of social consciousness. The mode of production in material life determines the social, political and intellectual life processes in general. It is not the consciousness of men that determines their being, but, on the contrary, their social being that determines their consciousness. At a certain stage of their development, the material forces of production in society come in conflict with the existing relations of production, or—what is but a legal expression for the same thing—with the property relations within which they have been at work before. From forms of development of the forces of production these relations turn into their fetters. Then begins an epoch of social revolution. With the change of the economic foundation the entire immense superstructure is more or less rapidly transformed. In considering such transformations a distinction should always be made between the material transformation of the economic conditions of production which can be determined with the precision of natural science, and the legal, political, religious, aesthetic or philosophic—in short, ideological forms in which men become conscious of this conflict and fight it out. Just as our opinion of an individual is not based on what he thinks of himself, so can we not judge of such a period of transformation by its own consciousness; on the contrary this consciousness must be explained rather from the contradictions of material life, from the existing conflict between the social forces of production and

From Marx, *Selected Works* (New York: International Publishers, n.d.) Edited by V. Adoratsky, Vol. I, Pp. 356-7 and 204-228. Section I is from Marx's Retrospective Preface to his work, *A Contribution to the Critique of Political Economy*, and is the most succinct summary of materialism available. Section II consists of Parts I & II of the *Manifesto of the Communist Party*—C. Wright Mills.

All the following footnotes signed "Ed." are by V. Adoratsky.

the relations of production. No social order ever disappears before all the productive forces for which there is room in it have been developed; and new higher relations of production never appear before the material conditions of their existence have matured in the womb of the old society itself. Therefore, mankind always sets itself only such tasks as it can solve; since, looking at the matter more closely, we will always find that the task itself arises only when the material conditions necessary for its solution already exist or are at least in the process of formation. In broad outlines we can designate the Asiatic, the ancient, the feudal, and the modern bourgeois modes of production as so many epochs in the progress of the economic formation of society. The bourgeois relations of production are the last antagonistic form of the social process of production—antagonistic not in the sense of individual antagonism, but of one arising from the social conditions of life of the individuals; at the same time the productive forces developing in the womb of bourgeois society create the material conditions for the solution of that antagonism. This social formation constitutes, therefore, the closing chapter of the prehistoric stage of human society.

II.

A spectre is haunting Europe—the spectre of communism. All the powers of old Europe have entered into a holy alliance to exorcise this spectre: Pope and tsar, Metternich and Guizot, French Radicals[1] and German police-spies.

Where is the party in opposition that has not been decried as communistic by its opponents in power? Where is the opposition that has not hurled back the branding reproach of communism, against the more advanced opposition parties, as well as against its reactionary adversaries?

Two things result from this fact:

1. Communism is already acknowledged by all European powers to be itself a power.

2. It is high time that Communists should openly, in the face of the whole world, publish their views, their aims, their tendencies, and meet this nursery tale of the spectre of communism with a manifesto of the party itself.

To this end, Communists of various nationalities have assembled in London, and sketched the following manifesto, to be published in the English, French, German, Italian, Flemish and Danish languages.

---

[1] The bourgeois-republicans of the time. Prominent writers and politicians, who fought socialism and communism, such as Marrast, were among their adherents.—*Ed.*

I. Bourgeois and Proletarians[1]

The history of all hitherto existing society[2] is the history of class struggles.

Freeman and slave, patrician and plebeian,[3] lord and serf, guild-master[4] and journeyman, in a word, oppressor and oppressed stood in constant opposition to one another, carried on an uninterrupted, now hidden, now open fight, a fight that each time ended, either in a revolutionary reconstitution of society at large, or in the common ruin of the contending classes.

In the earlier epochs of history, we find almost everywhere a complicated arrangement of society into various orders, a manifold gradation of social rank. In ancient Rome we have patricians, knights, plebeians, slaves; in the Middle Ages, feudal lords, vassals, guild-masters, journeymen, apprentices, serfs; in almost all of these classes, again, subordinate gradations.

The modern bourgeois society that has sprouted from the ruins of feudal society has not done away with class antagonisms. It has but established new classes, new conditions of oppression, new forms of struggle in place of the old ones.

Our epoch, the epoch of the bourgeoisie, possesses, however, this distinctive feature: It has simplified the class antagonisms. Society as a whole is more and more splitting up into two great hostile camps, into two great classes directly facing each other—bourgeoisie and proletariat.

---

[1] By bourgeoisie is meant the class of modern capitalists, owners of the means of social production and employers of wage labour. By proletariat, the class of modern wage labourers who, having no means of production of their own, are reduced to selling their labour power in order to live. [*Note by F. Engels to the English edition of 1888.*]

[2] That is, all *written* history. In 1847 the pre-history of society, the social organisation existing previous to recorded history, was all but unknown. Since then Haxthausen [August von, 1792-1866] discovered common ownership of land in Russia, Maurer [Georg Ludwig von] proved it to be the social foundation from which all Teutonic races started in history, and, by and by, village communities were found to be, or to have been, the primitive form of society everywhere from India to Ireland. The inner organisation of this primitive communistic society was laid bare, in its typical form, by Morgan's [Lewis Henry, 1818-81] crowning discovery of the true nature of the *gens* and its relation to the *tribe*. With the dissolution of these primæval communities, society begins to be differentiated into separate and finally antagonistic classes. I have attempted to retrace this process of dissolution in *Der Ursprung der Familie, des Privateigenthums und des Staats* [*The Origin of the Family, Private Property and the State*], second edition, Stuttgart, 1886. [*Note by F. Engels to the English edition of 1888.*]

[3] Patricians and plebeians—classes in ancient Rome. The patricians were the ruling class of big landowners, who held the land as well as state power. Plebeians were the class of citizens who were free, but did not possess full civic rights. For details of the classes in Rome, see Engels, *The Origin of the Family, Private Property and the State.—Ed.*

[4] Guild-master, that is a full member of a guild, a master within, not a head of a guild. [*Note by F. Engels to the English edition of 1888.*]

From the serfs of the Middle Ages sprang the chartered burghers of the earliest towns. From these burgesses the first elements of the bourgeoisie were developed.

The discovery of America, the rounding of the Cape, opened up fresh ground for the rising bourgeoisie. The East-Indian and Chinese markets, the colonisation of America, trade with the colonies, the increase in the means of exchange and in commodities generally, gave to commerce, to navigation, to industry, an impulse never before known, and thereby, to the revolutionary element in the tottering feudal society, a rapid development.

The feudal system of industry, in which industrial production was monopolised by closed guilds, now no longer sufficed for the growing wants of the new markets. The manufacturing system took its place. The guild-masters were pushed aside by the manufacturing middle class; division of labour between the different corporate guilds vanished in the face of division of labor in each single workshop.

Meantime the markets kept ever growing, the demand ever rising. Even manufacture no longer sufficed. Thereupon, steam and machinery revolutionised industrial production. The place of manufacture was taken by the giant, modern industry, the place of the industrial middle class by industrial millionaires, the leaders of whole industrial armies, the modern bourgeois.

Modern industry has established the world market, for which the discovery of America paved the way. This market has given an immense development to commerce, to navigation, to communication by land. This development has, in its turn, reacted on the extension of industry; and in proportion as industry, commerce, navigation, railways extended, in the same proportion the bourgeoisie developed, increased its capital, and pushed into the background every class handed down from the Middle Ages.

We see, therefore, how the modern bourgeoisie is itself the product of a long course of development, of a series of revolutions in the modes of production and of exchange.

Each step in the development of the bourgeoisie was accompanied by a corresponding political advance of that class. An oppressed class under the sway of the feudal nobility, an armed and self-governing association in the mediæval commune[1]; here independent urban republic (as in Italy and Germany), there taxable "third estate" of the monarchy (as in France); afterwards, in the period of manufacture proper, serving either the semi-

[1] This was the name given their urban communities by the townsmen of Italy and France, after they had purchased or conquered their initial rights of self-government from their feudal lords. [Note by F. Engels to the German edition of 1890.]

"Commune" was the name taken in France by the nascent towns even before they had conquered from their feudal lords and masters local self-government and political rights as the "Third Estate." Generally speaking, for the economical development of the bourgeoisie, England is here taken as the typical country, for its political development, France. [Note by F. Engels to the English edition of 1888.]

feudal or the absolute monarchy[1] as a counterpoise against the nobility, and, in fact, corner-stone of the great monarchies in general—the bourgeoisie has at last, since the establishment of modern industry and of the world market, conquered for itself, in the modern representative state, exclusive political sway. The executive of the modern state is but a committee for managing the common affairs of the whole bourgeoisie.

The bourgeoisie, historically, has played a most revolutionary part.

The bourgeoisie, wherever it has got the upper hand, has put an end to all feudal, patriarchal, idyllic relations. It has pitilessly torn asunder the motley feudal ties that bound man to his "natural superiors," and has left no other nexus between man and man than naked self-interest, than callous "cash payment." It has drowned the most heavenly ecstasies of religious fervour, of chivalrous enthusiasm, of philistine sentimentalism, in the icy water of egotistical calculation. It has resolved personal worth into exchange value, and in place of the numberless indefeasible chartered freedoms, has set up that single, unconscionable freedom—Free Trade. In one word, for exploitation, veiled by religious and political illusions, it has substituted naked, shameless, direct, brutal exploitation.

The bourgeoisie has stripped of its halo every occupation hitherto honoured and looked up to with reverent awe. It has converted the physician, the lawyer, the priest, the poet, the man of science, into its paid wage labourers.

The bourgeoisie has torn away from the family its sentimental veil, and has reduced the family relation to a mere money relation.

The bourgeoisie has disclosed how it came to pass that the brutal display of vigour in the Middle Ages, which reactionaries so much admire, found its fitting complement in the most slothful indolence. It has been the first to show what man's activity can bring about. It has accomplished wonders far surpassing Egyptian pyramids, Roman aqueducts, and Gothic cathedrals; it has conducted expeditions that put in the shade all former exoduses of nations[2] and crusades.[3]

The bourgeoisie cannot exist without constantly revolutionising the instruments of production, and thereby the relations of production, and with them the whole relations of society. Conservation of the old modes

---

[1] "Semi-feudal monarchy in the period of manufacture" signifies a monarchy with the estates (clergy, nobility, "Third Estate"—bourgeoisie) represented in the monarchy's organs.—*Ed.*

[2] Exodus of nations—in Europe from the fourth to the sixth century. Mass migrations of various peoples occurred during this period, extending to the territory of the Roman empire. Engels gives a characterisation of this exodus of nations in *The Origin of the Family, Private Property and the State*, chap. VII and VIII.—*Ed.*

[3] Crusades—big military and looting expeditions to the Near East under the leadership of the Catholic church, during the period from the eleventh century to the thirteenth, allegedly to "free" the Holy Land (Palestine). These expeditions arose on the basis of the increasing contradictions of European feudal society (especially the growing power of the big feudal lords, the rise of impoverished knights-errant, the increasing stratum of poor landless peasants), its motive-power was merchant capital, aiming to conquer the trade routes to the East.—*Ed.*

of production in unaltered form, was, on the contrary, the first condition of existence for all earlier industrial classes. Constant revolutionising of production, uninterrupted disturbance of all social conditions, everlasting uncertainty and agitation distinguish the bourgeois epoch from all earlier ones. All fixed, fast frozen relations, with their train of ancient and venerable prejudices and opinions, are swept away, all new-formed ones become antiquated before they can ossify. All that is solid melts into air, all that is holy is profaned, and man is at last compelled to face with sober senses his real conditions of life and his relations with his kind.

The need of a constantly expanding market for its products chases the bourgeoisie over the whole surface of the globe. It must nestle everywhere, settle everywhere, establish connections everywhere.

The bourgeoisie has through its exploitation of the world market given a cosmopolitan character to production and consumption in every country. To the great chagrin of reactionaries, it has drawn from under the feet of industry the national ground on which it stood. All old-established national industries have been destroyed or are daily being destroyed. They are dislodged by new industries, whose introduction becomes a life and death question for all civilised nations, by industries that no longer work up indigenous raw material, but raw material drawn from the remotest zones; industries whose products are consumed, not only at home, but in every quarter of the globe. In place of the old wants, satisfied by the production of the country, we find new wants, requiring for their satisfaction the products of distant lands and climes. In place of the old local and national seclusion and self-sufficiency, we have intercourse in every direction, universal inter-dependence of nations. And as in material, so also in intellectual production. The intellectual creations of individual nations become common property. National one-sidedness and narrow-mindedness become more and more impossible, and from the numerous national and local literatures there arises a world literature.

The bourgeoisie, by the rapid improvement of all instruments of production, by the immensely facilitated means of communication, draws all, even the most barbarian, nations into civilisation. The cheap prices of its commodities are the heavy artillery with which it batters down all Chinese walls, with which it forces the barbarians' intensely obstinate hatred of foreigners to capitulate. It compels all nations, on pain of extinction, to adopt the bourgeois mode of production; it compels them to introduce what it calls civilisation into their midst, *i.e.*, to become bourgeois themselves. In one word, it creates a world after its own image.

The bourgeois has subjected the country to the rule of the towns. It has created enormous cities, has greatly increased the urban population as compared with the rural, and has thus rescued a considerable part of the population from the idiocy of rural life. Just as it has made the country dependent on the towns, so it has made barbarian and semi-barbarian countries dependent on the civilised ones, nations of peasants on nations of bourgeois, the East on the West.

The bourgeoisie keeps more and more doing away with the scattered state of the population, of the means of production, and of property. It has agglomerated population, centralised means of production, and has concentrated property in a few hands. The necessary consequence of this was political centralisation. Independent, or but loosely connected provinces, with separate interests, laws, governments and systems of taxation, became lumped together into one nation, with one government, one code of laws, one national class interest, one frontier and one customs tariff.

The bourgeoisie, during its rule of scarce one hundred years, has created more massive and more colossal productive forces than have all preceding generations together. Subjection of nature's forces to man, machinery, application of chemistry to industry and agriculture, steam navigation, railways, electric telegraphs, clearing of whole continents for cultivation, canalisation of rivers, whole populations conjured out of the ground—what earlier century had even a presentiment that such productive forces slumbered in the lap of social labour?

We see then: the means of production and of exchange, on whose foundation the bourgeoisie built itself up, were generated in feudal society. At a certain stage in the development of these means of production and of exchange, the conditions under which feudal society produced and exchanged, the feudal organisation of agriculture and manufacturing industry, in one word, the feudal relations of property became no longer compatible with the already developed productive forces; they became so many fetters. They had to be burst asunder; they were burst asunder.

Into their place stepped free competition, accompanied by a social and political constitution adapted to it, and by the economic and political sway of the bourgeois class.

A similar movement is going on before our own eyes. Modern bourgeois society with its relations of production, of exchange and of property, a society that has conjured up such gigantic means of production and of exchange, is like the sorcerer who is no longer able to control the powers of the nether world whom he has called up by his spells. For many a decade past the history of industry and commerce is but the history of the revolt of modern productive forces against modern conditions of production, against the property relations that are the conditions for the existence of the bourgeoisie and of its rule. It is enough to mention the commercial crises that by their periodical return put the existence of the entire bourgeois society on its trial, each time more threateningly. In these crises a great part not only of the existing products, but also of the previously created productive forces, are periodically destroyed. In these crises there breaks out an epidemic that, in all earlier epochs, would have seemed an absurdity—the epidemic of over-production. Society suddenly finds itself put back into a state of momentary barbarism; it appears as if a famine, a universal war of devastation had cut off the supply of every means of subsistence; industry and commerce seem to be destroyed. And why? Because there is too much civilisation, too much means of subsistence, too much industry, too much commerce. The productive forces at the disposal of society no longer tend to further the development of the conditions of bourgeois property; on the contrary, they have become too powerful for these conditions, by which they are fettered, and so soon as they overcome these fetters, they bring disorder into the whole of bourgeois society, endanger the existence of bourgeois property. The conditions of bourgeois society are too narrow to comprise the wealth created by them. And how does the bourgeoisie get over these crises? On the one hand, by enforced destruction of a mass of productive forces; on the other, by the conquest of new markets, and by the more thorough exploitation of the old ones. That is to say, by paving the way for more extensive and more destructive crises, and by diminishing the means whereby crises are prevented.

The weapons with which the bourgeoisie felled feudalism to the ground are now turned against the bourgeoisie itself.

But not only has the bourgeoisie forged the weapons that bring death to itself; it has also called into existence the men who are to wield those weapons—the modern working class—the proletarians.

In proportion as the bourgeoisie, *i.e.*, capital, is developed, in the same proportion is the proletariat, the modern working class, developed—a class of labourers, who live only so long as they find work, and who find work only so long as their labour increases capital. These labourers, who must sell themselves piecemeal, are a commodity, like every other article of commerce, and are consequently exposed to all the vicissitudes of competition, to all the fluctuations of the market.

Owing to the extensive use of machinery and to division of labour, the work of the proletarians has lost all individual character, and, consequently, all charm for the workman. He becomes an appendage of the machine, and it is only the most simple, most monotonous, and most easily acquired knack, that is required of him. Hence, the cost of production of a workman is restricted, almost entirely, to the means of subsistence that he requires for his maintenance, and for the propagation of his race. But the price of a commodity, and therefore also of labour,[1] is equal to its cost of production. In proportion, therefore, as the repulsiveness of the work increases, the wage decreases. Nay more, in proportion as the use of machinery and division of labour increases, in the same proportion the burden of toil also increases, whether by prolongation of the working

---

[1] Marx made a correction subsequently, when he developed the theory of surplus value: he substituted "the value of labour power" for "the value of labour." See the explanation in Engels' Introduction to Marx's *Wage Labour and Capital*, p. 242 *et seq.* of the present volume.—*Ed.*

hours, by increase of the work exacted in a given time, or by increased speed of the machinery, etc.

Modern industry has converted the little workshop of the patriarchal master into the great factory of the industrial capitalist. Masses of labourers, crowded into the factory, are organised like soldiers. As privates of the industrial army they are placed under the command of a perfect hierarchy of officers and sergeants. Not only are they slaves of the bourgeois class, and of the bourgeois state; they are daily and hourly enslaved by the machine, by the overlooker, and, above all, by the individual bourgeois manufacturer himself. The more openly this despotism proclaims gain to be its end and aim, the more petty, the more hateful and the more embittering it is.

The less the skill and exertion of strength implied in manual labour, in other words, the more modern industry becomes developed, the more is the labour of men superseded by that of women. Differences of age and sex have no longer any distinctive social validity for the working class. All are instruments of labour, more or less expensive to use, according to their age and sex.

No sooner is the exploitation of the labourer by the manufacturer, so far at an end, that he receives his wages in cash, than he is set upon by the other portions of the bourgeoisie, the landlord, the shopkeeper, the pawnbroker, etc.

The lower strata of the middle class—the small tradespeople, shop-keepers, and retired tradesmen[1] generally, the handicraftsmen and peasants—all these sink gradually into the proletariat, partly because their diminutive capital does not suffice for the scale on which modern industry is carried on, and is swamped in the competition with the large capitalists, partly because their specialised skill is rendered worthless by new methods of production. Thus the proletariat is recruited from all classes of the population.

The proletariat goes through various stages of development. With its birth begins its struggle with the bourgeoisie. At first the contest is carried on by individual labourers, then by the work people of a factory, then by the operatives of one trade, in one locality, against the individual bourgeois who directly exploits them. They direct their attacks not against the bourgeois conditions of production, but against the instruments of production themselves; they destroy imported wares that compete with their labour, they smash to pieces machinery, they set factories ablaze, they seek to restore by force the vanished status of the workman of the Middle Ages.

At this stage the labourers still form an incoherent mass scattered over

---

[1] *Rentier* in the German original. This signifies a property owner (in this case a small property owner), living on the income of his capital invested in securities, such as domestic and foreign government bonds, or industrial shares.—Ed.

the whole country, and broken up by their mutual competition. If anywhere they unite to form more compact bodies, this is not yet the consequence of their own active union, but of the union of the bourgeoisie, which class, in order to attain its own political ends, is compelled to set the whole proletariat in motion, and is moreover yet, for a time, able to do so. At this stage, therefore, the proletarians do not fight their enemies, but the enemies of their enemies, the remnants of absolute monarchy, the landowners, the non-industrial bourgeois, the petty bourgeoisie. Thus the whole historical movement is concentrated in the hands of the bourgeoisie; every victory so obtained is a victory for the bourgeoisie.

But with the development of industry the proletariat not only increases in number; it becomes concentrated in greater masses, its strength grows, and it feels that strength more. The various interests and conditions of life within the ranks of the proletariat are more and more equalised, in proportion as machinery obliterates all distinctions of labour, and nearly everywhere reduces wages to the same low level. The growing competition among the bourgeois, and the resulting commercial crises, make the wages of the workers ever more fluctuating. The unceasing improvement of machinery, ever more rapidly developing, makes their livelihood more and more precarious; the collisions between individual workmen and individual bourgeois take more and more the character of collisions between two classes. Thereupon the workers begin to form combinations (trades unions) against the bourgeois; they club together in order to keep up the rate of wages; they found permanent associations in order to make provisions beforehand for these occasional revolts. Here and there the contest breaks out into riots.

Now and then the workers are victorious, but only for a time. The real fruit of their battles lies, not in the immediate result, but in the ever expanding union of the workers. This union is helped on by the improved means of communication that are created by modern industry, and that place the workers of different localities in contact with one another. It was just this contact that was needed to centralise the numerous local struggles, all of the same character, into one national struggle between classes. But every class struggle is a political struggle. And that union, to attain which the burghers of the Middle Ages, with their miserable highways, required centuries, the modern proletarians, thanks to railways, achieve in a few years.

This organization of the proletarians into a class, and consequently into a political party, is continually being upset again by the competition between the workers themselves. But it ever rises up again, stronger, firmer, mightier. It compels legislative recognition of particular interests of the workers, by taking advantage of the divisions among the bourgeoisie itself. Thus the ten-hours' bill in England was carried.

Altogether, collisions between the classes of the old society further in many ways the course of development of the proletariat. The bourgeoisie finds itself involved in a constant battle. At first with the aristocracy; later on, with those portions of the bourgeoisie itself, whose interests have become antagonistic to the progress of industry; at all times with the bourgeoisie of foreign countries. In all these battles it sees itself compelled to appeal to the proletariat, to ask for its help, and thus, to drag it into the political arena. The bourgeoisie itself, therefore, supplies the proletariat with its own elements of political and general education, in other words, it furnishes the proletariat with weapons for fighting the bourgeoisie.

Further, as we have already seen, entire sections of the ruling classes are, by the advance of industry, precipitated into the proletariat, or are at least threatened in their conditions of existence. These also supply the proletariat with fresh elements of enlightenment and progress.

Finally, in times when the class struggle nears the decisive hour, the process of dissolution going on within the ruling class, in fact within the whole range of old society, assumes such a violent, glaring character, that a small section of the ruling class cuts itself adrift, and joins the revolutionary class, the class that holds the future in its hands. Just as, therefore, at an earlier period, a section of the nobility went over to the bourgeoise, so now a portion of the bourgeoisie goes over to the proletariat, and in particular, a portion of the bourgeois ideologists, who have raised themselves to the level of comprehending theoretically the historical movement as a whole.

Of all the classes that stand face to face with the bourgeoisie today, the proletariat alone is a really revolutionary class. The other classes decay and finally disappear in the face of modern industry; the proletariat is its special and essential product. The lower middle class, the small manufacturer, the shopkeeeper, the artisan, the peasant, all these fight against the bourgeoisie, to save from extinction their existence as fractions of the middle class. They are therefore not revolutionary, but conservative. Nay more, they are reactionary, for they try to roll back the wheel of history. If by chance they are revolutionary, they are so only in view of their impending transfer into the proletariat; they thus defend not their present, but their future interests; they desert their own standpoint to place themselves at that of the proletariat.

The "dangerous class," the social scum, that passively rotting mass thrown off by the lowest layers of old society, may, here and there, be swept into the movement by a proletarian revolution; its conditions of life, however, prepare it far more for the part of a bribed tool of reactionary intrigue.

In the conditions of the proletariat, those of old society at large are already virtually swamped. The proletarian is without property; his relation to his wife and children has no longer anything in common with the bourgeois family relations: modern industrial labour, modern subjection to capital, the same in England as in France, in America as in

Germany, has stripped him of every trace of national character. Law, morality, religion, are to him so many bourgeois prejudices, behind which lurk in ambush just as many bourgeois interests.

All the preceding classes that got the upper hand, sought to fortify their already acquired status by subjecting society at large to their conditions of appropriation. The proletarians cannot become masters of the productive forces of society, except by abolishing their own previous mode of appropriation, and thereby also every other previous mode of appropriation. They have nothing of their own to secure and to fortify: their mission is to destroy all previous securities for, and insurances of, individual property.

All previous historical movements were movements of minorities, or in the interest of minorities. The proletarian movement is the self-conscious, independent movement of the immense majority, in the interest of the immense majority. The proletariat, the lowest stratum of our present society, cannot stir, cannot raise itself up, without the whole superincumbent strata of official society being sprung into the air.

Though not in substance, yet in form, the struggle of the proletariat with the bourgeoisie is at first a national struggle. The proletariat of each country must, of course, first of all settle matters with its own bourgeoisie.

In depicting the most general phases of the development of the proletariat, we traced the more or less veiled civil war, raging within existing society, up to the point where that war breaks out into open revolution, and where the violent overthrow of the bourgeoisie lays the foundation for the ways of the proletariat.

Hitherto, every form of society has been based, as we have already seen, on the antagonism of oppressing and oppressed classes. But in order to oppress a class, certain conditions must be assured to it under which it can, at least, continue its slavish existence. The serf, in the period of serfdom, raised himself to membership in the commune, just as the petty bourgeois, under the yoke of feudal absolutism, managed to developed into a bourgeois. The modern labourer, on the contrary, instead of rising with the progress of industry, sinks deeper and deeper below the conditions of existence of his own class. He becomes a pauper, and pauperism develops more rapidly than population and wealth. And here it becomes evident, that the bourgeoisie is unfit any longer to be the ruling class in society, and to impose its conditions of existence upon society as an over-riding law. It is unfit to rule because it is incompetent to assure an existence to its slave within his slavery, because it cannot help letting him sink into such a state, that it has to feed him, instead of being fed by him. Society can no longer live under this bourgeoisie, in other words, its existence is no longer compatible with society.

The essential condition for the existence and for the sway of the bourgeois class, is the formation and augmentation of capital; the condition for capital is wage labour. Wage labour rests exclusively on competition between the labourers. The advance of industry, whose involuntary promoter is the bourgeoisie, replaces the isolation of the labourers, due to competition, by their revolutionary combination, due to association. The development of modern industry, therefore, cuts from under its feet the very foundation on which the bourgeoisie produces and appropriates products. What the bourgeoisie therefore produces, above all, are its own grave-diggers. Its fall and the victory of the proletariat are equally inevitable.

II. PROLETARIANS AND COMMUNISTS

In what relation do the Communists stand to the proletarians as a whole?

The Communists do not form a separate party opposed to other working class parties.

They have no interests separate and apart from those of the proletariat as a whole.

They do not set up any sectarian principles of their own, by which to shape and mould the proletarian movement.

The Communists are distinguished from the other working class parties by this only: 1. In the national struggles of the proletarians of the different countries, they point out and bring to the front the common interests of the entire proletariat, independently of all nationality. 2. In the various stages of development which the struggle of the working class against the bourgeoisie has to pass through, they always and everywhere represent the interests of the movement as a whole.

The Communists, therefore, are on the one hand, practically, the most advanced and resolute section of the working class parties of every country, that section which pushes forward all others; on the other hand, theoretically, they have over the great mass of the proletariat the advantage of clearly understanding the line of march, the conditions, and the ultimate general results of the proletarian movement.

The immediate aim of the Communists is the same as that of all the other proletarian parties: Formation of the proletariat into a class, overthrow of the bourgeois supremacy, conquest of political power by the proletariat.

The theoretical conclusions of the Communists are in no way based on ideas or principles that have been invented, or discovered, by this or that would-be universal reformer.

They merely express, in general terms, actual relations springing from an existing class struggle, from a historical movement going on under our very eyes. The abolition of existing property relations is not at all a distinctive feature of communism.

All property relations in the past have continually been subject to historical change consequent upon the change in historical conditions.

The French Revolution, for example, abolished feudal property in favour of bourgeois property.[1]

The distinguishing feature of communism is not the abolition of property generally, but the abolition of bourgeois property. But modern bourgeois private property is the final and most complete expression of the system of producing and appropriating products that is based on class antagonisms, on the exploitation of the many by the few.

In this sense, the theory of the Communists may be summed up in the single sentence: Abolition of private property.

We Communists have been reproached with the desire of abolishing the right of personally acquiring property as the fruit of a man's own labour, which property is alleged to be the groundwork of all personal freedom, activity and independence.

Hard-won, self-acquired, self-earned property! Do you mean the property of the petty artisan and of the small peasant, a form of property that preceded the bourgeois form? There is no need to abolish that: the development of industry has to a great extent already destroyed it, and is still destroying it daily.

Or do you mean modern bourgeois private property?

But does wage labour create any property for the labourer? Not a bit. It creates capital, *i.e.*, that kind of property which exploits wage labour, and which cannot increase except upon condition of begetting a new supply of wage labour for fresh exploitation. Property, in its present form, is based on the antagonism of capital and wage labour. Let us examine both sides of this antagonism.

To be a capitalist, is to have not only a purely personal, but a social, *status* in production. Capital is a collective product, and only by the united action of many members, nay, in the last resort, only by the united action of all members of society, can it be set in motion.

Capital is therefore not a personal, it is a social power.

When, therefore, capital is converted into common property, into the property of all members of society, personal property is not thereby transformed into social property. It is only the social character of the property that is changed. It loses its class character.

Let us now take wage labour.

The average price of wage labour is the minimum wage, *i.e.*, that quantum of the means of subsistence which is absolutely requisite to keep the labourer in bare existence as a labourer. What, therefore, the wage labourer appropriates by means of his labour, merely suffices to prolong and reproduce a bare existence. We by no means intend to

[1] This refers to the Great French Revolution (1789-94) which overthrew the absolute monarchy and rule of the French nobility.—*Ed.*

abolish this personal appropriation of the products of labour, an appropriation that is made for the maintenance and reproduction of human life, and that leaves no surplus wherewith to command the labour of others. All that we want to do away with is the miserable character of this appropriation, under which the labourer lives merely to increase capital, and is allowed to live only in so far as the interest of the ruling class requires it.

In bourgeois society, living labour is but a means to increase accumulated labour. In communist society, accumulated labour is but a means to widen, to enrich, to promote the existence of the labourer.

In bourgeois society, therefore, the past dominates the present; in communist society, the present dominates the past. In bourgeois society capital is independent and has individuality, while the living person is dependent and has no individuality.

And the abolition of this state of things is called by the bourgeois, abolition of individuality and freedom! And rightly so. The abolition of bourgeois individuality, bourgeois independence, and bourgeois freedom is undoubtedly aimed at.

By freedom is meant, under the present bourgeois conditions of production, free trade, free selling and buying.

But if selling and buying disappears, free selling and buying disappears also. This talk about free selling and buying, and all the other "brave words" of our bourgeoisie about freedom in general, have a meaning, if any, only in contrast with restricted selling and buying, with the fettered traders of the Middle Ages, but have no meaning when opposed to the communist abolition of buying and selling, of the bourgeois conditions of production, and of the bourgeoisie itself.

You are horrified at our intending to do away with private property. But in your existing society, private property is already done away with for nine-tenths of the population; its existence for the few is solely due to its non-existence in the hands of those nine-tenths. You reproach us, therefore, with intending to do away with a form of property, the necessary condition for whose existence is the non-existence of any property for the immense majority of society.

In one word, you reproach us with intending to do away with your property. Precisely so; that is just what we intend.

From the moment when labour can no longer be converted into capital, money, or rent,[1] into a social power capable of being monopolised, *i.e.,* from the moment when individual property can no longer be transformed into bourgeois property, into capital, from that moment, you say, individuality vanishes.

---

[1] That part of the surplus value created by the workers' labour (and hence of the exploiters' income as well (which goes to the landowner as land rent or in the form of additional income, if he is his own entrepreneur.—*Ed.*

You must, therefore, confess that by "individual" you mean no other person than the bourgeois, than the middle-class owner of property. This person must, indeed, be swept out of the way, and made impossible.

Communism deprives no man of the power to appropriate the products of society; all that it does is to deprive him of the power to subjugate the labour of others by means of such appropriation.

It has been objected, that upon the abolition of private property all work will cease, and universal laziness will overtake us.

According to this, bourgeois society ought long ago to have gone to the dogs through sheer idleness; for those of its members who work, acquire nothing, and those who acquire anything, do not work. The whole of this objection is but another expression of the tautology: There can no longer be any wage labour when there is no longer any capital.

All objections urged against the communistic mode of producing and appropriating material products, have, in the same way, been urged against the communistic modes of producing and appropriating intellectual products. Just as to the bourgeois, the disappearance of class property is the disappearance of production itself, so the disappearance of class culture is to him identical with the disappearance of all culture.

That culture, the loss of which he laments, is, for the enormous majority, a mere training to act as a machine.

But don't wrangle with us so long as you apply, to our intended abolition of bourgeois property, the standard of your bourgeois notions of freedom, culture, law, etc. Your very ideas are but the outgrowth of the conditions of your bourgeois production and bourgeois property, just as your jurisprudence is but the will of your class made into a law for all, a will whose essential character and direction are determined by the economical conditions of existence of your class.

The selfish misconception that induces you to transform into eternal laws of nature and of reason, the social forms springing from your present mode of production and form of property—historical relations that rise and disappear in the progress of production—this misconception you share with every ruling class that has preceded you. What you see clearly in the case of ancient property,[1] what you admit in the case of feudal property, you are of course forbidden to admit in the case of your own bourgeois form of property.

Abolition of the family! Even the most radical flare up at this infamous proposal of the Communists.

On what foundation is the present family, the bourgeois family, based? On capital, on private gain. In its completely developed form this family exists only among the bourgeoisie. But this state of things finds it complement in the practical absence of the family among the proletarians, and in public prostitution.

[1] Property in the ancient world (Greece, Rome), based on the exploitation of slave labour.—Ed.

The bourgeois family will vanish as a matter of course when its complement vanishes, and both will vanish with the vanishing of capital.

Do you charge us with wanting to stop the exploitation of children by their parents? To this crime we plead guilty.

But, you will say, we destroy the most hallowed of relations, when we replace home education by social.

And your education! Is not that also social, and determined by the social conditions under which you educate, by the intervention direct or indirect, of society, by means of schools, etc.? The Communists have not invented the intervention of society in education; they do but seek to alter the character of that intervention, and to rescue education from the influence of the ruling class.

The bourgeois claptrap about the family and education, about the hallowed correlation of parent and child, becomes all the more disgusting, the more, by the action of modern industry, all family ties among the proletarians are torn asunder, and their children transformed into simple articles of commerce and instruments of labour.

But you Communists would introduce community of women, screams the whole bourgeoisie in chorus.

The bourgeois sees in his wife a mere instrument of production. He hears that the instruments of production are to be exploited in common, and, naturally, can come to no other conclusion than that the lot of being common to all will likewise fall to the women.

He has not even a suspicion that the real point aimed at is to do away with the status of women as mere instruments of production.

For the rest, nothing is more ridiculous than the virtuous indignation of our bourgeois at the community of women which, they pretend, is to be openly and officially established by the Communists. The Communists have no need to introduce community of women; it has existed almost from time immemorial.

Our bourgeois, not content with having the wives and daughters of their proletarians at their disposal, not to speak of common prostitutes, take the greatest pleasure in seducing each other's wives.

Bourgeois marriage is in reality a system of wives in common and thus, at the most, what the Communists might possibly be reproached with is that they desire to introduce, in substitution for a hypocritically concealed, an openly legalised community of women. For the rest, it is self-evident, that the abolition of the present system of production must bring with it the abolition of the community of women springing from that system, *i.e.*, of prostitution both public and private.

The Communists are further reproached with desiring to abolish countries and nationality.

The workingmen have no country. We cannot take from them what they have not got. Since the proletariat must first of all acquire political supremacy, must rise to be the leading class of the nation, must constitute itself *the* nation, it is, so far, itself national, though not in the bourgeois sense of the word.

National differences and antagonisms between peoples are daily more and more vanishing, owing to the development of the bourgeoisie, to freedom of commerce, to the world market, to uniformity in the mode of production and in the conditions of life corresponding thereto.

The supremacy of the proletariat will cause them to vanish still faster. United action of the leading civilised countries at least, is one of the first conditions for the emancipation of the proletariat.

In proportion as the exploitation of one individual by another is put an end to, the exploitation of one nation by another will also be put an end to. In proportion as the antagonism between classes within the nation vanishes, the hostility of one nation to another will come to an end.

The charges against communism made from a religious, a philosophical and, generally, from an ideological standpoint, are not deserving of serious examination.

Does it require deep intuition to comprehend that man's ideas, views, and conceptions, in one word, man's consciousness, changes with every change in the conditions of his material existence, in his social relations and in his social life?

What else does the history of ideas prove, than that intellectual production changes its character in proportion as material production is changed? The ruling ideas of each age have ever been the ideas of its ruling class.

When people speak of ideas that revolutionise society, they do but express the fact, that within the old society, the elements of a new one have been created, and that the dissolution of the old ideas keeps even pace with the dissolution of the old conditions of existence.

When the ancient world was in its last throes, the ancient religions were overcome by Christianty. When Christian ideas succumbed in the eighteenth century to rationalist ideas, feudal society fought its death battle with the then revolutionary bourgeoisie. The ideas of religious liberty and freedom of conscience, merely gave expression to the sway of free competition within the domain of knowledge.

"Undoubtedly," it will be said, "religious, moral, philosophical and juridical ideas have been modified in the course of historical development. But religion, morality, philosophy, political science, and law, constantly survived this change."

"There are, besides, eternal truths, such as Freedom, Justice, etc., that are common to all states of society. But communism abolishes eternal truths, it abolishes all religion, and all morality, instead of constituting them on a new basis; it therefore acts in contradiction to all past historical experience."

What does this accusation reduce itself to? The history of all past society has consisted in the development of class antagonisms, antagonisms that assumed different forms at different epochs.

But whatever form they may have taken, one fact is common to all past ages, *viz.*, the exploitation of one part of society by the other. No wonder, then, that the social consciousness of past ages, despite all the multiplicity and variety it displays, moves within certain common forms, or general ideas, which cannot completely vanish except with the total disappearance of class antagonisms.

The communist revolution is the most radical rupture with traditional property relations; no wonder that its development involves the most radical rupture with traditional ideas.

But let us have done with the bourgeois objections to communism.

We have seen above, that the first step in the revolution by the working class, is to raise the proletariat to the position of ruling class, to win the battle of democracy.

The proletariat will use its political supremacy to wrest, by degrees, all capital from the bourgeoisie, to centralise all instruments of production in the hands of the state, *i.e.*, of the proletariat organised as the ruling class;[1] and to increase the total of productive forces as rapidly as possible.

Of course, in the beginning, this cannot be effected except by means of despotic inroads on the rights of property, and on the conditions of bourgeois production; by means of measures, therefore, which appear economically insufficient and untenable, but which, in the course of the movement, outstrip themselves, necessitate further inroads upon the old social order, and are unavoidable as a means of entirely revolutionising the mode of production.

These measures will of course be different in different countries.

Nevertheless in the most advanced countries, the following will be pretty generally applicable.[2]

---

[1] Lenin makes the following comment on this passage of *The Communist Manifesto*: "*The state, i.e., the proletariat organised as the ruling class*, is precisely the dictatorship of the proletariat." When Marx spoke of "winning the battle of democracy" he meant "proletarian democracy"—the dictatorship of the proletariat. On the basis of the experiences of the 1848 Revolution, Marx in *The Eighteenth Brumaire* developed his doctrine on the dictatorship of the proletariat. Here he says that the proletariat cannot simply take possession of the bourgeois state machinery, but must "smash," must "destroy" it. On the basis of the experiences of the Paris Commune (see *The Civil War in France*), Marx gives a characterisation of the machinery of state (the state of the Commune type), with which the proletariat, during its dictatorship, will replace the oppressive bourgeois state machinery destroyed by it. (See Lenin, *The State and Revolution*.)—*Ed.*

[2] In the *Grundsätze des Kommunismus* [*Principles of Communism*], the draft of the Manifesto, Engels set forth his programme in twelve demands. Stalin, at the Fifteenth Conference of the C.P.S.U. in 1926, compared these demands with the achievements of the October Revolution, pointing out that "nine-tenths of this programme has already been realised by our revolution."—*Ed.*

1. Abolition of property in land and application of all rents of land to public purposes.

2. A heavy progressive or graduated income tax.

3. Abolition of all right of inheritance.

4. Confiscation of the property of all emigrants and rebels.

5. Centralisation of credit in the hands of the state, by means of a national bank with state capital and an exclusive monopoly.

6. Centralisation of the means of communication and transport in the hands of the state.

7. Extension of factories and instruments of production owned by the state; the bringing into cultivation of waste lands, and the improvement of the soil generally in accordance with a common plan.

8. Equal obligation of all to work. Establishment of industrial armies, especially for agriculture.

9. Combination of agriculture with manufacturing industries; gradual abolition of the distinction between town and country, by a more equable distribution of the population over the country.

10. Free education for all children in public schools. Abolition of children's factory labour in its present form. Combination of education with industrial production, etc.

When, in the course of development, class distinctions have disappeared, and all production has been concentrated in the hands of a vast association of the whole nation, the public power will lose its political character. Political power, properly so called, is merely the organised power of one class for oppressing another. If the proletariat during its contest with the bourgeoisie is compelled, by the force of circumstances, to organise itself as a class; if, by means of a revolution, it makes itself the ruling class, and, as such, sweeps away by force the old conditions of production, then it will, along with these conditions, have swept away the conditions for the existence of class antagonisms and of classes generally, and will thereby have abolished its own supremacy as a class.

In place of the old bourgeois society, with its classes and class antagonisms, we shall have an association, in which the free development of each is the condition for the free development of all.

5. Max Weber

Class, Status, Party

I. Economically Determined Power and the Social Order

Law exists when there is a probability that an order will be upheld by a specific staff of men who will use physical or psychical compulsion with the intention of obtaining conformity with the order, or of inflicting sanctions for infringement of it.* The structure of every legal order directly influences the distribution of power, economic or otherwise, within its respective community. This is true of all legal orders and not only that of the state. In general, we understand by 'power' the chance of a man or of a number of men to realize their own will in a communal action even against the resistance of others who are participating in the action.

'Economically conditioned' power is not, of course, identical with 'power' as such. On the contrary, the emergence of economic power may be the consequence of power existing on other grounds. Man does not strive for power only in order to enrich himself economically. Power, including economic power, may be valued 'for its own sake.' Very frequently the striving for power is also conditioned by the social 'honor' it entails. Not all power, however, entails social honor: The typical American Boss, as well as the typical big speculator, deliberately relinquishes social honor. Quite generally, 'mere economic' power, and especially 'naked' money power, is by no means a recognized basis of social honor. Nor is power the only basis of social honor. Indeed, social honor, or prestige, may even be the basis of political or economic power, and very frequently has been. Power, as well as honor, may be guaranteed by the legal order, but, at least normally, it is not their primary source. The

From *From Max Weber: Essays in Sociology*, translated, edited, and with an introduction by H. H. Gerth and C. Wright Mills. (New York: Oxford University Press, 1946), pp. 180-195. Copyright 1946 by Oxford University Press, Inc. Reprinted by permission.

* *Wirtschaft und Gesellschaft*, part III, chap. 4, pp. 631-40. The first sentence in paragraph one and the several definitions in this chapter which are in brackets do not appear in the original text. They have been taken from other contexts of *Wirtschaft und Gesellschaft*.

legal order is rather an additional factor that enhances the chance to hold power or honor; but it cannot always secure them.

The way in which social honor is distributed in a community between typical groups participating in this distribution we may call the 'social order.' The social order and the economic order are, of course, similarly related to the 'legal order.' However, the social and the economic order are not identical. The economic order is for us merely the way in which economic goods and services are distributed and used. The social order is of course conditioned by the economic order to a high degree, and in its turn reacts upon it.

Now: 'classes,' 'status groups,' and 'parties' are phenomena of the distribution of power within a community.

II. Determination of Class-Situation by Market-Situation

In our terminology, 'classes' are not communities; they merely represent possible, and frequent, bases for communal action. We may speak of a 'class' when (1) a number of people have in common a specific causal component of their life chances, in so far as (2) this component is represented exclusively by economic interests in the possession of goods and opportunities for income, and (3) is represented under the conditions of the commodity or labor markets. [These points refer to 'class situation,' which we may express more briefly as the typical chance for a supply of goods, external living conditions, and personal life experiences, in so far as this chance is determined by the amount and kind of power, or lack of such, to dispose of goods or skills for the sake of income in a given economic order. The term 'class' refers to any group of people that is found in the same class situation.]

It is the most elemental economic fact that the way in which the disposition over material property is distributed among a plurality of people, meeting competitively in the market for the purpose of exchange, in itself creates specific like chances. According to the law of marginal utility this mode of distribution excludes the non-owners from competing for highly valued goods; it favors the owners and, in fact, gives to them a monopoly to acquire such goods. Other things being equal, this mode of distribution monopolizes the opportunities for profitable deals for all those who, provided with goods, do not necessarily have to exchange them. It increases, at least generally, their power in price wars with those who, being propertyless, have nothing to offer but their services in native form or goods in a form constituted through their own labor, and who above all are compelled to get rid of these products in order barely to subsist. This mode of distribution gives to the propertied a monopoly on the possibility of transferring property from the sphere of use as a 'fortune,' to the sphere of 'capital goods'; that is, it gives them the entrepreneurial function and all chances to share directly or indirectly in returns on capital. All this holds true within the area in which pure market conditions prevail. 'Property' and 'lack of property' are, therefore, the basic categories of all class situations. It does not matter whether these two categories become effective in price wars or in competitive struggles.

Within these categories, however, class situations are further differentiated: on the one hand, according to the kind of property that is usable for returns; and, on the other hand, according to the kind of services that can be offered in the market. Ownership of domestic buildings; productive establishments; warehouses; stores; agriculturally usable land, large and small holdings—quantitative differences with possibly qualitative consequences—; ownership of mines; cattle; men (slaves); disposition over mobile instruments of production, or capital goods of all sorts, especially money or objects that can be exchanged for money easily and at any time; disposition over products of one's own labor or of others' labor differing according to their various distances from consumability; disposition over transferable monopolies of any kind—all these distinctions differentiate the class situations of the propertied just as does the 'meaning' which they can and do give to the utilization of property, especially to property which has money equivalence. Accordingly, the propertied, for instance, may belong to the class of rentiers or to the class of entrepreneurs.

Those who have no property but who offer services are differentiated just as much according to their kinds of services as according to the way in which they make use of these services, in a continuous or discontinuous relation to a recipient. But always this is the generic connotation of the concept of class: that the kind of chance in the *market* is the decisive moment which presents a common condition for the individual's fate. 'Class situation' is, in this sense, ultimately 'market situation.' The effect of naked possession *per se*, which among cattle breeders gives the non-owning slave or serf into the power of the cattle owner, is only a forerunner of real 'class' formation. However, in the cattle loan and in the naked severity of the law of debts in such communities, for the first time mere 'possession' as such emerges as decisive for the fate of the individual. This is very much in contrast to the agricultural communities based on labor. The creditor-debtor relation becomes the basis of 'class situations' only in those cities where a 'credit market,' however primitive, with rates of interest increasing according to the extent of dearth and a factual monopolization of credits, is developed by a plutocracy. Therewith 'class struggles' begin.

Those men whose fate is not determined by the chance of using goods or services for themselves on the market, e.g. slaves, are not, however, a 'class' in the technical sense of the term. They are, rather, a 'status group.'

III. Communal Action Flowing from Class Interest

According to our terminology, the factor that creates 'class' is unambiguously economic interest, and indeed, only those interests involved in the existence of the 'market.' Nevertheless, the concept of 'class-interest' is an ambiguous one: even as an empirical concept it is ambiguous as soon as one understands by it something other than the factual direction of interests following with a certain probability from the class situation for a certain 'average' of those people subjected to the class situation. The class situation and other circumstances remaining the same, the direction in which the individual worker, for instance, is likely to pursue his interests may vary widely, according to whether he is constitutionally qualified for the task at hand to a high, to an average, or to a low degree. In the same way, the direction of interests may vary according to whether or not a *communal* action of a larger or smaller portion of those commonly affected by the 'class situation,' or even an association among them, e.g. a 'trade union,' has grown out of the class situation from which the individual may or may not expect promising results. [Communal action refers to that action which is oriented to the feeling of the actors that they belong together. Societal action, on the other hand, is oriented to a rationally motivated adjustment of interests.] The rise of societal or even of communal action from a common class situation is by no means a universal phenomenon.

The class situation may be restricted in its effects to the generation of essentially *similar* reactions, that is to say, within our terminology, of 'mass actions.' However, it may not have even this result. Furthermore, often merely an amorphous communal action emerges. For example, the 'murmuring' of the workers known in ancient oriental ethics: the moral disapproval of the work-master's conduct, which in its practical significance was probably equivalent to an increasingly typical phenomenon of precisely the latest industrial development, namely, the 'slow down' (the deliberate limiting of work effort) of laborers by virtue of tacit agreement. The degree in which 'communal action' and possibly 'societal action,' emerges from the 'mass actions' of the members of a class is linked to general cultural conditions, especially to those of an intellectual sort. It is also linked to the extent of the contrasts that have already evolved, and is especially linked to the *transparency* of the connections between the causes and the consequences of the 'class situation.' For however different life chances may be, this fact in itself, according to all experience, by no means gives birth to 'class action' (communal action by the members of a class). The fact of being conditioned and the results of the class situation must be distinctly recognizable. For only then the contrast of life chances can be felt not as an absolutely given fact to be accepted, but as a resultant from either (1) the given distribution of property, or (2) the structure of the concrete economic order. It is only then that people may react against the class structure not only through acts of an intermittent and irrational protest, but in the form of rational association. There have been 'class situations' of the first category (1), of a specifically naked and transparent sort, in the urban centers of Antiquity and during the Middle Ages; especially then, when great fortunes were accumulated by factually monopolized trading in industrial products of these localities or in foodstuffs. Furthermore, under certain circumstances, in the rural economy of the most diverse periods, when agriculture was increasingly exploited in a profit-making manner. The most important historical example of the second category (2) is the class situation of the modern 'proletariat.'

IV. Types of 'Class Struggle'

Thus every class may be the carrier of any one of the possibly innumerable forms of 'class action,' but this is not necessarily so. In any case, a class does not in itself constitute a community. To treat 'class' conceptually as having the same value as 'community' leads to distortion. That men in the same class situation regularly react in mass actions to such tangible situations as economic ones in the direction of those interests that are most adequate to their average number is an important and after all simple fact for the understanding of historical events. Above all, this fact must not lead to that kind of pseudo-scientific operation with the concepts of 'class' and 'class interests' so frequently found these days, and which has found its most classic expression in the statement of a talented author, that the individual may be in error concerning his interests but that the 'class' is 'infallible' about its interests. Yet, if classes as such are not communities, nevertheless class situations emerge only on the basis of communalization. The communal action that brings forth class situations, however, is not basically action between members of the identical class; it is an action between members of different classes. Communal actions that directly determine the class situation of the worker and the entrepreneur are: the labor market, the commodities market, and the capitalistic enterprise. But, in its turn, the existence of a capitalistic enterprise presupposes that a very specific communal action exists and that it is specifically structured to protect the possession of goods *per se,* and especially the power of individuals to dispose, in principle freely, over the means of production. The existence of a capitalistic enterprise is preconditioned by a specific kind of 'legal order.' Each kind of class situation, and above all when it rests upon the power of property *per se,* will become most clearly efficacious when all other determinants of reciprocal relations are, as far as possible, eliminated in their significance. It is in this way that the utilization of the power of property in the market obtains its most sovereign importance.

Now 'status groups' hinder the strict carrying through of the sheer market principle. In the present context they are of interest to us only from this one point of view. Before we briefly consider them, note that not much of a general nature can be said about the more specific kinds of antagonism between 'classes' (in our meaning of the term). The great shift, which has been going on continuously in the past, and up to our times, may be summarized, although at the cost of some precision: the struggle in which class situations are effective has progressively shifted from consumption credit toward, first, competitive struggles in the commodity market and, then, toward price wars on the labor market. The 'class struggles' of antiquity—to the extent that they were genuine class struggles and not struggles between status groups—were initially carried on by indebted peasants, and perhaps also by artisans threatened by debt bondage and struggling against urban creditors. For debt bondage is the normal result of the differentiation of wealth in commercial cities, especially in seaport cities. A similar situation has existed among cattle breeders. Debt relationships as such produced class action up to the time of Cataline. Along with this, and with an increase in provision of grain for the city by transporting it from the outside, the struggle over the means of sustenance emerged. It centered in the first place around the provision of bread and the determination of the price of bread. It lasted throughout antiquity and the entire Middle Ages. The propertyless as such flocked together against those who actually and supposedly were interested in the dearth of bread. This fight spread until it involved all those commodities essential to the way of life and to handicraft production. There were only incipient discussions of wage disputes in antiquity and in the Middle Ages. But they have been slowly increasing up into modern times. In the earlier periods they were completely secondary to slave rebellions as well as to fights in the commodity market.

The propertyless of antiquity and of the Middle Ages protested against monopolies, pre-emption, forestalling, and the withholding of goods from the market in order to raise prices. Today the central issue is the determination of the price of labor.

This transition is represented by the fight for access to the market and for the determination of the price of products. Such fights went on between merchants and workers in the putting-out system of domestic handicraft during the transition to modern times. Since it is quite a general phenomenon we must mention here that the class antagonisms that are conditioned through the market situation are usually most bitter between those who actually and directly participate as opponents in price wars. It is not the rentier, the share-holder, and the banker who suffer the ill will of the worker, but almost exclusively the manufacturer and the business executives who are the direct opponents of workers in price wars. This is so in spite of the fact that it is precisely the cash boxes of the rentier, the share-holder, and the banker into which the more or less 'unearned' gains flow, rather than into the pockets of the manufacturers or of the business executives. This simple state of affairs has very frequently been decisive for the role the class situation has played in the formation of political parties. For example, it has made possible the varieties of patriarchal socialism and the frequent attempts—formerly, at least—of threatened status groups to form alliances with the proletariat against the 'bourgeoisie.'

V. Status Honor

In contrast to classes, *status groups* are normally communities. They are, however, often of an amorphous kind. In contrast to the purely economically determined 'class situation' we wish to designate as 'status situation' every typical component of the life fate of men that is determined by a specific, positive or negative, social estimation of *honor*. This honor may be connected with any quality shared by a plurality, and, of course, it can be knit to a class situation: class distinctions are linked in the most varied ways with status distinctions. Property as such is not always recognized as a status qualification, but in the long run it is, and with extraordinary regularity. In the subsistence economy of the organized neighborhood, very often the richest man is simply the chieftain. However, this often means only an honorific preference. For example, in the so-called pure modern 'democracy,' that is, one devoid of any expressly ordered status privileges for individuals, it may be that only the families coming under approximately the same tax class dance with one another. This example is reported of certain smaller Swiss cities. But status honor need not necessarily be linked with a 'class situation.' On the contrary, it normally stands in sharp opposition to the pretensions of sheer property.

Both propertied and propertyless people can belong to the same status group, and frequently they do with very tangible consequences. This 'equality' of social esteem may, however, in the long run become quite precarious. The 'equality' of status among the American 'gentlemen,' for instance, is expressed by the fact that outside the subordination determined by the different functions of 'business,' it would be considered strictly repugnant—wherever the old tradition still prevails—if even the richest 'chief,' while playing billiards or cards in his club in the evening, would not treat his 'clerk' as in every sense fully his equal in birthright. It would be repugnant if the American 'chief' would bestow upon his 'clerk' the condescending 'benevolence' marking a distinction of 'position,' which the German chief can never dissever from his attitude. This is one of the most important reasons why in America the German 'clubby-ness' has never been able to attain the attraction that the American clubs have.

VI. Guarantees of Status Stratification

In content, status honor is normally expressed by the fact that above all else a specific *style of life* can be expected from all those who wish to belong to the circle. Linked with this expectation are restrictions on 'social' intercourse (that is, intercourse which is not subservient to economic or any other of business's 'functional' purposes). These restrictions may confine normal marriages to within the status circle and may lead to complete endogamous closure. As soon as there is not a mere individual and socially irrelevant imitation of another style of life, but an agreed-upon communal action of this closing character, the 'status' development is under way.

In its characteristic form, stratification by 'status groups' on the basis of conventional styles of life evolves at the present time in the United States out of the traditional democracy. For example, only the resident of a certain street ('the street') is considered as belonging to 'society,' is qualified for social intercourse, and is visited and invited. Above all, this differentiation evolves in such a way as to make for strict submission to the fashion that is dominant at a given time in society. This submission to fashion also exists among men in America to a degree unknown in Germany. Such submission is considered to be an indication of the fact that a given man *pretends* to qualify as a gentleman. This submission decides, at least *prima facie,* that he will be treated as such. And this recognition becomes just as important for his employment chances in 'swank' establishments, and above all, for social intercourse and marriage with 'esteemed' families, as the qualification for dueling among Germans in the Kaiser's day. As for the rest: certain families resident for a long time, and, of course, correspondingly wealthy, e.g. 'F. F. V., i.e. First Families of Virginia,' or the actual or alleged descendants of the 'Indian Princess' Pocahontas, of the Pilgrim fathers, or of the Knickerbockers, the members of almost inaccessible sects and all sorts of circles setting themselves apart by means of any other characteristics and badges . . . all these elements usurp 'status' honor. The development of status is essentially a question of stratification resting upon usurpation. Such usurpation is the normal origin of almost all status honor. But the road from this purely conventional situation to legal privilege, positive or negative, is easily traveled as soon as a certain stratification of the social order has in fact been 'lived in' and has achieved stability by virtue of a stable distribution of economic power.

VII. 'Ethnic' Segregation and 'Caste'

Where the consequences have been realized to their full extent, the status group evolves into a closed 'caste.' Status distinctions are then guaranteed not merely by conventions and laws, but also by *rituals*. This occurs in such a way that every physical contact with a member of any caste that is considered to be 'lower' by the members of a 'higher' caste is considered as making for a ritualistic impurity and to be a stigma which must be expiated by a religious act. Individual castes develop quite distinct cults and gods.

In general, however, the status structure reaches such extreme consequences only where there are underlying differences which are held to be 'ethnic.' The 'caste' is, indeed, the normal form in which ethnic communities usually live side by side in a 'societalized' manner. These ethnic communities believe in blood relationship and exclude exogamous marriage and social intercourse. Such a caste situation is part of the phenomenon of 'pariah' peoples and is found all over the world. These people form communities, acquire specific occupational traditions of handicrafts or of other arts, and cultivate a belief in their ethnic community. They live in a 'diaspora' strictly segregated from all personal intercourse, except that of an unavoidable sort, and their situation is legally precarious. Yet, by virtue of their economic indispensability, they are tolerated, indeed, frequently privileged, and they live in interspersed political communities. The Jews are the most impressive historical example.

A 'status' segregation grown into a 'caste' differs in its structure from a mere 'ethnic' segregation: the caste structure transforms the horizontal and unconnected coexistences of ethnically segregated groups into a vertical social system of super- and subordination. Correctly formulated: a comprehensive societalization integrates the ethnically divided communities into specific political and communal action. In their consequences they differ precisely in this way: ethnic coexistences condition a mutual repulsion and disdain but allow each ethnic community to consider its own honor as the highest one; the caste structure brings about a social subordination and an acknowledgment of 'more honor' in favor of the privileged caste and status groups. This is due to the fact that in the caste structure ethnic distinctions as such have become 'functional' distinctions within the political societalization (warriors, priests, artisans that are politically important for war and for building, and so on). But even pariah people who are most despised are usually apt to continue cultivating in some manner that which is equally peculiar to ethnic and to status communities: the belief in their own specific 'honor.' This is the case with the Jews.

Only with the negatively privileged status groups does the 'sense of dignity' take a specific deviation. A sense of dignity is the precipitation in individuals of social honor and of conventional demands which a positively privileged status group raises for the deportment of its members. The sense of dignity that characterizes positively privileged status groups is naturally related to their 'being' which does not transcend itself, that is, it is to their 'beauty and excellence' (καλο-κἀγαδια). Their kingdom is 'of this world.' They live for the present and by exploiting their great past. The sense of dignity of the negatively privileged strata naturally refers to a future lying beyond the present, whether it is of this life or of another. In other words, it must be nurtured by the belief in a providential 'mission' and by a belief in a specific honor before God. The 'chosen people's' dignity is nurtured by a belief either that in the beyond 'the last will be the first,' or that in this life a Messiah will appear to bring forth into the light of the world which has cast them out the hidden honor of the pariah people. This simple state of affairs, and not the 'resentment' which is so strongly emphasized in Nietzsche's much admired construction in the *Genealogy of Morals*, is the source of the religiosity cultivated by pariah status groups. In passing, we may note that resentment may be accurately applied only to a limited extent; for one of Nietzsche's main examples, Buddhism, it is not at all applicable.

Incidentally, the development of status groups from ethnic segregations is by no means the normal phenomenon. On the contrary, since objective 'racial differences' are by no means basic to every subjective sentiment of an ethnic community, the ultimately racial foundation of status structure is rightly and absolutely a question of the concrete individual case. Very frequently a status group is instrumental in the production of a thoroughbred anthropological type. Certainly a status group is to a high degree effective in producing extreme types, for they select personally qualified individuals (e.g. the Knighthood selects those who are fit for warfare, physically and psychically). But selection is far from being the only, or the predominant, way in which status groups are formed: Political membership or class situation has at all times been at least as frequently decisive. And today the class situation is by far the predominant factor, for of course the possibility of a style of life expected for members of a status group is usually conditioned economically.

VIII. Status Privileges

For all practical purposes, stratification by status goes hand in hand with a monopolization of ideal and material goods or opportunities, in a manner we have come to know as typical. Besides the specific status honor, which always rests upon distance and exclusiveness, we find all sorts of material monopolies. Such honorific preferences may consist of the privilege of wearing special costumes, of eating special dishes taboo to others, of carrying arms—which is most obvious in its consequences—the right to pursue certain non-professional dilettante artistic practices, e.g. to play certain musical instruments. Of course, material monopolies provide the most effective motives for the exclusiveness of a status group; although, in themselves, they are rarely sufficient, almost always they come into play to some extent. Within a status circle there is the question of intermarriage: the interest of the families in the monopolization of potential bridegrooms is at least of equal importance and is parallel to the interest in the monopolization of daughters. The daughters of the circle must be provided for. With an increased inclosure of the status group, the conventional preferential opportunities for special employ-ment grow into a legal monopoly of special offices for the members. Certain goods become objects for monopolization by status groups. In the typical fashion these include 'entailed estates' and frequently also the possessions of serfs or bondsmen and, finally, special trades. This monopolization occurs positively when the status group is exclusively entitled to own and to manage them; and negatively when, in order to maintain its specific way of life, the status group must *not* own and manage them.

The decisive role of a 'style of life' in status 'honor' means that status groups are the specific bearers of all 'conventions.' In whatever way it may be manifest, all 'stylization' of life either originates in status groups or is at least conserved by them. Even if the principles of status conventions differ greatly, they reveal certain typical traits, especially among those strata which are most privileged. Quite generally, among privileged status groups there is a status disqualification that operates against the performance of common physical labor. This disqualification is now 'setting in' in America against the old tradition of esteem for labor. Very frequently every national economic pursuit, and especially: entrepreneurial activity,' is looked upon as a disqualification of status. Artistic and literary activity is also considered as degrading work as soon as it is exploited for income, or at least when it is connected with hard physical exertion. An example is the sculptor working like a mason in his dusty smock as over against the painter in his salon-like 'studio' and those forms of musical practice that are acceptable to the status group.

IX. Economic Conditions and Effects of Status Stratification

The frequent disqualification of the gainfully employed as such is a direct result of the principle of status stratification peculiar to the social order, and of course, of this principle's opposition to a distribution of power which is regulated exclusively through the market. These two factors operate along with various individual ones, which will be touched upon below.

We have seen above that the market and its processes 'knows no personal distinctions': 'functional' interests dominate it. It knows nothing of 'honor.' The status order means precisely the reverse, viz.: stratification in terms of 'honor' and of styles of life peculiar to status groups as such. If mere economic acquisition and naked economic power still bearing the stigma of its extra-status origin could bestow upon anyone who has won it the same honor as those who are interested in status by virtue of style of life claim for themselves, the status order would be threatened at its very root. This is the more so as, given equality of status honor, property *per se* represents an addition even if it is not overtly acknowledged to be such. Yet if such economic acquisition and power gave the agent any honor at all, his wealth would result in his attaining more honor than those who successfully claim honor by virtue of style of life. Therefore all groups having interests in the status order react with special sharpness precisely against the pretensions of purely economic acquisition. In most cases they react the more vigorously the more they feel themselves threatened. Calderon's respectful treatment of the peasant, for instance, as opposed to Shakespeare's simultaneous and ostensible disdain of the *canaille* illustrates the different way in which a firmly structured status order reacts as compared with a status order that has become economically precarious. This is an example of a state of affairs that recurs everywhere. Precisely because of the rigorous reactions against the claims of property *per se*, the 'parvenu' is never accepted, personally and without reservation, by the privileged status groups, no matter how completely his style of life has been adjusted to theirs. They will only accept his descendants who have been educated in the conventions of their status group and who have never besmirched its honor by their own economic labor.

As to the general *effect* of the status order, only one consequence can be stated, but it is a very important one: the hindrance of the free development of the market occurs first for those goods which status groups directly withheld from free exchange by monopolization. This monopolization may be effected either legally or conventionally. For example, in many Hellenic cities during the epoch of status groups, and also originally in Rome, the inherited estate (as is shown by the old formula for indiction against spendthrifts) was monopolized just as were the estates of knights, peasants, priests, and especially the clientele of the craft and merchant guilds. The market is restricted, and the power of naked property *per se*, which gives its stamp to 'class formation,' is pushed into the background. The results of this process can be most varied. Of course, they do not necessarily weaken the contrasts in the economic situation. Frequently they strengthen these contrasts, and in any case, where stratification by status permeates a community as strongly as was the case in all political communities of antiquity and of the Middle Ages, one can never speak of a genuinely free market competition as we understand it today. There are wider effects than this direct exclusion of special goods from the market. From the contrariety between the status order and the purely economic order mentioned above, it follows that in most instances the notion of honor peculiar to status absolutely abhors that which is essential to the market: higgling. Honor abhors higgling among peers and occasionally it taboos higgling for the members of a status group in general. Therefore, everywhere some status groups, and usually the most influential, consider almost any kind of overt participation in economic acquisition as absolutely stigmatizing.

With some over-simplification, one might thus say that 'classes' are stratified according to their relations to the production and acquisition of goods; whereas 'status groups' are stratified according to the principles of their *consumption* of goods as represented by special 'styles of life.'

An 'occupational group' is also a status group. For normally, it successfully claims social honor only by virtue of the special style of life which may be determined by it. The differences between classes and status groups frequently overlap. It is precisely those status communities most strictly segregated in terms of honor (viz. the Indian castes) who today show, although within very rigid limits, a relatively high degree of indifference to pecuniary income. However, the Brahmins seek such income in many different ways.

As to the general economic conditions making for the predominance of stratification by 'status,' only very little can be said. When the bases of the acquisition and distribution of goods are relatively stable, stratification by status is favored. Every technological repercussion and economic transformation threatens stratification by status and pushes the class situation into the foreground. Epochs and countries in which the naked class situation is of predominant significance are regularly the periods of technical and economic transformations. And every slowing down of the shifting of economic stratifications leads, in due course, to the growth of status structures and makes for a resuscitation of the important role of social honor.

X. Parties

Whereas the genuine place of 'classes' is within the economic order, the place of 'status groups' is within the social order, that is, within the sphere of the distribution of 'honor.' From within these spheres, classes and status groups influence one another and they influence the legal order and are in turn influenced by it. But 'parties' live in a house of 'power.'

Their action is oriented toward the acquisition of social 'power,' that is to say, toward influencing a communal action no matter what its content may be. In principle, parties may exist in a social 'club' as well as in a 'state.' As over against the actions of classes and status groups, for which this is not necessarily the case, the communal actions of 'parties' always mean a societalization. For party actions are always directed toward a goal which is striven for in planned manner. This goal may be a 'cause' (the party may aim at realizing a program for ideal or material purposes), or the goal may be 'personal' (sinecures, power, and from these, honor for the leader and the followers of the party). Usually the party action aims at all these simultaneously. Parties are, therefore, only possible within communities that are societalized, that is, which have some rational order and a staff of persons available who are ready to enforce it. For parties aim precisely at influencing this staff, and if possible, to recruit it from party followers.

In any individual case, parties may represent interests determined through 'class situation' or 'status situation,' and they may recruit their following respectively from one or the other. But they need be neither purely 'class' nor purely 'status' parties. In most cases they are partly class parties and partly status parties, but sometimes they are neither. They may represent ephemeral or enduring structures. Their means of attaining power may be quite varied, ranging from naked violence of any sort to canvassing for votes with coarse or subtle means: money, social influence, the force of speech, suggestion, clumsy hoax, and so on to the rougher or more artful tactics of obstruction in parliamentary bodies.

The sociological structure of parties differs in a basic way according to the kind of communal action which they struggle to influence. Parties also differ according to whether or not the community is stratified by status or by classes. Above all else, they vary according to the structure of domination within the community. For their leaders normally deal with the conquest of a community. They are, in the general concept which is maintained here, not only products of specially modern forms of domination. We shall also designate as parties the ancient and medieval 'parties,' despite the fact that their structure differs basically from the structure of modern parties. By virtue of these structural differences of domination it is impossible to say anything about the structure of parties without discussing the structural forms of social domination per se. Parties, which are always structures struggling for domination, are very frequently organized in a very strict 'authoritarian' fashion . . .

Concerning 'classes,' 'status groups,' and 'parties,' it must be said in general that they necessarily presuppose a comprehensive societalization, and especially a political framework of communal action, within which they operate. This does not mean that parties would be confined by the frontiers of any individual political community. On the contrary, at all times it has been the order of the day that the societalization (even when it aims at the use of military force in common) reaches beyond the frontiers of politics. This has been the case in the solidarity of interests among the Oligarchs and among the democrats in Hellas, among the Guelfs and among Ghibellines in the Middle Ages, and within the Calvinist party during the period of religious struggles. It has been the case up to the solidarity of the landlords (international congress of agrarian landlords), and has continued among princes (holy alliance, Karlsbad decrees), socialist workers, conservatives (the longing of Prussian conservatives for Russian intervention in 1850). But their aim is not necessarily the establishment of new international political, i.e. *territorial*, dominion. In the main they aim to influence the existing dominion.*

* The posthumously published text breaks off here. We omit an incomplete sketch of types of 'warrior estates.'

6. Thorstein Veblen

Status and Discontent

THE immediate occasion for the writing of this paper was given by the publication of Mr. Spencer's essay, "From Freedom to Bondage";[1] although it is not altogether a criticism of that essay. It is not my purpose to controvert the position taken by Mr. Spencer as regards the present feasibility of any socialist scheme. The paper is mainly a suggestion, offered in the spirit of the disciple, with respect to a point not adequately covered by Mr. Spencer's discussion, and which has received but very scanty attention at the hands of any other writer on either side of the socialist controversy. This main point is as to an economic ground, as a matter of fact, for the existing unrest that finds expression in the demands of socialist agitators.

I quote from Mr. Spencer's essay a sentence which does fair justice, so far as it goes, to the position taken by agitators: "In presence of obvious improvements, joined with that increase of longevity, which even alone yields conclusive proof of general amelioration, it is proclaimed, with increasing vehemence, that things are so bad that society must be pulled to pieces and reorganised on another plan." The most obtrusive feature of the change demanded by the advocates of socialism is governmental control of the industrial activities of society—the nationalisation of industry. There is also, just at present, a distinct movement in practice, towards a more extended control of industry by the government, as Mr. Spencer has pointed out. This movement strengthens the position of the advocates of a complete nationalisation of industry, by making it appear that the logic of events is on their side.

In America at least, this movement in the direction of a broader assertion of the paramount claims of the community, and an extension of corporate action on part of the community in industrial matters, has not

From Veblen, *The Place of Science in Modern Civilisation and Other Essays*. (New York: The Viking Press, 1932) p. 387-408. Copyright 1919 by B. W. Huebsch, 1947 by Ann B. Sims and Becky Myers. Reprinted by permission of the Viking Press, Inc. The original title of this essay is: "Some Neglected Points in the Theory of Socialism."

[1] Introductory paper of *A Plea for Liberty;* edited by Thomas Mackay.

generally been connected with or based on an adherence to socialistic dogmas. This is perhaps truer of the recent past than of the immediate present. The motive of the movement has been, in large part, the expediency of each particular step taken. Municipal supervision, and, possibly, complete municipal control, has come to be a necessity in the case of such industries—mostly of recent growth—as elementary education, street-lighting, water-supply, etc. Opinions differ widely as to how far the community should take into its own hands such industries as concern the common welfare, but the growth of sentiment may fairly be said to favor a wider scope of governmental control.

But the necessity of some supervision in the interest of the public extends to industries which are not simply of municipal importance. The modern development of industry and of the industrial organisation of society makes it increasingly necessary that certain industries—often spoken of as "natural monopolies"—should be treated as being of a semi-public character. And through the action of the same forces a constantly increasing number of occupations are developing into the form of "natural monopolies."

The motive of the movement towards corporate action on the part of the community—State control of industry—has been largely that of industrial expediency. But another motive has gone with this one, and has grown more prominent as the popular demands in this direction have gathered wider support and taken more definite form. The injustice, the inequality, of the existing system, so far as concerns these natural monopolies especially, are made much of. There is a distinct unrest abroad, a discontent with things as they are, and the cry of injustice is the expression of this more or less widely prevalent discontent. This discontent is the truly socialistic element in the situation.

It is easy to make too much of this popular unrest. The clamor of the agitators might be taken to indicate a wider prevalence and a greater acuteness of popular discontent than actually exists; but after all due allowance is made for exaggeration on the part of those interested in the agitation, there can still be no doubt of the presence of a chronic feeling of dissatisfaction with the working of the existing industrial system, and a growth of popular sentiment in favor of a leveling policy. The economic ground of this popular feeling must be found, if we wish to understand the significance, for our industrial system, of the movement to which it supplies the motive. If its causes shall appear to be of a transient character, there is little reason to apprehend a permanent or radical change of our industrial system as the outcome of the agitation; while if this popular sentiment is found to be the outgrowth of any of the essential features of the existing social system, the chances of its ultimately working a radical change in the system will be much greater.

The explanation offered by Mr. Spencer, that the popular unrest is due essentially to a feeling of *ennui*—to a desire for a change of posture on part of the social body, is assuredly not to be summarily rejected; but the analogy will hardly serve to explain the sentiment away. This may be a cause, but it can hardly be accepted as a sufficient cause.

Socialist agitators urge that the existing system is necessarily wasteful and industrially inefficient. That may be granted, but it does not serve to explain the popular discontent, because the popular opinion, in which the discontent resides, does notoriously not favor that view. They further urge that the existing system is unjust, in that it gives an advantage to one man over another. That contention may also be true, but it is in itself no explanation, for it is true only if it be granted that the institutions which make this advantage of one man over another possible are unjust, and that is begging the question. This last contention is, however, not so far out of line with popular sentiment. The advantage complained of lies, under modern conditions, in the possession of property, and there is a feeling abroad that the existing order of things affords an undue advantage to property, especially to owners of property whose possessions rise much above a certain rather indefinite average. This feeling of injured justice is not always distinguishable from envy; but it is, at any rate, a factor that works towards a leveling policy. With it goes a feeling of slighted manhood, which works in the same direction. Both these elements are to a great extent of a subjective origin. They express themselves in the general, objective form, but it is safe to say that on the average they spring from a consciousness of disadvantage and slight suffered by the person expressing them, and by persons whom he classes with himself. No flippancy is intended in saying that the rich are not so generally alive to the necessity of any leveling policy as are people of slender means. Any question as to the legitimacy of the dissatisfaction, on moral grounds, or even on grounds of expediency, is not very much to the point; the question is as to its scope and its chances of persistence.

The modern industrial system is based on the institution of private property under free competition, and it cannot be claimed that these institutions have heretofore worked to the detriment of the material interests of the average member of society. The ground of discontent cannot lie in a disadvantageous comparison of the present with the past, so far as material interests are concerned. It is notorious, and, practically, none of the agitators deny, that the system of industrial competition, based on private property, has brought about, or has at least co-existed with, the most rapid advance in average wealth and industrial efficiency that the world has seen. Especially can it fairly be claimed that the result of the last few decades of our industrial development has been to increase greatly the creature comforts within the reach of the average human being. And, decidedly, the result has been an amelioration of the lot of the less favored in a relatively greater degree than that of

those economically more fortunate. The claim that the system of competition has proved itself an engine for making the rich richer and the
poor poorer has the fascination of epigram; but if its meaning is that the
lot of the average, of the masses of humanity in civilised life, is worse
to-day, as measured in the means of livelihood, than it was twenty, or
fifty, or a hundred years ago, then it is farcical. The cause of discontent
must be sought elsewhere than in any increased difficulty in obtaining
the means of subsistence or of comfort. But there is a sense in which the
aphorism is true, and in it lies at least a partial explanation of the unrest
which our conservative people so greatly deprecate. The existing system
has not made, and does not tend to make, the industrious poor poorer as
measured absolutely in means of livelihood; but it does tend "to make
them relatively poorer, in their own eyes, as measured in terms of comparative economic importance," and, curious as it may seem at first
sight, that is what seems to count. It is not the abjectly poor that are
oftenest heard protesting; and when a protest is heard in their behalf it is
through spokesmen who are from outside their own class, and who are
not delegated to speak for them. They are not a negligible element in
the situation, but the unrest which is ground for solicitude does not
owe its importance to them. The protest comes from those who do not
habitually, or of necessity, suffer physical privation. The qualification
"of necessity," is to be noticed. There is a not inconsiderable amount of
physical privation suffered by many people in this country, which is
not physically necessary. The cause is very often that what might be the
means of comfort is diverted to the purpose of maintaining a decent
appearance, or even a show of luxury.

Man as we find him to-day has much regard to his good fame—to his
standing in the esteem of his fellowmen. This characteristic he always
has had, and no doubt always will have. This regard for reputation may
take the noble form of a striving after a good name; but the existing
organisation of society does not in any way preëminently foster that
line of development. Regard for one's reputation means, in the average of
cases, emulation. It is a striving to be, and more immediately to be thought
to be, better than one's neighbor. Now, modern society, the society in
which competition without prescription is predominant, is preëminently
an industrial, economic society, and it is industrial—economic—excellence
that most readily attracts the approving regard of that society. Integrity
and personal worth will, of course, count for something, now as always;
but in the case of a person of moderate pretentions and opportunities,
such as the average of us are, one's reputation for excellence in this
direction does not penetrate far enough into the very wide environment
to which a person is exposed in modern society to satisfy even a very
modest craving for respectability. To sustain one's dignity—and to sustain one's self-respect—under the eyes of people who are not socially one's

immediate neighbors, it is necessary to display the token of economic worth, which practically coincides pretty closely with economic success. A person may be well-born and virtuous, but those attributes will not bring respect to the bearer from people who are not aware of his possessing them, and these are ninety-nine out of every one hundred that one meets. Conversely, by the way, knavery and vulgarity in any person are not reprobated by people who know nothing of the person's shortcomings in those respects.

In our fundamentally industrial society a person should be economically successful, if he would enjoy the esteem of his fellowmen. When we say that a man is "worth" so many dollars, the expression does not convey the idea that moral or other personal excellence is to be measured in terms of money, but it does very distinctly convey the idea that the fact of his possessing many dollars is very much to his credit. And, except in cases of extraordinary excellence, efficiency in any direction which is not immediately of industrial importance, and does not redound to a person's economic benefit, is not of great value as a means of respectability. Economic success is in our day the most widely accepted as well as the most readily ascertainable measure of esteem. All this will hold with still greater force of a generation which is born into a world already encrusted with this habit of a mind.

But there is a further, secondary stage in the development of this economic emulation. It is not enough to possess the talisman of industrial success. In order that it may mend one's good fame efficiently, it is necessary to display it. One does not "make much of a showing" in the eyes of the large majority of the people whom one meets with, except by unremitting demonstration of ability to pay. That is practically the only means which the average of us have of impressing our respectability on the many to whom we are personally unknown, but whose transient good opinion we would so gladly enjoy. So it comes about that "the appearance of success" is very much to be desired, and is even in many cases preferred to the substance. We all know how nearly indispensable it is to afford whatever expenditure other people with whom we class ourselves can afford, and also that it is desirable to afford a little something more than others.

This element of human nature has much to do with the "standard of living." And it is of a very elastic nature, capable of an indefinite extension. After making proper allowance for individual exceptions and for the action of prudential restraints, it may be said, in a general way, that this emulation in expenditure stands ever ready to absorb any margin of income that remains after ordinary physical wants and comforts have been provided for, and, further, that it presently becomes as hard to give up that part of one's habitual "standard of living" which is due to the struggle for respectability, as it is to give up many physical comforts.

In a general way, the need of expenditure in this direction grows as fast as the means of satisfying it, and, in the long run, a large expenditure comes no nearer satisfying the desire than a smaller one.

It comes about through the working of this principle that even the creature comforts, which are in themselves desirable, and, it may even be, requisite to a life on a passably satisfactory plane, acquire a value as a means of respectability quite independent of, and out of proportion to, their simple utility as a means of livelihood. As we are all aware, the chief element of value in many articles of apparel is not their efficiency for protecting the body, but for protecting the wearer's respectability; and that not only in the eyes of one's neighbors but even in one's own eyes. Indeed, it happens not very rarely that a person chooses to go ill-clad in order to be well dressed. Much more than half the value of what is worn by the American people may confidently be put down to the element of "dress," rather than to that of "clothing." And the chief motive of dress is emulation—"economic emulation." The like is true, though perhaps in a less degree, of what goes to food and shelter.

This misdirection of effort through the cravings of human vanity is of course not anything new, nor is "economic emulation" a modern fact. The modern system of industry has not invented emulation, nor has even this particular form of emulation originated under that system. But the system of free competition has accentuated this form of emulation, both by exalting the industrial activity of man above the rank which it held under more primitive forms of social organisation, and by in great measure cutting off other forms of emulation from the chance of efficiently ministering to the craving for a good fame. Speaking generally and from the standpoint of the average man, the modern industrial organisation of society has practically narrowed the scope of emulation to this one line; and at the same time it has made the means of sustenance and comfort so much easier to obtain as very materially to widen the margin of human exertion that can be devoted to purposes of emulation. Further, by increasing the freedom of movement of the individual and widening the environment to which the individual is exposed—increasing the number of persons before whose eyes each one carries on his life, and, *pari passu*, decreasing the chances which such persons have of awarding their esteem on any other basis than that of immediate appearances, it has increased the relative efficiency of the economic means of winning respect through a show of expenditure for personal comforts.

It is not probable that further advance in the same direction will lead to a different result in the immediate future; and it is the *immediate* future we have to deal with. A further advance in the efficiency of our industry, and a further widening of the human environment to which the individual is exposed, should logically render emulation in this direction more intense. There are, indeed, certain considerations to be set off against this tendency, but they are mostly factors of slow action, and are hardly of sufficient consequence to reverse the general rule. On the whole, other things remaining the same, it must be admitted that, within wide limits, the easier the conditions of physical life for modern civilised man become, and the wider the horizon of each and the extent of the personal contact of each with his fellowmen, and the greater the opportunity of each to compare notes with his fellows, the greater will be the preponderance of economic success as a means of emulation, and the greater the straining after economic respectability. Inasmuch as the aim of emulation is not any absolute degree of comfort or of excellence, no advance in the average well being of the community can end the struggle or lessen the strain. A general amelioration cannot quiet the unrest whose source is the craving of everybody to compare favorably with his neighbor.

Human nature being what it is, the struggle of each to possess more than his neighbor is inseparable from the institution of private property. And also, human nature being what it is, one who possesses less will, on the average, be jealous of the one who possesses more; and "more" means not more than the average share, but more than the share of the person who makes the comparison. The criterion of complacency is, largely, the *de facto* possession or enjoyment; and the present growth of sentiment among the body of the people—who possess less—favors, in a vague way, a readjustment adverse to the interests of those who possess more, and adverse to the possibility of legitimately possessing or enjoying "more"; that is to say, the growth of sentiment favors a socialistic movement. The outcome of modern industrial development has been, so far as concerns the present purpose, to intensify emulation and the jealousy that goes with emulation, and to focus the emulation and the jealousy on the possession and enjoyment of material goods. The ground of the unrest with which we are concerned is, very largely, jealousy,—envy, if you choose; and the ground of this particular form of jealousy, that makes for socialism, is to be found in the institution of private property. With private property, under modern conditions, this jealousy and unrest are unavoidable.

The corner-stone of the modern industrial system is the institution of private property. That institution is also the objective point of all attacks upon the existing system of competitive industry, whether open or covert, whether directed against the system as a whole or against any special feature of it. It is, moreover, the ultimate ground—and, under modern conditions, necessarily so—of the unrest and discontent whose proximate cause is the struggle for economic respectability. The inference seems to be that, human nature being what it is, there can be no peace from this— it must be admitted—ignoble form of emulation, or from the discontent that goes with it, this side of the abolition of private property. Whether a larger measure of peace is in store for us after that event shall have come to pass, is of course not a matter to be counted on, nor is the question immediately to the point.

This economic emulation is of course not the sole motive, nor the most important feature, of modern industrial life; although it is in the foreground, and it pervades the structure of modern society more thoroughly perhaps than any other equally powerful moral factor. It would be rash to predict that socialism will be the inevitable outcome of a continued development of this emulation and the discontent which it fosters, and it is by no means the purpose of this paper to insist on such an inference. The most that can be claimed is that this emulation is one of the causes, if not the chief cause, of the existing unrest and dissatisfaction with things as they are; that this unrest is inseparable from the existing system of industrial organisation; and that the growth of popular sentiment under the influence of these conditions is necessarily adverse to the institution of private property, and therefore adverse to the existing industrial system of free competition.

The emulation to which attention has been called in the preceding section of this paper is not only a fact of importance to an understanding of the unrest that is urging us towards an untried path in social development, but it has also a bearing on the question of the practicability of any scheme for the complete nationalisation of industry. Modern industry has developed to such a degree of efficiency as to make the struggle of subsistence alone, under average conditions, relatively easy, as compared with the state of the case a few generations ago. As I have labored to show, the modern competitive system has at the same time given the spirit of emulation such a direction that the attainment of subsistence and comfort no longer fixes, even approximately, the limit of the required aggregate labor on the part of the community. Under modern conditions the struggle for existence has, in a very appreciable degree, been transformed into a struggle to keep up appearances. The ultimate ground of this struggle to keep up appearance by otherwise unnecessary expenditure, is the institution of private property. Under a régime which should allow no inequality of acquisition or of income, this form of emulation, which is due to the possibility of such inequality, would also tend to become obsolete. With the abolition of private property, the characteristic of human nature which now finds its exercise in this form of emulation, should logically find exercise in other, perhaps nobler and socially more serviceable, activities; it is at any rate not easy to imagine it running into any line of action more futile or less worthy of human effort.

Supposing the standard of comfort of the community to remain approximately at its present average, the abolition of the struggle to keep up economic appearances would very considerably lessen the aggregate amount of labor required for the support of the community. How great a saving of labor might be effected is not easy to say. I believe it is within the mark to suppose that the struggle to keep up appearances is chargeable, directly and indirectly, with one-half the aggregate labor, and abstinence from labor—for the standard of respectability requires us to shun labor as well as to enjoy the fruits of it—on the part of the American people. This does not mean that the same community, under a system not allowing private property, could make its way with half the labor we now put forth; but it means something more or less nearly approaching that. Any one who has not seen our modern social life from this point of view will find the claim absurdly extravagant, but the startling character of the proposition will wear off with longer and closer attention to this aspect of the facts of everyday life. But the question of the exact amount of waste due to this factor is immaterial. It will not be denied that this is a fact of considerable magnitude, and that is all that the argument requires.

It is accordingly competent for the advocates of the nationalisation of industry and property to claim that even if their scheme of organisation should prove less effective for production of goods than the present, as measured absolutely in terms of the aggregate output of our industry, yet the community might readily be maintained at the present average stand-ard of comfort. The required aggregate output of the nation's industry would be considerably less than at present, and there would therefore be less necessity for that close and strenuous industrial organisation and discipline of the members of society under the new régime, whose evils unfriendly critics are apt to magnify. The chances of practicability for the scheme should logically be considerably increased by this lessening of the necessity for severe application. The less irksome and exacting the new régime, the less chance of a reversion to the earlier system.

Under such a social order, where common labor would no longer be a mark of peculiar economic necessity and consequent low economic rank on part of the laborer, it is even conceivable that labor might practically come to assume that character of nobility in the eyes of society at large, which it now sometimes assumes in the speculations of the well-to-do, in their complacent moods. Much has sometimes been made of this pos-sibility by socialist speculators, but the inference has something of a utopian look, and no one, certainly, is entitled to build institutions for the coming social order on this dubious ground.

What there seems to be ground for claiming is that a society which has reached our present degree of industrial efficiency would not go into the Socialist or Nationalist state with as many chances of failure as a com-munity whose industrial development is still at the stage at which strenuous labor on the part of nearly all members is barely sufficient to make both ends meet.

In Mr. Spencer's essay, in conformity with the line of argument of his "Principles of Sociology," it is pointed out that, as the result of con-stantly operative social forces, all social systems, as regards the form of organisation, fall into the one or the other of Sir Henry Maine's two classes —the system of status or the system of contract. In accordance with this

generalisation it is concluded that whenever the modern system of contract or free competition shall be displaced, it will necessarily be replaced
by the only other known system—that of status; the type of which is the
military organisation, or, also, a hierarchy, or a bureaucracy. It is something after the fashion of the industrial organisation of ancient Peru that
Mr. Spencer pictures as the inevitable sequel of the demise of the existing
competitive system. Voluntary coöperation can be replaced only by compulsory coöperation, which is identified with the system of status and
defined as the subjection of man to his fellow-man.

Now, at least as a matter of speculation, this is not the only alternative.
These two systems, of status, or prescription, and of contract, or competition, have divided the field of social organisation between them in
some proportion or other in the past. Mr. Spencer has shown that, very
generally, where human progress in its advanced stages has worked towards the amelioration of the lot of the average member of society, the
movement has been away from the system of status and towards the
system of contract. But there is at least one, if not more than one exception to the rule, as concerns the recent past. The latest development of
the industrial organisation among civilised nations—perhaps in an especial
degree in the case of the American people—has not been entirely a
continuation of the approach to a régime of free contract. It is also, to say
the least, very doubtful if the movement has been towards a régime of
status, in the sense in which Sir Henry Maine uses the term. This is
especially evident in the case of the great industries which we call
"natural monopolies"; and it is to be added that the present tendency is
for a continually increasing proportion of the industrial activities of the
community to fall into the category of "natural monopolies." No revolution
has been achieved; the system of competition has not been discarded, but
the course of industrial development is not in the direction of an extension
of that system at all points; nor does the principle of status always replace that of competition wherever the latter fails.

The classification of methods of social organisation under the two heads
of status or of contract, is not logically exhaustive. There is nothing in the
meaning of the terms employed which will compel us to say that whenever man escapes from the control of his fellow man, under a system of
status, he thereby falls into a system of free contract. There is a conceivable escape from the dilemma, and it is this conceivable, though perhaps
impracticable, escape from both these systems that the socialist agitator
wishes to effect. An acquaintance with the aims and position of the more
advanced and consistent advocates of a new departure leaves no doubt
but that the principles of contract and of status, both, are in substance
familiar to their thoughts—though often in a vague and inadequate form
—and that they distinctly repudiate both. This is perhaps less true of
those who take the socialist position mainly on ethical grounds.

As bearing on this point it may be remarked that while the industrial system, in the case of all communities with whose history we are acquainted, has always in the past been organised according to a scheme of status or of contract, or of the two combined in some proportion, yet the social organisation has not in all cases developed along the same lines, so far as concerns such social functions as are not primarily industrial. Especially is this true of the later stages in the development of those communities whose institutions we are accustomed to contemplate with the most complacency, *e.g.*, the case of the English-speaking peoples. The whole system of modern constitutional government in its latest developed forms, in theory at least, and, in a measure, in practice, does not fall under the head of either contract or status. It is the analogy of modern constitutional government through an impersonal law and impersonal institutions, that comes nearest doing justice to the vague notions of our socialist propagandists. It is true, some of the most noted among them are fond of the analogy of the military organisation, as a striking illustration of one feature of the system they advocate, but that must after all be taken as an *obiter dictum*.

Further, as to the manner of the evolution of existing institutions and their relation to the two systems spoken of. So far as concerns the communities which have figured largely in the civilised world, the political organisation has had its origin in a military system of government. So, also, has the industrial organisation. But while the development of industry, during its gradual escape from the military system of status, has been, at least until lately, in the direction of a system of free contract, the development of the political organisation, so far as it has escaped from the régime of status, has not been in that direction. The system of status is a system of subjection to personal authority,—of prescription and class distinctions, and privileges and immunities; the system of constitutional government, especially as seen at its best among a people of democratic traditions and habits of mind, is a system of subjection to the will of the social organism, as expressed in an impersonal law. This difference between the system of status and the "constitutional system" expresses a large part of the meaning of the boasted free institutions of the English-speaking people. Here, subjection is not to the person of the public functionary, but to the powers vested in him. This has, of course, something of the ring of latter-day popular rhetoric, but it is after all felt to be true, not only speculatively, but in some measure also in practice.

The right of eminent domain and the power to tax, as interpreted under modern constitutional forms, indicate something of the direction of development of the political functions of society at a point where they touch the province of the industrial system. It is along the line indicated by these and kindred facts that the socialists are advancing; and it is along this line that the later developments made necessary by the exigencies of industry under modern conditions are also moving. The aim of the propagandists is to sink the industrial community in the political community; or perhaps better, to identify the two organisations; but always with insistence on the necessity of making the political organisation, in some further developed form, the ruling and only one in the outcome. Distinctly, the system of contract is to be done away with; and equally distinctly, no system of status is to take its place.

All this is pretty vague, and of a negative character, but it would quickly pass the limits of legitimate inference from the accepted doctrines of the socialists if it should attempt to be anything more. It does not have much to say as to the practicability of any socialist scheme. As a matter of speculation, there seems to be an escape from the dilemma insisted on by Mr. Spencer. We may conceivably have nationalism without status and without contract. In theory, both principles are entirely obnoxious to that system. The practical question, as to whether modern society affords the materials out of which an industrial structure can be erected on a system different from either of these, is a problem of constructive social engineering which calls for a consideration of details far too comprehensive to be entered on here. Still, in view of the past course of development of character and institutions on the part of the people to which we belong, it is perhaps not extravagant to claim that no form of organisation which should necessarily eventuate in a thorough-going system of status could endure among us. The inference from this proposition may be, either that a near approach to nationalisation of industry would involve a régime of status, a bureaucracy, which would be unendurable, and which would therefore drive us back to the present system before it had been entirely abandoned; or that the nationalisation would be achieved with such a measure of success, in conformity with the requirements of our type of character, as would make it preferable to what we had left behind. In either case the ground for alarm does not seem so serious as is sometimes imagined.

A reversion to the system of free competition, after it had been in large part discarded, would no doubt be a matter of great practical difficulty, and the experiment which should demonstrate the necessity of such a step might involve great waste and suffering, and might seriously retard the advance of the race toward something better than our present condition; but neither a permanent deterioration of human society, nor a huge catastrophe, is to be confidently counted on as the outcome of the movement toward nationalisation, even if it should prove necessary for society to retrace its steps.

It is conceivable that the application of what may be called the "constitutional method" to the organisation of industry—for that is essentially what the advocates of Nationalisation demand—would result in a course of development analogous to what has taken place in the case of the political organisation under modern constitutional forms. Modern constitutional government—the system of modern free institutions—is by no means an unqualified success, in the sense of securing to each the rights and immunities which in theory are guaranteed to him.

Our modern republics have hardly given us a foretaste of that political millennium whereof they proclaim the fruition. The average human nature is as yet by no means entirely fit for self-government according to the "constitutional method." Shortcomings are visible at every turn. These shortcomings are grave enough to furnish serious arguments against the practicability of our free institutions. On the continent of Europe the belief seems to be at present in the ascendant that man must yet, for a long time, remain under the tutelage of absolutism before he shall be fit to organise himself into an autonomous political body. The belief is not altogether irrational. Just how great must be the advance of society and just what must be the character of the advance, preliminary to its advantageously assuming the autonomous—republican—form of political organisation, must be admitted to be an open question. Whether we, or any people, have yet reached the required stage of the advance is also questioned by many. But the partial success which has attended the movement in this direction, among the English-speaking people for example, goes very far towards proving that the point in the development of human character at which the constitutional method may be advantageously adopted in the political field, lies far this side the point at which human nature shall have become completely adapted for that method. That is to say, it does not seem necessary, as regards the functions of society which we are accustomed to call political, to be entirely ready for nationalisation before entering upon it. How far the analogy of this will hold when applied to the industrial organisation of society is difficult to say, but some significance the analogy must be admitted to possess.

Certainly, the fact that constitutional government—the nationalisation of political functions—seems to have been a move in the right direction is not to be taken as proof of the advisability of forthwith nationalising the industrial functions. At the same time this fact does afford ground for the claim that a movement in this direction may prove itself in some degree advantageous, even if it takes place at a stage in the development of human nature at which mankind is still far from being entirely fit for the duties which the new system shall impose. The question, therefore, is not whether we have reached the perfection of character which would be necessary in order to achieve a perfect working of the scheme of nationalisation of industry, but whether we have reached such a degree of development as would make an imperfect working of the scheme possible.

7. Max Weber

Bureaucracy

I. Characteristics of Bureaucracy

Modern officialdom functions in the following specific manner:

I. There is the principle of fixed and official jurisdictional areas, which are generally ordered by rules, that is, by laws or administrative regulations.

1. The regular activities required for the purposes of the bureaucratically governed structure are distributed in a fixed way as official duties.

2. The authority to give the commands required for the discharge of these duties is distributed in a stable way and is strictly delimited by rules concerning the coercive means, physical, sacerdotal, or otherwise, which may be placed at the disposal of officials.

3. Methodical provision is made for the regular and continuous fulfilment of these duties and for the execution of the corresponding rights; only persons who have the generally regulated qualifications to serve are employed.

In public and lawful government these three elements constitute 'bureaucratic authority.' In private economic domination, they constitute bureaucratic 'management.' Bureaucracy, thus understood, is fully developed in political and ecclesiastical communities only in the modern state, and, in the private economy, only in the most advanced institutions of capitalism. Permanent and public office authority, with fixed jurisdiction, is not the historical rule but rather the exception. This is so even in large political structures such as those of the ancient Orient, the Germanic and Mongolian empires of conquest, or of many feudal structures of state. In all these cases, the ruler executes the most important measures through personal trustees, table-companions, or court-servants. Their commissions and authority are not precisely delimited and are temporarily called into being for each case.

II. The principles of office hierarchy and of levels of graded authority

From *From Max Weber: Essays in Sociology*, translated, edited, and with an introduction by H. H. Gerth and C. Wright Mills. (New York: Oxford University Press, 1946), pp. 196-244. Copyright 1946 by Oxford University Press, Inc. Reprinted by permission. Footnotes to the original essay have been eliminated.

mean a firmly ordered system of super- and subordination in which there is a supervision of the lower offices by the higher ones. Such a system offers the governed the possibility of appealing the decision of a lower office to its higher authority, in a definitely regulated manner. With the full development of the bureaucratic type, the office hierarchy is monocratically organized. The principle of hierarchical office authority is found in all bureaucratic structures: in state and ecclesiastical structures as well as in large party organizations and private enterprises. It does not matter for the character of bureaucracy whether its authority is called 'private' or 'public.'

When the principle of jurisdictional 'competency' is fully carried through, hierarchical subordination—at least in public office—does not mean that the 'higher' authority is simply authorized to take over the business of the 'lower.' Indeed, the opposite is the rule. Once established and having fulfilled its task, an office tends to continue in existence and be held by another incumbent.

III. The management of the modern office is based upon written documents ('the files'), which are preserved in their original or draught form. There is, therefore, a staff of subaltern officials and scribes of all sorts. The body of officials actively engaged in a 'public' office, along with the respective apparatus of material implements and the files, make up a 'bureau.' In private enterprise, 'the bureau' is often called 'the office.'

In principle, the modern organization of the civil service separates the bureau from the private domicile of the official, and, in general, bureaucracy segregates official activity as something distinct from the sphere of private life. Public monies and equipment are divorced from the private property of the official. This condition is everywhere the product of a long development. Nowadays, it is found in public as well as in private enterprises; in the latter, the principle extends even to the leading entrepreneur. In principle, the executive office is separated from the household, business from private correspondence, and business assets from private fortunes. The more consistently the modern type of business management has been carried through the more are these separations the case. The beginnings of this process are to be found as early as the Middle Ages.

It is the peculiarity of the modern entrepreneur that he conducts himself as the 'first official' of his enterprise, in the very same way in which the ruler of a specifically modern bureaucratic state spoke of himself as 'the first servant' of the state. The idea that the bureau activities of the state are intrinsically different in character from the management of private economic offices is a continental European notion and, by way of contrast, is totally foreign to the American way.

IV. Office management, at least all specialized office management—and such management is distinctly modern—usually presupposes thorough and expert training. This increasingly holds for the modern executive and employee of private enterprises, in the same manner as it holds for the state official.

V. When the office is fully developed, official activity demands the full working capacity of the official, irrespective of the fact that his obligatory time in the bureau may be firmly delimited. In the normal case, this is only the product of a long development, in the public as well as in the private office. Formerly, in all cases, the normal state of affairs was reversed: official business was discharged as a secondary activity.

VI. The management of the office follows general rules, which are more or less stable, more or less exhaustive, and which can be learned. Knowledge of these rules represents a special technical learning which the officials possess. It involves jurisprudence, or administrative or business management.

The reduction of modern office management to rules is deeply embedded in its very nature. The theory of modern public administration, for instance, assumes that the authority to order certain matters by decree—which has been legally granted to public authorities—does not entitle the bureau to regulate the matter by commands given for each case, but only to regulate the matter abstractly. This stands in extreme contrast to the regulation of all relationships through individual privileges and bestowals of favor, which is absolutely dominant in patrimonialism, at least in so far as such relationships are not fixed by sacred tradition.

II. The Position of the Official

All this results in the following for the internal and external position of the official:

I. Office holding is a 'vocation.' This is shown, first, in the requirement of a firmly prescribed course of training, which demands the entire capacity for work for a long period of time, and in the generally prescribed and special examinations which are prerequisites of employment. Furthermore, the position of the official is in the nature of a duty. This determines the internal structure of his relations, in the following manner: Legally and actually, office holding is not considered a source to be exploited for rents or emoluments, as was normally the case during the Middle Ages and frequently up to the threshold of recent times. Nor is office holding considered a usual exchange of services for equivalents, as is the case with free labor contracts. Entrance into an office, including one in the private economy, is considered an acceptance of a specific obligation of faithful management in return for a secure existence. It is decisive for the specific nature of modern loyalty to an office that, in the pure type, it does not establish a relationship to a *person*, like the vassal's or disciple's faith in feudal or in patrimonial relations of authority. Modern loyalty is devoted to impersonal and functional purposes. Behind the functional purposes, of course, 'ideas of culture-values' usually stand. These are *ersatz* for the earthly or supra-mundane personal master: ideas such as 'state,' 'church,' 'community,' 'party,' or 'enterprise' are thought of as being realized in a community; they provide an ideological halo for the master.

The political official—at least in the fully developed modern state—is not considered the personal servant of a ruler. Today, the bishop, the priest, and the preacher are in fact no longer, as in early Christian times, holders of purely personal charisma. The supra-mundane and sacred values which they offer are given to everybody who seems to be worthy of them and who asks for them. In former times, such leaders acted upon the personal command of their master; in principle, they were responsible only to him. Nowadays, in spite of the partial survival of the old theory, such religious leaders are officials in the service of a functional purpose, which in the present-day 'church' has become routinized and, in turn, ideologically hallowed.

II. The personal position of the official is patterned in the following way:

1. Whether he is in a private office or a public bureau, the modern official always strives and usually enjoys a distinct *social esteem* as compared with the governed. His social position is guaranteed by the prescriptive rules of rank order and, for the political official, by special definitions of the criminal code against 'insults of officials' and 'contempt' of state and church authorities.

The actual social position of the official is normally highest where, as in old civilised countries, the following conditions prevail: a strong demand for administration by trained experts; a strong and stable social differentiation, where the official predominantly derives from socially and economically privileged strata because of the social distribution of power; or where the costliness of the required training and status conventions are binding upon him. The possession of educational certificates—to be discussed elsewhere—are usually linked with qualification for office. Naturally, such certificates or patents enhance the 'status element' in the social position of the official. For the rest this status factor in individual cases is explicitly and impassively acknowledged; for example, in the prescription that the acceptance or rejection of an aspirant to an official career depends upon the consent ('election') of the members of the official body. This is the case in the German army with the officer corps. Similar phenomena, which promote this guild-like closure of officialdom, are typically found in patrimonial and, particularly, in prebendal officialdoms of the past. The desire to resurrect such phenomena in changed forms is by no means infrequent among modern bureaucrats. For instance, they have played a role among the demands of the quite proletarian and expert officials (the *tretyj* element) during the Russian revolution.

Usually the social esteem of the officials as such is especially low where the demand for expert administration and the dominance of status conventions are weak. This is especially the case in the United States; it is often the case in new settlements by virtue of their wide fields for profit-making and the great instability of their social stratification.

2. The pure type of bureaucratic official is *appointed* by a superior authority. An official elected by the governed is not a purely bureaucratic figure. Of course, the formal existence of an election does not by itself mean that no appointment hides behind the election—in the state, especially, appointment by party chiefs. Whether or not this is the case does not depend upon legal statutes but upon the way in which the party mechanism functions. Once firmly organized, the parties can turn a formally free election into the mere acclamation of a candidate designated by the party chief. As a rule, however, a formally free election is turned into a fight, conducted according to definite rules, for votes in favor of one of two designated candidates.

In all circumstances, the designation of officials by means of an election among the governed modifies the strictness of hierarchical subordination. In principle, an official who is so elected has an autonomous position opposite the superordinate official. The elected official does not derive his position 'from above' but 'from below,' or at least not from a superior authority of the official hierarchy but from powerful party men ('bosses'), who also determine his further career. The career of the elected official is not, or at least not primarily, dependent upon his chief in the administration. The official who is not elected but appointed by a chief normally functions more exactly, from a technical point of view, because, all other circumstances being equal, it is more likely that purely functional points of consideration and qualities will determine his selection and career. As laymen, the governed can become acquainted with the extent to which a candidate is expertly qualified for office only in terms of experience, and hence only after his service. Moreover, in every sort of selection of officials by election, parties quite naturally give decisive weight not to expert considerations but to the services a follower renders to the party boss. This holds for all kinds of procurement of officials by elections, for the designation of formally free, elected officials by party bosses when they determine the slate of candidates, or the free appointment by a chief who has himself been elected. The contrast, however, is relative: substantially similar conditions hold where legitimate monarchs and their subordinates appoint officials, except that the influence of the followings are then less controllable.

Where the demand for administration by trained experts is considerable, and the party followings have to recognize an intellectually developed, educated, and freely moving 'public opinion,' the use of unqualified officials falls back upon the party in power at the next election. Naturally, this is more likely to happen when the officials are appointed by the chief.

The demand for a trained administration now exists in the United States, but in the large cities, where immigrant votes are 'corraled,' there is, of course, no educated public opinion. Therefore, popular elections of the administrative chief and also of his subordinate officials usually endanger the expert qualification of the official as well as the precise functioning of the bureaucratic mechanism. It also weakens the dependence of the officials upon the hierarchy. This holds at least for the large administrative bodies that are difficult to supervise. The superior qualification and integrity of federal judges, appointed by the President, as over against elected judges in the United States is well known, although both types of officials have been selected primarily in terms of party considerations. The great changes in American metropolitan administrations demanded by reformers have proceeded essentially from elected mayors working with an apparatus of officials who were appointed by them. These reforms have thus come about in a 'Caesarist' fashion. Viewed technically, as an organized form of authority, the efficiency of 'Caesarism,' which often grows out of democracy, rests in general upon the position of the 'Caesar' as a free trustee of the masses (of the army or of the citizenry), who is unfettered by tradition. The 'Caesar' is thus the unrestrained master of a body of highly qualified military officers and officials whom he selects freely and personally without regard to tradition or to any other considerations. This 'rule of the personal genius,' however, stands in contradiction to the formally 'democratic' principle of a universally elected officialdom.

3. Normally, the position of the official is held for life, at least in public bureaucracies; and this is increasingly the case for all similar structures. As a factual rule, *tenure for life* is presupposed, even where the giving of notice or periodic reappointment occurs. In contrast to the worker in a private enterprise, the official normally holds tenure. Legal or actual life-tenure, however, is not recognized as the official's right to the possession of office, as was the case with many structures of authority in the past. Where legal guarantees against arbitrary dismissal or transfer are developed, they merely serve to guarantee a strictly objective discharge of specific office duties free from all personal considerations. In Germany, this is the case for all juridical and, increasingly, for all administrative officials.

Within the bureaucracy, therefore, the measure of 'independence,' legally guaranteed by tenure, is not always a source of increased status for the official whose position is thus secured. Indeed, often the reverse holds, especially in old cultures and communities that are highly differentiated. In such communities, the stricter the subordination under the arbitrary rule of the master, the more it guarantees the maintenance of the conventional seigneurial style of living for the official. Because of the very absence of these legal guarantees of tenure, the conventional

esteem for the official may rise in the same way as, during the Middle
Ages, the esteem of the nobility of office rose at the expense of esteem
for the freemen, and as the king's judge surpassed that of the people's
judge. In Germany, the military officer or the administrative official can
be removed from office at any time, or at least far more readily than
the 'independent judge,' who never pays with loss of his office for even
the grossest offense against the 'code of honor' or against social conventions of the salon. For this very reason, if other things are equal, in the
eyes of the master stratum the judge is considered less qualified for social
intercourse than are officers and administrative officials, whose greater
dependence on the master is a greater guarantee of their conformity with
status conventions. Of course, the average official strives for a civil-service
law, which would materially secure his old age and provide increased
guarantees against his arbitrary removal from office. This striving, however, has its limits. A very strong development of the 'right to the office'
naturally makes it more difficult to staff them with regard to technical
efficiency, for such a development decreases the career-opportunities
of ambitious candidates for office. This makes for the fact that officials,
on the whole, do not feel their dependency upon those at the top. This
lack of a feeling of dependency, however, rests primarily upon the inclination to depend upon one's equals rather than upon the socially inferior and governed strata. The present conservative movement among
the Badenia clergy, occasioned by the anxiety of a presumably threatening separation of church and state, has been expressly determined by the
desire not to be turned 'from a master into a servant of the parish.'

4. The official receives the regular *pecuniary* compensation of a
normally fixed *salary* and the old age security provided by a pension.
The salary is not measured like a wage in terms of work done, but according to 'status,' that is, according to the kind of function (the 'rank') and,
in addition, possibly, according to the length of service. The relatively
great security of the official's income, as well as the rewards of social
esteem, make the office a sought-after position, especially in countries
which no longer provide opportunities for colonial profits. In such countries, this situation permits relatively low salaries for officials.

5. The official is set for a *'career'* within the hierarchical order of the
public service. He moves from the lower, less important, and lower paid
to the higher positions. The average official naturally desires a mechanical
fixing of the conditions of promotion: if not of the offices, at least of the
salary levels. He wants these conditions fixed in terms of 'seniority,' or
possibly according to grades achieved in a developed system of expert
examinations. Here and there, such examinations actually form a character *indelebilis* of the official and have lifelong effects on his career. To
this is joined the desire to qualify the right to office and the increasing
tendency toward status group closure and economic security. All of this

makes for a tendency to consider the offices as 'prebends' of those who are qualified by educational certificates. The necessity of taking general personal and intellectual qualifications into consideration, irrespective of the often subaltern character of the educational certificate, has led to a condition in which the highest political offices, especially the positions of 'ministers,' are principally filled without reference to such certificates.

III. The Presuppositions and Causes of Bureaucracy

The social and economic presuppositions of the modern structure of the office are as follows:

The development of the *money economy,* in so far as a pecuniary compensation of the officials is concerned, is a presupposition of bureaucracy. Today it not only prevails but is predominant. This fact is of very great importance for the whole bearing of bureaucracy, yet by itself it is by no means decisive for the existence of bureaucracy.

Historical examples of rather distinctly developed and quantitatively large bureaucracies are: (a) Egypt, during the period of the new Empire which, however, contained strong patrimonial elements; (b) the later Roman Principate, and especially the Diocletian monarchy and the Byzantine polity which developed out of it and yet retained strong feudal and patrimonial elements; (c) the Roman Catholic Church, increasingly so since the end of the thirteenth century; (d) China, from the time of Shi Hwangti until the present, but with strong patrimonial and prebendal elements; (e) in ever purer forms, the modern European states and, increasingly, all public corporations since the time of princely absolutism; (f) the large modern capitalist enterprise, the more so as it becomes greater and more complicated.

To a very great extent, partly even predominantly, cases (a) to (d) have rested upon compensation of the officials in kind. Yet they have displayed many other traits and effects characteristic of bureaucracy. The historical model of all later bureaucracies—the new Empire of Egypt— is at the same time one of the most grandiose examples of an organized subsistence economy. Yet this coincidence of bureaucracy and subsistence economy is understandable in view of the quite unique conditions that existed in Egypt. And the reservations—and they are quite considerable —which one must make in classifying this Egyptian structure as a bureaucracy are conditioned by the subsistence economy. A certain measure of a developed money economy is the normal precondition for the unchanged and continued existence, if not for the establishment, of pure bureaucratic administrations.

According to historical experience, without a money economy the bureaucratic structure can hardly avoid undergoing substantial internal changes, or indeed, turning into another type of structure. The allocation of fixed income in kind, from the magazines of the lord or from his current intake, to the officials easily means a first step toward appropriation of the sources of taxation and their exploitation as private property. This kind of allocation has been the rule in Egypt and China for thousands of years and played an important part in the later Roman monarchy as well as elsewhere. The income in kind has protected the official against the often sharp fluctuations in the purchasing power of money. Whenever the lord's prerogatives have relaxed, the taxes in kind, as a rule, have been irregular. In this case, the official has direct recourse to the tributaries of his bailiwick, whether or not he is authorized. Close at hand is the idea of securing the official against such oscillations by mortgaging or transferring the levies and therewith the power to tax, or by leasing profitable lands of the lord to the official for his own use. Every central authority which is not strictly organized is tempted to take this course either voluntarily or because the officials compel it to do so. The official may satisfy himself with the use of these levies or loans up to the level of his salary claim and then hand over the surplus. This implies strong temptation and therefore yields results chiefly unsatisfactory to the lord. Another process involves fixing the official's salary: This often occurred in the early history of German officialdom; and it happened on the largest scale in all Eastern Satrap administrations: the official hands over a stipulated amount and retains the surplus.

In such cases the official is economically in a position rather similar to that of the entrepreneurial tax-farmer. Indeed, office-farming including even the leasing of offices to the highest bidder is regularly found. On the soil of a private economy, the transformation of the statutes of villenage into tenancy relations is one of the most important among numerous examples. By tenancy arrangements the lord can transfer the trouble of changing his income-in-kind into money-income to the office tenant or to the official who is to be given a fixed sum. This was plainly the case with some Oriental regents in Antiquity. And above all, the farming out of public collection of taxes in lieu of the lord's own management of tax-gathering served this purpose. From this procedure there develops the possibility for the lord to progress in the ordering of his finances into a systematic budget. This is a very important advance, for it means that a fixed estimate of the income, and correspondingly of the expenses, can take the place of a hand-to-mouth living from incalculable incomes in kind, a condition typical of all the early states of public households. On the other hand, in systematizing his budget in this way, the lord renounces the control and full exploitation of his capacity to tax for his own use. According to the measure of freedom left to the official, to the office, or to the tax-farmer, the lasting capacity to pay taxes is endangered by inconsiderate exploitation. For, unlike the political overlord, the capitalist is not in the same way permanently interested in the subject's ability to pay.

The lord seeks to safeguard himself against this loss of control by regulations. The mode of tax-farming or the transfer of taxes can thus vary widely, according to the distribution of power between the lord and the tenant. Either the tenant's interest in the free exploitation of capacity to pay taxes or the lord's interest in the permanence of this capacity prevails. The nature of the tax-farming system rests essentially upon the joint or the opposing influence of these motives: the elimination of oscillations in the yields, the possibility of a budget, the safeguarding of the subjects' capacity to pay by protecting them against uneconomical exploitation, and a state control of the tax-farmer's yields for the sake of appropriating the maximum possible. In the Ptolemaic empire, as in Hellas and in Rome, the tax-farmer was still a private capitalist. The raising of taxes, however, was bureaucratically executed and controlled by the Ptolemaic state. The tenant's profit consisted in only a share of the respective surplus over and above the tax-farmer's fee, which was, in fact, only a guarantee. The tax-farmer's risk consisted in the possibility of yields that were lower than this sum.

The purely economic conception of the office as a source of the official's private income can also lead to the direct purchase of offices. This occurs when the lord finds himself in a position in which he requires not only a current income but money capital—for instance, for warfare or for debt payments. The purchase of office as a regular institution has existed in modern states, in the church state as well as in that of France and England; it has existed in the cases of sinecures as well as of very serious offices; and, in the case of officers' commissions, it lagged over until the early nineteenth century. In individual cases, the economic meaning of such a purchase of office can be altered so that the purchasing sum is partly or wholly in the nature of bail deposited for faithful service, but this has not been the rule.

Every sort of assignment of usufructs, tributes and services which are due to the lord himself or to the official for personal exploitation, always means a surrender of the pure type of bureaucratic organization. The official in such positions has a personal right to the possession of his office. This is the case to a still higher degree when official duty and compensation are interrelated in such a way that the official does not transfer to the lord any yields gained from the objects left to him, but handles these objects for his private ends and in turn renders to the lord services of a personal or a military, political, or ecclesiastical character.

We wish to speak of 'prebends' and of a 'prebendal' organization of office, wherever the lord assigns to the official rent payments for life, payments which are somehow fixed to objects or which are essentially *economic* usufruct from lands or other sources. They must be compensations for the fulfilment of actual or fictitious office duties; they are goods permanently set aside for the economic assurance of the office.

The transition from such prebendal organization of office to salaried officialdom is quite fluid. Very often the economic endowment of priesthoods has been 'prebendal,' as in Antiquity and the Middle Ages, and even up to the modern period. But in almost all periods the same form has been found in other areas. In Chinese sacerdotal law, the prebendal character of all offices forced the mourning official to resign his office. For during the ritual mourning period for the father or other household authorities abstention from the enjoyment of possessions was prescribed. Originally this prescription was aimed at avoiding the ill-will of the deceased master of the house, for the house belonged to this master and the office was considered purely as a prebend, a source for rent.

When not only economic rights but also lordly prerogatives are leased for personal execution with the stipulation of *personal* services to the lord, a further step away from salaried bureaucracy is taken. These leased prerogatives vary; for instance, with the political official, they may be in the nature of landlordism or in the nature of office authority. In both instances, and certainly in the latter, the specific nature of bureaucratic organization is completely destroyed and we enter the organizational realm of *feudal* dominion. All kinds of assignments of services and usufructs in kind as endowments for officials tend to loosen the bureaucratic mechanism, and especially to weaken hierarchic subordination. This subordination is most strictly developed in the discipline of modern officialdom. A precision similar to the precision of the contractually employed official of the modern Occident can only be attained—at least under very energetic leadership—where the subjection of the officials to the lord is personally absolute, where slaves, or employees treated like slaves, are used for administration.

The Egyptian officials were slaves of the Pharaoh, if not legally, at least in fact. The Roman latifundia owners liked to commission slaves with the direct management of money matters, because of the possibility of subjecting them to torture. In China, similar results have been sought by the prodigal use of the bamboo as a disciplinary instrument. The chances, however, for such direct means of coercion to function with *steadiness* are extremely unfavorable. According to experience, the relative optimum for the success and maintenance of a strict mechanization of the bureaucratic apparatus is offered by a secured money salary connected with the opportunity of a career that is not dependent upon mere accident and arbitrariness. Strict discipline and control, which at the same time has consideration for the official's sense of honor, and the development of prestige sentiments of the status group, as well as the possibility of public criticism, work in the direction of strict mechanization. With all this, the bureaucratic apparatus functions more assuredly than does any legal enslavement of functionaries. A strong status sentiment among officials not only agrees with the official's readiness to subordinate himself to the chief without any will of his own, but—just as is the case with the officer—status sentiments are the consequence of such subordination, for internally they balance the official's self-feeling. The purely impersonal character of office work, with its principled separation of the private sphere of the official from that of the office, facilitates the official's integration into the given functional conditions of a fixed mechanism based upon discipline.

Even though the full development of a money economy is not an indispensable precondition for bureaucratization, bureaucracy as a permanent structure is knit to the one presupposition of a constant income for maintaining it. Where such an income cannot be derived from private profits, as is the case with the bureaucratic organization of large modern enterprises, or from fixed land rents, as with the manor, a stable system of *taxation* is the precondition for the permanent existence of bureaucratic administration. For well-known and general reasons, only a fully developed money economy offers a secure basis for such a taxation system. The degree of administrative bureaucratization in urban communities with fully developed money economies has not infrequently been relatively greater in the contemporary far larger states of plains. Yet as soon as these plain states have been able to develop orderly systems of tribute, bureaucracy has developed more comprehensively than in city states. Whenever the size of the city states has remained confined to moderate limits, the tendency for a plutocratic and collegial administration by notables has corresponded most adequately to their structure.

IV. The Quantitative Development of Administrative Tasks

The proper soil for the bureaucratization of an administration has always been the specific developments of administrative tasks. We shall first discuss the quantitative extension of such tasks. In the field of politics, the great state and the mass party are the classic soil for bureaucratization.

This does not mean that every historically known and genuine formation of great states has brought about a bureaucratic administration. The permanence of a once-existing great state, or the homogeneity of a culture borne by such a state, has not always been attached to a bureaucratic structure of state. However, both of these features have held to a great extent, for instance, in the Chinese empire. The numerous great Negro empires, and similar formations, have had only an ephemerical existence primarily because they have lacked an apparatus of officials. And the unity of the Carolingian empire disintegrated when its organization of officials disintegrated. This organization, however, was predominantly patrimonial rather than bureaucratic in nature. From a purely temporal view, however, the empire of the Caliphs and its predecessors on Asiatic soil have lasted for considerable periods of time, and the organization of office was essentially patrimonial and prebendal. Also, the Holy Roman

Empire lasted for a long time in spite of the almost complete absence of bureaucracy. All these realms have represented a cultural unity of at least approximately the same strength as is usually created by bureaucratic polities.

The ancient Roman Empire disintegrated internally in spite of increasing bureaucratization and even during its very execution. This was because of the way the tax burdens were distributed by the bureaucratic state, which favored the subsistence economy. Viewed with regard to the intensity of their purely *political* unities, the temporal existences of the empires of the Caliphs, Carolingian and other medieval emperors were essentially unstable, nominal, and cohesive conglomerates. On the whole, the capacity for political action steadily diminished, and the relatively great unity of *culture* flowed from ecclesiastic structures that were in part strictly unified and, in the Occidental Middle Ages, increasingly bureaucratic in character. The unity of their cultures resulted partly from the far-going homogeneity of their social structures, which in turn was the aftermath and transformation of their former political unity. Both are phenomena of the traditional stereotyping of culture, which favors an unstable equilibrium. Both of these factors proved so strong a foundation that even grandiose attempts at expansion, such as the Crusades, could be undertaken in spite of the lack of intensive political unity; they were, one might say, performed as 'private undertakings.' The failure of the Crusades and their often irrational political course, however, is associated with the absence of a unified and intensive state power to back them up. And there is no doubt that the nuclei of intensive 'modern' states in the Middle Ages developed concomitantly with bureaucratic structures. Furthermore, in the end these quite bureaucratic political structures undoubtedly shattered the social conglomerates, which rested essentially upon unstable equilibriums.

The disintegration of the Roman Empire was partly conditioned by the very bureaucratization of its army and official apparatus. This bureaucratization could only be realized by carrying through at the same time a method of taxation which by its distribution of burdens was bound to lead to relative increase in the importance of a subsistence economy. Individual factors of this sort always enter the picture. Also the 'intensity' of the external and the internal state activities play their part. Quite apart from the relation between the state influence upon culture and the degree of bureaucratization, it may be said that 'normally'— though not without exception—the vigor to expand is directly related to the degree of bureaucratization. For two of the most expansive polities, the Roman Empire and the British world empire, during their most expansive periods, rested upon bureaucratic foundations only to a small extent. The Norman state in England carried through a strict organization on the basis of a feudal hierarchy. To a large extent, it received its unity and its push through the bureaucratization of the royal exchequer, which, in comparison to other political structures of the feudal period, was extremely strict. Later on, the English state did not share in the continental development towards bureaucratization, but remained an administration of notables. Just as in the republican administration of Rome, this English rule by notables was a result of the relative absence of a continental character, as well as of absolutely unique preconditions, which at the present time are disappearing. The dispensability of the large standing armies, which a continental state with equally expansive tendencies requires for its land frontiers, is among these special preconditions. In Rome, bureaucratization advanced with the transition from a coastal to a continental ring of frontiers. For the rest, in the domination structure of Rome, the strictly military character of the magistrate authorities—in the Roman manner unknown to any other people—made up for the lack of a bureaucratic apparatus with its technical efficiency, its precision and unity of administrative functions, especially outside the city limits. The continuity of administration was safeguarded by the unique position of the Senate. In Rome, as in England, one presupposition for this dispensability of bureaucracy which should not be forgotten was that the state authorities increasingly 'minimized' the scope of their functions at home. They restricted their functions to what was absolutely demanded for direct 'reasons of state.'

At the beginning of the modern period, all the prerogatives of the continental states accumulated in the hands of those princes who most relentlessly took the course of administrative bureaucratization. It is obvious that technically the great modern state is absolutely dependent upon a bureaucratic basis. The larger the state, and the more it is or the more it becomes a great power state, the more unconditionally is this the case.

The United States still bears the character of a polity which, at least in the technical sense, is not fully bureaucratized. But the greater the zones of friction with the outside and the more urgent the needs for administrative unity at home become, the more this character is inevitably and gradually giving way formally to the bureaucratic structure. Moreover, the partly unbureaucratic form of the state structure of the United States is materially balanced by the more strictly bureaucratic structures of those formations which, in truth, dominate politically, namely, the parties under the leadership of professionals or experts in organization and election tactics. The increasingly bureaucratic organization of all genuine mass parties offers the most striking example of the role of sheer quantity as a leverage for the bureaucratization of a social structure. In Germany, above all, the Social Democratic party, and abroad both of the 'historical' American parties are bureaucratic in the greatest possible degree.

V. Qualitative Changes of Administrative Tasks

Bureaucratization is occasioned more by intensive and qualitative enlargement and internal deployment of the scope of administrative tasks than by their extensive and quantitative increase. But the direction bureaucratization takes and the reasons that occasion it vary widely.

In Egypt, the oldest country of bureaucratic state administration, the public and collective regulation of waterways for the whole country and from the top could not be avoided because of technical economic factors. This regulation created the mechanism of scribes and officials. Once established, this mechanism, even in early times, found its second realm of business in the extraordinary construction activities which were organized militarily. As mentioned before, the bureaucratic tendency has chiefly been influenced by needs arising from the creation of standing armies as determined by power politics and by the development of public finance connected with the military establishment. In the modern state, the increasing demands for administration rest on the increasing complexity of civilization and push towards bureaucratization.

Very considerable expansions, especially overseas, have, of course, been managed by states ruled by notables (Rome, England, Venice), as will become evident in the appropriate context. Yet the 'intensity' of the administration, that is, the transfer of as many tasks as possible to the organization of the state proper for continuous management and discharge, has been only slightly developed among the great states ruled by notables, especially Rome and England, if we compare them with bureaucratic polities.

Both in notable and bureaucratic administrations the *structure* of state power has influenced culture very strongly. But it has done so relatively slightly in the form of management and control by the state. This holds from justice down to education. The growing demands on culture, in turn, are determined, though to a varying extent, by the growing wealth of the most influential strata in the state. To this extent increasing bureaucratization is a function of the increasing possession of goods used for consumption, and of an increasingly sophisticated technique of fashioning external life—a technique which corresponds to the opportunities provided by such wealth. This reacts upon the standard of living and makes for an increasing subjective indispensability of organized, collective, inter-local, and thus bureaucratic, provision for the most varied wants, which previously were either unknown, or were satisfied locally or by a private economy.

Among purely political factors, the increasing demand of a society, accustomed to absolute pacification, for order and protection ('police') in all fields exerts an especially persevering influence in the direction of bureaucratization. A steady road leads from modifications of the blood feud, sacerdotally, or by means of arbitration, to the present position of the policeman as the 'representative of God on earth.' The former means placed the guarantees for the individual's rights and security squarely upon the members of his sib, who are obligated to assist him with oath and vengeance. Among other factors, primarily the manifold tasks of the so-called 'policy of social welfare' operate in the direction of bureaucratization, for these tasks are, in part, saddled upon the state by interest groups and, in part, the state usurps them, either for reasons of power policy or for ideological motives. Of course, these tasks are to a large extent economically determined.

Among essentially technical factors, the specifically modern means of communication enter the picture as pacemakers of bureaucratization. Public land and water-ways, railroads, the telegraph, et cetera—they must, in part, necessarily be administered in a public and collective way; in part, such administration is technically expedient. In this respect, the contemporary means of communication frequently play a role similar to that of the canals of Mesopotamia and the regulation of the Nile in the ancient Orient. The degree to which the means of communication have been developed is a condition of decisive importance for the possibility of bureaucratic administration, although it is not the only decisive condition. Certainly in Egypt, bureaucratic centralization, on the basis of an almost pure subsistence economy, could never have reached the actual degree which it did without the natural trade route of the Nile. In order to promote bureaucratic centralization in modern Persia, the telegraph officials were officially commissioned with reporting all occurrences in the provinces to the Shah, over the heads of the local authorities. In addition, everyone received the right to remonstrate directly by telegraph. The modern Occidental state can be administered the way it actually is only because the state controls the telegraph network and has the mails and railroads at its disposal.

Railroads, in turn, are intimately connected with the development of an inter-local traffic of mass goods. This traffic is among the causal factors in the formation of the modern state. As we have already seen, this does not hold unconditionally for the past.

VI. Technical Advantages of Bureaucratic Organization

The decisive reason for the advance of bureaucratic organization has always been its purely technical superiority over any other form of organization. The fully developed bureaucratic mechanism compares with other organizations exactly as does the machine with the non-mechanical modes of production.

Precision, speed, unambiguity, knowledge of the files, continuity, discretion, unity, strict subordination, reduction of friction and of material and personal costs—these are raised to the optimum point in the strictly bureaucratic administration, and especially in its monocratic form. As compared with all collegiate, honorific, and avocational forms of administration, trained bureaucracy is superior on all these points. And as far as complicated tasks are concerned, paid bureaucratic work is not only more precise but, in the last analysis, it is often cheaper than even formally unremunerated honorific service.

Honorific arrangements make administrative work an avocation and, for this reason alone, honorific service normally functions more slowly; being less bound to schemata and being more formless. Hence it is less precise and less unified than bureaucratic work because it is less dependent upon superiors and because the establishment and exploitation of the apparatus of subordinate officials and filing services are almost unavoidably less economical. Honorific service is less continuous than bureaucratic and frequently quite expensive. This is especially the case if one thinks not only of the money costs to the public treasury—costs which bureaucratic administration, in comparison with administration by notables, usually substantially increases—but also of the frequent economic losses of the governed caused by delays and lack of precision. The possibility of administration by notables normally and permanently exists only where official management can be satisfactorily discharged as an avocation. With the qualitative increase of tasks the administration has to face, administration by notables reaches its limits—today, even in England. Work organized by collegiate bodies causes friction and delay and requires compromises between colliding interests and views. The administration, therefore, runs less precisely and is more independent of superiors; hence, it is less unified and slower. All advances of the Prussian administrative organization have been and will in the future be advances of the bureaucratic, and especially of the monocratic, principle.

Today, it is primarily the capitalist market economy which demands that the official business of the administration be discharged precisely, unambiguously, continuously, and with as much speed as possible. Normally, the very large, modern capitalist enterprises are themselves unequalled models of strict bureaucratic organization. Business management throughout rests on increasing precision, steadiness, and, above all, the speed of operations. This, in turn, is determined by the peculiar nature of the modern means of communication, including, among other things, the news service of the press. The extraordinary increase in the speed by which public announcements, as well as economic and political facts, are transmitted exerts a steady and sharp pressure in the direction of speeding up the tempo of administrative reaction toward various situations. The optimum of such reaction time is normally attained only by a strictly bureaucratic organization.*

Bureaucratization offers above all the optimum possibility for carrying through the principle of specializing administrative functions according to purely objective considerations. Individual performances are allocated to functionaries who have specialized training and who by constant practice learn more and more. The 'objective' discharge of business primarily means a discharge of business according to *calculable rules* and 'without regard for persons.'

'Without regard for persons' is also the watchword of the 'market' and, in general, of all pursuits of naked economic interests. A consistent execution of bureaucratic domination means the leveling of status 'honor.' Hence, if the principle of the free-market is not at the same time restricted, it means the universal domination of the 'class situation.' That this consequence of bureaucratic domination has not set in everywhere, parallel to the extent of bureaucratization, is due to the differences among possible principles by which polities may meet their demands.

The second element mentioned, 'calculable rules,' also is of paramount importance for modern bureaucracy. The peculiarity of modern culture, and specifically of its technical and economic basis, demands this very 'calculability' of results. When fully developed, bureaucracy also stands, in a specific sense, under the principle of *sine ira ac studio*. Its specific nature, which is welcomed by capitalism, develops the more perfectly the more the bureaucracy is 'dehumanized,' the more completely it succeeds in eliminating from official business love, hatred, and all purely personal, irrational, and emotional elements which escape calculation. This is the specific nature of bureaucracy and it is appraised as its special virtue.

The more complicated and specialized modern culture becomes, the more its external supporting apparatus demands the personally detached and strictly 'objective' *expert,* in lieu of the master of older social structures, who was moved by personal sympathy and favor, by grace and gratitude. Bureaucracy offers the attitudes demanded by the external apparatus of modern culture in the most favorable combination. As a rule, only bureaucracy has established the foundation for the administration of a rational law conceptually systematized on the basis of such enactments as the latter Roman imperial period first created with a high degree of technical perfection. During the Middle Ages, this law was received along with the bureaucratization of legal administration, that is to say, with the displacement of the old trial procedure which was

---

* Here we cannot discuss in detail how the bureaucratic apparatus may, and actually does, produce definite obstacles to the discharge of business in a manner suitable for the single case.

bound to tradition or to irrational presuppositions, by the rationally trained and specialized expert.

VII. Bureaucracy and Law

The 'rational' interpretation of law on the basis of strictly formal conceptions stands opposite the kind of adjudication that is primarily bound to sacred traditions. The single case that cannot be unambiguously decided by tradition is either settled by concrete 'revelation' (oracle, prophetic dicta, or ordeal—that is, by 'charismatic' justice) or—and only these cases interest us here—by informal judgments rendered in terms of concrete ethical or other practical valuations. This is 'Kadi-justice,' as R. Schmidt has fittingly called it. Or, formal judgments are rendered, though not by subsumption under rational concepts, but by drawing on 'analogies' and by depending upon and interpreting concrete 'precedents.' This is 'empirical justice.'

Kadi-justice knows no reasoned judgment whatever. Nor does empirical justice of the pure type give any reasons which in our sense could be called rational. The concrete valuational character of Kadi-justice can advance to a prophetic break with all tradition. Empirical justice, on the other hand, can be sublimated and rationalized into a 'technology.' All non-bureaucratic forms of domination display a peculiar coexistence: on the one hand, there is a sphere of strict traditionalism, and, on the other, a sphere of free arbitrariness and lordly grace. Therefore, combinations and transitional forms between these two principles are very frequent; they will be discussed in another context.

Even today in England, as Mendelssohn has demonstrated, a broad substratum of justice is actually Kadi-justice to an extent that is hardly conceivable on the Continent. The justice of German juries which preclude a statement of the reasons for their verdict often functions in practice in the same way as this English justice. In general, one has to beware of believing that 'democratic' principles of justice are identical with 'rational' adjudication (in the sense of formal rationality). Indeed, the contrary holds, as will be shown in another context. The English and American adjudication of the highest courts is still to a great extent empirical; and especially is it adjudication by precedents. In England, the reason for the failure of all efforts at a rational codification of law, as well as the failure to borrow Roman law, was due to the successful resistance against such rationalization offered by the great and centrally organized lawyers' guilds. These guilds formed a monopolistic stratum of notables from whose midst the judges of the high courts of the realm were recruited. They retained in their hands juristic training as an empirical and highly developed technology, and they successfully fought all moves towards rational law that threatened their social and material position. Such moves came especially from the ecclesiastical courts and, for a time, also from the universities.

The fight of the common law advocates against the Roman and ecclesiastical law and the power of the church in general was to a considerable degree economically caused by the lawyer's interest in fees; this is distinctly evidenced by the way in which the king intervened in this struggle. But the power position of the lawyers, who emerged victoriously from this struggle, was conditioned by political centralization. In Germany, primarily for political reasons, a socially powerful estate of notables was lacking. There was no estate which, like the English lawyers, could have been the carriers of a national administration of law, which could have raised national law to the level of a technology with regulated apprenticeship, and which could have offered resistance to the intrusion of the technically superior training of jurists in Roman law.

That fact that Roman law was substantively better adjusted to the needs of emerging capitalism did not decide its victory on the Continent. All legal institutions specific for modern capitalism are alien to Roman law and are medieval in origin. What was decisive was the rational form of Roman law and, above all, the technical necessity to place the trial procedure in the hands of rationally trained experts, which meant men trained in the universities and learned in Roman law. This training was necessary because the increasing complexity of practical legal cases and the increasingly rationalized economy demanded a rational procedure of evidence rather than the ascertainment of true facts by concrete revelation or sacerdotal guarantee, which, of course, are the ubiquitous and primeval means of proof. This legal situation was also determined to a large extent by structural changes in the economy. This factor, however, was efficacious everywhere, including England, where the royal power introduced the rational procedure of evidence for the sake of the merchants. The predominant reasons for the differences, which still exist, in the development of substantive law in England and Germany do not rest upon this economic factor. As is already obvious, these differences have sprung from the lawfully autonomous development of the respective structures of domination.

In England centralized justice and notable rule have been associated; in Germany, at the same time, there is bureaucratization and an absence of political centralization. England, which in modern times was the first and most highly developed capitalist country, thereby retained a less rational and less bureaucratic judicature. Capitalism in England, however, could quite easily come to terms with this, especially because the nature of the court constitution and of the trial procedure up to the modern period amounted in effect to a far-going denial of justice to the economically weak groups. This fact exerted a profound influence upon the distribution of landholdings in England by favoring the accumulation and immobilization of landed wealth. The length and expense of real estate transfers, determined by the economic interests of the lawyers, also worked in the same direction.

During the time of the Republic, Roman law represented a unique mixture of rational and empirical elements, and even of elements of Kadi-justice. The appointment of a jury as such, and the *praetor's actiones in factum,* which at first undoubtedly occurred 'from one given case to another,' contained an element of Kadi-justice. The bailing system of Roman justice and all that grew out of it, including even a part of the classic jurists' practice of responses, bore an 'empirical' character. The decisive turn of juridical thought toward rational thinking was first prepared by the technical nature of the instruction for trial procedure at the hands of the praetorian edict's formula, which were geared to legal conceptions. Today, under the dominance of the principle of substantiation, the presentation of facts is decisive, no matter from what legal point of view they may make the complaint seem justified. A similar compulsion to bring out the scope of the concepts unambiguously and formally is now lacking; but such a compulsion was produced by the technical culture of Roman law at its very height. Technical factors of trial procedure thus played their part in the development of rational law, factors which resulted only indirectly from the structure of the state. The rationalization of Roman law into a closed system of concepts to be scientifically handled was brought to perfection only during the period when the polity itself underwent bureaucratization. This rational and systematic quality sets off Roman law sharply from all law produced by the Orient or by Hellenic Greece.

The rabbinic responses of the *Talmud* is a typical example of empirical justice that is not rational but 'rationalist,' and at the same time strictly *fettered* by tradition. Every prophetic verdict is in the end pure Kadi-justice, *unfettered* by tradition, and follows the schema: 'It is written . . . but I say unto you.' The more strongly the religious nature of the Kadi's (or a similar judge's) position is emphasized, the more freely the judgment of the single case prevails and the less it is encumbered by rules within that sphere of its operation which is not fettered by sacred tradition. For a generation after the occupation of Tunisia by the French, for instance, a very tangible handicap for capitalism remained in that the ecclesiastic court (the *Chara*) decided over land holdings by 'free discretion,' as the Europeans put it. We shall become acquainted with the sociological foundation of these older types of justice when we discuss the structures of domination in another context.

It is perfectly true that 'matter-of-factness' and 'expertness' are not necessarily identical with the rule of general and abstract norms. Indeed, this does not even hold in the case of the modern administration of justice. In principle, the idea of 'a law without gaps' is, of course, vigorously disputed. The conception of the modern judge as an automaton into which the files and the costs are thrown in order that it may spill forth the verdict at the bottom along with the reasons, read mechanically from codified paragraphs—this conception is angrily rejected, perhaps because a certain approximation to this type is implied by a consistent bureaucratization of justice. In the field of court procedure there are areas in which the bureaucratic judge is directly held to 'individualizing' procedures by the legislator.

For the field of administrative activity proper, that is, for all state activities that fall outside the field of law creation and court procedure, one is accustomed to claiming the freedom and paramountcy of individual circumstances. General norms are held to play primarily a negative role as barriers to the official's positive and 'creative' activity, which should never be regulated. The bearing of this thesis may be disregarded here. Yet the point that this 'freely' creative administration (and possibly judicature) does not constitute a realm of *free*, arbitrary action, of mercy, and of *personally* motivated favor and valuation, as we shall find to be the case among pre-bureaucratic forms, is a very decisive point. The rule and the rational estimation of 'objective' purposes, as well as devotion to them, always exist as a norm of conduct. In the field of executive administration, especially where the 'creative' arbitrariness of the official is most strongly built up, the specifically modern and strictly 'objective' idea of 'reasons of state' is upheld as the supreme and ultimate guiding star of the official's behavior.

Of course, and above all, the sure instincts of the bureaucracy for the conditions of maintaining its power in its own state (and through it, in opposition to other states) are inseparably fused with the canonization of the abstract and 'objective' idea of 'reasons of state.' In the last analysis, the power interests of the bureaucracy only give a concretely exploitable content to this by no means unambiguous ideal; and, in dubious cases, power interests tip the balance. We cannot discuss this further here. The only decisive point for us is that in principle a system of rationally debatable 'reasons' stands behind every act of bureaucratic administration, that is, either subsumption under norms or a weighing of ends and means.

The position of all 'democratic' currents, in the sense of currents that would minimize 'authority,' is necessarily ambiguous. 'Equality before the law' and the demand for legal guarantees against arbitrariness demand a formal and rational 'objectivity' of administration, as opposed to the personally free discretion flowing from the 'grace' of the old patrimonial domination. If, however, an 'ethos'—not to speak of instincts— takes hold of the masses on some individual question, it postulates *substantive* justice oriented toward some concrete instance and person; and such an 'ethos' will unavoidably collide with the formalism and the rule-bound and cool 'matter-of-factness' of bureaucratic administration. For this reason, the ethos must emotionally reject what reason demands.

The propertyless masses especially are not served by a formal 'equality before the law' and a 'calculable' adjudication and administration, as demanded by 'bourgeois' interests. Naturally, in their eyes justice and administration should serve to compensate for their economic and social life-opportunities in the face of the propertied classes. Justice and administration can fulfil this function only if they assume an informal character to a far-reaching extent. It must be informal because it is substantively 'ethical' ('Kadi-justice'). Every sort of 'popular justice'—which usually does not ask for reasons and norms—as well as every sort of intensive influence on the administration by so-called public opinion, crosses the rational course of justice and administration just as strongly, and under certain conditions far more so, as the 'star chamber' proceedings of an 'absolute' ruler has been able to do. In this connection, that is, under the conditions of mass democracy, public opinion is communal conduct born of irrational 'sentiments.' Normally it is staged or directed by party leaders and the press.

VIII. The Concentration of the Means of Administration

The bureaucratic structure goes hand in hand with the concentration of the material means of management in the hands of the master. This concentration occurs, for instance, in a well-known and typical fashion, in the development of big capitalist enterprises, which find their essential characteristics in this process. A corresponding process occurs in public organizations.

The bureaucratically led army of the Pharaohs, the army during the later period of the Roman republic and the principate, and, above all, the army of the modern military state are characterized by the fact that their equipment and provisions are supplied from the magazines of the war lord. This is in contrast to the folk armies of agricultural tribes, the armed citizenry of ancient cities, the militias of early medieval cities, and all feudal armies; for these, the self-equipment and the self-provisioning of those obliged to fight was normal.

War in our time is a war of machines. And this makes magazines technically necessary, just as the dominance of the machine in industry promotes the concentration of the means of production and management. In the main, however, the bureaucratic armies of the past, equipped and provisioned by the lord, have risen when social and economic development has absolutely or relatively diminished the stratum of citizens who were economically able to equip themselves, so that their number was no longer sufficient for putting the required armies in the field. They were reduced at least relatively, that is, in relation to the range of power claimed for the polity. Only the bureaucratic army structure allowed for the development of the professional standing armies which are necessary for the constant pacification of large states of the plains, as well as for warfare against far-distant enemies, especially enemies overseas. Specifically, military discipline and technical training can be normally and fully developed, at least to its modern high level, only in the bureaucratic army.

Historically, the bureaucratization of the army has everywhere been realized along with the transfer of army service from the propertied to the propertyless. Until this transfer occurs, military service is an honorific privilege of propertied men. Such a transfer was made to the native-born unpropertied, for instance, in the armies of the generals of the late Roman republic and the empire, as well as in modern armies up to the nineteenth century. The burden of service has also been transferred to strangers, as in the mercenary armies of all ages. This process typically goes hand in hand with the general increase in material and intellectual culture. The following reason has also played its part everywhere: the increasing density of population, and therewith the intensity and strain of economic work, makes for an increasing 'indispensability' of the acquisitive strata for purposes of war. Leaving aside periods of strong ideological fervor, the propertied strata of sophisticated and especially of urban culture as a rule are little fitted and also little inclined to do the coarse war work of the common soldier. Other circumstances being equal, the propertied strata of the open country are at least usually better qualified and more strongly inclined to become professional officers. This difference between the urban and the rural propertied is balanced only where the increasing possibility of mechanized warfare requires the leaders to qualify as 'technicians.'

The bureaucratization of organized warfare may be carried through in the form of private capitalist enterprise, just like any other business. Indeed, the procurement of armies and their administration by private capitalists has been the rule in mercenary armies, especially those of the Occident up to the turn of the eighteenth century. During the Thirty Years' War, in Brandenburg the soldier was still the predominant owner of the material implements of his business. He owned his weapons, horses, and dress, although the state, in the role, as it were, of the merchant of the 'putting-out system,' did supply him to some extent. Later on, in the standing army of Prussia, the chief of the company owned the material means of warfare, and only since the peace of Tilsit has the concentration of the means of warfare in the hands of the state definitely come about. Only with this concentration was the introduction of uniforms generally carried through. Before then, the introduction of uniforms had been left to a great extent to the arbitrary discretion of the regimental officer, with the exception of individual categories of troops to whom the king had 'bestowed' certain uniforms, first, in 1620, to the royal bodyguard, then, under Frederick II, repeatedly.

Such terms as 'regiment' and 'battalion' usually had quite different meanings in the eighteenth century from the meanings they have today. Only the battalion was a tactical unit (today both are); the 'regiment' was then a managerial unit of an economic organization established by the colonel's position as an 'entrepreneur.' 'Official' maritime ventures (like the Genoese *maonae*) and army procurement belong to private capitalism's first giant enterprises of far-going bureaucratic character. In this respect, the 'nationalization' of these enterprises by the state has its modern parallel in the nationalization of the railroads, which have been controlled by the state from their beginnings.

In the same way as with army organizations, the bureaucratization of administration goes hand in hand with the concentration of the means of organization in other spheres. The old administration by satraps and regents, as well as administration by farmers of office, purchasers of office, and, most of all, administration by feudal vassals, decentralize the material means of administration. The local demand of the province and the cost of the army and of subaltern officials are regularly paid for in advance from local income, and only the surplus reaches the central treasure. The enfeoffed official administers entirely by payment out of his own pocket. The bureaucratic state, however, puts its whole administrative expense on the budget and equips the lower authorities with the current means of expenditure, the use of which the state regulates and controls. This has the same meaning for the 'economics' of the administration as for the large centralized capitalist enterprise.

In the field of scientific research and instruction, the bureaucratization of the always existing research institutes of the universities is a function of the increasing demand for material means of management. Liebig's laboratory at Giessen University was the first example of big enterprise in this field. Through the concentration of such means in the hands of the privileged head of the institute, the mass of researchers and docents are separated from their 'means of production,' in the same way as capitalist enterprise has separated the workers from theirs.

In spite of its indubitable technical superiority, bureaucracy has everywhere been a relatively late development. A number of obstacles have contributed to this, and only under certain social and political conditions have they definitely receded into the background.

IX. The Leveling of Social Differences

Bureaucratic organization has usually come into power on the basis of a leveling of economic and social differences. This leveling has been at least relative, and has concerned the significance of social and economic differences for the assumption of administrative functions.

Bureaucracy inevitably accompanies modern *mass democracy* in contrast to the democratic self-government of small homogeneous units.

This results from the characteristic principle of bureaucracy: the abstract regularity of the execution of authority, which is a result of the demand for 'equality before the law' in the personal and functional sense—hence, of the horror of 'privilege,' and the principled rejection of doing business 'from case to case.' Such regularity also follows from the social preconditions of the origin of bureaucracies. The non-bureaucratic administration of any large social structure rests in some way upon the fact that existing social, material, or honorific preferences and ranks are connected with administrative functions and duties. This usually means that a direct or indirect economic exploitation or a 'social' exploitation of position, which every sort of administrative activity gives to its bearers, is equivalent to the assumption of administrative functions.

Bureaucratization and democratization within the administration of the state therefore signify and increase the cash expenditures of the public treasury. And this is the case in spite of the fact that bureaucratic administration is usually more 'economical' in character than other forms of administration. Until recent times—at least from the point of view of the treasury—the cheapest way of satisfying the need for administration was to leave almost the entire local administration and lower judicature to the landlords of Eastern Prussia. The same fact applies to the administration of sheriffs in England. Mass democracy makes a clean sweep of the feudal, patrimonial, and—at least in intent—the plutocratic privileges in administration. Unavoidably it puts paid professional labor in place of the historically inherited avocational administration by notables.

This not only applies to structures of the state. For it is no accident that in their own organizations, the democratic mass parties have completely broken with traditional notable rule based upon personal relationships and personal esteem. Yet such personal structures frequently continue among the old conservative as well as the old liberal parties. Democratic mass parties are bureaucratically organized under the leadership of party officials, professional party and trade union secretaries, et cetera. In Germany, for instance, this has happened in the Social Democratic party and in the agrarian mass-movement; and in England, for the first time, in the caucus democracy of Gladstone-Chamberlain, which was originally organized in Birmingham and since the 1870's has spread. In the United States, both parties since Jackson's administration have developed bureaucratically. In France, however, attempts to organize disciplined political parties on the basis of an election system that would compel bureaucratic organization have repeatedly failed. The resistance of local circles of notables against the ultimately unavoidable bureaucratization of the parties, which would encompass the entire country and break their influence, could not be overcome. Every advance of the simple election techniques, for instance the system of proportional elections, which calculates with figures, means a strict and inter-local bureaucratic organization of the parties and therewith an increasing domination of party bureaucracy and discipline, as well as the elimination of the local circles of notables—at least this holds for great states.

The progress of bureaucratization in the state administration itself is a parallel phenomenon of democracy, as is quite obvious in France, North America, and now in England. Of course one must always remember that the term 'democratization' can be misleading. The *demos* itself, in the sense of an inarticulate mass, never 'governs' larger associations; rather, it is governed, and its existence only changes the way in which the executive leaders are selected and the measure of influence which the *demos*, or better, which social circles from its midst are able to exert upon the content and the direction of administrative activities by supplementing what is called 'public opinion.' 'Democratization,' in the sense here intended, does not necessarily mean an increasingly active share of the governed in the authority of the social structure. This may be a result of democratization, but it is not necessarily the case.

We must expressly recall at this point that the political concept of democracy, deduced from the 'equal rights' of the governed, includes these postulates: (1) prevention of the development of a closed status group of officials in the interest of a universal accessibility of office, and (2) minimization of the authority of officialdom in the interest of expanding the sphere of influence of 'public opinion' as far as practicable. Hence, wherever possible, political democracy strives to shorten the term of office by election and recall and by not binding the candidate to a special expertness. Thereby democracy inevitably comes into conflict with the bureaucratic tendencies which, by its fight against notable rule, democracy has produced. The generally loose term 'democratization' cannot be used here, in so far as it is understood to mean the minimization of the civil servants' ruling power in favor of the greatest possible 'direct' rule of the *demos*, which in practice means the respective party leaders of the *demos*. The most decisive thing here—indeed it is rather exclusively so—is the *leveling of the governed* in opposition to the ruling and bureaucratically articulated group, which in its turn may occupy a quite autocratic position, both in fact and in form.

In Russia, the destruction of the position of the old landed nobility through the regulation of the Mjeshtshitelstvo (rank order) and the permeation of the old nobility by an office nobility were characteristic transitional phenomena in the development of bureaucracy. In China, the estimation of rank and the qualification for office according to the number of examinations passed mean something similar, but they have had consequences which, in theory at least, are still sharper. In France, the Revolution and still more Bonapartism have made the bureaucracy all-powerful. In the Catholic Church, first the feudal and then all independent local intermediary powers were eliminated. This was begun by Gregory VII and continued through the Council of Trent, the Vatican Council, and it was completed by the edicts of Pius X. The transformation of these local powers into pure functionaries of the central authority was connected with the constant increase in the factual significance of the formally quite dependent chaplains, a process which above all was based on the political party organization of Catholicism. Hence this process meant an advance of bureaucracy and at the same time of 'passive democratization,' as it were, that is, the leveling of the governed. The substitution of the bureaucratic army for the self-equipped army of notables is everywhere a process of 'passive' democratization, in the sense in which every establishment of an absolute military monarchy in the place of a feudal state or of a republic of notables is. This has held, in principle, even for the development of the state in Egypt in spite of all the peculiarities involved. Under the Roman principate the bureaucratization of the provincial administration in the field of tax collection, for instance, went hand in hand with the elimination of the plutocracy of a capitalist class, which, under the Republic, had been all-powerful. Ancient capitalism itself was finally eliminated with this stroke.

It is obvious that almost always economic conditions of some sort play their part in such 'democratizing' developments. Very frequently we meet with the influence of an economically determined origin of new classes, whether plutocratic, petty bourgeois, or proletarian in character. Such classes may call on the aid of, or they may only call to life or recall to life, a political power, no matter whether it is of legitimate or of Caesarist stamp. They may do so in order to attain economic or social advantages by political assistance. On the other hand, there are equally possible and historically documented cases in which initiative came 'from on high' and was of a purely political nature and drew advantages from political constellations, especially in foreign affairs. Such leadership exploited economic and social antagonisms as well as class interests merely as a means for their own purpose of gaining purely political power. For this reason, political authority has thrown the antagonistic classes out of their almost always unstable equilibrium and called their latent interest conflicts into battle. It seems hardly possible to give a general statement of this.

The extent and direction of the course along which economic influences have moved, as well as the nature in which political power relations exert influence, vary widely. In Hellenic Antiquity, the transition to disciplined combat by Hoplites, and in Athens, the increasing importance of the navy laid the foundation for the conquest of political power by the strata on whose shoulders the military burden rested. In Rome, however, the same development shook the rule of the office nobility only temporarily and seemingly. Although the modern mass army has everywhere been a means of breaking the power of notables, by itself it has in no way served as a leverage for active, but rather for merely passive, democratization. One contributing factor, however, has been the fact that the ancient citizen army rested economically upon self-equipment, whereas the modern army rests upon the bureaucratic procurement of requirements.

The advance of the bureaucratic structure rests upon 'technical' superiority. This fact leads here, as in the whole field of technique, to the following: the advance has been realized most slowly where older structural forms have been technically well developed and functionally adjusted to the requirements at hand. This was the case, for instance, in the administration of notables in England and hence England was the slowest of all countries to succumb to bureaucratization or, indeed, is still only partly in the process of doing so. The same general phenomenon exists when highly developed systems of gaslight or of steam railroads with large and fixed capital offer stronger obstacles to electrification than in completely new areas which are opened up for electrification.

X. The Permanent Character of the Bureaucratic Machine

Once it is fully established, bureaucracy is among those social structures which are the hardest to destroy. Bureaucracy is *the* means of carrying 'community action' over into rationally ordered 'societal action.' Therefore, as an instrument for 'societalizing' relations of power, bureaucracy has been and is a power instrument of the first order—for the one who controls the bureaucratic apparatus.

Under otherwise equal conditions, a 'societal action,' which is methodically ordered and led, is superior to every resistance of 'mass' or even of 'communal action.' And where the bureaucratization of administration has been completely carried through, a form of power relation is established that is practically unshatterable.

The individual bureaucrat cannot squirm out of the apparatus in which he is harnessed. In contrast to the honorific or avocational 'notable,' the professional bureaucrat is chained to his activity by his entire material and ideal existence. In the great majority of cases, he is only a single cog in an ever-moving mechanism which prescribes to him an essentially fixed route of march. The official is entrusted with specialized tasks and normally the mechanism cannot be put into motion or arrested by him, but only from the very top. The individual bureaucrat is thus forged to the community of all the functionaries who are integrated into the mechanism. They have a common interest in seeing that the mechanism continues its functions and that the societally exercised authority carries on.

The ruled, for their part, cannot dispense with or replace the bureaucratic apparatus of authority once it exists. For this bureaucracy rests upon expert training, a functional specialization of work, and an attitude set for habitual and virtuoso-like mastery of single yet methodically integrated functions. If the official stops working, or if his work is forcefully interrupted, chaos results, and it is difficult to improvise replacements from among the governed who are fit to master such chaos. This holds for public administration as well as for private economic management. More and more the material fate of the masses depends upon the steady and correct functioning of the increasingly bureaucratic organizations of private capitalism. The idea of eliminating these organizations becomes more and more utopian.

The discipline of officialdom refers to the attitude-set of the official for precise obedience within his *habitual* activity, in public as well as in private organizations. This discipline increasingly becomes the basis of all order, however great the practical importance of administration on the basis of the filed documents may be. The naive idea of Bakuninism of destroying the basis of 'acquired rights' and 'domination' by destroying public documents overlooks the settled orientation of *man* for keeping to the habitual rules and regulations that continue to exist independently of the documents. Every reorganization of beaten or dissolved troops, as well as the restoration of administrative orders destroyed by revolt, panic, or other catastrophes, is realized by appealing to the trained orientation of obedient compliance to such orders. Such compliance has been conditioned into the officials, on the one hand, and, on the other hand, into the governed. If such an appeal is successful it brings, as it were, the disturbed mechanism into gear again.

The objective indispensability of the once-existing apparatus, with its peculiar, 'impersonal' character, means that the mechanism—in contrast to feudal orders based upon personal piety—is easily made to work for anybody who knows how to gain control over it. A rationally ordered system of officials continues to function smoothly after the enemy has occupied the area; he merely needs to change the top officials. This body of officials continues to operate because it is to the vital interest of everyone concerned, including above all the enemy.

During the course of his long years in power, Bismarck brought his ministerial colleagues into unconditional bureaucratic dependence by eliminating all independent statesmen. Upon his retirement, he saw to his surprise that they continued to manage their offices unconcerned and undismayed, as if he had not been the master mind and creator of these creatures, but rather as if some single figure had been exchanged for some other figure in the bureaucratic machine. With all the changes of masters in France since the time of the First Empire, the power machine has remained essentially the same. Such a machine makes 'revolution,' in the sense of the forceful creation of entirely new formations of authority, technically more and more impossible, especially when the apparatus controls the modern means of communication (telegraph, et cetera) and also by virtue of its internal rationalized structure. In classic fashion, France has demonstrated how this process has substituted *coups d'état* for 'revolutions': all successful transformations in France have amounted to *coups d'état*.

XI. Economic and Social Consequences of Bureaucracy

It is clear that the bureaucratic organization of a social structure, and especially of a political one, can and regularly does have far-reaching economic consequences. But what sort of consequences? Of course in any individual case it depends upon the distribution of economic and social power, and especially upon the sphere that is occupied by the emerging bureaucratic mechanism. The consequences of bureaucracy depend therefore upon the direction which the powers using the apparatus give to it. And very frequently a crypto-plutocratic distribution of power has been the result.

In England, but especially in the United States, party donors regularly stand behind the bureaucratic party organizations. They have financed those parties and have been able to influence them to a large extent. The breweries in England, the so-called 'heavy industry,' and in Germany the Hansa League with their voting funds are well enough known as political donors to parties. In modern times bureaucratization and social leveling within political, and particularly within state organizations in connection with the destruction of feudal and local privileges, have very frequently benefited the interests of capitalism. Often bureaucratization has been carried out in direct alliance with capitalist interests, for example, the great historical alliance of the power of the absolute prince with capitalist interests. In general, a legal leveling and destruction of firmly established local structures ruled by notables has usually made for a wider range of capitalist activity. Yet one may expect as an effect of bureaucratization, a policy that meets the petty bourgeois interest in a secured traditional 'subsistence,' or even a state socialist policy that strangles opportunities for private profit. This has occurred in several cases of historical and far-reaching importance, specifically during antiquity; it is undoubtedly to be expected as a future development. Perhaps it will occur in Germany.

The very different effects of political organizations which were, at least in principle, quite similar—in Egypt under the Pharaohs and in Hellenic and Roman times—show the very different economic significances of bureaucratization which are possible according to the direction of other factors. The mere fact of bureaucratic organization does not unambiguously tell us about the concrete direction of its economic effects, which are always in some manner present. At least it does not tell us as much as can be told about its relatively leveling effect socially. In this respect, one has to remember that bureaucracy as such is a precision instrument which can put itself at the disposal of quite varied interests in domination purely political as well as purely economic ones, or any other sort. Therefore the measure of its parallelism with democratization must not be exaggerated, however typical it may be. Under certain conditions, strata of feudal lords have also put bureaucracy into their service. There is also the possibility—and often it has become a fact, for instance, in the Roman principate and in some forms of absolutist state structures—that a bureaucratization of administration is deliberately connected with the formation of *estates*, or is entangled with them by the force of the existing groupings of social power. The express reservation of offices for certain status groups is very frequent, and actual reservations are even more frequent. The democratization of society in its totality, and in the *modern* sense of the term, whether actual or perhaps merely formal, is an especially favorable basis of bureaucratization, but by no means the only possible one. After all, bureaucracy strives merely to level those powers that stand in its way and in those areas that, in the individual case, it seeks to occupy. We must remember this fact—which we have encountered several times and which we shall have to discuss repeatedly: that 'democracy' as such is opposed to the 'rule' of bureaucracy, in spite and perhaps because of its unavoidable yet unintended promotion of bureaucratization. Under certain conditions, democracy creates obvious ruptures and blockages to bureaucratic organization. Hence, in every individual historical case, one must observe in what special direction bureaucratization has developed.

XII. The Power Position of Bureaucracy

Everywhere the modern state is undergoing bureaucratization. But whether the *power* of bureaucracy within the polity is universally increasing must here remain an open question.

The fact that bureaucratic organization is technically the most highly developed means of power in the hands of the man who controls it does not determine the weight that bureaucracy as such is capable of having in a particular social structure. The ever-increasing 'indispensability' of the officialdom, swollen to millions, is no more decisive for this question than is the view of some representatives of the proletarian movement that the economic indispensability of the proletarians is decisive for the measure of their social and political power position. If 'indispensability' were decisive, then where slave labor prevailed and where freemen usually abhor work as a dishonor, the 'indispensable' slaves ought to have held the positions of power, for they were at least as indispensable as officials and proletarians are today. Whether the power of bureaucracy as such increases cannot be decided *a priori* from such reasons. The drawing in of economic interest groups or other non-official experts, or the drawing in of non-expert lay representatives, the establishment of local, inter-local, or central parliamentary or other representative bodies, or of occupational associations—these *seem* to run directly against the bureaucratic tendency. How far this appearance is the truth must be discussed in another chapter rather than in this purely formal and typological discussion. In general, only the following can be said here:

Under normal conditions, the power position of a fully developed bureaucracy is always overtowering. The 'political master' finds himself in the position of the 'dilettante' who stands opposite the 'expert,' facing the trained official who stands within the management of administration. This holds whether the 'master' whom the bureaucracy serves is a 'people,' equipped with the weapons of 'legislative initiative,' the 'referendum,' and the right to remove officials, or a parliament, elected on a more aristocratic or more 'democratic' basis and equipped with the right to vote a lack of confidence, or with the actual authority to vote it. It holds whether the master is an aristocratic, collegiate body, legally or actually based on self-recruitment, or whether he is a popularly elected president, a hereditary and 'absolute' or a 'constitutional' monarch.

Every bureaucracy seeks to increase the superiority of the professionally informed by keeping their knowledge and intentions secret. Bureaucratic administration always tends to be an administration of 'secret sessions': in so far as it can, it hides its knowledge and action from criticism. Prussian church authorities now threaten to use disciplinary measures against pastors who make reprimands or other admonitory measures in any way accessible to third parties. They do this because the pastor, in making such criticism available, is 'guilty' of facilitating a possible criticism of the church authorities. The treasury officials of the Persian shah have made a secret doctrine of their budgetary art and even use secret script. The official statistics of Prussia, in general, make public only what cannot do any harm to the intentions of the power-wielding bureaucracy. The tendency toward secrecy in certain administrative fields follows their material nature: everywhere that the power interests of the domination structure toward *the outside* are at stake, whether it is an economic competitor of a private enterprise, or a foreign, potentially hostile polity, we find secrecy. If it is to be successful, the management of diplomacy can only be publicly controlled to a very limited extent. The military administration must insist on the concealment of its most important measures; with the increasing significance of purely technical aspects, this is all the more the case. Political parties do not proceed differently, in spite of all the ostensible publicity of Catholic congresses and party conventions. With the increasing bureaucratization of party organizations, this secrecy will prevail even more. Commercial policy, in Germany for instance, brings about a concealment of production statistics. Every fighting posture of a social structure toward the outside tends to buttress the position of the group in power.

The pure interest of the bureaucracy in power, however, is efficacious far beyond those areas where purely functional interests make for secrecy. The concept of the 'official secret' is the specific invention of bureaucracy, and nothing is so fanatically defended by the bureaucracy as this attitude, which cannot be substantially justified beyond these specifically qualified areas. In facing a parliament, the bureaucracy, out of a sure power instinct, fights every attempt of the parliament to gain knowledge by means of its own experts or from interest groups. The so-called right of parliamentary investigation is one of the means by which parliament seeks such knowledge. Bureaucracy naturally welcomes a poorly informed and hence a powerless parliament—at least in so far as ignorance somehow agrees with the bureaucracy's interests.

The absolute monarch is powerless opposite the superior knowledge of the bureaucratic expert—in a certain sense more powerless than any other political head. All the scornful decrees of Frederick the Great concerning the 'abolition of serfdom' were derailed, as it were, in the course of their realization because the official mechanism simply ignored them as the occasional ideas of a dilettante. When a constitutional king agrees with a socially important part of the governed, he very frequently exerts a greater influence upon the course of administration than does the absolute monarch. The constitutional king can control these experts better because of what is, at least relatively, the public character of criticism, whereas the absolute monarch is dependent for information solely upon the bureaucracy. The Russian czar of the old regime was seldom able to accomplish permanently anything that displeased his bureaucracy and hurt the power interests of the bureaucrats. His ministerial departments, placed directly under him as the autocrat, represented a conglomerate of satrapies, as was correctly noted by Leroy-Beaulieu. These satrapies constantly fought against one another by all the means of personal intrigue, and, especially, they bombarded one another with voluminous 'memorials,' in the face of which, the monarch, as a dilettante, was helpless.

With the transition to constitutional government, the concentration of the power of the central bureaucracy in one head became unavoidable. Officialdom was placed under a monocratic head, the prime minister, through whose hands everything had to go before it got to the monarch. This put the latter, to a large extent, under the tutelage of the chief of the bureaucracy. Wilhelm II, in his well-known conflict with Bismarck, fought against this principle, but he had to withdraw his attack very soon. Under the rule of expert knowledge, the actual influence of the monarch can attain steadiness only by a continuous communication with the bureaucratic chiefs; this intercourse must be methodically planned and directed by the head of the bureaucracy.

At the same time, constitutionalism binds the bureaucracy and the ruler into a community of interests against the desires of party chiefs for power in the parliamentary bodies. And if he cannot find support in parliament the constitutional monarch is powerless against the bureaucracy. The desertion of the 'Great of the Reich,' the Prussian ministers and top officials of the Reich in November 1918, brought a monarch into approximately the same situation as existed in the feudal state in 1056. However, this is an exception, for, on the whole, the power position of a monarch opposite bureaucratic officials is far stronger than it was in any feudal state or in the 'stereotyped' patrimonial state. This is because of the constant presence of aspirants for promotion, with whom the monarch can easily replace inconvenient and independent officials. Other circumstances being equal, only economically independent officials, that is, officials who belong to the propertied strata, can permit themselves to risk the loss of their offices. Today as always, the recruitment of officials from among propertyless strata increases the power of the rulers. Only officials who belong to a socially influential stratum, whom the monarch believes he must take into account as personal supporters, like the so-called *Kanalrebellen* in Prussia can permanently and completely paralyse the substance of his will.

Only the expert knowledge of private economic interest groups in the field of 'business' is superior to the expert knowledge of the bureaucracy. This is so because the exact knowledge of facts in their field is vital to the economic existence of businessmen. Errors in official statistics do not have direct economic consequences for the guilty official, but errors in the calculation of a capitalist enterprise are paid for by losses, perhaps by its existence. The 'secret,' as a means of power, is, after all, more safely hidden in the books of an enterpriser than it is in the files of public authorities. For this reason alone authorities are held within narrow barriers when they seek to influence economic life in the capitalist epoch. Very frequently the measures of the state in the field of capitalism take unforeseen and unintended courses, or they are made illusory by the superior expert knowledge of interest groups.

XIII. Stages in the Development of Bureaucracy

More and more the specialized knowledge of the expert became the foundation for the power position of the officeholder. Hence an early concern of the ruler was how to exploit the special knowledge of experts without having to abdicate in their favor but preserve his dominant position. With the qualitative extension of administrative tasks and

therewith the indispensability of expert knowledge, it typically happens
that the lord no longer is satisfied by occasional consultation with individual and proved confidants or even with an assembly of such men called
together intermittently and in difficult situations. The lord begins to
surround himself with *collegiate* bodies who deliberate and resolve in
continuous session.* The *Räte von Haus aus* is a characteristic transitional
phenomenon in this development.

The position of such collegiate bodies naturally varies according to
whether they become the highest administrative authority, or whether a
central and monocratic authority, or several such authorities stand at
their side. In addition, a great deal depends upon their procedure. When
the collegiate type is fully developed, such bodies, in principle or in fiction, meet with the lord in the chair and all important matters are
elucidated from all points of view in the papers of the respective experts
and their assistants and by the reasoned votes of the other members.
The matter is then settled by a resolution, which the lord will sanction or
reject by an edict. This kind of collegiate body is the typical form in
which the ruler, who increasingly turns into a 'dilettante,' at the same
time exploits expert knowledge and—what frequently remains unnoticed
—seeks to fend off the overpowering weight of expert knowledge and
to maintain his dominant position in the face of experts. He keeps one
expert in check by others and by such cumbersome procedures he seeks
personally to gain a comprehesive picture as well as the certainty that
nobody prompts him to arbitrary decisions. Often the prince expects to
assure himself a maximum of personal influence less from personally
presiding over the collegiate bodies than from having written memo-
randa submitted to him. Frederick William I of Prussia actually exerted a
very considerable influence on the administration, but he almost never
attended the collegiately organized sessions of the cabinet ministers! He
rendered his decisions on written presentations by means of marginal
comments or edicts. These decisions were delivered to the ministers by
the *Feldjaeger* of the *Cabinett*, after consultation with those servants who
belonged to the cabinet and were personally attached to the king.

The hatred of the bureaucratic departments turns against the cabinet
just as the distrust of the subjects turns against the bureaucrats in case of
failure. The cabinet in Russia, as well as in Prussia and in other states,
thus developed into a personal fortress in which the ruler, so to speak,
sought refuge in the face of expert knowledge and the impersonal and
functional routinization of administration.

By the collegiate principle the ruler furthermore tries to fashion a sort
of synthesis of *specialized experts* into a collective unit. His success in
doing this cannot be ascertained in general. The phenomenon itself,

* *Conseil d'Etat*, Privy Council, *Generaldirektorium, Cabinett, Divan, Tsung-li
Yamen, Wai-wu pu*, etc.

however, is common to very different forms of state, from the patrimonial and feudal to the early bureaucratic, and it is especially typical for early princely absolutism. The collegiate principle has proved itself to be one of the strongest educative means for 'matter-of-factness' in administration. It has also made possible the drawing in of socially influential private persons and thus to combine in some measure the authority of notables and the practical knowledge of private enterprisers with the specialized expertness of professional bureaucrats. The collegiate bodies were one of the first institutions to allow the development of the modern concept of 'public authorities,' in the sense of enduring structures independent of the person.

As long as an expert knowledge of administrative affairs was the exclusive product of a long empirical practice, and administrative norms were not regulations but elements of tradition, the council of *elders*—in a manner typical often with priests, 'elder statesmen,' and notables participating—was the adequate form for collegiate authorities, which in the beginning merely gave advice to the ruler. But as such bodies continued to exist in the face of changing rulers, they often usurped actual power. The Roman Senate and the Venetian Council, as well as the Athenian *Areopag* until its downfall and replacement by the rule of the *demagogos* acted in this manner. We must of course sharply distinguish such authorities from the corporate bodies under discussion here.

In spite of manifold transitions, collegiate bodies, as a type, emerge on the basis of the rational specialization of functions and the rule of expert knowledge. On the other hand, they must be distinguished from advisory bodies selected from among private and *interested* circles, which are frequently found in the modern state and whose nucleus is not formed of officials or of former officials. These collegiate bodies must also be distinguished sociologically from the boards of control found in the bureaucratic structures of the modern private economy (economic corporations). This distinction must be made in spite of the fact that such corporate bodies not infrequently complete themselves by drawing in notables from among disinterested circles for the sake of their expert knowledge or in order to exploit them for representation and advertising. Normally, such bodies do not unite holders of special expert knowledge but rather the decisive representatives of paramount economic interest groups, especially the bank creditors of the enterprise—and such men by no means hold merely advisory positions. They have at least a controlling voice, and very often they occupy an actually dominant position. They are to be compared (not without some distortion) to the assemblies of the great independent holders of feudal fiefs and offices and other socially powerful interest groups of patrimonial or feudal polities. Occasionally, however, these have been the precursors of the 'councilors' who have emerged in consequence of an increased intensity of administration. And even more frequently they have been precursors of corporations of legally privileged estates.

With great regularity the bureaucratic collegiate principle has been transferred from the central authority to the most varied lower authorities. Within locally closed, and especially within urban units, collegiate administration is the original form of the rule of notables, as was indicated at the beginning of this discussion. Originally it worked through elected, later on, usually, or at least in part, through co-opted 'councilors,' collegiate bodies of 'magistrates,' *decuriones,* and 'jurors.' Such bodies are a normal element of organized 'self-government,' that is, the management of administrative affairs by local interest groups under the control of the bureaucratic authorities of the state. The above-mentioned examples of the Venetian Council and even more so of the Roman Senate represent transfers of notable rule to great overseas empires. Normally such a rule of notables is rooted in local political associations. Within the bureaucratic state, collegiate administration disappears as soon as progress in the means of communication and the increasing technical demands of administration necessitate quick and unambiguous decisions, and as soon as the dominant motives for full bureaucratization and monocracy, which we discussed above, push to the fore. Collegiate administration disappears when from the point of view of the ruler's interests a strictly unified administrative leadership appears to be more important than thoroughness in the preparation of administrative decisions. This is the case as soon as parliamentary institutions develop and—usually at the same time—as criticism from the outside and publicity increase.

Under these modern conditions the thoroughly rationalized system of departmental ministers and prefects, as in France, offers significant opportunities for pushing the old forms into the background. Probably the system is supplemented by the calling in of interest groups as advisory bodies recruited from among the economically and socially most influential strata. This practice, which I have mentioned above, is increasingly frequent and gradually may well be ordered more formally.

This latter development seeks especially to put the concrete experience of interest groups into the service of a rational administration of expertly trained officials. It will certainly be important in the future and it further increases the power of bureaucracy. It is known that Bismarck sought to realize the plan of a 'national economic council' as a means of power against parliament. Bismarck, who would never have given the Reichstag the right of investigation in the sense of the British Parliament, reproached the majority, who rejected his proposal, by stating that in the interest of parliamentary power the majority sought to protect officialdom from becoming 'too prudent.' Discussion of the position of organized interest groups within the administration, which may be in the offing, does not belong in this context.

Only with the bureaucratization of the state and of law in general can one see a definite possibility of separating sharply and conceptually an 'objective' legal order from the 'subjective rights' of the individual which it guarantees; of separating 'public' law from 'private' law. Public law regulates the interrelationships of public authorities and their relationships with the 'subjects'; private law regulates the relationships of the governed individuals among themselves. This conceptual separation presupposes the conceptual separation of the 'state,' as an abstract bearer of sovereign prerogatives and the creator of 'legal norms,' from all personal 'authorizations' of individuals. These conceptual forms are necessarily remote from the nature of pre-bureaucratic, and especially from patrimonial and feudal, structures of authority. This conceptual separation of private and public was first conceived and realized in urban communities; for as soon as their officeholders were secured by periodic *elections,* the individual power-holder, even if he was in the highest position, was obviously no longer identical with the man who possessed authority 'in his own right.' Yet it was left to the complete depersonalization of administrative management by bureaucracy and the rational systematization of law to realize the separation of public and private fully and in principle.

XIV. The 'Rationalization' of Education and Training

We cannot here analyze the far-reaching and general cultural effects that the advance of the rational bureaucratic structure of domination, as such, develops quite independently of the areas in which it takes hold. Naturally, bureaucracy promotes a 'rationalist' way of life, but the concept of rationalism allows for widely differing contents. Quite generally, one can only say that the bureaucratization of all domination very strongly furthers the development of 'rational matter-of-factness' and the personality type of the professional expert. This has far-reaching ramifications, but only one important element of the process can be briefly indicated here: its effect upon the nature of training and education.

Educational institutions on the European continent, especially the institutions of higher learning—the universities, as well as technical academies, business colleges, gymnasiums, and other middle schools—are dominated and influenced by the need for the kind of 'education' that produces a system of special examinations and the trained expertness that is increasingly indispensable for modern bureaucracy.

The 'special examination,' in the present sense, was and is found also outside of bureaucratic structures proper; thus, today it is found in the 'free' professions of medicine and law and in the guild-organized trades. Expert examinations are neither indispensable to nor concomitant phenomena of bureaucratization. The French, English, and American bureaucracies have for a long time foregone such examinations entirely or to a large extent, for training and service in party organizations have made up for them.

'Democracy' also takes an ambivalent stand in the face of specialized examinations, as it does in the face of all the phenomena of bureaucracy —although democracy itself promotes these developments. Special examinations, on the one hand, mean or appear to mean a 'selection' of those who qualify from all social strata rather than a rule by notables. On the other hand, democracy fears that a merit system and educational certificates will result in a privileged 'caste.' Hence, democracy fights against the special-examination system.

The special examination is found even in pre-bureaucratic or semi-bureaucratic epochs. Indeed, the regular and earliest locus of special examinations is among prebendally organized dominions. Expectancies of prebends, first of church prebends—as in the Islamite Orient and in the Occidental Middle Ages—then, as was especially the case in China, secular prebends, are the typical prizes for which people study and are examined. These examinations, however, have in truth only a partially specialized and expert character.

The modern development of full bureaucratization brings the system of rational, specialized, and expert examinations irresistibly to the fore. The civil-service reform gradually imports expert training and specialized examinations into the United States. In all other countries this system also advances, stemming from its main breeding place, Germany. The increasing bureaucratization of administration enhances the importance of the specialized examination in England. In China, the attempt to replace the semi-patrimonial and ancient bureaucracy by a modern bureaucracy brought the expert examination; it took the place of a former and quite differently structured system of examinations. The bureaucratization of capitalism, with its demand for expertly trained technicians, clerks, et cetera, carries such examinations all over the world. Above all, the development is greatly furthered by the social prestige of the educational certificates acquired through such specialized examinations. This is all the more the case as the educational patent is turned to economic advantage. Today, the certificate of education becomes what the test for ancestors has been in the past, at least where the nobility has remained powerful: a prerequisite for equality of birth, a qualification for a canonship, and for state office.

The development of the diploma from universities, and business and engineering colleges, and the universal clamor for the creation of educational certificates in all fields make for the formation of a privileged stratum in bureaus and in offices. Such certificates support their holders' claims for intermarriages with notable families (in business offices people naturally hope for preferment with regard to the chief's daughter), claims to be admitted into the circles that adhere to 'codes of honor,' claims for a 'respectable' remuneration rather than remuneration for work done, claims for assured advancement and old-age insurance, and, above all, claims to monopolize socially and economically advantageous positions. When we hear from all sides the demand for an introduction of regular curricula and special examinations, the reason behind it is, of course, not a suddenly awakened 'thirst for education' but the desire for restricting the supply for these positions and their monopolization by the owners of educational certificates. Today, the 'examination' is the universal means of this monopolization, and therefore examinations irresistibly advance. As the education prerequisite to the acquisition of the educational certificate requires considerable expense and a period of waiting for full remuneration, this striving means a setback for talent (charisma) in favor of property. For the 'intellectual' costs of educational certificates are always low, and with the increasing volume of such certificates, their intellectual costs do not increase, but rather decrease.

The requirement of a chivalrous style of life in the old qualification for fiefs in Germany is replaced by the necessity of participating in its present rudimental form as represented by the dueling corps of the universities which also distribute the educational certificates. In Anglo-Saxon countries, athletic and social clubs fulfil the same function. The bureaucracy, on the other hand, strives everywhere for a 'right to the office' by the establishment of a regular disciplinary procedure and by removal of the completely arbitrary disposition of the 'chief' over the subordinate official. The bureaucracy seeks to secure the official position, the orderly advancement, and the provision for old age. In this, the bureaucracy is supported by the 'democratic' sentiment of the governed, which demands that domination be minimized. Those who hold this attitude believe themselves able to discern a weakening of the master's prerogatives in every weakening of the arbitrary disposition of the master over the officials. To this extent, bureaucracy, both in business offices and in public service, is a carrier of a specific 'status' development, as have been the quite differently structured officeholders of the past. We have already pointed out that these status characteristics are usually also exploited, and that by their nature they contribute to the technical usefulness of the bureaucracy in fulfilling its specific tasks.

'Democracy' reacts precisely against the unavoidable 'status' character of bureaucracy. Democracy seeks to put the election of officials for short terms in the place of appointed officials; it seeks to substitute the removal of officials by election for a regulated procedure of discipline. Thus, democracy seeks to replace the arbitrary disposition of the hierarchically superordinate 'master' by the equally arbitrary disposition of the governed and the party chiefs dominating them.

Social prestige based upon the advantage of special education and training as such is by no means specific to bureaucracy. On the contrary! But educational prestige in other structures of domination rests upon substantially different foundations.

Expressed in slogan-like fashion, the 'cultivated man,' rather than the 'specialist,' has been the end sought by education and has formed the basis of social esteem in such various systems as the feudal, theocratic, and patrimonial structures of dominion: in the English notable administration, in the old Chinese patrimonial bureaucracy, as well as under the rule of demagogues in the so-called Hellenic democracy.

The term 'cultivated man' is used here in a completely value-neutral sense; it is understood to mean solely that the goal of education consists in the quality of a man's bearing in life which was *considered* 'cultivated,' rather than in a specialized training for expertness. The 'cultivated' personality formed the educational ideal, which was stamped by the structure of domination and by the social condition for membership in the ruling stratum. Such education aimed at a chivalrous or an ascetic type; or, at a literary type, as in China; a gymnastic-humanist type, as in Hellas; or it aimed at a conventional type, as in the case of the Anglo-Saxon gentleman. The qualification of the ruling stratum as such rested upon the possesion of 'more' cultural quality (in the absolutely changeable, value-neutral sense in which we use the term here), rather than upon 'more' expert knowledge. Special military, theological, and juridical ability was of course intensely practiced; but the point of gravity in Hellenic, in medieval, as well as in Chinese education, has rested upon educational elements that were entirely different from what was 'useful' in one's specialty.

Behind all the present discussions of the foundations of the educational system, the struggle of the 'specialist type of man' against the older type of 'cultivated man' is hidden at some decisive point. This fight is determined by the irresistibly expanding bureaucratization of all public and private relations of authority and by the ever-increasing importance of expert and specialized knowledge. This fight intrudes into all intimate cultural questions.

During its advance, bureaucratic organization has had to overcome those essentially negative obstacles that have stood in the way of the leveling process necessary for bureaucracy. In addition, administrative structures based on different principles intersect with bureaucratic organizations. Since these have been touched upon above, only some especially important structural *principles* will be briefly discussed here in a very simplified schema. We would be led too far afield were we to discuss all the actually existing types. We shall proceed by asking the following questions:

1. How far are administrative structures subject to economic determination? Or, how far are opportunities for development created by other circumstances, for instance, the purely political? Or, finally, how far are

developments created by an 'autonomous' logic that is solely of the technical structure as such?

2. We shall ask whether or not these structural principles, in turn, release specific economic effects, and if so, what effects. In doing this, one of course from the beginning has to keep his eye on the fluidity and the overlapping transitions of all these organizational principles. Their 'pure' types, after all, are to be considered merely as border cases which are especially valuable and indispensable for analysis. Historical realities, which almost always appear in mixed forms, have moved and still move between such pure types.

The bureaucratic structure is everywhere a late product of development. The further back we trace our steps, the more typical is the absence of bureaucracy and officialdom in the structure of domination. Bureaucracy has a 'rational' character: rules, means, ends, and matter-of-factness dominate its bearing. Everywhere its origin and its diffusion have therefore had 'revolutionary' results, in a special sense, which has still to be discussed. This is the same influence which the advance of *rationalism* in general has had. The march of bureaucracy has destroyed structures of domination which had no rational character, in the special sense of the term. Hence, we may ask: What were these structures?*

---

* In chapters following the present one in *Wirtschaft und Gesellschaft*, Weber discusses Patriarchialism, Patrimonialism, Feudalism, and Charismatic Authority.

8. Gaetano Mosca

The Ruling Class

AMONG THE constant facts and tendencies that are to be found in all political organisms, one is so obvious that it is apparent to the most casual eye. In all societies—from societies that are very meagerly developed and have barely attained the dawnings of civilization, down to the most advanced and powerful societies—two classes of people appear—a class that rules and a class that is ruled. The first class, always the less numerous, performs all political functions, monopolizes power and enjoys the advantages that power brings, whereas the second, the more numerous class, is directed and controlled by the first, in a manner that is now more or less legal, now more or less arbitrary and violent, and supplies the first, in appearance at least, with material means of subsistence and with the instrumentalities that are essential to the vitality of the political organism.

In practical life we all recognize the existence of this ruling class (or political class, as we have elsewhere chosen to define it).[1] We all know that, in our own country, whichever it may be, the management of public affairs is in the hands of a minority of influential persons, to which management, willingly or unwillingly, the majority defer. We know that the same thing goes on in neighboring countries, and in fact we should be put to it to conceive of a real world otherwise organized—a world in which all men would be directly subject to a single person without relationships of superiority or subordination, or in which all men would share equally in the direction of political affairs. If we reason otherwise in theory, that is due partly to inveterate habits that we follow in our thinking and partly to the exaggerated importance that we attach to two political facts that loom far larger in appearance than they are in reality.

The first of these facts—and one has only to open one's eyes to see it—is that in every political organism there is one individual who is chief

From Mosca, *The Ruling Class* (New York: McGraw-Hill Book Company, Inc., 1939), p. 50-102. Copyright 1939 by the McGraw-Hill Book Company, Inc. Used with the permission of the publisher. Cross references have been omitted.

[1] Mosca, *Teorica dei governi e governo parlamentare*, chap. I.

among the leaders of the ruling class as a whole and stands, as we say, at the helm of the state. That person is not always the person who holds supreme power according to law. At times, alongside of the hereditary king or emperor there is a prime minister or a major-domo who wields an actual power that is greater than the sovereign's. At other times, in place of the elected president the influential politician who has procured the president's election will govern. Under special circumstances there may be, instead of a single person, two or three who discharge the functions of supreme control.

The second fact, too, is readily discernible. Whatever the type of political organization, pressures arising from the discontent of the masses who are governed, from the passions by which they are swayed, exert a certain amount of influence on the policies of the ruling, the political, class.

But the man who is at the head of the state would certainly not be able to govern without the support of a numerous class to enforce respect for his orders and to have them carried out; and granting that he can make one individual, or indeed many individuals, in the ruling class feel the weight of his power, he certainly cannot be at odds with the class as a whole or do away with it. Even if that were possible, he would at once be forced to create another class, without the support of which action on his part would be completely paralyzed. On the other hand, granting that the discontent of the masses might succeed in deposing a ruling class, inevitably, as we shall later show, there would have to be another organized minority within the masses themselves to discharge the functions of a ruling class. Otherwise all organization, and the whole social structure, would be destroyed.

From the point of view of scientific research the real superiority of the concept of the ruling, or political, class lies in the fact that the varying structure of ruling classes has a preponderant importance in determining the political type, and also the level of civilization, of the different peoples. According to a manner of classifying forms of government that is still in vogue, Turkey and Russia were both, up to a few years ago, absolute monarchies, England and Italy were constitutional, or limited, monarchies, and France and the United States were classed as republics. The classification was based on the fact that, in the first two countries mentioned, headship in the state was hereditary and the chief was nominally omnipotent; in the second two, his office is hereditary but his powers and prerogatives are limited; in the last two, he is elected.

That classification is obviously superficial. Absolutisms though they were, there was little in common between the manners in which Russia and Turkey were managed politically, the levels of civilization in the two countries and the organization of their ruling classes being vastly different. On the same basis, the regime in Italy, a monarchy, is much more similar to the regime in France, a republic, than it is to the regime in

England, also a monarchy; and there are important differences between the political organizations of the United States and France, though both countries are republics.

As we have already suggested, ingrained habits of thinking have long stood, as they still stand, in the way of scientific progress in this matter. The classification mentioned above, which divides governments into absolute monarchies, limited monarchies and republics, was devised by Montesquieu and was intended to replace the classical categories of Aristotle, who divided governments into monarchies, aristocracies and democracies. What Aristotle called a democracy was simply an aristocracy of fairly broad membership. Aristotle himself was in a position to observe that in every Greek state, whether aristocratic or democratic, there was always one person or more who had a preponderant influence. Between the day of Polybius and the day of Montesquieu, many writers perfected Aristotle's classification by introducing into it the concept of "mixed" governments. Later on the modern democratic theory, which had its source in Rousseau, took its stand upon the concept that the majority of the citizens in any state can participate, and in fact *ought* to participate, in its political life, and the doctrine of popular sovereignty still holds sway over many minds in spite of the fact that modern scholarship is making it increasingly clear that democratic, monarchical and aristocratic principles function side by side in every political organism. We shall not stop to refute this democratic theory here, since that is the task of this work as a whole. Besides, it would be hard to destroy in a few pages a whole system of ideas that has become firmly rooted in the human mind. As Las Casas aptly wrote in his life of Christopher Columbus, it is often much harder to unlearn than to learn.

We think it may be desirable, nevertheless, to reply at this point to an objection which might very readily be made to our point of view. If it is easy to understand that a single individual cannot command a group without finding within the group a minority to support him, it is rather difficult to grant, as a constant and natural fact, that minorities rule majorities, rather than majorities minorities. But that is one of the points— so numerous in all the other sciences—where the first impression one has of things is contrary to what they are in reality. In reality the dominion of an organized minority, obeying a single impulse, over the unorganized majority is inevitable. The power of any minority is irresistible as against each single individual in the majority, who stands alone before the totality of the organized minority. At the same time, the minority is organized for the very reason that it is a minority. A hundred men acting uniformly in concert, with a common understanding, will triumph over a thousand men who are not in accord and can therefore be dealt with one by one. Meanwhile it will be easier for the former to act in concert and have a mutual understanding simply because they are a hundred and not a thousand. It follows that the larger the political community, the smaller will the proportion of the governing minority to the governed majority be, and the more difficult will it be for the majority to organize for reaction against the minority.

However, in addition to the great advantage accruing to them from the fact of being organized, ruling minorities are usually so constituted that the individuals who make them up are distinguished from the mass of the governed by qualities that give them a certain material, intellectual or even moral superiority; or else they are the heirs of individuals who possessed such qualities. In other words, members of a ruling minority regularly have some attribute, real or apparent, which is highly esteemed and very influential in the society in which they live.

In primitive societies that are still in the early stages of organization, military valor is the quality that most readily opens access to the ruling, or political, class. In societies of advanced civilization, war is the exceptional condition. It may be regarded as virtually normal in societies that are in the initial stages of their development; and the individuals who show the greatest ability in war easily gain supremacy over their fellows—the bravest become chiefs. The fact is constant, but the forms it may assume, in one set of circumstances or another, vary considerably.

As a rule the dominance of a warrior class over a peaceful multitude is attributed to a superposition of races, to the conquest of a relatively un-warlike group by an aggressive one. Sometimes that is actually the case—we have examples in India after the Aryan invasions, in the Roman Empire after the Germanic invasions and in Mexico after the Aztec conquest. But more often, under certain social conditions, we note the rise of a warlike ruling class in places where there is absolutely no trace of a foreign conquest. As long as a horde lives exclusively by the chase, all individuals can easily become warriors. There will of course be leaders who will rule over the tribe, but we will not find a warrior class rising to exploit, and at the same time to protect, another class that is devoted to peaceful pursuits. As the tribe emerges from the hunting stage and enters the agricultural and pastoral stage, then, along with an enormous increase in population and a greater stability in the means of exerting social influence, a more or less clean-cut division into two classes will take place, one class being devoted exclusively to agriculture, the other class to war. In this event, it is inevitable that the warrior class should little by little acquire such ascendancy over the other as to be able to oppress it with impunity.

Poland offers a characteristic example of the gradual metamorphosis of a warrior class into an absolutely dominant class. Originally the Poles had the same organization by rural villages as prevailed among all the Slavic peoples. There was no distinction between fighters and farmers—in other words, between nobles and peasants. But after the Poles came to settle on the broad plains that are watered by the Vistula and the Niemen, agriculture began to develop among them. However, the necessity of fighting with warlike neighbors continued, so that the tribal chiefs, or voivodes, gathered about themselves a certain number of picked men whose special occupation was the bearing of arms. These warriors were distributed among the various rural communities. They were exempt from agricultural duties, yet they received their share of the produce of the soil, along with the other members of the community. In early days their position was not considered very desirable, and country dwellers sometimes waived exemption from agricultural labor in order to avoid going to war. But gradually as this order of things grew stabilized, as one class became habituated to the practice of arms and military organization while the other hardened to the use of the plow and the spade, the warriors became nobles and masters, and the peasants, once companions and brothers, became villeins and serfs. Little by little the warrior lords increased their demands to the point where the share they took as members of the community came to include the community's whole produce minus what was absolutely necessary for subsistence on the part of the cultivators; and when the latter tried to escape such abuses they were constrained by force to stay bound to the soil, their situation taking on all the characteristics of serfdom pure and simple.

In the course of this evolution, around the year 1333, King Casimir the Great tried vainly to curb the overbearing insolence of the warriors. When peasants came to complain of the nobles, he contented himself with asking whether they had no sticks and stones. Some generations later, in 1537, the nobility forced all tradesmen in the cities to sell such real estate as they owned, and landed property became a prerogative of nobles only. At the same time the nobility exerted pressure upon the king to open negotiations with Rome, to the end that thenceforward only nobles should be admitted to holy orders in Poland. That barred townsmen and peasants almost completely from honorific positions and stripped them of any social importance whatever.[1]

We find a parallel development in Russia. There the warriors who formed the druzhina, or escort, of the old knezes (princes descended from Rurik) also received a share in the produce of the mirs (rural peasant communities) for their livelihood. Little by little this share was increased. Since land abounded and workers were scarce, the peasants often had an eye to their advantage and moved about. At the end of the sixteenth century, accordingly, the czar Boris Godunov empowered the nobles to hold peasants to their lands by force, so establishing serfdom. However, armed forces in Russia were never composed exclusively of nobles. The muzhiks, or peasants, went to war as common soldiers under the droujina.

[1] Mickiewicz, *Les Slaves*, vol. I, leçon XXIV, pp. 376-380; *Histoire populaire de Pologne*, chaps. I-II.

As early as the sixteenth century, Ivan the Terrible established the order of strelitzes which amounted practically to a standing army, and which lasted until Peter the Great replaced it with regiments organized along western European lines. In those regiments members of the old druzhina, with an intermixture of foreigners, became officers, while the muzhiks provided the entire contingent of privates.[1]

Among peoples that have recently entered the agricultural stage and are relatively civilized, it is the unvarying fact that the strictly military class is the political, or ruling, class. Sometimes the bearing of arms is reserved exclusively to that class, as happened in India and Poland. More often the members of the governed class are on occasion enrolled—always, however, as common soldiers and in the less respected divisions. So in Greece, during the war with the Medes, the citizens belonging to the richer and more influential classes formed the picked corps (the cavalry and the hoplites), the less wealthy fought as peltasts or as slingers, while the slaves, that is the laboring masses, were almost entirely barred from military service. We find analogous arrangements in republican Rome, down to the period of the Punic Wars and even as late as the day of Marius; in Latin and Germanic Europe during the Middle Ages; in Russia, as just explained, and among many other peoples. Caesar notes repeatedly that in his time the backbone of the Gallic armies was formed by cavalrymen recruited from the nobility. The Aedui, for example, could not hold out against Ariovistus after the flower of their cavalry had been killed in battle.

Everywhere—in Russia and Poland, in India and medieval Europe— the ruling warrior classes acquire almost exclusive ownership of the land. Land, as we have seen, is the chief source of production and wealth in countries that are not very far advanced in civilization. But as civilization progresses, revenue from land increases proportionately. With the growth of population there is, at least in certain periods, an increase in rent, in the Ricardian sense of the term, largely because great centers of consumption arise—such at all times have been the great capitals and other large cities, ancient and modern. Eventually, if other circumstances permit, a very important social transformation occurs. Wealth rather than military valor comes to be the characteristic feature of the dominant class: the people who rule are the rich rather than the brave.

The condition that in the main is required for this transformation is that social organization shall have concentrated and become perfected to such an extent that the protection offered by public authority is considerably more effective than the protection offered by private force. In other words, private property must be so well protected by the practical and real efficacy of the laws as to render the power of the proprietor himself superfluous. This comes about through a series of gradual alterations in the

[1] Leroy-Beaulieu, *L'Empire des tzars et les Russes,* vol. I, pp. 338 f.

social structure whereby a type of political organization, which we shall call the "feudal state," is transformed into an essentially different type, which we shall term the "bureaucratic state." We are to discuss these types at some length hereafter, but we may say at once that the evolution here referred to is as a rule greatly facilitated by progress in pacific manners and customs and by certain moral habits which societies contract as civilization advances.

Once this transformation has taken place, wealth produces political power just as political power has been producing wealth. In a society already somewhat mature—where, therefore, individual power is curbed by the collective power—if the powerful are as a rule the rich, to be rich is to become powerful. And, in truth, when fighting with the mailed fist is prohibited whereas fighting with pounds and pence is sanctioned, the better posts are inevitably won by those who are better supplied with pounds and pence.

There are, to be sure, states of a very high level of civilization which in theory are organized on the basis of moral principles of such a character that they seem to preclude this overbearing assertiveness on the part of wealth. But this is a case—and there are many such—where theoretical principles can have no more than a limited application in real life. In the United States all powers flow directly or indirectly from popular elections, and suffrage is equal for all men and women in all the states of the Union. What is more, democracy prevails not only in institutions but to a certain extent also in morals. The rich ordinarily feel a certain aversion to entering public life, and the poor a certain aversion to choosing the rich for elective office. But that does not prevent a rich man from being more influential than a poor man, since he can use pressure upon the politicians who control public administration. It does not prevent elections from being carried on to the music of clinking dollars. It does not prevent whole legislatures and considerable numbers of national congressmen from feeling the influence of powerful corporations and great financiers.[1]

In China, too, down to a few years ago, though the government had not accepted the principle of popular elections, it was organized on an essentially equalitarian basis. Academic degrees gave access to public office, and degrees were conferred by examination without any apparent regard for family or wealth. According to some writers, only barbers and certain classes of boatmen, together with their children, were barred from competing for the various grades of the mandarinate.[2] But though the moneyed class in China was less numerous, less wealthy, less powerful than the moneyed class in the United States is at present, it was none the less able to modify the scrupulous application of this system to a very considerable

---

[1] Jannet, *Le istituzioni politiche e sociali degli Stati Uniti d'America,* part II, chap. X f.

[2] Rousset, *À travers la Chine.*

extent. Not only was the indulgence of examiners often bought with money. The government itself sometimes sold the various academic degrees and allowed ignorant persons, often from the lowest social strata, to hold public office.[1]

In all countries of the world those other agencies for exerting social influence—personal publicity, good education, specialized training, high rank in church, public administration, and army—are always readier of access to the rich than to the poor. The rich invariably have a considerably shorter road to travel than the poor, to say nothing of the fact that the stretch of road that the rich are spared is often the roughest and most difficult.

In societies in which religious beliefs are strong and ministers of the faith form a special class a priestly aristocracy almost always arises and gains possession of a more or less important share of the wealth and the political power. Conspicuous examples of that situation would be ancient Egypt (during certain periods), Brahman India and medieval Europe. Oftentimes the priests not only perform religious functions. They possess legal and scientific knowledge and constitute the class of highest intellectual culture. Consciously or unconsciously, priestly hierarchies often show a tendency to monopolize learning and hamper the dissemination of the methods and procedures that make the acquisition of knowledge possible and easy. To that tendency may have been due, in part at least, the painfully slow diffusion of the demotic alphabet in ancient Egypt, though that alphabet was infinitely more simple than the hieroglyphic script. The Druids in Gaul were acquainted with the Greek alphabet but would not permit their rich store of sacred literature to be written down, requiring their pupils to commit it to memory at the cost of untold effort. To the same outlook may be attributed the stubborn and frequent use of dead languages that we find in ancient Chaldea, in India, and in medieval Europe. Sometimes, as was the case in India, lower classes have been explicitly forbidden to acquire knowledge of sacred books.

Specialized knowledge and really scientific culture, purged of any sacred or religious aura, become important political forces only in a highly advanced stage of civilization, and only then do they give access to membership in the ruling class to those who possess them. But in this case too, it is not so much learning in itself that has political value as the practical applications that may be made of learning to the profit of the public or the state. Sometimes all that is required is mere possession of the mechanical processes that are indispensable to the acquisition of a higher culture. This may be due to the fact that on such a basis it is easier to ascertain and measure the skill which a candidate has been able to acquire—it is easier to "mark" or grade him. So in certain periods in

[1] Mas y Sans, *La Chine et les puissances chrétiennes,* vol. II, pp. 332-334, Huc, *L'Empire chinois.*

ancient Egypt the profession of scribe was a road to public office and power, perhaps because to have learned the hieroglyphic script was proof of long and patient study. In modern China, again, learning the number-less characters in Chinese script has formed the basis of the mandarin's education.[1] In present-day Europe and America the class that applies the findings of modern science to war, public administration, public works and public sanitation holds a fairly important position, both socially and politically, and in our western world, as in ancient Rome, an altogether privileged position is held by lawyers. They know the complicated legisla-tion that arises in all peoples of long-standing civilization, and they be-come especially powerful if their knowledge of law is coupled with the type of eloquence that chances to have a strong appeal to the taste of their contemporaries.

There are examples in abundance where we see that long-standing practice in directing the military and civil organization of a community creates and develops in the higher reaches of the ruling class a real art of governing which is something better than crude empiricism and better than anything that mere individual experience could suggest. In such circumstances aristocracies of functionaries arise, such as the Roman senate, the Venetian nobility and to a certain extent the English aristo-cracy. Those bodies all stirred John Stuart Mill to admiration and certainly they all three developed governments that were distinguished for care-fully considered policies and for great steadfastness and sagacity in carry-ing them out. This art of governing is not political science, though it has, at one time or another, anticipated applications of a number of the postu-lates of political science. However, even if the art of governing has now and again enjoyed prestige with certain classes of persons who have long held possession of political functions, knowledge of it has never served as an ordinary criterion for admitting to public offices persons who were barred from them by social station. The degree of mastery of the art of governing that a person possesses is, moreover, apart from exceptional cases, a very difficult thing to determine if the person has given no practi-cal demonstration that he possesses it.

In some countries we find hereditary castes. In such cases the governing class is explicitly restricted to a given number of families, and birth is the one criterion that determines entry into the class or exclusion from it. Examples are exceedingly common. There is practically no country of long-standing civilization that has not had a hereditary aristocracy at one period or another in its history. We find hereditary nobilities during certain periods in China and ancient Egypt, in India, in Greece before the wars with the Medes, in ancient Rome, among the Slavs, among the Latins and Germans of the Middle Ages, in Mexico at the time of the Discovery and in Japan down to a few years ago.

[1] This was true up to a few years ago, the examination of a mandarin covering only literary and historical studies—as the Chinese understood such studies, of course.

In this connection two preliminary observations are in point. In the first place, all ruling classes tend to become hereditary in fact if not in law. All political forces seem to possess a quality that in physics used to be called the force of inertia. They have a tendency, that is, to remain at the point and in the state in which they find themselves. Wealth and military valor are easily maintained in certain families by moral tradition and by heredity. Qualification for important office—the habit of, and to an extent the capacity for, dealing with affairs of consequence—is much more readily acquired when one has had a certain familiarity with them from childhood. Even when academic degrees, scientific training, special aptitudes as tested by examinations and competitions, open the way to public office, there is no eliminating that special advantage in favor of certain individuals which the French call the advantage of *positions déjà prises.* In actual fact, though examinations and competitions may theoretically be open to all, the majority never have the resources for meeting the expense of long preparation, and many others are without the connections and kinships that set an individual promptly on the right road, enabling him to avoid the gropings and blunders that are inevitable when one enters an unfamiliar environment without any guidance or support.

The democratic principle of election by broad-based suffrage would seem at first glance to be in conflict with the tendency toward stability which, according to our theory, ruling classes show. But it must be noted that candidates who are successful in democratic elections are almost always the ones who possess the political forces above enumerated, which are very often hereditary. In the English, French and Italian parliaments we frequently see the sons, grandsons, brothers, nephews and sons-in-law of members and deputies, ex-members and ex-deputies.

In the second place, when we see a hereditary caste established in a country and monopolizing political power, we may be sure that such a status de jure was preceded by a similar status de facto. Before proclaiming their exclusive and hereditary right to power the families or castes in question must have held the scepter of command in a firm grasp, completely monopolizing all the political forces of that country at that period. Otherwise such a claim on their part would only have aroused the bitterest protests and provoked the bitterest struggles.

Hereditary aristocracies often come to vaunt supernatural origins, or at least origins different from, and superior to, those of the governed classes. Such claims are explained by a highly significant social fact, namely that every governing class tends to justify its actual exercise of power by resting it on some universal moral principle. This same sort of claim has come forward in our time in scientific trappings. A number of writers, developing and amplifying Darwin's theories, contend that upper classes represent a higher level in social evolution and are therefore superior to lower classes by organic structure. Gumplowicz we have already quoted. That writer goes to the point of maintaining that the divisions of populations into trade groups and professional classes in modern civilized countries are based on ethnological heterogeneousness.[1]

Now history very definitely shows the special abilities as well as the special defects—both very marked—which have been displayed by aristocracies that have either remained absolutely closed or have made entry into their circles difficult. The ancient Roman patriciate and the English and German nobilities of modern times give a ready idea of the type we refer to. Yet in dealing with this fact, and with the theories that tend to exaggerate its significance, we can always raise the same objection—that the individuals who belong to the aristocracies in question owe their special qualities not so much to the blood that flows in their veins as to their very particular upbringing, which has brought out certain intellectual and moral tendencies in them in preference to others.

Among all the factors that figure in social superiority, intellectual superiority is the one with which heredity has least to do. The children of men of highest mentality often have very mediocre talents. That is why hereditary aristocracies have never defended their rule on the basis of intellectual superiority alone, but rather on the basis of their superiorities in character and wealth.

It is argued, in rebuttal, that education and environment may serve to explain superiorities in strictly intellectual capacities but not differences of a moral order—will power, courage, pride, energy. The truth is that social position, family tradition, the habits of the class in which we live, contribute more than is commonly supposed to the greater or lesser development of the qualities mentioned. If we carefully observe individuals who have changed their social status, whether for better or for worse, and who consequently find themselves in environments different from the ones they have been accustomed to, it is apparent that their intellectual capacities are much less sensibly affected than their moral ones. Apart from a greater breadth of view that education and experience bring to anyone who is not altogether stupid, every individual, whether he remains a mere clerk or becomes a minister of state, whether he reaches the rank of sergeant or the rank of general, whether he is a millionaire or a beggar, abides inevitably on the intellectual level on which nature has placed him. And yet with changes of social status and wealth the proud man often becomes humble, servility changes to arrogance, an honest nature learns to lie, or at least to dissemble, under pressure of need, while the man who has an ingrained habit of lying and bluffing makes himself over and puts on an outward semblance at least of honesty and firmness of character. It is true, of course, that a man fallen from high estate often acquires powers of resignation, self-denial and resourcefulness, just as one who rises in the world sometimes gains in sentiments of justice and

[1] *Der Rassenkampf.* This notion transpires from Gumplowicz's whole volume. It is explicitly formulated in book II, chap. XXXIII.

fairness. In short, whether a man change for the better or for the worse, he has to be exceptionally level-headed if he is to change his social status very appreciably and still keep his character unaltered. Mirabeau remarked that, for any man, any great climb on the social ladder produces a crisis that cures the ills he has and creates new ones that he never had before.[1]

Courage in battle, impetuousness in attack, endurance in resistance—such are the qualities that have long and often been vaunted as a monopoly of the higher classes. Certainly there may be vast natural and—if we may say so—innate differences between one individual and another in these respects; but more than anything else traditions and environmental influences are the things that keep them high, low or just average, in any large group of human beings. We generally become indifferent to danger or, perhaps better, to a given type of danger, when the persons with whom we daily live speak of it with indifference and remain cool and imperturbable before it. Many mountaineers or sailors are by nature timid men, yet they face unmoved, the ones the dangers of the precipice, the others the perils of the storm at sea. So peoples and classes that are accustomed to warfare maintain military virtues at the highest pitch.

So true is this that even peoples and social classes which are ordinarily unaccustomed to arms acquire the military virtues rapidly when the individuals who compose them are made members of organizations in which courage and daring are traditional, when—if one may venture the metaphor—they are cast into human crucibles that are heavily charged with the sentiments that are to be infused into their fiber. Mohammed II recruited his terrible Janizaries in the main from boys who had been kidnapped among the degenerate Greeks of Byzantium. The much despised Egyptian fellah, unused for long centuries to war and accustomed to remaining meek and helpless under the lash of the oppressor, became a good soldier when Mehemet Ali placed him in Turkish or Albanian regiments. The French nobility has always enjoyed a reputation for brilliant valor, but down to the end of the eighteenth century that quality was not credited in anything like the same degree to the French bourgeoisie. However, the wars of the Republic and the Empire amply proved that nature had been uniformly lavish in her endowments of courage upon all the inhabitants of France. Proletariat and bourgeoisie both furnished good soldiers and, what is more, excellent officers, though talent for command had been considered an exclusive prerogative of the nobility. Gumplowicz's theory that differentiation in social classes depends very largely on ethnological antecedents requires proof at the very least. Many facts to the contrary readily occur to one—among others the obvious

[1] *Correspondance entre le comte de Mirabeau et le comte de La Marck*, vol. II, p. 223.

fact that branches of the same family often belong to widely different social classes.

Finally, if we were to keep to the idea of those who maintain the exclusive influence of the hereditary principle in the formation of ruling classes, we should be carried to a conclusion somewhat like the one to which we were carried by the evolutionary principle: The political history of mankind ought to be much simpler than it is. If the ruling class really belonged to a different race, or if the qualities that fit it for dominion were transmitted primarily by organic heredity, it is difficult to see how, once the class was formed, it could decline and lose its power. The peculiar qualities of a race are exceedingly tenacious. Keeping to the evolutionary theory, acquired capacities in the parents are inborn in their children and, as generation succeeds generation, are progressively accentuated. The descendants of rulers, therefore, ought to become better and better fitted to rule, and the other classes ought to see their chances of challenging or supplanting them become more and more remote. Now the most commonplace experience suffices to assure one that things do not go in that way at all.

What we see is that as soon as there is a shift in the balance of political forces—when, that is, a need is felt that capacities different from the old should assert themselves in the management of the state, when the old capacities, therefore, lose some of their importance or changes in their distribution occur—then the manner in which the ruling class is constituted changes also. If a new source of wealth develops in a society, if the practical importance of knowledge grows, if an old religion declines or a new one is born, if a new current of ideas spreads, then, simultaneously, far-reaching dislocations occur in the ruling class. One might say, indeed, that the whole history of civilized mankind comes down to a conflict between the tendency of dominant elements to monopolize political power and transmit possession of it by inheritance, and the tendency toward a dislocation of old forces and an insurgence of new forces; and this conflict produces an unending ferment of endosmosis and exosmosis between the upper classes and certain portions of the lower. Ruling classes decline inevitably when they cease to find scope for the capacities through which they rose to power, when they can no longer render the social services which they once rendered, or when their talents and the services they render lose in importance in the social environment in which they live. So the Roman aristocracy declined when it was no longer the exclusive source of higher officers for the army, of administrators for the commonwealth, of governors for the provinces. So the Venetian aristocracy declined when its nobles ceased to command the galleys and no longer passed the greater part of their lives in sailing the seas and in trading and fighting.

In inorganic nature we have the example of our air, in which a tendency

to immobility produced by the force of inertia is continuously in conflict
with a tendency to shift about as the result of inequalities in the distribution of heat. The two tendencies, prevailing by turn in various regions
on our planet, produce now calm, now wind and storm. In much the same
way in human societies there prevails now the tendency that produces
closed, stationary, crystallized ruling classes, now the tendency that
results in a more or less rapid renovation of ruling classes.

The Oriental societies which we consider stationary have in reality
not always been so, for otherwise, as we have already pointed out, they
could not have made the advances in civilization of which they have left
irrefutable evidence. It is much more accurate to say that we came to
know them at a time when their political forces and their political classes
were in a period of crystallization. The same thing occurs in what we
commonly call "aging" societies, where religious beliefs, scientific knowledge, methods of producing and distributing wealth have for centuries
undergone no radical alteration and have not been disturbed in their
everyday course by infiltrations of foreign elements, material or intellectual. In such societies political forces are always the same, and the
class that holds possession of them holds a power that is undisputed.
Power is therefore perpetuated in certain families, and the inclination to
immobility becomes general through all the various strata in that society.

So in India we see the caste system become thoroughly entrenched
after the suppression of Buddhism. The Greeks found hereditary castes
in ancient Egypt, but we know that in the periods of greatness and renaissance in Egyptian civilization political office and social status were
not hereditary. We possess an Egyptian document that summarizes the
life of a high army officer who lived during the period of the expulsion of
the Hyksos. He had begun his career as a simple soldier. Other documents
show cases in which the same individual served successively in army, civil
administration and priesthood.[1]

The best-known and perhaps the most important example of a society
tending toward crystallization is the period in Roman history that used
to be called the Low Empire. There, after several centuries of almost
complete social immobility, a division between two classes grew sharper
and sharper, the one made up of great landowners and high officials, the
other made up of slaves, farmers and urban plebeians. What is even more
striking, public office and social position became hereditary by custom
before they became hereditary by law, and the trend was rapidly generalized during the period mentioned.[2]

On the other hand it may happen in the history of a nation that commerce with foreign peoples, forced emigrations, discoveries, wars, create

[1] Lenormant, Maspero, Brugsch.
[2] Marquardt, *Manuel des antiquités romaines;* Fustel de Coulanges, *Nouvelles
recherches sur quelques problèmes d'histoire.*

new poverty and new wealth, disseminate knowledge of things that were previously unknown or cause infiltrations of new moral, intellectual and religious currents. Or again—as a result of such infiltrations or through a slow process of inner growth, or from both causes—it may happen that a new learning arises, or that certain elements of an old, long forgotten learning return to favor so that new ideas and new beliefs come to the fore and upset the intellectual habits on which the obedience of the masses has been founded. The ruling class may also be vanquished and destroyed in whole or in part by foreign invasions, or, when the circumstances just mentioned arise, it may be driven from power by the advent of new social elements who are strong in fresh political forces. Then, naturally, there comes a period of renovation, or, if one prefer, of revolution, during which individual energies have free play and certain individuals, more passionate, more energetic, more intrepid or merely shrewder than others, force their way from the bottom of the social ladder to the topmost rungs.

Once such a movement has set in, it cannot be stopped immediately. The example of individuals who have started from nowhere and reached prominent positions fires new ambitions, new greeds, new energies, and this molecular rejuvenation of the ruling class continues vigorously until a long period of social stability slows it down again. We need hardly mention examples of nations in such periods of renovation. In our age that would be superfluous. Rapid restocking of ruling classes is a frequent and very striking phenomenon in countries that have been recently colonized. When social life begins in such environments, there is no ready-made ruling class, and while such a class is in process of formation, admittance to it is gained very easily. Monopolization of land and other agencies of production is, if not quite impossible, at any rate more difficult than elsewhere. That is why, at least during a certain period, the Greek colonies offered a wide outlet for all Greek energy and enterprise. That is why, in the United States, where the colonizing of new lands continued through the whole nineteenth century and new industries were continually springing up, examples of men who started with nothing and have attained fame and wealth are still frequent—all of which helps to foster in the people of that country the illusion that democracy is a fact.

Suppose now that a society gradually passes from its feverish state to calm. Since the human being's psychological tendencies are always the same, those who belong to the ruling class will begin to acquire a group spirit. They will become more and more exclusive and learn better and better the art of monopolizing to their advantage the qualities and capacities that are essential to acquiring power and holding it. Then, at last, the force that is essentially conservative appears—the force of habit. Many people become resigned to a lowly station, while the members of certain privileged families or classes grow convinced that they have almost an absolute right to high station and command.

A philanthropist would certainly be tempted to inquire whether mankind is happier—or less unhappy—during periods of social stability and crystallization, when everyone is almost fated to remain in the social station to which he was born, or during the directly opposite periods of renovation and revolution, which permit all to aspire to the most exalted positions and some to attain them. Such an inquiry would be difficult. The answer would have to take account of many qualifications and exceptions, and might perhaps always be influenced by the personal preferences of the observer. We shall therefore be careful not to venture on any answer of our own. Besides, even if we could reach an undebatable conclusion, it would have a very slight practical utility; for the sad fact is that what the philosophers and theologians call free will—in other words, spontaneous choice by individuals—has so far had, and will perhaps always have, little influence, if any at all, in hastening either the ending or the beginning of one of the historical periods mentioned.

As WE have just seen, in fairly populous societies that have attained a certain level of civilization, ruling classes do not justify their power exclusively by de facto possession of it, but try to find a moral and legal basis for it, representing it as the logical and necessary consequence of doctrines and beliefs that are generally recognized and accepted. So if a society is deeply imbued with the Christian spirit the political class will govern by the will of the sovereign, who, in turn, will reign because he is God's anointed. So too in Mohammedan societies political authority is exercised directly in the name of the caliph, or vicar, of the Prophet, or in the name of someone who has received investiture, tacit or explicit, from the caliph. The Chinese mandarins ruled the state because they were supposed to be interpreters of the will of the Son of Heaven, who had received from heaven the mandate to govern paternally, and in accordance with the rules of the Confucian ethic, "the people of the hundred families." The complicated hierarchy of civil and military functionaries in the Roman Empire rested upon the will of the emperor, who, at least down to Diocletian's time, was assumed by a legal fiction to have received from the people a mandate to rule the commonwealth. The powers of all lawmakers, magistrates and government officials in the United States emanate directly or indirectly from the vote of the voters, which is held to be the expression of the sovereign will of the whole American people.

This legal and moral basis, or principle, on which the power of the political class rests, is what we have elsewhere called, and shall continue here to call, the "political formula." (Writers on the philosophy of law generally call it the "principle of sovereignty."[1]) The political formula

[1] Mosca, *Teorica dei governi e governo parlamentare*, chap. I; see also Mosca, *Le constituzioni moderne*.

can hardly be the same in two or more different societies; and fundamental or even notable similarities between two or more political formulas appear only where the peoples professing them have the same type of civilization (or—to use an expression which we shall shortly define—belong to the same social type). According to the level of civilization in the peoples among whom they are current, the various political formulas may be based either upon supernatural beliefs or upon concepts which, if they do not correspond to positive realities, at least appear to be rational. We shall not say that they correspond in either case to scientific truths. A conscientious observer would be obliged to confess that, if no one has ever seen the authentic document by which the Lord empowered certain privileged persons or families to rule his people on his behalf, neither can it be maintained that a popular election, however liberal the suffrage may be, is ordinarily the expression of the will of a people, or even of the will of the majority of a people.

And yet that does not mean that political formulas are mere quackeries aptly invented to trick the masses into obedience. Anyone who viewed them in that light would fall into grave error. The truth is that they answer a real need in man's social nature; and this need, so universally felt, of governing and knowing that one is governed not on the basis of mere material or intellectual force, but on the basis of a moral principle, has beyond any doubt a practical and a real importance.

Spencer wrote that the divine right of Kings was the great superstition of past ages, and that the divine right of elected assemblies is the great superstition of our present age. The idea cannot be called wholly mistaken, but certainly it does not consider or exhaust all aspects of the question. It is further necessary to see whether a society can hold together without one of these "great superstitions"—whether a universal illusion is not a social force that contributes powerfully to consolidating political organization and unifying peoples or even whole civilizations.

Mankind is divided into social groups each of which is set apart from other groups by beliefs, sentiments, habits and interests that are peculiar to it. The individuals who belong to one such group are held together by a consciousness of common brotherhood and held apart from other groups by passions and tendencies that are more or less antagonistic and mutually repellent. As we have already indicated, the political formula must be based upon the special beliefs and the strongest sentiments of the social group in which it is current, or at least upon the beliefs and sentiments of the particular portion of that group which holds political preeminence.

This phenomenon—the existence of social groups each of which has characteristics peculiar to itself and often presumes absolute superiority over other groups (the *boria nazionale*, the national conceit, that Vico talks about!) has been recognized and studied by many writers, and

particularly by modern scholars, in dealing with the principle of nationality. Gumplowicz, for instance, pointed to its importance in political
science, or in sociology if you will. We should be quite ready to adopt the
word that Gumplowicz uses to designate it—syngenism—did the term
not imply, in conformity with the fundamental ideas of that writer, an
almost absolute preponderance of the ethnological element, of community of blood and race, in the formation of each separate social group.[1]
We do think that, in a number of primitive civilizations, not so much
community of blood as a belief that such community existed—belief in
a common ancestor, often arising, as Gumplowicz himself admits, after
the social type had been formed—may have helped to cement group
unities. But we also think that certain modern anthropological and
philological doctrines have served to awaken between social groups and
between fractions within one group antipathies that use racial differences
as mere pretexts. Actually, moreover, in the formation of the group, or
social type, many other elements besides a more or less certain racial
affinity figure—for example, community of language, of religion, of interests, and the recurring relationships that result from geographical
situation. It is not necessary that all these factors be present at one
and the same time, for community of history—a life that is lived for
centuries in common, with identical or similar experiences, engendering
similar moral and intellectual habits, similar passions and memories—
often becomes the chief element in the development of a conscious social
type.[2]

Once such a type is formed, we get, to return to a metaphor which we
have earlier used, a sort of crucible that fuses all individuals who enter it
into a single alloy. Call it suggestion, call it imitation or mimetism, call it
education pure and simple, it nevertheless comes about that a man feels,
believes, loves, hates, according to the environment in which he lives.
With exceedingly rare exceptions, we are Christians or Jews, Mohammedans or Buddhists, Frenchmen or Italians, for the simple reason that
such were the people among whom we were born and bred.

In the early dawn of history each of the civilized peoples was virtually
an oasis in a desert of barbarism, and the various civilizations, therefore,
had either scant intercourse with one another or none whatever. That
was the situation of ancient Egypt during the early dynasties and of
China down to a day far less remote. Under these circumstances, naturally,
each social type had an absolute originality that was virtually unaffected
by infiltrations and influences from outside.[3] And yet, though this isolation must have contributed considerably to strengthening the tendency

[1] Gumplowicz, *Der Rassenkampf*, book II, chap. XXXVII.
[2] Mosca, "Fattori della nazionalità."
[3] We are thinking here of moral and intellectual influences. Physical mixtures with
neighboring barbarians must always have occurred, if only for the reason that outsiders were hunted for the purpose of procuring slaves.

that every social type manifests to consolidate into a single political organism, nevertheless even in those early days that tendency prevailed only sporadically. To keep to the examples mentioned: China, in the day of Confucius, was broken up into many quasi-independent feudal states; and in Egypt the various hiqs, or viceroys, of the individual nomes often acquired full independence, and sometimes upper Egypt and lower Egypt were separate kingdoms.

Later on, in highly advanced and very complex civilizations such as the Hellenic, we see an opposite tendency coming more prominently to the fore, a tendency on the part of a social type to divide into separate, and almost always rival, political organisms. The hegemony that one Greek state or another tried to impose on the other Hellenic peoples was always a concept far removed from what we moderns think of as political unity; and the attempts of Athens and Sparta, and later on of Macedonia, to establish such a hegemony in a permanent and effective form never quite succeeded.

The trait that is truly characteristic of many ancient peoples, and in general of civilizations that we may call primitive because foreign elements have exerted hardly any influence upon them, is the simpleness and unity of the whole system of ideas and beliefs on which a people's existence and its political organization are based. Among ancient peoples the political formula not only rested upon religion but was wholly identified with it. Their god was preeminently a national god. He was the special protector of the territory and the people. He was the fulcrum of its political organization. A people existed only as long as its god was strong enough to sustain it, and in his turn the god survived only as long as his people did.

The ancient Hebrews are the best-known example of a people organized according to the system just described. We must not assume, however, that the kingdoms of Israel and Judah were any exception in the periods in which they flourished. The role that Jehovah played in Jerusalem was played by Chemosh at Moab,[1] by Marduk (Merodach) at Babylon, by Ashur at Nineveh, by Ammon at Thebes. Just as the God of Israel commanded Saul, David and Solomon to fight to the bitter end against the Ammonites and the Philistines, so Ammon ordered the Egyptian Pharaohs to smite the barbarians to east and west and Ashur incited the sovereigns of Nineveh to exterminate all foreigners and assured them of victory. The speech that the Assyrian ambassador, Rab-shakeh, addressed to the Jews assembled on the walls of Jerusalem, illustrates the conceptions mentioned.[2] "Yield to my Lord," he argues, "for just as other gods have been powerless to save their peoples from Assyrian conquest, so will

[1] See the famous stele of Mesha, king of Moab. A translation of it may be found in Lenormant.
[2] II Kings 18:19 f.

Jehovah be powerless to save you." In other words, Jehovah was a god, but he was less powerful than Ashur, since Ashur's people had conquered other peoples. The Syrians of Damascus are said to have once avoided joining battle with the Kings of Israel in the mountains because they believed that Jehovah fought better on a mountainous terrain than their god did.[1]

But little by little contacts between relatively civilized peoples became more frequent. Vast empires were founded, and these could not always be based upon complete assimilation and destruction of vanquished peoples. The conquerors often had to rest content with merely subduing them. In such cases the victor often found it politic to recognize and worship the god of the vanquished. The Assyrian kings who conquered Babylon paid homage to Marduk, and Cyrus seems to have done the same. Alexander the Great sacrificed to Ammon, and in general to all the deities of the peoples he conquered. The Romans admitted all conquered deities into their pantheon. At that point in history, long interludes of peace, and the lulling of national rivalries that follows upon the establishment of great political organisms, had prepared the ground for a relatively recent phenomenon—the rise of great religions which were humanitarian and universal and which, without distinction of race, language or political system, sought to extend the influence of their doctrines indiscriminately over the whole world.

Buddhism, Christianity and Mohammedanism are the three great humanitarian religions that have so far appeared in history.[2] Each of them possesses a complete body of doctrine, the basis being predominantly metaphysical in Buddhism and dogmatic in Christianity and Mohammedanism. Each of them claims that its doctrine contains the absolute truth and that it offers a trustworthy and infallible guide to welfare in this world and salvation in the next. Common acceptance of one of these religions constitutes a very close bond between most disparate peoples who differ widely in race and language. It gives them a common and special manner of viewing morality and life and, more than that, political customs and private habits of such a nature as to cause the formation of a real social type with conspicuous characteristics that are often so profound as to become virtually indelible. From the appearance of these great religions dates a clean-cut distinction between social type and national type that had scarcely existed before. There had once been Egyptian, Chaldean and Greek civilizations, but no Christian or Mohammedan civilization—in other words, there had never been aggregations

---

[1] I Kings 20:28: "The Lord is God of the hills."

[2] The Jewish religion, parent of Christianity and Mohammedanism, has also become preponderantly humanitarian through a long process of evolution that can be traced as far back as the Prophets. Judaism, however, has never had any very wide following. There may have been humanitarian tendencies in the religion of Zoroaster, though that was just a national religion in origin.

of peoples who were different in language and race and were divided into many political organisms but were nevertheless united by beliefs, sentiments and a common culture.

Of all religions Mohammedanism is the one, perhaps, that leaves its imprint most deeply on individuals who have embraced it, or better, who have been born into a society over which it has secured control. Christianity, and Judaism too, have been and still are forms that are exceedingly well adapted to molding the soft clay of the human spirit in accordance with certain definite patterns. The influence of Buddhism is more bland, but it is still effective.

It is to be noted, however, that if these great religions, with their closely knit doctrines and their strongly organized religious hierarchies, do serve wonderfully to bind their cobelievers together in brotherhood and assimilate them to a common type, they also act as estranging forces of great potency between populations that cherish different beliefs. They create almost unbridgeable gulfs between peoples who are otherwise close kin in race and language and who live in adjoining territories or even within one country. Differences in religion have rendered any fusion between the populations inhabiting the Balkan peninsula almost impossible, and the same is true of India. In India, as is known, the religions prevailing at present are Mohammedanism and Brahmanism. The latter is not a humanitarian religion, but it is strongly organized. Minute precepts create cases of impurity at the least contact between persons of different castes. The caste, therefore, becomes a powerful estranging force, and greatly hampers any ferment of impulses toward social assimilation.

Amazing indeed is the skill that the Romans showed in assimilating subject peoples, in the face of the very considerable obstacles that arose from differences in race, language and level of civilization. They might not have succeeded so well had they encountered the resistance of hostile, exclusive and strongly organized religions. Druidism in Gaul and Britain had a very rudimentary organization, but it offered a certain amount of resistance nevertheless. The Jews allowed themselves to be killed and dispersed, but they were never assimilated. In North Africa, Rome succeeded in Latinizing the ancestors of the modern Moors, Arabs and Kabyles and in converting them to her civilization, at least up to a certain point; but she never had to deal with the Mussulman religion, as the French and Italians of our day are obliged to do. Jugurtha and Tacfarinas could not appeal to religious passions as Abd-el-Kader and Bou-Maza have done in our time. As Karamzin so aptly remarks, the Christian religion saved Moscow from becoming wholly Asiatic under the long dominion of the Mongols. On the other hand, though the Russians in their turn are efficient assimilators, and though Finnish and Mongol blood are blended in large proportions with the Slavic in White Russia, the units of Mohammedan Tatars in Kazan, Astrakhan and the Crimea have never been absorbed. Either they have emigrated or else they have stayed on as a people apart, subject, to be sure, but sharply distinguished from the rest of the Russian people.[1] The children of the Celestial Empire have been fairly successful in assimilating the inhabitants of the southern provinces, alien by race and language, but they have not succeeded so well with the Roui-Tze, descendants of Turkish tribes who have dwelt for a thousand years or more in provinces in the northwest of China proper. These have taken on the language and the external appearance of the real Chinese, and mingle with the latter in the same cities, but they have been kept in spiritual isolation by Mohammedanism, which their fathers had embraced before passing the Great Wall. The Turkish tribes in question established themselves in the provinces of Shensi and Kansu under the Tang dynasty, on being summoned thither to check invasions by the Tibetans. In 1861 the antipathies that had always existed between the Mohammedans and their Buddhist fellow countrymen gave rise to a terrible insurrection, in which the Mohammedans waged a war of extermination against the Buddhists. After the provinces mentioned had been reduced to ghastly desolation, the civil war became localized in the Kashgar, beyond the Great Wall. It did not end until 1877, when the Mohammedan leader, Jakoub-beg, was assassinated.[2]

With the appearance of the great universal religions, the history of mankind becomes complicated by new factors. We have already seen that even before those religions arose, a social type, in spite of its tendency toward unity, might split up into different political systems. With the advent of the great religions, this fact becomes more general and less avoidable, and the ground is prepared for the emergence of a phenomenon which, as regards Europe, is called the struggle between church and state.

The complication arises primarily from the fact that the tendency of the social type toward unity remains but is hampered by far stronger forces. The political organization still tries to justify its own existence by the tenets of the prevailing religion, but the religion, on its side, is always trying to obtain control of, and to identify itself with, political power in order to use the latter as an instrument for its own ends and propaganda.

Religion and politics are most closely united in Mohammedan countries. The head of a Mohammedan state has almost always been the high priest of one of the great Islamic sects, or else has received his investiture from the hands of a high priest. In past centuries this investiture was often an empty formality which the caliph, by that time stripped of temporal power, could not withhold from the powerful. In the period between the fall of the Abbassids of Bagdad and the rise of the great Ottoman Empire

[1] Leroy-Beaulieu, *L'Empire des tzars et les Russes.*
[2] Rousset, *À travers la Chine.*

Mussulman fanaticism was less violent than it is today. Even a superficial familiarity with the history of the Mohammedan countries convinces one of that. Heirs of the Persian civilization of the age of the Sassanids, and thanks to their study of ancient Greek authors, the Mussulmans were for several centuries during the Middle Ages much less prejudiced than the Christians of the same period.[1] It is certain, moreover, that almost every great revolution in the Mohammedan world, the birth of almost every state, is accompanied and justified by a new religious schism. So it was in the Middle Ages, when the new empires of the Almoravides and the Almohades arose; and that was also the case in the nineteenth century with the insurrection of the Wahabis and the revolt led by the Mahdi of Omdurman.

In China, Buddhism lives meekly on under the protection of the state, the latter showing that it recognizes and fosters the creed as a gesture of deference toward the lower classes, which really believe in it. Down to a few years ago the Grand Lama, who is the high authority of the Buddhists in Tibet, Mongolia and certain provinces of China proper, scrupulously followed the suggestions of the Chinese resident at Lhasa. The bonzes, who are scattered over the greater part of China, have no centralized organization—in a way they are the Protestants of Buddhism. The government tolerates them and often spends a certain amount of money on Buddhist festivals in order to humor popular beliefs. The higher classes in China follow the agnostic positivism of Confucius, which is not clearly distinguishable from a vague sort of deism. In Japan the same religion is tolerated, but the government has of late been trying to rehabilitate the ancient national cult of Shinto.

The various Christian sects have met widely varying conditions in Europe. In Russia the czar was the head of the orthodox religion and the church authority was practically one with the state authority. In the eyes of a loyal Russian a good subject of the czar had to be an orthodox Greek Catholic.[2] In Protestant countries, too, the dominant sect often has a more or less official character. Since the fall of the Roman empire, Catholicism has had greater independence. In the Middle Ages it aspired to control over lay authority in all the countries that had entered the Catholic orbit, and there was a time when the pope could reasonably hope that a realization of the vast papal project of uniting all Christianity —in other words a whole social type—under his more or less direct influence was near at hand. Today the pope gets along by compromises, lending his support to secular powers and receiving theirs. In one country or another he is in open conflict with them.

But a political organism, which has a population that follows one of the universal religions, or is divided among several sects of one of them,

[1] Amari, *Storia dei Musulmani in Sicilia.*
[2] Leroy-Beaulieu, *L'Empire des tzars et les Russes.*

must have a legal and moral basis of its own on which the ruling class may take its stand. It must, therefore, be founded on a national feeling, on a long tradition of independence, on historic memories, on an age-old loyalty to a dynasty—on something, in short, that is peculiar to itself. Alongside of the general humanitarian cult, there must somehow be a, so to say, national cult that is more or less satisfactorily reconciled and coordinated with the other. The duties of the two cults are often simultaneously observed by the same individuals, for human beings are not always strictly consistent in reconciling the various principles that inspire their conduct. In practice one may be a good Catholic and at the same time a good German, or a good Italian, or a good Frenchman, or a loyal subject of a Protestant sovereign, or a good citizen of a republic that makes official profession of anticlericalism. Sometimes, as frequently happened in an older Italy, one can be a good patriot and an ardent socialist at the same time, though socialism, like Catholicism, is in essence antagonistic to national particularisms. These compromises occur, however, when passions are not very keen. In point of strict consistency, the eighteenth century English were right when they thought that, since the king was the head of the Anglican Church and every good Catholic owed his prime obedience to the pope, no good Catholic could be a good Englishman.

When there is a more or less masked antagonism between a doctrine, or a creed, that aspires to universality, and the sentiments and traditions that support the particularism of a state, what is really essential is that those sentiments and traditions should be really vigorous, that they should also be bound up with many material interests and that a considerable portion of the ruling class should be strongly imbued with them and should propagate and keep them alive in the masses. If, in addition, this element in the ruling class is soundly organized, it can resist all the religious or doctrinary currents that are exerting an influence in the society that it rules. But if it is lukewarm in its sentiments, if it is feeble in moral and intellectual forces, if its organization is defective, then the religious and doctrinary currents prevail and the state ends by becoming a plaything of some one of the universal religions or doctrines—for example of Catholicism or of social democracy.

Before we proceed any further, it might be wise to linger briefly on the two types into which, in our opinion, all political organisms may be classified, the feudal and the bureaucratic.

This classification, it should be noted, is not based upon essential, unchanging criteria. It is not our view that there is any psychological law peculiar to either one of the two types and therefore alien to the other. It seems to us, rather, that the two types are just different manifestations, different phases, of a single constant tendency whereby human societies become less simple, or, if one will, more complicated in political organization, as they grow in size and are perfected in civilization. Level of civilization is, on the whole, more important in this regard than size, since, in actual fact, a literally huge state may once have been feudally organized. At bottom, therefore, a bureaucratic state is just a feudal state that has advanced and developed in organization and so grown more complex; and a feudal state may derive from a once bureaucratized society that has decayed in civilization and reverted to a simpler, more primitive form of political organization, perhaps falling to pieces in the process.

By "feudal state" we mean that type of political organization in which all the executive functions of society—the economic, the judicial, the administrative, the military—are exercised simultaneously by the same individuals, while at the same time the state is made up of small social aggregates, each of which possesses all the organs that are required for self-sufficiency. The Europe of the Middle Ages offers the most familiar example of this type of organization—that is why we have chosen to designate it by the term "feudal"; but as one reads the histories of other peoples or scans the accounts of travelers of our own day one readily perceives that the type is widespread. Just as the medieval baron was simultaneously owner of the land, military commander, judge and administrator of his fief, over which he enjoyed both a pure and a mixed sovereignty, so the Abyssinian ras dispensed justice, commanded the soldiery and levied taxes—or rather extorted from the farmer everything over and above the bare necessaries of subsistence. In certain periods of ancient Egypt the hiq, or local governor, saw to the upkeep of the canals, supervised agriculture, administered justice, exacted tribute, commanded his warriors. This was more especially the case during the earliest known periods and under some of the more recent dynasties. It must not be forgotten that the history of ancient Egypt covers about thirty centuries, a period long enough, in spite of the alleged immobility of the East, for a society to pass back and forth between feudalism and bureaucracy any number of times. So too the curaca of Peru, under Inca rule, was the head of his village, and in that capacity administered the collective rural property, exercised all judiciary functions and, at the request of the Son of the Sun, commanded the armed quotas that the village contributed. China also passed through a feudal period, and in Japan that type of organization lasted down to the end of the sixteenth century, its last traces not vanishing till after the revolution of 1868. Afghanistan is still feudally organized, and so was India to a great extent at the time of the European conquest. We may go so far as to say that every great society must have passed one or more times through a feudal period.

Sometimes religious functions also are exercised by the leader who has charge of other social activities. This was true of Europe in medieval times, when abbots and bishops were holders of fiefs. A feudal order may exist, furthermore, even when land, the almost exclusive source of wealth in societies of low-grade civilization, is not by law the absolute property of the governing class. Even granting that the cultivators are not legally vassals and slaves, or indeed are nominally owners of the soil they cultivate, the local leader and his satellites, having full power to exact tribute and require forced labor, will leave the workers of the land no more than is indispensable for a bare subsistence.

Even small political units, in which the production of wealth rests not upon agriculture but upon commerce and industry, sometimes show markedly feudal characteristics, exhibiting a concentration of political and economic management in the same persons that is characteristically feudal. The political heads of the medieval communes were at the same time heads of the craft and trade guilds. The merchants of Tyre and Sidon, like the merchants of Genoa and Venice, Bremen and Hamburg, managed banks, superintended the trading posts that were established in barbarian countries, commanded ships which served now as merchantmen, now as war vessels, and governed their cities. That was the case especially when the cities lived by maritime commerce, in the exercise of which anyone who commanded a vessel readily combined his functions as a merchant with political or military leadership. In other places, in Florence for example, where a large part of the municipal wealth was derived from industry and banking, the ruling class soon lost its warlike habits and therewith direction of military affairs. To that fact may have been partly due the troubled career of the commercial oligarchy in Florence after the expulsion of the Duke of Athens and down to the time of Cosimo dei Medici. The year 1325 saw the last of the cavallate, or military expeditions, in which the nobles and wealthy merchants of Florence personally participated.[1]

In the bureaucratic state not all the executive functions need to be concentrated in the bureaucracy and exercised by it. One might even declare that so far in history that has never been the case. The main characteristic of this type of social organization lies, we believe, in the fact that, wherever it exists, the central power conscripts a considerable portion of the social wealth by taxation and uses it first to maintain a military establishment and then to support a more or less extensive number of public services. The greater the number of officials who perform public duties and receive their salaries from the central government or from its local agencies, the more bureaucratic a society becomes.

In a bureaucratic state there is always a greater specialization in the functions of government than in a feudal state. The first and most elementary division of capacities is the withdrawal of administrative and judiciary powers from the military element. The bureaucratic state, furthermore, assures a far greater discipline in all grades of political, ad-

[1] Capponi, *Storia della Republica di Firenze.*

ministrative and military service. To gain some conception of what this means, one has only to compare a medieval count, hedged about by armed retainers and by vassals who have been attached for centuries to his family and supported by the produce of his lands, with a modern French or Italian prefect or army general, whom a telegram can suddenly shear of authority and even of stipend. The feudal state, therefore, demands great energy and a great sense of statesmanship in the man, or men, who stand on the top rung of the social ladder, if the various social groups, which would otherwise tend to disorganization and autonomy, are to be kept organized, compact and obedient to a single impulse. So true is this that often with the death of an influential leader the power of a feudal state itself comes to an end. Only great moral unity —the presence of a sharply defined social type—can long save the political existence of a people that is feudally organized. Nothing less than Christianity was required to hold the Abyssinian tribes together amid the masses of pagans and Mohammedans that encircled them, and to preserve their autonomy for over two thousand years. But when the estranging force is feeble, or when the feudal state comes into contact with more soundly organized peoples, then such a state may very easily be absorbed and vanish in one of the frequent periodical crises to which its central power is irremediably exposed—the example of Poland comes immediately to mind. On the other hand, the personal qualities of the supreme head exert relatively little influence on the destinies of a bureaucratic state. A society that is bureaucratically organized may retain its freedom even if it repudiates an old political formula and adopts a new one, or even if it subjects its social type to very far-reaching modifications. This was the case with the Roman Empire. It survived the adoption of Christianity in the West for a century and a half, and in the East for more than eleven centuries. So our modern nations have nearly all shifted at one time or another from a divine-right formula to parliamentary systems of government.

Bureaucratic organization need not necessarily be centralized, in the sense commonly given to that expression. Often bureaucratization is compatible with a very liberal provincial autonomy, as in China, where the eighteen strictly Chinese provinces preserved broad autonomous privileges and the capital city of each province looked after almost all provincial affairs.[1]

States of European civilization—even the most decentralized of them— are all bureaucratized. As we have already indicated, the chief characteristic of a bureaucratic organization is that its military functions, and other public services in numbers more or less large, are exercised by salaried employees. Whether salaries are paid exclusively by the central government or in part by local bodies more or less under the control of

[1] Huc, Réclus, Rousset.

the central government is a detail that is not as important as it is often supposed to be. History is not lacking in cases of very small political organisms which have accomplished miracles of energy in every branch of human activity with the barest rudiments of bureaucratic organization or with practically none at all. The ancient Hellenic cities and the Italian communes of the Middle Ages are examples that flock to mind. But when vast human organisms, spreading over huge territories and comprising millions and millions of individuals, are involved, nothing short of bureaucratic organization seems capable of uniting under a single impulse the immense treasures of economic power and moral and intellectual energy with which a ruling class can in a measure modify conditions within a society and make its influence effective and powerful beyond its own frontiers. Under a feudal organization the authority which a given member of the ruling class exerts over individuals of the subject class, few or many, may be more direct, oppressive, and arbitrary. Under a bureaucratic organization society is influenced less by the given individual leader than by the ruling class as a whole.

Egypt was bureaucratized in the golden ages of the seventeenth and eighteenth dynasties, when the civilization of the Pharaohs had one of its most lustrous periods of renascence, and the Egyptian battalions pushed their conquests from the Blue Nile to the foothills of the Caucasus. In ancient Egypt, as in China, the coinage of precious metals was unknown. Taxes therefore were collected in kind or were calculated in precious metals, which were weighed out on scales. This was no inconsiderable obstacle to the functioning of the bureaucratic system. The difficulty was overcome by a complicated and very detailed system of bookkeeping. It is interesting also to note, on the psychological side, that with social conditions equal, man is always the same, even in little things, through the ages. Letters surviving from those days[1] show Egyptian officers detailing the hardships of their faraway garrisons in Syria, and functionaries who are bored in their little provincial towns soliciting the influence of their superiors to procure transfers to the gayer capital. Such letters could be drawn from the archives of almost any department in any modern European government.

The Roman empire was a highly bureaucratized state, and its sound social organism was able to spread Greco-Roman civilization and the language of Italy over large portions of the ancient world, accomplishing a most difficult task of social assimilation. Another bureaucracy was czarist Russia, which, despite a number of serious internal weaknesses, had great vitality and carried its expansion deep into the remote fastnesses of Asia.

In spite of these examples, and not a few others that might readily occur to one, we should not forget a very important fact to which we

[1] Texts and translations by Lenormant and Maspero.

have already alluded: namely, that history shows no instance of a great society in which all human activities have been completely bureaucratized. This, perhaps, is one of the many indications of the great complexity of social laws, for a type of political organization may produce good results when applied up to a certain point, but become impracticable and harmful when it is generalized and systematized. Justice is quite generally bureaucratized, and so is public administration. Napoleon I, great bureaucratizer that he was, succeeded in bureaucratizing education and even the Catholic priesthood. We often see bureaucracies building roads, canals, railways and all sorts of public works that facilitate the production of wealth. But production itself we never see entirely bureaucratized. It would seem as though that very important branch of social activity, like so many other branches, lends itself ill to bureaucratic regulation, individual profit being a far more effective spur to the classes engaged in production than any government salary could be.

What is more, we have fairly strong evidence that the extension of bureaucratic control to the production and distribution of wealth as a whole would be fatal. We are not thinking here of the economic evils of protectionism, of governmental control of banking and finance, of the overdevelopment of public works. We are merely pointing to a well-established fact. In a bureaucratic system both the manager of economic production and the individual worker are protected against arbitrary confiscations on the part of the strong and powerful, and all private warfare is sternly suppressed. Human life and property are therefore relatively secure. Under a bureaucratic regime, the producer pays over a fixed quota to the social organization and secures tranquil enjoyment of the rest of his product. This permits an accretion of wealth, public and private, that is unknown to barbarous or primitively organized countries. But the amount of wealth that is absorbed and consumed by the class that fulfills other than economic functions may become too great, either because the demands of the military class, and of other bureaucrats, are excessive, or because the bureaucracy tries to perform too many services, or because of wars and the debts that result from wars. Under these circumstances the taxes that are levied upon the wealth-producing classes become so heavy that the profit that an individual can earn in the field of production is markedly reduced. In that event production itself inevitably falls off. As wealth declines, emigration and higher death rates thin out the poorer classes, and finally the exhaustion of the entire social body ensues. These phenomena are observable whenever a bureaucratic state declines. We see them in the epoch that followed upon the maximum development of bureaucracy in ancient Egypt, and more strikingly still during the decay of the Roman Empire. At the end of the long reign of Ramese II, with which the decline of the third Egyptian civilization begins, taxes had become intolerable, as is attested by numbers of private documents that have been deciphered by Maspero, Lenormant and others. We know that the real reason for the decline of the Roman Empire was a falling-off in population and wealth, which in turn must have been caused in the main by the burden of taxes and the unthinking greed with which they were collected.[1] In France, too, population and wealth dwindled at the end of the long reign of the Great King. They were put into good condition again under the administration of the peace-loving Cardinal de Fleury.

It would take us too far afield to respond seriatim to all the theories and doctrines that diverge from our point of view concerning the classification of governmental types in human societies. Among such doctrines, however, two are so important, in view of the vogue that they are having today, that we can hardly ignore them. We allude to the closely related theories of Comte and Spencer. Large numbers of writers on the social and political sciences make the concepts of those famous sociologists the cornerstones of their reasonings and their systems.

Comte, as is well known, stressed three stages in the evolution of human intelligence, the theological, the metaphysical and the positive, with three different types of social organization corresponding to them, the military, the feudal and the industrial.

Little fault need be found with this classification of the intellectual processes of man in general. Man may, in fact, explain to himself all phenomena in the organic and inorganic universe, even social phenomena, by attributing them to supernatural beings, to the intervention of God or of gods or of spirits beneficent or maleficent, whom he takes to be the authors of victory and defeat, of abundance and famine, of good health and pestilence; and if one assumes that there was a stage in history in which man reasoned exclusively in this fashion, the stage may well be called theological. Man may also explain the same phenomena by ascribing them to prime, or first, causes which are products of his imagination or of a superficial or fanciful observation of facts, as when he believed that the destinies of individuals and nations depended upon the motions and conjunctions of the planets, or that the health of the human body depended upon combinations of humors, or that the wealth of nations corresponded to the quantities of precious metals that they possessed. In this case man may well be said to be in a metaphysical, or aprioristic stage. Finally, man can give up trying to discover the prime causes of phenomena and try instead, with rigorous methods of observation, to formulate the natural laws with which phenomena conform and so enable himself to take all possible advantage of them. In this frame of mind man can be said to be in a scientific or positive stage.

Objections to Comte's system begin when he sets out to ascribe the three processes mentioned to definite historical periods and then to clas-

[1] Marquardt, *Organisation financière chez les Romains.*

sify human societies by assigning them to one or another of the periods
so obtained. All three intellectual processes go on in all human societies,
from the maturest down to those which are still, so to speak, in the savage
state. Ancient Greece gave us Hippocrates and Aristotle, and Rome
Lucretius. Modern European civilization has given us physics, chemistry
and political economy. It has invented the telescope and the microscope.
It has tamed electricity and discovered the bacteria that cause epidemics
and diseases. Yet we cannot help recognizing that in Athens as in ancient
Rome, in Paris as in Berlin, in London as in New York, the majority of
individuals were and are in the full midst of the theological stage, or at
best in the metaphysical stage. Just as there was no time in classical
antiquity when soothsayers and oracles were not consulted, or when
sacrifices were not offered and omens believed, so revealed religions
continue to play important roles in the lives of our contemporaries, and
wherever religion weakens we witness growths of spiritualistic superstitions or of the absurd metaphysics of social democracy. On the other
hand the savage who sees a fetish in a plant or a stone, or who believes
that his tribe's medicine man produces rain and makes the lightning,
could not live in this world if he did not possess a certain amount of
soundly positive information. When he studies the habits of the animals
he hunts, when he learns to identify their tracks and takes account of
the direction of the wind in order to surprise and capture them, he is
utilizing observations that have been accumulated and systematized by
himself and his fathers, and is acting therefore in accord with the dictates
of sound science.[1]

But that is not all. Comte's three intellectual processes go on simultaneously—to use his curious language, his three periods coexist—not
only in one historical epoch and in one people, but also in one individual.
We may say, with examples by the hundreds before our eyes, that this
is the general rule and that the contrary is the exception. What Italian,
in fact, has not known some God-fearing ship's captain who in religion
believes in the miracles of Our Lady of Lourdes or of the Madonna of
Pompeii, who in politics or in economics believes in universal suffrage or
in the class struggle, but who, when it comes to running his ship, handles
his tiller according to the compass and trims his sails according to the
direction of the wind? All, or virtually all, physicians down to two centuries ago believed in religion and so did not deny the efficacy of prayer
and votive offerings in the treatment of the sick. As regards the functioning of the different organs in the human body and the virtues of certain
simples, they held various metaphysical beliefs, derived in large part

[1] This objection to Comte's theory was seen by Comte himself, for he wrote: "This
ephemeral coexistence of the three intellectual stages today is the only plausible explanation for the resistance that outdated thinkers are still offering to my law."
Système, vol. III, p. 41.

from Galen or from Arab doctors. But at the same time they were not without a certain fund of scientific information that went back to Hippocrates and which, slowly enriched by the experience of many centuries, permitted rational treatments in some few cases. So prayers for victory and *Te Deums* of thanksgiving were offered in Europe to the Most High long after Gustavus Adolphus, Turenne and Montecuccoli had begun to fight wars on scientific principles. To mention one other case: When Xenophon believed that a dream was a warning from the gods he was in a full theological period. As to the shape of the earth and the composition of matter he had ideas that the geographers and chemists of our day would characterize as metaphysical. But, in leading the famous retreat of the Ten Thousand, he found it necessary to protect his main column, which was marching with the baggage train, from continuous raids by the Persian cavalry. He flanked it with two lines of light-armed troops—so guiding himself by principles which, given the armaments then in use, a modern tactician would judge thoroughly scientific and positive. In the *Cyropaedia* Xenophon is primarily theological and metaphysical. He turns positive again in his treatise on the art of horseback riding. On this topic he draws his precepts, as any modern writer would, from study of the nature of the horse.

The truth is that, in this as in so many other cases, over-simplification is not well suited to the sciences that deal with the psychology of man. Man is an exceedingly complex animal, full of contradictions. He is not always considerate enough to be logical and consistent and so, even when he believes and hopes that God is going to interfere in his behalf, he is careful to keep his powder dry—careful to take advantage, in other words, both of his own and of other people's intelligence and experience. The one really valid argument that can be adduced in favor of Comte's classification is that although the three intellectual stages coexist in all human societies and can be detected in the majority of individuals who compose those societies, they may, according to the case, be very unequally distributed. A people may have an equipment of scientific knowledge that is unquestionably superior to that of another people, and in the various periods of its history it may progress or decline greatly in respect of scientific knowledge; and it is just as certain that metaphysical doctrines and supernatural beliefs generally have a stronger hold on scientifically backward nations and individuals and exert a greater influence on them. But subjected to those limitations Comte's theory comes down to something like the rather commonplace doctrine that the farther a society progresses in scientific thinking, the less room it has left for aprioristic or metaphysical thinking, and the less influence the supernatural has upon it.

"*Natio est omnium Gallorum admodum dedita religionibus* (the whole race of Gauls is extraordinarily devoted to religious rites)," wrote Caesar

—a judgment that an individual belonging to a more civilized people always makes of a less civilized people.[1] It is a curious fact that if believers in revealed religions have a certain amount of scientific training they are careful not to attribute everything that happens in this world to the continuous interference of supernatural beings, as cruder peoples and more ignorant individuals usually do.

But the ideas of the father of modern sociology seem to go even wider of the mark in the matter of the parallel that he sets up between his three intellectual stages and his three types of political organization, the military, the feudal and the industrial, the first corresponding to the infancy, the second to the adolescence, the third to the maturity of human societies.

The military function, in other words the organization of an armed force for the defense of a people at home and abroad (and, for that matter, for offense too, according as human interests, prejudices and passions chance to determine) has so far been a necessity in all human societies. The greater or lesser predominance of the military element in political life depends partly upon factors which we have already examined—on whether the military element is a more or less indispensable and comprehensive political force, and whether it is more or less balanced by other political forces—and partly on other factors which we shall not fail to consider in due course. For the time being we see no necessity for the indissoluble union that Comte insists on establishing between the predominance of militarism in political life and the prevalence of the theological period in the intellectual and moral worlds. We can even go on and say that we do not consider it in any way proved that the type of organization that Comte calls military can prevail only in societies that are in the first stage of their development, or, to use the language of the modern positivists, in a state of infancy.

Hellenic society, after Alexander the Great, was evidently organized according to a pattern that any sociologist would define as military. After the Macedonian conquest the republican leagues of Greece proper had only a very limited political importance. Down to the Roman conquest they were always in the position of clients or vassals to the great Hellenized kingdoms of Egypt, Syria and, particularly, Macedonia, which were real military absolutisms based on the support of armies. Yet those were the days when Greek society was in anything but a state of infancy, or a theological period. The philosophical schools that represent the greatest effort of Hellenic thought in the direction of positive science had been formed shortly before and were flourishing at that time. The same thing may be observed in Roman society when, after Caesar, an imperial absolutism resting on the praetorian guards and the legions came to be established.

[1] *De bello Gallico*, VI, 16.

When religious beliefs are widespread and a people has ardent faith in them we inevitably get a political predominance of the priestly classes. Now those classes and the military classes are not always one and the same, nor do they always have the same sentiments and interests. The union of throne and altar that took place in Europe early in the nineteenth century, after the Holy Alliance, was due to the peculiar circumstance that both throne and altar were directly threatened by the same rationalistic and revolutionary currents. But far from constituting a general rule which might be taken as a universal law, that case is to be regarded rather as one of the many transitory phenomena that develop in history. There is no lack of examples to the contrary—the case of India, for instance, where, at one time, the Brahman caste found itself in conflict with the warrior caste. In Europe there is the celebrated struggle between papacy and empire.

Going on, we can find no justification in fact whatever for that portion of Comte's doctrine which correlates the predominance of the feudal system in political organization with the predominance of metaphysics in human thought. In Comte's system, medieval monotheism and medieval ontology represent a transition between polytheism—in other words a full-fledged theological period—and modern science, just as feudalism, which Comte regards as a defensive type of militarism, is a bridge between the military and industrial periods. "In fact," he says, "monotheism fits in with defense as well as polytheism fits in with conquest. The feudal lords formed just as complete a transition between military commanders and industrial leaders as ontology formed between theology and science."[1] Now to hold that monotheism is best adapted to defense, just as polytheism is best adapted to conquest, is to take no account whatever of large portions of the world's history—the history of the Mussulman world, for example.

We have already seen (chap. III, §6) that what is commonly called feudal organization is a relatively simple political type that is often encountered in the early stages of great human societies and appears again as great bureaucratic states degenerate. Political progress and scientific progress do not always go hand in hand, as is shown by the history of Italy in the Renaissance. We may nevertheless grant, with reservations, that periods of general ignorance and intellectual prostration correspond on the whole to primitive stages in political life or to periods of political decadence and dissolution. But what we cannot see is why such periods should be characterized by the prevalence of metaphysical rather than theological thinking—any more than we can see that there can necessarily be no scientific activity during the flowering of a feudal organization. Confucius lived in a period when China was feudally organized, and he certainly was no metaphysician. On the other

[1] *Système*, vol. III, p. 66.

hand the trivium and the quadrivium are unknown to the Afghans and Abyssinians of our day—as well, for that matter, as anything more than the very elementary forms of culture.

Comte bases his argument largely upon the example of medieval Europe, and that period undoubtedly had its great metaphysicians, as did classical antiquity. But to think of medieval thought as a sort of bridge between ancient theology and modern scientific thought is a mistake, just as it is a mistake to imagine that feudalism was an organically intermediary political form between the ancient hieratic empires and the modern state.

One has only to read a medieval writer—a writer, preferably, who is somewhat posterior to the fall of the western Empire and not too close to the Renaissance—to perceive at once how much more profoundly, how much more basically theological, medieval thinking was than the thinking of antiquity. Medieval writers and the people about them are immensely more remote, immensely more different, from us, than the contemporaries of Aristotle or Cicero ever were. And the feudal order developed and flourished in the very centuries when continuous fear of famine and pestilence, and frequent apparitions of celestial and infernal beings tormented and utterly moronized the human mind; when terror of the devil was a permanent mental state in wretched souls in whom reason had languished for want of any cultural sustenance, and to whom the marvelous and the supernatural were elements as familiar as the air they breathed.

One of the most characteristic writers of the period was the monk Raoul Glaber (Radulfus) who wrote a chronicle that comes down to almost the middle of the eleventh century.[1] According to that monk the ancient classical writers, Vergil included, appeared to their readers in the guise of devils. Glaber's faith is steadfast but unwarmed by brotherly love, and in it fear of the Evil One probably plays a larger role than love and worship of the good, the merciful God of the Christians. In Glaber's eyes, Satan is at all times present and has a finger in everything that happens to human beings. There is perhaps no living person who has not seen him. In spite of an energetic piety and zealous compliance with the rule of his order, Glaber himself has seen the Devil three or four times.

Not all writers of that era, to be sure, show the same derangement of the intellectual faculties, but no one is altogether immune to it. A Norman, Goffredo Malaterra, tells the story of Count Roger's conquest of Sicily from the Saracens with considerable discernment and balance of judgment, and at times he evinces a certain capacity for observing human events with an unprejudiced eye. Yet in describing a battle that was fought at Cerami between the Count and the infidels, he ascribes the victory of the Christians to the direct interposition of St. George,

[1] Émile Gebhart, "L'État d'âme d'un moine de l'an 1000."

who fought in person in the ranks of the Normans. In proof of the miracle Malaterra records that a white flag emblazoned with a cross was seen to appear on the lance of the Christian leader and flutter in the wind.

The epidemic of demonolatry even spread to the Byzantine East. Georgius Cedrenus and the chronicler Constantine Porphyrogenitus relate that the capture of Syracuse by the Saracens was known in the Peloponnesus long before any refugees arrived, because some demons were chatting together in a wood one night and were overheard recounting the details of that disaster.

In justification of his theory Comte writes: "Noteworthy as characterizing the true spirit of Catholicism is the fact that it reduces theological life to the domain of the strictly necessary."[1] But that is failing to take account of the fact that the supernatural is "reduced to the strictly necessary" not only in Catholicism but in all monotheistic religions when they are professed by civilized peoples who possess broad scientific cultures—the modern English for instance. No such reduction occurs when monotheistic religions are professed by barbarous peoples of low cultural levels. In such cases the sway of the supernatural over the minds of men may be much greater than it is among polytheistic peoples of higher levels of civilization.

The third necessary correspondence that Comte sets up, the relation between the industrial system and positive science, is also fallacious. We may dispense with proof of that because, in this third section of Comte's political positivism, his ideas have had no great resonance, being too divergent from the ideas that are now most in vogue among our contemporaries, and not offering sufficient leverage for justifying with a semblance of scientific method the passions and interests that have so far been most to the fore in our day. Comte regarded industrialism as a type of social organization that would be realized in a remote future when the managerial functions of society would be entrusted to a priesthood of positivistic scientists and to a patriciate of bankers and businessmen, to which, it would seem, the members of the lower classes were not to gain ready admittance. Foreseeing that this question might arise, Comte did not forget to write that "the priesthood will prevail upon the proletarians to scorn any temptation to leave their own class as contrary to the majesty of the people's function and fatal to the righteous aspirations of the masses, who have always been betrayed by deserters from their ranks."[2] Another fundamental idea of Comte's is that the entire intellectual and political movement at the end of the eighteenth century and in the first half of the nineteenth was a revolutionary movement that resulted in moral and political anarchy because the feudal monotheistic system had been destroyed and nobody had been able to find a substitute for it. In line with this idea Comte severely condemned the parliamentary

[1] *Système,* vol. III, p. 434.
[2] *Ibid.,* vol. IV, p. 83.

system as a manifestation of the anarchic period (in which we are still living); and the representative function itself, whereby inferiors choose their superiors, Comte defined as a revolutionary function.[1]

It will be more to our purpose to dwell on the second theory mentioned (§9), that is to say, on the modification that Spencer, and a host of modern sociologists after him, made in Comte's doctrines. Spencer divided human societies into two types, the militant (*i.e.*, military), based upon force, and the industrial, based upon contract and the free consent of the citizens. This dual classification is propounded more especially in Spencer's *Principles of Sociology,* but it is regularly assumed in most of his other writings, as well as in the works of his numerous followers.

Any classification has to be based upon distinctive traits that are clear and definite, and Spencer, in fact, does not fail to serve warning at the outset that, although "during social evolution there has habitually been a mingling of the two types [the militant and the industrial], we shall find that, alike in theory and in fact, it is possible to trace with due clearness these opposite characters which distinguish them in their respective complete developments."[2] Spencer's fundamental criterion is that the militant society is based on *status*, on "regimentation," "the members standing towards one another in successive grades of subordination,"[3] and on the supervision, therefore, and the coercion, which the governors exercise over the governed. His industrial society is based upon contract, upon the free consent of its members, in exactly the same way as a literary society, or an industrial or commercial partnership, is based on the free consent of the associated members and could not exist without such consent.

Now, for a first general objection, this classification is based upon eminently aprioristic assumptions which do not stand the test of facts. Any political organization is both voluntary and coercive at one and the same time—voluntary because it arises from the very nature of man, as was long ago noted by Aristotle, and coercive because it is a necessary fact, the human being finding himself unable to live otherwise. It is natural, therefore, and at the same time indispensable, that where there are men there should automatically be a society, and that when there is a society there should also be a state—that is to say, a minority that rules and a majority that is ruled by the ruling minority.

It might be objected that, although the existence of a social organization is natural and necessary wherever human groups or multitudes form, there are states that receive the assent, or at least the tacit acquiescence,

---

[1] *Ibid.,* vol. IV, chap. 5, especially pp. 368, 382, 393-94.

[2] *Principles of Sociology,* vol. II, chap. XVII ("The Militant Type of Society"), §547, p. 568. "The Industrial Type of Society" is discussed in chap. XVIII. Chapter XIX, "Political Retrospect and Prospect," relates to the past and future of the two types.

[3] *Ibid.,* vol. II, chap. XVII, §553.

of the great majority of the individuals who belong to them, and states that do not attain that condition. We do not deny that things stand exactly that way, but still we do not see why the former should be called industrial states and the latter militant states, in the sense that Spencer attaches to the terms. The majority of a people consents to a given governmental system solely because the system is based upon religious or philosophical beliefs that are universally accepted by them. To use a language that we prefer, the amount of consent depends upon the extent to which, and the ardor with which, the class that is ruled believes in the political formula by which the ruling class justifies its rule. Now, in general, faith of that kind is certainly greater not in Spencer's industrial states but in states that Spencer classifies as militant, or which present all the characteristics that he attributes to militant states—states where an absolute and arbitrary government is based on divine right.

In the monarchies of the Near East there are often conspiracies against the persons of sovereigns, but down to a few years ago attempts to set up new forms of government were very rare. Among all the nations of modern Europe before the World War, Turkey and Russia were the ones where governmental systems were most in harmony with the political ideals of the great majority in their populations. Only small educated minorities were systematically opposed to the rule of the czar and the sultan. In all barbarous countries populations may be dissatisfied with their rulers, but ordinarily they neither conceive of better political systems nor desire any.

We can hardly agree, either, with certain applications that Spencer makes of his categories to particular cases. Spencer seems to have thought of an industrial state as a sort of democratic state, a state, at any rate, in which government is based on representation, or in which there is at least a tendency not to recognize any authority as legitimate unless it emanates from some public assembly. He says: "Such control as is required under the industrial type can be exercised only by an appointed agency for ascertaining and executing the average will; and a representative agency is the one best fitted for doing this."[1] He therefore classifies the Pueblo Indians of New Mexico and Arizona with societies of the industrial type because, "sheltering in their walled villages and fighting only when invaded, they . . . united with their habitually industrial life a free form of government: . . . 'the governor and his council were annually elected by the people.' "[2] Now Spencer could not have been unaware how widely common the elective system was in the republics of ancient Greece, in Rome, and even among the ancient Germans, who chose their leaders by acclamation, raising them on high on their shields. Nevertheless, all those peoples, according to Spencer's own criteria, would

[1] *Ibid.*, §566, p. 508.
[2] *Ibid.*, vol. II, chap. XVIII, §513, p. 616.

be classified as militant peoples. On the other hand, we should hardly be able to call them industrial peoples, in Spencer's sense. The fact that a people participates in electoral assemblies does not meant that it directs its government or that the class that is governed chooses its governors. It means merely that when the electoral function operates under favorable social conditions it is a tool by which certain political forces are enabled to control and limit the activity of other political forces.

Spencer finds certain distinguishing characteristics in his militant and industrial types that seem to us exceedingly vague and indefinite. He writes that as militarism decreases and industrialism increases proportionately, a social organization in which the individual exists for the benefit of the state develops into another organization in which the state exists for the benefit of the individual.[1] That is a subtle distinction. It reminds one of the debate as to whether the brain exists for the benefit of the rest of the body or the rest of the body for the benefit of the brain.

Spencer elsewhere finds that the militant state is "positively regulative," in the sense that it requires the performance of certain acts, while the industrial state is "negatively regulative only,"[2] since it confines itself to specifying acts that must not be performed, and he gives his blessing to states of the negatively regulative variety. As a matter of fact, no social organization has ever existed in which control is not simultaneously positive and negative. Furthermore, since human activity has its limits, multiplication of negative injunctions is almost as bad, as regards fettering individual initiative, as excessive regulation in a positive sense.

Spencer relates to his two types of state traits that we would explain and classify otherwise. In ancient Peru, for instance, public officials superintended agriculture and distributed water (probably for purposes of regular irrigation or else in areas and at times of extreme drought). Spencer finds that trait characteristic of militant states. We should think of it simply as a phenomenon of over-bureaucratization. Then again, Spencer, quoting Brantôme, finds the practice of the private vendetta still common in France in the late Middle Ages, even among the clergy, and he regards the institution as a symptom of militancy. We, for our part, should expect to find such phenomena as the vendetta conspicuous in peoples among whom social authority is weak, or recently has been weak—peoples, in other words, who are in the period of crude and primitive organization which we defined as feudal, or who have recently emerged from it. Wherever the vendetta flourishes, and therefore among almost all barbarous peoples, or peoples whose social organization has greatly decayed, it is natural that personal courage should be a much esteemed quality. In fact, the same thing occurs in any society which, for one reason or another, has had to fight many wars of defense and offense. It is natural that bravery and bombast should be the attributes

[1] *Ibid.*, chap. XVIII.
[2] *Ibid.*, §569, pp. 611-612.

that confer prestige and influence in barbarous societies, the low level of culture not permitting aptitudes for science or for the production of wealth to develop and to win esteem.

Spencer believes that militant societies are protectionist societies and vice versa. He finds in them a tendency to live on their own economic resources with the least possible resort to international exchange. In our opinion that tendency is, more than anything else, a consequence of crudeness and isolation in primitive peoples. In modern civilized nations it results from popular prejudices that are exploited in the interests of a few individuals, who are expert in the arts of serving their own advantage at the expense of the many. It is very probable that the tribes which are so often mentioned by Spencer as typical of primitive industrial societies profited very little from exchange with other tribes; and in our day protectionist doctrines have, alas, no less influence in "industrial" North America than in "militant" Germany.

It would be a mistake, according to Spencer, to identify industrial societies by the degree of economic development that they attain, or militant societies by the energy they develop and the success they achieve in war. Now superficial as such criteria might be, they would have the advantage of being very simple and easily applied. But Spencer himself directly or indirectly warns that they are to be rejected. With regard to the first, he notes that "industrialism must not be confounded with industriousness" and that "the social relations which characterize the industrial type may coexist with but very moderate productive activities."[1] As regards the second, Spencer would allow one to assume that the Roman Republic was less militant than the Near Eastern empires which were subdued by Rome, and following the same reasoning, the English would be less advanced toward the industrial type than the Hindus whom they conquered in India.

Despite these objections and still others that might be urged against Spencer's classification, it cannot be denied that with its aid he glimpsed a great truth—but as through a cloud, so to speak, of misunderstanding. If we follow not so much Spencer's criteria of classification as the mass of his incidental assertions, and especially the spirit that animates his work as a whole, we cannot fail to see that by a "militant state" he means a state in which juridical defense has made little progress and by an "industrial state" another type of society in which justice and social morality are much better safeguarded.

The misunderstanding that kept Spencer from going farther than he went in the discovery of a great scientific principle lay in this: impressed by the fact that material violence has been, as it still is, one of the greatest obstacles to progress in juridical defense, he believed that war and the need of military organization were the causes of all violence. But to view the problem in that light is to confuse the cause with one of its

[1] *Ibid.*, §562, pp. 603-604.

effects. It means taking war as the sole origin of the tendency in human nature to tyrannize over one's fellows, whereas war is just one of the many manifestations of that tendency. Now in the external relations between people and people, that tendency can be curbed only by the greater and greater prevalence of material interests rightly understood. The curb operates only among peoples that have attained high economic and scientific levels, because it is only under highly civilized conditions that war infallibly harms, though still in varying degrees, both victors and vanquished. In internal relations between individual members of one people the tendency in question can be to an extent neutralized, as we have seen, only by a multifarious interplay of such political forces as are able to assert themselves in a society, and by the control they are able to exercise over one another reciprocally.

How is it that among the various ruling cliques, among the various political forces, the section that represents material force, in other words the army, is not always upsetting the juridical equilibrium in its own favor and forcing its will systematically upon the state? Certainly the possibility that that may occur is a standing danger to which all societies are exposed. It is a danger especially to societies that are rapidly rejuvenating their political forces or hastily overhauling their political formulas. We are, therefore, obliged to examine the relations that obtain between military organization and juridical defense in order to discover, if possible, the best methods for dealing with that danger. It is a most important subject, and we shall later go into it in some detail.

For the present we might simply remark that the foregoing criticism of Spencer's conception of war and military power was made from a theoretical point of view. But neither can we approve of his doctrine in respect of a number of practical applications that he more or less directly suggests. Of the various forms of military organization Spencer shows a predilection for forms in which the soldier, "volunteering on specified terms, acquires in so far the position of a free worker"; and he thinks that such an organization is best suited to a society "where the industrial type is much developed."[1] That means, in other terms, that those elements in a society which have a greater inclination toward the bearing of arms ought voluntarily to assume responsibility for military defense both at home and abroad, for a compensation which, in the military trade as in any other, would be fixed by market conditions. Now it seems to us— and so it seemed to Machiavelli and to many others after him—that, apart from special and exceptional circumstances, that is the system that yields the positively worst results among peoples of high cultural levels. It is the one that develops most readily in the military class the tendency to oppress other classes, while it deprives the latter of any chance of effective resistance and strips them of any protection.

[1] *Ibid.*, §562, p. 603.

9. Robert Michels

The Iron Law of Oligarchy

I. The Sovereign Masses

It is a fact of everyday experience that enormous public meetings commonly carry resolutions by acclamation or by general assent, whilst these same assemblies, if divided into small sections, say of fifty persons each, would be much more guarded in their assent. Great party congresses, in which are present the *élite* of the membership, usually act in this way. Words and actions are far less deliberately weighed by the crowd than by the individuals or the little groups of which this crowd is composed. The fact is incontestable—a manifestation of the pathology of the crowd. The individual disappears in the multitude, and therewith disappears also personality and sense of responsibility.

The most formidable argument against the sovereignty of the masses is, however, derived from the mechanical and technical impossibility of its realization.

The sovereign masses are altogether incapable of undertaking the most necessary resolutions. The impotence of direct democracy, like the power of indirect democracy, is a direct outcome of the influence of number. In a polemic against Proudhon (1849), Louis Blanc asks whether it is possible for thirty-four millions of human beings (the population of France at that time) to carry on their affairs without accepting what the pettiest man of business finds necessary, the intermediation of representatives. He answers his own question by saying that one who declares direct action on this scale to be possible is a fool, and that one who denies its possibility need not be an absolute opponent of the idea of the state. The same question and the same answer could be repeated to-day in respect of party organization. Above all in the great industrial centres, where the labour party sometimes numbers its adherents by tens of thousands, it is impossible to carry on the affairs of this gigantic body without a system of representation. The great socialist organization of Berlin, which embraces the six constituencies of the city, as well as the

From Michels, *Political Parties* (Glencoe, Illinois: The Free Press, 1949), pp. 25-36, 78-79, 365-374, 382-392, 400-408. Reprinted with the permission of the publisher.

two outlying areas of Niederbarnim and Teltow-Beeskow-Charlottenburg, has a member-roll of more than ninety thousand.

It is obvious that such a gigantic number of persons belonging to a unitary organization cannot do any practical work upon a system of direct discussion. The regular holding of deliberative assemblies of a thousand members encounters the gravest difficulties in respect of room and distance; while from the topographical point of view such an assembly would become altogether impossible if the members numbered ten thousand. Even if we imagined the means of communication to become much better than those which now exist, how would it be possible to assemble such a multitude in a given place, at a stated time, and with the frequency demanded by the exigencies of party life? In addition must be considered the physiological impossibility even for the most powerful orator of making himself heard by a crowd of ten thousand persons. There are, however, other reasons of a technical and administrative character which render impossible the direct self-government of large groups. If Peter wrongs Paul, it is out of the question that all the other citizens should hasten to the spot to undertake a personal examination of the matter in dispute, and to take the part of Paul against Peter. By parity of reasoning, in the modern democratic party, it is impossible for the collectivity to undertake the direct settlement of all the controversies that may arise.

Hence the need for delegation, for the system in which delegates represent the mass and carry out its will. Even in groups sincerely animated with the democratic spirit, current business, the preparation and the carrying out of the most important actions, is necessarily left in the hands of individuals. It is well known that the impossibility for the people to exercise a legislative power directly in popular assemblies led the democratic idealists of Spain to demand, as the least of evils, a system of popular representation and a parliamentary state.

Originally the chief is merely the servant of the mass. The organization is based upon the absolute equality of all its members. Equality is here understood in its most general sense, as an equality of like men. In many countries, as in idealist Italy (and in certain regions in Germany where the socialist movement is still in its infancy), this equality is manifested, among other ways, by the mutual use of the familiar "thou," which is employed by the most poorly paid wage-labourer in addressing the most distinguished intellectual. This generic conception of equality is, however, gradually replaced by the idea of equality among comrades belonging to the same organization, all of whose members enjoy the same rights. The democratic principle aims at guaranteeing to all an equal influence and an equal participation in the regulation of the common interests. All are electors, and all are eligible for office. The fundamental postulate of the *Déclaration des Droits de l'Homme* finds here its theoretical application. All the offices are filled by election. The officials, executive organs of the general will, play a merely subordinate part, are always dependent upon the collectivity, and can be deprived of their office at any moment. The mass of the party is omnipotent.

At the outset, the attempt is made to depart as little as possible from pure democracy by subordinating the delegates altogether to the will of the mass, by tying them hand and foot. In the early days of the movement of the Italian agricultural workers, the chief of the league required a majority of four-fifths of the votes to secure election. When disputes arose with the employers about wages, the representative of the organization, before undertaking any negotiations, had to be furnished with a written authority, authorized by the signature of every member of the corporation. All the accounts of the body were open to the examination of the members, at any time. There were two reasons for this. First of all, the desire was to avoid the spread of mistrust through the mass, "this poison which gradually destroys even the strongest organism." In the second place, this usage allowed each one of the members to learn bookkeeping, and to acquire such a general knowledge of the working of the corporation as to enable him at any time to take over its leadership. It is obvious that democracy in this sense is applicable only on a very small scale. In the infancy of the English labour movement, in many of the trade-unions, the delegates were either appointed in rotation from among all the members, or were chosen by lot. Gradually, however, the delegates' duties become more complicated; some individual ability becomes essential, a certain oratorical gift, and a considerable amount of objective knowledge. It thus becomes impossible to trust to blind chance, to the fortune of alphabetic succession, or to the order of priority, in the choice of a delegation whose members must possess certain peculiar personal aptitudes if they are to discharge their mission to the general advantage.

Such were the methods which prevailed in the early days of the labour movement to enable the masses to participate in party and trade-union administration. To-day they are falling into disuse, and in the development of the modern political aggregate there is a tendency to shorten and stereotype the process which transforms the led into a leader—a process which has hitherto developed by the natural course of events. Here and there voices make themselves heard demanding a sort of official consecration for the leaders, insisting that it is necessary to constitute a class of professional politicians, of approved and registered experts in political life. Ferdinand Tönnies advocates that the party should institute regular examinations for the nomination of socialist parliamentary candidates, and for the appointment of party secretaries. Heinrich Herkner goes even farther. He contends that the great trade-unions cannot long maintain their existence if they persist in entrusting the management of their affairs to persons drawn from the rank and file, who have risen to command stage by stage solely in consequence of practical aptitudes acquired in the service of the organization. He refers, in this connection, to the unions that are controlled by the employers, whose officials are for the most part university men. He foresees that in the near future all the labour organizations will be forced to abandon proletarian exclusiveness, and in the choice of their officials to give the preference to persons of an education that is superior alike in economic, legal, technical, and commercial respects.

Even to-day, the candidates for the secretaryship of a trade-union are subject to examination as to their knowledge of legal matters and their capacity as letter-writers. The socialist organizations engaged in political action also directly undertake the training of their own officials. Everywhere there are coming into existence "nurseries" for the rapid supply of officials possessing a certain amount of "scientific culture." Since 1906 there has existed in Berlin a Party-School in which courses of instruction are given for the training of those who wish to take office in the socialist party or in the trade-unions. The instructors are paid out of the funds of the socialist party, which was directly responsible for the foundation of the school. The other expenses of the undertaking, including the maintenance of the pupils, are furnished from a common fund supplied by the party and the various trade-unions interested. In addition, the families of the pupils, in so far as the attendance of these at the school deprives the families of their bread-winners, receive an allowance from the provincial branch of the party or from the local branch of the union to which each pupil belongs. The third course of this school, from October 1, 1908, to April 3, 1909, was attended by twenty-six pupils, while the first year there had been thirty-one and the second year thirty-three. As pupils, preference is given to comrades who already hold office in the party or in one of the labour unions. Those who do not already belong to the labour bureaucracy make it their aim to enter that body, and cherish the secret hope that attendance at the school will smooth their path. Those who fail to attain this end are apt to exhibit a certain discontent with the party which, after having encouraged their studies, has sent them back to manual labour. Among the 141 students of the year 1910-11, three classes were to be distinguished: one of these consisted of old and tried employees in the different branches of the labour movement (fifty-two persons); a second consisted of those who obtained employment in the party or the trade-unions directly the course was finished (forty-nine persons); the third consisted of those who had to return to manual labour (forty persons).

In Italy, L'Umanitaria, a philanthropic organization run by the socialists, founded at Milan in 1905 a "Practical School of Social Legislation," whose aim it is to give to a certain number of workers an education which will fit them for becoming factory inspectors, or for taking official positions in the various labour organizations, in the friendly societies, or in the labour exchanges. The course of instruction lasts for two years, and at its close the pupils receive, after examination, a diploma which entitles them to the title of "Labour Expert." In 1908 there were two hundred and two pupils, thirty-seven of whom were employees of trade unions or of co-operative societies, four were secretaries of labour exchanges, forty-five employees in or members of the liberal professions, and a hundred and twelve working men. At the outset most of the pupils came to the school as a matter of personal taste, or with the aim of obtaining the diploma in order to secure some comparatively lucrative private employment. But quite recently the governing body has determined to suppress the diploma, and to institute a supplementary course open to those only who are already employed by some labour organization or who definitely intend to enter such employment. For those engaged upon this special course of study there will be provided scholarships of £2 a week, the funds for this purpose being supplied in part by *L'Umanitaria* and in part by the labour organizations which wish to send their employees to the school. In the year 1909, under the auspices of the *Bourse du Travail,* there was founded at Turin a similar school (*Scuola Pratica di Cultura e Legislazione Sociale*), which, however, soon succumbed.

In England the trade-unions and co-operative societies make use of Ruskin College, Oxford, sending thither those of their members who aspire to office in the labour organizations, and who have displayed special aptitudes for this career. In Austria it is proposed to found a party school upon the German model.

It is undeniable that all these educational institutions for the officials of the party and of the labour organizations tend, above all, towards the artificial creation of an *élite* of the working-class, of a caste of cadets composed of persons who aspire to the command of the proletarian rank and file. Without wishing it, there is thus effected a continuous enlargement of the gulf which divides the leaders from the masses.

The technical specialization that inevitably results from all extensive organization renders necessary what is called expert leadership. Consequently the power of determination comes to be considered one of the specific attributes of leadership, and is gradually withdrawn from the masses to be concentrated in the hands of the leaders alone.* Thus the leaders, who were at first no more than the executive organs of the

* "In intimate connection with these theoretical tendencies, there results a change in the relationship between the leaders and the mass. For the comradely leadership of local committees with all its undeniable defects there is substituted the professional leadership of the trade-union officials. Initiative and capacity for decision thus become what may be called a professional speciality, whilst for the rank and file is left the passive virtue of discipline. There can be no doubt that this seamy side of officialism involves serious dangers for the party. The latest innovation in this direction, in the German social democratic party, is the appointment of salaried secretaries to the local branches. Unless the rank and file of the party keep very much on the alert, unless they are careful that these secretaries shall be restricted to purely executive functions,

collective will, soon emancipate themselves from the mass and become independent of its control.

Organization implies the tendency to oligarchy. In every organization, whether it be a political party, a professional union, or any other association of the kind, the aristocratic tendency manifests itself very clearly. The mechanism of the organization, while conferring a solidity of structure, induces serious changes in the organized mass, completely inverting the respective position of the leaders and the led. As a result of organization, every party or professional union becomes divided into a minority of directors and a majority of directed.

It has been remarked that in the lower stages of civilization tyranny is dominant. Democracy cannot come into existence until there is attained a subsequent and more highly developed stage of social life. Freedoms and privileges, and among these latter the privilege of taking part in the direction of public affairs, are at first restricted to the few. Recent times have been characterized by the gradual extension of these privileges to a widening circle. This is what we know as the era of democracy. But if we pass from the sphere of the state to the sphere of party, we may observe that as democracy continues to develop, a backwash sets in. With the advance of organization, democracy tends to decline. Democratic evolution has a parabolic course. At the present time, at any rate as far as party life is concerned, democracy is in the descending phase. It may be enunciated as a general rule that the increase in the power of the leaders is directly proportional with the extension of the organization. In the various parties and labour organizations of different countries the influence of the leaders is mainly determined (apart from racial and individual grounds) by the varying development of organization. Where organization is stronger, we find that there is lesser degree of applied democracy.

Every solidly constructed organization, whether it be a democratic state, a political party, or a league of proletarians for the resistance of

---

the secretaries will come to be regarded as the natural and sole depositaries of all power of initiative, and as the exclusive leaders of local party life. In the socialist party, however, by the nature of things, by the very character of the political struggle, narrower limits are imposed upon bureaucracy than in the case of the trade-unions. In these latter, the technical specialization of the wage-struggle (the need, for example, for the drafting of complicated sliding scales and the like) often leads the chiefs to deny that the mass of organized workers can possess "a general view of the economic life of the country as a whole," and to deny, therefore, their capacity of judgment in such matters. The most typical outcome of this conception is afforded by the argument with which the leaders are accustomed to forbid all theoretical criticism of the prospects and possibilities of practical trade-unionism, asserting that such criticism involves a danger for the spirit of organization. This reasoning starts from the assumption that the workers can be won for organization and can be induced to remain faithful to their trade-unions only by a blind and artless belief in the saving efficacy of the trade-union struggle" (Rosa Luxemburg, *Massenstreik, Partei u. Gewerkschaften,* Erdmann Dubber, Hamburg, 1906, p. 61).

economic oppression, presents a soil eminently favourable for the differentiation of organs and of functions. The more extended and the more ramified the official apparatus of the organization, the greater the number of its members, the fuller its treasury, and the more widely circulated its press, the less efficient becomes the direct control exercised by the rank and file, and the more is this control replaced by the increasing power of committees. Into all parties there insinuates itself that indirect electoral system which in public life the democratic parties fight against with all possible vigour. Yet in party life the influence of this system must be more disastrous than in the far more extensive life of the state. Even in the party congresses, which represent the party-life seven times sifted, we find that it becomes more and more general to refer all important questions to committees which debate in camera.

As organization develops, not only do the tasks of the administration become more difficult and more complicated, but, further, its duties become enlarged and specialized to such a degree that it is no longer possible to take them all in at a single glance. In a rapidly progressive movement, it is not only the growth in the number of duties, but also the higher quality of these, which imposes a more extensive differentiation of function. Nominally, and according to the letter of the rules, all the acts of the leaders are subject to the ever vigilant criticism of the rank and file. In theory the leader is merely an employee bound by the instructions he receives. He has to carry out the orders of the mass, of which he is no more than the executive organ. But in actual fact, as the organization increases in size, this control becomes purely fictitious. The members have to give up the idea of themselves conducting or even supervising the whole administration, and are compelled to hand these tasks over to trustworthy persons specially nominated for the purpose, to salaried officials. The rank and file must content themselves with summary reports, and with the appointment of occasional special committees of inquiry. Yet this does not derive from any special change in the rules of the organization. It is by very necessity that a simple employee gradually becomes a "leader," acquiring a freedom of action which he ought not to possess. The chief then becomes accustomed to despatch important business on his own responsibility, and to decide various questions relating to the life of the party without any attempt to consult the rank and file. It is obvious that democratic control thus undergoes a progressive diminution, and is ultimately reduced to an infinitesimal minimum. In all the socialist parties there is a continual increase in the number of functions withdrawn from the electoral assemblies and transferred to the executive committees. In this way there is constructed a powerful and complicated edifice. The principle of division of labour coming more and more into operation, executive authority undergoes division and subdivision. There is thus constituted a rigorously defined and hierarchical bureaucracy. In the

catechism of party duties, the strict observance of hierarchical rules becomes the first article. This hierarchy comes into existence as the outcome
of technical conditions, and its constitution is an essential postulate of
the regular functioning of the party machine.

It is indisputable that the oligarchical and bureaucratic tendency of
party organization is a matter of technical and practical necessity. It is
the inevitable product of the very principle of organization. Not even the
most radical wing of the various socialist parties raises any objection to
this retrogressive evolution, the contention being that democracy is only a
form of organization and that where it ceases to be possible to harmonize
democracy with organization, it is better to abandon the former than the
latter. Organization, since it is the only means of attaining the ends of
socialism, is considered to comprise within itself the revolutionary content
of the party, and this essential content must never be sacrificed for the
sake of form.

In all times, in all phases of development, in all branches of human
activity, there have been leaders. It is true that certain socialists, above
all the orthodox Marxists of Germany, seek to convince us that socialism
knows nothing of "leaders," that the party has "employees" merely, being a
democratic party, and the existence of leaders being incompatible with
democracy. But a false assertion such as this cannot override a sociological
law. Its only result is, in fact, to strengthen the rule of the leaders, for it
serves to conceal from the mass a danger which really threatens democracy.

For technical and administrative reasons, no less than for tactical
reasons, a strong organization needs an equally strong leadership. As long
as an organization is loosely constructed and vague in its outlines, no
professional leadership can arise. The anarchists, who have a horror of all
fixed organization, have no regular leaders. In the early days of German
socialism, the *Vertrauensmann* (homme de confiance) continued to exercise his ordinary occupation. If he received any pay for his work for
the party, the remuneration was on an extremely modest scale, and was no
more than a temporary grant. His function could never be regarded by
him as a regular source of income. The employee of the organization was
still a simple workmate, sharing the mode of life and the social condition
of his fellows. To-day he has been replaced for the most part by the
professional politician, *Berzirksleiter* (U.S. ward-boss), etc. The more
solid the structure of an organization becomes in the course of the evolution of the modern political party, the more marked becomes the tendency
to replace the emergency leader by the professional leader. Every party
organization which has attained to a considerable degree of complication
demands that there should be a certain number of persons who devote
all their activities to the work of the party. The mass provides these by

delegation, and the delegates, regularly appointed, become permanent representatives of the mass for the direction of its affairs.

To enable us to understand and properly to appreciate the superiority of the leaders over the mass it is necessary to turn our attention to the characteristics of the rank and file. The question arises, what are these masses?

It has already been shown that a general sentiment of indifference towards the management of its own affairs is natural to the crowd, even when organized to form political parties.

The very composition of the mass is such as to render it unable to resist the power of an order of leaders aware of its own strength. An analysis of the German trade unions in respect of the age of their members gives a sufficiently faithful picture of the composition also of the various socialist parties. The great majority of the membership ranges in age from 25 to 39 years. Quite young men find other ways of employing their leisure; they are heedless, their thoughts run in erotic channels, they are always hoping that some miracle will deliver them from the need of passing their whole lives as simple wage-earners, and for these reasons they are slow to join a trade union. The men over forty, weary and disillusioned, commonly resign their membership (unless retained in the union by purely personal interest, to secure out-of-work pay, insurance against illness, and the like). Consequently there is lacking in the organization the force of control of ardent and irreverent youth and also that of experienced maturity. In other words, the leaders have to do with a mass of members to whom they are superior in respect of age and experience of life, whilst they have nothing to fear from the relentless criticism which is so peculiarly characteristic of men who have just attained to virility.

Another important consideration as to the composition of the rank and file who have to be led is its fluctuating character. It seems, at any rate, that this may be deduced from a report of the socialist section of Munich for the year 1906. It contains statistics, showing analytically the individual duration of membership. . . .

The fluctuating character of the membership is manifest in even greater degree in the German trade unions. This has given rise to the saying that a trade union is like a pigeon-house where the pigeons enter and leave at their caprice. The German Metalworkers' Federation (Deutscher Metallarbeiterverband) had, during the years 1906 to 1908, 210,561 new members. But the percentage of withdrawals increased in 1906 to 60, in 1907 to 83, and in 1908 to 100. This shows us that the bonds connecting the bulk of the masses to their organization are extremely slender, and that it is only a small proportion of the organized workers who feel themselves really at one with their unions. Hence the leaders, when compared with the masses, whose composition varies from moment to moment, constitute a more stable and more constant element of the organized membership.

II. The Conservative Basis of Organization

At this point in our inquiry two decisive questions present themselves. One of these is whether the oligarchical disease of the democratic parties is incurable. This will be considered in the next chapter. The other question may be formulated in the following terms. Is it impossible for a democratic party to practise a democratic policy, for a revolutionary party to pursue a revolutionary policy? Must we say that not *socialism* alone, but even a socialistic *policy*, is utopian? The present chapter will attempt a brief answer to this inquiry.

Within certain narrow limits, the democratic party, even when subjected to oligarchical control, can doubtless act upon the state in the democratic sense.* The old political caste of society, and above all the "state" itself, are forced to undertake the revaluation of a considerable number of values—a revaluation both ideal and practical. The importance attributed to the masses increases, even when the leaders are demagogues. The legislature and the executive become accustomed to yield, not only to claims proceeding from above, but also to those proceeding from below. This may give rise, in practice, to great inconveniences, such as we recognize in the recent history of all the states under a parliamentary regime; in theory, however, this new order of things signifies an incalculable progress in respect of public rights, which thus come to conform better with the principles of social justice. This evolution will, however, be arrested from the moment when the governing classes succeed in attracting within the governmental orbit their enemies of the extreme left, in order to convert them into collaborators. Political organization leads to power. But power is always conservative. In any case, the influence exercised upon the governmental machine by an energetic opposition party is necessarily slow, is subject to frequent interruptions, and is always restricted by the nature of oligarchy.

The recognition of this consideration does not exhaust our problem, for we have further to examine whether the oligarchical nature of organization be not responsible for the creation of the external manifestations of oligarchical activity, whether it be not responsible for the production of an oligarchical policy. The analysis here made shows clearly that the internal policy of the party organizations is to-day absolutely conservative, or is on the way to become such. Yet it might happen that the external

* Especially where there exists universal, equal, and direct suffrage, and where the working-class is strongly organized and is awake to its own interests. (Cf. Franco Savorgnan, *Soziologische Fragmente*, Wagner, Innsbruck, 1909, p. 105). In this case the leaders have every interest in exercising upon the state all the pressure they can to render it more democratic.

policy of these conservative organisms would be bold and revolutionary; that the anti-democratic centralization of power in the hands of a few leaders is no more than a tactical method adopted to effect the speedier overthrow of the adversary; that the oligarchs fulfil the purely provisional function of educating the masses for the revolution, and that organization is after all no more than a means employed in the service of an amplified Blanquist conception.

This development would conflict with the nature of party, with the endeavour to organize the masses upon the vastest scale imaginable. As the organization increases in size, the struggle for great principles becomes impossible. It may be noticed that in the democratic parties of to-day the great conflicts of view are fought out to an ever-diminishing extent in the field of ideas and with the weapons of pure theory, that they therefore degenerate more and more into personal struggles and invectives, to be settled finally upon considerations of a purely superficial character. The efforts made to cover internal dissensions with a pious veil are the inevitable outcome of organization based upon bureaucratic principles, for, since the chief aim of such an organization is to enrol the greatest possible number of members, every struggle on behalf of ideas within the limits of the organization is necessarily regarded as an obstacle to the realization of its ends, an obstacle, therefore, which must be avoided in every possible way. This tendency is reinforced by the parliamentary character of the political party. "Party organization" signifies the aspiration for the greatest number of members. "Parliamentarism" signifies the aspiration for the greatest number of votes. The principal fields of party activity are electoral agitation and direct agitation to secure new members. What, in fact, is the modern political party? It is the methodical organization of the electoral masses. The socialist party, as a political aggregate endeavouring simultaneously to recruit members and to recruit votes, finds here its vital interests, for every decline in membership and every loss in voting strength diminishes its political prestige. Consequently great respect must be paid, not only to new members, but also to possible adherents, to those who in Germany are termed *mitläufer*, in Italy *simpatizzanti*, in Holland *geestverwanten*, and in England *sympathizers*. To avoid alarming these individuals, who are still outside the ideal worlds of socialism or democracy, the pursuit of a policy based on strict principle is shunned, while the consideration is ignored whether the numerical increase of the organization thus effected is not likely to be gained at the expense of its quality.

The last link in the long chain of phenomena which confer a profoundly conservative character upon the intimate essence of the political party (even upon that party which boasts itself revolutionary) is found in the relationships between party and state. Generated to overthrow the centralized power of the state, starting from the idea that the working

class need merely secure a sufficiently vast and solid organization in order
to triumph over the organization of the state, the party of the workers
has ended by acquiring a vigorous centralization of its own, based upon
the same cardinal principles of authority and discipline which characterize the organization of the state.* It thus becomes a governmental
party, that is to say, a party which, organized itself like a government
on the small scale, hopes some day to assume the reins of government
upon the large scale. The revolutionary political party is a state within
the state, pursuing the avowed aim of destroying the existing state in
order to substitute for it a social order of a fundamentally different character.** To attain this essentially political end, the party avails itself of
the socialist organization, whose sole justification is found precisely in its

* Albert Schäffle believes that socialism needs merely to produce a great general
at the right moment in order to inherit the power of the centralized military organization (Schäffle, *Quintessenz des Sozialismus*, Perthes, Gotha, 1879, 7th ed., p. 68).
** Devoting all its energies to the imitation of the outward apparatus of power
characteristic of the "class-state," the socialist party allots no more than a secondary
importance to psychological enfranchisement from the mentality which dominates this
same class-state. This neglect of the psychical factor is disastrous to the democratic
principle, especially in so far as it springs from psychological sources. Raphael Friedeberg, who finds fault with historical materialism because it "starts from the monstrous
error that the mode of production of material life is the sole cause of all sociological
happenings," because it leads to the atrophy of all spiritual faculties, and consequently
to the decay of socialist thought, has opposed this doctrine by that which he calls the
doctrine of historical psychism, namely, "the psychical enfranchisement of the proletariat from all the intrinsic conditions of class dominion" (see his preface to the
German edition of Gustave Hervé's work, *Leur Patrie* [*Das Vaterland der Reichen*],
Zurich, 1907, p. vii). But Friedeberg's charge against historical materialism is un-
sound, for the following reason. This doctrine, based upon the idea of class, teaches
the masses of the workers that just as they exist in a state of economic antagonism to
the dominant class, so also their spiritual and psychical life (the "superstructure") is
(or at least ought to be) in irreconcilable conflict with the spiritual and psychic life
of the bourgeoisie. Another argument against historical materialism is adduced elsewhere by Friedeberg. It conflicts, he says, with the class struggle, which depends
upon the fact that those who are removed from the mental environment of their
material sphere of production become psychical *déclassés*. He goes so far as to maintain that the more independent the human brain becomes, the more manifest is the
fallacy of Marxism (R. Friedeberg, *Historische Materialismus und Klassenkampf*,
"Polis," a review published at Zurich, 1907, i, No. 5). But this reasoning is erroneous,
for in the class situation of the proletariat, a situation clearly recognized by Marxism,
there exist all the elements which combine to make the proletariat the natural enemy
(in the intellectual sphere) of the bourgeoisie, and thus lead to the "class struggle."
Ideologically to remove the members of the working class from the world of their
material sphere of production could not mean anything else than to impose upon them
an essentially strange mentality, to *embourgeoiser* them. In actual fact this process
occurs to-day upon a large scale, not in consequence, however, of historical materialism, but in opposition to it, being due above all to the suggestive influence exercised
upon the masses by leaders who have themselves become *embourgeoisés*. It is true
that the process of embourgeoisement can itself be explained in conformity with the
doctrine of historical materialism, on the ground that it depends upon the changed
mode of life and changed position in life of the leaders, upon the organization that is
necessary for the conduct of the class struggle, and upon the consequences inherent in
this organization which have been studied in the text.

patient but systematic preparation for the destruction of the organization of the state in its existing form. The subversive party organizes the *framework* of the social revolution. For this reason it continually endeavours to strengthen its positions, to extend its bureaucratic mechanism, to store up its energies and its funds.

Every new official, every new secretary, engaged by the party is in theory a new agent of the revolution; in the same way every new section is a new battalion; and every additional thousand francs furnished by the members' subscriptions, by the profits of the socialist press, or by the generous donations of sympathetic benefactors, constitute fresh additions to the war-chest for the struggle against the enemy. In the long run, however, the directors of this revolutionary body existing within the authoritarian state, sustained by the same means as that state and inspired by the like spirit of discipline, cannot fail to perceive that the party organization, whatever advances it may make in the future, will never succeed in becoming more than an ineffective and miniature copy of the state organization. For this reason, in all ordinary circumstances, and as far as prevision is humanly possible, every attempt of the party to measure its forces with those of its antagonists is foredoomed to disastrous failure. The logical consequence of these considerations is in direct conflict with the hopes entertained by the founders of the party. Instead of gaining revolutionary energy as the force and solidity of its structure has increased, the precise opposite has occurred; there has resulted, *pari passu* with its growth, a continued increase in the prudence, the timidity even, which inspires its policy. The party, continually threatened by the state upon which its existence depends, carefully avoids (once it has attained to maturity) everything which might irritate the state to excess. The party doctrines are, whenever requisite, attenuated and deformed in accordance with the external needs of the organization.* Organization

* A classical example of the extent to which the fear of injuring the socialist organization will lead even the finest intelligences of the party to play tricks with socialist theory is afforded by the history of that celebrated preface which in 1895 Frederick Engels wrote for a posthumous edition of Marx's book, *Die Klassenkämpfe in Frankreich, 1848-9*. This preface became the subject of great international discussions, and has been justly considered as the first vigorous manifestation of reformism in German socialism. For Engels here declares that socialist tactics will have more success through the use of legal than of illegal and revolutionary means, and thus expressly repudiates the Marxist conception of the socialist revolution. It was not till some years later that Kautsky published a letter from Engels in which the latter disavowed his preface, saying: "My text had to suffer from the timid legalism of our friends in Berlin, who dreaded a second edition of the anti-socialist laws—a dread to which I was forced to pay attention at the existing political juncture" (Karl Kautsky, *Der Weg zur Macht*, Buchhandlung "Vorwärts," 1909, p. 42). From this it would appear that the theory (at that time brand-new) that socialism could attain to its ends by parliamentary methods—and this was the quintessence of Engels' preface—came into existence from a fear lest the socialist party organization (which should be a means, and not an end in itself) might suffer at the hands of the state. Thus Engels was fêted, on the one hand, as a man of sound judgment and one willing to look facts in the face

becomes the vital essence of the party. During the first years of its existence, the party did not fail to make a parade of its revolutionary character, not only in respect of its ultimate ends, but also in respect of the means employed for their attainment—although not always in love with these means. But as soon as it attained to political maturity, the party did not hesitate to modify its original profession of faith and to affirm itself revolutionary only "in the best sense of the word," that is to say, no longer on lines which interest the police, but only in theory and on paper.* This same party, which at one time did not hesitate, when the triumphant guns of the bourgeois governors of Paris were still smoking, to proclaim with enthusiasm its solidarity with the communards, now announces to the whole world that it repudiates anti-militarist propaganda in any form which may bring its adherents into conflict with the penal code, and that it will not assume any responsibility for the consequences that may result from such a conflict. A sense of responsibility is suddenly becoming active in the socialist party. Consequently it reacts with all the authority at its disposal against the revolutionary currents which exist within its own organization, and which it has hitherto regarded with an indulgent eye. In the name of the grave responsibilities attaching to its position it now disavows anti-militarism, repudiates the general strike, and denies all the logical audacities of its past.

The history of the international labour movement furnishes innumerable examples of the manner in which the party becomes increasingly inert as the strength of its organization grows; it loses its revolutionary impetus, becomes sluggish, not in respect of action alone, but also in the sphere of thought.** More and more tenaciously does the party cling to

---

(cf. W. Sombart, *Friedrich Engels, Ein Blatt zur Entwicklungsgeschichte des Sozialismus,* Separat-Abdruck der "Zukunft," Berlin, 1895, p. 32), and was attacked, on the other hand, as a pacifist utopist (cf. Arturo Labriola, *Riforme e Rivoluzione sociale,* ed. cit., pp. 181 and 224); whereas in reality Engels would seem to have been the victim of an opportunist sacrifice of principles to the needs of organization, a sacrifice made for love of the party and in opposition to his own theoretical convictions.

* Maximilian Harden is not far wrong when he compares the revolutionary parties in their attitude towards the state authorities to a cock which is as it were glued to its place because a chalk-line has been drawn in front of its beak, a line which to the bird represents an insuperable obstacle.

** In this connection it may be observed that the intellectual decadence of the socialist party, and its incapacity for producing men of talent, or at least for attracting such men to its ranks, are often demonstrated by critics who dwell upon the contrast between the present and the past. Ludwig Stein writes (*Die soziale Frage, im Lichte der Philosophie,* Encke, Stuttgart, 1897, p. 438): "The intellectual growth of the socialist party is in inverse ratio to its geographical extension. What an intellectual vacuum has existed since the death of Engels. Millions of votes, but not a single man. A vast number of respectabilities, but not one leading intelligence. The columns of the 'Neue Zeit' are largely filled with matter which is nothing better than an insipid Alexandrianism." A similar opinion by Sombart has been previously quoted (cf. p. 63, note 2).—There is at least this amount of truth in such accusations, that everywhere in the socialist parties the new generation is weakly and intellectually insignificant.

what it calls the "ancient and glorious tactics," the tactics which have led to a continued increase in membership. More and more invincible becomes its aversion to all aggressive action.

The dread of the reaction by which the socialist party is haunted paralyses all its activities, renders impossible all manifestation of force, and deprives it of all energy for the daily struggle. It attempts to justify its misoneism by the false pretence that it must reserve its strength for the final struggle. Thus we find that the conservative tendencies inherent in all forms of possession manifest themselves also in the socialist party. For half a century the socialists have been working in the sweat of their brow to create a model organization. Now, when three million workers have been organized—a greater number than was supposed necessary to secure complete victory over the enemy—the party is endowed with a bureaucracy which, in respect of its consciousness of its duties, its zeal, and its submission to the hierarchy, rivals that of the state itself; the treasuries are full; a complex ramification of financial and moral interests extends all over the country. A bold and enterprising tactic would endanger all this: the work of many decades, the social existence of thousands of leaders and sub-leaders, the entire party, would be compromised. For these reasons the idea of such a tactic becomes more and more distasteful. It conflicts equally with an unjustified sentimentalism and a justified egoism. It is opposed by the artist's love of the work he has created with so much labour, and also by the personal interest of thousands of honest bread-winners whose economic life is so intimately associated with the life of the party and who tremble at the thought of losing their employment and the consequences they would have to endure if the government should proceed to dissolve the party, as might readily happen in case of war.

Thus, from a means, organization becomes an end. To the institutions and qualities which at the outset were destined simply to ensure the good working of the party machine (subordination, the harmonious co-operation of individual members, hierarchical relationships, discretion, propriety of conduct), a greater importance comes ultimately to be attached than to the productivity of the machine. Henceforward the sole preoccupation is to avoid anything which may clog the machinery. Should the party be attacked, it will abandon valuable positions previously conquered, and will renounce ancient rights rather than reply to the enemy's offensive by methods which might "compromise" its position. Naumann writes sarcastically: "The war-cry 'Proletarians of all countries unite!' has had its due effect. The forces of the organized proletariat have gained a strength which no one believed possible when that war-cry was first sounded. There is money in the treasuries. Is the signal for the final assault never to be given? . . . Is the work of preliminary organization to go on for ever?" As the party's need for tranquillity increases, its revolutionary talons atrophy. We have now a finely conservative party which (since the effect survives the cause) continues to employ revolutionary terminology, but which in actual practice fulfils no other function than that of a constitutional opposition.

All this has deviated far from the ideas of Karl Marx, who, were he still alive, ought to be the first to revolt against such a degeneration of Marxism. Yet it is quite possible that, carried away by the spectacle of an army of three million men acting in his name, swearing on solemn occasions *in verba magistri*, he also would find nothing to say in reprobation of so grave a betrayal of his own principles. There were incidents in Marx's life which render such a view possible. He certainly knew how to close his eyes, in public at any rate, to the serious faults committed by the German social democracy in 1876.

III. The Iron Law

The Marxist theory of the state, when conjoined with a faith in the revolutionary energy of the working class and in the democratic effects of the socialization of the means of production, leads logically to the idea of a new social order which to the school of Mosca appears utopian. According to the Marxists the capitalist mode of production transforms the great majority of the population into proletarians, and thus digs its own grave. As soon as it has attained maturity, the proletariat will seize political power, and will immediately transform private property into state property. "In this way it will eliminate itself, for it will thus put an end to all social differences, and consequently to all class antagonisms. In other words, the proletariat will annul the state, *qua* state. Capitalist society, divided into classes, has need of the state as an organization of the ruling class, whose purpose it is to maintain the capitalist system of production in its own interest and in order to effect the continued exploitation of the proletariat. Thus to put an end to the state is synonymous with putting an end to the existence of the dominant class." But the new collectivist society, the society without classes, which is to be established upon the ruins of the ancient state, will also need elective elements. It may be said that by the adoption of the preventive rules formulated by Rousseau in the *Contrat Sociale,* and subsequently reproduced by the French revolutionists in the *Déclaration des Droits de l'Homme,* above all by the strict application of the principle that all offices are to be held on a revocable tenure, the activity of these representatives may be confined within rigid limits. It is none the less true that social wealth cannot be satisfactorily administered in any other manner than by the creation of an extensive bureaucracy. In this way we are led by an inevitable logic to the flat denial of the possibility of a state without classes. The administration of an immeasurably large capital, above all when this capital is collective property, confers upon the administrator influence at least equal to that possessed by the private owner of capital. Consequently the critics in advance of the Marxist social order ask whether the instinct which to-day leads the members of the possessing classes to transmit to their children the wealth which they (the parents) have amassed, will not exist also in the administrators of the public wealth of the socialist state, and whether these administrators will not utilize their immense influence in order to secure for their children the succession to the offices which they themselves hold.

The constitution of a new dominant minority would, in addition, be especially facilitated by the manner in which, according to the Marxist conception of the revolution, the social transformation is to be effected. Marx held that the period between the destruction of capitalist society and the establishment of communist society would be bridged by a period of revolutionary transition in the economic field, to which would correspond a period of political transition, "when the state could not be anything other than the revolutionary dictatorship of the proletariat." To put the matter less euphemistically, there will then exist a dictatorship in the hands of those leaders who have been sufficiently astute and sufficiently powerful to grasp the sceptre of dominion in the name of socialism, and to wrest it from the hands of the expiring bourgeois society.

A revolutionary dictatorship was also foreshadowed in the minimum programme of Mazzini's republican party, and this led to a rupture between Young Italy and the socialist elements of the carbonari. Filippo Buonarroti, the Florentine, friend and biographer of Gracchus Babeuf, a man who at one time played a heroic part in the French Revolution, and who had had opportunities for direct observation of the way in which the victorious revolutionists maintained inequality and endeavoured to found a new aristocracy, resisted with all his might the plan of concentrating the power of the carbonari in the hands of a single individual. Among the theoretical reasons he alleged against this concentration, the principal was that individual dictatorship was merely a stage on the way to monarchy. To Mazzini and his friends, Buonarroti objected that all the political changes they had in view were purely formal in character, aiming simply at the gratification of personal needs, and above all at the acquirement and exercise of unrestricted authority. For this reason Buonarroti opposed the armed rising organized by Mazzini in 1833, issuing a secret decree in which he forbade his comrades of the carbonari to give any assistance to the insurgents, whose triumph, he said, could not fail to give rise to the creation of a new ambitious aristocracy. "The ideal republic of Mazzini," he wrote, "differs from monarchy in this respect alone, that it possesses a dignity the less and an elective post the more."

There is little difference, as far as practical results are concerned, be-

tween individual dictatorship and the dictatorship of a group of oligarchs.
Now it is manifest that the concept *dictatorship* is the direct antithesis of
the concept *democracy*. The attempt to make dictatorship serve the ends
of democracy is tantamount to the endeavour to utilize war as the most
efficient means for the defence of peace, or to employ alcohol in the
struggle against alcoholism. It is extremely probable that a social group
which had secured control of the instruments of collective power would
do all that was possible to retain that control. Theophrastus noted long
ago that the strongest desire of men who have attained to leadership in a
popularly governed state is not so much the acquirement of personal
wealth as the gradual establishment of their own sovereignty at the expense of popular sovereignty. The danger is imminent lest the social
revolution should replace the visible and tangible dominant classes which
now exist and act openly, by a clandestine demagogic oligarchy, pursuing
its ends under the cloak of equality.

The Marxist economic doctrine and the Marxist philosophy of history
cannot fail to exercise a great attraction upon thinkers. But the defects
of Marxism are patent directly we enter the practical domains of administration and public law, without speaking of errors in the psychological field and even in more elementary spheres. Wherever socialist theory
has endeavoured to furnish guarantees for personal liberty, it has in the
end either lapsed into the cloudland of individualist anarchism, or else
has made proposals which (doubtless in opposition to the excellent intentions of their authors) could not fail to enslave the individual to the
mass. Here is an example: to ensure that the literature of socialist society
shall be elevated and moral, and to exclude *a priori* all licentious books,
August Bebel proposed the nomination of a committee of experts to
decide what might and what might not be printed. To obviate all danger
of injustice and to secure freedom of thought and expression, Bebel added
that every author must have the right of appeal to the collectivity. It is
hardly necessary to point out the impracticability of this proposal, which
is in effect that the books, however large, regarding which an appeal is
made, must be printed by the million and distributed to the public in
order that the public may decide whether they are or are not fit for
publication!

The problem of socialism is not merely a problem in economics. In
other words, socialism does not seek merely to determine to what extent
it is possible to realize a distribution of wealth which shall be at once
just and economically productive. Socialism is also an administrative problem, a problem of democracy, and this not in the technical and administrative sphere alone, but also in the sphere of psychology. In the individualist
problem is found the most difficult of all that complex of questions which
socialism seeks to answer. Rudolf Goldscheid, who aims at a renascence of
the socialist movement by the strengthening of the more energetic ele-

ments in that movement, rightly draws attention to a danger which socialism incurs, however brilliantly it may handle the problems of economic organization. If socialism, he says, fails to study the problem of individual rights, individual knowledge, and individual will, it will suffer shipwreck from a defective understanding of the significance of the problem of freedom for the higher evolution of our species—will suffer shipwreck no less disastrous than that of earlier conceptions of world reform which, blinded by the general splendour of their vision, have ignored the individual light-sources which combine to produce that splendour.

The youthful German labour party had hardly succeeded in detaching itself, at the cost of severe struggles, from the bourgeois democracy, when one of its sincerest friends drew attention to certain urgent dangers. In an open letter to the Leipzig committee of the Allgemeine Deutsche Arbeiterverein, Rodbertus wrote: "You are separating yourselves from a political party because, as you rightly believe, this political party does not adequately represent your social interests. But you are doing this in order to found a new political party. Who will furnish you with guarantees against the danger that in this new party the adversaries of your class (*die antisozialen Elemente*) may some day gain the upper hand?" In this observation Rodbertus touches the very essence of the political party. An analysis of the elements which enter into the composition of a party will show the perfect justice of his criticism. A party is neither a social unity nor an economic unity. It is based upon its programme. In theory this programme may be the expression of the interests of a particular class. In practice, however, anyone may join a party, whether his interests coincide or not with the principles enunciated in the party programme. The socialist party, for example, is the ideological representative of the proletariat. This, however, does not make it a class organism. From the social point of view it is a mixture of classes, being composed of elements fulfilling diverse functions in the economic process. But since the programme has a class origin, an ostensible social unity is thereby conferred upon the party. All socialists as such, whatever their economic position in private life, admit in theory the absolute pre-eminence of one great class, the proletariat. Those non-proletarians affiliated to the party, and those who are but partial proletarians, "adopt the outlook of the working class, and recognize this class as predominant." It is tacitly presupposed that those members of a party who do not belong to the class which that party represents will renounce their personal interests whenever these conflict with the interests of the proletarian class. On principle, the heterogeneous elements will subordinate themselves to the "idea" of a class to which they themselves do not belong. So much for theory. In practice, the acceptance of the programme does not suffice to abolish the conflict of interests between capital and labour. Among the members belonging to higher social strata who have made their adhesion to the political organization of the working class, there will be some who will, when the occasion demands it, know how to sacrifice themselves, who will be able to unclass themselves. The majority of such persons, however, notwithstanding their outward community of ideas with the proletariat, will continue to pursue economic interests opposed to those of the proletariat. There is, in fact, a conflict of interests, and the decision in this conflict will be determined by the relationship which the respective interests bear towards the principal necessities of life. Consequently it is by no means impossible that an economic conflict may arise between the bourgeois members and the proletarian members of the party, and that as this conflict extends it will culminate in political dissensions. Economic antagonism stifles the ideological superstructure. The programme then becomes a dead letter, and beneath the banner of "socialism" and within the bosom of the party, a veritable class struggle goes on. We learn from actual experience that in their conduct towards persons in their employ the bourgeois socialists do not always subordinate personal interests to those of their adoptive class. When the party includes among its members the owners of factories and workshops, it may be noticed that these, notwithstanding personal goodwill and notwithstanding the pressure which is exercised on them by the party, have the same economic conflict with their employees as have those employers whose convictions harmonize with their economic status, and who think not as socialists but as bourgeois.

But there exists yet another danger. The leadership of the socialist party may fall into the hands of persons whose practical tendencies are in opposition with the programme of the working class, so that the labour movement will be utilized for the service of interests diametrically opposed to those of the proletariat. This danger is especially great in countries where the working-class party cannot dispense with the aid and guidance of capitalists who are not economically dependent upon the party; it is least conspicuous where the party has no need of such elements, or can at any rate avoid admitting them to leadership.

When the leaders, whether derived from the bourgeoisie or from the working class, are attached to the party organism as employees, their economic interest coincides as a rule with the interest of the party. This, however, serves to eliminate only one aspect of the danger. Another aspect, graver because more general, depends upon the opposition which inevitably arises between the leaders and the rank and file as the party grows in strength.

The party, regarded as an entity, as a piece of mechanism, is not necessarily identifiable with the totality of its members, and still less so with the class to which these belong. The party is created as a means to secure an end. Having, however, become an end in itself, endowed with aims and interests of its own, it undergoes detachment, from the teleological point of view, from the class which it represents. In a party, it is far from obvious that the interests of the masses which have combined to form the party will coincide with the interests of the bureaucracy in which the party becomes personified. The interests of the body of employees are always conservative, and in a given political situation these interests may dictate a defensive and even a reactionary policy when the interests of the working class demand a bold and aggressive policy; in other cases, although these are very rare, the rôles may be reversed. By a universally applicable social law, every organ of the collectivity, brought into existence through the need for the division of labour, creates for itself, as soon as it becomes consolidated, interests peculiar to itself. The existence of these special interests involves a necessary conflict with the interests of the collectivity. Nay, more, social strata fulfilling peculiar functions tend to become isolated, to produce organs fitted for the defence of their own peculiar interests. In the long run they tend to undergo transformation into distinct classes.

The sociological phenomena whose general characteristics have been discussed in this chapter and in preceding ones offer numerous vulnerable points to the scientific opponents of democracy. These phenomena would seem to prove beyond dispute that society cannot exist without a "dominant" or "political" class, and that the ruling class, whilst its elements are subject to a frequent partial renewal, nevertheless constitutes the only factor of sufficiently durable efficacy in the history of human development. According to this view, the government, or, if the phrase be preferred, the state, cannot be anything other than the organization of a minority. It is the aim of this minority to impose upon the rest of society a "legal order," which is the outcome of the exigencies of dominion and of the exploitation of the mass of helots effected by the ruling minority, and can never be truly representative of the majority. The majority is thus permanently incapable of self-government. Even when the discontent of the masses culminates in a successful attempt to deprive the bourgeoisie of power, this is after all, so Mosca contends, effected only in appearance; always and necessarily there springs from the masses a new organized minority which raises itself to the rank of a governing class. Thus the majority of human beings, in a condition of eternal tutelage, are predestined by tragic necessity to submit to the dominion of a small minority, and must be content to constitute the pedestal of an oligarchy.

The principle that one dominant class inevitably succeeds to another, and the law deduced from that principle that oligarchy is, as it were, a preordained form of the common life of great social aggregates, far from conflicting with or replacing the materialist conception of history, completes that conception and reinforces it. There is no essential contradiction between the doctrine that history is the record of a continued series of class struggles and the doctrine that class struggles invariably culminate in the creation of new oligarchies which undergo fusion with the old. The existence of a political class does not conflict with the essential content of Marxism, considered not as an economic dogma but as a philosophy of history; for in each particular instance the dominance of a political class arises as the resultant of the relationships between the different social forces competing for supremacy, these forces being of course considered dynamically and not quantitatively.

The Russian socialist Alexandre Herzen, whose chief permanent claim to significance is found in the psychological interest of his writings, declared that from the day in which man became accessory to property and his life a continued struggle for money, the political groups of the bourgeois world underwent division into two camps: the owners, tenaciously keeping hold of their millions; and the dispossessed, who would gladly expropriate the owners, but lack the power to do so. Thus historical evolution merely represents an uninterrupted series of oppositions (in the parliamentary sense of this term), "attaining one after another to power, and passing from the sphere of envy to the sphere of avarice."

Thus the social revolution would not effect any real modification of the internal structure of the mass. The socialists might conquer, but not socialism, which would perish in the moment of its adherents' triumph. We are tempted to speak of this process as a tragicomedy in which the masses are content to devote all their energies to effecting a change of masters. All that is left for the workers is the honour "de participer au recrutement gouvernemental." The result seems a poor one, especially if we take into account the psychological fact that even the purest of idealists who attains to power for a few years is unable to escape the corruption which the exercise of power carries in its train. In France, in working-class circles, the phrase is current, *homme élu, homme foutu.* The social revolution, like the political revolution, is equivalent to an operation by which, as the Italian proverb expresses it: "Si cambia il maestro di cappella, ma la musica è sempre quella."*

Fourier defined modern society as a mechanism in which the extremest individual licence prevailed, without affording any guarantee to the individual against the usurpations of the mass, or to the mass against the usurpations of the individual. History seems to teach us that no popular movement, however energetic and vigorous, is capable of producing profound and permanent changes in the social organism of the civilized world. The preponderant elements of the movement, the men who lead and nourish it, end by undergoing a gradual detachment from the masses, and are attracted within the orbit of the "political class." They perhaps contribute to this class a certain number of "new ideas," but they also endow it with more creative energy and enhanced practical intelligence,

* There is a new conductor but the music is just the same.

thus providing for the ruling class an ever-renewed youth. The "political class" (continuing to employ Mosca's convenient phrase) has unquestionably an extreme fine sense of its possibilities and its means of defence. It displays a remarkable force of attraction and a vigorous capacity for absorption which rarely fail to exercise an influence even upon the most embittered and uncompromising of its adversaries. From the historical point of view, the anti-romanticists are perfectly right when they sum up their scepticism in such caustic phraseology as this: "Qu'est ce qu'une révolution? Des gens qui se tirent des coups de fusil dans une rue: cela casse beaucoup de carreaux; il n'y a guère que les vitriers qui trouvent du profit. Le vent emporte la fumée. Ceux qui reste dessus mettent les autres dessous. . . . C'est bien la peine de remuer tant d'honnêtes pavés qui n'en pouvaient mais!" Or we may say, as the song runs in *Madame Angot*: "Ce n'est pas la peine de changer de gouvernement!" In France, the classic land of social theories and experiments, such pessimism has struck the deepest roots.

IV. Final Considerations

"A prendre le terme dans la rigueur de l'acception il n'a jamais existé de véritable démocratie, et il n'en existera jamais. Il est contre l'ordre naturel que le grand nombre gouverne, et que le petit soit gouverné."—J. J. Rousseau, *Contrat Social*.

Leadership is a necessary phenomenon in every form of social life. Consequently it is not the task of science to inquire whether this phenomenon is good or evil, or predominantly one or the other. But there is great scientific value in the demonstration that every system of leadership is incompatible with the most essential postulates of democracy. We are now aware that the law of the historic necessity of oligarchy is primarily based upon a series of facts of experience. Like all other scientific laws, sociological laws are derived from empirical observation. In order, however, to deprive our axiom of its purely descriptive character, and to confer upon it that status of analytical explanation which can alone transform a formula into a law, it does not suffice to contemplate from a unitary outlook those phenomena which may be empirically established; we must also study the determining causes of these phenomena. Such has been our task.

Now, if we leave out of consideration the tendency of the leaders to organize themselves and to consolidate their interests, and if we leave also out of consideration the gratitude of the led towards the leaders, and the general immobility and passivity of the masses, we are led to conclude that the principal cause of oligarchy in the democratic parties is to be found in the technical indispensability of leadership.

The process which has begun in consequence of the differentiation of functions in the party is completed by a complex of qualities which the leaders acquire through their detachment from the mass. At the outset, leaders arise SPONTANEOUSLY; their functions are ACCESSORY and GRATUITOUS. Soon, however, they become PROFESSIONAL leaders, and in this second stage of development they are STABLE and IRREMOVABLE.

It follows that the explanation of the oligarchical phenomenon which thus results is partly PSYCHOLOGICAL; oligarchy derives, that is to say, from the psychical transformations which the leading personalities in the parties undergo in the course of their lives. But also, and still more, oligarchy depends upon what we may term the PSYCHOLOGY OF ORGANIZATION ITSELF, that is to say, upon the tactical and technical necessities which result from the consolidation of every disciplined political aggregate. Reduced to its most concise expression, the fundamental sociological law of political parties (the term "political" being here used in its most comprehensive significance) may be formulated in the following terms: "It is organization which gives birth to the dominion of the elected over the electors, of the mandataries over the mandators, of the delegates over the delegators. Who says organization, says oligarchy."

Every party organization represents an oligarchical power grounded upon a democratic basis. We find everywhere electors and elected. Also we find everywhere that the power of the elected leaders over the electing masses is almost unlimited. The oligarchical structure of the building suffocates the basic democratic principle. That which IS oppresses THAT WHICH OUGHT TO BE. For the masses, this essential difference between the reality and the ideal remains a mystery. Socialists often cherish a sincere belief that a new *élite* of politicians will keep faith better than did the old. The notion of the representation of popular interests, a notion to which the great majority of democrats, and in especial the working-class masses of the German-speaking lands, cleave with so much tenacity and confidence, is an illusion engendered by a false illumination, is an effect of mirage. In one of the most delightful pages of his analysis of modern Don Quixotism, Alphonse Daudet shows us how the "brav' commandant" Bravida, who has never quitted Tarascon, gradually comes to persuade himself, influenced by the burning southern sun, that he has been to Shanghai and has had all kinds of heroic adventures. Similarly the modern proletariat, enduringly influenced by glib-tongued persons intellectually superior to the mass, ends by believing that by flocking to the poll and entrusting its social and economic cause to a delegate, its direct participation in power will be assured.

The formation of oligarchies within the various forms of democracy is the outcome of organic necessity, and consequently affects every organization, be it socialist or even anarchist. Haller long ago noted that in every form of social life relationships of dominion and of dependence are created by Nature herself. The supremacy of the leaders in the democratic and revolutionary parties has to be taken into account in every historic situation present and to come, even though only a few and exceptional minds will be fully conscious of its existence. The mass will never rule except *in abstracto*. Consequently the question we have to discuss is not whether ideal democracy is realizable, but rather to what point and in what degree democracy is desirable, possible, and realizable at a given moment. In the problem as thus stated we recognize the fundamental problem of politics as a science. Whoever fails to perceive this must, as Sombart says, either be so blind and fanatical as not to see that the democratic current daily makes undeniable advance, or else must be so inexperienced and devoid of critical faculty as to be unable to understand that all order and all civilization must exhibit aristocratic features. The great error of socialists, an error committed in consequence of their lack of adequate psychological knowledge, is to be found in their combination of pessimism regarding the present, with rosy optimism and immeasurable confidence regarding the future. A realistic view of the mental condition of the masses shows beyond question that even if we admit the possibility of moral improvement in mankind, the human materials with whose use politicians and philosophers cannot dispense in their plans of social reconstruction are not of a character to justify excessive optimism. Within the limits of time for which human provision is possible, optimism will remain the exclusive privilege of utopian thinkers.

The socalist parties, like the trade unions, are living forms of social life. As such they react with the utmost energy against any attempt to analyse their structure or their nature, as if it were a method of vivisection. When science attains to results which conflict with their apriorist ideology, they revolt with all their power. Yet their defence is extremely feeble. Those among the representatives of such organizations whose scientific earnestness and personal good faith make it impossible for them to deny outright the existence of oligarchical tendencies in every form of democracy, endeavour to explain these tendencies as the outcome of a kind of atavism in the mentality of the masses, characteristic of the youth of the movement. The masses, they assure us, are still infected by the oligarchic virus simply because they have been oppresed during long centuries of slavery, and have never yet enjoyed an autonomous existence. The socialist regime, however, will soon restore them to health, and will furnish them with all the capacity necessary for self-government. Nothing could be more anti-scientific than the supposition that as soon as socialists have gained possession of governmental power it will suffice for the masses to exercise a little control over their leaders to secure that the interests of these leaders shall coincide perfectly with the interests of the led. This idea may be compared with the view of Jules Guesde, no less anti-scientific than anti-Marxist (though Guesde proclaims himself a Marxist), that

whereas Christianity has made God into a man, socialism will make man
into a god.

The objective immaturity of the mass is not a mere transitory phenomenon which will disappear with the progress of democratization *au
lendemain du socialisme*. On the contrary, it derives from the very nature
of the mass as mass, for this, even when organized, suffers from an incurable incompetence for the solution of the diverse problems which
present themselves for solution—because the mass *per se* is amorphous,
and therefore needs division of labour, specialization, and guidance.
"L'espèce humaine veut être gouvernée; elle le sera. J'ai honte de mon
espèce," wrote Proudhon from his prison in 1850. Man as individual is
by nature predestined to be guided, and to be guided all the more in
proportion as the functions of life undergo division and subdivision. To
an enormously greater degree is guidance necessary for the social group.

From this chain of reasoning and from these scientific convictions it
would be erroneous to conclude that we should renounce all endeavours
to ascertain the limits which may be imposed upon the powers exercised
over the individual by oligarchies (state, dominant class, party, etc.). It
would be an error to abandon the desperate enterprise of endeavouring
to discover a social order which will render possible the complete realization of the idea of popular sovereignty. In the present work, as the writer
said at the outset, it has not been his aim to indicate new paths. But it
seemed necessary to lay considerable stress upon the pessimist aspect of
democracy which is forced on us by historical study. We had to inquire
whether, and within what limits, democracy must remain purely ideal,
possessing no other value than that of a moral criterion which renders
it possible to appreciate the varying degrees of that oligarchy which is
immanent in every social regime. In other words, we have had to inquire
if, and in what degree, democracy is an ideal which we can never hope
to realize in practice. A further aim of this work was the demolition of
some of the facile and superficial democratic illusions which trouble
science and lead the masses astray. Finally, the author desired to throw
light upon certain sociological tendencies which oppose the reign of
democracy, and to a still greater extent oppose the reign of socialism.

The writer does not wish to deny that every revolutionary working-
class movement, and every movement sincerely inspired by the democratic
spirit, may have a certain value as contributing to the enfeeblement of
oligarchic tendencies. The peasant in the fable, when on his death-bed,
tells his sons that a treasure is buried in the field. After the old man's
death the sons dig everywhere in order to discover the treasure. They
do not find it. But their indefatigable labour improves the soil and secures
for them a comparative well-being. The treasure in the fable may well
symbolize democracy. Democracy is a treasure which no one will ever
discover by deliberate search. But in continuing our search, in labouring

indefatigably to discover the indiscoverable, we shall perform a work which will have fertile results in the democratic sense. We have seen, indeed, that within the bosom of the democratic working-class party are born the very tendencies to counteract which that party came into existence. Thanks to the diversity and to the unequal worth of the elements of the party, these tendencies often give rise to manifestations which border on tyranny. We have seen that the replacement of the traditional legitimism of the powers-that-be by the brutal plebiscitary rule of Bonapartist parvenus does not furnish these tendencies with any moral or æsthetic superiority. Historical evolution mocks all the prophylactic measures that have been adopted for the prevention of oligarchy. If laws are passed to control the dominion of the leaders, it is the laws which gradually weaken, and not the leaders. Sometimes, however, the democratic principle carries with it, if not a cure, at least a palliative, for the disease of oligarchy. When Victor Considérant formulated his "democratico-pacificist" socialism, he declared that socialism signified, not the rule of society by the lower classes of the population, but the government and organization of society in the interest of all, through the intermediation of a group of citizens; and he added that the numerical importance of this group must increase *pari passu* with social development. This last observation draws attention to a point of capital importance. It is, in fact, a general characteristic of democracy, and hence also of the labour movement, to stimulate and to strengthen in the individual the intellectual aptitudes for criticism and control. We have seen how the progressive bureaucratization of the democratic organism tends to neutralize the beneficial effects of such criticism and such control. None the less it is true that the labour movement, in virtue of the theoretical postulates it proclaims, is apt to bring into existence (in opposition to the will of the leaders) a certain number of free spirits who, moved by principle, by instinct, or by both, desire to revise the base upon which authority is established. Urged on by conviction or by temperament, they are never weary of asking an eternal "Why?" about every human institution. Now this predisposition towards free inquiry, in which we cannot fail to recognize one of the most precious factors of civilization, will gradually increase in proportion as the economic status of the masses undergoes improvement and becomes more stable, and in proportion as they are admitted more effectively to the advantages of civilization. A wider education involves an increasing capacity for exercising control. Can we not observe every day that among the well-to-do the authority of the leaders over the led, extensive though it be, is never so unrestricted as in the case of the leaders of the poor? Taking in the mass, the poor are powerless and disarmed vis-à-vis their leaders. Their intellectual and cultural inferiority makes it impossible for them to see whither the leader is going, or to estimate in advance the significance of his actions. It is, consequently, the great task of social education to raise the intellectual level of the masses, so that they may be enabled, within the limits of what is possible, to counteract the oligarchical tendencies of the working-class movement.

In view of the perennial incompetence of the masses, we have to recognize the existence of two regulative principles:—

1. The *ideological* tendency of democracy towards criticism and control;

2. The *effective* counter-tendency of democracy towards the creation of parties ever more complex and ever more differentiated—parties, that is to say, which are increasingly based upon the competence of the few.

To the idealist, the analysis of the forms of contemporary democracy cannot fail to be a source of bitter deceptions and profound discouragement. Those alone, perhaps, are in a position to pass a fair judgment upon democracy who, without lapsing into dilettantist sentimentalism, recognize that all scientific and human ideals have relative values. If we wish to estimate the value of democracy, we must do so in comparison with its converse, pure aristocracy. The defects inherent in democracy are obvious. It is none the less true that as a form of social life we must choose democracy as the least of evils. The ideal government would doubtless be that of an aristocracy of persons at once morally good and technically efficient. But where shall we discover such an aristocracy? We may find it sometimes, though very rarely, as the outcome of deliberate selection; but we shall never find it where the hereditary principle remains in operation. Thus monarchy in its pristine purity must be considered as imperfection incarnate, as the most incurable of ills; from the moral point of view it is inferior even to the most revolting of demagogic dictatorships, for the corrupt organism of the latter at least contains a healthy principle upon whose working we may continue to base hopes of social resanation. It may be said, therefore, that the more humanity comes to recognize the advantages which democracy, however imperfect, presents over aristocracy, even at its best, the less likely is it that a recognition of the defects of democracy will provoke a return to aristocracy. Apart from certain formal differences and from the qualities which can be acquired only by good education and inheritance (qualities in which aristocracy will always have the advantage over democracy—qualities which democracy either neglects altogether, or, attempting to imitate them, falsifies them to the point of caricature), the defects of democracy will be found to inhere in its inability to get rid of its aristocratic scoriæ. On the other hand, nothing but a serene and frank examination of the oligarchical dangers of democracy will enable us to minimize these dangers, even though they can never be entirely avoided.

The democratic currents of history resemble successive waves. They break ever on the same shoal. They are ever renewed. This enduring spectacle is simultaneously encouraging and depressing. When democracies have gained a certain stage of development, they undergo a gradual transformation, adopting the aristocratic spirit, and in many cases also the aristocratic forms, against which at the outset they struggled so fiercely. Now new accusers arise to denounce the traitors; after an era of glorious combats and of inglorious power, they end by fusing with the old dominant class; whereupon once more they are in their turn attacked by fresh opponents who appeal to the name of democracy. It is probable that this cruel game will continue without end.

10. Vilfredo Pareto

Elites, Force and Governments

I. The Idea of the Elite and of Class Circulation

We have more than once found ourselves called upon to consider the heterogeneous character of society, and we shall have to consider it all the more closely now that we are coming to our investigation of the conditions that determine the social equilibrium. To have a clear road ahead of us, it would be wise to go into that matter somewhat thoroughly at this point.

Whether certain theorists like it or not, the fact is that human society is not a homogeneous thing, that individuals are physically, morally, and intellectually different. Here we are interested in things as they actually are. Of that fact, therefore, we have to take account. And we must also take account of another fact: that the social classes are not entirely distinct, even in countries where a caste system prevails; and that in modern civilized countries circulation among the various classes is exceedingly rapid. To consider at all exhaustively here this matter of the diversity of the vastly numerous social groups and the numberless ways in which they mix is out of the question. As usual, therefore, since we cannot have the more, we must rest content with the less and try to make the problem easier in order to have it the more manageable. That is a first step along a path that others may go on following. We shall consider the problem only in its bearing on the social equilibrium and try to reduce as far as possible the numbers of the groups and the modes of circulation, putting under one head phenomena that prove to be roughly and after a fashion similar.

Suppose we begin by giving a theoretical definition of the thing we are dealing with, making it as exact as possible, and then go on to see what practical considerations we can replace it with to get a first approximation. Let us for the moment completely disregard considerations as to the good or bad, useful or harmful, praiseworthy or reprehensible

From Pareto, *The Mind and Society* (Translated by A. Bongiorno and A. Livingston; edited by Arthur Livingston.) Four Volumes (New York: Harcourt, Brace & Company, 1935), pp. 1419-1432, 1512-1527, 1566-1591. Reprinted by permission of Harcourt, Brace and Company, Inc. Most footnotes and all cross-references have been omitted.

character of the various traits in individuals, and confine ourselves to degrees—to whether, in other words, the trait in a given case be slight, average, intense, or more exactly, to the index that may be assigned to each individual with reference to the degree, or intensity, in him of the trait in question.

Let us assume that in every branch of human activity each individual is given an index which stands as a sign of his capacity, very much the way grades are given in the various subjects in examinations in school. The highest type of lawyer, for instance, will be given 10. The man who does not get a client will be given 1—reserving zero for the man who is an out-and-out idiot. To the man who has made his millions—honestly or dishonestly as the case may be—we will give 10. To the man who has earned his thousands we will give 6; to such as just manage to keep out of the poor-house, 1, keeping zero for those who get in. To the woman "in politics," such as the Aspasia of Pericles, the Maintenon of Louis XIV, the Pompadour of Louis XV, who has managed to infatuate a man of power and play a part in the man's career, we shall give some higher number, such as 8 or 9; to the strumpet who merely satisfies the senses of such a man and exerts no influence on public affairs, we shall give zero. To a clever rascal who knows how to fool people and still keep clear of the penitentiary, we shall give 8, 9, or 10, according to the number of geese he has plucked and the amount of money he has been able to get out of them. To the sneak-thief who snatches a piece of silver from a restaurant table and runs away into the arms of a policeman, we shall give 1. To a poet like Carducci we shall give 8 or 9 according to our tastes; to a scribbler who puts people to rout with his sonnets we shall give zero. For chess-players we can get very precise indices, noting what matches, and how many, they have won. And so on for all the branches of human activity.

We are speaking, remember, of an actual, not a potential, state. If at an English examination a pupil says: "I could know English very well if I chose to; I do not know any because I have never seen fit to learn," the examiner replies: "I am not interested in your alibi. The grade for what you know is zero." If, similarly, someone says: "So-and-so does not steal, not because he couldn't, but because he is a gentleman," we reply: "Very well, we admire him for his self-control, but his grade as a thief is zero."

There are people who worship Napoleon Bonaparte as a god. There are people who hate him as the lowest of criminals. Which are right? We do not choose to solve that question in connexion with a quite different matter. Whether Napoleon was a good man or a bad man, he was certainly not an idiot, nor a man of little account, as millions of others are. He had exceptional qualities, and that is enough for us to give him a high ranking, though without prejudice of any sort to questions that might be raised as to the ethics of his qualities or their social utility.

In short, we are here as usual resorting to scientific analysis, which distinguishes one problem from another and studies each one separately. As usual, again, we are replacing imperceptible variations in absolutely exact numbers with the sharp variations corresponding to groupings by class, just as in examinations those who are passed are sharply and arbitrarily distinguished from those who are "failed," and just as in the matter of physical age we distinguish children from young people, the young from the aged.

So let us make a class of the people who have the highest indices in their branch of activity, and to that class give the name of *élite*.*

For the particular investigation with which we are engaged, a study of the social equilibrium, it will help if we further divide that class into two classes: a *governing élite*, comprising individuals who directly or indirectly play some considerable part in government, and a *non-governing élite*, comprising the rest.

A chess champion is certainly a member of the *élite*, but it is no less certain that his merits as a chess-player do not open the doors to political influence for him; and hence unless he has other qualities to win him that distinction, he is not a member of the governing *élite*. Mistresses of absolute monarchs have oftentimes been members of the *élite*, either because of their beauty or because of their intellectual endowments; but only a few of them, who have had, in addition, the particular talents required by politics, have played any part in government.

So we get two strata in a population: (1) A lower stratum, the *non-élite*, with whose possible influence on government we are not just here concerned; then (2) a higher stratum, *the élite*, which is divided into two: (*a*) a governing *élite*; (*b*) a non-governing *élite*.

In the concrete, there are no examinations whereby each person is assigned to his proper place in these various classes. That deficiency is made up for by other means, by various sorts of labels that serve the purpose after a fashion. Such labels are the rule even where there are examinations. The label "lawyer" is affixed to a man who is supposed to know something about the law and often does, though sometimes again he is an ignoramus. So, the governing *élite* contains individuals who

---

* Kolabinska, *La circulation des élites en France*, p. 5: "The outstanding idea in the term '*élite*' is 'superiority.' That is the only one I keep. I disregard secondary connotations of appreciation or as to the utility of such superiority. I am not interested here in what is desirable. I am making a simple study of what is. In a broad sense I mean by the *élite* in a society people who possess in marked degree qualities of intelligence, character, skill, capacity, of whatever kind. . . . On the other hand I entirely avoid any sort of judgment on the merits and uility of such classes." [The phrase "circulation of *élites*" is well established in Continental literature. Pareto himself renders it in Italian as "circulation of the élite (selected, chosen, ruling, "better") classes." It is a cumbersome phrase and not very exact, and I see no reason for preferring it to the more natural and, in most connexions, the more exact, English phrase, class-circulation.—A.L.]

wear labels appropriate to political offices of a certain altitude—ministers, Senators, Deputies, chief justices, generals, colonels, and so on—making the apposite exceptions for those who have found their way into that exalted company without possessing qualities corresponding to the labels they wear.

Such exceptions are much more numerous than the exceptions among lawyers, physicians, engineers, millionaires (who have made their own money), artists of distinction, and so on; for the reason, among others, that in these latter departments of human activity the labels are won directly by each individual, whereas in the *élite* some of the labels—the label of wealth, for instance—are hereditary. In former times there were hereditary labels in the governing *élite* also—in our day hardly more than the label of king remains in that status; but if direct inheritance has disappeared, inheritance is still powerful indirectly; and an individual who has inherited a sizable patrimony can easily be named Senator in certain countries, or can get himself elected to the parliament by buying votes or, on occasion, by wheedling voters with assurances that he is a democrat of democrats, a Socialist, an Anarchist. Wealth, family, or social connexions also help in many other cases to win the label of the *élite* in general, or of the governing *élite* in particular, for persons who otherwise hold no claim upon it.

In societies where the social unit is the family the label worn by the head of the family also benefits all other members. In Rome, the man who became Emperor generally raised his freedmen to the higher class, and oftentimes, in fact, to the governing *élite*. For that matter, now more, now fewer, of the freedmen taking part in the Roman government possessed qualities good or bad that justified their wearing the labels which they had won through imperial bounty. In our societies, the social unit is the individual; but the place that the individual occupies in society also benefits his wife, his children, his connexions, his friends.

If all these deviations from type were of little importance, they might be disregarded, as they are virtually disregarded in cases where a diploma is required for the practice of a profession. Everyone knows that there are persons who do not deserve their diplomas, but experience shows that on the whole such exceptions may be overlooked.

One might, further, from certain points of view at least, disregard deviations if they remained more or less constant quantitatively—if there were only a negligible variation in proportions between the total of a class and the people who wear its label without possessing the qualities corresponding.

As a matter of fact, the real cases that we have to consider in our societies differ from those two. The deviations are not so few that they can be disregarded. Then again, their number is variable, and the variations give rise to situations having an important bearing on the social equilibrium. We are therefore required to make a special study of them.

Furthermore, the manner in which the various groups in a population intermix has to be considered. In moving from one group to another an individual generally brings with him certain inclinations, sentiments, attitudes, that he has acquired in the group from which he comes, and that circumstance cannot be ignored.

To this mixing, in the particular case in which only two groups, the *élite* and the non-*élite*, are envisaged, the term "circulation of élites" has been applied[1]—in French, *circulation des élites* [or in more general terms "class-circulation"].

In conclusion we must pay special attention (1), in the case of one single group, to the proportions between the total of the group and the number of individuals who are nominally members of it but do not possess the qualities requisite for effective membership; and then (2), in the case of various groups, to the ways in which transitions from one group to the other occur, and to the intensity of that movement—that is to say, to the velocity of the circulation.

Velocity in circulation has to be considered not only absolutely but also in relation to the supply of and the demand for certain social elements. A country that is always at peace does not require many soldiers in its governing class, and the production of generals may be overexuberant as compared with the demand. But when a country is in a state of continuous warfare many soldiers are necessary, and though production remains at the same level it may not meet the demand. That, we might note in passing, has been one of the causes for the collapse of many aristocracies.[2]

Another example. In a country where there is little industry and little commerce, the supply of individuals possessing in high degree the qualities requisite for those types of activity exceeds the demand. Then industry and commerce develop and the supply, though remaining the same, no longer meets the demand.

We must not confuse the state of law with the state of fact. The latter alone, or almost alone, has a bearing on the social equilibrium. There are many examples of castes that are legally closed, but into which, in

---

[1] [And most inappropriately, for, in this sense, the phrase never meant more than circulation within the *élite*. Furthermore, the *élite* is not the only class to be considered, and the principles that apply to circulation within the *élite* apply to circulation within such lower classes as one may choose for one purpose or another to consider.—A.L.]

[2] Kolabinska, *Op. cit.*, p. 10: "Inadequate recruiting in the *élite* does not result from a mere numerical proportion beween new members and old. Account has to be taken of the number of persons who possess the qualities required for membership in the governing *élite* but are refused admittance; or else, in an opposite direction, the number of new members the *élite* might require but does not get. In the first case, the production of persons possessing unusual qualities as regards education may far surpass the number of such persons that the *élite* can accommodate, and then we get what has been called an 'intellectual proletariat.'"

point of fact, new-comers make their way, and often in large numbers. On the other hand, what difference does it make if a caste is legally open, but conditions *de facto* prevent new accessions to it? If a person who acquires wealth thereby becomes a member of the governing class, but no one gets rich, it is as if the class were closed; and if only a few get rich, it is as if the law erected serious barriers against access to the caste. Something of that sort was observable towards the end of the Roman Empire. People who acquired wealth entered the order of the curials. But only a few individuals made any money. Theoretically we might examine any number of groups. Practically we have to confine ourselves to the more important. We shall proceed by successive approximations, starting with the simple and going on to the complex.

Higher class and lower class in general. The least we can do is to divide society into two strata: a higher stratum, which usually contains the rulers, and a lower stratum, which usually contains the ruled. That fact is so obvious that it has always forced itself even upon the most casual observation, and so for the circulation of individuals between the two strata. Even Plato had an inkling of class-circulation and tried to regulate it artificially. The "new man," the upstart, the *parvenu*, has always been a subject of interest, and literature has analyzed him unendingly. Here, then, we are merely giving a more exact form to things that have long been perceived more or less vaguely. Above . . . we noted a varying distribution of residues in the various social groupings, and chiefly in the higher and the lower class. Such heterogeneousness is a fact perceived by the most superficial glance. . . .

The upper stratum of society, the *élite*, nominally contains certain groups of peoples, not always very sharply defined, that are called aristocracies. There are cases in which the majority of individuals belonging to such aristocracies actually possess the qualities requisite for remaining there; and then again there are cases where considerable numbers of the individuals making up the class do not possess those requisites. Such people may occupy more or less important places in the governing *élite* or they may be barred from it.

In the beginning, military, religious, and commercial aristocraries and plutocracies—with a few exceptions not worth considering—must have constituted parts of the governing *élite* and sometimes have made up the whole of it. The victorious warrior, the prosperous merchant, the opulent plutocrat, were men of such parts, each in his own field, as to be superior to the average individual. Under those circumstances the label corresponded to an actual capacity. But as time goes by, considerable, sometimes very considerable, differences arise between the capacity and the label; while on the other hand, certain aristocracies originally figuring prominently in the rising *élite* end by constituting an insignificant element in it. That has happened especially to military aristocracies.

Aristocracies do not last. Whatever the causes, it is an incontestable fact that after a certain length of time they pass away. History is a grave-yard of aristocracies. The Athenian "People" was an aristocracy as compared with the remainder of a population of resident aliens and slaves. It vanished without leaving any descent. The various aristocracies of Rome vanished in their time. So did the aristocracies of the Barbarians. Where, in France, are the descendants of the Frankish conquerors? The genealogies of the English nobility have been very exactly kept; and they show that very few families still remain to claim descent from the comrades of William the Conqueror. The rest have vanished. In Germany the aristocracy of the present day is very largely made up of descendants of vassals of the lords of old. The populations of European countries have increased enormously during the past few centuries. It is as certain as certain can be that the aristocracies have not increased in proportion.

They decay not in numbers only. They decay also in quality, in the sense that they lose their vigour, that there is a decline in the proportions of the residues which enabled them to win their power and hold it. The governing class is restored not only in numbers, but—and that is the more important thing—in quality, by families rising from the lower classes and bringing with them the vigour and the proportions of residues necessary for keeping themselves in power. It is also restored by the loss of its more degenerate members.

If one of those movements comes to an end, or worse still, if they both come to an end, the governing class crashes to ruin and often sweeps the whole of a nation along with it. Potent cause of disturbance in the equilibrium is the accumulation of superior elements in the lower classes and, conversely, of inferior elements in the higher classes. If human aristocracies were like thorough-breds among animals, which reproduce themselves over long periods of time with approximately the same traits, the history of the human race would be something altogether different from the history we know.

In virtue of class-circulation, the governing *élite* is always in a state of slow and continuous transformation. It flows on like a river, never being today what it was yesterday. From time to time sudden and violent disturbances occur. There is a flood—the river overflows its banks. Afterwards, the new governing *élite* again resumes its slow transformation. The flood has subsided, the river is again flowing normally in its wonted bed.

Revolutions come about through accumulations in the higher strata of society—either because of a slowing-down in class-circulation, or from other causes—of decadent elements no longer possessing the residues suitable for keeping them in power, and shrinking from the use of force; while meantime in the lower strata of society elements of superior quality are coming to the fore, possessing residues suitable for exercising the functions of government and willing enough to use force.

In general, in revolutions the members of the lower strata are captained by leaders from the higher strata, because the latter possess the intellectual qualities required for outlining a tactic, while lacking the combative residues supplied by the individuals from the lower strata.

Violent movements take place by fits and starts, and effects therefore do not follow immediately on their causes. After a governing class, or a nation, has maintained itself for long periods of time on force and acquired great wealth, it may subsist for some time still without using force, buying off its adversaries and paying not only in gold, but also in terms of the dignity and respect that it had formerly enjoyed and which constitute, as it were, a capital. In the first stages of decline, power is maintained by bargainings and concessions, and people are so deceived into thinking that the policy can be carried on indefinitely. So the decadent Roman Empire bought peace of the Barbarians with money and honours. So Louis XVI, in France, squandering in a very short time an ancestral inheritance of love, respect, and almost religious reverence for the monarchy, managed, by making repeated concessions, to be the King of the Revolution. So the English aristocracy managed to prolong its term of power in the second half of the nineteenth century down to the dawn of its decadence, which was heralded by the "Parliament Bill" in the first years of the twentieth.

II. The Use of Force in Society

To ask whether or not force ought to be used in a society, whether the use of force is or is not beneficial, is to ask a question that has no meaning; for force is used by those who wish to preserve certain uniformities and by those who wish to overstep them; and the violence of the ones stands in contrast and in conflict with the violence of the others. In truth, if a partisan of a governing class disavows the use of force, he means that he disavows the use of force by insurgents trying to escape from the norms of the given uniformity. On the other hand, if he says he approves of the use of force, what he really means is that he approves of the use of force by the public authority to constrain insurgents to conformity. Conversely, if a partisan of the subject class says he detests the use of force in society, what he really detests is the use of force by constituted authorities in forcing dissidents to conform; and if, instead, he lauds the use of force, he is thinking of the use of force by those who would break away from certain social uniformities.*

Nor is there any particular meaning in the question as to whether the use of violence to enforce existing uniformities is beneficial to society,

---

* In the Zabern incident the same newspapers evinced the greatest indignation at the "browbeating" by the military authorities but were very lenient towards the "browbeating" and the acts of "sabotage" for which the strikers were responsible at the same time. Conversely, newspapers that approved the use of force by the military waxed indignant at acts of violence on the part of their adversaries.

or whether it is beneficial to use force in order to overstep them; for the various uniformities have to be distinguished to see which of them are beneficial and which deleterious to society. Nor, indeed, is that enough; for it is further necessary to determine whether the utility of the uniformity is great enough to offset the harm that will be done by using violence to enforce it, or whether detriment from the uniformity is great enough to overbalance the damage that will be caused by the use of force in subverting it; in which detriment and damage we must not forget to reckon the very serious drawback involved in the anarchy that results from any frequent use of violence to abolish existing uniformities, just as among the benefits and utilities of maintaining frankly injurious uniformities must be counted the strength and stability they lend to the social order. So, to solve the problem as to the use of force, it is not enough to solve the other problem as to the utility, in general, of certain types of social organization; it is essential also and chiefly to compute all the advantages and all the drawbacks, direct and indirect. Such a course leads to the solution of a scientific problem; but it may not be and oftentimes is not the course that leads to an increase in social utility. It is better, therefore, if it be followed only by people who are called upon to solve a scientific problem or, to some limited extent, by certain individuals belonging to the ruling class; whereas social utility is oftentimes best served if the members of the subject class, whose function it is not to lead but to act, accept one of the two theologies according to the case— either the theology that enjoins preservation of existing uniformities, or the theology that counsels change.

What we have just said serves to explain, along with the theoretical difficulties, how it comes about that the solutions that are usually found for the general problem have so little and sometimes no bearing on realities. Solutions of particular problems come closer to the mark because, situate as they are in specific places and times, they present fewer theoretical difficulties; and because practical empiricism implicitly takes account of many circumstances that theory, until it has been carried to a state of high perfection, cannot explicitly appraise.

Considering violations of material conformities among modern civilized peoples, we see that, in general, the use of violence in repressing them is the more readily condoned in proportion as the violation can be regarded as an individual anomaly designed to attain some individual advantage, and the less readily condoned in proportion as the violation appears as a collective act aiming at some collective advantage, and especially if its apparent design be to replace general norms prevailing with certain other general norms.*

* It would be hardly in point here to review the whole history of the use of force from ancient down to modern times, or to go into too many details. We shall confine ourselves to the present, and try to find a formula that will give a rough and general

That states all that there is in common between the large numbers of facts in which a distinction is drawn between so-called private and so-called political crimes. A distinction, and often a very sharp distinction, is drawn between the individual who kills or steals for his own benefit and the individual who commits murder or theft with the intent of benefiting a party. In general, civilized countries grant extradition for the former, but refuse it for the latter. In the same way one notes a continually increasing leniency towards crimes committed during labour strikes or in the course of other economic, social, or political struggles. There is a more and more conspicuous tendency to meet such aggressions with merely passive resistance, the police power being required not to use arms, or else permitted to do so only in cases of extreme necessity. Such cases never arise in practice. So long as the policeman is alive, the necessity is held not to be extreme, and it is bootless, after all, to recognize the extremity after he is in his grave and no longer in a position to profit by the considerate permission to use his revolver. Punishment by judicial process is also becoming less and less vigorous. Criminals are either not convicted or, being convicted, are released in virtue of some probation law, failing of which, they can still rely on commutations, individual pardons, or general amnesties, so that, sum total, they have little or nothing to fear from the courts. In a word, in a vague, cloudy, confused sort of way, the notion is coming to the fore that an existing government may make some slight use of force against its enemies, but no great amount of force, and that it is under all circumstances to be condemned if it carries the use of force so far as to cause the death of considerable numbers, of a small number, a single one, of its enemies; nor can it rid itself of them, either, by putting them in prison or otherwise.

What now are the correlations that subsist between this method of applying force and other social facts? We note, as usual, a sequence of actions and reactions, in which the use of force appears now as cause, now as effect. As regards the governing class, one gets, in the main, five groups of facts to consider: 1. A mere handful of citizens, so long as they are willing to use violence, can force their will upon public officials who are not inclined to meet violence with equal violence. If the reluctance of the officials to resort to force is primarily motivated by humanitarian sentiments, that result ensues very readily; but if they refrain from violence because they deem it wiser to use some other means, the effect is often the following: 2. To prevent or resist violence, the governing class

picture of the facts observable. If we were dealing with a recent past, we should have to regard violations of the norms of intellectual uniformity as on a par with violations of a material order. Not so long ago they were actually so regarded, and often indeed the former were regarded as more serious than the latter. But in our day, barring some few exceptions, proportions have been inverted, and the norms of intellectual uniformity that public authority sets out to enforce are relatively few. They may therefore be better considered apart from norms of a material order.

resorts to "diplomacy," fraud, corruption—governmental authority passes, in a word, from the lions to the foxes. The governing class bows its head under the threat of violence, but it surrenders only in appearances, trying to turn the flank of the obstacle it cannot demolish in frontal attack. In the long run that sort of procedure comes to exercise a far-reaching influence on the selection of the governing class, which is now recruited only from the foxes, while the lions are blackballed. The individual who best knows the arts of sapping the strength of the foes of "graft" and of winning back by fraud and deceit what seemed to have been surrendered under pressure of force, is now leader of leaders. The man who has bursts of rebellion, and does not know how to crook his spine at the proper times and places, is the worst of leaders, and his presence is tolerated among them only if other distinguished endowments offset that defect. 3. So it comes about that the residues of the combination-instinct (Class I) are intensified in the governing class, and the residues of group-persistence (Class II) debilitated; for the combination-residues supply, precisely, the artistry and resourcefulness required for evolving ingenious expedients as substitutes for open resistance, while the residues of group-persistence stimulate open resistance, since a strong sentiment of group-persistence cures the spine of all tendencies to curvature.* 4. Policies of the governing class are not planned too far ahead in time. Predominance of the combination instincts and enfeeblement of the sentiments of group-persistence result in making the governing class more satisfied with the present and less thoughtful of the future. The individual comes to prevail, and by far, over family, community, nation. Material interests and interests of the present or a near future come to prevail over the ideal interests of community or nation and interests of the distant future. The impulse is to enjoy the present without too much thought for the morrow. 5. Some of these phenomena become observable in international relations as well. Wars become essentially economic. Efforts are made to avoid conflicts with the powerful and the sword is rattled only before the weak. Wars are regarded more than anything else as speculations. A country is often unwittingly edged towards war by nursings of economic conflicts which, it is expected, will never get out of control and turn into armed conflicts. Not seldom, however, a war will be forced upon a country by peoples who are not so far advanced in the evolution that leads to the predominance of Class I residues.

* The term "residues," as used by Pareto, seems to refer to individualistic psychological elements that are non-logical and immutable, and which somehow lie behind—as instincts are supposed to do, in a blind way—a variety of social actions. Pareto classifies them into some six groups with many sub-classifications. They are used by him as explanations, but are not themselves explainable. His development of the idea seems to me quite unsatisfactory. "Derivations" refer to "semi-logical" explanations by which people justify their actions but hide their true feelings. In brief, they are cover-ups, rationalizations, ideologies. For a careful and brief account of Pareto's terminology, see Franz Borkenau, *Pareto* (London, Chapman & Hall, 1936).

As regards the subject class, we get the following relations, which correspond in part to the preceding: 1. When the subject class contains a number of individuals disposed to use force and with capable leaders to guide them, the governing class is, in many cases, overthrown and another takes its place. That is easily the case where governing classes are inspired by humanitarian sentiments primarily, and very very easily if they do not find ways to assimilate the exceptional individuals who come to the front in the subject classes. A humanitarian aristocracy that is closed or stiffly exclusive represents the maximum of insecurity. 2. It is far more difficult to overthrow a governing class that is adept in the shrewd use of chicanery, fraud, corruption; and in the highest degree difficult to overthrow such a class when it successfully assimilates most of the individuals in the subject class who show those same talents, are adept in those same arts, and might therefore become the leaders of such plebeians as are disposed to use violence. Thus left without leadership, without talent, disorganized, the subject class is almost always powerless to set up any lasting régime. 3. So the combination-residues (Class I) become to some extent enfeebled in the subject class. But that phenomenon is in no way comparable to the corresponding reinforcement of those same residues in the governing class; for the governing class, being composed, as it is, of a much smaller number of individuals, changes considerably in character from the addition to it or withdrawal from it of relatively small numbers of individuals; whereas shifts of identical numbers produce but slight effects in the enormously greater total of the subject class. For that matter the subject class is still left with many individuals possessed of combination-instincts that are applied not to politics or activities connected with politics but to arts and trades independent of politics. That circumstance lends stability to societies, for the governing class is required to absorb only a small number of new individuals in order to keep the subject class deprived of leadership. However, in the long run the differences in temperament between the governing class and the subject class become gradually accentuated, the combination-instincts tending to predominate in the ruling class, and instincts of group-persistence in the subject class. When that difference becomes sufficiently great, revolution occurs. 4. Revolution often transfers power to a new governing class, which exhibits a reinforcement in its instincts of group-persistence and so adds to its designs of present enjoyment aspirations towards ideal enjoyments presumably attainable at some future time—scepticism in part gives way to faith. 5. These considerations must to some extent be applied to international relations. If the combination-instincts are reinforced in a given country beyond a certain limit, as compared with the instincts of group-persistence, that country may be easily vanquished in war by another country in which that change in relative proportions has not occurred. The potency of an ideal as a pilot to victory is observable in both civil and international strife. People who lose the habit of applying force, who acquire the habit of considering policy from a commercial standpoint and of judging it only in terms of profit and loss, can readily be induced to purchase peace; and it may well be that such a transaction taken by itself is a good one, for war might have cost more money than the price of peace. Yet experience shows that in the long run, and taken in connexion with the things that inevitably go with it, such practice leads a country to ruin. The combination-instincts rarely come to prevail in the whole of a population. More commonly that situation arises in the upper strata of society, there being few if any traces of it in the lower and more populous classes. So when a war breaks out one gazes in amazement on the energies that are suddenly manifested by the masses at large, something that could in no way have been foreseen by studying the upper classes only. Sometimes, as happened in the case of Carthage, the burst of energy may not be sufficient to save a country, because a war may have been inadequately prepared for and be incompetently led by the ruling classes, and soundly prepared for and wisely led by the ruling classes of the enemy country. Then again, as happened in the wars of the French Revolution, the energy in the masses may be great enough to save a country because, though the war may have been badly prepared for by its ruling classes, preparations and leadership have been even worse in the ruling classes of the enemy countries, a circumstance that gives the constituent members of the lower strata of society time to drive their ruling class from power and replace it with another of greater energy and possessing the instincts of group-persistence in greater abundance. Still again, as happened in Germany after the disaster at Jena, the energy of the masses may spread to the higher classes and spur them to an activity that proves most effective as combining able leadership with enthusiastic faith.

These, then, are the main, the outstanding phenomena, but other phenomena of secondary or incidental importance also figure. Notable among such is the fact that if a ruling class is unable or unwilling or incompetent to use force to eradicate violations of uniformities in private life, anarchic action on the part of the subject class tends to make up for the deficiency. It is well known to history that the private vendetta languishes or recurs in proportion as public authority continues or ceases to replace it. It has been seen to recur in the form of lynchings in the United States, and even in Europe. Whenever the influence of public authority declines, little states grow up within the state, little societies within society. So, whenever judicial process fails, private or group justice replaces it, and vice versa. In international relations, the tinselling of humanitarian and ethical declamation is just a dressing for an underlying force. The Chinese considered themselves the superiors in civilization of the Japanese, and perhaps they were, but they lacked a military aptitude that the Japanese, in virtue of a surviving remnant of feudal "barbarism," possessed in abundance. So the poor Chinese were attacked by hordes of Europeans —whose exploits in China, as Sorel well says, remind one of the feats of the Spanish *conquistadores* in the Americas. They suffered murder, rapine, and pillage at European hands, and then paid an indemnity into the bargain; whereas the Japanese came off victorious over the Russians and now exact respect from everybody. A few centuries back, the subtle diplomacy of the Christian lords of Constantinople did not save them from ruin under the impact of the fanaticism and might of the Turks; and now, in this year 1913, on the very same spot, the victors show that they have deteriorated in their fanaticism and in their power and, in their turn reposing illusory hopes in the diplomatic arts, are defeated and overthrown by the vigour of their sometime subjects. Grievous the hallucination under which those statesmen labour who imagine that they can replace the use of force with unarmed law. Among the many examples that one might point to are Sulla's constitution in ancient Rome and the conservative constitution of the Third Republic in France. Sulla's constitution fell because the armed force that might have compelled respect for it was not maintained. The constitution of Augustus endured because his successors were in a position to rely on the might of the legions. When the Commune had been defeated and overthrown, Thiers decided that his government ought to find its support rather in the law than in armed force. As a result his laws were scattered like leaves before the hurricane of democratic plutocracy.* We need say nothing of Louis XVI of France, who thought he could halt the Revolution with his royal veto, for his was the illusion of a spineless weakling who was soon to lose what little head he had.

All such facts as a rule present themselves in the guise of derivations. In one direction we get theories that condemn the use of violence by the subject class in whatever case, in the other direction theories that censure its use by public authority.

Ruling-class theories, when the requirement of logic is not too keenly felt, appeal simply to sentiments of veneration for holders of power, or for abstractions such as "the state," and to sentiments of disapprobation for individuals who try to disturb or subvert existing orders. Then when it is deemed advisable to satisfy the need of logic, the effort is to create a confusion between the violation of an established uniformity for the individual's exclusive profit and a violation designed to further some collective interest or some new uniformity. The aim in such a derivation

---

* Humanitarians are fond of repeating the aphorism: "*On peut tout faire avec des baïonnettes excepté s'asseoir dessus.*" ("One can do anything with bayonets except sit on them"); but it would be interesting if they would tell us whether, in their opinion, the power of Augustus and his successors did or did not rest to an extent at least on the power of the praetorians and the legionaries. To be sure, the praetorians used swords and not bayonets, but if that is not pap, it is pudding.

is to carry over to the social or political act the reprobation that is generally visited upon common crime. Frequent in our day are reasonings in some way connected with the theology of Progress. Not a few of our modern governments have revolutionary origins. How condemn the revolutions that might be tried against them without repudiating the forefathers? That is attended to by invoking a new divine right: Insurrection was legitimate enough against governments of the past, where authority was based on force; it is not legitimate against modern governments, where the authority is based on "reason." Or else: Insurrection was legitimate against kings and oligarchies; it is never legitimate against "the People." Or again: Rebellion is justifiable where there is no universal suffrage, but not where that panacea is the law of the land. Or again: Revolt is useless and therefore reprehensible in all countries where "the People" are able to express their "will." Then finally—just to give some little satisfaction to their Graces, the Metaphysicists: Insurrection cannot be tolerated where a "state of law" exists. I hope I shall be excused if I do not define that very sweet entity here. For all of most painstaking researchers on my part, it remains an entity altogether unknown to me, and I should much rather be asked to give the zoological pedigree of the Chimaera.

Again as usual, no one of these derivations has any exact meaning. All governments use force, and all assert that they are founded on reason. In the fact, whether universal suffrage prevails or not, it is always an oligarchy that governs, finding ways to give to the "will of the people" that expression which the few desire, from the "royal law" that bestowed the *imperium* on the Roman Emperors down to the votes of a legislative majority elected in one way or another, from the plebiscite that gave the empire to Napoleon III down to the universal suffrage that is shrewdly bought, steered, and manipulated by our "speculators." Who is this new god called Universal Suffrage? He is no more exactly definable, no less shrouded in mystery, no less beyond the pale of reality, than the hosts of other divinities; nor are there fewer and less patent contradictions in his theology than in theirs. Worshippers of Universal Suffrage are not led by their god. It is they who lead him—and by the nose, determining the forms in which he must manifest himself. Oftentimes, proclaiming the sanctity of "majority rule," they resist "majority rule" by obstructionist tactics, even though they form but small minorities, and burning incense to the goddess Reason, they in no wise disdain, in certain cases, alliances with Chicanery, Fraud, and Corruption.

Substantially such derivations express the sentiments felt by people who have climbed into the saddle and are willing to stay there—along with the far more general sentiment that social stability is a good thing. If, the moment a group, large or small, ceased to be satisfied with certain norms established in the community of which it is a part, it flew to arms to abolish them, organized society would fall to pieces. Social stability is so beneficial a thing that to maintain it it is well worth while to enlist the aid of fantastic ideals and this or that theology—among the others, the theology of universal suffrage—and be resigned to putting up with certain actual disadvantages. Before it becomes advisable to disturb the public peace, such disadvantages must have grown very very serious; and since human beings are effectively guided not by the sceptical reasonings of science but by "living faiths" expressed in ideals, theories such as the divine right of kings, the legitimacy of oligarchies, of "the people," of "majorities," of legislative assemblies, and other such things, may be useful within certain limits, and have in fact proved to be, however absurd they may be from the scientific standpoint.

Theories designed to justify the use of force by the governed are almost always combined with theories condemning the use of force by the public authority. A few dreamers reject the use of force in general, on whatever side; but their theories either have no influence at all or else serve merely to weaken resistance on the part of people in power, so clearing the field for violence on the part of the governed.

III. On Forms of Government

Among the complex phenomena that are observable in a society, of very great importance is the system of government. That is closely bound up with the character of the governing class, and both stand in a relationship of interdependence with all other social phenomena.

Oftentimes, as usual, too much importance has been attached to forms at the expense, somewhat, of substance; and the thing chiefly considered has been the form that the political régime assumed. However, in France, especially during the reign of Napoleon III, and more particularly among economists, a tendency developed to ascribe little or no importance to forms of government, and not only that, to substance as well. That was going to another extreme, and exclusively "political" theories of society were met with exclusively "economic" theories, among them the theory of economic determinism—the usual mistake of disregarding mutual correlations in social phenomena.

Those who attach supreme significance to forms of government find it very important to answer the question, "What is the best form of government?" But that question has little or no meaning unless the society to which the government is to be applied is specified and unless some explanation is given of the term "best," which alludes in a very indefinite way to the various individual and social utilities. Although that has now and then been sensed, consideration of governmental forms has given rise to countless derivations leading up to this or that political myth, both derivations and myths being worth exactly zero from the logico-experimental standpoint, but both of them—or, rather the sentiments that they manifest—having, it may be, effects of great consequence in the way of influencing human conduct. It cannot be doubted that the sentiments manifested by the monarchical, republican, oligarchic, democratic, and still other faiths, have played and continue to play no mean part in social phenomena, as is the case with the sentiments underlying other religions. The "divine rights" of the prince, of the aristocracy, of the people, the proletariat, the majority—or any other divine right that might be imagined—have not the slightest experimental validity. We must therefore consider them extrinsically only, as facts, as manifestations of sentiments, operating, like other traits in the human beings that go to make up a given society, to determine its mode of being, its form. To say that no one of these "rights" has any experimental foundation does not, of course, in any way impugn the utility to society with which it may be credited. Such an inference would be justified if the statement were a derivation, since in such reasonings it is generally taken for granted that anything that is not rational is harmful. But the question of utility is left untouched when the statement is rigorously logico-experimental, since then it contains no such implicit premise.

Here, as in dealing with other subjects of the kind, we stumble at the very first step on difficulties of terminology. That is natural enough: the objective investigations that we are trying to make require an objective terminology, whereas the subjective discussions that are commonly conducted can get along with the subjective terminology of ordinary parlance. Everyone recognizes that in our day "democracy" is tending to become the political system of all civilized peoples. But what is the exact meaning of the term "democracy"? It is even more vague than that vaguest of terms, "religion." We must therefore leave it to one side and turn to the facts that it covers.*

One observes at the outset a pronounced tendency on the part of modern civilized peoples to use a form of government where legislative power rests largely with an assembly elected by a part at least of the citizens. One further notes a tendency to augment that power and increase the number of citizens electing the assembly.

In Switzerland, by way of exception, the legislative powers of the elective assembly are limited by the popular referendum, and in the United States they are to some extent checked by the federal courts. An attempt to limit them by plebiscite was made in France at the instance of Napoleon III. It met with no success, though one could not definitely assert that that was due to any inherent defect in the scheme itself, since the

---

* The best government now in existence, and also better than countless others that have so far been observable in history, is the government of Switzerland, especially in the forms it takes on in the small cantons—forms of direct democracy. It is a democratic government, but it has nothing but the name in common with the governments, also called democratic, of other countries such as France or the United States

government that was created by it was destroyed by the armed forces of a foreign enemy. The tendency to increase numbers of voters is general, and along that road, for the time being, there is no going back. The franchise is continually being extended. After giving it to adult men, the idea is now to grant it to women. It is not beyond the range of possibility that it may be extended as regards age.

Underlying such forms, which are more or less the same with all civilized peoples, there are great differences in substance, like names being given to unlike things. The power of the legislative assembly varies all the way from a maximum to a minimum. In France both the Chamber of Deputies and the Senate are elective. For the purposes of our investigation, therefore, they may be regarded as a single assembly, which is, one may say, absolutely sovereign and has no limits to its power. In Italy, the power of the Chamber has a theoretical check in the Senate, an actual check in the monarchy. In England, once upon a time, the power of the House of Commons found in the House of Lords an actual check that is now very much attenuated, and in the monarchy another that has likewise become largely nominal. In the United States the President is elected independently of the Congress and effectively limits its power. In Germany the States' Council and, to a still greater extent, the Emperor, supported by the military caste, constituted very considerable checks on the power of the Reichstag. So gradually we come to Russia, where the Duma has very little power, and to Japan, where the elective assembly has almost none at all. We may overlook Turkey and the republics of Central America, where the legislative assemblies are more or less fanciful entities.

We need not linger on the fiction of "popular representation"—poppycock grinds no flour. Let us go on and see what substance underlies the various forms of power in the governing classes. Ignoring exceptions, which are few in number and of short duration, one finds everywhere a governing class of relatively few individuals that keeps itself in power partly by force and partly by the consent of the subject class, which is much more populous. The differences lie principally, as regards substance, in the relative proportions of force and consent; and as regards forms, in the manners in which the force is used and the consent obtained.

As we have elsewhere observed, if the consent were unanimous there would be no need to use force; but that extreme is unknown to fact. Another extreme has a few concrete illustrations—the case where a despot keeps himself in power by armed force against a hostile population (such cases all belong to the past); and then the case where a foreign power holds a reluctant people in subjection—of that there are still quite a few examples in the present. The reason why the equilibrium is much more unstable in the first case than in the other has to be sought in the prevalence of differing residues. The residues working in the satellites of the despot are not essentially different from those working in the despot's subjects, so that there is no faith available to inspire, and at the same time to restrain, the use of force; and as was the case with the praetorians, the janissaries, and the Mamelukes, satellites are readily tempted to make capricious use of their power, or else to abandon defence of the despot against the people. The ruling nation, on the other hand, generally differs in usages and customs, and sometimes in language and religion, from the subject nation. There is a difference in residues, therefore, and so plenty of faith to inspire use of force. But there may be plenty of faith in the subject nation to inspire resistance to oppression; and that is how, in the long run, the equilibrium may chance to be upset.

It is in fear of that very outcome that conquering peoples try to assimilate their subject peoples, and when that can be done, it is by all odds the best way for them to assure their dominion. They often fail because they try to change residues by violence instead of taking advantage of existing residues. Rome had the faculty for this latter in pre-eminent degree, and so was able to assimilate the many peoples about her in Latium, Italy, and the Mediterranean basin.

We have had incidental occasion already to remark that the policies of governments are the more effective, the more adept they are at utilizing existing residues, the less effective, the less skilful, and in general total failures when they set out to change residues by force; and to tell the truth, almost all explanations as to the success or failure of certain policies of this or that government come down in the end to that principle.

Many people are prevented by derivations from recognizing the principle. If A, for instance, is the derivation that expresses certain sentiments of the subject class, another derivation, B, is readily found, which at bottom expresses the sentiments of the dominant class but which the latter regards as a valid and convincing refutation of A. In that confidence it concludes that it will be an easy matter to force B upon the subject class, since that will be a mere question of opening their eyes to a truth so obvious. So the conflict between sentiments becomes a conflict between derivations or, in other terms, a mere battle of words. Others see the realities a little more clearly but use sophistries. They dwell at length on the advantages of a people's having unity of faith in certain matters, but neglect entirely to consider whether that can be accomplished without incurring very serious disadvantages that would offset or more than offset the advantages. Still others implicitly assume that for a person to take advantage of the sentiments of others without sharing them, he must necessarily have a purpose that is dishonest and detrimental to society, and so they condemn such conduct outright as worthy only of a wicked hypocrite.*

To utilize the sentiments prevalent in a society for attaining a given

* However, that mode of reasoning is peculiar to a small number of moralists. One rarely notes it in practical men.

purpose is in itself neither beneficial nor detrimental to society. The utility, or the detriment, depends upon the result achieved. If the result is beneficial, one gets a utility; if harmful, a detriment. Nor can it be said that when a governing class works for a result that will be advantageous to itself regardless of whether it will be beneficial, or the reverse, to its subject class, the latter is necessarily harmed. Countless the cases where a governing class working for its own exclusive advantage has further promoted the welfare of a subject class. In a word, utilization of the residues prevailing in a society is just a means, and its value the value of the results achieved.

Along with residues, considered as instruments of governing, come interests, and at times these are the only available agents for modifying residues. It is important, however, not to forget that naked interests alone, taken apart from sentiments, may indeed be a powerful instrument for influencing individuals showing a predominance of Class I residues and so for influencing numerous elements in a governing class; but that taken in that way by themselves, apart from sentiments, they have very little influence upon individuals showing a predominance of Class II residues, and consequently upon the subject class as a whole. One may say, in general and speaking very roughly, that the governing class has a clearer view of its own interests because its vision is less obscured by sentiments, whereas the subject class is less aware of its interests because its vision is more clouded by sentiments; and that, as a result, the governing class is in a position to mislead the subject class into serving the interests of the governing class; but that those interests are not necessarily opposite to the interests of the subject class, often in fact coincide with them, so that in the end the deception may prove beneficial to the subject class.

Consent and force appear in all the course of history as instruments of governing. They come forward in the legendary days of the *Iliad* and *Odyssey* to make the power of the Greek kings secure. They are discernible in the legends of the Roman kings. Later on, in historical times, in Rome they are busy under both Republic and Empire; and it is by no means to be taken for granted that the government of Augustus enjoyed any less support in the subject class than the various governments the last years of the Republic managed to secure. And so coming on through the Barbarian kings and the mediaeval republics down to the divine-right potentates of two or three centuries ago, and finally to our modern democratic régimes, we find all along the same mixture of force and consent.

Just as derivations are much more variable than the residues that underlie them, so the forms in which force and consent express themselves are much more variable than the sentiments and interests in which they originate; and the differences in the relative proportions of force and consent are in large part due to varying relative proportions of sentiments and interests. The parallel between derivations and forms of government goes farther still. They both have less influence upon the social equilibrium than do the sentiments and interests that underlie them. That fact has also been perceived by many scholars, but they have tended to go a little too far in asserting that forms of government are altogether matters of indifference.

A governing class is present everywhere, even where there is a despot, but the forms under which it appears are widely variable. In absolute governments a sovereign occupies the stage alone. In so called democratic governments it is the parliament. But behind the scenes in both cases there are always people who play a very important rôle in actual government. To be sure they must now and again bend the knee to the whims of ignorant and domineering sovereigns or parliaments, but they are soon back at their tenacious, patient, never-ending work, which is of much the greater consequence. In the Roman *Digesta* one may read truly splendid constitutions bearing the names of very wretched Emperors, just as in our day we have very fair legal codes that have been enacted by fairly brainless parliaments. The cause in both cases is the same: The sovereign leaves everything to his legal advisers, in some cases not even divining what they are having him do—and parliaments today even less than many a shrewd leader or king. And least of all King Demos! And such blindness on his part has at times helped to effect betterments in conditions of living in the face of his prejudices, not to mention much-needed steps in behalf of national defence. King Demos, good soul, thinks he is following his own devices. In reality he is following the lead of his rulers. But that very very often turns out to the advantage of his rulers only, for they, from the days of Aristotle down to our own, have made lavish use of the arts of bamboozling King Demos. Our plutocrats, like those of the late Roman Republic, are at all times busy making money, either on their own account or to sate the hungry maws of their partisans and accomplices; and for anything else they care little or nothing. Among the derivations which they use to show that their rule is to the advantage of a country, interesting is the assertion that the public is better qualified to pass on general questions than on special ones. The fact, in reality, is the precise opposite. One has to talk only for a very brief time with an uneducated person to see that he grasps special questions, which are usually concrete, much more clearly than general questions, which as a rule are abstract. But abstract questions have the advantage for people in power that whatever the answers that are given them by the public, they will be able to draw any inference they choose from them. The people sends to parliament men who are pledged to abolish interest on capital and "surplus value" in industry, and check the "greed" of the "speculators" (general questions); and those representatives now directly, now indirectly by helping others, increase the public debt beyond all bounds and consequently the interest paid to capital, maintain and in fact increase the "surplus value" enjoyed by manufacturers (many of whom fatten on political demagoguery), and put the government of the nation into the hands of speculators such as Volpi, who concluded the Peace of Lausanne, or of cabinet ministers such as Caillaux and Lloyd George.

The governing class is not a homogeneous body. It too has a government—a smaller, choicer class (or else a leader, or a committee) that effectively and practically exercises control. Sometimes that fact is visible to the eye, as in the case of the Ephors of Sparta, the Council of Ten in Venice, the favourite ministers of absolute sovereigns, or the "bosses" in parliaments. At other times it is more or less hidden from view, as in the "caucus" in England, the political convention in the United States, the cliques of "speculator" chieftains who function in France and Italy, and so on. The tendency to personify abstractions or merely to think of them as objective realities inclines many people to picture the governing class as a person, or at least as a concrete unit, and imagine that it knows what it wants and executes by logical procedures designs which it had conceived in advance. In just such terms do anti-Semites think of the Jews, and many Socialists of the "*bourgeoisie*" (though others, coming closer to realities, think of the middle class as a "system" functioning to some extent quite aside from any design on the part of its members). Ruling classes, like other social groups, perform both logical and non-logical actions, and the chief element in what happens is in fact the order, or system, not the conscious will of individuals, who indeed may in certain cases be carried by the system to points where they would never have gone of deliberate choice. In speaking of "speculators," we must not think of them as actors in a melodrama who administer and rule the world, executing wicked designs by stratagem dark. Such a conception of them would be no more real than a fairy-story. Speculators are just people who keep their minds on their business, and being well supplied with Class I residues, take advantage of them to make money, following lines of least resistance, as after all everybody else does. They hold no meetings where they congregate to plot common designs, nor have they any other devices for reaching a common accord. That accord comes about automatically; for if in a given set of circumstances there is one line of procedure where the advantage is greatest and the resistance least, the majority of those who are looking for it will find it, and though each of them will be following it on his own account, it will seem, without being so, that they are all acting in common accord. But at other times they will be carried along by the sheer force of the system to which they belong, involuntarily, and indeed against their wills, following the course that is required of the system. Fifty years ago "speculators" had no conception whatever of the state of affairs that prevails today and to which their activities have brought them. The road they have followed has been the resultant of an infinitude of minor acts, each determined by the present advantage. As is the case with all social phenomena, it has been the resultant of certain forces operating in conjunction with certain ties and in the face of certain obstacles. When we say that at the present time our speculators are laying the foundations for a war by continually increasing public expenditures, we in no sense mean that they are doing that deliberately—quite to the contrary! They are continually increasing public expenditures and fanning economic conflicts not in order to bring on a war, but in order to make a direct profit in each little case. But that cause, though an important one, is not the main cause. There is another of greater importance—their appeal to sentiments of patriotism in the masses at large, as a device for governing. Furthermore, the speculators in the various countries are in competition with each other and are using armaments to exact concessions from rivals. Other similar causes are operating, and they all are leading to increases in armaments without that's being in any sense the consequence of preconceived design. Not only that. Those men who are rich in Class I residues sense intuitively, without needing to reason or theorize, that if a great and terrible war should occur, one of its possible consequences might be that they would have to give way to men who are rich in Class II residues. To such a war they are opposed in virtue of the same instinct that prompts the stag to run from the lion, though they are glad to take on little colonial wars, which they can superintend without any danger to themselves. It is on such interests and sentiments, not on any deliberate, premeditated resolve, that their activities depend, and these accordingly may eventually carry them to some objective that they may be aiming at, but also quite as readily to points where they would never have dreamed of going. Some day the war they have made way for but not wanted may break out; and then it will be a consequence of the past activities of the speculators, but not of any intent they have had either at that time or ever. So the speculators of ancient Rome brought on the fall of the Republic and the dictatorships of Caesar and Augustus, but without knowing that they were headed in those directions and without the slightest desire to reach those goals.

In dealing with speculators, as with other elements in the social order, the ethical aspect and the aspect of social utility have to be kept sharply distinguished. The speculators are not to be condemned from the standpoint of social utility because they do things that are censured by one or another of the current ethical systems; nor are they to be absolved from any given ethical standpoint because they have proved socially beneficial. The utility depends upon the circumstances in which the activities of the speculators are carried on, and specifically upon the relative proportions of speculators to persons strong in Class II residues, either in the population at large or in the governing classes. To determine and appraise such utility is a quantitative, not a qualitative, problem. In our day, for instance, the enormous development of economic production, the spread of civilization to new countries, the remarkable rise in standards of living among all civilized peoples, are in large part the work of speculators. But they have been able to do that work because they came from populations in which Class II residues were numerous and strong: and it is doubtful, indeed it is hardly probable, that benefits such as these could be realized if there were any great decline in the Class II residues in our masses at large or even merely in our governing classes.

To have a concrete instance of the applications of the instruments of governing just described, one might consider the case of Italy during the Depretis régime. How could that politician ever have been master of the Italian Chamber and the country for so many years? He was not the leader of a victorious army. He had none of the eloquence that stirs the emotions of men. He had none of the prestige born of high achievement. He was not forced upon the country by a king. What, then, the source of his strength? Only one answer is possible: He was a past master at utilizing the sentiments and interests then prevailing in the country, and more especially the interests, and so becoming really the leader of the syndicate of speculators that was then ruling the country and to a large extent holding the substance of the power of which he enjoyed only the semblance. He made many speculators rich men by protective tariffs, railway deals, government contracts in which the state was robbed right and left, banking irregularities that were later exposed. Never was bandit chieftain more lavish towards his confederates in pillage and plunder. Crispi was an interlude. His was an administration that set out to modify residues and cared little for the interests of speculators. He aspired to creating sentiments of nationalism in a people that had no sense of country, and his work, like the work of all men who have tried what he tried, came to nothing. Instead of using the Socialists, he fought them and so had their more intelligent and active leaders against him. And hostile or indifferent were the speculators, to whom he tossed few if any bones to pick. In a word, the conditions of the economic period in which he ruled were all in his disfavour. He fell incidentally as the result of a defeat in Abyssinia, but he could not have lasted long in power in any event. Remarkable the contrast between him and his successor, Giolitti, who was truly a master in the art of using interests and sentiments. He, no less than Depretis, made himself the leader of the speculator class and the protector of "big business"; and since money was required for helping the latter, and the banks had their money tied up in government loans, he provided the government with funds by founding the insurance monopoly, so making the money in the banks available for "big business." Sentiments he had a gift for using in a truly marvellous way, never overlooking a single one. Crispi had striven to create nation-

alist sentiments in the country, and he had striven in vain. Giolitti found
them ready-made, and exploited them lavishly and ever with success.
He never dreamed of fighting Socialism. He billed and cooed with its
leaders till he got them—as he himself said—to "pack Marx away in the
attic." Others he tamed to such an extent that they came to deserve their
nickname as "the King's Socialists." He lavished money on the Socialist
cooperatives, and that he was in a position to do, because economic
conditions were in his favour, just as they had been unfavourable to
Crispi; and those same conditions allowed him to carry the Libyan adventure to a successful conclusion and defer to the Greek calends the
liquidation of the huge public debt that was incurred in connexion with
his policies. Friendly with the Socialists, at least with such among them
as were not too savage and staunch, he was not unfriendly to the Cleri-
cals, and if he did not tame them, he at least made them more tractable,
and could depend on them extensively at election time. Taking advantage
of an enthusiastic public consensus in sentiments of nationalism, he broke
up the close-knit body of Republicans and reduced that party to a small
nucleus of zealots blindly keeping faith with their principles. He extended the franchise to strike terror into the hearts of the *bourgeoisie*
and make himself its protector, meanwhile doing his utmost to look like
the patron of the popular parties. In a word, there was not a sentiment
nor an interest in Italy of which he failed to make clever use for his
purposes, so piling success on success and going through with the Libyan
enterprise, which was something far more costly and dangerous than
the Abyssinian venture that had proved so fatal to Crispi. It is said that
he did not want the war with Turkey and fought it only as a sop to
certain sentiments, using it as an instrument of governing. Like all men
preponderantly endowed with Class I residues, he could use sentiments,
but he did not understand them. He could never see how they could
still be strong in the masses at large when they showed themselves so
pliant in the popular leaders whom he flattered and cajoled. He therefore
had no accurate perception of their social significance. That was no great
hindrance to him in his deft manoeuvres from moment to moment; but it
prevented him from having any broad view of the future that he was
meantime preparing. But that, after all, did not worry him greatly—his
eye was wholly on the present. In fighting the Libyan War, he was
striking a grievous blow at the Ottoman Empire and so bringing on the
Balkan War, and as a result profoundly altering the balance in Europe.
Yet he made no efforts to strengthen the military and naval forces of
his country with a view to oncoming wars. He refused to increase army
and navy appropriations in the degree required because he did not care
to exasperate the taxpayers, and especially because he needed the votes
of the Socialists. On the other hand, he made loud boast of the fact
that in spite of his war he had maintained or increased expenditures on

public works and in subventions of various kinds to voters. He concealed the amounts the war had cost by disguising them in his budget reports, postponing payment of them to the future. He increased the public debt clandestinely by issuing long-term treasury bonds, so filling the coffers of commercial and savings-banks but with grave risks of danger to come. By such devices he made ready to have his war and yet conceal its costs. The policy was momentarily convenient, for by those devices he was able to satisfy both the elements who wanted the war and the elements who were unwilling to shoulder its inevitable consequences. But it postponed and aggravated the difficulties that it failed to solve.

In this particular case one sees, as under a magnifying lens, the kind of thing that speculators generally tend to do. The great predominance of Class I and the virtual absence of Class II residues in Giolitti and his followers first was a great help and then ended by being a great handicap to their power, which was all but shattered by fifty or more Socialist Deputies who were sent to the parliament by the elections of 1913 and who were strong in Class II residues. Before that campaign the Socialist party had had to choose between "transformism" and "intransigence" (non-compromise), in other words, between following a course more particularly featured by Class I residues and a course prevailingly featured by Class II residues. As usually happens with both nations and parties, the Socialist leaders were inclined to follow the first course; but a great tidal wave came surging up from the masses and bore new leaders to the fore, and then swept them, with a few survivors from among the old, along the second course, where sentiments predominated. That was fortunate for the Socialist party, for it was in that way placed in a favourable position for giving battle to a government that had no convictions and no faith. And in that we have a particular instance of a development that is general and with which we shall have to deal at some length. In other words, we discover that the greatest strength of a party lies not in the exclusive predominance of Class I residues or of Class II residues, but in a combination of residues from the two classes in certain relative proportions.

The interlude provided by the administration of Luzzatti confirms these inferences. Luzzatti had been of great help to elements that profited by protective tariffs, but they had no further need of him when he became Prime Minister—at that time protection was in no danger, and once water has gone over the dam it comes no more to the mill. Furthermore, Luzzatti was far from being as good a representative of the speculators as Giolitti had been, nor did he have Giolitti's faculty for using sentiments without sharing them. For that reason Giolitti remained the actual "boss" during Luzzatti's turn in power and took power away from him with the greatest ease when he judged the moment opportune. Likewise Sonnino, who is far superior to many another statesman in Italy so far as education and political thinking are concerned, has never been able to last long in power, because he lacks either the ability or the inclination to act as a faithful agent of the band of speculators. In France, Rouvier was frequently "boss" of the parliament simply because of his merits as leader of a similar band, and his last ministry came to an end not because of difficulties at home but because of difficulties abroad. Caillaux's strength lies altogether in the speculators who are gathered about him. But it would be wiser for us not to stop at these names or any other list of the kind and imagine that we are dealing with situations peculiar to certain individuals, certain political systems, certain countries. They are closely bound up with a social system in which speculators make up the governing *élite.** In England the election campaigns against the House of Lords were backed financially by speculators led by so-called Liberal ministers. In Germany the great manufacturing and financial interests reach the very foot of the throne, though that choice spot is still to some extent disputed by the military caste. In the United States Wilson and Bryan went into

* Descriptions given by technicians who follow the ways of empiricism without any cluttering of theory are very useful for getting facts in a clear light. Such men are immune to the ever present danger of reshaping fact to conform with theory, even unwittingly. I will quote in point such a description from the *Financial Times*, Mar. 27, 1914. It relates to the things that we have just been discussing. I will merely note that the description applies not only to France, but to other countries where speculators are in the saddle. As regards the United States, a good deal would have to be added to the description, but nothing taken away. "*Paris, March 24.* We have heard a good deal of late about 'plutocratic democrats' and 'democratic plutocrats,' by which is meant either a wealthy financier who becomes a demagogue for the sake of political influence rather than from any real conviction or, as is more widely the case in France, a demagogue who has no objection to becoming a wealthy financier if circumstances permit. M. Barthou, M. Briand, and their friends have freely used the expression in connexion with M. Caillaux, to whom they are politically opposed, and it is a fact that certain prominent Republican politicians belonging to all sections of the Republican party have of late years turned their political influence to considerable personal advantage." A long account follows of things various statesmen had done in collusion with financiers. We omit it because we prefer not to cite proper names, their presence easily diverting attention from general uniformities to considerations of ethics, party, or particular sympathies or antipathies. The conclusion of the article takes us back to facts of general bearing, which are of greater importance in a scientific study. "*Need of a political protector*: As a matter of fact, it has long been the fashion with French financial and other companies to provide themselves with a '*paratonnerre*' or 'lightning-rod,' in the shape of a person of political influence who can act more or less as a mediator in high places, and who, on occasion, can help to shield financiers who may be liable to get into trouble, or protect interests that may be in danger from threatened legislation. As a rule politicians are very chary of being openly connected with any but concerns of very high reputation; but there are others. Thus, there are many barristers who are both clever pleaders and brilliant politicians. Many are the concerns that willingly pay huge annual fees to a political barrister in order to secure his services as 'legal adviser.' The legal adviser is paid quite as much for his political influence as for his legal advice, and he runs no risk, not being openly connected with the concern. It is natural, perhaps, in a country where kissing goes by favour—and show me the country in which it does not!—that people interested in important business schemes should endeavour to obtain a hearing with the powers that be by securing as influential a political intermediary as they can get, but the practice undoubtedly has its drawbacks."

power as professed and probably sincere opponents of trusts and financiers, but actually they worked in their favour in maintaining anarchy in Mexico with a view to securing a President there who would be subservient to American finance. And those pacifists carried their self-composure to the extent of inviting Mexico to attend the Peace Congress at The Hague at the very moment when the American navy was attacking Vera Cruz, killing men, women and children! The recent past is very much like the present. In France Louis Napoleon Bonaparte was able to become Napoleon III only because he had become the leader of the speculators, while in Italy administrations of the past have fallen through unawareness of the importance of speculators or through disregarding or neglecting them. It would perhaps be going too far, though not very much too far, to say that if the governments of the King of Naples and his other neighbours had made a concession of the "Railways of the South" to private interests, and promoted other similar enterprises, they would not have been overthrown. For years and years French and Italian liberals have tired our ear-drums with their praises of the English parliamentary system, which they have held up as a model before the whole world. Some of them may possibly have been ignorant of the extraordinary corruption which features that system and has been so excellently described by Ostrogorski. But others must certainly have known of it, and if they have held their peace, it has been in deference to the principle that wolf does not eat wolf.

For purposes of maintaining its power the governing class uses individuals from the subject class, who may be grouped in two divisions corresponding to the two principal instruments for holding power secure. The one group uses force, and is made up of soldiers, police of one sort or another, and the *bravi* of a day gone by; the other uses skill, and ranges in character and in time all the way from the clientage of the old Roman politicians to the clientèles of our contemporary politicians. Those two groups are always with us, but never in the same actual proportions, nor, much less, in the same visible proportions. One extreme is marked by the Rome of the praetorians, where the chief *de facto* instrument of governing, and even more so the visible instrument, was armed force. The other extreme is represented by the United States of America, where the chief actual instrument of governing, and to a somewhat lesser extent the apparent instrument, is the political "machine." These cliques work in various ways. The principal way is the least conspicuous. The administration in power "looks after" the interests of the speculators, and often without any explicit understanding with them. A protectionist government, for instance, gets the confidence and the support of the manufacturers it protects without having to come to explicit terms with all of them, though it may have some agreement with outstanding individuals. The situation is the same with public works, though agreement with the big contractors is becoming the rule. Other ways are better known—they are less important from the social standpoint, but are commonly regarded as more important from the ethical standpoint. Among them is the bribery of voters, elected officials, government ministers, newspaper-owners, and other such persons, which has its counterpart under systems of absolutism in the bribery of courtiers, favourites, male and female, officials, generals, and so on—an old form of corruption that has not altogether disappeared. Such means have been employed in all periods of history, from the days of ancient Athens and republican Rome down to our own; but they are really the consequences of government by a class that forces its way into power by cunning and rules by cunning. And that is why the numberless attempts which have been made to "purify" politics have been failures and still remain such. Witch-grass may be cut as often as one chooses, but it sprouts only the more rankly if the roots are left untouched. Our democracies in France, Italy, England, and the United States are tending more and more to become demagogic plutocracies and may be following that road on the way to one of those radical transformations that have been witnessed in the past.

Barring some few exceptions, chief among them the conferring of honours and decorations by governments, money has to be spent to secure the support both of armed force and of political "machines." It is not enough, therefore, to be willing to use such instruments—one has to be able to. That capacity is correlated with the production of wealth, and the production of wealth, in its turn, is not independent of the manner in which armed force and the political following are utilized. The problem therefore is a complex one and has to be considered synthetically. Analytically, one may say that armed force in many cases costs less than the "machine," but in certain other cases the "machine" may prove to be more favourable to the production of wealth; and that has to be taken into account in striking the balance.

Evolution towards "democracy" seems to stand in strict correlation with the increased use of that instrument of governing which involves resort to artifice and to the "machine," as against the instrument of force. In ancient times that was clearly observable toward the end of the Republic in Rome, where there was a conflict between precisely those two instrumentalities, force winning the final victory in the Empire. It is even more apparent in our own day, when the régimes in many "democratic" countries might be defined as a sort of feudalism that is primarily economic and in which the principal instrument of governing is the manipulation of political followings, whereas the military feudalism of the Middle Ages used force primarily as embodied in vassalage. A political system in which "the people" expresses its "will"—given but not granted that it has one—without cliques, intrigues, "combines," "gangs," exists only as a pious wish of theorists. It is not to be observed in reality, either in the past or in the present, either in our Western countries or in any others.

Such phenomena, long the subject of remark, are usually described as aberrations, or "degenerations," of "democracy"; but when and where one may be introduced to the perfect, or even the merely decent, state from which said aberration or "degeneration" has occurred, no one ever manages to tell. The best that can be said is that when democracy was an opposition party it did not show as many blemishes as it does at present; but that is a trait common to almost all opposition parties, which lack not so much the will as the chance to go wrong.

It is further to be noted that the defects in various systems of government may differ from each other, but, taking things as a whole, it cannot be held that one type of régime is very different in that respect from any other. The criticisms that are levelled at modern democracy are not greatly different from those that were levelled at ancient democracies, the Athenian, for instance; and if there are cases of corruption in democracies old and new, it would not be difficult to find cases just as bad in absolute and constitutional monarchies, in oligarchical governments, and in any other sort of régime.

11. Herbert Spencer

Militant and Industrial Societies

I. The Militant Type of Society

Preceding chapters have prepared the way for framing conceptions of
the two fundamentally-unlike kinds of political organization, proper to
the militant life and the industrial life, respectively. It will be instructive
here to arrange in coherent order, those traits of the militant type already
incidentally marked, and to join with them various dependent traits;
and in the next chapter to deal in like manner with the traits of the
industrial type.

During social evolution there has habitually been a mingling of the two.
But we shall find that, alike in theory and in fact, it is possible to trace
with due clearness those opposite characters which distinguish them in
their respective complete developments. Especially is the nature of the
organization which accompanies chronic militancy, capable of being
inferred à priori and proved à posteriori to exist in numerous cases. While
the nature of the organization accompanying pure industrialism, of which
at present we have little experience, will be made clear by contrast;
and such illustrations as exist of progress towards it will become recognizable.

Two liabilities to error must be guarded against. We have to deal with
societies compounded and re-compounded in various degrees; and we
have to deal with societies which, differing in their stages of culture, have
their structures elaborated to different extents. We shall be misled, therefore, unless our comparisons are such as take account of unlikenesses in
size and in civilization. Clearly, characteristics of the militant type which
admit of being displayed by a vast nation, may not admit of being displayed by a horde of savages, though this is equally militant. Moreover,
as institutions take long to acquire their finished forms, it is not to be
expected that all militant societies will display the organization appropriate to them in its completeness. Rather may we expect that in most cases
it will be incompletely displayed.

In face of these difficulties the best course will be to consider, first,

From Spencer, *The Principles of Sociology* (New York: D. Appleton and Co. 1896)
Vol. II, Part V, p. 568-640.

what are the several traits which of necessity militancy tends to produce; and then to observe how far these traits are conjointly shown in past and present nations distinguished by militancy. Having contemplated the society ideally organized for war, we shall be prepared to recognize in real societies the characters which war has brought about.

For preserving its corporate life, a society is impelled to corporate action; and the preservation of its corporate life is the more probable in proportion as its corporate action is the more complete. For purposes of offence and defence, the forces of individuals have to be combined; and where every individual contributes his force, the probability of success is greatest. Numbers, natures, and circumstances being equal, it is clear that of two tribes or two larger societies, one of which unites the actions of all its capable members while the other does not, the first will ordinarily be the victor. There must be an habitual survival of communities in which militant cooperation is universal.

This proposition is almost a truism. But it is needful here, as a preliminary, consciously to recognize the truth that the social structure evolved by chronic militancy, is one in which all men fit for fighting act in concert against other societies. Such further actions as they carry on they can carry on separately; but this action they must carry on jointly.

A society's power of self-preservation will be great in proportion as, besides the direct aid of all who can fight, there is given the indirect aid of all who cannot fight. Supposing them otherwise similar, those communities will survive in which the efforts of combatants are in the greatest degree seconded by those of non-combatants. In a purely militant society, therefore, individuals who do not bear arms have to spend their lives in furthering the maintenance of those who do. Whether, as happens at first, the non-combatants are exclusively the women; or whether, as happens later, the class includes enslaved captives; or whether, as happens later still, it includes serfs; the implication is the same. For if, of two societies equal in other respects, the first wholly subordinates its workers in this way, while the workers in the second are allowed to retain for themselves the produce of their labour, or more of it than is needful for maintaining them; then, in the second, the warriors, not otherwise supported, or supported less fully than they might else be, will have partially to support themselves, and will be so much the less available for war purposes. Hence in the struggle for existence between such societies, it must usually happen that the first will vanquish the second. The social type produced by survival of the fittest, will be one in which the fighting part includes all who can bear arms and be trusted with arms, while the remaining part serves simply as a permanent commissariat.

An obvious implication, of a significance to be hereafter pointed out, is that the non-combatant part, occupied in supporting the combatant part, cannot with advantage to the self-preserving power of the society increase beyond the limit at which it efficiently fulfils its purpose. For, otherwise, some who might be fighters are superfluous workers; and the fighting power of the society is made less than it might be. Hence, in the militant type, the tendency is for the body of warriors to bear the largest practicable ratio to the body of workers.

Given two societies of which the members are all either warriors or those who supply the needs of warriors, and, other things equal, supremacy will be gained by that in which the efforts of all are most effectually combined. In open warfare joint action triumphs over individual action. Military history is a history of the successes of men trained to move and fight in concert.

Not only must there be in the fighting part a combination such that the powers of its units may be concentrated, but there must be a combination of the subservient part with it. If the two are so separated that they can act independently, the needs of the fighting part will not be adequately met. If to be cut off from a temporary base of operations is dangerous, still more dangerous is it to be cut off from the permanent base of operations; namely, that constituted by the body of noncombatants. This has to be so connected with the body of combatants that its services may be fully available. Evidently, therefore, development of the militant type involves a close binding of the society into a whole. As the loose group of savages yields to the solid phalanx, so, other things equal, must the society of which the parts are but feebly held together, yield to one in which they are held together by strong bonds.

But in proportion as men are compelled to cooperate, their self-prompted actions are restrained. By as much as the unit becomes merged in the mass, by so much does he lose his individuality as a unit. And this leads us to note the several ways in which evolution of the militant type entails subordination of the citizen.

His life is not his own, but is at the disposal of his society. So long as he remains capable of bearing arms he has no alternative but to fight when called on; and, where militancy is extreme, he cannot return as a vanquished man under penalty of death.

Of course, with this there goes possession of such liberty only as military obligations allow. He is free to pursue his private ends only when the tribe or nation has no need of him; and when it has need of him, his actions from hour to hour must conform, not to his own will but to the public will.

So, too, with his property. Whether, as in many cases, what he holds as private he so holds by permission only, or whether private ownership is recognized, it remains true that in the last resort he is obliged to surrender whatever is demanded for the community's use.

Briefly, then, under the militant type the individual is owned by the State. While preservation of the society is the primary end, preservation of each member is a secondary end—an end cared for chiefly as subserving the primary end.

Fulfilment of these requirements, that there shall be complete corporate action, that to this end the non-combatant part shall be occupied in providing for the combatant part, that the entire aggregate shall be strongly bound together, and that the units composing it must have their individualities in life, liberty, and property, thereby subordinated, presupposes a coercive instrumentality. No such union for corporate action can be achieved without a powerful controlling agency. On remembering the fatal results caused by division of counsels in war, or by separation into factions in face of an enemy, we see that chronic militancy tends to develop a despotism; since, other things equal, these societies will habitually survive in which, by its aid, the corporate action is made complete.

And this involves a system of centralization. The trait made familiar to us by an army, in which, under a commander-in-chief there are secondary commanders over large masses, and under these tertiary ones over smaller masses, and so on down to the ultimate divisions, must characterize the social organization at large. A militant society requires a regulative structure of this kind, since, otherwise, its corporate action cannot be made most effectual. Without such grades of governing centres diffused throughout the non-combatant part as well as the combatant part, the entire forces of the aggregate cannot be promptly put forth. Unless the workers are under a control akin to that which the fighters are under, their indirect aid cannot be insured in full amount and with due quickness.

And this is the form of a society characterized by *status*—a society, the members of which stand one towards another in successive grades of subordination. From the despot down to the slave, all are masters of those below and subjects of those above. The relation of the child to the father, of the father to some superior, and so on up to the absolute head, is one in which the individual of lower status is at the mercy of one of higher status.

Otherwise described, the process of militant organization is a process of regimentation, which, primarily taking place in the army, secondarily affects the whole community.

The first indication of this we trace in the fact everywhere visible, that the military head grows into a civil head—usually at once, and, in exceptional cases, at last, if militancy continues. Beginning as leader in war he becomes ruler in peace; and such regulative policy as he pursues in the one sphere, he pursues, so far as conditions permit, in the other. Being, as the non-combatant part is, a permanent commissariat, the principle of graduated subordination is extended to it. Its members come to be directed in a way like that in which the warriors are directed—not literally, since by dispersion of the one and concentration of the other exact parallelism is prevented; but, nevertheless, similarly in principle.

Labour is carried on under coercion; and supervision spreads everywhere.

To suppose that a despotic military head, daily maintaining regimental control in conformity with inherited traditions, will not impose on the producing classes a kindred control, is to suppose in him sentiments and ideas entirely foreign to his circumstances.

The nature of the militant form of government will be further elucidated on observing that it is both positively regulative and negatively regulative. It does not simply restrain; it also enforces. Besides telling the individual what he shall not do, it tells him what he shall do.

That the government of an army is thus characterised needs no showing. Indeed, commands of the positive kind given to the soldier are more important than those of the negative kind: fighting is done under the one, while order is maintained under the other. But here it chiefly concerns us to note that not only the control of military life but also the control of civil life, is, under the militant type of government, thus characterized. There are two ways in which the ruling power may deal with the private individual. It may simply limit his activities to those which he can carry on without aggression, direct or indirect, upon others; in which case its action is negatively regulative. Or, besides doing this, it may prescribe the how, and the where, and the when, of his activities—may force him to do things which he would not spontaneously do—may direct in greater or less detail his mode of living; in which case its action is positively regulative. Under the militant type this positively regulative action is widespread and peremptory. The civilian is in a condition as much like that of the soldier as difference of occupation permits.

And this is another way of expressing the truth that the fundamental principle of the militant type is compulsory cooperation. While this is obviously the principle on which the members of the combatant body act, it no less certainly must be the principle acted on throughout the non-combatant body, if military efficiency is to be great; since, otherwise, the aid which the non-combatant body has to furnish cannot be insured.

That binding together by which the units of a militant society are made into an efficient fighting structure, tends to fix the position of each in rank, in occupation, and in locality.

In a graduated regulative organization there is resistance to change from a lower to a higher grade. Such change is made difficult by lack of the possessions needed for filling superior positions; and it is made difficult by the opposition of those who already fill them, and can hold inferiors down. Preventing intrusion from below, these transmit their respective places and ranks to their descendants; and as the principle of inheritance becomes settled, the rigidity of the social structure becomes decided. Only where an "egalitarian despotism" reduces all subjects to the same political status—a condition of decay rather than of development—does the converse state arise.

The principle of inheritance, becoming established in respect of the classes which militancy originates, and fixing the general functions of their members from generation to generation, tends eventually to fix also their special functions. Not only do men of the slave-classes and the artizan-classes succeed to their respective ranks, but they succeed to the particular occupations carried on in them. This, which is a result of the tendency towards regimentation, is ascribable primarily to the fact that a superior, requiring from each kind of worker his particular product, has an interest in replacing him at death by a capable successor; while the worker, prompted to get aid in executing his tasks, has an interest in bringing up a son to his own occupation: the will of the son being powerless against these conspiring interests. Under the system of compulsory cooperation, therefore, the principle of inheritance, spreading through the producing organization, causes a relative rigidity in this also.

A kindred effect is shown in the entailed restraints on movement from place to place. In proportion as the individual is subordinated in life, liberty, and property, to his society, it is needful that his whereabouts shall be constantly known. Obviously the relation of the soldier to his officer, and of this officer to his superior, is such that each must be ever at hand; and where the militant type is fully developed the like holds throughout the society. The slave cannot leave his appointed abode; the serf is tied to his allotment; the master is not allowed to absent himself from his locality without leave.

So that the corporate action, the combination, the cohesion, the regimentation, which efficient militancy necessitates, imply a structure which strongly resists change.

A further trait of the militant type, naturally accompanying the last, is that organizations other than those forming parts of the State-organization, are wholly or partially repressed. The public combination occupying all fields, excludes private combinations.

For the achievement of complete corporate action there must, as we have seen, be a centralized administration, not only throughout the combatant part but throughout the non-combatant part; and if there exist unions of citizens which act independently, they in so far diminish the range of this centralized administration. Any structures which are not portions of the State-structure, serve more or less as limitations to it, and stand in the way of the required unlimited subordination. If private combinations are allowed to exist, it will be on condition of submitting to an official regulation such as greatly restrains independent action; and since private combinations officially regulated are inevitably hindered from doing things not conforming to established routine, and are thus debarred from improvement, they cannot habitually thrive and grow. Obviously, indeed, such combinations, based on the principle of voluntary cooperation, are incongruous with social arrangements based on the principle of compulsory cooperation. Hence the militant type is characterized by the absence, or comparative rarity, of bodies of citizens associated for commercial purposes, for propagating special religious views, for achieving philanthropic ends, &c.

Private combinations of one kind, however, are congruous with the militant type—the combinations, namely, which are formed for minor defensive or offensive purposes. We have, as examples, those which constitute factions, very general in militant societies; those which belong to the same class as primitive guilds, serving for mutual protection; and those which take the shape of secret societies. Of such bodies it may be noted that they fulfil on a small scale ends like those which the whole society fulfills on a large scale—the ends of self-preservation, or aggression, or both. And it may be further noted that these small included societies are organized on the same principle as the large including society—the principle of compulsory cooperation. Their governments are coercive: in some cases even to the extent of killing those of their members who are disobedient.

A remaining fact to be set down is that a society of the militant type tends to evolve a self-sufficient sustaining organization. With its political autonomy there goes what we may call an economic autonomy. Evidently if it carries on frequent wars against surrounding societies, its commercial intercourse with them must be hindered or prevented: exchange of commodities can go on to but a small extent between those who are continually fighting. A militant society must, therefore, to the greatest degree practicable, provide internally the supplies of all articles needful for carrying on the lives of its members. Such an economic state as that which existed during early feudal times, when, as in France, "the castles made almost all the articles used in them," is a state evidently entailed on groups, small or large, which are in constant antagonism with surrounding groups. If there does not already exist within any group so circumstanced, an agency for producing some necessary article, inability to obtain it from without will lead to the establishment of an agency for obtaining it within.

Whence it follows that the desire "not to be dependent on foreigners" is one appropriate to the militant type of society. So long as there is constant danger that the supplies of needful things derived from other countries will be cut off by the breaking out of hostilities, it is imperative that there shall be maintained a power of producing these supplies at home, and that to this end the required structures shall be maintained. Hence there is a manifest direct relation between militant activities and a protectionist policy.

And now having observed the traits which may be expected to establish themselves by survival of the fittest during the struggle for existence among societies, let us observe how these traits are displayed in actual societies, similar in respect of their militancy but otherwise dissimilar.

Of course in small primitive groups, however warlike they may be, we must not look for more than rude outlines of the structure proper to the militant type. Being loosely aggregated, definite arrangement of their parts can be carried but to a small extent. Still, so far as it goes, the evidence is to the point.

The ancient Peruvian empire, gradually established by the conquering Yncas, may next be instanced. Here the ruler, divinely descended, sacred, absolute, was the centre of a system which minutely controlled all life. His headship was at once military, political, ecclesiastical, judicial; and the entire nation was composed of those who, in the capacity of soldiers, labourers, and officials, were slaves to him and his deified ancestors. Military service was obligatory on all taxable Indians who were capable; and those of them who had served their prescribed terms, formed into reserves, had then to work under State-superintendence. The army having heads over groups of ten, fifty, a hundred, five hundred, a thousand, ten thousand, had, besides these, its superior commanders of Ynca blood. The community at large was subject to a parallel regimentation: the inhabitants registered in groups, being under the control of officers over tens, fifties, hundreds, and so on. And through these successive grades of centres, reports ascended to the Ynca-governors of great divisions, passing on from them to the Ynca; while his orders descended "from rank to rank till they reached the lowest." There was an ecclesiastical organization similarly elaborate, having, for example, five classes of diviners; and there was an organization of spies to examine and report upon the doings of the other officers. Everything was under public inspection. There were village-officers who overlooked the ploughing, sowing, and harvesting. When there was a deficiency of rain, measured quantities of water were supplied by the State. All who travelled without authority were punished as vagabonds; but for those who were authorized to travel for public purposes, there were establishments supplying lodging and necessaries. "It was the duty of the decurions to see that the people were clothed"; and the kinds of cloth, decorations, badges, &c., to be worn by the different ranks were prescribed. Besides this regulation of external life there was regulation of domestic life. The people were required to "dine and sup with open doors, that the judges might be able to enter freely;" and these judges had to see that the house, clothes, furniture, &c., were kept clean and in order, and the children properly disciplined: those who mismanaged their houses being flogged. Subject to this minute control, the people laboured to support this elaborate State-organization. The political, religious, and military classes were exempt from tribute; while the labouring classes when not serving in the army, had to yield up all produce beyond that required for their bare sustenance. Of the whole empire, one-third was alloted for supporting the State, one-third for supporting the priesthood who ministered to the manes of ancestors, and the remaining third had to support the workers. Besides giving tribute by tilling the lands of the Sun and the King, the workers had to till the lands of the soldiers on duty, as well as those of incapables. And they also had to pay tribute of clothes, shoes, and arms. Of the lands on which the people maintained themselves, a tract was apportioned to each man according to the size of his family. Similarly with the produce of the flocks. Such moiety of this in each district as was not required for supplying public needs, was periodically shorn, and the wool divided by officials. These arrangements were in pursuance of the principle that "the private property of each man was held by favour of the Ynca, and according to their laws he had no other title to it." Thus the people, completely possessed by the State in person, property, and labour, transplanted to this or that locality as the Ynca directed, and, when not serving as soldiers, living under a discipline like that within the army, were units in a centralized regimented machine, moved throughout life to the greatest practicable extent by the Ynca's will, and to the least practicable extent by their own wills. And, naturally, along with militant organization thus carried to its ideal limit, there went an almost entire absence of any other organization. They had no money; "they neither sold clothes, nor houses, nor estates;" and trade was represented among them by scarcely anything more than some bartering of articles of food.

Take, now, another ancient society, which, strongly contrasted in sundry respects, shows us, along with habitual militancy, the assumption of structural traits allied in their fundamental characters to those thus far observed. I refer to Sparta. That warfare did not among the Spartans evolve a single despotic head, while in part due to causes which, as before shown, favour the development of compound political heads, was largely due to the accident of their double kingship: the presence of two divinely-descended chiefs prevented the concentration of power. But though from this cause there continued an imperfectly centralized government, the relation of this government to members of the community was substantially like that of militant governments in general. Notwithstanding the serfdom, and in towns the slavery, of the Helots, and notwithstanding the political subordination of the Periœki, they all, in common with the Spartans proper, were under obligation to military service: the working function of the first, and the trading function, so far as it existed, which was carried on by the second, were subordinate to the militant function, with which the third was exclusively occupied. And the civil divisions thus marked re-appeared in the military divisions: "at the battle of Platæa every Spartan hoplite had seven Helots, and every Periœki hoplite one Helot to attend him." The extent to which, by the daily military discipline, prescribed military mess, and fixed contributions of food, the individual life of the Spartan was subordinated to public demands, from seven years upwards, needs mention only to show the rigidity of the restraints which here, as elsewhere, the militant type imposes—restraints which were further shown in the prescribed age for marriage, the prevention of domestic life, the forbidding of industry or any money-seeking occupation, the interdict on going abroad without leave, and the authorized censorship under which his days and nights were passed. There was fully carried out in Sparta the Greek theory of society, that "the citizen belongs neither to himself nor to his family, but to his city." So that though in this exceptional case, chronic militancy was prevented from developing a supreme head, owning the individual citizen in body and estate, yet it developed an essentially identical relation between the community as a whole and its units. The community, exercising its power through a compound head instead of through a simple head, completely enslaved the individual. While the lives and labours of the Helots were devoted exclusively to the support of those who formed the military organization, the lives and labours of those who formed the military organization were exclusively devoted to the service of the State: they were slaves with a difference.

Of modern illustrations, that furnished by Russia will suffice. Here, again, with the wars which effected conquests and consolidations, came the development of the victorious commander into the absolute ruler, who, if not divine by alleged origin, yet acquired something like divine *prestige*. "All men are equal before God, and the Russians' God is the Emperor," says De Custine: "the supreme governor is so raised above earth, that he sees no difference between the serf and the lord." Under the stress of Peter the Great's wars, which, as the nobles complained, took them away from their homes, "not, as formerly, for a single campaign, but for long years," they became "servants of the State, without privileges, without dignity, subjected to corporal punishment, and burdened with onerous duties from which there was no escape." "Any noble who refused to serve ['the State in the Army, the Fleet, or the Civil Administration, from boyhood to old age,'] was not only deprived of his estate, as in the old times, but was declared to be a traitor, and might be condemned to capital punishment." "Under Peter," says Wallace, "all offices, civil and military," were "arranged in fourteen classes or ranks;" and he "defined the obligations of each with microscopic minuteness. After his death the work was carried on in the same spirit, and the tendency reached its climax in the reign of Nicholas." In the words of De Custine, "the tchinn [the name for this organization] is a nation formed into a regiment; it is the military system applied to all classes of society, even to those who never go to war." With this universal regimentation in structure went a regimental discipline. The conduct of life was dictated to the citizens at large in the same way as to soldiers. In the reign of Peter and his successors, domestic entertainments were appointed and regulated; the people were compelled to change their costumes; the clergy to cut off their beards; and even the harnessing of horses was according to pattern.

Occupations were controlled to the extent that "no boyard could enter any profession, or forsake it when embraced, or retire from public to private life, or dispose of his property, or travel into any foreign country, without the permission of the Czar." This omnipresent rule is well expressed in the close of certain rhymes, for which a military officer was sent to Siberia:—

> "Tout se fait par ukase ici;
> C'est par ukase que l'on voyage,
> C'est par ukase que l'on rit."

. . . we have before us cases in which such similarities of social structure as exist, cannot be ascribed to inheritance of a common character by the social units. The immense contrasts between the populations of these several societies, too, varying from millions at the one extreme to thousands at the other, negative the supposition that their common structural traits are consequent on size. Nor can it be supposed that likenesses of conditions in respect of climate, surface, soil, flora, fauna, or likenesses of habits caused by such conditions, can have had anything to do with the likenesses of organization in these societies; for their respective habitats present numerous marked unlikenesses. Such traits as they one and all exhibit, not ascribable to any other cause, must thus be ascribed to the habitual militancy characteristic of them all. The results of induction alone would go far to warrant this ascription; and it is fully warranted by their correspondence with the results of deduction, as set forth above.

Any remaining doubts must disappear on observing how continued militancy is followed by further development of the militant organization. . . .

An example under our immediate observation may . . . be taken—that of the German Empire. Such traits of the militant type in Germany as were before manifest, have, since the late war, become still more manifest. The army, active and passive, including officers and attached functionaries, has been increased by about 100,000 men; and changes in 1875 and 1880, making certain reserves more available, have practically caused a further increase of like amount. Moreover, the smaller German States, having in great part surrendered the administration of their several contingents, the German army has become more consolidated; and even the armies of Saxony, Würtemberg, and Bavaria, being subject to Imperial supervision, have in so far ceased to be independent. Instead of each year granting military supplies, as had been the practice in Prussia before the formation of the North German Confederation, the Parliament of the Empire was, in 1871, induced to vote the required annual sum for three years thereafter; in 1874 it did the like for the succeeding seven years; and again in 1880 the greatly increased amount for the augmented army was authorized for the seven years then following: steps obviously surrendering popular checks on Imperial power. Simultaneously, military officialism has been in two ways replacing civil officialism. Subaltern officers are rewarded for long services by appointments to civil posts—local communes being forced to give them the preference to civilians; and not a few members of the higher civil service, and of the universities, as well as teachers in the public schools, having served as "volunteers of one year," become commissioned officers of the Landwehr. During the struggles of the so-called Kulturkampf, the ecclesiastical organization became more subordinated by the political. Priests suspended by bishops were maintained in their offices; it was made penal for a clergyman publicly to take part against the government; a recalcitrant bishop had his salary stopped; the curriculum for ecclesiastics was prescribed by the State, and examination by State-officials required; church discipline was subjected to State-approval; and a power of expelling rebellious clergy from the country was established. Passing to the industrial activities we may note, first, that through sundry steps, from 1873 onwards, there has been a progressive transfer of railways into the hands of the State; so that, partly by original construction (mainly of lines for military purposes), and partly by purchase, three-fourths of all Prussian railways have been made government property; and the same percentage holds in the other German States: the aim being eventually to make them all Imperial. Trade interferences have been extended in various ways—by protectionist tariffs, by revival of the usury laws, by restrictions on Sunday labour. Through its postal service the State has assumed industrial functions—presents acceptances, receives money on bills of exchange that are due, as also on ordinary bills, which it gets receipted; and until stopped by shopkeepers' protests, undertook to procure books from publishers. Lastly there come the measures for extending, directly and indirectly, the control over popular life. On the one hand there are the laws under which, up to the middle of last year, 224 socialist societies have been closed, 180 periodicals suppressed, 317 books, &c., forbidden; and under which sundry places have been reduced to a partial state of siege. On the other hand may be named Prince Bismarck's scheme for re-establishing guilds (bodies which by their regulations coerce their members), and his scheme of State-insurance, by the help of which the artizan would, in a considerable degree, have his hands tied. Though these measures have not been carried in the forms proposed, yet the proposal of them sufficiently shows the general tendency. In all which changes we see progress towards a more integrated structure, towards increase of the militant part as compared with the industrial part, towards the replacing of civil organization by military organization, towards the strengthening of restraints over the individual and regulation of his life in greater detail.*

* This chapter was originally published in the *Contemporary Review* for Sept., 1881. Since that date a further movement of German society in the same general direction has been shown by the pronounced absolutism of the imperial rescript of Jan., 1882, endorsing Prince Bismarck's scheme of State-socialism.

The remaining example to be named is that furnished by our own society since the revival of military activity—a revival which has of late been so marked that our illustrated papers are, week after week, occupied with little else than scenes of warfare. Already in the first volume of *The Principles of Sociology*, I have pointed out many ways in which the system of compulsory cooperation characterizing the militant type, has been trenching on the system of voluntary cooperation characterizing the industrial type; and since those passages appeared (July, 1876), other changes in the same direction have taken place. Within the military organization itself, we may note the increasing assimilation of the volunteer forces to the regular army, now going to the extent of proposing to make them available abroad, so that instead of defensive action for which they were created, they can be used for offensive action; and we may also note that the tendency shown in the army during the past generation to sink the military character whenever possible, by putting on civilian dresses, is now checked by an order to officers in garrison towns to wear their uniforms when off duty, as they do in more militant countries. Whether, since the date named, usurpations of civil functions by military men (which had in 1873–4 gone to the extent that there were 97 colonels, majors, captains, and lieutenants employed from time to time as inspectors of science and art classes) have gone further, I cannot say; but there has been a manifest extension of the militant spirit and discipline among the police, who, wearing helmet-shaped hats, beginning to carry revolvers, and looking upon themselves as half soldiers, have come to speak of the people as "civilians." To an increasing extent the executive has been overriding the other governmental agencies; as in the Cyprus business, and as in the doings of the Indian Viceroy under secret instructions from home. In various minor ways are shown endeavours to free officialism from popular checks; as in the desire expressed in the House of Lords that the hanging of convicts in prisons, entrusted entirely to the authorities, should have no other witnesses; and as in the advice given by the late Home Secretary (on 11th May, 1878) to the Derby Town Council, that it should not interfere with the chief constable (a military man) in his government of the force under him—a step towards centralizing local police control in the Home Office. Simultaneously we see various actual or prospective extensions of public agency, replacing or restraining private agency. There is the "endowment of research," which, already partially carried out by a government fund, many wish to carry further; there is the proposed act for establishing a registration of authorized teachers; there is the bill which provides central inspection for local public libraries; there is the scheme for compulsory insurance—a scheme showing us in an instructive manner the way in which the regulating policy extends itself: compulsory charity having generated improvidence, there comes compulsory insurance as a remedy for the improvidence. Other proclivities towards institutions belonging to the militant type, are seen in the increasing demand for some form of protection, and in the lamentations uttered by the "society papers" that duelling has gone out. Nay, even though the party which by position and function is antagonistic to militancy, we see that militant discipline is spreading; for the caucus-system, established for the better organization of liberalism, is one which necessarily, in a greater or less degree, centralizes authority and controls individual action.

Besides seeing, then, that the traits to be inferred *à priori* as characterizing the militant type, constantly exist in societies which are permanently militant in high degrees, we also see that in other societies increase of militant activity is followed by development of such traits.

In some places I have stated, and in other places implied, that a necessary relation exists between the structure of a society and the natures of its citizens. Here it will be well to observe in detail the characters proper to, and habitually exemplified by, the members of a typically militant society.

Other things equal, a society will be successful in war in proportion as its members are endowed with bodily vigour and courage. And, on the average, among conflicting societies there will be a survival and spread of those in which the physical and mental powers called for in battle, are not only most marked but also most honoured. Egyptian and Assyrian sculptures and inscriptions, show us that prowess was the thing above all others thought most worthy of record. Of the words good, just, &c., as used by the ancient Greeks, Grote remarks that they "signify the man of birth, wealth, influence and daring, whose arm is strong to destroy or to protect, whatever may be the turn of his moral sentiments; while the opposite epithet, bad, designates the poor, lowly, and weak, from whose dispositions, be they ever so virtuous society has little to hope or to fear." In the identification of virtue with bravery among the Romans, we have a like implication. During early turbulent times throughout Europe, the knightly character, which was the honourable character, primarily included fearlessness: lacking this, good qualities were of no account; but with this, sins of many kinds, great though they might be, were condoned.

If, among antagonist groups of primitive men, some tolerated more than others the killing of their members—if, while some always retaliated others did not; those which did not retaliate, continually aggressed on with impunity, would either gradually disappear or have to take refuge in undesirable habitats. Hence there is a survival of the unforgiving. Further, the *lex talionis,* primarily arising between antagonist groups, becomes the law within the group; and chronic feuds between component families and clans, everywhere proceed upon the general principle of life for life. Under the militant *régime* revenge becomes a virtue, and failure to revenge a disgrace. Among the Fijians, who foster anger in their

children, it is not infrequent for a man to commit suicide rather than
live under an insult; and in other cases the dying Fijian bequeathes the
duty of inflicting vengeance to his children. This sentiment and the resulting practices we trace among peoples otherwise wholly alien, who
are, or have been, actively militant. In the remote East may be instanced
the Japanese. They are taught that "with the slayer of his father a man
may not live under the same heaven; against the slayer of his brother a
man must never have to go home to fetch a weapon; with the slayer of
his friend a man may not live in the same State." And in the West may be
instanced France during feudal days, when the relations of one killed or
injured were required by custom to retaliate on any relations of the
offender—even those living at a distance and knowing nothing of the
matter. Down to the time of the Abbé Brantôme, the spirit was such
that ecclesiastic, enjoining on his nephews by his will to avenge any
unredressed wrongs done to him in his old age, says of himself—"I may
boast, and I thank God for it, that I never received an injury without
being revenged on the author of it." That where militancy is active,
revenge, private as well as public, becomes a duty, is well shown at the
present time among the Montenegrins—a people who have been at war
with the Turks for centuries. "Dans le Montenegro," says Boué, "on dira
d'un homme d'une natrie [clan] ayant tué un individu d'une autre: Cette
natrie nous doit une tête, et il faut que cette dette soit acquittée, car qui
ne se venge pas ne se sancitie pas."

Where activity in destroying enemies is chronic, destruction will become a source of pleasure; where success in subduing fellow-men is above
all things honoured, there will arise delight in the forcible exercise of
mastery; and with pride in spoiling the vanquished, will go disregard for
the rights of property at large. As it is incredible that men should be
courageous in face of foes and cowardly in face of friends, so it is
incredible that the other feelings fostered by perpetual conflicts abroad
should not come into play at home. We have just seen that with the
pursuit of vengeance outside the society, there goes the pursuit of
vengeance inside the society; and whatever other habits of thought and
action constant war necessitates, must show their effects on the social
life at large. Facts from various places and times prove that in militant
communities the claims to life, liberty, and property, are little regarded.
The Dahomans, warlike to the extent that both sexes are warriors, and by
whom slave-hunting invasions are, or were, annually undertaken "to
furnish funds for the royal exchequer," show their bloodthirstiness by their
annual "customs," at which multitudinous victims are publicly slaughtered
for the popular gratification. The Fijians, again, highly militant in their
activities and type of organization, who display their recklessness of life
not only by killing their own people for cannibal feasts, but by destroying
immense numbers of their infants and by sacrificing victims on such trivial

occasions as launching a new canoe, so much applaud ferocity that to commit a murder is a glory. Early records of Asiatics and Europeans show us the like relation. What accounts there are of the primitive Mongols, who, when united, massacred western peoples wholesale, show us a chronic reign of violence, both within and without their tribes; while domestic assassinations, which from the beginning have characterized the militant Turks, continue to characterize them down to our own day. In proof that it was so with the Greek and Latin races it suffices to instance the slaughter of the two thousand helots by the Spartans, whose brutality was habitual, and the murder of large numbers of suspected citizens by jealous Roman emperors, who also, like their subjects, manifested their love of bloodshed in their arenas. That where life is little regarded there can be but little regard for liberty, follows necessarily. Those who do not hesitate to end another's activities by killing him, will still less hesitate to restrain his activities by holding him in bondage. Militant savages, whose captives, when not eaten, are enslaved, habitually show us this absence of regard for fellow-men's freedom, which characterizes the members of militant societies in general. How little, under the *régime* of war, more or less markedly displayed in all early historic societies, there was any sentiment against depriving men of their liberties, is sufficiently shown by the fact that even in the teachings of primitive Christianity there was no express condemnation of slavery. Naturally the like holds with the right of property. Where mastery established by force is honourable, claims to possession by the weaker are likely to be little respected by the stronger. In Fiji it is considered chief-like to seize a subject's goods; and theft is virtuous if undiscovered. Among the Spartans "the ingenious and successful pilferer gained applause with his booty." In mediæval Europe, with perpetual robberies of one society by another there went perpetual robberies within each society. Under the Merovingians "the murders and crimes it [*The Ecclesiastical History of the Franks*] relates, have almost all for their object the possession of the treasure of the murdered persons." And under Charlemagne plunder by officials was chronic: the moment his back was turned, "the provosts of the king appropriated the funds intended to furnish food and clothing for the artisans."

Where warfare is habitual, and the required qualities most needful and therefore most honoured, those whose lives do not display them are treated with contempt, and their occupations regarded as dishonourable. In early stages labour is the business of women and of slaves—conquered men and the descendants of conquered men; and trade of every kind, carried on by subject classes, long continues to be identified with lowness of origin and nature. In Dahomey, "agriculture is despised because slaves are employed in it." "The Japanese nobles and placemen, even of secondary rank, entertain a sovereign contempt for traffic." Of the ancient Egyptians

Wilkinson says, "their prejudices against mechanical employments, as far as regarded the soldier, were equally strong as in the rigid Sparta." "For trade and commerce the [ancient] Persians were wont to express extreme contempt," writes Rawlinson. That progress of class-differentiation which accompanied the conquering wars of the Romans, was furthered by establishment of the rule that it was disgraceful to take money for work, as also by the law forbidding senators and senators' sons from engaging in speculation. And how great has been the scorn expressed by the militant classes for the trading classes throughout Europe, down to quite recent times, needs no showing.

That there may be willingness to risk life for the benefit of the society, there must be much of the feeling called patriotism. Though the belief that it is glorious to die for one's country cannot be regarded as essential, since mercenaries fight without it; yet it is obvious that such a belief conduces greatly to success in war; and that entire absence of it is so unfavourable to offensive and defensive action that failure and subjugation will, other things equal, be likely to result. Hence the sentiment of patriotism is habitually established by the survival of societies the members of which are most characterized by it.

With this has to be united the sentiment of obedience. The possibility of that united action by which, other things equal, war is made successful, depends on the readiness of individuals to subordinate their wills to the will of a commander or ruler. Loyalty is essential. In early stages the manifestation of it is but temporary; as among the Araucanians who, ordinarily showing themselves "repugnant to all subordination, are then [when war is impending] prompt to obey, and submissive to the will of their military sovereign" appointed for the occasion. And with development of the militant type this sentiment becomes permanent. Erskine tells us that the Fijians are intensely loyal: men buried alive in the foundations of a king's house, considered themselves honoured by being so sacrificed; and the people of a slave district "said it was their duty to become food and sacrifice for the chiefs." So in Dahomey, there is felt for the king "a mixture of love and fear, little short of adoration." In ancient Egypt again, where "blind obedience was the oil which caused the harmonious working of the machinery" of social life, the monuments on every side show with wearisome iteration the daily acts of subordination—of slaves and others to the dead man, of captives to the king, of the king to the gods. Though for reasons already pointed out, chronic war did not generate in Sparta a supreme political head, to whom there could be shown implicit obedience, yet the obedience shown to the political agency which grew up was profound: individual wills were in all things subordinate to the public will expressed by the established authorities. Primitive Rome, too, though without a divinely-descended king to whom submission could be shown, displayed great submission to an appointed king, qualified only by expressions of opinion on special occasions; and the principle of absolute obedience, slightly mitigated in the relations of the community as a whole to its ruling agency, was unmitigated within its component groups. That throughout European history, alike on small and on large scales, we see the sentiment of loyalty dominant where the militant type of structure is pronounced, is a truth that will be admitted without detailed proof.

From these conspicuous traits of nature, let us turn to certain consequent traits which are less conspicuous and which have results of less manifest kinds. Along with loyalty naturally goes faith—the two being, indeed, scarcely separable. Readiness to obey the commander in war, implies belief in his military abilities; and readiness to obey him during peace, implies belief that his abilities extend to civil affairs also. Imposing on men's imaginations, each new conquest augments his authority. There come more frequent and more decided evidences of his regulative action over men's lives; and these generate the idea that his power is boundless. Unlimited confidence in governmental agency is fostered. Generations brought up under a system which controls all affairs, private and public, tacitly assume that affairs can only thus be controlled. Those who have experience of no other *régime* are unable to imagine any other *régime*. In such societies as that of ancient Peru, for example, where, as we have seen, regimental rule was universal, there were no materials for framing the thought of an industrial life spontaneously carried on and spontaneously regulated.

By implication there results repression of individual initiative, and consequent lack of private enterprise. In proportion as an army becomes organized, it is reduced to a state in which the independent action of its members is forbidden. And in proportion as regimentation pervades the society at large, each member of it, directed or restrained at every turn, has little or no power of conducting his business otherwise than by established routine. Slaves can do only what they are told by their masters; their masters cannot do anything that is unusual without official permission; and no permission is to be obtained from the local authority until superior authorities through their ascending grades have been consulted. Hence the mental state generated is that of passive acceptance and expectancy. Where the militant type is fully developed, everything must be done by public agencies; not only for the reason that these occupy all spheres, but for the further reason that did they not occupy them, there would arise no other agencies: the prompting ideas and sentiments having been obliterated.

There must be added a concomitant influence on the intellectual nature, which cooperates with the moral influences just named. Personal causation is alone recognized, and the conception of impersonal causation is prevented from developing. The primitive man has no idea of cause in the modern sense. The only agents included in his theory of things are living persons and the ghosts of dead persons. All unusual occurrences, together with those usual ones liable to variation, he ascribes to supernatural beings. And this system of interpretation survives through early stages of civilization; as we see, for example, among the Homeric Greeks, by whom wounds, deaths, and escapes in battle, were ascribed to the enmity or the aid of the gods, and by whom good and bad acts were held to be divinely prompted. Continuance and development of militant forms and activities maintain this way of thinking. In the first place, it indirectly hinders the discovery of causal relations. The sciences grow out of the arts—begin as generalizations of truths which practice of the arts makes manifest. In proportion as processes of production multiply in their kinds and increase in their complexities, more numerous uniformities come to be recognized; and the ideas of necessary relation and physical cause arise and develop. Consequently, by discouraging industrial progress, militancy checks the replacing of ideas of personal agency by ideas of impersonal agency. In the second place, it does the like by direct repression of intellectual culture. Naturally a life occupied in acquiring knowledge, like a life occupied in industry, is regarded with contempt by a people devoted to arms. The Spartans clearly exemplified this relation in ancient times; and it was again exemplified during feudal ages in Europe, when learning was scorned as proper only for clerks and the children of mean people. And obviously, in proportion as warlike activities are antagonistic to study and the spread of knowledge, they further retard that emancipation from primitive ideas which ends in recognition of natural uniformities. In the third place, and chiefly, the effect in question is produced by the conspicuous and perpetual experience of personal agency which the militant *régime* yields. In the army, from the commander-in-chief down to the private undergoing drill, every movement is directed by a superior; and throughout the society, in proportion as its regimentation is elaborate, things are hourly seen to go thus or thus according to the regulating wills of the ruler and his subordinates. In the interpretation of social affairs, personal causation is consequently alone recognized. History comes to be made up of the doings of remarkable men; and it is tacitly assumed that societies have been formed by them. Wholly foreign to the habit of mind as is the thought of impersonal causation, the course of social evolution is unperceived. The natural genesis of social structures and functions is an utterly alien conception, and appears absurd when alleged. The notion of a self-regulating social process is unintelligible. So that militancy moulds the citizen into a form not only morally adapted but intellectually adapted—a form which cannot think away from the entailed system.

In three ways, then, we are shown the character of the militant type of social organization. Observe the congruities which comparison of results discloses.

Certain conditions, manifest *à priori*, have to be fulfilled by a society fitted for preserving itself in presence of antagonist societies. To be in the highest degree efficient, the corporate action needed for preserving the corporate life must be joined in by every one. Other things equal, the fighting power will be greatest where those who cannot fight, labour exclusively to support and help those who can: an evident implication being that the working part shall be no larger than is required for these ends. The efforts of all being utilized directly or indirectly for war, will be most effectual when they are most combined; and, besides union among the combatants, there must be such union of the non-combatants with them as renders the aid of these fully and promptly available. To satisfy these requirements, the life, the actions, and the possessions, of each individual must be held at the service of the society. This universal service, this combination, and this merging of individual claims, pre-suppose a despotic controlling agency. That the will of the soldier-chief may be operative when the aggregate is large, there must be sub-centres and sub-sub-centres in descending grades, through whom orders may be conveyed and enforced, both throughout the combatant part and the non-combatant part. As the commander tells the soldier both what he shall not do and what he shall do; so, throughout the militant community at large, the rule is both negatively regulative and positively regulative: it not only restrains, but it directs: the citizen as well as the soldier lives under a system of compulsory cooperation. Development of the militant type involves increasing rigidity, since the cohesion, the combination, the subordination, and the regulation, to which the units of a society are subjected by it, inevitably decrease their ability to change their social positions, their occupations, their localities.

On inspecting sundry societies, past and present, large and small, which are, or have been, characterized in high degrees by militancy, we are shown, *à posteriori*, that amid the differences due to race, to circumstances, and to degrees of development, there are fundamental similarities of the kinds above inferred *à priori*. Modern Dahomey and Russia, as well as ancient Peru, Egypt, and Sparta, exemplify that owning of the individual by the State in life, liberty, and goods, which is proper to a social system adapted for war. And that with changes further fitting a society for war-like activities, there spread throughout it an officialism, a dictation, and a superintendence, akin to those under which soldiers live, we are shown by imperial Rome, by imperial Germany, and by England since its late aggressive activities.

Lastly comes the evidence furnished by the adapted characters of the men who compose militant societies. Making success in war the highest glory, they are led to identify goodness with bravery and strength. Revenge becomes a sacred duty with them; and acting at home on the law of retaliation which they act on abroad, they similarly, at home as abroad, are ready to sacrifice others to self: their sympathies, continually deadened during war, cannot be active during peace. They must have a patriotism which regards the triumph of their society as the supreme end of action; they must possess the loyalty whence flows obedience to authority; and that they may be obedient they must have abundant faith. With faith in authority and consequent readiness to be directed, naturally goes relatively little power of initiation. The habit of seeing everything officially controlled fosters the belief that official control is everywhere needful; while a course of life which makes personal causation familiar and negatives experience of impersonal causation, produces an inability to conceive of any social processes as carried on under self-regulating arrangements. And these traits of individual nature, needful concomitants as we see of the militant type, are those which we observe in the members of actual militant societies.

II. The Industrial Type

Having nearly always to defend themselves against external enemies, while they have to carry on internally the processes of sustentation, societies, as remarked in the last chapter, habitually present us with mixtures of the structures adapted to these diverse ends. Disentanglement is not easy. According as either structure predominates it ramifies through the other: instance the fact that where the militant type is much developed, the worker, ordinarily a slave, is no more free than the soldier; while, where the industrial type is much developed, the soldier, volunteering on specified terms, acquires in so far the position of a free worker. In the one case the system of status, proper to the fighting part, pervades the working part; while in the other the system of "contract," proper to the working part, affects the fighting part. Especially does the organization adapted for war obscure that adapted for industry. While, as we have seen, the militant type as theoretically constructed, is so far displayed in many societies as to leave no doubt about its essential nature, the "industrial type" has its traits so hidden by those of the still-dominant militant type, that its nature is nowhere more than very partially exemplified. Saying thus much to exclude expectations which cannot be fulfilled, it will be well also to exclude certain probable misconceptions.

In the first place, "industrialism" must not be confounded with "industriousness." Though the members of an industrially-organized society are habitually industrious, and are, indeed, when the society is a developed one, obliged to be so; yet it must not be assumed that the industrially-organized society is one in which, of necessity, much work is done. Where the society is small, and its habitat so favourable that life may be comfortably maintained with but little exertion, the social relations which characterize the industrial type may co-exist with but very moderate productive activities. It is not the diligence of its members which constitutes the society an industrial one in the sense here intended, but the "form of cooperation" under which their labours, small or great in amount, are carried on. This distinction will be best understood on observing that, conversely, there may be, and often is, great industry in societies framed on the militant type. In ancient Egypt there was an immense labouring population and a large supply of commodities, numerous in their kinds, produced by it. Still more did ancient Peru exhibit a vast community purely militant in its structure, the members of which worked unceasingly. We are here concerned, then, not with the quantity of labour but with the mode of organization of the labourers. A regiment of soldiers can be set to construct earth-works; another to cut down wood; another to bring in water; but they are not thereby reduced for the time being to an industrial society. The united individuals do these several things under command; and having no private claims to the products, are, though industrially occupied, not industrially organized. And the same holds throughout the militant society as a whole, in proportion as the regimentation of it approaches completeness.

The industrial type of society, properly so called, must also be distinguished from a type very likely to be confounded with it—the type, namely, in which the component individuals, while exclusively occupied in production and distribution, are under a regulation such as that advocated by socialists and communists. For this, too, involves in another form the principle of compulsory cooperation. Directly or indirectly, individuals are to be prevented from severally and independently occupying themselves as they please; are to be prevented from competing with one another in supplying goods for money; are to be prevented from hiring themselves out on such terms as they think fit. There can be no artificial system for regulating labour which does not interfere with the natural system. To such extent as men are debarred from making whatever engagements they like, they are to that extent working under dictation. No matter in what way the controlling agency is constituted, it stands towards those controlled in the same relation as does the controlling agency of a militant society. And how truly the *régime* which those who declaim against competition would establish, is thus characterized, we see both in the fact that communistic forms of organization existed in early societies which were predominantly warlike, and in the fact that at the present time communistic projects chiefly originate among, and are most favoured by, the more warlike societies.

A further preliminary explanation may be needful. The structures proper to the industrial type of society must not be looked for in distinct forms when they first appear. Contrariwise, we must expect them to begin in vague unsettled forms. Arising, as they do, by modification of pre-existing structures, they are necessarily long in losing all trace of these. For example, transition from the state in which the labourer, owned like a beast, is maintained that he may work exclusively for his master's benefit, to the condition in which he is completely detached from master, soil, and locality, and free to work anywhere and for anyone, is through gradations. Again, the change from the arrangement proper to militancy, under which subject-persons receive, in addition to maintenance, occasional presents, to the arrangement under which, in place of both, they received fixed wages, or salaries, or fees, goes on slowly and unobtrusively. Once more it is observable that the process of exchange, originally indefinite, has become definite only where industrialism is considerably developed. Barter began, not with a distinct intention of giving one thing for another thing equivalent in value, but it began by making a present and receiving a present in return; and even now in the East there continue traces of this primitive transaction. In Cairo the purchase of articles from a shopkeeper is preceded by his offer of coffee and cigarettes; and during the negotiation which ends in the engagement of a *dahabeah*, the dragoman brings gifts and expects to receive them. Add to which that there exists under such conditions none of that definite equivalence which characterizes exchange among ourselves: prices are not fixed, but vary widely with every fresh transaction. So that throughout our interpretations we must keep in view the truth, that the structures and functions proper to the industrial type distinguish themselves but gradually from those proper to the militant type.

Having thus prepared the way, let us now consider what are, *à priori*, the traits of that social organization which, entirely unfitted for carrying on defence against external enemies, is exclusively fitted for maintaining the life of the society by subserving the lives of its units. As before in treating of the militant type, so here in treating of the industrial type, we will consider first its ideal form.

While corporate action is the primary requirement in a society which has to preserve itself in presence of hostile societies, conversely, in the absence of hostile societies, corporate action is no longer the primary requirement.

The continued existence of a society implies, first, that it shall not be destroyed bodily by foreign foes, and implies, second, that it shall not be destroyed in detail by failure of its members to support and propagate themselves. If danger of destruction from the first cause ceases, there remains only danger of destruction from the second cause. Sustentation of the society will now be achieved by the self-sustentation and multiplication of its units. If his own welfare and the welfare of his offspring is fully achieved by each, the welfare of the society is by implication achieved. Comparatively little corporate activity is now required. Each man may maintain himself by labour, may exchange his products for the products of others, may give aid and receive payment, may enter into this or that combination for carrying on an undertaking, small or great, without the direction of the society as a whole. The remaining end to be achieved by public action is to keep private actions within due bounds; and the amount of public action needed for this becomes small in proportion as private actions become duly self-bounded.

So that whereas in the militant type the demand for corporate action is intrinsic, such demand for corporate action as continues in the industrial type is mainly extrinisic—is called for by those aggressive traits of human nature which chronic warfare has fostered, and may gradually diminish as, under enduring peaceful life, these decrease.

In a society organized for militant action, the individuality of each member has to be so subordinated in life, liberty, and property, that he is largely, or completely, *owned* by the State; but in a society industrially organized, no such subordination of the individual is called for. There remain no occasions on which he is required to risk his life while destroying the lives of others; he is not forced to leave his occupation and submit to a commanding officer; and it ceases to be needful that he should surrender for public purposes whatever property is demanded of him.

Under the industrial *régime* the citizen's individuality, instead of being sacrificed by the society, has to be defended by the society. Defence of his individuality becomes the society's essential duty. That after external protection is no longer called for, internal protection must become the cardinal function of the State, and that effectual discharge of this function must be a predominant trait of the industrial type, may be readily shown.

For it is clear that, other things equal, a society in which life, liberty, and property, are secure, and all interests justly regarded, must prosper more than one in which they are not; and, consequently, among competing industrial societies, there must be a gradual replacing of those in which personal rights are imperfectly maintained, by those in which they are perfectly maintained. So that by survival of the fittest must be produced a social type in which individual claims, considered as sacred, are trenched on by the State no further than is requisite to pay the cost of maintaining them, or rather, of arbitrating among them. For the aggressiveness of nature fostered by militancy having died out, the corporate function becomes that of deciding between those conflicting claims, the equitable adjustment of which is not obvious to the persons concerned.

With the absence of need for that corporate action by which the efforts of the whole society may be utilized for war, there goes the absence of need for a despotic controlling agency.

Not only is such an agency unnecessary, but it cannot exist. For since, as we see, it is an essential requirement of the industrial type, that the individuality of each man shall have the fullest play compatible with the like play of other men's individualities, despotic control, showing itself as it must by otherwise restricting men's individualities, is necessarily excluded. Indeed, by his mere presence an autocratic ruler is an aggressor on citizens. Actually or potentially exercising power not given by them, he in so far restrains their wills more than they would be restrained by mutual limitation merely.

Such control as is required under the industrial type, can be exercised only by an appointed agency for ascertaining and executing the average will; and a representative agency is the one best fitted for doing this.

Unless the activities of all are homogeneous in kind, which they cannot be in a developed society with its elaborate division of labour, there arises a need for conciliation of divergent interests; and to the end of insuring an equitable adjustment, each interest must be enabled duly to express itself. It is, indeed, supposable that the appointed agency should be a single individual. But no such single individual could arbitrate justly among numerous classes variously occupied, without hearing evidence: each would have to send representatives setting forth its claims. Hence the choice would lie between two systems, under one of which the representatives privately and separately stated their cases to an arbitrator on whose single judgment decisions depended; and under the other of which these representatives stated their cases in one another's presence, while judgments were openly determined by the general *consensus*. Without insisting on the fact that a fair balancing of class-interests is more likely to be effected by this last form of representation than by the first, it is sufficient to remark that it is more congruous with the nature of the industrial type; since men's individualities are in the smallest degree trenched upon. Citizens who, appointing a single ruler for a prescribed time, may have a majority of their wills traversed by his during this time, surrender their individualities in a greater degree than do those who, from their local groups, depute a number of rulers; since these, speaking and acting under public inspection and mutually restrained, habitually conform their decisions to the wills of the majority.

The corporate life of the society being no longer in danger, and the remaining business of government being that of maintaining the conditions requisite for the highest individual life, there comes the question —What are these conditions?

Already they have been implied as comprehended under the administration of justice; but so vaguely is the meaning of this phrase commonly conceived, that a more specific statement must be made. Justice then, as here to be understood, means preservation of the normal connexions between acts and results—the obtainment by each of as much benefit as his efforts are equivalent to—no more and no less. Living and working within the restraints imposed by one another's presence, justice requires that individuals shall severally take the consequences of their conduct, neither increased nor decreased. The superior shall have the good of his superiority; and the inferior the evil of his inferiority. A veto is therefore put on all public action which abstracts from some men part of the advantages they have earned, and awards to other men advantages they have not earned.

That from the developed industrial type of society there are excluded all forms of communistic distribution, the inevitable trait of which is that they tend to equalize the lives of good and bad, idle and diligent, is readily proved. For when, the struggle for existence between societies by war having ceased, there remains only the industrial struggle for existence, the final survival and spread must be on the part of those societies which produce the largest number of the best individuals—individuals best adapted for life in the industrial state. Suppose two societies, otherwise equal, in one of which the superior are allowed to retain, for their own benefit and the benefit of their offspring, the entire proceeds of their labour; but in the other of which the superior have taken from them part of these proceeds for the benefit of the inferior and their offspring. Evidently the superior will thrive and multiply more in the first than in the second. A greater number of the best children will be reared in the first; and eventually it will outgrow the second. It must not be inferred that private and voluntary aid to the inferior is negatived, but only public and enforced aid. Whatever effects the sympathies of the better for the worse spontaneously produce, cannot, of course, be interfered with; and will, on the whole, be beneficial. For while, on the average, the better will not carry such efforts so far as to impede their own multiplication, they will carry them far enough to mitigate the ill-fortunes of the worse without helping them to multiply.

Otherwise regarded, this system under which the efforts of each bring neither more nor less than their natural returns, is the system of contract.

We have seen that the *régime* of status is in all ways proper to the militant type. It is the concomitant of that graduated subordination by which the combined action of a fighting body is achieved, and which must pervade the fighting society at large to insure its corporate action. Under this *régime*, the relation between labour and produce is traversed by authority. As in the army, the food, clothing, &c., received by each soldier are not direct returns for work done, but are arbitrarily apportioned, while duties are arbitrarily enforced; so throughout the rest of the militant society, the superior dictates the labour and assigns such share of the returns as he pleases. But as, with declining militancy and growing industrialism, the power and range of authority decrease while uncontrolled action increases, the relation of contract becomes general; and in the fully-developed industrial type it becomes universal.

Under this universal relation of contract when equitably administered, there arises that adjustment of benefit to effort which the arrangements of the industrial society have to achieve. If each as producer, distributor, manager, adviser, teacher, or aider of other kind, obtains from his fellows such payment for his service as its value, determined by the demand, warrants; then there results that correct apportioning of reward to merit which ensures the prosperity of the superior.

Again changing the point of view, we see that whereas public control in the militant type is both positively regulative and negatively regulative, in the industrial type it is negatively regulative only. To the slave, to the soldier, or to other member of a community organized for war, authority says—"Thou shalt do this; thou shalt not do that." But to the member of the industrial community, authority gives only one of these orders—"Thou shalt not do that."

For people who, carrying on their private transactions by voluntary cooperation, also voluntarily cooperate to form and support a governmental agency, are, by implication, people who authorize it to impose on their respective activities, only those restraints which they are all interested in maintaining—the restraints which check aggressions. Omitting criminals (who under the assumed conditions must be very few, if not a vanishing quantity), each citizen will wish to preserve uninvaded his sphere of action, while not invading others' spheres, and to retain whatever benefits are achieved within it. The very motive which prompts all to unite in upholding a public protector of their individualities, will also prompt them to unite in preventing any interference with their indivdualities beyond that required for this end.

Hence it follows that while, in the militant type, regimentation in the army is paralleled by centralized administration throughout the society at large; in the industrial type, administration, becoming decentralized, is at the same time narrowed in its range. Nearly all public organizations save that for administering justice, necessarily disappear; since they have the common character that they either aggress on the citizen by dictating his actions, or by taking from him more property than is needful for protecting him, or by both. Those who are forced to send their children to this or that school, those who have, directly or indirectly, to help in supporting a State priesthood, those from whom rates are demanded that parish officers may administer public charity, those who are taxed to provide gratis reading for people who will not save money for library subscriptions, those whose businesses are carried on under regulation by inspectors, those who have to pay the costs of State science-and-art-teaching, State emigration, &c., all have their individualities trenched upon, either by compelling them to do what they would not spontaneously do, or by taking away money which else would have furthered their private ends. Coercive arrangements of such kinds, consistent with the militant type, are inconsistent with the industrial type.

With the relatively narrow range of public organizations, there goes, in the industrial type, a relatively wide range of private organizations. The spheres left vacant by the one are filled by the other.

Several influences conspire to produce this trait. Those motives which, in the absence of that subordination necessitated by war, make citizens unite in asserting their individualities subject only to mutual limitations, are motives which make them unite in resisting any interference with their freedom to form such private combinations as do not involve aggression. Moreover, beginning with exchanges of goods and services under agreements between individuals, the principle of voluntary co-operation is simply carried out in a larger way by individuals who, in-corporating themselves, contract with one another for jointly pursuing this or that business or function. And yet again, there is entire congruity between the representative constitutions of such private combinations, and that representative constitution of the public combination which we see is proper to the industrial type. The same law of organization pervades the society in general and in detail. So that an inevitable trait of the industrial type is the multiplicity and heterogeneity of associations, politi-cal, religious, commercial, professional, philanthropic, and social, of all sizes.

Two indirectly resulting traits of the industrial type must be added. The first is its relative plasticity.

So long as corporate action is necessitated for national self-preservation —so long as, to effect combined defence or offence, there is maintained that graduated subordination which ties all inferiors to superiors, as the soldier is tied to his officer—so long as there is maintained the relation of status, which tends to fix men in the positions they are severally born to; there is insured a comparative rigidity of social organization. But with the cessation of those needs that initiate and preserve the militant type of structure, and with the establishment of contract as the universal relation under which efforts are combined for mutual advantage, social organization loses its rigidity. No longer determined by the principle of inheritance, places and occupations are now determined by the principle of efficiency; and changes of structure follow when men, not bound to prescribed functions, acquire the functions for which they have proved themselves most fit. Easily modified in its arrangements, the industrial type of society is therefore one which adapts itself with facility to new requirements.

The other incidental result to be named is a tendency towards loss of economic autonomy.

While hostile relations with adjacent societies continue, each society has to be productively self-sufficing; but with the establishment of peace-ful relations, this need for self-sufficingness ceases. As the local divisions composing one of our great nations, had, while they were at feud, to produce each for itself almost everything it required, but now permanently at peace with one another, have become so far mutually dependent that no one of them can satisfy its wants without aid from the rest; so the great nations themselves, at present forced in large measure to maintain their economic autonomies, will become less forced to do this as war decreases, and will gradually become necessary to one another. While, on the one hand, the facilities possessed by each for certain kinds of production, will render exchange mutually advantageous; on the other hand, the citizens of each will, under the industrial *régime*, tolerate no such restraints on their individualities as are implied by interdicts on exchange or impediments to exchange.

With the spread of industrialism, therefore, the tendency is towards the breaking down of the divisions between nationalities, and the running through them of a common organization: if not under a single government, then under a federation of governments.

Such being the constitution of the industrial type of society to be inferred from its requirements, we have now to inquire what evidence is furnished by actual societies that approach towards this constitution accompanies the progress of industrialism.

As, during the peopling of the Earth, the struggle for existence among societies, from small hordes up to great nations, has been nearly everywhere going on; it is, as before said, not to be expected that we should readily find examples of the social type appropriate to an exclusively industrial life. Ancient records join the journals of the day in proving that thus far no civilized or semi-civilized nation has fallen into circumstances making needless all social structures for resisting aggression; and from every region travellers' accounts bring evidence that almost universally among the uncivilized, hostilities between tribes are chronic. Still, a few examples exist which show, with tolerable clearness, the outline of the industrial type in its rudimentary form—the form which it assumes where culture has made but little progress. . . .

Difficulties meet us when, turning to civilized societies, we seek in them for traits of the industrial type. Consolidated and organized as they have all been by wars actively carried on throughout the earlier periods of their existence, and mostly continued down to recent times; and having simultaneously been developing within themselves organizations for producing and distributing commodities, which have little by little become contrasted with those proper to militant activities; the two are everywhere presented so mingled that clear separation of the first from the last is, as said at the outset, scarcely practicable. Radically opposed, however, as is compulsory cooperation, the organizing principle of the militant type, to voluntary cooperation, the organizing principle of the industrial type, we may, by observing that the decline of institutions exhibiting the one, recognize, by implication, the growth of institutions exhibiting the other. Hence if, in passing from the first states of civilized nations in which war is the business of life, to states in which hostilities are but occasional, we simultaneously pass to states in which the ownership of the individual by his society is not so constantly and strenuously enforced, in which the subjection of rank to rank is mitigated, in which political rule is no longer autocratic, in which the regulation of citizens' lives is diminished in range and rigour, while the protection of them is increased; we are, by implication, shown the traits of a developing industrial type. Comparisons of several kinds disclose results which unite in verifying this truth.

Take, first, the broad contrast between the early condition of the more civilized European nations at large, and their later condition. Setting out from the dissolution of the Roman empire, we observe that for many centuries during which conflicts were effecting consolidations, and dissolutions, and re-consolidations in endless variety, such energies as were not directly devoted to war were devoted to little else than supporting the organizations which carried on war: the working part of each community did not exist for its own sake, but for the sake of the fighting part. While militancy was thus high and industrialism undeveloped, the reign of superior strength, continually being established by societies one over another, was equally displayed within each society. From slaves and serfs, through vassals of different grades up to dukes and kings, there was an enforced subordination by which the individualities of all were greatly restricted. And at the same time that, to carry on external aggression or resistance, the ruling power in each group sacrificed the personal claims of its members, the function of defending its members from one another was in but small degree discharged by it: they were left to defend themselves. If with these traits of European societies in mediæval times, we compare their traits in modern times, we see the following essential differences. First, with the formation of nations covering large areas, the perpetual wars within each area have ceased; and though the wars between nations which from time to time occur are on larger scales, they are less frequent, and they are no longer the business of all freemen. Second, there has grown up in each country a relatively large population which carries on production and distribution for its own maintenance; so that whereas of old, the working part existed for the benefit of the fighting part, now the fighting part exists mainly for the benefit of the working part—exists ostensibly to protect it in the quiet pursuit of its ends. Third, the system of status, having under some of its forms disappeared and under others become greatly mitigated, has been almost universally replaced by the system of contract. Only among those who, by choice or by conscription, are incorporated in the military organization, does the system of status in its primitive rigour still hold so long as they remain in this organization. Fourth, with this decrease of compulsory cooperation and increase of voluntary cooperation, there have diminished or ceased many minor restraints over individual actions. Men are less tied to their localities than they were; they are not obliged to profess certain religious opinions; they are less debarred from expressing their political views; they no longer have their dresses and modes of living dictated to them; they are comparatively little restrained from forming private combinations and holding meetings for one or other purpose—political, religious, social. Fifth, while the individualities of citizens are less aggressed upon by public agency, they are more protected by public agency against aggression. Instead of a *régime* under which individuals rectified their private wrongs by force as well as they could, or else bribed the ruler, general or local, to use his power in their behalf, there has come a *régime* under which, while much less self-protection is required, a chief function of the ruling power and its agents is to administer justice. In all ways, then, we are shown that with this relative decrease of militancy and relative increase of industrialism, there has been a change from a social order in which individuals exist for the benefit of the State, to a social order in which the State exists for the benefit of individuals.

When, instead of contrasting early European communities at large with European communities at large as they now exist, we contrast the one in which industrial development has been less impeded by militancy with those in which it has been more impeded by militancy, parallel results are apparent. Between our own society and continental societies, as for example, France, the differences which have gradually arisen may be cited in illustration. After the conquering Normans had spread over England, there was established here a much greater subordination of local rulers to the general ruler than existed in France; and, as a result, there was not nearly so much internal dissension. Says Hallam, speaking of this period, "we read very little of private wars in England." Though from time to time, as under Stephen, there were rebellions, and though there were occasional fights between nobles, yet for some hundred and fifty years, up to the time of King John, the subjection maintained secured comparative order. Further, it is to be noted that such general wars as occurred were mostly carried on abroad. Descents on our coasts were few and unimportant, and conflicts with Wales, Scotland, and Ireland, entailed but few intrusions on English soil. Consequently, there was a relatively small hindrance to industrial life and the growth of social forms appropriate to it. Meanwhile, the condition of France was widely different. During this period and long after, besides wars with England (mostly fought out on French soil) and wars with other countries, there were going on everywhere local wars. From the 10th to the 14th century perpetual fights between suzerains and their vassals occurred, as well as fights of vassals with one another. Not until towards the middle of the 14th century did the king begin greatly to predominate over the nobles; and only in the 15th century was there established a supreme ruler strong enough to prevent the quarrels of local rulers. How great was the repression of industrial development caused by internal conflicts, may be inferred from the exaggerated language of an old writer, who says of this period, during which the final struggle of monarchy with feudalism was going on, that "agriculture, traffic, and all the mechanical arts ceased." Such being the contrast between the small degree in which industrial life was impeded by war in England, and the great degree in which it was impeded by war in France, let us ask—what were the political contrasts which arose. The first fact to be noted is that in the middle of the 13th century there began in England a mitigation of villeinage, by limitation of labour-services and commutation of them for money, and that in the 14th century the transformation of a servile into a free population had in great measure taken place; while in France, as in other continental countries, the old condition survived and became worse. As Mr. Freeman says of this period —"in England villeinage was on the whole dying out, while in many other countries it was getting harder and harder." Besides this spreading sub-stitution of contract for status, which, taking place first in the industrial centres, the towns, afterwards went on in the rural districts, there was going on an analogous enfranchisemen of the noble class. The enforced military obligations of vassals were more and more replaced by money payments or scutages; so that by King John's time, the fighting services of the upper class had been to a great extent compounded for, like the labour services of the lower class. After diminished restraints over persons, there came diminished invasions of property. By the Charter, arbitrary tallages on towns and non-military king's tenants were checked; and while the aggressive actions of the State were thus decreased, its protective actions were extended: provisions were made that justice should be neither sold, delayed, nor denied. All which changes were towards those social arrangements which we see characterize the industrial type. Then, in the next place, we have the subsequently-occurring rise of a representative government; which, as shown in a preceding chapter by another line of inquiry, is at once the product of industrial growth and the form proper to the industrial type. But in France none of these changes took place. Villeinage remaining unmitigated continued to comparatively late times; compounding for military obligation of vassal to suzerain was less general; and when there arose tendencies towards the establishment of an assembly expressing the popular will, they proved abortive. Detailed comparisons of subsequent periods and their changes would detain us too long: it must suffice to indicate the leading facts. Beginning with the date at which, under the influences just indicated, parliamentary government was finally established in England, we find that for a century and a half, down to the Wars of the Roses, the internal disturbances were few and unim-portant compared with those which took place in France; and at the same time (remembering that the wars between England and France, habitually taking place on French soil, affected the state of France more than that of England) we note that France carried on serious wars with Flanders, Castille and Navarre besides the struggle with Burgundy: the result being that while in England popular power as expressed by the House of Commons became settled and increased, such power as the States General had acquired in France, dwindled away. Not forgetting that by the Wars of the Roses, lasting over thirty years, there was initiated a return towards absolutism; let us contemplate the contrasts which subsequently arose. For a century and a half after these civil conflicts ended, there were but few and trivial breaches of internal peace; while such wars as went on with foreign powers, not numerous, took place as usual out of England. During this period the retrograde movement which the Wars of the Roses set up, was reversed, and popular power greatly increased; so that in the words of Mr. Bagehot, "the slavish parliament of Henry VIII, grew into the murmuring parliament of Queen Elizabeth, the mutinous Parliament of James I., and the rebellious parliament of Charles I." Meanwhile France, during the first third of this period, had been engaged in almost continuous external wars with Italy, Spain, and Austria; while during the remaining two-thirds, it suffered from almost continuous internal wars, religious and political: the accompanying result being that, notwithstanding resistances from time to time made, the monarchy became increasingly despotic. Fully to make manifest the different social types which had been evolved under these different conditions, we have to compare not only the respective political constitutions but also the respective systems of social control. Observe what these were at the time when there commenced that reaction which ended in the French revolution. In harmony with the theory of the militant type, that the individual is in life, liberty, and property, owned by the State, the monarch was by some held to be the universal proprietor. The burdens he imposed upon landowners were so grievous that a part of them preferred abandoning their estates to paying. Then besides the taking of property by the State, there was the taking of labour. One-fourth of the working days in the year went to the *corvées*, due now to the king and now to the feudal lord. Such liberties as were allowed, had to be paid for and again paid for: the municipal privileges of towns being seven times in twenty-eight years withdrawn and re-sold to them. Military services of nobles and people were imperative to whatever extent the king demanded; and conscripts were drilled under the lash. At the same time that the subjection of the individual to the State was pushed to such an extreme by exactions of money and services that the impoverished people cut the grain while it was green, ate grass, and died of starvation in multitudes, the State did little to guard their persons and homes. Contemporary writers enlarge on the immense numbers of highway robberies, burglaries, assassinations, and torturings of people to discover their hoards. Herds of vagabonds, levying blackmail, roamed about; and when, as a remedy, penalties were imposed, innocent persons denounced as vagabonds were sent to prison without evidence. No personal security could be had either against the ruler or against powerful enemies. In Paris there were some thirty prisons where untried and unsentenced people might be incarcerated; and the "brigandage of justice" annually cost suitors forty to sixty millions of francs. While the State, aggressing on citizens to such extremes, thus failed to protect them against one another, it was active in regulating their private lives and labours. Religion was dictated to the extent that Protestants were imprisoned, sent to the galleys, or whipped, and their ministers hanged. The quantity of salt (on which there was a heavy tax) to be consumed by each person was prescribed; as were also the modes of its use. Industry of every kind was supervised. Certain crops were prohibited; and vines destroyed that were on soils considered unfit. The wheat that might be bought at market was limited to two bushels; and sales took place in presence of dragoons. Manufacturers were regulated in their processes and products to the extent that there was destruction of improved appliances and of goods not made according to law, as well as penalties upon inventors. Regulations succeeded one another so rapidly that amid their multiplicity, government agents found it difficult to carry them out; and with increasing official orders there came increasing swarms of public functionaries. Turning now to England at the same period, we see that along with progress towards the industrial type of political structure, carried to the extent that the House of Commons had become the predominant power, there had gone a progress towards the accompanying social system. Though the subjection of the individual to the State was considerably greater than now, it was far less than in France. His private rights were not sacrificed in the same unscrupulous way; and he was not in danger of a *lettre de cachet*. Though justice was very imperfectly administered, still it was not administered so wretchedly: there was a fair amount of personal security, and aggressions on property were kept within bounds. The disabilities of Protestant dissenters were diminished early in the century; and, later on, those of Catholics. Considerable freedom of the press was acquired, showing itself in the discussion of political questions, as well as in the publication of parliamentary debates; and, about the same time, there came free speech in public meetings. While thus the State aggressed on the individual less and protected him more, it interfered to a smaller extent with his daily transactions. Though there was much regulation of commerce and industry, yet it was pushed to no such extreme as that which in France subjected agriculturists, manufacturers, and merchants, to an army of officials who directed their acts at every turn. In brief, the contrast between our state and that of France was such as to excite the surprise and admiration of various French writers of the time; from whom Mr. Buckle quotes numerous passages showing this.

Most significant of all, however, are the changes in England itself, first retrogressive and then progressive, that occurred during the war-period which extended from 1775 to 1815, and during the subsequent period of peace. At the end of the last century and the beginning of this, reversion towards ownership of the individual by the society had gone a long way. "To statesmen, the State, as a unit, was all in all, and it is really difficult to find any evidence that the people were thought of at all, except in the relation of obedience." "The Government regarded the people with little other view than as a taxable and soldier-yielding mass." While the militant part of the community had greatly developed, the industrial part had approached towards the condition of a permanent commissariat. By conscription and by press-gangs, was carried to a rela-tively vast extent that sacrifice of the citizen in life and liberty which war entails; and the claims to property were trenched on by merciless taxation, weighing down the middle classes so grievously that they had greatly to lower their rate of living, while the people at large were so distressed (partly no doubt by bad harvests) that "hundreds ate nettles and other weeds." With these major aggressions upon the individual by the State, went numerous minor aggressions. Irresponsible agents of the executive were empowered to suppress public meetings and seize their leaders: death being the punishment for those who did not disperse when ordered. Libraries and news-rooms could not be opened without licence; and it was penal to lend books without permission. There were "strenuous attempts made to silence the press;" and booksellers dared not publish works by obnoxious authors. "Spies were paid, witnesses were suborned, juries were packed, and the *habeas corpus* Act being constantly sus-pended, the Crown had the power of imprisoning without inquiry and without limitation." While the Government taxed and coerced and re-strained the citizen to this extent, its protection of him was inefficient. It is true that the penal code was made more extensive and more severe. The definition of treason was enlarged, and numerous offences were made capital which were not capital before; so that there was "a vast and absurd variety of offences for which men and women were sentenced to death by the score:" there was "a devilish levity in dealing with human life." But at the same time there was not an increase, but rather a de-crease, of security. As says Mr. Pike in his *History of Crime in England,* "it became apparent that the greater the strain of the conflict the greater is the danger of a reaction towards violence and lawlessness." Turn now to the opposite picture. After recovery from the prostration which pro-longed wars had left, and after the dying away of those social perturba-tions caused by impoverishment, there began a revival of traits proper to the industrial type. Coercion of the citizen by the State decreased in various ways. Voluntary enlistment replaced compulsory military service; and there disappeared some minor restraints over personal freedom, as instance the repeal of laws which forbade artizans to travel where they pleased, and which interdicted trades-unions. With these manifestations of greater respect for personal freedom, may be joined those shown in the amelioration of the penal code: the public whipping of females being first abolished; then the long list of capital offences being reduced until there finally remained but one; and, eventually, the pillory and imprisonment for debt being abolished. Such penalties on religious independence as remained disappeared; first by removal of those directed against Protestant Dissenters, and then of those which weighed on Catholics, and then of some which told specially against Quakers and Jews. By the Parliamentary Reform Bill and the Municipal Reform Bill, vast numbers were removed from the subject classes to the governing classes. Interferences with the business-transactions of citizens were diminished by allowing free trade in bullion, by permitting joint-stock banks, by abolishing multitudinous restrictions on the importation of commodities—leaving eventually but few which pay duty. Moreover while these and kindred changes, such as the removal of restraining burdens on the press, decreased the impediments to free actions of citizens, the protective action of the State was increased. By a greatly-improved police system, by county courts, and so forth, personal safety and claims to property were better secured.

Not to elaborate the argument further by adding the case of the United States, which repeats with minor differences the same relations of phenomena, the evidence given adequately supports the proposition laid down. Amid all the complexities and perturbations, comparisons show us with sufficient clearness that in actually-existing societies those attributes which we inferred must distinguish the industrial type, show themselves clearly in proportion as the social activities are predominantly characterized by exchange of services under agreement.

As, in the last chapter, we noted the traits of character proper to the members of a society which is habitually at war; so here, we have to note the traits of character proper to the members of a society occupied exclusively in peaceful pursuits. Already in delineating above, the rudiments of the industrial type of social structure as exhibited in certain small groups of unwarlike peoples, some indications of the accompanying personal qualities have been given; but it will be well now to emphasize these and add to them, before observing the kindred personal qualities in more advanced industrial communities.

Absence of a centralized coercive rule, implying as it does feeble political restraints exercised by the society over its units, is accompanied by a strong sense of individual freedom, and a determination to maintain it. The amiable Bodo and Dhimáls, as we have seen, resist "injunctions injudiciously urged with dogged obstinacy." The peaceful Lepchas "undergo great privations rather than submit to oppression or injustice." The "simple-minded Santál" has a "strong natural sense of justice, and should any attempt be made to coerce him, he flies the country." Similarly of a tribe not before mentioned, the Jakuns of the South Malayan Peninsula, who, described as "entirely inoffensive," personally brave but peaceful, and as under no control but that of popularly-appointed heads who settle their disputes, are also described as "extremely proud:" the so-called pride being exemplified by the statement that their remarkably good qualities "induced several persons to make attempts to domesticate them, but such essays have generally ended in the Jakuns' disappearance on the slightest coercion."

With a strong sense of their own claims, these unwarlike men display unusual respect for the claims of others. This is shown in the first place by the rarity of personal collisions among them. Hodgson says that the Bodo and the Dhimáls "are void of all violence towards their own people or towards their neighbours." Of the peaceful tribes of the Neilgherry Hills, Colonel Ouchterlony writes:—"drunkenness and violence are unknown amongst them." Campbell remarks of the Lepchas, that "they rarely quarrel among themselves." The Jakuns, too, "have very seldom quarrels among themselves;" and such disputes as arise are settled by their popularly-chosen heads "without fighting or malice." In like manner the Arafuras "live in peace and brotherly love with one another." Further, in the accounts of these peoples we read nothing about the *lex talionis*. In the absence of hostilities with adjacent groups there does not exist within each group that "sacred duty of blood-revenge" universally recognized in military tribes and nations. Still more significantly, we find evidence of the opposite doctrine and practice. Says Campbell of the Lepchas—"they are singularly forgiving of injuries . . . making mutual amends and concessions."

Naturally, with respect for others' individualities thus shown, goes respect for their claims to property. Already in the preliminary chapter I have quoted testimonies to the great honesty of the Bodo and the Dhimáls, the Lepchas, the Santáls, the Todas, and other peoples kindred in their form of social life; and here I may add further ones. Of the Lepchas, Hooker remarks:—"in all my dealings with these people, they proved scrupulously honest." "Among the pure Santáls," writes Hunter, "crime and criminal officers are unknown;" while of the Hos, belonging to the same group as the Santáls, Dalton says, "a reflection on a man's honesty or veracity may be sufficient to send him to self-destruction." Shortt testifies that "the Todas, as a body, have never been convicted of heinous crimes of any kind;" and concerning other tribes of the Shervaroy Hills, he states that "crime of a serious nature is unknown amongst them." Again of the Jakuns we read that "they are never known to steal anything, not even the most insignificant trifle." And so of certain natives of Malacca who "are naturally of a commercial turn," Jukes writes:—"no part of the world is freer from crime than the district of Malacca;" "a few petty cases of assault, or of disputes about property . . . are all that occur."

Thus free from the coercive rule which warlike activities necessitate, and without the sentiment which makes the needful subordination possible—thus maintaining their own claims while respecting the like claims of others—thus devoid of the vengeful feelings which aggressions without and within the tribe generate; these peoples, instead of the blood-thirstiness, the cruelty, the selfish trampling upon inferiors, characterizing militant tribes and societies, display, in unusual degrees, the humane sentiments. Insisting on their amiable qualities, Hodgson describes the Bodo and the Dhimáls as being "almost entirely free from such as are unamiable." Remarking that "while courteous and hospitable he is firm and free from cringing," Hunter tells us of the Santál that he thinks "uncharitable men" will suffer after death. Saying that the Lepchas are "ever foremost in the forest or on the bleak mountain, and ever ready to help, to carry, to encamp, collect, or cook," Hooker adds—"they cheer on the traveller by their unostentatious zeal in his service;" and he also adds that, "a present is divided equally amongst many, without a syllable of discontent or grudging look or word." Of the Jakuns, too, Favre tells us that "they are generally kind, affable, inclined to gratitude and to beneficence:" their tendency being not to ask favours but to confer them. And then of the peaceful Arafuras we learn from Kolff that—

"They have a very excusable ambition to gain the name of rich men by paying the debts of their poorer villagers. The officer [M. Bik], whom I quoted above, related to me a very striking instance of this. At Affara he was present at the election of the village chiefs, two individuals aspiring to the station of Orang Tua. The people chose the elder of the two, which greatly afflicted the other, but he soon afterwards expressed himself satisfied with the choice the people had made, and said to M. Bik, who had been sent there on a commission, 'What reason have I to grieve; whether I am Orang Tua or not, I still have it in my power to assist my fellow villagers.' Several old men agreed to this, apparently to comfort him. Thus the only use they make of their riches is to employ it in settling differences."

With these superiorities of the social relations in permanently peaceful tribes, go superiorities of the domestic relations. As I have before pointed out, while the status of women is habitually very low in tribes given to war and in more advanced militant societies, it is habitually very high in these primitive peaceful societies. The Bodo and the Dhimáls, the Kocch, the Santáls, the Lepchas, are monogamic, as were also the Pueblos; and along with their monogamy habitually goes a superior sexual morality. Of the Lepchas Hooker says—"the females are generally chaste, and the marriage tie is strictly kept." Among the Santáls "unchastity is almost unknown," and "divorce is rare." By the Bodo and the Dhimáls, "polygamy, concubinage and adultery are not tolerated;" "chastity is prized in man and woman, married and unmarried." Further it is to be noted that the behaviour to women is extremely good. "The Santál treats the female members of his family with respect;" the Bodo and the Dhimáls "treat

their wives and daughters with confidence and kindness; they are free
from all out-door work whatever." And even among the Todas, low as are
the forms of their sexual relations, "the wives are treated by their hus-
bands with marked respect and attention." Moreover, we are told concerning sundry of these unwarlike peoples that the status of children is also
high; and there is none of that distinction of treatment between boys and
girls which characterizes militant peoples.

Of course on turning to the civilized to observe the form of individual
character which accompanies the industrial form of society, we encounter
the difficulty that the personal traits proper to industrialism, are, like the
social traits, mingled with those proper to militancy. It is manifestly
thus with ourselves. A nation which, besides its occasional serious wars,
is continually carrying on small wars with uncivilized tribes—a nation
which is mainly ruled in Parliament and through the press by men whose
school-discipline led them during six days in the week to take Achilles
for their hero, and on the seventh to admire Christ—a nation which, at
its public dinners, habitually toasts its army and navy before toasting
its legislative bodies; has not so far emerged out of militancy that we
can expect either the institutions or the characteristics proper to industrialism to be shown with clearness. In independence, in honesty, in
truthfulness, in humanity, its citizens are not likely to be the equals of
the uncultured but peaceful peoples above described. All we may anticipate is an approach to those moral qualities appropriate to a state undisturbed by international hostilities; and this we find.

In the first place, with progress of the *régime* of contract has come
growth of independence. Daily exchange of services under agreement,
involving at once the maintenance of personal claims and respect for the
claims of others, has fostered a normal self-assertion and consequent
resistance to unauthorized power. The facts that the word "independence," in its modern sense, was not in use among us before the middle
of the last century and that on the continent independence is less markedly displayed, suggest the connexion between this trait and a developing
industrialism. The trait is shown in the multitudinousness of religious
sects, in the divisions of political parties, and, in minor ways, by the
absence of those "schools" in art, philosophy, &c., which, among continental peoples, are formed by the submission of disciples to an adopted
master. That Englishmen show, more than their neighbours, a jealousy
of dictation, and a determination to act as they think fit, will not, I think,
be disputed.

The diminished subordination to authority, which is the obverse of
this independence, of course implies decrease of loyalty. Worship of the
monarch, at no time with us reaching the height it did in France early
in the last century, or in Russia down to recent times, has now changed

into a respect depending very much on the monarch's personal character. Our days witness no such extreme servilities of expression as were used by ecclesiasties in the dedication of the Bible to King James, nor any such exaggerated adulations as those addressed to George III. by the House of Lords. The doctrine of divine right has long since died away; belief in an indwelling supernatural power (implied by the touching for king's evil, &c.) is named as a curiosity of the past; and the monarchical institution has come to be defended on grounds of expediency. So great has been the decrease of this sentiment which, under the militant *régime*, attaches subject to ruler, that now-a-days the conviction commonly expressed is that, should the throne be occupied by a Charles II. or a George IV., there would probably result a republic. And this change of feeling is shown in the attitude towards the Government as a whole. For not only are there many who dispute the authority of the State in respect of sundry matters besides religious beliefs, but there are some who passively resist what they consider unjust exercises of its authority, and pay fines or go to prison rather than submit.

As this last fact implies, along with decrease of loyalty has gone decrease of faith, not in monarchs only but in governments. Such belief in royal omnipotence as existed in ancient Egypt, where the power of the ruler was supposed to extend to the other world, as it is even now supposed to do in China, has had no parallel in the West; but still, among European peoples in past times, that confidence in the soldier-king essential to the militant type, displayed itself among other ways in exaggerated conceptions of his ability to rectify mischiefs, achieve benefits, and arrange things as he willed. If we compare present opinion among ourselves with opinion in early days, we find a decline in these credulous expectations. Though, during the late retrograde movement towards militancy, State-power has been invoked for various ends, and faith in it has increased; yet, up to the commencement of this reaction, a great change had taken place in the other direction. After the repudiation of a State-enforced creed, there came a denial of the State's capacity for determining religious truth, and a growing movement to relieve it from the function of religious teaching; held to be alike needless and injurious. Long ago it had ceased to be thought that Government could do any good by regulating people's food, clothing, and domestic habits; and over the multitudinous processes carried on by producers and distributors, constituting immensely the larger part of our social activities, we no longer believe that legislative dictation is beneficial. Moreover, every newspaper by its criticisms on the acts of ministers and the conduct of the House of Commons, betrays the diminished faith of citizens in their rulers. Nor is it only by contrasts between past and present among ourselves that we are shown this trait of a more developed industrial state. It is shown by kindred contrasts between opinion here and opinion abroad. The speculations of social reformers in France and in Germany, prove that the hope for benefits to be achieved by State-agency is far higher with them than with us.

Along with decrease of loyalty and concomitant decrease of faith in the powers of governments, has gone decrease of patriotism—patriotism, that is, under its original form. To fight "for king and country" is an ambition which now-a-days occupies but a small space in men's minds; and though there is among us a majority whose sentiment is represented by the exclamation—"Our country, right or wrong!" yet there are large numbers whose desire for human welfare at large, so far overrides their desire for national prestige, that they object to sacrificing the first to the last. The spirit of self-criticism, which in sundry respects leads us to make unfavourable comparisons between ourselves and our continental neighbours, leads us more than heretofore to blame ourselves for wrong conduct to weaker peoples. The many and strong reprobations of our dealings with the Afghans, the Zulus, and the Boers, show that there is a large amount of the feeling reprobated by the "Jingo"-class as unpatriotic.

That adaptation of individual nature to social needs, which, in the militant state, makes men glory in war and despise peaceful pursuits, has partially brought about among us a converse adjustment of the sentiments. The occupation of the soldier has ceased to be so much honoured, and that of the civilian is more honoured. During the forty years' peace, the popular sentiment became such that "soldiering" was spoken of contemptuously; and those who enlisted, habitually the idle and the dissolute, were commonly regarded as having completed their disgrace. Similarly in America before the late civil war, such small military gatherings and exercises as from time to time occurred, excited general ridicule. Meanwhile we see that labours, bodily and mental, useful to self and others, have come to be not only honourable but in a considerable degree imperative. In America the adverse comments on a man who does nothing, almost force him into some active pursuit; and among ourselves the respect for industrial life has become such that men of high rank put their sons into business.

While, as we saw, the compulsory cooperation proper to militancy, forbids, or greatly discourages, individual initiative, the voluntary cooperation which distinguishes industrialism, gives free scope to individual initiative, and develops it by letting enterprise bring its normal advantages. Those who are successfully original in idea and act, prospering and multiplying in a greater degree than others, produce, in course of time, a general type of nature ready to undertake new things. The speculative tendencies of English and American capitalists, and the extent to which large undertakings, both at home and abroad, are carried out by them, sufficiently indicate this trait of character. Though, along with considerable qualifications of militancy by industrialism on the continent, there has occurred there, too, an extension of private enterprise; yet the fact that while many towns in France and Germany have been supplied with gas and water by English companies, there is in England but little of kindred achievement by foreign companies, shows that among the more industrially-modified English, individual initiative is more decided.

There is evidence that the decline of international hostilities associated as it is with the decline of hostilities between families and between individuals, is followed by a weakening of revengeful sentiments. This is implied by the fact that in our own country the more serious of these private wars early ceased, leaving only the less serious in the form of duels, which also have at length ceased: their cessation coinciding with the recent great development of industrial life—a fact with which may be joined the fact that in the more militant societies, France and Germany, they have not ceased. So much among ourselves has the authority of the *lex talionis* waned, that a man whose actions are known to be prompted by the wish for vengeance on one who has injured him, is reprobated rather than applauded.

With decrease of the aggressiveness shown in acts of violence and consequent acts of retaliation, has gone decrease of the aggressiveness shown in criminal acts at large. That this change has been a concomitant of the change from a more militant to a more industrial state, cannot be doubted by one who studies the history of crime in England. Says Mr. Pike in his work on that subject, "the close connexion between the military spirit and those actions which are now legally defined to be crimes, has been pointed out, again and again, in the course of this history." If we compare a past age in which the effects of hostile activities had been less qualified by the effects of peaceful activities than they are in our own age, we see a marked contrast in respect of the numbers and kinds of offences against person and property. We have no longer any English buccaneers; wreckers have ceased to be heard of; and travellers do not now prepare themselves to meet highwaymen. Moreover, that flagitiousness of the governing agencies themselves, which was shown by the venality of ministers and members of Parliament, and by the corrupt administration of justice, has disappeared. With decreasing amount of crime has come increasing reprobation of crime. Biographies of pirate captains, suffused with admiration of their courage, no longer find a place in our literature; and the sneaking kindness for "gentlemen of the road," is, in our days, but rarely displayed. Many as are the transgressions which our journals report, they have greatly diminished; and though in trading transactions there is much dishonesty (chiefly of the indirect sort) it needs but to read Defoe's *English Tradesman,* to see how marked has been the improvement since his time. Nor must we forget that the change of character which has brought a decrease of unjust actions, has brought an increase of beneficent actions; as seen in paying for slave-emancipation, in nursing the wounded soldiers of our fighting neighbours, in philanthropic efforts of countless kinds.

As with the militant type then, so with the industrial type, three lines of evidence converge to show us its essential nature. Let us set down briefly the several results, that we may observe the correspondences among them.

On considering what must be the traits of a society organized exclusively for carrying on internal activities, so as most efficiently to subserve the lives of citizens, we find them to be these. A corporate action subordinating individual actions by uniting them in joint effort, is no longer requisite. Contrariwise, such corporate action as remains has for its end to guard individual actions against all interferences not necessarily entailed by mutual limitation: the type of society in which this function is best discharged, being that which must survive, since it is that of which the members will most prosper. Excluding, as the requirements of the industrial type do, a despotic controlling agency, they imply, as the only congruous agency for achieving such corporate action as is needed, one formed of representatives who serve to express the aggregate will. The function of this controlling agency, generally defined as that of administering justice, is more specially defined as that of seeing that each citizen gains neither more nor less of benefit than his activities normally bring; and there is thus excluded all public action involving any artificial distribution of benefits. The *régime* of status proper to militancy having disappeared, the *régime* of contract which replaces it has to be universally enforced; and this negatives interferences between efforts and results by arbitrary apportionment. Otherwise regarded, the industrial type is distinguished from the militant type as being not both positively regulative and negatively regulative, but as being negatively regulative only. With this restricted sphere for corporate action comes an increased sphere for individual action; and from that voluntary cooperation which is the fundamental principle of the type, arise multitudinous private combinations, akin in their structures to the public combination of the society which includes them. Indirectly it results that a society of the industrial type is distinguished by plasticity; and also that it tends to lose its economic autonomy, and to coalesce with adjacent societies.

The question next considered was, whether these traits of the industrial type as arrived at by deduction are inductively verified; and we found that in actual societies they are visible more or less clearly in proportion as industrialism is more or less developed. Glancing at those small groups of uncultured people who, wholly unwarlike, display the industrial type in its rudimentary form, we went on to compare the structures of European nations at large in early days of chronic militancy, with their structures in modern days characterized by progressing industrialism; and we saw the differences to be of the kind implied. We next compared two of these societies, France and England, which were once in kindred states, but of which the one has had its industrial life much more repressed by its militant life than the other; and it became manifest that the contrasts which, age after age, arose between their institutions, were such as answer to the hypothesis. Lastly, limiting ourselves to England itself, and first noting how recession from such traits of the industrial type as had shown themselves, occurred during a long war-period, we observed how, during the subsequent long period of peace beginning in 1815, there were numerous and decided approaches to that social structure which we concluded must accompany developed industrialism.

We then inquired what type of individual nature accompanies the industrial type of society; with the view of seeing whether, from the character of the unit as well as from the character of the aggregate, confirmation is to be derived. Certain uncultured peoples whose lives are passed in peaceful occupations, proved to be distinguished by independence, resistance to coercion, honesty, truthfulness, forgivingness, kindness. On contrasting the characters of our ancestors during more warlike periods with our own characters, we see that, with an increasing ratio of industrialism to militancy, have come a growing independence, a less-marked loyalty, a smaller faith in governments, and a more qualified patriotism; and while, by enterprising action, by diminished faith in authority, by resistance to irresponsible power, there has been shown a strengthening assertion of individuality, there has accompanied it a growing respect for the individualities of others, as is implied by the diminution of aggressions upon them and the multiplication of efforts for their welfare.

To prevent misapprehension it seems needful, before closing, to explain that these traits are to be regarded less as the immediate results of industrialism than as the remote results of non-militancy. It is not so much that a social life passed in peaceful occupations is positively moralizing, as that a social life passed in war is positively demoralizing. Sacrifice of others to self is in the one incidental only; while in the other it is necessary. Such aggressive egoism as accompanies the industrial life is extrinsic; whereas the aggressive egoism of the militant life is intrinsic. Though generally unsympathetic, the exchange of services under agreement is now, to a considerable extent, and may be wholly, carried on with a due regard to the claims of others—may be constantly accompanied by a sense of benefit given as well as benefit received; but the slaying of antagonists, the burning of their houses, the appropriation of their territory, cannot but be accompanied by vivid consciousness of injury done them, and a consequent brutalizing effect on the feelings—an effect wrought, not on soldiers only, but on those who employ them and contemplate their deeds with pleasure. The last form of social life, therefore, inevitably deadens the sympathies and generates a state of mind which prompts crimes of trespass; while the first form, allowing the sympathies free play if it does not directly exercise them, favours the growth of altruistic sentiments and the resulting virtues.

12. Thorstein Veblen

The Main Drift

I.

In recent times absentee ownership has come to be the main and immediate controlling interest in the life of civilised men. It is the paramount issue between the civilised nations, and guides the conduct of their affairs at home and abroad. The Great War arose out of a conflict of absentee interests and the Peace was negotiated with a view to stabilise them.

This state of things is not precisely new, nor has it come on suddenly. It is a growth out of the past, but it has reached something like a culmination during these opening decades of the century; and it is an outcome of cumulative changes which have been directed to no such end. The years of the Great War and the Armistice have brought many things to a head, and among other things they have also thrown this factor into the foreground of the situation. And the experience of the War and after has stirred men to a crude and uneasy realisation of this state of things. Under one form of words or another, issues which arise out of the sovereign rights of absentee ownership are stirring the popular sentiment and engaging the attention of the officials with an ever increasing urgency. These issues are the substance of all those desperate perplexities that beset the constituted authorities and they underlie all those dissensions that continually trouble the nation's industry and business. With the result that popular attention and sentiment are gathering about the issues of absentee ownership more and more directly and consciously with each further move,—questions of its aims and uses, its necessary limitations, its

From Veblen, *Absentee Ownership and Business Enterprise in Recent Times: The Case of America* (New York: The Viking Press, 1938 edition), pp. 3-10, 398-445. Copyright 1923 by B. W. Huebsch, 1951 by Ann B. Sims. Reprinted with the permission of The Viking Press, Inc.

Clarence Ayres—probably the foremost authority on Veblen—once remarked that Veblen was a very systematic thinker but a very unsystematic writer. I am tempted to "organise" these materials but refrain from doing so. If one has to wander about, what better guide than Veblen? No footnote has been omitted and there is no need to say that they are Veblen's own—C. W. Mills.

continued security, its rightful claims, and its possible eventual abridgment or disallowance.

It is true, this particular form of words—"Absentee Ownership"—has not been commonly employed to describe this peculiar institution which now engrosses public policy and about which controversy is beginning to gather. But that only marks a deficiency of speech. It is only within the last few decades, and only by degrees, that the facts in the case have been changing in such a way as to call for the habitual use of such a phrase as "absentee ownership." It is only within the last few decades, and only by degrees, that absentee ownership has visibly come to be the main controlling factor in the established order of things. Yet it is no less true that this peculiar institution which this form of words is fit to describe has now plainly come to be the prime institutional factor that underlies and governs the established order of society. At the same time and in the same degree it has, as a matter of course, become the chief concern of the constituted authorities in all the civilised nations to safeguard the security and gainfulness of absentee ownership. This state of things is now plain to be seen, and it is therefore beginning to cloud the sentiments of the underlying population at whose cost this security and gainfulness are maintained.

So, by degrees the drift of changing conditions has been heading up in a new alignment of economic forces and of economic classes. So that the dominant considerations which now govern the material fortunes of the community are no longer the same as they have been in the recent past; nor indeed such as they are alleged to be in the present. These matters are still spoken of in terms handed down from the past, and law and custom still run in terms that are fit to describe a past situation and conform to the logic of a bygone alignment of forces. As always, the language employed and the principles acted on lag behind the facts. But when, as now, the facts have been changing at an unexampled rate the language and the principles will lag behind the facts by an unexampled interval. Yet under the urgent pressure of new material conditions some degree of adjustment or derangement of these ancient principles is due to follow. Continued "lag, leak and friction" is bound to count for something in the outcome. Continued irritation and defeat begot of a system of law and custom that no longer fits the material conditions of life will necessarily be an agency of unrest, particularly as touches the frame of mind of that fraction of the community on whom the irritation and defeat continue chiefly to fall.

Therefore these time-worn principles of ownership and control, which are now coming to a head in a system of absentee ownership and control, are beginning to come in for an uneasy and reluctant reconsideration; particularly at the hands of that underlying population who have no absentee ownership to safeguard. Their questioning of these matters habitually takes the shape of personal recrimination and special pleading, but the drift of it all is no less evident. Those traditions that underlie the established order and that guide legal and administrative policy, proceed on an assumed community of class interests, a national solidarity of interests, and an international conflict of interests; none of which is borne out by material facts. Therefore these traditional policies that still govern the conduct of affairs, civil and political, legal and administrative, are also falling under suspicion of being incompetent, irrelevant and impertinent, if not downright mischievous. The losers under these rules of the game are beginning to see that law and politics, too, serve the needs of the absentee owners at the cost of the underlying population.

So, popular interest and sentiment no longer cluster about these respectable heirlooms of civil liberty and national rivalry with the same enthusiastic bigotry as in the recent past. Among these unblest classes who have to pay its cost, patriotic animosity is no longer so unreflectingly self-sufficient as it once was, and as perhaps it always should be. Among these classes of the underlying population the new alignment of material interests is beginning to threaten the continued life of the patriotic spirit. The effectual division of interest and sentiment is beginning visibly to run on class lines, between the absentee owners and the underlying population. In material effect, the national frontiers no longer divide anything but national groups of special interests, and these special interests are quite uniformly interests of absentee owners. National rivalries are useful to these special interests; hence the feverish urgency with which the constituted authorities and the substantial citizens are concerned to foment national animosity and to penalise backsliders.

Of course these matters are not currently spoken of in these terms. The new alignment of interest and sentiment is not formally recognised, not yet. A decent respect for the obsolete amenities of Natural Liberty forbids it, and there is always the human propensity to hold fast that which once was good. And more particularly, the bygone issues of national ambition still continue to hold the affections of the substantial citizens, and the spirit of national rivalry still continues to serve the needs of the special interests. Therefore national ambitions must and shall be preserved and all conflict of class interests must and shall be ignored.

But all the while the drift of circumstances goes forward and cuts the lines of the new cleavage of interest and sentiment no less deep and with no less intractable ill-will on both sides, for all their being decently covered over with patriotic invective and authentic verbiage about the common good. And all the while, under one form of words or another, men's everyday interest and attention gathers more and more consciously about this ill-defined and shifty issue of absentee ownership, and about its place and value in the country's industry, to the slowly increasing neglect of obsolete political ambitions. And all the while it is increasingly evident that patriotic sentiment and national ambitions are no longer of any material consequence, except as ways and means by which the statesmen are enabled to further the material interests of the substantial citizens. A "substantial citizen" is an absentee owner of much property.

This summary description of things as they are may seem overdrawn. But it is intended to describe the present drift of things, rather than the accomplished facts hitherto. It is drawn from current observation rather than from the historical records; so that it aims to describe the current facts rather than the current talk about these facts. Of course there is no intention to intimate that the ancient and honorable habits of national conceit and patriotic intolerance have been forgotten or even that they are by way of becoming inoperative; nor is it that the rightful claims of absentee ownership are being neglected or being formally questioned and required to show cause why. Those cardinal realities of the established order have not gone out of date or out of mind, neither the one nor the other. Nor is there an effectual resolution anywhere being taken to put either of them away; not yet. But these ancient and honorable pillars of the old order are by way of becoming holdovers, both the one and the other; and the spokesmen of both are beginning to find themselves on the defensive. As witness the Treaty of Peace, which foots up to little if anything else than a plan of defense for the vested interests, concerted between the several custodians of the old order, at any cost to the world's peace or to the underlying population. As witness also the later conferences of the Powers at Genoa, at The Hague, and at Lausanne, which have turned on little else than measures designed to stabilise the rightful claims of absentee owners as against the defection of the Russians and other recusants, together with the equitable distribution of absentee perquisites among the several groups of vested interests represented by the several governments concerned.

In effect, and notoriously, it has been the chief and engrossing business of all the statesmen of the Armistice and the Treaty, on the winning and the losing side alike, to safeguard these two essential holdovers that go to make up the *status quo ante.* National rivalry is a necessary means of making things safe and profitable for the absentee owners, as will appear more in detail in the further argument. All this is a traditional matter of course and has consequently aroused no particular discussion. Indeed, it is so much a matter of course as to be taken for granted. But the defensive measures concerted by these statesmen, and their continued manœuvres for the stabilisation of absentee interests, go to show which way the cleavage of interests runs. Statesmen do not resort to counsels of desperation, such as underlie the Treaty and the later negotiations concerning partition of colonies and military establishments, except to save a precarious situation. And the same defensive purpose, it must be admitted, runs through that desperate recourse to the strong arm of repression which today engages the energies of the civilised governments, all and several, with the clamorous approval of their substantial citizens whose pecuniary interests are sought to be safeguarded by these measures.

Now, this red line of cleavage, in material interest and in sentiment, runs not between those who own something and those who own nothing, as has habitually been set out in the formulas of the doctrinaires, but between those who own more than they personally can use and those who have urgent use for more than they own. The issue now is turning not on a question of ownership, as such, but on absentee ownership. The standard formalities of "Socialism" and "Anti-socialism" are obsolete in face of the new alignment of economic forces. It is now not so much a question of equity in the distribution of incomes, but rather a question of expediency as regards the absentee management of productive industry, at large and in detail. It is not a matter of moral revulsion. It may be said, of course, and perhaps truthfully, that the absentee owners of the country's industrial equipment come in for a disproportionate share of the "national dividend," and that they and their folks habitually consume their share in superfluities; but no urgent moral indignation appears to be aroused by all that. All that has long been a familiar matter of course, and no substantial question as to the merits of that arrangement has yet been seriously entertained. Efforts to capitalise such a sentiment for purposes of disturbance have uniformly failed.

What the material circumstances are bringing to men's attention is a question of how to get the work done rather than of what to do with the output. It is a question of the effectual use of the country's industrial resources, man-power, and equipment.* Investment and corporation finance have taken such a turn and reached such a growth that, between them, the absentee owners large and small have come to control the ways and means of production and distribution, at large and in detail, in what is to be done and what is to be left undone. And the business interests of these absentee owners no longer coincide in any passable degree with the material interests of the underlying population, whose livelihood is bound up with the due working of this industrial system, at large and in detail. The material interest of the underlying population is best served by a maximum output at a low cost, while the business interests of the industry's owners may best be served by a moderate output at an enhanced price.

II.

As has been explained in earlier chapters, and as will readily be seen by any intelligent person who takes an interest in these matters, secular

* Cf., e.g., Walther Rathenau, "Die neue Wirtschaft," *Schriften*, vol. V.

life among the peoples of Christendom is governed in recent times by three several systems of use and wont, sovereign action-patterns induced by the run of past habituation:—the mechanical system of industry; the price-system; and the national establishment. The existing industrial system is dominated by the technology of physics and chemistry, and is a product of recent times, a profoundly modified derivative of the handicraft industry. The current price-system is dominated by absentee ownership and is also a greatly altered outgrowth of the handicraft industry and its petty trade; its continued growth in recent times has, in effect, changed it into a credit-price system. The nation, considered as a habit of thought, is a residual form of the predatory dynastic State of early modern times, superficially altered by a suffusion of democratic and parliamentary institutions in recent times.

By continued growth of use and wont in recent times the price-system has in effect become a credit-price system; and driven by the same growth the system of ownership has to all intents and purposes become a system of absentee ownership, in all that concerns any effectual initiative and authority in the conduct of economic affairs. The effectual control of the economic situation, in business, industry, and civil life, rests on the control of credit. Therefore the effectual exercise of initiative, discretion, and authority is perforce vested in those massive aggregations of absentee ownership that make up the Interests. Within certain wide limits of tolerance, therefore, the rest of the community, the industrial system and the underlying population, are at the disposal of the Interests, as ways and means of business, to be managed in a temperate spirit of usufruct for the continued and cumulative benefit of the major Interests and their absentee owners. The nation, both as a habit of thought and as a governmental going concern, comes into the case, in effect and in the main, as an auxiliary agency the function of which is to safeguard, extend and facilitate this work of surveillance and usufruct which has by drift of circumstances become incumbent on the Interests.

Such appears to be the state of the case, in the large and in so far as the forces engaged have yet fallen into definite lines and groupings, in those respects which come in question here.

It will be seen, accordingly, that the current economic situation is drawn on lines of a two-sided division of its forces or elements:—the Interests; and the underlying population. Such is the situation, typically, in the case of America; and such is also the state of things in the other civilised countries, in much the same measure in which they are civilised according to the same pattern. The Interests, properly speaking, are made up of those blocks of absentee ownership which are sufficiently massive to come into the counsels of the One Big Union of the Interests. Associated with these in their work, as copartners, auxiliaries, subsidiaries, extensions, purveyors of traffic, are the minor Interests and the business community at large; primarily the banking community. The work which they have in hand is to do business for a profit by use of the industrial system and the underlying population. For the purposes of business the underlying population has two uses:—as industrial man-power; and as ultimate consumers,—that is to say as ultimate purchasers, since the business interest does not extend beyond the ultimate sale of the goods.

To do a profitable business one should buy cheap and sell dear, as all reasonable men know. In its dealings with the underlying population the business community buys their man-power and sells them their livelihood. So it is incumbent on the business men in the case to buy the industrial man-power as cheap as may be, and to sell the means of living to the ultimate consumer as dear as may be. All of which is a platitudinous matter of course.

The source of profits is the margin of sales-price over production-cost (or purchase-cost). In earlier chapters it has already been explained how this margin is widened by raising the level of sales-prices; both by efficient salesmanship in the merchandising trades and by a continued expansion of the outstanding volume of purchasing-power through a continued creation of credits at the hands of the investment bankers and similar credit-establishments. In the same connection something has also been said of the service which the agencies of government render, in the way of enhancing prices by contributing to the security of this expanded volume of credit and so helping to make it indefinitely expansible without risk.

On the side of costs the underlying population comes into the case as being the industrial man-power that is to be bought, including the skill and technical knowledge that makes up the state of the industrial arts. On this side this population comes in as vendors of the ways and means of production. For the present purpose they may be classed loosely under two heads:—the industrial workmen; and the farmers. Also loosely and with a negligible fringe of exceptions it may be said that both of these groups of industrial man-power come into the negotiations on a businesslike footing, governed by the principles of the price-system and aiming to sell as dear as may be.

In these endeavours to sell dear the farmers have hitherto met with no measurable success, apparently for want of effectual collusion. In effect and in the common run the farm population and its work and livelihood are a species of natural resources which the business community holds in usufruct, in the nature of inert materials exposed to the drift of circumstances over which they have no control, somewhat after the analogy of bacteria employed in fermentation.

The case of the industrial man-power in the narrower sense is somewhat different, the case of the specialised workman engaged in the mechanical industries. In great part, and more or less effectually, these have been drawn together in craft-unions to do their bargaining on a collusive plan for the more profitable sale of their manpower. In the typical case these unions are businesslike coalitions endeavoring to drive a bargain and establish a vested interest, governed by the standard aims and methods of the price-system.[1] The unions habitually employ the standard methods of the merchandising business, endeavoring to sell their vendible output at the best price obtainable; their chief recourse in these negotiations being a limitation of the supply, a strategic withdrawal of efficiency by means of strikes, union rules, apprenticeship requirements, and devices for consuming time unproductively. The nature of the business does not admit the use of sales-publicity in this traffic in anything like the same measure in which that expedient is employed in ordinary merchandising. Hence the strategic stress of their salesmanship falls all the more insistently and effectually on the limitation of the vendible supply; a running balance of unemployment and orderly inefficiency under union rules, rising promptly to the proportions of an embargo on productive work in any emergency. The aim being a scarcity-price for work done, quite in the spirit of business-as-usual.

Meantime the continued flow of credits and capitalisations continues to expand the volume of purchasing-power in the market, and so continues to enhance the price-cost of living for the workmen, along with the rising level of general prices. Which provokes the organised workmen to a more assiduous bargaining for higher wages; which calls for a more exacting insistence on mediocrity and obstruction in the day's work and a more instant mobilisation in the way of strikes. On sound business principles, the organised workmen's remedy for scarcity of livelihood is a persistent curtailment of output.

As a secondary effect—which may presently, in the course of further habituation, turn out to be its gravest consequence—this struggle for existence by way of sabotage fosters a rising tide of hostility and distrust between the parties to the bargain. There would seem to be in prospect a progressively settled and malevolent hostility on the part of the embattled workmen over against their employers and the absentee owners for whose ease and gain they are employed; which should logically be counted on to rise in due course to that pitch of vivacity where it will stick at nothing. But in the meantime the logical recourse of the workmen in their negotiations for wages and livelihood, according to the logic of sound business under the price-system, is a strategic withdrawal of

[1] The American Federation of Labor may be taken as a typeform; although it goes perhaps to an extreme in its adherence to the principles and procedure of merchandising, in all its aims and negotiations, its constant aim being an exclusive market and a limitation of supply.

efficiency, of a passive sort, increasing in frequency and amplitude to keep pace with the increasing urgency of their case.

And the urgency of their case is increasing progressively, in the nature of things. The increasing stability of the credit system, such as it has attained during the past decade, enables the price-level to rise progressively, and thereby progressively to increase the price-cost of living. At the same time the business community, the absentee owners with whom the workmen are carrying on their acrimonious argument about wages and livelihood, are in a progressively stronger position and a progressively more determined frame of mind. They have learned to act in concert and have also learned that, in a business way, the industrial man-power is their common enemy, against which it is for them to make common cause, within reason,—that is to say within the bounds of profitable business.

While the business men are endeavoring to enhance the reasonable gains of business by expanding the volume of capital and lifting the level of prices, and so widening the margin of sales-prices over production-costs, the organised workmen are forever cutting in on the same margin by pushing up the labor-cost. And on this employers' side of the argument, as well as on the side of the embattled workmen, the standard and reasonable recourse by which to bring their opponents to reason is a strategic use of unemployment, a conscientious withdrawal of efficiency, carried to such a point as will bring an effectual degree of privation on the ultimate consumers, including the workmen, without reducing the net aggregate sales-price of the decreased output when sold at the resulting enhanced price per unit. In all these negotiations there is, on the employers' side also, relatively little effectual use to be made of salesmanlike publicity. The ordinary and effectual means employed is privation brought on by unemployment. So also, in these endeavors to economise on labor-cost as well as in the flotation of credits, capitalisations, and overhead charges, a more intelligent concert of action and a wider solidarity of interests on the side of the employers and owners is of great service; in that it enables the business of strategic unemployment to be carried out with a wider sweep and with increased confidence and security.[1]

At this point the national establishment, federal and local, comes into the case, by way of constituted authority exercising surveillance and punitive powers. In effect and ordinarily the intervention of governmental agencies in these negotiations between the owners and the workmen redounds to the benefit of the former. Such is necessarily the case in the nature of things. In the nature of things, as things go in any democratic community, these governmental agencies are administered by a business-

[1] As has appeared, e.g., in the wide-concerted campaign lately carried on for the suppression of the unions, spoken of by courtesy as a "campaign for the open shop."

like personnel, imbued with the habitual bias of business principles,—the principles of ownership; that is to say, under current conditions, the rights, powers, and immunities of absentee ownership. In the nature of the case, the official personnel is drawn from the business community,—lawyers, bankers, merchants, contractors, etc.; in the main and ordinarily drawn from the country towns and the trading-centers; "practical men," whose preconceptions and convictions are such as will necessarily emerge from continued and successful experience in the conduct of business of that character. Lawyers and magistrates who have proved their fitness by their successful conduct of administrative duties and litigations turning on the legal niceties of ownership, and in whom the logic of ownership has become second nature.[1]

In the negotiations between owners and workmen there is little use for the ordinary blandishments of salesmanship. The two parties to the quarrel—for it is after all a quarrel—have learned to know what to count

[1] There is no fault to be found with all this, of course; but it is necessary to note the fact. It is one of the substantial factors in the case, and it lies in the nature of things in any democratic community. Life and experience in these democratic communities is governed by the price-system. Efficiency, practical capacity, popular confidence, in these communities are rateable only in terms of price. "Practical" means "businesslike." Driven by this all-pervading bias of business principles in all that touches their practical concerns, no such democratic community is capable of entrusting the duties of responsible office to any other than business men. Hence, in increasing measure as the situation has moved forward and approached the current highly businesslike order of things, the incumbents of office are necessarily persons of businesslike antecedents, dominated by the logic of ownership, essentially absentee ownership. Legislators, executives, and judiciary are of the same derivation in respect of the bias which their habits of life have engendered and in respect of the drift to which their bias subjects them in their further conduct of affairs. There need of course be no question of the good faith or the intelligence of these responsible incumbents of office. It is to be presumed that in these respects they will commonly grade up to the general average, or something not far short of that point. But by force of the businesslike personal equation that is ingrained by habit in the official personnel, the growth of use and wont, of law and custom, of precedent and enactment, during recent times has fallen into lines drawn on considerations of expediency for business; it has followed that line of least resistance which the sound bias of legislators, executives, and judiciary has made easy and reasonable, at the same time that it has conformed to the logical bent of the substantial citizens. Doubtless in good faith and on sound principles, the ceaseless proliferation of statutes, decisions, precedents, and constitutional interpretations, has run, in the main and with increasing effect, on these lines that converge on the needs and merits of absentee ownership.

As a late and notable illustrative instance of this logical bias, it has been found on judicial consideration that such corporate income as is distributed under the absentee form of a stock-dividend is legally exempt from the income tax.

So again, in the main and ordinarily, the "injunction" which has lately come into extensive application in American practice is an expedient for the conservation and enforcement of the rights and immunities of absentee ownership in case of controversy between owners and workmen. The injunction has other uses, but in practical effect this is its main and ordinary use. Effectual recourse to the injunction to enforce the demands of the workmen is of rare occurrence and of doubtful legitimacy. In effectual scope and force the injunction has grown with the growth of the scope and range of absentee ownership and at the call of issues which have arisen out of its administration and safe-keeping.

on. And the bargaining between them therefore settles down without much circumlocution into a competitive use of unemployment, privation, restriction of work and output, strikes, shut-downs and lockouts, espionage, pickets, and similar manœuvres of mutual derangement, with a large recourse to menacing language and threats of mutual sabotage. The colloquial word for it is "labor troubles." The business relations between the two parties are of the nature of hostilities, suspended or active, conducted in terms of mutual sabotage; which will on occasion shift from the footing of such obstruction and disallowance as is wholly within the law and custom of business, from the footing of legitimate sabotage in the way of passive resistance and witholding of efficiency, to that illegitimate phase of sabotage that runs into violent offenses against persons and property. The negotiations have habitually and increasingly taken on this character of a businesslike dissension. So much so that they have come to be spoken of habitually in terms of conflict, armed forces, and warlike strategy. It is a conflict of hostile forces which is conducted on the avowed strategic principle that either party stands to gain at the cost of the other.[1]

[1] Many public spirited citizens, and many substantial citizens with an interest in business, deplore this spirit of division and cross purposes that pervades the ordinary relations between owners and workmen in the large industries. And in homiletical discourse bearing on this matter it is commonly insisted that such division of sentiment is uncalled for, at the same time that it works mischief to the common good, that "the interests of labor and capital are substantially identical," that dilatory and obstructionist tactics bring nothing better than privation and discontent to both parties in controversy, as well as damage and discomfort to the community at large.

Such homiletical discourse is commonly addressed to the workmen. It is a plain fact of common sense, embedded in immemorial habit, that the business men who have the management of industrial production must be free to limit their output and restrain employment with a view to what the traffic will bear. That is a matter of sound business, authentic and meritorious. Whereas unemployment brought to bear by collusion among the workmen in pursuit of their special advantage will interfere with the orderly earnings of business and thereby bring discouragement and adversity upon the business community, and so will derange and retard the processes of industry from which the earnings are drawn. As things go, because the continued subsistence and material comforts of the community are contingent upon the continued profits of the business men in charge, prosperity is a function of earnings, not of wages; and the material fortunes of the community at large are in practical fact bound up with the continued peace of mind of the absentee owners of the industries, which in turn is bound up with the continued run of free income from the business. This is commonplace and familiar, an habitual fact of common sense, to which no sound man has a right or an inclination to take exception; for settled usage makes all things right. The workmen are not similarly within the familiar bounds of common sense in applying unemployment and restriction of output to enforce their notions of what the traffic will bear in the way of wages. Their assumption of a business standing in an argument with their employers and owners violates common sense; that is to say it is not their right according to the precedents of use and wont, however securely it may be within the statutory formalities. It is not sound common sense, because it has not been ingrained by workday habituation into the action-pattern of the community. By use and wont hitherto the workmen have in practical effect been free to take or leave the terms offered by their owner-employers; and by use and wont the employer-owners have been free to offer such terms as the traffic would bear in the way of earnings. But

It is of the essence of the new order in business that the tactical units now run larger than before, in larger parcels and with a greater degree of compactness and solidarity in action. In industrial business this is exemplified in the growth of corporations and in the tactical grouping of corporations under the surveillance of those massive Interests that govern the pitch and volume of business activity. In effect, as tactical units in the conduct of industrial business, the corporations are associations of absentee owners who are working together on a joint plan in a joint pursuit of gain. So that in effect such a corporation is a method of collusion and concerted action for the joint conduct of transactions designed to benefit the allied and associated owners at the cost of any whom it may concern. In effect, therefore, the joint-stock corporation is a conspiracy of owners; and as such it transgresses that principle of individual self-help that underlies the system of Natural Rights; in which democratic institutions as well as the powers and immunities of ownership are grounded. But the exigencies of business enterprise in recent times, as conditioned by the wide-reaching articulations of trade and industry, call for such large tactical units as will necessarily be composite in point of personnel and collusive in point of ownership.

And the official personnel of civil government, the constituted authorities who have had the making and surveillance of precedents and statutory regulations touching these matters in recent times, have necessarily been persons of businesslike antecedents, imbued with an inveterate businesslike bias, governed by business principles, if not also by business interests. Business exigencies, borne along on this habitual bent of the legislators and judiciary, and enforced by the workday needs of the substantial citizens, have decided that such collusion, conspiracy, or coalition as takes the form of (absentee) ownership is right and good, to be safeguarded in all the powers and immunities of ownership by the constituted authorities at any cost to the community at large. So that any strategic withdrawal of efficiency incident to the conduct of business by such an organisation of collusive ownership, any restriction of output to what the traffic

___

increasingly for some time past the workmen have been drawing together on a businesslike plan of demanding all that the traffic will bear in the way of wages, and of enforcing their demands by the same businesslike recourse to unemployment and retardation that has long served the needs of the employer-owners in their dealings with the market and the livelihood of the ultimate consumers. In its character of industrial man-power, this organised fraction of the underlying population is endeavoring to negotiate for terms on the footing of a *de-facto* Business Interest. (The agricultural manpower, and the population at large as a body of consumers, have not yet made an effectual move of the kind.) And right lately the organisation, animus, and tactics of these industrial workmen have been brought to such a point of businesslike efficiency as to constitute a menace to reasonable earnings and to a reasonable balanced return on the outstanding capitalisation. Therefore, since prosperity depends on a continued free run of earnings on the outstanding capitalisation, the businesslike attitude and tactics of the organised workmen are also a menace to the prosperity of the community at large.

will bear, any unemployment of equipment and man-power with a view to increased earnings on capital, has the countenance of the constituted authorities and will be defended by a suitable use of force in case of need.

It is otherwise, in a degree, with the collusive organisations of workmen. Being not grounded in ownership, their legal right of conspiracy in restraint of trade is doubtful at the best. It has also not the countenance of the substantial citizens[1] or of the minor business men, of the pulpit, or the public press. The effectual limits on strikes are somewhat narrower than on lockouts. Boycotts in support of strikes are illegal, and the more effectual methods of picketing are disallowed by courts and police, except in negligible cases. Since the striking workmen are not owners of the plant that is to be laid idle by their striking, they are excluded from the premises, and they are therefore unable to watch over the unemployment which they have precipitated, and to see to its unbroken continuance. This is a grave disability. The owners are more fortunate in this respect. The power to dispose of matters in the conduct of industry commonly attaches to ownership, and is not legally to be claimed on other grounds. The employer-owners are in a much better position to take care of any desired unemployment, as in case of a lockout. In the same connection it should be recalled that effectual collusion and concert of action is more a matter of routine and takes effect in a more compact and complete fashion on the side of the owners, who are already organised as a corporate unit. The block of ownership embodied in any ordinary business corporation of the larger sort covers a larger segment of the industrial processes involved in any given strike or lockout than does the body of industrial man-power with which the corporation is contending. This will more particularly be the case where and in so far as the old-fashioned craft-unions have not been displaced by an industrial union. It comes to a conflict between a corporate whole on the side of the owners against a fragment of the working forces on the side of the workmen.

So again, in any eventual resort to force, the workmen are under a handicap as against the owners,—a handicap due to law and precedent as well as to the businesslike predilections that are habitual among the personnel of the constituted authorities. Labor troubles are disorders of business, and business is a matter of ownership, while work and livelihood are not. The presumption, in law and custom and official predilection, is against the use of force or the possession or disposal of arms by persons or associations of persons who are not possessed of appreciable property. It is assumed, in effect, that the use of weapons is to protect property and guard its rights; and the assumption applies to the use of weapons by private persons as well as to the armed forces of government. Under the statutes regulating the possession and use of weapons,

[1] As has been remarked in an earlier passage, a "substantial citizen" is an absentee owner of much property.

such, e.g., as the so-called "Sullivan Law" of New York, it will be found that permits to carry weapons are issued in the main to substantial citizens, corporations, and to those incorporations of mercenaries that are known by courtesy as detective agencies; these latter being in the nature of auxiliary forces employed on occasion by corporations which may be involved in strikes or lockouts. All this is doubtless as it should be, and doubtless the intention of it is salutary. So also it will be found that the state constabularies, as well as any units of the National Guards that may be called out on occasion of labor troubles, are, quite habitually and as a matter of routine, employed in safeguarding corporation property and guarding against trespassers on the corporation's premises or interference with the corporation's employees.[1]

This is not to be construed as partisanship, but rather as defensive measures for the preservation of things as they are, or as they recently have been. But the effect is much the same, by and large. It signifies that other than peaceable methods are not effectually at the disposal of the organised workmen in the recurring quarrel with their owner-employers. Of late years the difficulties in the way of any recourse to forcible measures, or even of preparation for demonstrations in force on the part of the unions, have been appreciably increased by the judicial use of the injunction. The injunction has been applied with increasing frequency and an ampler sweep and scope, and its restraint has fallen on the organised workmen, as a rule, rather than on the owners. In effect, the use of the injunction as a means of creating an actionable "contempt of court" enables the authorities to penalise by anticipation; which has visibly turned the endeavours of the unions into channels of passive resistance in preference to anything in the way of overt action. There can be no question but that, in its bearing on the rights and immunities of absentee ownership, this freer use of the injunction has had a notably salutary effect. In one way and another the organised workmen are perforce and progressively reduced to tactics of passive resistance, to tactics of unemployment and retardation by a strategic withdrawal of efficiency, after the same general pattern of inconspicuous restriction and retardation which the owners of industry habitually employ in adjusting the rate and volume of output to what the traffic will bear. And such undivided attention to the strategy of inaction on the part of the workmen is already giving them a visibly increasing proficiency, and is hastening the adoption of a standard routine of retardation. That is to say, the industrial man-power is by force of circumstances taking the same businesslike position as their owner-employers; prudently seeking their own advantage at the cost of any whom it may concern, unmoved by passion, except the passion for the main chance.

[1] Cf. e.g., *Report on the Steel Strike of 1919*, by the Interchurch Movement, pp. 235-248.

In so meeting their owner-employers on their own businesslike ground of graduated curtailment and abeyance the organised workmen are still somewhat at a disadvantage. They have not the countenance of popular sympathy in any unreserved way, inasmuch as they do not speak for a recognised businesslike vested interest. Morally the workmen are still in a precarious position, according to the common sense of a community which is by unbroken habit bound to rate all economic actions and claims in terms of price and ownership. The workmen are under a moral disability at this point, in that the industrial man-power has not been formally capitalised and written into an issue of corporation securities or similar credit-instruments bearing a fixed charge. It is not covered with negotiable paper, such as would invest it with a morally defensible claim to an undiminished income, and would therefore justify any conduct which may serve to make good such a claim. This ethical infirmity of the embattled workmen's case should logically be remedied in some measure by habituation; by their getting used to it and getting their fellow-citizens used to it. In a degree such an effect of habituation is already visible, in the greater tolerance with which the community puts up with the inconveniences that result from the obstructive tactics employed in labor troubles.

But whatever may be the relative strength of the two parties to this controversy, present or prospective, the negotiations between them are visibly falling into more tangible and more standardised shape and are conducted on increasingly businesslike principles of what the traffic will bear, and on both sides alike the negotiations as to what the traffic will bear are carried on in terms of competitive unemployment, mutual defeat, designed to hold the work and output down to such a minimum as will yield the most profitable price per unit to one party or the other. In due consequence, as the contending forces achieve a more effectual mobilisation on a larger scale, and as these tactics of inaction and retardation take effect with greater alacrity and consistency, the practicable minimum of work and output should logically become the ordinary standard practice. So that in "ordinary times" the effectual volume of work and output should run at a minimum.

So soon as the contending forces achieve a sufficiently alert and inclusive mobilisation on both sides, and bring their strategy to a finished and consistent routine, this ordinary balanced minimum of work and output should logically fall somewhat short of the ordinary consumptive needs of the underlying population. The fluctuations should run under, as a general rule. It is reasonable to expect that any fluctuations in excess would be curbed with all due dispatch by a watchful businesslike application of unemployment on one side and the other. In effect, the contending forces are doing team-work in the strategic use of unemployment. Business principles worked out on conservative lines of "watchful waiting" and "safety first" may be counted on with some confidence to keep the run of current production temperately short of current consumptive needs, so soon as these businesslike dispositions have been completed,—in the absence of disturbing causes; and fluctuations in deficiency would come in as workday incidents of the tactical routine. This follows in the nature of the case. The conflict of interests in the case is a conflict of business interests, in which each of the contending parties endeavors to bring the other to terms by as unremitting a pressure of privation as the traffic will bear, leaving the benefit of the doubt quite consistently on the side of deficiency.

The manner in which this routine of deficiency is expected to work out, on business principles consistently applied, is shown in a concrete way in the situation of American industrial business as it has been running during the interval since the Armistice. The dispositions on both sides of the controversy have not yet been perfected, but the results already achieved are enough to serve as notice of what may eventually be looked for. Strategic unemployment of plant and man-power results in a depletion of stocks on hand; a deficiency of maintenance, repairs and replacements; resulting in an impairment of the means of production, a consequent lowering of the practicable level of production and output, and a correspondingly lowered base-line on which further tactics of competitive unemployment will run. The logic of the case, as well as the object-lessons of current experience, appears to say somewhat unequivocally that these mutual businesslike negotiations in unemployment will in all reason work out in so closely-shorn a withdrawal of productive efficiency as to yield but a scant margin for maintenance and necessary extensions and a still more dubious margin for necessary repairs and replacements.[1]

A further line of considerations runs to the same general effect. The several tactical units engaged in this business of strategic unemployment for a revenue, the concerns which do business in industry and its output as well as the associations of workmen that negotiate with them for a division of the proceeds, are, each and several, fractional segments of a larger

[1] An illustrative instance is that of the American railways, which have been suffering a shrinkage of physical assets for want of due repairs and replacements. The commitments of the railway corporations in the way of fixed charges hinder their applying an adequate proportion of their earnings to repairs and replacements, at the same time that the rigidity of their outstanding capitalisation hinders their writing off the resulting depreciation and obsolescence of the plant; whereby they are driven to charging more than the traffic will bear in the way of freight and passenger rates as well as in the way of retrenchment on wages and dismissal of workmen. All of which works together cumulatively toward a progressive decline of efficiency and a more accentuated policy of strategic unemployment.

The remedy which is ordinarily applied in such a case is that universal solvent of business exigencies, the creation of new credit obligations, with which to provide needed working capital, and which are duly capitalised with the due complement of fixed charges, payable out of an advance of prices due to the resulting increased volume of outstanding purchasing-power helped out by a temperate limitation of output.

composite industrial mechanism and of the industrial system at large. Each unit large or small, composite or single, pursues its own ends, negotiates for its own differential advantage at the cost of any whom it may concern, by a strategic retardation of the industrial process within that segment of the whole which is subject to its particular jurisdiction as a business concern, in detachment from the rest of the system or with slight and contingent regard for any ulterior consequences which its tactics of unemployment may have for the rest. Such is the nature of that system and canon of free competition which has stood over out of the eighteenth century as an axiomatic fact of Natural Right, and which still underlies the law and morals of business enterprise.

As business concerns, and therefore as tactical units in the management of industrial business, these several segments of the business community go about their business on a competitive basis, on the principle of "putting it over"; also called *caveat emptor*. But as industrial factors, and therefore as technological units engaged in the conduct of industrial production, they are members of a close-knit industrial system, bound in a comprehensive fabric of interlocking processes of work, in such a way that the continued working of any one member is conditioned on the due working of the rest. Technologically each member of the system, each of these tactical units, is bound to bear its due part in the ceaseless give and take of interlocking industrial processes. So that any retardation or suspension of the rate and volume of output at any point in the industrial system will check the work throughout a series of industrial plants and processes that go before and that follow after in the balanced sequence of operations, and it will therefore cripple the industrial system at large by that much.

Owing to this articulated character of industrial work as carried on by the methods of the mechanical industry, the ulterior (systemic) consequences of any strategic suspension or retardation of work at any point are likely to be more serious than the direct waste and loss incurred at the initial point, where the strategic unemployment is applied. This applies with especial force, of course, in the case of unemployment initiated in the key industries; but it will apply in only a lessening degree outward from the key industries throughout that fabric of "continuation industries" whose interlocking processes of work play into one another to maintain the due rate and volume of output, and it will apply with increasing urgency and effect as the industrial system takes on more of the character of the mechanical industry and is organised on the lines of quantity production.[1]

In recent times, and especially in recent years, the balance, articulation,

---

[1] The case has latterly been well illustrated by what happens in the way of ulterior consequences for industry at large when work is suspended or seriously abridged (for strategic purposes), in coal-mining, railroad transportation, or steel production.

and interdependence of industrial processes has been growing visibly greater, wider, more delicate, and more imperative. At the same time the facilities for instant and drastic suspension of work in the various mechanical industries are being greatly perfected; both in the way of a swift and resolute mobilisation of the workmen and in the way of loyal concert of action and standard methods of unemployment among the owner-employers and the governmental agencies of surveillance and enforcement. The work of industrial confusion by recourse to unemployment in the pursuit of business has been greatly facilitated and abridged. The recourse to unemployment is readier and more sweeping, and the articulations of industry are growing progressively more extensive and more exacting, resulting in a wider and profounder effect in the way of derangement and deficiency due to suspension of work at any point. These two lines of improvement in methods—in business and in technology—converge and concur in such a way that the ceaseless, though fluctuating, application of unemployment entailed by the current exigencies of business will have presently—if not rather, has already—brought the industrial system to such a state of chronic, though fluctuating, derangement as will result in a chronic, though fluctuating, margin of deficiency; whereby the rate and volume of output of those goods and services that make up the livelihood of the community will fall short of current needs by a progressively widening margin of deficiency. The eventual outcome of such progressive disallowance of work, disability, and privation, can, of course, not be predicted; although it seems plain that there should be an eventual limit to its continuance.[1]

Over against this orderly drift into retardation and industrial paralysis there are, of course, other factors at work running to the contrary effect.

[1] All the while there need, also of course, result no decline in the community's total wealth, as counted in money-values. Business should presumably continue on a conservatively prosperous footing, with fluctuating variations, and with an increasing devotion to salesmanship and overhead. Any shrinkage in physical possessions, in the current output of goods and services, or in the available means of subsistence and physical comfort, could and presumably would be offset, or more than offset, by a conservative creation and capitalisation of new credits, with new and valuable fixed charges. Such a running creation of capitalised wealth will be all the more imperatively called for, in that the progressively widening deficiency in the material supply, coupled with rising prices and rising costs, will entail an urgent and progressive need of additional funds to serve as working capital.

It is perhaps unnecessary to note that such a view of these matters will not have the countenance of the certified economic experts. Those economists and public men who still faithfully construe the current situation in terms of the nineteenth century, as defined by formulas which have stood over from the eighteenth century, will scarcely see these matters in this light. By received preconception, credit is deferred payment, capital is assembled "production goods," business is the helper of productive industry, salesmanship is the facility of the "middleman," money is "the great wheel of circulation" employed in a "refined system of barter," and absentee ownership is a rhetorical solecism.

There is a continued run of discoveries, inventions, adaptations, and short-cuts in the industrial arts, new ways and means and new uses of the old. With the result that the coefficient of productive capacity per unit of man-power continues to gain in a cumulative fashion. New processes, new materials from near and far, are continually being turned to account, and new methods of turning old materials to account and of coördinating known processes for the more efficient use of old resources, as well as for incorporating new resources into the routine of the day's work,—these improvements and accelerations in the industrial arts continue to insinuate themselves into the fabric of the industrial system, in spite of the uniformly conservative management on the part of the business community as touches all new projects and project-makers in the industrial field.

But all such advances in the mechanic arts bring new complications in the working structure of the industrial system; whether the innovations come by way of an increased scale of operation or by way of a new procedure in the mechanics of production and distribution; whether they draw into the complex of industry material and power-resources previously unknown or unused,—as, e.g., petroleum and the obscure industrial metals, or power transmission by electricity; or they facilitate and abridge the work in hand—as, e.g., the Bessemer and the basic processes in steel production, or the internal combustion engine for use in vehicles, or the synthetic production of drugs, dyes, and condiments. At every move the network of technological interrelations will be drawn to a finer mesh, a more close-knit and more widely inclusive web of give and take, within which the working balance of coordinations runs on a continually closer margin of tolerance. With the result that a disturbance, in the nature of retardation or deficiency at any critical point, will carry derangement and sabotage farther and faster than before through the main lines and into the intricate working details of production. With every further move along the lines on which the industrial arts are advancing, therefore, sabotage—that is to say strategic unemployment at the instance of the owner-employers or of the workmen—becomes a swifter and more widely corrosive agency of miscarriage and decay.

At the same time, and in great part by help of these same technical appliances and powers, the business community is able, also in a progressive fashion, to bring sound conservative business principles to bear on industry in a swifter and more comprehensive way and with a slighter margin of error. That is to say, novelties will be disallowed with a freer hand and the tactical manœuvres of unemployment will gain something in frequency and amplitude; measures to suppress or disable the organisations of workmen and malcontents will take on added scope, assurance, vigor, and despatch. And the organised workmen, too, are coming to realise the increasing need as well as the increasing facilities for meeting their owners on a business footing and carrying on their negotiations in strategic unemployment and retardation with a wider and more effectual coördination and manœuvres and a more provident attention to their needful financial resources.[1]

Under these circumstances it seems reasonable to expect that the systematic retardation and derangement of productive industry which is entailed by the current businesslike management will work out in a progressive abatement of the margin of net output of the industrial system at large; that this progressive abatement of the net industrial output will presently reach and pass the critical point of no net return—as counted in physical units of livelihood; and that in the calculable future the industrial system, so managed on sound business principles, will run on lines of a progressively "diminishing return," converging to an eventual limit of tolerance in the way of a reduced subsistence minimum; beyond which the situation at large should apparently be liable to revision by an intrusion of some sort of "disturbing cause."[2]

[1] Right lately, since 1920, certain of the more businesslike unions have gone into banking with a view to financing their own affairs. So far the plan appears to be practicable. It is expected that by this means these unions will be able to extend, consolidate and standardise those measures of unemployment and retardation that are advisable in their business. It should greatly "facilitate and abridge the labor" of concientiously withdrawing efficiency in those lines of work with which these unions have to do. The farmers, too, are looking hopefully, and desperately, in the same direction with a similar end in view.

[2] All the while there is not, at least not for the time being, any reason to apprehend that this progressive deficit of industrial production will cause a shrinkage in the country's aggregate wealth—as counted in money-values; or even that the current rate of increase of such wealth will fall off. All that is in the main a question of capitalisation, and therefore it is a question of the continued creation of credit and overhead charges. The aggregate of possessions, as counted in terms of "production goods" and livelihood, should presumably continue to fall off, as during the past few years; but wealth, as counted in money-values, should presumably continue to increase, perhaps at an accelerated rate, as during the past years. And as a matter of course the wealth in hand should continue, perhaps at an accelerated rate, to gravitate into progressively larger blocks of absentee ownership.

Just now (1923) the appearances would seem to say that the critical point of no net aggregate product has been reached and passed within recent years, since the Armistice. Yet it is quite possible that these appearances are transient and misleading. There is no reasonable doubt but that the countries of Europe have been running on a deficit, industrially speaking, during these years; and indeed on a progressively widening margin of deficit.

In effect, these Europeans have also curtailed their technological personnel by uncovered consumption of technical manpower during the War; while the production and upkeep of technological personnel and facilities are now running short of current needs, in rate, volume and quality, due to the present state of Peace. So that the Europeans, and by consequence the Americans also, face a technological deficit, and therefore a foresumptive disintegration of their industrial system.

Nor need it be doubted that the Americans have also been running slightly short of a net balance in their industrial output, as counted in physical units. But a cautious appraisal would perhaps say that this net industrial deficiency may be a transient effect due to transient causes connected with the War and the inordinately businesslike terms of the Peace; and that so soon as the international bargaining between the Interests has been concluded, and so soon as the earnings of the "profiteers," past and prospective, shall have been duly stabilised and capitalised, this businesslike embargo on industry and livelihood will be lifted. Such appears to be the expectation of the statesmen. It is a point in doubt.

It is conceivable that the civilised peoples might yet save themselves alive out of this impasse, in spite of their addiction to business, if it were not for their national integrity.

Business-as-usual, helped out by its later extensions and facilities, may be counted on to hold the ordinary level of employment and output down to the minimum of what the traffic will bear, with a reasonable degree of consistency, and with something of a conservative downward trend to a lower minimum. Frequent and substantial oscillations below the ordinary level are to be looked for, due to repeated and inconclusive trials of endurance between the owners and the workmen, in their businesslike endeavors to bring one another to terms in a struggle of mutual discomfort. These persistent excursions below the ordinary level should have a cumulative effect and establish a downward trend in the average run, such as to depress the practicable minimum. Provided always that a partial failure, or abrupt recession, of the state of the industrial arts, due to curtailment of technological instruction and personnel at home or abroad, does not bring the whole case to a precipitate liquidation.

As is the current practice, these manœuvres of strategic deficiency will continue to be financed by a conservative but effectual creation of capitalised credits, in great part if not in the main. Such is, in effect, the established practice on the side of the owners, and such is now beginning to be the recourse also of the organised workmen. By this means these recurring depressions of the ordinary level of employment and output will, in some measure and progressively, be incorporated in the routine and will progressively lower the minimum which the traffic will bear. Such will necessarily be the case, inasmuch as any deficiency brought about in this way in the physical output will not count as a deficiency in money-values and will therefore not disturb the course of the businesslike negotiations on which the whole matter turns. Money-values are the conclusive realities of business, and the outstanding money-values will not suffer so long as the price per unit is suitably enhanced by a limitation of the output and an enlargement of the outstanding volume of purchasing-power. The progressive reduction of output through unemployment will take effect in physical terms of goods and services, not in terms of price, as current experience goes to show; price being a function of scarcity and purchasing-power.

In the long run, so soon as the privation and chronic derangement which follows from this application of business principles has grown unduly irksome and becomes intolerable, there is due to come a sentimental revulsion and a muttering protest that "something will have to be done about it,"—as, e.g., in the case which has arisen in the coal industry. Thoughtful persons will then devise remedial measures. As a matter of course, in a community which is addicted to business principles, the remedial measures which are brought under advisement in such a case by

responsible citizens and officials are bound to be of a businesslike nature;
designed in all reason to safeguard the accomplished facts of absentee
ownership in the natural resources involved and in the capitalised overhead charges which have been incorporated in the business. Necessarily
so, for the community at large is addicted to business principles, and the
official personnel is so addicted in an especial degree, in the nature of
things.

Yet all the while there are certain loose ends in this fabric of business
convictions which binds the mentality of these peoples. There is always
the chance, more or less imminent, that in time, after due trial and error,
on duly prolonged and intensified irritation, some sizable element of the
underlying population, not intrinsically committed to absentee ownership, will forsake or forget their moral principles of business-as-usual, and
will thereupon endeavor to take this businesslike arrangement to pieces
and put the works together again on some other plan, for better or worse.

"Other things remaining the same," some such shifting of the economic
base should be due to follow, eventually. Not because a better plan than
the present businesslike one has been projected or is likely to be conceived; but because, "human nature being such as it is," the present businesslike management of the industrial system is incompetent, irrelevant,
and not germane to the livelihood of the underlying population. It is
not that absentee ownership is wrong, in principle. "The law allows it,
and the court awards it." It is only that its concrete working-out is incompatible with the current state of the industrial arts, and that the material
welfare of the civilised peoples is conditioned on the full and orderly
operation of the industrial system in which this state of the arts is embodied.

This precarious state of the case is now beginning to engage the attention of the substantial citizens and of their constituted authorities,—on
whom it is incumbent, through good report and evil report, to guard the
status quo of capitalised overhead charges. Being "practical men," they
bend their energies to the preservation of an arrangement which will
not work, lest a worse evil befall. The accomplished facts of absentee
ownership must and shall be preserved; and it is for the authorities and
the substantial citizens to take measures to that end. The national integrity
of the civilised peoples comes into the case as a pivotal factor at this point.

Whatever will bear the appearance of being a national interest, of being
bound up with the fortunes of the national establishment, will find a
ready lodgment in the popular sentiment as an article of patriotic in-
fatuation. Such things become right and good, and it becomes the dutiful
privilege of all citizens to cherish these things and to devote their substance and energies to the furtherance of them, without scrutiny or after-

thought. Indeed, further scrutiny of any article of belief or practice which has found lodgment in the community's habits of thought as a standard item of national aspiration or national pretension will be odious, to the point of presumptive criminality So also, whatever can be made to bear the appearance of hindering or trifling with those aspirations that are covered by the habitual canons of national integrity in force at a given time and place are presumptively treasonable. Such treason is the gravest of crimes,—next after lèse majesté. Indeed, the spirit of national integrity touches the skirts of divinity and carries more than a trace of religious intolerance. So that the crime of treason comes near to the unique atrocity of sin against the Holy Ghost. In both cases there is the same dutiful renunciation of sobriety and reason in dealing with delinquents, and the same presumption of guilt in the accused.

Uncritical devotion to the national pretensions being a meritorious habit, it is also a useful article of camouflage, a shelter for gainful enterprises and transactions which might otherwise be open to doubt, a means of avoiding unfavorable notice and of procuring a profitable line of goodwill. In this sense it has come to have a merchantable value, so that professions of such devotion have become a businesslike matter-of-course among those who follow "gainful pursuits." Which weeds out profitless argument and reflection in these premises and dispenses with any irritating afterthought. And men will commonly believe and live up to those things which they habitually profess. That is the meaning of autosuggestion. "Auto-intoxication" can not properly be applied in this connection, since the term has been assigned a specific meaning in medical usage.

What is yet more to the point is the secondary effect of these businesslike professions of national faith, in that the young are taught to believe what their elders profess to believe. This indoctrination of the young by undeviating habituation in word and deed, precept and example, is very much in the foreground of their schooling just now, and it should logically bring grave consequences in the way of an accentuated nationalist bias in the incoming generation. It is something like drill in the manual of arms, both in respect of the mental qualities involved and in respect of the automatic responses induced in persons subjected to it. The resulting action-pattern of national animation runs on much the same lines as the habitual use of the Paternoster and Rosary, and carries the like uncritical assurance of well-doing.

In an earlier chapter something has already been said of the salesmanlike piety that is habitually professed by those who do business in the country towns. They and all their folks and ways are given to blamelessly devout observances and professions, by routine of the day's work in pursuit of salesmanlike gains. There is no especial degree of hypocrisy and no appreciable mental strain involved in their so professing and acting on a belief in religious verities of which they neither have nor seek an understanding. It is all a foregone conclusion, a businesslike matter-of-course incident to their "gainful pursuit." But in this as in other matters men (and women) come to believe what they habitually profess, and with a jealous solicitude they train their offspring, by precept, example, and systematic schooling, into due conformity with these canons of salvation and profitable respectability. So also as regards the secular faith and observances of national integrity. And in an eminent sense the country towns have the making of the community's ideals and mentality, beyond any other one agency. In much the same measure they have also the making of the country's official personnel and their mentality. National integrity, religious intolerance, and business principles march together under the banners of the country town in a co-partnership of means and ends, for the Glory of God and the good of man.

In any democratic community, such as the American, the official personnel which is vested with jurisdiction and initiative will be, in the main, such as the country town has made them, by exacting habituation and by selective elimination of the unfit. Fitness for responsible office being, on the whole, tested by conformity to these three canonical articles: national integrity, devout observance, and business-as-usual. A democratic community addicted to business enterprise and devout observances will not tolerate an official personnel endowed with a different equipment of habitual predilections. Exceptions may occur, but they are sporadic and negligible, and they fall into abeyance at any juncture of national exigency. Such a community will trust no one but its substantial citizens; which is another way of saying the same thing. Anyone may assure himself of the truth of this statement, as a general proposition, by a cursory survey of the case as it presents itself at large or at any point.

These persons who make up this official personnel, and in whose hands is the power to act, locally, departmentally, and at large, will go into action as practical men, faithful to the joint governance of these settled habits of thought whose creatures they are. With a mentality compounded of national integrity and business principles they will devoutly follow out the drift of the two conjointly; to such effect that in the official apprehension the community's fortunes are bound up with the pursuit of its business enterprise; that is to say, with the continued gains of its absentee owners. It lies in the nature of democratic institutions that any such community will select its official personnel from among its absentee owners, that is to say its substantial citizens. And it lies in the nature of the substantial citizen-official to let business interests coalesce with the national integrity in such a way as to make the safe-keeping of business-as-usual the first and constant care of the official establishment. So that any conjunction of circumstances which may threaten to encroach on the accomplished facts of absentee ownership or of capitalised overhead charges at any point will forthwith be rated as a menace to the national integrity and a call for official measures of repression to guard the public's safety.

Business-as-usual and the national integrity are joint and integral factors in that complex of habits of thought that makes up the official mentality; so that any irritation of the official sensibilities along either line will unavoidably bring a response along the two together and indiscriminately. In that parallelogram of forces in which business principles and the sense of national integrity combine jointly to move and direct the democratic officials there is no distinguishing the two joint factors. The fact may also be worth noting, although it is essentially of secondary consequence, that since any given democratic official is also in effect a substantial citizen, his pecuniary interests as an owner in his own right will fall into line with his civic principles at large in this matter, and will therefore coalesce with his civic virtue and give urgency and singleness of purpose; with the result that the weight of the official establishment, national and local, will in the nature of things be brought to bear on the side of ownership at any juncture of doubt or dissension.

The point of immediate interest here is not any merit or demerit that may attach to this run of the facts, but only the fact that such is the run of them.

So far as concerns the argument at this point, the upshot of this run of the facts is that the habit of thinking in terms of national solidarity and civic allegiance, ingrained in the community at large as well as in its official personnel, comes into the case as an effectual bar to any departure from the standard routine. Faithful adherence to business principles and to the businesslike management of industry is second nature to the substantial citizen. But by process of growth, such businesslike management of the industrial system has become incompatible with the current state of the industrial arts; so that the continued management of industry for business purposes results in an industrial stalemate.

In that intractable dissension which divides the owner-employers and the organised workmen, the resources and appliances of constituted authority are brought into action on the side of the employer-owners, in effect and in the main. That such should be the case lies in the nature of things; partly for reasons reflected in the last few paragraphs above. Also in great part this run of the facts is grounded in ancient and standard law and custom, as well as in current statute and precedent.

The rights, powers, and immunities of ownership, including the incidents of free contract, are grounded in principles of law and usage which are by ancient habit deeply embedded in the popular common sense as well as in the common law. This body of law and usage grew out of habituation to an earlier order of things, and has therefore stood over from some time before anything like the present system of industry and business had come into action; before ownership and its share in the management of industry had passed over into absentee ownership and engendered the current credit system. So that these ancient principles of law and of common sense, in which the rights, powers, and immunities of ownership are grounded, are by way of being holdovers. The material circumstances have moved out of their way. But all the while that the shift to absentee ownership and credit has been going forward, the ancient principles have been progressively construed, adapted, and amplified to meet the newly arisen exigencies; and the work of construction and amplification has been carried on by men whose immersion in business affairs has imbued them with a steadfast bias; to such effect that, as a matter of formal scope and authority, the ancient principles have been enabled to sanction whatever arrangements may be expedient for absentee ownership and its administration. In point of statutory provision and constructive precedent, the rights, powers, and immunities of absentee ownership and capitalised overhead charges have all that sanction and stability that belong to habits of thought which are embedded in immemorial common sense. They are right and good, in point of statutory provision and constructive precedent, before the law; indeed, the law and the lawgivers have been busy with their enforcement and reënforcement, for some time past.

But they are not equally secure in point of common sense; that is to say, the grounds of habitual morality are not similarly stable. The material exigencies of life and the habituation enforced by them have not been running on precisely the same lines as those exigencies of business which have given rise to these statutory provisions and constructive precedents. At any juncture where a discrepancy arises between law and common sense it is incumbent on the constituted authorities to take precautionary measures and guard the provisions of law against inroads of common sense. Under the circumstances, therefore, it has become the prime and particular duty of the constituted authorities to safeguard the rights, powers, and immunities of absentee ownership, at any cost to the underlying population.

Under "the majestic equality of the law," the organised workmen enjoy the same rights, powers, and immunities of absentee ownership and capitalised overhead charges as their owner-employers with whom they are forever at odds. But their circumstances are different, and the incidence of these legal provisions is therefore different in their case. They have, in effect, no enforceable absentee rights and powers, and they have been unable to capitalise their income into fixed overhead charges on industry, collectible *in absentia*. They and their claims and circumstances do not fit into the legal framework of business-as-usual conducted on the current plan; which is their misfortune, if not their fault. The legal validity of any of those demands and perquisites for which they contend is of a slight and dubious nature. Being not capitalised into a corporate entity with fixed charges and limited liability, as their absentee owners are, any concerted action on their part is likely to be obnoxious to the law which penalises conspiracy. A few hundred or a few thousand absentee owners acting in collusion as stockholders in a corporation, on the other side of the controversy, are not guilty of conspiracy in the eyes of the law. So also, since the workmen are not owners of the plant about the use or unemployment of which the controversy turns, they have no right of access to the premises and are therefore unable to supervise and enforce the unemployment of the works in support of their contention. It is otherwise with the employer-owners. By and large, the legitimate powers of the workmen in such a controversy extend no farther than to take or leave the terms offered them by the employer-owners. Even a boycott is obnoxious to the law.

In effect it is recognised as a matter of common sense that this right of individual and passive unemployment is scarcely adequate to serve the turn in their negotiations with their owner-employers. Quite visibly the substantial citizens and the constituted authorities are of that mind. Indeed they are animated with a lively apprehension on that score, and precautionary measures are taken to guard against anticipated excesses on the part of the workmen at this point. There is no similar apprehension and no similar precautions are taken as regards the owner-employers. It is quite plainly the persuasion of the substantial citizens and the official personnel that the organised workmen may, at any juncture, be provoked by these disabilities into exceeding the limits of sabotage countenanced by the law—the passive withdrawal of efficiency—and that they will be likely, on due provocation, to resort to such "direct action" as will jeopardise the rightful holdings and incomes of the absentee owners in the case. The substantial citizens and the official personnel are moved by no serious apprehension that precautionary measures are necessary to restrain the employer-owners within the law. The ordinary legal correctives and remedies are sufficient for that purpose. Whereas such precautionary measures of forcible repression to keep recalcitrant workmen within due bounds and to safeguard the interests of the owners belong in the standard routine of things to be done. No doubt, all this is as it should be, in view of the relevant facts.[1]

---

[1] It has been said, with a disquieting verisimilitude though perhaps with unwarranted breadth, that "The Intelligence Service of the Army has for its primary purpose" a surveillance of certain obnoxious civil organisations; and the organisations enumerated as obnoxious are organisations of workmen and farmers,—the list includes the American Federation of Labor. It is to be presumed that such an avowal will not be found formally correct. It is at least inexpedient; but there is a disquieting verisimilitude about it, in view of the known facts.

Apart from international intrigue and intimidation, almost wholly in pursuit of business interests, the workday use of the administration's military arm is to keep the domestic peace. In practical effect and in the common run, the enforcement of domestic peace works out in restraining unruly workmen and safeguarding the interests of property and business, in the recurrent cases of dispute between owners and employees. The like will apply generally to measures of "preparedness" in the way of armed force; whether under the auspices of the Federal administration or as carried

By force of ancient law and custom and by the later drift of circumstances it has come about that the resources and apparatus of constituted authority, whether by administrative direction or permissively, will in the main serve the needs of the employer-owners in their controversial dealings with their industrial man-power. It will not be denied that this state of the case has a very appreciable dramatic and sentimental value; but the merits of the arrangement, whether as a question of public morals or of class interest, will not engage the argument at this point. What is of immediate interest is the objective consequences of the arrangement. One of these immediate consequences is an abiding sense of grievance and hostility on both sides of the negotiations, but more pronounced perhaps on the side of the workmen. Mutual distrust and sharp practice has come to be of the essence of the case; working out in a standard policy of mutual defeat.

By force of law and custom, as progressively construed and amplified by successive generations of businesslike officials, any manœuvres which violate or exceed the immunities and powers of ownership are disallowed in this strategy of mutual defeat by which the working of the industrial system is governed. This bears on the manœuvres of the workmen in a peculiarly drastic way, since they are vested with none of the powers and immunities of ownership,—except in that Pickwickian sense in which "the majestic equality of the law" deals impartially with rich and poor. In effect, their powers and immunities in these premises are wholly of a negative order, such as will enable them to do nothing, to withhold

---

on in the several states; whether they come under the name of the National Guard, State Militia, State Constabulary, or Municipal Police,—although some substantial reservation is to be entered as regards the last mentioned. The like is also true of those private enterprises in preparedness, the so-called Detective Agencies, which make a business of supplying mercenaries and "under-cover men." These mercenary fighting men are used by the employer-owners, almost wholly, as against the workmen. This private traffic in mercenaries is presumably quite right and proper, being permitted by the authorities and approved by the substantial citizens; although with some demur from the side of the organised workmen.

To complete the sketch at this point it is necessary to note that in those states or municipalities where the carriage or possession of firearms is subject to "Permit," the prohibition of arms will chiefly affect the workmen and others who have no substantial standing as owners or custodians of property: the need of guarding valuable property rights being the usual ground on which such permits are issued. Whether by intention or not, this regulation has the effect of leaving the employer-owners and their retainers armed, while the workmen are not armed except by evasion of the law. In the same connection, and as a characteristic circumstance, it appears that the larger industrial corporations come somewhat habitually into the market for firearms and ammunition, as good and valuable customers. This corporate preparedness includes rifles and machine-guns; whereas there appears to be little demand on the part of the same concerns for guns of such calibre as would be at all properly called artillery, such as "quick-firers" and "trench-mortars."

What has just been said is no more than a *pro forma* recital of obvious facts, of course. It is a description of the state of the case at large, and is to be taken with such qualifications as may be called for in detail.

efficiency, to lie idle and to put in their working-time as wastefully and ineffectively as the circumstances will permit; in short to go in for that negative sabotage which is of the essence of business management in industry. So they concentrate their endeavors and ingenuity on this line. Bent on defeating their owner-employers by such ways and means as are at their disposal, they apply themselves with all diligence to delivering as nearly nothing as may be in return for such wages as their latest manœuvres in unemployment have enabled them to carry off, for the transient time being. So that by what foots up to a concerted policy of mutual defect the two parties in interest work together to pare the effectual work and output of industry down to whatever level of deficiency the traffic will bear in the short run.

In the short run, under the spur of tactical necessity, the traffic will bear and the exigencies will enjoin so effectual a disallowance of work and output as to leave a margin of livelihood and maintenance uncovered, and to entail a shrinkage of the available man-power and material equipment. Under the hands of a businesslike official personnel, supported by a like-minded body of substantial citizens, the vindication of property rights coalesces in principle with the vindication of the national integrity, to such effect that any proposal to disallow or abridge the sovereign rights of absentee ownership in the conduct of industry will be constructive sedition. So that the spur of tactical necessity will drive with an unmitigated incentive to the one line of strategy which this posture of things leaves open,—an alert and obstinate disallowance of work and output. Short runs of intensified strategic sabotage come therefore to predominate in the contest between employers and employees; succeeding one another with increasing urgency and decreasing intervals; so that the long run falls into shape as a discontinuous chain of deficits, with scant and vanishing internodes of recovery. This describes the present rather than the future. And since the several lines of productive industry are bound by the state of the industrial arts into an increasingly intricate and exacting network of give and take, they will each and several be subject to undesigned and unforeseen stoppages induced by tactical stoppages in related lines of industry, with increasing frequency and amplitude as business principles take the upperhand and the spirit of salesmanship finally displaces workmanship in the conduct of industry. All the while any shrinkage in the rate and volume of output and any curtailment of the material factors engaged is to be covered over and made good on the books with a capitalisation of credits and a rising level of prices, due to an increased volume of purchasing-power thereby thrown on the market. A progressively increasing volume of working capital is required for the conduct of an increasingly stubborn campaign of labor troubles and an increasingly large and exacting expenditure on sales-publicity; which is to be covered with a running creation of credits, duly capitalised and thrown on the market as an addition to the outstanding purchasing-power.

In recent times, and in a progressively increasing measure, the national establishments and the spirit of national integrity among the peoples of Christendom have been an agency of dissension and distress, a means of curtailing and impairing the material conditions of life for the underlying population, and an arrangement for the increase and diffusion of ill-will among men. Such is their major and ordinary outcome. Coupled with this is commonly some slight differential advantage to some special Interest in whose service these agencies are employed. In recent times the differential gains which so accrue from this usufruct of national ill-will, inure in the main, to certain commercial and financial Interests sheltered under the national Flag.

The net aggregate amount of these differential gains which so accrue to these special Interests at the cost of such ill-will and distress to the common run will ordinarily foot up to no more than a vanishing percentage of their net aggregate cost to the underlying populations that are employed in the traffic. In the material respect these institutional holdovers work out in a formidable aggregate loss of life and livelihood; while in the spiritual respect their staple output is a tissue of dissension, distrust, dishonesty, servility, and bombast. The net product is mutual and collective defeat and grief.[1]

[1] As has been remarked in an earlier passage, this characterisation has nothing to say as regards the moral or æsthetic excellence of these institutional holdovers, as to the righteousness, goodness, or beauty of national integrity, patriotic intolerance, or political intrigue. These are questions of taste and fashion, about which there is no disputing. Nor do these questions touch the present argument, which has to do with the objective consequences of these institutional factors.

By derivation, in point of institutional pedigree, the democratic nations of Christendom are a "filial generation" of those dynastic and territorial monarchies which filled Europe with a muddle of war and politics in early modern times. And these national establishments, and the spirit of national integrity on which they trade, are still essentially warlike and political. That is to say, predation is still the essence of the thing. The ways and means of the traffic are still force and fraud, at home and abroad. The actualities of that "self-determination of nations" which has so profoundly engaged the sentiments of thoughtful persons, always foots up to a self-determination in respect of warlike adventures, political jobbery, and territorial aggrandisement. Witness the newly self-determining nations, Poland, Czechoslovakia, Jugoslavia.

There are, doubtless, many mitigating circumstances, and many fanciful card-houses of cultural and linguistic conceits erected in good faith by the apologists of Chauvinism. But in point of fact, "realpolitik" continues to make satisfactory use of the chauvinists in a pursuit of its own ends by force and fraud. So also the universal type-form of national solemnities, even when staged by the mildest mannered and most amiable curators of the spiritual antiquities, continues to be a worshipful magnification of past warlike adventures, backed with a staging of histrionic obsequies of war-heroes, with parade of guns, uniforms and battle standards. "Breathes there a man with soul so dead, Who never to himself hath said, 'This is my own, my native land,' " when the national anniversary is being magnified with warlike fireworks and bombast,

Apart from any glamor of national prowess, in the way of blood and wounds, the nations have also a certain sentimental value as standard containers, each of its distinctive cultural tincture, very precious to persons of cultivated tastes in these matters. So also, as a matter of history these national commonwealths, as well as the territorial states in their time, have served to alleviate local animosities, each within its jurisdiction, and to bring consistency and correlation into the process of industry and of civil life within their several territories. But all that is beside the point today. The work of correlation, standardisation, and concatenation of local units and of the processes of work and life has been taken over, irretrievably, by the industrial arts, which do not go by favor of nationalities. The industrial arts, and the industrial system in which they go into action, have no use for and no patience with local tinctures of culture and the obstructive routine of statecraft. The mechanistic system of industry is of a collective and coöperative nature, essentially and of necessity a joint enterprise of all the civilised peoples, in so far as their civilisation is of the occidental pattern; and there is substantially only one such pattern. This industrial system runs on a balanced specialisation of work among its working members; standardised quantity production, which is always and of necessity in excess of the local needs; free draught on a limitless range of material resources from far and near. No isolated industrial undertaking and no isolated cultural activity is self-sufficient within the sweep of this industrial system of Christendom. And any degree of wilful isolation is straitway and automatically penalised by a corresponding degree of impotence, under the impassive run of the industrial system at large, which draws impartially on far and near. In this new industrial order of things the national establishments and their frontiers and functionaries come in as an extraneous apparatus of deflection and obstruction, employed to perpetuate animosities and generate lag, leak, and friction.

Of this nature are customs-duties, shipping-subsidies, trade-concessions, consular service, passport regulations, national protection and enforcement of claims in foreign parts. Much has been said in censure of these and the like contrivances of discrimination, and much more in the way of censure is doubtless merited. The closer the scrutiny of this apparatus and its working, the more deplorable it all proves to be, in its material consequences. But this notorious imbecility of it all does after all not immediately concern the argument at this point. It is of more immediate interest to note that in all these diplomatic, legislative, and administrative

---

while veterans, Red Cross nurses and Boy Scouts parade their uniforms to martial music under banners? In any one of these democratic commonwealths the acid test of sound and serviceable citizenship still is the good old propensity to fight for the flag without protest or afterthought. There is no question but this is a meritorious frame of mind. It is also the frame of mind which is sedulously drilled into the incoming generation.

measures in restraint of trade and industry, the measures are taken for the benefit of business, to stabilise, fortify and enhance the gains of one and another among the special business Interests that are domiciled in the country; that the national establishment is in this way employed in the service of these business concerns, at the cost of the national community at large; that in this way the national interests have come to be identified with the gainful traffic of these business Interests; that the sense of national integrity is by habituation to this routine of subservience made to cover the maintenance of business-as-usual and the insurance of capitalised earnings. The subservience of the national establishment and the official personnel to the aims and manœuvres of business becomes a fact of prescriptive use and wont, passes into law and custom, and is embedded in the community's common sense as a matter of workday routine.

In the last analysis the nation remains a predatory organism, in practical effect an association of persons moved by a community interest in getting something for nothing by force and fraud. There is, doubtless, also much else of a more genial nature to be said for the nation as an institutional factor in recent times. The voluminous literature of patriotic encomium and apology has already said all that is needed on that head. But the irreducible core of national life, what remains when the non-essentials are deducted, still is of this nature; it continues to be self-determination in war and politics. Such is the institutional pedigree of the nation. It is a residual derivative of the predatory dynastic State, and as such it still continues to be, in the last resort, an establishment for the mobilisation of force and fraud as against the outside, and for a penalised subservience of its underlying population at home.

In recent times, owing to the latterday state of the industrial arts, this national pursuit of warlike and political ends has come to be a fairly single-minded chase after unearned income to be procured by intimidation and intrigue. It has been called Imperialism; it might also, in a colloquial phrasing, be called national graft. By and large, it takes the two typical forms of graft: official salaries (The White Man's Burden), as in the British crown colonies and the American dependencies; and of special concessions and advantageous bargains in the way of trade, credits and investments, as, e.g., the British interests in Africa and Mesopotamia or the American transactions in Nicaragua and Haiti. The official salaries which are levied by this means on the underlying population in foreign parts inure directly to the nation's kept classes, in their rôle of official personnel, being in the nature of perquisites of gentility and of political suction. The special benefits in the way of profitable trade and investment under national tutelage in foreign parts inure to those special Interests which are in close touch with the nation's official personnel and do business in foreign parts with their advice and consent.

All the while, of course, all this trading on the national integrity is carried on as inconspicuously as may be, quite legally and morally under democratic forms, by night and cloud, and is covered over with such decently voluble prevarication as the case may require, prevarication of a decently statesmanlike sort; such a volume and texture of prevarication as may serve to keep the national left hand from knowing what the right hand is doing, the left hand in these premises being the community at large, as contrasted with the Interests and the official personnel. In all such work of administrative prevarication and democratic camouflage the statesmen are greatly helped out by the newspapers and the approved agencies that gather and purvey such news as is fit to print for the purpose in hand. The pulpit, too, has its expedient uses as a publicity agency in furtherance of this gainful pursuit of national enterprise in foreign parts.

However, the present argument is not concerned with the main facts and material outcome of this imperial statecraft considered as a "gainful pursuit," but only with the ulterior and residual consequences of the traffic in the way of a heightened sense of national integrity and a closer coalescence of this national integrity with the gainful pursuits of all these dominant business Interests that engage the sympathies of the official personnel. By this means the national integrity becomes ever more closely identified, in the popular apprehension, with the security and continued enlargement of the capitalised overhead charges of those concerns which do business in foreign parts; whereby the principles of business and absentee ownership come in for an added sanction; so that the official personnel which has these matters in charge is enabled to give a more undivided attention and a more headlong support to any manœuvres of strategic sabotage on industrial production which the exigencies of gainful business may dictate, whether at home or abroad.

Statecraft as a gainful pursuit has always been a furtive enterprise. And in due proportion as the nation's statecraft is increasingly devoted to the gainful pursuit of international intrigue it will necessarily take on a more furtive character, and will conduct a larger proportion of its ordinary work by night and cloud. Which leads to a substitution of coercion in the place of consultation in the dealings of the official personnel with their underlying population, whether in domestic or foreign policy; and such coercion is increasingly accepted in a complaisant, if not a grateful, spirit by the underlying population, on a growing conviction that the national integrity is best provided for by night and cloud. So therefore it also follows that any overt expression of doubt as to the national expediency of any obscure transaction or line of transactions entered into by the official personnel in the course of this clandestine traffic in gainful politics, whether at home or abroad, will presumptively be seditious; and unseasonable inquiry into the furtive movements of the official personnel is by way of becoming an actionable offense; since it is to be presumed that, for the good of the nation, no one outside of the official personnel and the business Interests in collusion can bear any intelligent part in the management of these delicate negotiations, and any premature intimation of what is going on is likely to be "information which may be useful to the enemy." Any pronounced degree of skepticism touching the expediency of any of the accomplished facts of political intrigue or administrative control is due to be penalised as obnoxious to the common good. In the upshot of it all, the paramount rights, powers, aims, and immunities of ownership, or at least those of absentee ownership, come in for a closer identification with the foundations of the national establishment and are hedged about with a double conviction of well-doing.

In that strategy of businesslike curtailment of output, debilitation of industry, and capitalisation of overhead charges, which is entailed by the established system of ownership and bargaining, the constituted authorities in all the democratic nations may, therefore, be counted on to lend their unwavering support to all manœuvres of business-as-usual, and to disallow any transgression of or departure from business principles. Nor should there seem any probability that the effectual run of popular sentiment touching these matters will undergo any appreciable change in the calculable future. The drift of workday discipline, as well as of deliberate instruction, sets in the conservative direction. For the immediate future the prospect appears to offer a fuller confirmation in the faith that business principles answer all things. The outlook should accordingly be that the businesslike control of the industrial system in detail should presently reach, if it has not already reached, and should speedily pass beyond that critical point of chronic derangement in the aggregate beyond which a continued pursuit of the same strategy on the same businesslike principles will result in a progressively widening margin of deficiency in the aggregate material output and a progressive shrinkage of the available means of life.

13. Joseph A. Schumpeter

On Capitalism

BUT I AM not going to sum up as the reader presumably expects me to. That is to say, I am not going to invite him, before he decides to put his trust in an untried alternative advocated by untried men, to look once more at the impressive economic and the still more impressive cultural achievement of the capitalist order and at the immense promise held out by both. I am not going to argue that that achievement and that promise are in themselves sufficient to support an argument for allowing the capitalist process to work on and, as it might easily be put, to lift poverty from the shoulders of mankind.

There would be no sense in this. Even if mankind were as free to choose as a businessman is free to choose between two competing pieces of machinery, no determined value judgment necessarily follows from the facts and relations between facts that I have tried to convey. As regards the economic performance, it does not follow that men are "happier" or even "better off" in the industrial society of today than they were in a medieval manor or village. As regards the cultural performance, one may accept every word I have written and yet hate it—its utilitarianism and the wholesale destruction of Meanings incident to it—from the bottom of one's heart. Moreover, as I shall have to emphasize again in our discussion of the socialist alternative, one may care less for the efficiency of the capitalist process in producing economic and cultural values than for the kind of human beings that it turns out and then leaves to their own devices, free to make a mess of their lives. There is a type of radical whose adverse verdict about capitalist civilization rests on nothing except stupidity, ignorance or irresponsibility, who is unable or unwilling to grasp the most obvious facts, let alone their wider implications. But a completely adverse verdict may also be arrived at on a higher plane.

However, whether favorable or unfavorable, value judgments about capitalist performance are of little interest. For mankind is not free to

From Schumpeter, *Capitalism, Socialism, and Democracy* (New York: Harper & Brothers, 1947—3rd edition), pp. 129-163. Copyright 1942, 1947 by Joseph A. Schumpeter. Reprinted by permission of Harper & Brothers.

choose. This is not only because the mass of people are not in a position
to compare alternatives rationally and always accept what they are being
told. There is a much deeper reason for it. Things economic and social
move by their own momentum and the ensuing situations compel individuals and groups to behave in certain ways whatever they may wish
to do—not indeed by destroying their freedom of choice but by shaping
the choosing mentalities and by narrowing the list of possibilities from
which to choose. If this is the quintessence of Marxism then we all of
us have got to be Marxists. In consequence, capitalist performance is not
even relevant for prognosis. Most civilizations have disappeared before
they had time to fill to the full the measure of their promise. Hence I
am not going to argue, on the strength of that performance, that the
capitalist intermezzo is likely to be prolonged. In fact, I am now going
to draw the exactly opposite inference.

I. The Obsolescence of the Entrepreneurial Function

In our discussion of the theory of vanishing investment opportunity, a
reservation was made in favor of the possibility that the economic wants
of humanity might some day be so completely satisfied that little motive
would be left to push productive effort still further ahead. Such a state of
satiety is no doubt very far off even if we keep within the present scheme
of wants; and if we take account of the fact that, as higher standards of
life are attained, these wants automatically expand and new wants emerge
or are created,[1] satiety becomes a flying goal, particularly if we include
leisure among consumers' goods. However, let us glance at that possibility,
assuming, still more unrealistically, that methods of production have
reached a state of perfection which does not admit of further improvement.

A more or less stationary state would ensue. Capitalism, being essentially
an evolutionary process, would become atrophic. There would be nothing
left for entrepreneurs to do. They would find themselves in much the
same situation as generals would in a society prefectly sure of permanent
peace. Profits and along with profits the rate of interest would converge
toward zero. The bourgeois strata that live on profits and interest would
tend to disappear. The management of industry and trade would become
a matter of current administration, and the personnel would unavoidably
acquire the characteristics of a bureaucracy. Socialism of a very sober
type would almost automatically come into being. Human energy would
turn away from business. Other than economic pursuits would attract the
brains and provide the adventure.

For the calculable future this vision is of no importance. But all the
greater importance attaches to the fact that many of the effects on the

[1] Wilhelm Wundt called this the Heterogony of Aims (*Heterogonie der Zwecke*).

structure of society and on the organization of the productive process that we might expect from an approximately complete satisfaction of wants or from absolute technological perfection can also be expected from a development that is clearly observable already. Progress itself may be mechanized as well as the management of a stationary economy, and this mechanization of progress may affect entrepreneurship and capitalist society nearly as much as the cessation of economic progress would. In order to see this it is only necessary to restate, first, what the entrepreneurial function consists in and, secondly, what it means for bourgeois society and the survival of the capitalist order.

We have seen that the function of entrepreneurs is to reform or revolutionize the pattern of production by exploiting an invention or, more generally, an untried technological possibility for producing a new commodity or producing an old one in a new way, by opening up a new source of supply of materials or a new outlet for products, by reorganizing an industry and so on. Railroad construction in its earlier stages, electrical power production before the First World War, steam and steel, the motorcar, colonial ventures afford spectacular instances of a large genus which comprises innumerable humbler ones—down to such things as making a success of a particular kind of sausage or toothbrush. This kind of activity is primarily responsible for the recurrent "prosperities" that revolutionize the economic organism and the recurrent "recessions" that are due to the disequilibrating impact of the new products or methods. To undertake such new things is difficult and constitutes a distinct economic function, first, because they lie outside of the routine tasks which everybody understands and, secondly, because the environment resists in many ways that vary, according to social conditions, from simple refusal either to finance or to buy a new thing, to physical attack on the man who tries to produce it. To act with confidence beyond the range of familiar beacons and to overcome that resistance requires aptitudes that are present in only a small fraction of the population and that define the entrepreneurial type as well as the entrepreneurial function. This function does not essentially consist in either inventing anything or otherwise creating the conditions which the enterprise exploits. It consists in getting things done.

This social function is already losing importance and is bound to lose it at an accelerating rate in the future even if the economic process itself of which entrepreneurship was the prime mover went on unabated. For, on the one hand, it is much easier now than it has been in the past to do things that lie outside familiar routine—innovation itself is being reduced to routine. Technological progress is increasingly becoming the business of teams of trained specialists who turn out what is required and make it work in predictable ways. The romance of earlier commercial adventure is rapidly wearing away, because so many more things can be strictly calculated that had of old to be visualized in a flash of genius.

On the other hand, personality and will power must count for less in environments which have become accustomed to economic change—best instanced by an incessant stream of new consumers' and producers' goods—and which, instead of resisting, accept it as a matter of course. The resistance which comes from interests threatened by an innovation in the productive process is not likely to die out as long as the capitalist order persists. It is, for instance, the great obstacle on the road toward mass production of cheap housing which presupposes radical mechanization and wholesale elimination of inefficient methods of work on the plot. But every other kind of resistance—the resistance, in particular, of consumers and producers to a new kind of thing because it is new—has well-nigh vanished already.

Thus, economic progress tends to become depersonalized and automatized. Bureau and committee work tends to replace individual action. Once more, reference to the military analogy will help to bring out the essential point.

Of old, roughly up to and including the Napoleonic Wars, generalship meant leadership and success meant the personal success of the man in command who earned corresponding "profits" in terms of social prestige. The technique of warfare and the structure of armies being what they were, the individual decision and driving power of the leading man—even his actual presence on a showy horse—were essential elements in the strategical and tactical situations. Napoleon's presence was, and had to be, actually felt on his battlefields. This is no longer so. Rationalized and specialized office work will eventually blot out personality, the calculable result, the "vision." The leading man no longer has the opportunity to fling himself into the fray. He is becoming just another office worker—and one who is not always difficult to replace.

Or take another military analogy. Warfare in the Middle Ages was a very personal affair. The armored knights practiced an art that required lifelong training and every one of them counted individually by virtue of personal skill and prowess. It is easy to understand why this craft should have become the basis of a social class in the fullest and richest sense of that term. But social and technological change undermined and eventually destroyed both the function and the position of that class. Warfare itself did not cease on that account. It simply became more and more mechanized—eventually so much so that success in what now is a mere profession no longer carries that connotation of individual achievement which would raise not only the man but also his group into a durable position of social leadership.

Now a similar social process—in the last analysis the same social process—undermines the role and, along with the role, the social position of the capitalist entrepreneur. His role, though less glamorous than that of medieval warlords, great or small, also is or was just another form of individual leadership acting by virtue of personal force and personal responsibility for success. His position, like that of warrior classes, is threatened as soon as this function in the social process loses its importance, and no less if this is due to the cessation of the social needs it served than if those needs are being served by other, more impersonal, methods.

But this affects the position of the entire bourgeois stratum. Although entrepreneurs are not necessarily or even typically elements of that stratum from the outset, they nevertheless enter it in case of success. Thus, though entrepreneurs do not *per se* form a social class, the bourgeois class absorbs them and their families and connections, thereby recruiting and revitalizing itself currently while at the same time the families that sever their active relation to "business" drop out of it after a generation or two. Between, there is the bulk of what we refer to as industrialists, merchants, financiers and bankers; they are in the intermediate stage between "entrepreneurial venture" and mere "current administration of an inherited domain." The returns on which the class lives are produced by, and the social position of the class rests on, the success of this more or less active sector—which of course may, as it does in this country, form over 90 per cent of the bourgeois stratum—and of the individuals who are in the act of rising into that class. Economically and sociologically, directly and indirectly, the bourgeoisie therefore depends on the entrepreneur and, as a class, lives and will die with him, though a more or less prolonged transitional stage—eventually a stage in which it may feel equally unable to die and to live—is quite likely to occur, as in fact it did occur in the case of the feudal civilization.

To sum up this part of our argument: if capitalist evolution—"progress" —either ceases or becomes completely automatic, the economic basis of the industrial bourgeoisie will be reduced eventually to wages such as are paid for current administrative work excepting remnants of quasi-rents and monopoloid gains that may be expected to linger on for some time. Since capitalist enterprise, by its very achievements, tends to automatize progress, we conclude that it tends to make itself superfluous —to break to pieces under the pressure of its own success. The perfectly bureaucratized giant industrial unit not only ousts the small or medium-sized firm and "expropriates" its owners, but in the end it also ousts the entrepreneur and expropriates the bourgeoisie as a class which in the process stands to lose not only its income but also what is infinitely more important, its function. The true pacemakers of socialism were not the intellectuals or agitators who preached it but the Vanderbilts, Carnegies and Rockefellers. This result may not in every respect be to the taste of Marxian socialists, still less to the taste of socialists of a more popular (Marx would have said, vulgar) description. But so far as prognosis goes, it does not differ from theirs.

II. The Destruction of the Protecting Strata

So far we have been considering "the effects of the capitalist process upon the economic bases of the upper strata of capitalist society and upon their social position and prestige." But effects further extend to the institutional framework that protected them. In showing this we shall take the term in its widest acceptance so as to include not only legal institutions but also attitudes of the public mind and policies.

1. Capitalist evolution first of all destroyed, or went far toward destroying, the institutional arrangements of the feudal world—the manor, the village, the craft guild. The facts and mechanisms of this process are too familiar to detain us. Destruction was wrought in three ways. The world of the artisan was destroyed primarily by the automatic effects of the competition that came from the capitalist entrepreneur; political action in removing atrophic organizations and regulations only registered results. The world of the lord and the peasant was destroyed primarily by political —in some cases revolutionary—action and capitalism merely presided over adaptive transformations say, of the German manorial organizations into large-scale agricultural units of production. But along with these industrial and agrarian revolutions went a no less revolutionary change in the general attitude of legislative authority and public opinion. Together with the old economic organization vanished the economic and political privileges of the classes or groups that used to play the leading role in it, particularly the tax exemptions and the political prerogatives of the landed nobility and gentry and of the clergy.

Economically all this meant for the bourgeoisie the breaking of so many fetters and the removal of so many barriers. Politically it meant the replacement of an order in which the bourgeois was a humble subject by another that was more congenial to his rationalist mind and to his immediate interests. But, surveying that process from the standpoint of today, the observer might well wonder whether in the end such complete emancipation was good for the bourgeois and his world. For those fetters not only hampered, they also sheltered. Before proceeding further we must carefully clarify and appraise this point.

2. The related processes of the rise of the capitalist bourgeoisie and of the rise of national states produced, in the sixteenth, seventeenth and eighteenth centuries, a social structure that may seem to us amphibial though it was no more amphibial or transitional than any other. Consider the outstanding instance that is afforded by the monarchy of Louis XIV. The royal power had subjugated the landed aristocracy and at the same time conciliated it by proffering employment and pensions and by conditionally accepting its claim to a ruling or leading class position. The same royal power had subjugated and allied itself with the clergy.[1] It had

---

[1] Gallicanism was nothing else but the ideological reflex of this.

finally strengthened its sway over the bourgeoisie, its old ally in the struggle with the territorial magnates, protecting and propelling its enterprise in order to exploit it the more effectively in turn. Peasants and the (small) industrial proletariat were likewise managed, exploited and protected by public authority—though the protection was in the case of the French *ancien régime* very much less in evidence than for instance in the Austria of Maria Theresa or of Joseph II—and, vicariously, by landlords or industrialists. This was not simply a government in the sense of nineteenth-century liberalism, i.e., a social agency existing for the performance of a few limited functions to be financed by a minimum of revenue. On principle, the monarchy managed everything, from consciences to the patterns of the silk fabrics of Lyons, and financially it aimed at a maximum of revenue. Though the king was never really absolute, public authority was all-comprehensive.

Correct diagnosis of this pattern is of the utmost importance for our subject. The king, the court, the army, the church and the bureaucracy lived to an increasing extent on revenue created by the capitalist process, even purely feudal sources of income being swelled in consequence of contemporaneous capitalist developments. To an increasing extent also, domestic and foreign policies and institutional changes were shaped to suit and propel that development. *As far as that goes,* the feudal elements in the structure of the so-called absolute monarchy come in only under the heading of atavisms which in fact is the diagnosis one would naturally adopt at first sight.

Looking more closely, however, we realize that those elements meant more than that. The steel frame of that structure still consisted of the human material of feudal society and this material still behaved according to precapitalist patterns. It filled the offices of state, officered the army, devised policies—it functioned as a *classe dirigente* and, though taking account of bourgeois interests, it took care to distance itself from the bourgeoisie. The centerpiece, the king, was king by the grace of God, and the root of his position was feudal, not only in the historical but also in the sociological sense, however much he availed himself of the economic possibilities offered by capitalism. All this was more than atavism. It was an active symbiosis of two social strata, one of which no doubt supported the other economically but was in turn supported by the other politically. Whatever we may think of the achievements or shortcomings of this arrangement, whatever the bourgeois himself may have thought of it at the time or later—and of the aristocratic scapegrace or idler—it was of the essence of that society.

3. Of *that* society only? The subsequent course of things, best exemplified by the English case, suggests the answer. The aristocratic element continued to rule the roost *right to the end of the period of intact and vital capitalism.* No doubt that element—though nowhere so effec-

tively as in England—currently absorbed the brains from other strata that drifted into politics; it made itself the representative of bourgeois interests and fought the battles of the bourgeoisie; it had to surrender its last legal privileges; but with these qualifications, and for ends no longer its own, it continued to man the political engine, to manage the state, to govern.

The economically operative part of the bourgeois strata did not offer much opposition to this. On the whole, that kind of division of labor suited them and they liked it. Where they did revolt against it or where they got into the political saddle without having to revolt, they did not make a conspicuous success of ruling and did not prove able to hold their own. The question arises whether it is really safe to assume that these failures were merely due to lack of opportunity to acquire experience and, with experience, the attitudes of a politically ruling class.

It is not. There is a more fundamental reason for those failures such as are instanced by the French or German experiences with bourgeois attempts at ruling—a reason which again will best be visualized by contrasting the figure of the industrialist or merchant with that of the medieval lord. The latter's "profession" not only qualified him admirably for the defense of his own class interest—he was not only able to fight for it physically—but it also cast a halo around him and made of him a ruler of men. The first was important, but more so were the mystic glamour and the lordly attitude—that ability and habit to command and to be obeyed that carried prestige with all classes of society and in every walk of life. That prestige was so great and that attitude so useful that the class position outlived the social and technological conditions which had given rise to it and proved adaptable, by means of a transformation of the class function, to quite different social and economic conditions. With the utmost ease and grace the lords and knights metamorphosed themselves into courtiers, administrators, diplomats, politicians and into military officers of a type that had nothing whatever to do with that of the medieval knight. And—most astonishing phenomenon when we come to think of it —a remnant of that old prestige survives even to this day, and not only with our ladies.

Of the industrialist and merchant the opposite is true. There is surely no trace of any mystic glamour about him which is what counts in the ruling of men. The stock exchange is a poor substitute for the Holy Grail. We have seen that the industrialist and merchant, as far as they are entrepreneurs, also fill a function of leadership. But economic leadership of this type does not readily expand, like the medieval lord's military leadership, into the leadership of nations. On the contrary, the ledger and the cost calculation absorb and confine.

I have called the bourgeois rationalist and unheroic. He can only use rationalist and unheroic means to defend his position or to bend a nation to his will. He can impress by what people may expect from his economic performance, he can argue his case, he can promise to pay out money or threaten to withhold it, he can hire the treacherous services of a *condottiere* or politician or journalist. But that is all and all of it is greatly overrated as to its political value. Nor are his experiences and habits of life of the kind that develop personal fascination. A genius in the business office may be, and often is, utterly unable outside of it to say boo to a goose—both in the drawing room and on the platform. Knowing this he wants to be left alone and to leave politics alone.

Again exceptions will occur to the reader. But again they do not amount to much. Aptitude for, and interest and success in, city management is the only important exception in Europe, and this will be found to strengthen our case instead of weakening it. Before the advent of the modern metropolis, which is no longer a bourgeois affair, city management was akin to business management. Grasp of its problems and authority within its precincts came naturally to the manufacturer and trader, and the local interests of manufacturing and trading supplied most of the subject matter of its politics which therefore lent itself to treatment by the methods and in the spirit of the business office. Under exceptionally favorable conditions, exceptional developments sprouted from those roots, such as the developments of the Venetian or Genoese republics. The case of the Low Countries enters into the same pattern, but it is particularly instructive by virtue of the fact that the merchants' republic invariably failed in the great game of international politics and that in practically every emergency it had to hand over the reins to a warlord of feudal complexion. As regards the United States, it would be easy to list the uniquely favorable circumstances—rapidly waning—that explain its case.[1]

4. The inference is obvious: barring such exceptional conditions, the bourgeois class is ill equipped to face the problems, both domestic and international, that have normally to be faced by a country of any importance. The bourgeois themselves feel this in spite of all the phraseology that seems to deny it, and so do the masses. Within a protecting framework not made of bourgeois material, the bourgeoisie may be successful, not only in the political defensive but also in the offensive, especially as an opposition. For a time it felt so safe as to be able to afford the luxury of attacking the protective frame itself; such bourgeois opposition as there was in imperial Germany illustrates this to perfection. But without protection by some non-bourgeois group, the bourgeoisie is politically helpless and unable not only to lead its nation but even to take care of its particular class interest. Which amounts to saying that it needs a master.

But the capitalist process, both by its economic mechanics and by its

[1] This line of reasoning will be taken up again in Part IV.

psycho-sociological effects, did away with this protecting master or, as in this country, never gave him, or a substitute for him, a chance to develop. The implications of this are strengthened by another consequence of the same process. Capitalist evolution eliminates not only the king *Dei Gratia* but also the political entrenchments that, had they proved tenable, would have been formed by the village and the craft guild. Of course, neither organization was tenable in the precise shape in which capitalism found it. But capitalist policies wrought destruction much beyond what was unavoidable. They attacked the artisan in reservations in which he could have survived for an indefinite time. They forced upon the peasant all the blessings of early liberalism—the free and unsheltered holding and all the individualist rope he needed in order to hang himself.

In breaking down the pre-capitalist framework of society, capitalism thus broke not only barriers that impeded its progress but also flying buttresses that prevented its collapse. That process, impressive in its relentless necessity, was not merely a matter of removing institutional deadwood, but of removing partners of the capitalist stratum, symbiosis with whom was an essential element of the capitalist schema. Having discovered this fact which so many slogans obscure, we might well wonder whether it is quite correct to look upon capitalism as a social form *sui generis* or, in fact, as anything else but the last stage of the decomposition of what we have called feudalism. On the whole, I am inclined to believe that its peculiarities suffice to make a type and to accept that symbiosis of classes which owe their existence to different epochs and processes as the rule rather than as an exception—at least it has been the rule these 6000 years, i.e., ever since primitive tillers of the soil became the subjects of mounted nomads. But there is no great objection that I can see against the opposite view alluded to.

III. The Destruction of the Institutional Framework of Capitalist Society

We return from our digression with a load of ominous facts. They arc almost, though not quite, sufficient to establish our next point, viz., that the capitalist process in much the same way in which it destroyed the institutional framework of feudal society also undermines its own.

It has been pointed out above that the very success of capitalist enterprise paradoxically tends to impair the prestige or social weight of the class primarily associated with it and that the giant unit of control tends to oust the bourgeoisie from the function to which it owed that social weight. The corresponding change in the meaning, and the incidental loss in vitality, of the institutions of the bourgeois world and of its typical attitudes are easy to trace.

On the one hand, the capitalist process unavoidably attacks the economic standing ground of the small producer and trader. What it did to the pre-capitalist strata it also does—and by the same competitive mechanism—to the lower strata of capitalist industry. Here of course Marx scores. It is true that the facts of industrial concentration do not quite live up to the ideas the public is being taught to entertain about it (see Chapter XIX). The process has gone less far and is less free from setbacks and compensatory tendencies than one would gather from many a popular exposition. In particular, large-scale enterprise not only annihilates but also, to some extent, creates space for the small producing, and especially trading, firm. Also, in the case of the peasants and farmers, the capitalist world has at last proved both willing and able to pursue an expensive but on the whole effective policy of conservation. In the long run, however, there can be little doubt about the fact we are envisaging, or about its consequences. Outside of the agrarian field, moreover, the bourgeoisie has shown but little awareness of the problem[1] or its importance for the survival of the capitalist order. The profits to be made by rationalizing the organization of production and especially by cheapening the tortuous way of commodities from the factory to the ultimate consumer are more than the mind of the typical businessman can resist.

Now it is important to realize precisely what these consequences consist in. A very common type of social criticism which we have already met laments the "decline of competition" and equates it to the decline of capitalism because of the virtues it attributes to competition and the vices it attributes to modern industrial "monopolies." In this schema of interpretation, monopolization plays the role of arteriosclerosis and reacts upon the fortunes of the capitalist order through increasingly unsatisfactory economic performance. We have seen the reasons for rejecting this view. Economically neither the case for competition nor the case against concentration of economic control is anything like as strong as this argument implies. And, whether weak or strong, it misses the salient point. Even if the giant concerns were all managed so perfectly as to call forth applause from the angels in heaven, the political consequences of concentration would still be what they are. The political structure of a nation is profoundly affected by the elimination of a host of small and medium-sized firms the owner-managers of which, together with their dependents, henchmen and connections, count quantitatively at the polls and have a hold on what we may term the foreman class that no management of a large unit can ever have; the very foundation of private property and free contracting wears away in a nation in which its most vital, most concrete, most meaningful types disappear from the moral horizon of the people.

---

[1] Although some governments did; the government of imperial Germany did much to fight this particular kind of rationalization, and there is now a strong tendency to do the same in this country.

On the other hand, the capitalist process also attacks its own institutional framework—let us continue to visualize "property" and "free contracting" as *partes pro toto*—within the precincts of the big units. Excepting the cases that are still of considerable importance in which a corporation is practically owned by a single individual or family, the figure of the proprietor and with it the specifically proprietary interest have vanished from the picture. There are the salaried executives and all the salaried managers and submanagers. There are the big stockholders. And then there are the small stockholders. The first group tends to acquire the employee attitude and rarely if ever identifies itself with the stockholding interest even in the most favorable cases, i.e., in the cases in which it identifies itself with the interest of the concern as such. The second group, even if it considers its connection with the concern as permanent and even if it actually behaves as financial theory would have stockholders behave, is at one remove from both the functions and the attitudes of an owner. As to the third group, small stockholders often do not care much about what for most of them is but a minor source of income and, whether they care or not, they hardly ever bother, unless they or some representatives of theirs are out to exploit their nuisance value; being often very ill used and still more often thinking themselves ill used, they almost regularly drift into an attitude hostile to "their" corporations, to big business in general and, particularly when things look bad, to the capitalist order as such. No element of any of those three groups into which I schematized the typical situation unconditionally takes the attitude characteristic of that curious phenomenon, so full of meaning and so rapidly passing, that is covered by the term Property.

Freedom of contracting is in the same boat. In its full vitality it meant individual contracting regulated by individual choice between an indefinite number of possibilities. The stereotyped, unindividual, impersonal and bureaucratized contract of today—this applies much more generally, but *a potiori* we may fasten upon the labor contract—which presents but restricted freedom of choice and mostly turns on a *c'est à prendre ou à laisser,* has none of the old features the most important of which become impossible with giant concerns dealing with other giant concerns or impersonal masses of workmen or consumers. The void is being filled by a tropical growth of new legal structures—and a little reflection shows that this could hardly be otherwise.

Thus the capitalist process pushes into the background all those institutions, the institutions of property and free contracting in particular, that expressed the needs and ways of the truly "private" economic activity. Where it does not abolish them, as it already has abolished free contracting in the labor market, it attains the same end by shifting the relative importance of existing legal forms—the legal forms pertaining to corporate business for instance as against those pertaining to the partnership or individual firm—or by changing their contents or meanings. The capitalist process, by substituting a mere parcel of shares for the walls of and the machines in a factory, takes the life out of the idea of property. It loosens the grip that once was so strong—the grip in the sense of the legal right and the actual ability to do as one pleases with one's own; the grip also in the sense that the holder of the title loses the will to fight, economically, physically, politically, for "his" factory and his control over it, to die if necessary on its steps. And this evaporation of what we may term the material substance of property—its visible and touchable reality—affects not only the attitude of holders but also that of the workmen and of the public in general. Dematerialized, defunctionalized and absentee ownership does not impress and call forth moral allegiance as the vital form of property did. Eventually there will be *nobody* left who really cares to stand for it—nobody within and nobody without the precincts of the big concerns.

IV. The Social Atmosphere of Capitalism

From the analysis of the two preceding chapters, it should not be difficult to understand how the capitalist process produced that atmosphere of almost universal hostility to its own social order to which I have referred at the threshold of this part. The phenomenon is so striking and both the Marxian and the popular explanations are so inadequate that it is desirable to develop the theory of it a little further.

1. The capitalist process, so we have seen, eventually decreases the importance of the function by which the capitalist class lives. We have also seen that it tends to wear away protective strata, to break down its own defenses, to disperse the garrisons of its entrenchments. And we have finally seen that capitalism creates a critical frame of mind which, after having destroyed the moral authority of so many other institutions, in the end turns against its own; the bourgeois finds to his amazement that the rationalist attitude does not stop at the credentials of kings and popes but goes on to attack private property and the whole scheme of bourgeois values.

The bourgeois fortress thus becomes politically defenseless. Defenseless fortresses invite aggression especially if there is rich booty in them. Aggressors will work themselves up into a state of rationalizing hostility[1]— aggressors always do. No doubt it is possible, for a time, to buy them off. But this last resource fails as soon as they discover that they can have all. In part, this explains what we are out to explain. So far as it goes—it does

---

[1] It is hoped that no confusion will arise from my using the verb "to rationalize" in two different meanings. An industrial plant is being "rationalized" when its productive efficiency per unit of expenditure is being increased. We "rationalize" an action of ours when we supply ourselves and others with reasons for it that satisfy our standard of values regardless of what our true impulses may be.

not go the whole way of course—this element of our theory is verified by the high correlation that exists historically between bourgeois defense-lessness and hostility to the capitalist order: there was very little hostility on principle as long as the bourgeois position was safe, although there was then much more reason for it; it spread *pari passu* with the crumbling of the protecting walls.

2. But, so it might well be asked—in fact, so it is being asked in naïve bewilderment by many an industrialist who honestly feels he is doing his duty by all classes of society—why should the capitalist order need any protection by extra-capitalist powers or extra-rational loyalties? Can it not come out of the trial with flying colors? Does not our own previous argument sufficiently show that it has plenty of utilitarian credentials to present? Cannot a perfectly good case be made out for it? And those industrialists will assuredly not fail to point out that a sensible workman, in weighing the pro's and con's of his contract with, say, one of the big steel or automobile concerns, might well come to the conclusion that, everything considered, he is not doing so badly and that the advantages of this bargain are not all on one side. Yes—certainly, only all that is quite irrelevant.

For, first, it is an error to believe that political attack arises primarily from grievance and that it can be turned by justification. Political criticism cannot be met effectively by rational argument. From the fact that the criticism of the capitalist order proceeds from a critical attitude of mind, i.e., from an attitude which spurns allegiance to extra-rational values, it does not follow that rational refutation will be accepted. Such refutation may tear the rational garb of attack but can never reach the extra-rational driving power that always lurks behind it. Capitalist rationality does not do away with sub- or super-rational impulses. It merely makes them get out of hand by removing the restraint of sacred or semi-sacred tradition. In a civilization that lacks the means and even the will to discipline and to guide them, they will revolt. And once they revolt it matters little that, in a rationalist culture, their manifestations will in general be rationalized somehow. Just as the call for utilitarian credentials has never been addressed to kings, lords and popes in a judicial frame of mind that would accept the possibility of a satisfactory answer, so capitalism stands its trial before judges who have the sentence of death in their pockets. They are going to pass it, whatever the defense they may hear; the only success victorious defense can possibly produce is a change in the indictment. Utilitarian reason is in any case weak as a prime mover of group action. In no case is it a match for the extra-rational determinants of conduct.

Second, the success of the indictment becomes quite understandable as soon as we realize what acceptance of the case for capitalism would imply. That case, were it even much stronger than it actually is, could never be made simple. People at large would have to be possessed of an insight and a power of analysis which are altogether beyond them. Why, practically every nonsense that has ever been said about capitalism has been championed by some professed economist. But even if this is disregarded, rational recognition of the economic performance of capitalism and of the hopes it holds out for the future would require an almost impossible moral feat by the have-not. That performance stands out only if we take a long-run view; any procapitalist argument must rest on long-run considerations. In the short run, it is profits and inefficiencies that dominate the picture. In order to accept his lot, the leveler or the chartist of old would have had to comfort himself with hopes for his great-grand-children. In order to identify himself with the capitalist system, the unemployed of today would have completely to forget his personal fate and the politician of today his personal ambition. The long-run interests of society are so entirely lodged with the upper strata of bourgeois society that it is perfectly natural for people to look upon them as the interests of that class only. For the masses, it is the short-run view that counts. Like Louis XV, they feel *après nous le déluge,* and from the standpoint of individualist utilitarianism they are of course being perfectly rational if they feel like that.

Third, there are the daily troubles and expectations of trouble everyone has to struggle with in any social system—the frictions and disappointments, the greater and smaller unpleasant events that hurt, annoy and thwart. I suppose that every one of us is more or less in the habit of attributing them wholly to that part of reality which lies without his skin, and *emotional* attachment to the social order—i.e., the very thing capitalism is constitutionally unable to produce—is necessary in order to overcome the hostile impulse by which we react to them. If there is no emotional attachment, then that impulse has its way and grows into a permanent constituent of our psychic setup.

Fourth, the ever-rising standards of life and particularly the leisure that modern capitalism provides for the fully employed workman . . . well, there is no need for me to finish the sentence or to elaborate one of the tritest, oldest and most stodgy of all arguments which unfortunately is but too true. Secular improvement that is taken for granted and coupled with individual insecurity that is acutely resented is of course the best recipe for breeding social unrest.

V. The Sociology of the Intellectual

Nevertheless, neither the opportunity of attack nor real or fancied grievances are in themselves sufficient to produce, however strongly they may favor, the emergence of active hostility against a social order. For such an atmosphere to develop it is necessary that there be groups to whose interest it is to work up and organize resentment, to nurse it, to voice it and to lead it. As will be shown in Part IV, the mass of people never develops definite opinions on its own initiative. Still less is it able to articulate them and to turn them into consistent attitudes and actions. All it can do is to follow or refuse to follow such group leadership as may offer itself. Until we have discovered social groups that will qualify for that role our theory of the atmosphere of hostility to capitalism is incomplete.

Broadly speaking, conditions favorable to general hostility to a social system or specific attack upon it will in any case tend to call forth groups that will exploit them. But in the case of capitalist society there is a further fact to be noted: unlike any other type of society, capitalism inevitably and by virtue of the very logic of its civilization creates, educates and subsidizes a vested interest in social unrest.[1] Explanation of this phenomenon, which is as curious as it is important, follows from our argument in Chapter XI, but may be made more telling by an excursion into the Sociology of the Intellectual.

1. This type is not easy to define. The difficulty is in fact symptomatic of the character of the species. Intellectuals are not a social class in the sense in which peasants or industrial laborers constitute social classes; they hail from all the corners of the social world, and a great part of their activities consist in fighting each other and in forming the spearheads of class interests not their own. Yet they develop group attitudes and group interests sufficiently strong to make large numbers of them behave in the way that is usually associated with the concept of social classes. Again, they cannot be simply defined as the sum total of all the people who have had a higher education; that would obliterate the most important features of the type. Yet anyone who had—and, save exceptional cases, nobody who had not—is a potential intellectual; and the fact that their minds are all similarly furnished facilitates understanding between them and constitutes a bond. Nor would it serve our purpose to make the concept coextensive with the membership of the liberal professions; physicians or lawyers for instance are not intellectuals in the relevant sense unless they talk or write about subjects outside of their professional competence which no doubt they often do—particularly the lawyers. Yet there is a close connection between the intellectuals and the professions. For *some* professions—especially if we count in journalism—actually do belong almost wholly to the domain of the intellectual type; the members of *all* professions have the opportunity of becoming intel-

---

[1] Every social system is sensitive to revolt and in every social system stirring up revolt is a business that pays in case of success and hence alway attracts both brain and brawn. It did in feudal times—very much so. But warrior nobles who revolted against their superiors attacked individual persons or positions. They did not attack the feudal system as such. And feudal society as a whole displayed no tendencies to encourage—intentionally or unintentionally—attacks upon its own social system as a whole.

lectuals; and many intellectuals take to some profession for a living. Finally, a definition by means of the contrast to manual labor would be much too wide.[1] Yet the Duke of Wellington's "scribbling set" seems to be too narrow.[2] So is the meaning of *hommes de lettres*.

But we might do worse than take our lead from the Iron Duke. Intellectuals are in fact people who wield the power of the spoken and the written word, and one of the touches that distinguish them from other people who do the same is the absence of direct responsibility for practical affairs. This touch in general accounts for another—the absence of that first-hand knowledge of them which only actual experience can give. The critical attitude, arising no less from the intellectual's situation as an onlooker—in most cases also as an outsider—than from the fact that his main chance of asserting himself lies in his actual or potential nuisance value, should add a third touch. The profession of the unprofessional? Professional dilettantism? The people who talk about everything because they understand nothing? Bernard Shaw's journalist in *The Doctor's Dilemma*? No, no. I have not said that and I do not mean that. That sort of thing would be still more untrue than it would be offensive. Let us give up trying to define by words and instead define "epideiktically": in the Greek museum we can see the object, nicely labeled. The sophists, philosophers and rhetors—however strongly they objected to being thrown together, they were all of the same genus—of the fifth and fourth centuries B.C. illustrate ideally what I mean. That practically all of them were teachers does not destroy the value of the illustration.

2. When analyzing the rationalist nature of capitalist civilization (Chapter XI) I pointed out that the development of rational thought of course precedes the rise of the capitalist order by thousands of years; all that capitalism did was to give a new impulse and a particular bend to the process. Similarly—leaving aside the Graeco-Roman world—we find intellectuals in thoroughly pre-capitalist conditions, for instance in the Kingdom of the Franks and in the countries into which it dissolved. But they were few in number; they were clergymen, mostly monks; and their written performance was accessible to only an infinitesimal part of the population. No doubt strong individuals were occasionally able to develop unorthodox views and even to convey them to popular audiences. This however in general implied antagonizing a very strictly organized environment—from which at the same time it was difficult to get away—and risking the lot of the heretic. Even so it was hardly possible without the support or connivance of some great lord or chieftain, as the tactics of

---

[1] To my sorrow, I have found that the Oxford English Dictionary does not list the meaning I wish to attach to the term. It does give the turn of phrase "a dinner of intellectuals," but in connection with "superior powers of intellect" which points in a very different direction. I have been duly disconcerted, yet have not been able to discover another term that would serve my purpose equally well.

[2] The Duke's phrase occurs in *The Croker Papers* (ed. L. J. Jennings, 1884).

missionaries suffice to show. On the whole, therefore, intellectuals were well in hand, and kicking over the traces was no joke, even in times of exceptional disorganization and license, such as during the Black Death (in and after 1348).

But if the monastery gave birth to the intellectual of the medieval world, it was capitalism that let him loose and presented him with the printing press. The slow evolution of the lay intellectual was merely an aspect of this process: the coincidence of the emergence of humanism with the emergence of capitalism is very striking. The humanists were primarily philologists but—excellently illustrating a point made above—they quickly expanded into the fields of manners, politics, religion and philosophy. This was not alone due to the contents of the classic works which they interpreted along with their grammar—from the criticism of a text to the criticism of a society, the way is shorter than it seems. Nevertheless, the typical intellectual did not relish the idea of the stake which still awaited the heretic. As a rule, honors and comfort suited him a great deal better. And these were after all to be had only from princes, temporal or spiritual, though the humanists were the first intellectuals to have a public in the modern sense. The critical attitude grew stronger every day. But *social* criticism—beyond what was implied in certain attacks on the Catholic Church and in particular its head—did not flourish under such conditions.

Honors and emoluments can however be had in more than one way. Flattery and subservience are often less remunerative than are their opposites. This discovery was not made by the Aretino[1] but no mortal ever surpassed him in exploiting it. Charles V was a devoted husband but, during his campaigns which kept him from home for many months at a time, he lived the life of a gentleman of his time and class. Very well, the public—and what particularly mattered to Charles, his empress—need never know, provided arguments of the right kind and weight were duly handed to the great critic of politics and morals. Charles paid up. But the point is that this was not simple blackmail which in general benefits one party only and inflicts uncompensated loss on the other. Charles knew why he paid though doubtless it would have been possible to secure silence by cheaper if more drastic methods. He did not display resentment. On the contrary he even went out of his way to honor the man. Obviously he wanted more than silence and, as a matter of fact, he received full value for his gifts.

3. In a sense, therefore, the Aretino's pen was indeed stronger than the sword. But, perhaps through ignorance, I do not know of comparable instances of that type for the next hundred and fifty years,[2] during which intellectuals do not seem to have played any great role outside and in-

[1] Pietro Aretino, 1492-1556.
[2] In England, however, the scope and importance of pamphleteering increased greatly in the seventeenth century.

dependently of the established professions, mainly the law and the church. Now this setback roughly coincides with the setback in capitalist evolution which in most countries of continental Europe occurred in that troubled period. And the subsequent recovery of capitalist enterprise was similarly shared by the intellectuals. The cheaper book, the cheap newspaper or pamphlet, together with the widening of the public that was in part their product but partly an independent phenomenon due to the access of wealth and weight which came to the industrial bourgeoisie and to the incident increase in the political importance of an anonymous public opinion—all these boons, as well as increasing freedom from restraint, are by-products of the capitalist engine.

In the first three-quarters of the eighteenth century the individual patron was slow to lose the paramount importance in the intellectual's career that he had held at the beginning. But in the peak successes at least, we clearly discern the growing importance of the new element—the support of the collective patron, the bourgeois public. In this as in every other respect, Voltaire affords an invaluable instance. His very superficiality that made it possible for him to cover everything from religion to Newtonian optics, allied to indomitable vitality and an insatiable curiosity, a perfect absence of inhibitions, an unerring instinct for and a wholesale acceptance of the humors of his time, enabled that uncritical critic and mediocre poet and historian to fascinate—and to sell. He also speculated, cheated, accepted gifts and appointments, but there was always the independence founded on the solid base of his success with the public. Rousseau's case and type, though entirely different, would be still more instructive to discuss.

In the last decades of the eighteenth century a striking episode displayed the nature of the power of a free-lance intellectual who has nothing to work with but the socio-psychological mechanism called Public Opinion. This happened in England, the country that was then farthest advanced on the road of capitalist evolution. John Wilkes' attacks on the political system of England, it is true, were launched under uniquely favorable circumstances; moreover, it cannot be said that he actually upset the Earl of Bute's government which never had any chance and was bound to fall for a dozen other reasons: but Wilkes' *North Briton* was nevertheless the last straw that broke . . . Lord Bute's political back. No. 45 of the *North Briton* was the first discharge in a campaign that secured the abolition of general warrants and made a great stride toward the freedom of the press and of elections. This does not amount to making history or to creating the conditions for a change in social institutions, but it does amount to playing, say, the role of a midwife's assistant.[1] The in-

---

[1] I do not fear that any historian of politics will find that I have exaggerated the importance of Wilkes' success. But I do fear objection to my calling him a free lance and to the implication that he owed everything to the collective, and nothing to any

ability of Wilkes' enemies to thwart him is the most significant fact about it all. They evidently had all the power of organized government at their command. Yet something drove them back.

In France, the years preceding the revolution and the revolution itself brought the rabble-raising tabloid (Marat, Desmoulins), which however did not, like ours, completely jettison style and grammar. But we must hurry on. The Terror and, more systematically, the First Empire put an end to this. Then followed a period, interrupted by the rule of the *roi burgeois*, of more or less resolute repression that lasted until the Second Empire felt compelled to loosen the reins—about the middle sixties. In central and southern Europe this period also lasted about as long, and in England analogous conditions prevailed from the beginning of the revolutionary wars to Canning's accession to power.

4. How impossible it is to stem the tide within the framework of capitalist society is shown by the failure of the attempts—some of them prolonged and determined—made during that period by practically all European governments to bring the intellectuals to heel. Their histories were nothing but so many different versions of Wilkes' exploits. In capitalist society—or in a society that contains a capitalist element of decisive importance—any attack on the intellectuals must run up against the private fortresses of bourgeois business which, or some of which, will shelter the quarry. Moreover such an attack must proceed according to bourgeois principles of legislative and administrative practice which no doubt may be stretched and bent but will checkmate prosecution beyond a certain point. Lawless violence the bourgeois stratum may accept or even applaud when thoroughly roused or frightened, but only temporarily. In a purely bourgeois regime like that of Louis Philippe, troops may fire on strikers, but the police cannot round up intellectuals or must release them forthwith; otherwise the bourgeois stratum, however strongly disapproving some of their doings, will rally behind them because the freedom it disapproves cannot be cushed without also crushing the freedom it approves.

Observe that I am not crediting the bourgeoisie with an unrealistic dose of generosity or idealism. Nor am I unduly stressing what people think and feel and want—on the importance of which I almost, though not quite, agree with Marx. In defending the intellectuals as a group—not of course every individual—the bourgeoisie defends itself and its scheme of life. Only a government of non-bourgeois nature and non-bourgeois creed—under modern circumstances only a socialist or fascist one—is

---

individual patron. In his beginnings he was no doubt encouraged by a *coterie*. On examination it will however be conceded, I think, that this was not of decisive importance and that all the support and all the money and honors he got afterwards were but a consequence of and tribute to previous success and to a position independently acquired with the public.

strong enough to discipline them. In order to do that it would have to change typically bourgeois institutions and drastically reduce the individual freedom of *all* strata of the nation. And such a government is not likely—it would not even be able—to stop short of private enterprise.

From this follows both the unwillingness and the inability of the capitalist order to control its intellectual sector effectively. The unwillingness in question is unwillingness to use methods consistently that are uncongenial to the mentality shaped by the capitalist process; the inability is the inability to do so within the frame of institutions shaped by the capitalist process and without submitting to nonbourgeois rule. Thus, on the one hand, freedom of public discussion involving freedom to nibble at the foundations of capitalist society is inevitable in the long run. On the other hand, the intellectual group cannot help nibbling, because it lives on criticism and its whole position depends on criticism that stings; and criticism of persons and of current events will, in a situation in which nothing is sacrosanct, fatally issue in criticism of classes and institutions.

5. A few strokes will complete the modern picture. There are the increasing means. There is the increase in the standard of life and in the leisure of the masses that changed and is still changing the composition of the collective patron for the tastes of whom the intellectuals have to provide. There was and is the further cheapening of the book and newspaper and the large-scale newspaper concern.[1] There is now the radio. And there was and is the tendency toward complete removal of restraints, steadily breaking down those short-run attempts at resistance by which

---

[1] The emergence and the career up to date of the large-scale newspaper concern illustrate two points which I am anxious to stress: the manifold aspects, relations and effects of *every* concrete element of the social pattern that preclude simple and one-way propositions, and the importance of distinguishing short-run and long-run phenomena for which different, sometimes opposite, propositions hold true. The *large*-scale newspaper concern is in most cases simply a capitalist business enterprise. This does not *imply* that it espouses capitalist or any other class interests. It *may* do so, but only from one or more of the following motives, the limited importance of which is obvious: because it is subsidized by a capitalist group for the very purpose of advocating its interests or views—the larger the concern and its sales, the less important this element; because it intends to sell to a public of bourgeois tastes—this, very important until about 1914, now increasingly cuts the other way: because advertisers prefer to use a congenial medium—but mostly they take a very businesslike view of the matter; because the owners insist on a certain course irrespective of their interest in sales—to a certain extent, they do and especially did, but experience teaches that they do not hold out if the conflict with their pecuniary interest in sales is too severe. In other words, the large-scale newspaper concern is a most powerful tool for raising the position and increasing the influence of the intellectual group, but it is even now not completely in its control. It means employment and a wider public, but it also means "strings." These are mainly of importance in the short run: in fighting for greater freedom to do as he pleases, the individual journalist may easily meet defeat. But this short-run aspect—and the group's recollection of past conditions—are what enters the intellectual's mind and what determines the colors of the picture of slavery and martyrdom he draws for the public. In reality, it should be a picture of conquest. Conquest and victory are in this, as in so many other cases, a mosaic composed of defeats.

bourgeois society proves itself so incompetent and occasionally so childish a disciplinarian.

There is, however, another factor. One of the most important features of the later stages of capitalist civilization is the vigorous expansion of the educational apparatus and particularly of the facilities for higher education. This development was and is no less inevitable than the development of the largest-scale industrial unit,[1] but, unlike the latter, it has been and is being fostered by public opinion and public authority so as to go much further than it would have done under its own steam. Whatever we may think of this from other standpoints and whatever the precise causation, there are several consequences that bear upon the size and attitude of the intellectual group.

First, inasmuch as higher education thus increases the supply of services in professional, quasi-professional and in the end all "white collar" lines beyond the point determined by cost-return considerations, it may create a particularly important case of sectional unemployment.

Second, along with or in place of such unemployment, it creates unsatisfactory conditions of employment—employment in substandard work or at wages below those of the better-paid manual workers.

Third, it may create unemployability of a particularly disconcerting type. The man who has gone through a college or university easily becomes psychically unemployable in manual occupations without necessarily acquiring employability in, say, professional work. His failure to do so may be due either to lack of natural ability—perfectly compatible with passing academic tests—or to inadequate teaching; and both cases will, absolutely and relatively, occur more frequently as ever larger numbers are drafted into higher education and as the required amount of teaching increases irrespective of how many teachers and scholars nature chooses to turn out. The results of neglecting this and of acting on the theory that schools, colleges and universities are just a matter of money, are too obvious to insist upon. Cases in which among a dozen applicants for a job, all formally qualified, there is not one who can fill it satisfactorily, are known to everyone who has anything to do with appointments—to everyone, that is, who is himself qualified to judge.

All those who are unemployed or unsatisfactorily employed or unem-

---

[1] At present this development is viewed by most people from the standpoint of the ideal of making educational facilities of any type available to all who can be induced to use them. This ideal is so strongly held that any doubts about it are almost universally considered to be nothing short of indecent, a situation not improved by the comments, all too often flippant, of dissentients. Actually, we brush here against a set of extremely complex problems of the sociology of education and educational ideals which we cannot attack within the limits of this sketch. This is why I have confined the above paragraph to two incontestable and noncommittal trivialities that are all we want for the purpose in hand. But of course they do not dispose of the larger problems which must be left aside to testify to the incompleteness of my exposition.

ployable drift into the vocations in which standards are least definite or in which aptitudes and acquirements of a different order count. They swell the host of intellectuals in the strict sense of the term whose numbers hence increase disproportionately. They enter it in a thoroughly discontented frame of mind. Discontent breeds resentment. And it often rationalizes itself into that social criticism which as we have seen before is in any case the intellectual spectator's typical attitude toward men, classes and institutions especially in a rationalist and utilitarian civilization. Well, here we have numbers; a well-defined group situation of proletarian hue; and a group interest shaping a group attitude that will much more realistically account for hostility to the capitalist order than could the theory—itself a rationalization in the psychological sense—according to which the intellectual's righteous indignation about the wrongs of capitalism simply represents the logical inference from outrageous facts and which is no better than the theory of lovers that their feelings represent nothing but the logical inference from the virtues of the beloved.[1] Moreover our theory also accounts for the fact that this hostility increases, instead of diminishing, with every achievement of capitalist evolution.

Of course, the hostility of the intellectual group—amounting to moral disapproval of the capitalist order—is one thing, and the general hostile atmosphere which surrounds the capitalist engine is another thing. The latter is the really significant phenomenon; and it is not simply the product of the former but flows partly from independent sources, some of which have been mentioned before; so far as it does, it is raw material for the intellectual group to work on. There are give-and-take relations between the two which it would require more space to unravel than I can spare. The general contours of such an analysis are however sufficiently obvious and I think it safe to repeat that the role of the intellectual group consists primarily in stimulating, energizing, verbalizing and organizing this material and only secondarily in adding to it. Some particular aspects will illustrate the principle.

6. Capitalist evolution produces a labor movement which obviously is not the creation of the intellectual group. But it is not surprising that such an opportunity and the intellectual demiurge should find each other. Labor never craved intellectual leadership but intellectuals invaded labor politics. They had an important contribution to make: they verbalized the movement, supplied theories and slogans for it—class war is an excellent example—made it conscious of itself and in doing so changed its meaning.

[1] The reader will observe that any such theories would be unrealistic even if the facts of capitalism or the virtues of the beloved were actually all that the social critic or the lover believes them to be. It is also important to note that in the overwhelming majority of cases both critics and lovers are obviously sincere: neither psycho-sociological nor psycho-physical mechanisms enter as a rule into the limelight of the Ego, except in the mask of sublimations.

In solving this task from their own standpoint, they naturally radicalized it, eventually imparting a revolutionary bias to the most bourgeois trade-union practices, a bias most of the non-intellectual leaders at first greatly resented. But there was another reason for this. Listening to the intellectual, the workman is almost invariably conscious of an impassable gulf if not of downright distrust. In order to get hold of him and to compete with non-intellectual leaders, the intellectual is driven to courses entirely unnecessary for the latter who can afford to frown. Having no genuine authority and feeling always in danger of being unceremoniously told to mind his own business, he must flatter, promise and incite, nurse left wings and scowling minorities, sponsor doubtful or submarginal cases, appeal to fringe ends, profess himself ready to obey—in short, behave toward the masses as his predecessors behaved first toward their ecclesiastical superiors, later toward princes and other individual patrons, still later toward the collective master of bourgeois complexion.[1] Thus, though intellectuals have not created the labor movement, they have yet worked it up into something that differs substantially from what it would be without them.

The social atmosphere, for the theory of which we have been gathering stones and mortar, explains why public policy grows more and more hostile to capitalist interests, eventually so much so as to refuse on principle to take account of the requirements of the capitalist engine and to become a serious impediment to its functioning. The intellectual group's activities have however a relation to anti-capitalist policies that is more direct than what is implied in their share in verbalizing them. Intellectuals rarely enter professonal politics and still more rarely conquer responsible office. But they staff political bureaus, write party pamphlets and speeches, act as secretaries and advisers, make the individual politician's newspaper reputation which, though it is not everything, few men can afford to neglect. In doing these things they to some extent impress their mentality on almost everything that is being done.

The actual influence exerted varies greatly with the state of the political game from mere formulation to making a measure politically possible or impossible. But there is always plenty of scope for it. When we say that individual politicians and parties are exponents of class interests we are at best emphasizing one-half of the truth. The other half, just as important if not more so, comes into view when we consider that politics is a profession which evolves interests of its own—interests that may clash with as well as conform to the interests of the groups that a man or party "represents."[2] Individual and party opinion is, more than anything else,

---

[1] All this will be illustrated and further developed in Part V.

[2] This of course is just as true of the intellectuals themselves with respect to the class from which they come or to which, economically and culturally, they belong. The subject will be taken up again in ch. xxiii.

sensitive to those factors in the political situation that directly affect the career or the standing of the individual or party. Some of these are controlled by the intellectual group in much the same sense as is the moral code of an epoch that exalts the cause of some interests and puts the cause of others tacitly out of court.

Finally, that social atmosphere or code of values affects not only policies—the spirit of legislation—but also administrative practice. But again there is also a more direct relation between the intellectual group and bureaucracy. The bureaucracies of Europe are of pre- and extra-capitalist origin. However much they may have changed in composition as the centuries rolled on, they never identified themselves wholly with the bourgeoisie, its interests or its scheme of values, and never saw much more in it than an asset to be managed in the interest of the monarch or of the nation. Except for inhibitions due to professional training and experience, they are therefore open to conversion by the modern intellectual with whom, through a similar education, they have much in common,[1] while the tinge of gentility that in many cases used to raise a barrier has been fading away from the modern civil servant during the last decades. Moreover, in times of rapid expansion of the sphere of public administration, much of the additional personnel required has to be taken directly from the intellectual group—witness this country.

VI. Decomposition

1. Faced by the increasing hostility of the environment and by the legislative, administrative and judicial practice born of that hostility, entrepreneurs and capitalists—in fact the whole stratum that accepts the bourgeois scheme of life—will eventually cease to function. Their standard aims are rapidly becoming unattainable, their efforts futile. The most glamorous of these bourgeois aims, the foundation of an industrial dynasty, has in most countries become unattainable already, and even more modest ones are so difficult to attain that they may cease to be thought worth the struggle as the permanence of these conditions is being increasingly realized.

Considering the role of bourgeois motivation in the explanation of the economic history of the last two or three centuries, its smothering by the unfavorable reactions of society or its weakening by disuse no doubt constitutes a factor adequate to explain a flop in the capitalist process —should we ever observe it as a permanent phenomenon—and one that is much more important than any of those that are presented by the Theory of Vanishing Investment Opportunity. It is hence interesting to observe that that motivation not only is threatened by forces external to the bourgeois mind but that it also tends to die out from internal causes.

[1] For examples see ch. xxvi.

There is of course close interdependence between the two. But we cannot get at the true diagnosis unless we try to disentangle them.

One of those "internal causes" we have already met with. I have dubbed it Evaporation of the Substance of Property. We have seen that, normally, the modern businessman, whether entrepreneur or mere managing administrator, is of the executive type. From the logic of his position he acquires something of the psychology of the salaried employee working in a bureaucratic organization. Whether a stockholder or not, his will to fight and to hold on is not and cannot be what it was with the man who knew ownership and its responsibilities in the fullblooded sense of those words. His system of values and his conception of duty undergo a profound change. Mere stockholders of course have ceased to count at all—quite independently of the clipping of their share by a regulating and taxing state. Thus the modern corporation, although the product of the capitalist process, socializes the bourgeois mind; it relentlessly narrows the scope of capitalist motivation; not only that, it will eventually kill its roots.[1]

2. Still more important however is another "internal cause," viz., the disintegration of the bourgeois family. The facts to which I am referring are too well known to need explicit statement. To men and women in modern capitalist societies, family life and parenthood mean less than they meant before and hence are less powerful molders of behavior; the rebellious son or daughter who professes contempt for "Victorian" standards is, however incorrectly, expressing an undeniable truth. The weight of these facts is not impaired by our inability to measure them statistically. The marriage rate proves nothing because the term Marriage covers as many sociological meanings as does the term Property, and the kind of alliance that used to be formed by the marriage contract may completely die out without any change in the legal construction or in the frequency of the contract. Nor is the divorce rate more significant. It does not matter how many marriages are dissolved by judical decree—what matters is how many lack the content essential to the old pattern. If in our statistical age readers insist on a statistical measure, the proportion of marriages that produce no children or only one child, though still inadequate to quantify the phenomenon I mean, might come as near as we can hope to come to indicating its numerical importance. The phenomenon by now extends, more or less, to all classes. But it first appeared in the bourgeois (and

---

[1] Many people will deny this. This is due to the fact that they derive their impression from past history and from the slogans generated by past history during which the institutional change brought about by the big corporation had not yet asserted itself. Also they may think of the scope which corporate business used to give for illegal satisfactions of the capitalist motivation. But that would cut my way: the fact that personal gain beyond salary and bonus cannot, in corporate business, be reaped by executives except by illegal or semi-illegal practices shows precisely that the structural idea of the corporation is averse to it.

intellectual) stratum and its symptomatic as well as causal value for our purposes lies entirely there. It is wholly attributable to the rationalization of everything in life, which we have seen is one of the effects of capitalist evolution. In fact, it is but one of the results of the spread of that rationalization to the sphere of private life. All the other factors which are usually adduced in explanation can be readily reduced to that one.

As soon as men and women learn the utilitarian lesson and refuse to take for granted the traditional arrangements that their social environment makes for them, as soon as they acquire the habit of weighing the individual advantages and disadvantages of any prospective course of action—or, as we might also put it, as soon as they introduce into their private life a sort of inarticulate system of cost accounting—they cannot fail to become aware of the heavy personal sacrifices that family ties and especially parenthood entail under modern conditions and of the fact that at the same time, excepting the cases of farmers and peasants, children cease to be economic assets. These sacrifices do not consist only of the items that come within the reach of the measuring rod of money but comprise in addition an indefinite amount of loss of comfort, of freedom from care, and opportunity to enjoy alternatives of increasing attractiveness and variety—alternatives to be compared with joys of parenthood that are being subjected to a critical analysis of increasing severity. The implication of this is not weakened but strengthened by the fact that the balance sheet is likely to be incomplete, perhaps even fundamentally wrong. For the greatest of the assets, the contribution made by parenthood to physical and moral health—to "normality" as we might express it—particularly in the case of women, almost invariably escapes the rational searchlight of modern individuals who, in private as in public life, tend to focus attention on ascertainable details of immediate utilitarian relevance and to sneer at the idea of hidden necessities of human nature or of the social organism. The point I wish to convey is, I think, clear without further elaboration. It may be summed up in the question that is so clearly in many potential parents' minds: "Why should we stunt our ambitions and impoverish our lives in order to be insulted and looked down upon in our old age?"

While the capitalist process, by virtue of the psychic attitudes it creates, progressively dims the values of family life and removes the conscientious inhibitions that an old moral tradition would have put in the way toward a different scheme of life, it at the same time implements the new tastes. As regards childlessness, capitalist inventiveness produces contraceptive devices of ever-increasing efficiency that overcome the resistance which the strongest impulse of man would otherwise have put up. As regards the style of life, capitalist evolution decreases the desirability of, and provides alternatives to, the bourgeois family home. I have previously adverted to the Evaporation of Industrial Property; I have now to advert to the Evaporation of Consumers' Property.

Until the later decades of the ninteenth century, the town house and the country place were everywhere not only pleasant and convenient shells of private life on the higher levels of income, but they were indispensable. Not only hospitality on any scale and in any style, but even the comfort, dignity, repose and refinement of the family depended upon its having an adequate *foyer* of its own that was adequately staffed. The arrangements summarized by the term Home were accordingly accepted as a matter of course by the average man and woman of bourgeois standing, exactly as they looked upon marriage and children—the "founding of a family"—as a matter of course.

Now, on the one hand, the amenities of the bourgeois home are becoming less obvious than are its burdens. To the critical eye of a critical age it is likely to appear primarily as a source of trouble and expense which frequently fail to justify themselves. This would be so even independently of modern taxation and wages and of the attitude of modern household personnel, all of which are typical results of the capitalist process and of course greatly strengthen the case against what in the near future will be almost universally recognized as an outmoded and uneconomical way of life. In this respect as in others we are living in a transitional stage. The average family of bourgeois standing tends to reduce the difficulties of running the big house and the big country place by substituting for it small and mechanized establishments plus a maximum of outside service and outside life—hospitality in particular being increasingly shifted to the restaurant or club.

On the other hand, the home of the old type is no longer an indispensable requirement of comfortable and refined living in the bourgeois sphere. The apartment house and the apartment hotel represent a rationalized type of abode and another style of life which when fully developed will no doubt meet the new situation and provide all the essentials of comfort and refinement. To be sure, neither that style nor its shell are fully developed anywhere as yet and they proffer cost advantage only if we count in the trouble and annoyance incident to running a modern home. But other advantages they proffer already—the facility of using to the full the variety of modern enjoyments, of travel, of ready mobility, of shifting the load of the current little things of existence to the powerful shoulders of highly specialized organizations.

It is easy to see how this in turn bears, in the upper strata of capitalist society, upon the problems of the child. Again there is interaction: the passing of the spacious home—in which alone the rich life of a numerous family can unfold[1]—and the increasing friction with which it functions supply another motive for avoiding the cares of parenthood; but the decline of philoprogenitivity in turn renders the spacious home less worth while.

[1] Modern relations between parents and children are of course partly conditioned by the crumbling of that steady frame of family life.

I have said that the new style of bourgeois life does not as yet offer any decisive cost advantage. But this refers only to the current or prime costs of servicing the wants of private life. As to overhead, even the purely pecuniary advantage is obvious already. And inasmuch as the outlay on the most durable elements of home life—especially the house, the pictures, the furniture—used to be financed mainly from previous earnings we may say that the need for accumulation of "consumers' capital" is drastically reduced by that process. This does not mean of course that demand for "consumers' capital" is at present, even relatively, smaller than it was; the increasing demand for durable consumers' goods from small and medium incomes more than counterbalances this effect. But it does mean that, so far as the hedonistic component in the pattern of acquisitive motives is concerned, the desirability of incomes beyond a certain level is reduced. In order to satisfy himself of this, the reader need only visualize the situation in a thoroughly practical spirit: the successful man or couple or the "society" man or couple who can pay for the best available accommodation in hotel, ship and train, and for the best available qualities of the objects of personal consumption and use—which qualities are increasingly being turned out by the conveyor of mass production[1]—will, things being what they are, as a rule have all they want with any intensity *for themselves*. And it is easy to see that a budget framed on those lines will be far below the requirements of a "seignioral" style of life.

3. In order to realize what all this means for the efficiency of the capitalist engine of production we need only recall that the family and the family home used to be the mainspring of the typically bourgeois kind of profit motive. Economists have not always given due weight to this fact. When we look more closely at their idea of the self-interest of entrepreneurs and capitalists we cannot fail to discover that the results it was supposed to produce are really not at all what one would expect from the rational self-interest of the detached individual or the childless couple who no longer look at the world through the windows of a family home. Consciously or unconsciously they analyzed the behavior of the man whose views and motives are shaped by such a home and who means to work and to save primarily for wife *and children*. As soon as these fade out from the moral vision of the businessman, we have a different kind of *homo oeconomicus* before us who cares for different things and acts in different ways. For him and from the standpoint of his individualistic utilitarianism, the behavior of that old type would in fact be completely irrational. He loses the only sort of romance and heroism that is left in the unromantic and unheroic civilization of capitalism—the heroism of

[1] Effects on consumers' budgets of the increasing eligibility of mass-produced articles are enhanced by the price difference between them and the corresponding custom-made articles which increases owing to the increase in wages *pari passu* with the decrease in the relative desirability of the latter; the capitalist process democratizes consumption.

navigare necesse est, vivere non necesse est.[1] And he loses the capitalist ethics that enjoins working for the future irrespective of whether or not one is going to harvest the crop oneself.

The last point may be put more tellingly. In the preceding chapter it was observed that the capitalist order entrusts the long-run interests of society to the upper strata of the bourgeoisie. They are really entrusted to the family motive operative in those strata. The bourgeoisie worked primarily in order to invest, and it was not so much a standard of consumption as a standard of accumulation that the bourgeoisie struggled for and tried to defend against governments that took the short-run view.[2] With the decline of the driving power supplied by the family motive, the businessman's time-horizon shrinks, roughly, to his life expectation. And he might now be less willing than he was to fulfill that function of earning, saving and investing even if he saw no reason to fear that the results would but swell his tax bills. He drifts into an anti-saving frame of mind and accepts with an increasing readiness anti-saving *theories* that are indicative of a short-run *philosophy*.

But anti-saving theories are not all that he accepts. With a different attitude to the concern he works for and with a different scheme of private life he tends to acquire a different view of the values and standards of the capitalist order of things. Perhaps the most striking feature of the picture is the extent to which the bourgeoisie, besides educating its own enemies, allows itself in turn to be educated by them. It absorbs the slogans of current radicalism and seems quite willing to undergo a process of conversion to a creed hostile to its very existence. Haltingly and grudgingly it concedes in part the implications of that creed. This would be most astonishing and indeed very hard to explain were it not for the fact that the typical bourgeois is rapidly losing faith in his own creed. And this again becomes fully understandable as soon as we realize that the social conditions which account for its emergence are passing.

This is verified by the very characteristic manner in which particular capitalist interests and the bourgeoisie as a whole behave when facing direct attack. They talk and plead—or hire people to do it for them; they snatch at every chance of compromise; they are ever ready to give in; they never put up a fight under the flag of their own ideals and interests—in this country there was no real resistance anywhere against the imposition of crushing financial burdens during the last decade or against labor legislation incompatible with the effective management of industry. Now, as the reader will surely know by this time, I am far from overestimating the political power of either big business or the bourgeoisie in general.

[1] "Seafaring is necessary, living is not necessary." Inscription on an old house in Bremen.

[2] It has been said that in economic matters "the state can take the longer view." But excepting certain matters outside of party politics such as conservation of natural resources, it hardly ever does.

Moreover, I am prepared to make large allowances for cowardice. But still, means of defense were not entirely lacking as yet and history is full of examples of the success of small groups who, believing in their cause, were resolved to stand by their guns. The only explanation for the meekness we observe is that the bourgeois order no longer makes any sense to the bourgeoisie itself and that, when all is said and nothing is done, it does not really care.

Thus the same economic process that undermines the position of the bourgeoisie by decreasing the importance of the functions of entrepreneurs and capitalists, by breaking up protective strata and institutions, by creating an atmosphere of hostility, also decomposes the motor forces of capitalism from within. Nothing else shows so well that the capitalist order not only rests on props made of extra-capitalist material but also derives its energy from extra-capitalist patterns of behavior which at the same time it is bound to destroy.

We have rediscovered what from different standpoints and, so I believe, on inadequate grounds has often been discovered before: there is inherent in the capitalist system a tendency toward self-destruction which, in its earlier stages, may well assert itself in the form of a tendency toward retardation of progress.

I shall not stay to repeat how objective and subjective, economic and extra-economic factors, reinforcing each other in imposing accord, contribute to that result. Nor shall I stay to show what should be obvious and in subsequent chapters will become more obvious still, viz., that those factors make not only for the destruction of the capitalist but for the emergence of a socialist civilization. They all point in that direction. The capitalist process not only destroys its own institutional framework but it also creates the conditions for another. Destruction may not be the right word after all. Perhaps I should have spoken of transformation. The outcome of the process is not simply a void that could be filled by whatever might happen to turn up; things and souls are transformed in such a way as to become increasingly amenable to the socialist form of life. With every peg from under the capitalist structure vanishes an impossibility of the socialist plan. In both these respects Marx's *vision* was right. We can also agree with him in linking the particular social transformation that goes on under our eyes with an economic process as its prime mover. What our analysis, if correct, disproves is after all of secondary importance, however essential the role may be which it plays in the socialist credo. In the end there is not so much difference as one might think between saying that the decay of capitalism is due to its success and saying that it is due to its failure.

But our answer to the question that heads this part posits far more problems than it solves. In view of what is to follow in this book, the reader should bear in mind:

First, that so far we have not learned anything about the kind of socialism that may be looming in the future. For Marx and for most of his followers—and this was and is one of the most serious shortcomings of their doctrine—socialism meant just one definite thing. But the definiteness really goes no further than nationalization of industry would carry us and with this an indefinite variety of economic and cultural possibilities will be seen to be compatible.

Second, that similarly we know nothing as yet about the precise way by which socialism may be expected to come except that there must be a great many possibilities ranging from a gradual bureaucratization to the most picturesque revolution. Strictly speaking we do not even know whether socialism will actually come to stay. For to repeat: perceiving a tendency and visualizing the goal of it is one thing and predicting that this goal will actually be reached and that the resulting state of things will be workable, let alone permanent, is quite another thing. Before humanity chokes (or basks) in the dungeon (or paradise) of socialism it may well burn up in the horrors (or glories) of imperialist wars.[1]

Third, that the various components of the tendency we have been trying to describe, while everywhere discernible, have as yet nowhere fully revealed themselves. Things have gone to different lengths in different countries but in no country far enough to allow us to say with any confidence precisely how far they will go, or to assert that their "underlying trend" has grown too strong to be subject to anything more serious than temporary reverses. Industrial integration is far from being complete. Competition, actual and potential, is still a major factor in any business situation. Enterprise is still active, the leadership of the bourgeois group still the prime mover of the economic process. The middle class is still a political power. Bourgeois standards and bourgeois motivations though being increasingly impaired are still alive. Survival of traditions—and family ownership of controlling parcels of stock—still make many an executive behave as the owner-manager did of old. The bourgeois family has not yet died; in fact, it clings to life so tenaciously that no responsible politician has as yet dared to touch it by any method other than taxation. From the standpoint of immediate practice as well as for the purposes of short-run forecasting—and in these things, a century is a "short run"[2]—all this surface may be more important than the tendency toward another civilization that slowly works deep down below.

[1] Written in the summer of 1935.

[2] This is why the facts and arguments presented in this and the two preceding chapters do not invalidate my reasoning about the possible economic results of another fifty years of capitalist evolution. The thirties may well turn out to have been the last gasp of capitalism—the likelihood of this is of course greatly increased by the current war. But again they may not. In any case there are no *purely economic* reasons why capitalism should not have another successful run which is all I wished to establish.

III

The Crisis of Individuality

14. William I. Thomas and Florian Znaniecki

·Three Types of Personality

. . . the human personality is both a continually producing factor and a continually produced result of social evolution, and this double relation expresses itself in every elementary social fact; there can be for social science no change of social reality which is not the common effect of pre-existing social values and individual attitudes acting upon them, no change of individual consciousness which is not the common effect of pre-existing individual attitudes and social values acting upon them. When viewed as a factor of social evolution the human personality is a ground of the causal explanation of social happenings; when viewed as a product of social evolution it is causally explicable by social happenings. In the first case individual attitudes toward pre-existing social values serve to explain the appearance of new social values; in the second case social values acting upon pre-existing individual attitudes serve to explain the appearance of new individual attitudes.

The essential points, which cannot be here sufficiently emphasized, are that the social personality as a whole manifests itself only in the course of its total life and not at any particular moment of its life, and that its life is not a mere empirical manifestation of a timeless metaphysical essence, always the same, but is a continuous evolution in which nothing remains unchanged. This evolution often tends toward a stabilization as its ultimate limit, but never attains this limit completely; and even then it is not this limit as such, but the very course of evolution tending to this limit, that constitutes the main object-matter of socio-psychological synthesis.

An individual with nothing but his biological formation, or—in social terms—with nothing but his temperamental attitudes, is not yet a social personality, but is able to become one. In the face of the world of social meanings he stands powerless; he is not even conscious of the existence of

From Thomas and Znaniecki, *The Polish Peasant in Europe and America.* "The Introduction" of Vol. II, Part IV: Life-record of an Immigrant. (New York: Dover Publications, 1958 edition), pp. 1831, 1837-38, 1850-1903.

this reality, and when the latter manifests itself to him in changes of the material reality upon which his instincts bear, he is quite lost and either passively submits to the unexpected, or aimlessly revolts. Such is the position of the animal or the infant in human society; and a similar phenomenon repeats itself on a smaller scale whenever an individual on a low level of civilization gets in touch with a higher civilized environment, a worldling with a body of specialists, a foreigner with an autochthonic society, etc. In fact, human beings for the most part never suspect the existence of innumerable meanings—scientific, artistic, moral, political, economic—and a field of social reality whose meanings the individual does not know, even if he can observe its sensual contents, is as much out of the reach of his practical experience as the other side of the moon.

In order to become a social personality in any domain the individual must therefore not only realize the existence of the social meanings which objects possess in this domain, but also learn how to adapt himself to the demands which society puts upon him from the standpoint of these meanings and how to control these meanings for his personal purposes; and since meanings imply conscious thought, he must do this by conscious reflection, not by mere instinctive adaptations of reflexes. In order to satisfy the social demands put upon his personality he must reflectively organize his temperamental attitudes; in order to obtain the satisfaction of his own demands, he must develop intellectual methods for the control of social reality in place of the instinctive ways which are sufficient to control natural reality. And this effective reorganization of temperamental attitudes leads, as we have seen, to character, while the parallel development of intellectual methods of controlling social reality leads to a life-organization, which is nothing but the totality of these methods at work in the individual's social career.

The practical problem which the individual faces in constructing a life-organization has only in so far a similarity with the problem of biological control of the living being's natural environment as the solution of both implies a certain stabilization of individual experiences, the realization of a certain more or less permanent order within that sphere of reality which the individual controls. But the nature of this stability, of this permanent order, is essentially different in both cases—a difference which has been obliterated by the indistinct use of the term "habit" to indicate any uniformities of behavior. This term should be restricted to the biological field. A habit, inherited or acquired, is the tendency to repeat the same act in similar material conditions. The stabilization reached through habit involves no conscious, purposeful regulation of new experiences, but merely the tendency to find in new experiences old elements which will enable the living being to react to them in an old way. This tendency is unreflective; reflection arises only when there is disappointment, when new experiences cannot be practically assimilated to the old ones. But this form of stability can work only when the reality to which the individual has to adjust is entirely constituted by sensually given contents and relations. It is evidently insufficient when he has to take social meanings into account, interpret his experience not exclusively in terms of his own needs and wishes, but also in terms of the traditions, customs, beliefs, aspirations of his social milieu. Thus the introduction of any stable order into experience requires continual reflection, for it is impossible even to realize whether a certain experience is socially new or old without consciously interpreting the given content—an object, a movement, a word—and realizing what social meaning it possesses. However stable a social milieu may be, its stability can never be compared with that of a physical milieu; social situations never spontaneously repeat themselves, every situation is more or less new, for every one includes new human activities differently combined. The individual does not find passively ready situations exactly similar to past situations; he must consciously define every situation as similar to certain past situations, if he wants to apply to it the same solution applied to those situations. And this is what society expects him to do when it requires of him a stable life-organization; it does not want him to react instinctively in the same way to the same material conditions, but to construct reflectively similar social situations even if material conditions vary. The uniformity of behavior it tends to impose upon the individual is not a uniformity of organic habits but of consciously followed *rules*. The individual, in order to control social reality for his needs, must develop not series of uniform reactions, but general *schemes* of situations; his life-organization is a set of rules for definite situations, which may be even expressed in abstract formulas. Moral principles, legal prescription, economic forms, religious rites, social customs, etc., are examples of schemes.

The definiteness of attitudes attained in character and the corresponding schematization of social data in life-organization admit, however, a wide scale of gradation with regard to one point of fundamental importance,—the range of possibilities of further development remaining open to the individual after the stabilization. This depends on the nature of the attitudes involved in the character and of the schemes of life-organization, and also on the way in which both are unified and systematized. And here three typical cases can be distinguished.

The set of attitudes constituting the character may be such as practically to exclude the development of any new attitude in the given conditions of life, because the reflective attitudes of an individual have attained so great a fixity that he is accessible to only a certain class of influences—those constituting the most permanent part of his social milieu. The only possibilities of evolution then remaining open to the individual are the slow changes brought by age in himself and by time in his social milieu, or a change of conditions so radical as to destroy at once the values to whose influence he was adapted and presumably his own character. This is the type which has found its expression in literature as the "Philistine." It is opposed to the "Bohemian," whose possibilities of evolution are not closed, simply because his character remains unformed. Some of his temperamental attitudes are in their primary form, others may have become intellectualized but remain unrelated to each other, do not constitute a stable and systematized set, and do not exclude any new attitude, so that the individual remains open to any and all influences. As opposed to both these types we find the third type of the individual whose character is settled and organized but involves the possibility and even the necessity of evolution, because the reflective attitudes constituting it include a tendency to change, regulated by plans of productive activity, and the individual remains open to such influences as will be in line of his preconceived development. This is the type of the creative individual.

A parallel distinction must be made with regard to the schemes of social situations constituting the life-organization. The ability to define every situation which the individual meets in his experience is not necessarily a proof of intellectual superiority; it may mean simply a limitation of claims and interests and a stability of external conditions which do not allow any radically new situations to be noticed, so that a few narrow schemes are sufficient to lead the individual through life, simply because he does not see problems on his way which demand new schemes. This type of schemes constitutes the common stock of social traditions in which every class of situation is defined in the same way once and forever. These schemes harmonize perfectly with the Philistine's character and therefore the Philistine is always a conformist, usually accepting social tradition in its most stable elements. Of course every important and unexpected change in the conditions of life results for such an individual in a disorganization of activity. As long as he can he still applies the old schemes, and up to a certain point his old definition of new situations may be sufficient to allow him to satisfy his claims if the latter are low, although he cannot compete with those who have higher claims and more efficient schemes. But as soon as the results of his activity become unsuccessful even in his own eyes, he is entirely lost; the situation becomes for him completely vague and undetermined, he is ready to accept any definition that may be suggested to him and is unable to keep any permanent line of activity. This is the case with any conservative and intellectually limited member of a stable community, whatever may be his social class, when he finds himself transferred into another community or when his own group undergoes some rapid and sudden change.

Opposed to this type we find an undetermined variation of schemes in the life of all the numerous species of the Bohemian. The choice of the scheme by a Bohemian depends on his momentary standpoint, and this may be determined either by some outburst of a primary temperamental attitude or by some isolated character-attitude which makes him subject to some indiscriminately accepted influence. In either case inconsistency is the essential feature of his activity. But on the other hand he shows a degree of adaptability to new conditions quite in contrast with the Philistine, though his adaptability is only provisional and does not lead to a new systematic life-organization.

But adaptability to new situations and diversity of interest are even compatible with a consistency of activity superior to that which tradition can give if the individual builds his life-organization not upon the presumption of the immutability of his sphere of social values, but upon the tendency to modify and to enlarge it according to some definite aims. These may be purely intellectual or æsthetic, and in this case the individual searches for new situations to be defined simply in order to widen and to perfect his knowledge or his æsthetic interpretation and appreciation; or his aims may be "practical," in any sense of the term —hedonistic, economical, political, moral, religious—and then the individual searches for new situations in order to widen the control of his environment, to adapt to his purposes a continually increasing sphere of social reality. This is the creative man.

The Philistine, the Bohemian and the creative man are the three fundamental forms of personal determination toward which social personalities tend in their evolution. None of these forms is ever completely and absolutely realized by a human individual in all lines of activity; there is no Philistine who lacks completely Bohemian tendencies, no Bohemian who is not a Philistine in certain respects, no creative man who is fully and exclusively creative and does not need some Philistine routine in certain lines to make creation in other lines practically possible, and some Bohemianism in order to be able to reject occasionally such fixed attitudes and social regulations as hinder his progress, even if he should be unable at the time to substitute for them any positive organization in the given line. But while pure Philistinism, pure Bohemianism and pure creativeness represent only ideal limits of personal evolution, the process of personal evolution grows to be more and more definite as it progresses, so that, while the form which a human personality will assume is not determined in advance, either by the individual's temperament or by his social milieu, his future becomes more and more determined by the very course of his development; he approaches more and more to Philistinism, Bohemianism or creativeness and thereby his possibilities of becoming something else continually diminish.

These three general types—limits of personal evolution—include, of course, an indefinite number of variations, depending on the nature of the attitudes by which characters are constituted and on the schemes composing the life-organization of social individuals. If we wished therefore to classify human personalities on the ground of the limits of development to which they tend, our task would be very difficult, if not impossible, for we should have to take characters and life-organizations separately in all their varieties into account. In each of these three fundamental types similar characters may correspond to indefinitely varying life-organizations and similar life-organizations to indefinitely varying characters. But, as we have seen, the problem is to study characters and life-organizations not in their static abstract form, but in their dynamic concrete development. And both character and life-organization—the subjective and the objective side of the personality—develop together. For an attitude can become stabilized as a part of the reflective character only under the influence of a scheme of behavior, and *vice versa*, the construction or acceptance of a scheme demands that an attitude be stabilized as a part of character. Every process of personal evolution consists, therefore, in a complex evolutionary series in which social schemes, acting upon pre-existing attitudes, produce new attitudes in such a way that the latter represent a determination of the temperamental tendencies with regard to the social world, a realization in a conscious form of the character-possibilities which the individual brings with him; and these new attitudes, with their intellectual continuity, acting upon pre-existing sets of social values in the sphere of individual experiences produce new values in such a way that every production of a value represents at the same time a definition of some vague situation, and this is a step toward the constitution of some consistent scheme of behavior. In the continual interaction between the individual and his environment we can say neither that the individual is the product of his milieu nor that he produces his milieu; or rather, we can say both. For the individual can indeed develop only under the influence of his environment, but on the other hand during his development he modifies this environment by defining situations and solving them according to his wishes and tendencies. His influence upon the environment may be scarcely noticeable socially, may have little importance for others, but it is important for himself, since, as we have said, the world in which he lives is not the world as society or the scientific observer sees it but as he sees it himself. In various cases we may find various degrees of dependence upon the environment, conditioned by the primary qualities of the individual and the type of social organization. The individual is relatively dependent upon society in his evolution, if he develops mainly such attitudes as lead to dependence, which is then due both to his temperamental dispositions and to the fact that the organization of society is such as to enforce by various means individual subjection; he is relatively independent if in his evolution he develops attitudes producing independence, which again results from certain primary tendencies determined by a social organization which favors individual spontaneity. And thus both dependence and independence are gradual products of an evolution which is due originally to reciprocal interaction; the individual cannot become exclusively dependent upon society without the help of his own disposition, nor become independent of society without the help of social influences. The fundamental principles of personal evolution must be sought therefore both in the individual's own nature and in his social milieu.

We find, indeed, two universal traits manifested in all individual attitudes, instinctive or intellectual, which form the condition of both development and conservatism. In the reflex system of all the higher organisms are two powerful tendencies which in their most distinct and explicit form manifest themselves as curiosity and fear. Without curiosity, that is, an interest in new situations in general, the animal would not live; to neglect the new situation might mean either that he was about to be eaten or that he was missing his chance for food. And fear with its contrary tendency to avoid certain experiences for the sake of security is equally essential to life. To represent these two permanent tendencies as they become parts of character in the course of the social development of a personality we shall use the terms *"desire for new experience"* and *"desire for stability."* These two tendencies in every permanent attitude manifest themselves in the rythmical form which conscious life assumes in every line. When consciousness embraces only a short span of activities, the rhythm expresses itself in the alternation of single wishes or appetites with repose. The satisfaction of hunger or of sexual desire and the subsequent wish for uninterrupted calm are the most general examples. On a higher level these tendencies manifest themselves with regard to much more complex and longer series of facts. The desire for stability extends to a whole period of regular alternations of activity and rest from which new experiences are relatively excluded; the desire for new experience finds its expression in the break of such a whole line of regulated activities. And the range and complexity of both stability and change may have many degrees. Thus, for example, stability may mean the possibility of a single series of satisfactions of hunger in a certain restaurant, of a week's relation with an individual of the other sex, of a few days' stay in one place during travel, of a certain kind of work in an office; or it may lie in the possibility of such an organization of money-affairs as gives the certainty of always getting food, of a permanent marriage-relation, settling permanently in one place, a life career, etc. And new experience may mean change of restaurant, change of the temporary sexual relation, change of the kind of work within the same office, the resuming of travel, the acquiring of wealth, getting a divorce, developing a Don Juan attitude toward women, change of career or speciality, development of amateur or sporting interests, etc.

On the individual side, then, alternation of the desire for new experience and of the desire for security is the fundamental principle of personal evolution, as including both the development of a character and of a life-organization. On the social side the essential point of this evolution lies in the fact that the individual living in society has to fit into a pre-existing social world, to take part in the hedonistic, economic, political, religious, moral, æsthetic, intellectual activities of the group. For these activities the group has objective *systems*, more or less complex sets of schemes, organized either by traditional association or with a conscious regard to the greatest possible efficiency of the result, but with only a secondary, or even with no interest in the particular desires, abilities and experiences of the individuals who have to perform these activities. The latter feature of the social systems results, of course, from the fact that the systems have to regulate identically the activities of many individuals at once, and that they usually last longer than the period of activity of an individual, passing from generation to generation. The gradual establishment of a determined relation between these systems which constitute together the social organization of the civilized life of a group, and individual character and life-organization in the course of their progressive formation, is the central problem of the social control of personal evolution. And social control—which, when applied to personal evolution, may be called "social education"—manifests itself also in the duality of two opposite tendencies: the tendency to suppress in the course of personal evolution, any attitudes or values which are either directly in disharmony with the existing social organization or seem to be the starting-points of lines of genesis which are expected to lead to socially disharmonious consequences; and the tendency to develop by adequately influencing personal evolution features of character and schemes of situations required by the existing social systems.

There is, of course, no pre-existing harmony whatever between the individual and the social factors of personal evolution, and the fundamental tendencies of the individual are always in some disaccordance with the fundamental tendencies of social control. Personal evolution is always a struggle between the individual and society—a struggle for self-expression on the part of the individual, for his subjection on the part of society—and it is in the total course of this struggle that the personality —not as a static "essence" but as a dynamic, continually evolving set of activities—manifests and constructs itself. The relative degree of the desire for new experience and the desire for stability necessary for and compatible with the progressive incorporation of a personality into a social organization is dependent on the nature of individual interests and of the social systems. Thus, different occupations allow for more or less change, as in the cases of the artist and the factory workman; and a many-sided dilletante needs and can obtain more new experiences than a specialist; single life usually makes more new experiences along certain lines possible and demands less stabilization than married life; political co-operation with the conservative part of a group brings less change than taking part in a revolutionary movement. And in modern society in general there is an increasing tendency to appreciate change, as compared with the appreciation of stability in the ancient and mediæval worlds. For every system within a given group and at a certain time there is a maximum and a minimum of change and of stability permissible and required. The widening of this range and the increase of the variety of systems are, of course, favorable to individual self-expression within the socially permitted limits. Thus, the whole process of development of the personality as ruled in various proportions by the desire for new experience and the desire for stability on the individual side, by the tendency to suppress and the tendency to develop personal possibilities on the social side, includes the following parallel and interdependent processes:

(1) Determination of the character on the ground of the temperament;

(2) Constitution of a life-organization which permits a more or less complete objective expression of the various attitudes included in the character;

(3) Adaptation of the character to social demands put upon the personality;

(4) Adaptation of individual life-organization to social organization.

1. We know already that the development of temperamental attitudes into character-attitudes can assume many different directions, so that, if the proper influences were exercised from the beginning, a wide range of characters, theoretically any possible character, might be evolved out of any temperament. But the directions which evolution must take in order to produce a determined attitude out of a pre-existing one become more and more limited with the fixation of character; in a systematically unified "consistent" character every fixed attitude would exclude the contrary one, and some degree of consistency appears as soon as the character begins to be formed. With the progressive evolution of the personality the means of developing a given character become therefore less and less numerous and it may be finally practically impossible to carry the development of certain attitudes to their end, for the process necessary to develop them might be so long and complicated as to be impracticable. Thus, it might be possible to produce a sweet and even a meek character out of an irascible temperament by developing first, for example, a strong altruistic disposition, to which in turn the way might lead through the desire for social response. But if in the develop-

ment of the personality other attitudes were gradually formed contrary to the desire for response or to altruism, such as desire for solitude, pride, etc., the original irascibility might be still subdued by other influences, but certainly it would be impossible to produce sweetness. Assuming now that we are determined to produce the latter, then we must be careful not to allow any temperamental possibilities to realize themselves which may be contrary either to this attitude itself or to any of the attitudes which the individual must evolve in order to attain this stage. The more opposition there is between the original temperamental attitude and the one that we want to develop, the longer the process, the more the intermediary stages to be passed, and the greater the number of necessary suppressions.

But in actual social life the mechanism of suppression is not used in this detailed way and the motives of suppression are not in the main those which we have outlined. The possible attitudes which the members of the group wish to suppress are usually those whose direct expression in action would, in the social opinion, be harmful, rather than those which are contrary to the development of other useful ones. The control exercised by the group is negative much more than positive, tends to destroy much more than to construct, for reasons which we shall investigate presently. And even when it wishes to construct, it often assumes, implicitly or explicitly, that when an undesirable attitude is suppressed, the contrary desirable one will develop. And, of course, if there is in individual temperament a possibility of the desirable attitude, this supposition may be true. But the point is that by suppressing an attitude, whether for the sake of some other more desirable one or through fear of its undesirable manifestations, we suppress at the same time all the possible lines of a further evolution that may have started from the suppressed attitude and resulted in something very desirable. The earlier the suppression, the greater the number of possibilities destroyed and the greater the resulting limitation of the personality. Well-known examples are the suppression of the adventurous spirit and of the critical tendency in children.

The mechanism of suppression is double. A temperamental possibility not yet conscious is suppressed if given no opportunity to manifest itself in any situation, for only through such manifestations can it become explicit and be evolved into a character-attitude. This form of suppression is attained by an isolation of the individual from all experiences that may give stimulation to endeavors to define situations by the undesirable tendency. The suppression of sexual attitudes and of free thought in religious matters are good examples of this mechanism. The second course, used when an attitude is already manifested, in order to prevent its further development and stabilization, is suppression by negative sanction; a negative value—punishment or blame—is attached to the manifestation of the attitude, and by lack of manifestation the attitude cannot evolve. But both mechanisms are in fact only devices for postponing the development of the undesirable attitude until a character is fixed including the contrary attitudes, and it is only this fixation which does suppress the undesirable attitude definitively.

But suppression is not always a necessary consequence of the evolution of character from temperament. Attitudes need to be suppressed only when they are inadequately qualified and thus interfere with more desirable ones when meeting in the same field of social experience. For example, unqualified spirit of adventure and a tendency to regulated life, unqualified sexual desire and claims of social respectability, unqualified wish for pleasures and recognition of familial obligations are, indeed, more or less irreconcilable with each other. But one of the fundamental points of the development of character from temperament is precisely the qualification of attitudes with respect to definite social contents, and if this qualification begins in time and the attitudes are determined with sufficient precision, there may be no opposition between them at all and none of them needs to be socially harmful.

The principle that permits the harmonizing of opposite attitudes without impairing the consistency of character is, in general, distinction of applicability of attitudes. The situations involved must, of course, be classed in advance so that certain features of a given complex of values may be a sufficient criterion for the application of one attitude or another. Many criteria are given by social tradition; the conventionalization of certain attitudes in certain circumstances permits of their preservation together with others to which they are opposed. The criteria are of various kinds. They may consist, for example, in a time-limitation. Vacation is considered a time when some of the spirit of adventure suppressed during the year may be expressed. Or it may be a limitation in space, as when certain behavior is permitted at a certain place, like the dropping of social forms and the relative freedom of relations between the sexes at bathing resorts. Sometimes the occasion is ceremonial, as in the hilarity of evening parties and the drinking at social meetings. On other occasions a certain attitude is assumed to be excluded from situations to which without the conventionalization it would apply. Thus, the sexual attitude is theoretically not applied to passages in the Bible bearing on sexual questions, or to an artist's model, or in medical studies and investigations and in legal works. More important cases of conventionalization are found when a whole line of organized activities, with the corresponding attitudes, is permitted under circumstances carefully circumscribed and usually designated by some social symbol. Thus, marriage is a conventionalization of the woman's—to some extent also the man's—system of sexual attitudes, besides being a familial organization. War is the conventionalization of murder, plundering and arson, diplomacy a conventionalization of cheating and treachery. Freedom of theoretic investigation has attained a social conventionalization in the physical sciences but not yet in human sciences—philosophy, sociology, history, history of literature, economics.

In every case the dividing line between the fields of applicability of two contrary attitudes can be drawn by or for the individual even if no general rules of division are laid down by society. The only difficulty is that every attitude if allowed to develop freely tends to an exclusive domination of the whole field of experience to which it can be applied. Of course this is not true of every attitude of every individual, but there is probably not a single attitude which does not in somebody tend to assume such an importance as to conflict with others. The principle of right measure and harmony of virtues, developed by Greek ethics, expressed precisely the need of such a limitation of attitudes. But it is evident that with a proper limitation no attitude needs to be suppressed and all the temperamental possibilities can be allowed to develop without leading to internal contradictions and impairing the consistency of character. The principle through which any attitude can be made not only socially harmless but even useful, is *sublimation*. It consists in turning the attitude exclusively toward situations that have in them an element endowed with social sacredness. We cannot analyze the latter concept now; we shall do it another time. At present it is enough to point out that an object is socially sacred when it provokes in members of the group an attitude of reverence and when it can be profaned in the eyes of social opinion, by being connected with some other object. There are many degrees of social sacredness; an object that may appear as sacred in comparison with another may be itself a source of profanation of a third. Thus, business has a feature of sacredness which becomes manifest when it is interfered with by frivolous things like drinking or the company of women of the demi-monde; but its sacredness is not very high since it can easily appear as profane when it interferes with scientific or religious interests. And even so highly sacred an object as a scientific congress or a formal religious meeting may seem profane as compared with a particularly eager and difficult pursuit by the individual of the solution of a great theoretic problem, the ecstasy of a mystic, or the preservation of the society itself from destruction or devastation by an alien enemy. And of course the degree of sacredness attached to different objects varies from group to group and from time to time, and some still current contrarieties, such as the fight for superiority of sacredness between art and morality, religion and science, patriotism and internationalism, show that in certain lines a general understanding even within a single group may be hardly possible at a given moment. But in spite of all these variations of sacredness there are, from this point of view, higher and lower forms possible for every attitude, dependent on the relative degree of sacredness of the situations which it defines. Thus, the spirit of adventure may manifest itself in a criminal's career, in a cow-boy's or trapper's life, in the activity of a detective, in geographical or ethnographical exploration; the desire for money, in stealing, gambling, "living by one's wits," commercial activity, great industrial organization; the sexual attitude may manifest itself in association with prostitutes, in relations, short but not devoid of individualization, with many girls and married women, in an ordinary marriage for the sake of the regulation of sexual life; in romantic love, in artistic creation, in religious mysticism. Even such attitudes as seem essentially harmful, as the desire of shedding blood, may become sublimated; the butcher's activity represents a lower degree of sublimation, surgery the highest.

To sublimate an attitude we must develop an appreciation of its higher forms, which then becomes a factor of evolution and eventually results in a depreciation of its lower manifestations. The feeling of social sacredness can arise in the individual only in close contact with a group which has definite standards of sacredness; more than any other feeling it needs a continual and permeating influence of social opinion and is likely to be lost without the support of the environment. But the social group does not always provide ready methods for the sublimation of all the attitudes which need this stimulation; its standards of sacredness are incomplete, often contradictory, and not extended to *all* the values to which they ought to be applied. The individual's own initiative must therefore supplement the social influences. When the feeling of social sacredness is once strongly developed with regard to a larger number of values the individual will be able to sublimate spontaneously social attitudes whose sublimation is not provided for by social tradition, by extending old standards of social sacredness to new values or by creating new standards. And as he needs social support to maintain his new valuations, he will try to convert his environment, to impart to others his reverence for things whose sacredness they have failed to recognize.

The principles of discrimination of situations to which contrary attitudes should be applied and of sublimation of socially forbidden attitudes allow a rich and consistent character to develop without suppressions from any source, temperamental or social. The individual spontaneously tries to preserve his temperamental attitudes, and as he can do this only by removing contradictions between attitudes contending for supremacy and by sublimating attitudes that can find no expression in his milieu, and since society never gives him all the ready conventions and the whole hierarchy of sacredness that he needs, he is naturally led to create new discriminations and new valuations, and becomes a creative type simply by fully developing all of his possibilities. The only task of social culture is to prepare him for this creation by teaching him the mechanism of discrimination and sublimation in general, and not interfering with his efforts to preserve all that he is able to preserve of his individuality. It is the suppression that produces the two other fundamental characters, the Philistine and the Bohemian. If society is successful in repressing all the possibilities that seem directly or indirectly dangerous until a character is formed which excludes them once and forever, then the product tends to be an individual for whom there are no problems of self-development left, no internal contradictions to solve, no external oppositions to overcome—a limited, stable, self-satisfied Philistine. If, on the contrary, the suppression is unsuccessful and the rebellious attitudes break out before a sufficiently stable set of contrary attitudes is formed, the individual is unprepared to meet the problems that arise, unable to discriminate or to sublimate, and an inconsistent, non-conformist, Bohemian type develops, which in its highest form, as artist, thinker, religious reformer, social revolutionist, may even succeed in producing, but whose products will always lack the internal harmony and social importance of the true creative type.

2. The construction of a life-organization in conformity with individual character may go on in two typically different ways. There may be ready social schemes which are imposed upon the individual, or the latter may develop his schemes himself, in agreement or non-agreement with those prevailing in his social environment. In the first case the scheme is usually given to the individual in an abstract form or through concrete examples, and then he is taught to apply it to the various situations which he meets by chance or which are especially created for him. In the second case he works out himself a definition of every new situation in conformity with his existing attitude, which grows in definiteness as the solved situation acts back upon it, and out of these definitions he gradually constructs a schematism.

Education gives us many examples of the first method. The inculcation of every moral norm, precept of behavior, logical rule, etc., follows this course. The formula or example is easily communicated; the difficulty begins with its application. It may happen that the individual has already defined situations spontaneously as the rule demands; then he accepts gladly the formulation of his own behavior which solves in advance the problem of reconciling this part of his life-organization with the social organization of the group. The well-known educational device is precisely to find among the individual's own actions such as are in accordance with the rule and then to state the rule as an induction from his own behavior. This is really an introduction of the second method, the one of spontaneous development, into the field of education. More frequently it happens that the individual has the attitude necessary to define situations in accordance with the rule, but the attitude lacks the determination that it needs to express itself in action, has not attained the consciousness of its social object enabling it to pass from the sphere of temperament into that of character. If then the individual has one or two situations defined for him it is enough to make him imitate this definition in the future and accept the scheme as a rule of behavior.

But the most common case is the one where the individual lacks the attitude which the social scheme demands. This is very general in the education of youth, where attitudes are developed progressively and the social group does not wait—and frequently cannot wait—for their spontaneous development, but forces the process so as to fit young people promptly into a social framework and have as little trouble with them as possible. Another general cause of the frequent failure of the social schemes to find ready response in the individual is their uniformity and stiffness. The social schematism is not adapted to the variety of individuals but to the artificial production of a minimum of uniformity. And even when this is successful the attitudes tend to evolve, not only in single individuals but also in the whole group, and this evolution is continuous, while the schemes can be changed only discontinuously, and so they remain behind—occasionally run ahead of—the social reality which they tend to express. From all these causes comes the continual and in a large measure fruitless effort to adapt the content of social life to its form—to produce attitudes to fit the schemes, while the contrary and more important process must be left largely to the individuals themselves.

The adaptation of attitudes to schemes may be pursued by two methods. The representatives of the social environment can try to develop the attitude on the basis of some existing attitude by applying such social laws as may be known. This would be the normal and successful method, but though it is sometimes applied, its success is now quite accidental, because, as we have indicated in the methodological note to Volume I, social technique is at present in a purely empirical stage, for there are scarcely any social laws definitely demonstrated. The only domain in which some consistent success has been obtained by this method is theoretic instruction. There at least it is clearly recognized that it is vain to try to force the individual to accept schemes, to define situations, to state and solve problems for which he has not yet the necessary preparation, and that new mental attitudes must be developed in a certain determined order and gradually. By the second and more usual method the individual is forced to define situations according to the imposed scheme, because to every situation coming under the scheme some sanction is added, some value which appeals to an existing attitude of the individual. But if the sanction is a more or less successful device in suppressing temporarily the manifestation of undesirable attitudes until character is formed, it proves quite unsuccessful in developing desirable ones. The situation to which the sanction is added is quite different from what it would have been without the sanction; the scheme accepted is really not the scheme that society wanted to impose, but a different one, consisting fundamentally in an adaptation to the sanction, and the individual develops not the attitude demanded, but another one, a modification of the attitude provoked by the sanction. Thus—to take a familiar type of case—by inducing the individual to comply with a moral norm through the fear of punishment or the hope of reward the idea of punishment or reward is added to every situation which demands the application of the moral norm. Then the situation is not the moral situation as such, but the moral situation *plus* the idea of punishment or reward; the scheme is not a moral scheme, but a scheme of prudence, a solution of the problem of avoiding punishment or of meriting reward; the attitude developed is not the moral attitude, but the fear of punishment or the hope of reward qualified by the given moral part of the situation.

When the individual constructs his life-organization himself instead of having it imposed upon him by society, his problem always consists, as we have already seen, in the determination of the vague. Any new situation is always vague and its definition demands not only intellectual analysis of the objective data but determination of the attitude itself, which becomes explicit and distinct only by manifesting itself in action. The definition of the new situation is therefore possible only if a new corresponding attitude can directly arise out of some preceding one, as its qualification or modification in view of the new values, and this determination of the attitude is in turn possible only if the new situation can be defined on the ground of some analogy with known situations—as an old problem viewed from a new standpoint. This explains why an entirely new situation which has no analogies in the past experience of the individual remains practically undefined even if it is understood theoretically; the individual may know all the values that are there, he may know how others define such a situation, and still all this remains practically meaningless to him. But when the scheme has once been formed it becomes itself a great help in developing new attitudes and defining situations in a new way. As long as the scheme is not there the new elements appearing in individual character and experience are not sufficiently noticed. There is still a lingering of the past, a conscious or unconscious effort to interpret the new in terms of the old, to consider the recently formed type of behavior as a mere variation of the preexisting type. The constitution of a new scheme at once makes conscious the evolution that has been accomplished—sometimes even makes the subject exaggerate its importance. In its light the recent changes appear as examples of a new general line of behavior, acquire an objectivity that they did not possess, for the scheme can be communicated to others, compared with social rules of behavior and can even become a social rule of behavior—for such is the source of every social reform.

The factor making the individual perceive and define new situations is always his own, conscious or subconscious, desire for new experience.

There is no external power capable of forcing him to work out a new definition. Even the influence of natural or social sanctions, of punishment following an unsuccessful definition, presupposes some active effort on the part of the individual tending to define the situation in view of the punishment. Even the mere defense against an aggression disturbing a state of security would be impossible without a latent power making the individual face the new situation instead of running away. The usual doctrine that new ways of behavior, new definitions, appear as a result of adaptation to new external conditions is based upon a quite inadequate conception of adaptation. The common idea is that adaptation marks a certain fixed limit to which the individual has to approach, because as long as he has not reached it he is misadapted, and various calamities force him to adapt himself. But where is such a limit? It must be different for various individuals. Napoleon was adapted to the conditions of French life after the revolution, and so was any one of his guards; the honest and solid real estate owner is as well adapted to the conditions of city life as is the successful pick-pocket. And it must change for every individual; the errand-boy who becomes a millionaire is no less adapted to his environment during his youth than in his later life. If adaptation means anything, it can be only a harmonious relation between individual claims and individual control of the environment; the harmony can be perfect whatever the range of claims and of control. But then the concept of readaptation to a changed environment loses its seeming precision. By an analogy with biological theories, the meaning that is given to readaptation in sociology is usually this, that the individual attains in the new conditions a range of control and claims relatively equal to those he had in the old conditions. This equality is not particularly difficult to determine in biology where for every organism a certain minimum can be fixed and the living being seldom goes far beyond this minimum. But how shall we fix a minimum of claims and control in social life? And without this the meaning of equality of range of adaptation becomes very unclear.

The real point is not adaptation as a state reached at a certain moment, but the process of the widening or narrowing of the sphere of adaptation. And this depends essentially upon the individual himself, not upon his environment. If the individual is satisfied with what he can get out of the given conditions he will not try to set and solve new problems, to see more in the situations he meets than he used to see or to find in his environment a greater complexity of situations than he used to find. The dissatisfaction which the individual feels with what he can get out of given conditions arises frequently, indeed, when an external change makes it impossible to get the same results with the same efforts, but even then the individual may as well resign the results as increase his efforts. The course he selects depends on the prevalence of the desire for new experience over the desire for stability, the first pushing him to find new methods and to widen the sphere of activity in order to preserve the old claims, the second tending to preserve the old form and range of activity in spite of the changed conditions and to be satisfied with the results that can be obtained in this way. But in modern human society dissatisfaction with the given is far more frequently expressed as desire for the new, and even external changes in the given conditions are often only an unconscious or conscious pretext to satisfy this desire by justifying the individual in leaving these conditions for others. A typical example is emigration. Thus, in Poland the conditions of the peasants' life are now much better, in spite of the rapid increase of population with which the growth of cities does not keep pace, than they were fifty years ago. But the subjective tendencies are not the same. A desire for economic progress has arisen, the opening of new fields for the satisfaction of this desire provokes a latent dissatisfaction with the old life, and the slightest change for the worse, which could be remedied with a little effort, is often enough to make the peasant start to America.

With the formation of schemes it is different. A new scheme which the individual finds to express his new way of defining situations is not the result of the desire for new experience, but, on the contrary, the result of the desire for stability. Behavior that is not schematized, not generalized, but is or seems to be different from moment to moment and in disaccordance with the previously recognized rules calls after a time for recognition and justification, provokes a desire for a settlement. Moreover there are always plans to be made for the future requiring a conscious stabilization of the individual's own activity. And thus, even independently of social demands which make the individual search for security in determined systems and which we shall study presently, the individual, after a longer or shorter period during which new forms of behavior are developed, wants to fix his acquisition in a stable formula. And when such a moment comes, if the individual is unable to create his own scheme, he is ready to accept any one that is given to him and expresses more or less adequately his new way of defining situations. This explains such striking cases as the sudden "conversion" of individuals whose intellectual level is much above the doctrine to which they are converted, the influence that people of a limited intellectual power but of strong convictions can occasionally exercise over much more profound, but doubting personalities, and the incomprehensible social success of self-satisfied mediocrities during periods of intellectual unrest. Anything may become preferable to mental uncertainty.

Although there seems to be little difference between the schemes spontaneously created or selected by the individual and the schemes imposed by society, in the sense that both correspond to the way in which the individual actually does define situations, the different processes of development lead to the formation of quite opposite life-organizations. It is clear that if the individual learns to adapt his attitudes to the schemes given him he will always be dependent upon society and its ready schemes, and if society succeeds in imposing upon him a complete life-organization and in adapting his character to this, no further development will be possible for him unless his environment works out some new scheme; but even then it will be difficult for him to adapt himself to this new scheme in the degree that his life-organization and character have become stabilized. Or if he is temperamentally inclined to change he will pass from one form of behavior to another according to the schemes that actually happen to come in his way. A Philistine or Bohemian life-organization is thus the necessary result of this process in which schemes are imposed and attitudes are made to fit them. Bolshevism is really nothing but the disorganization of a society that was organized exclusively for Philistinism. On the contrary the individual who has learned to work out new schemes spontaneously will not be stopped in his evolution by the non-existence of a ready scheme nor disorganized at periods of social crisis, but will be able to construct progressively better schemes to suit his spontaneous evolution. His desire for stability itself will lead him not to a limitation of his desire for new experience in conformity with a fixed, externally-given scheme, but to the elaboration of schemes that will be wide and dynamic enough to permit a development of behavior within their limits; we shall study presently the nature of these schemes. Thus an organization of life in view of creation is the result of the spontaneity of the process in which the individual elaborates schemes to fit his developing attitudes.

3. We pass now to the social aspect of the problem of personal evolution. We have seen that the social group tends to fit the individual perfectly into the existing organization and to produce a definite character as rapidly as possible. This character must also be stable, so that no surprises need be anticipated from its future development; simple, so that any member of the group, however limited his mental capacities, can understand it at once; presenting a perfect unity, in spite of the multiplicity of individual activities; based on attitudes common to all members and socially desirable, so that each member shall appreciate it positively. In other words, in its demands upon personal character society aims to stop individual evolution as early as possible, to limit the complexity of each personality as much as is compatible with the variety of interests which it is required to possess, to exclude all real or apparent irrationality of its manifestations in different fields of social civilization, to reduce the differences between personalities to a minimum compatible with the social division of classes and professions.

The tendency of society to produce such characters in its members is most efficient when the social environment is a primary group in which all his activities are enclosed. In such a group, as, for instance, a peasant community, all the individual interests are supposed to be subordinated to the predominant social interest, because all the values—hedonistic, economic, intellectual, æsthetic—which are within the reach of the individual are included in the stock of civilization of his primary group and controlled by it. Every cultural problem reaches the individual only through the mediacy of this group, which, because of the immediate character of the relations between its members, is for each member the primary and fundamental complex of values; all other values are continually referred to this complex and draw their positive or negative character directly from this reference. The continual tendency of social education in such a group is to have each individual appreciate every object from the standpoint of the attitude of the group toward this object. Every situation is first of all treated as a social situation and only secondarily as an economic, religious, sexual, æsthetic intellectual one.

The adaptation of the individual to the primary group requires, therefore, that all his attitudes be subordinated to those by which the group itself becomes for him a criterion of all values. These fundamental social attitudes are the *desire for response,* corresponding to the family system in the primary group-organization, and the *desire for recognition,* corresponding to the traditionally standardized systems of social values upon which the social opinion of the community bases its appreciations. The desire for response is the tendency to obtain a direct positive personal reaction to an action whose object is another individual; the desire for recognition is the tendency to obtain a direct or indirect positive appreciation of any action, whatever may be its object. The desire for response is the common socio-psychological element of all those attitudes by which an individual tends to adapt himself to the attitudes of other individuals —family affection, friendship, sexual love, humility, personal subordination and imitation, flattery, admirative attachment of inferior to superior, etc. Of course each of the attitudes indicated by these terms is usually more or less compound and contains other elements besides the desire for response. Those other elements may range with regard to their social bearing from the most altruistic and self-sacrificing love of another personality, becoming almost independent of the response actually obtained, to the most calculating and egotistic tendency to use the responses of the other personality as mere instruments for the attainment of social ends; and yet the desire for response as such and independently of its further consequences is hardly ever absent even in the most radical examples of these contradictory attitudes. It is clearly an egotistic attitude and yet it contains a minimum of altruistic considerations. Its egotistic side makes it the most general and on the average the strongest of all those attitudes by which harmony is maintained and dissension avoided between the members of a group; it may be qualified, therefore, as representing the lowest possible, and yet precisely, therefore, in the large mass of mankind, the most efficient positive type of *emotional morality.*

The desire for recognition is the common element of all those attitudes by which the individual tends to impose the positive appreciation of his personality upon the group by adapting his activities to the social standards of valuation recognized by the group. It is found, more or less connected with other attitudes, in showing-off, pride, honor, feeling of self-righteousness, protection of inferiors, snobbishness, cabotinism, vanity, ambition, etc. It is the most common and most elementary, and probably the strongest factor pushing the individual to realize the highest demands which the group puts upon personal conduct, and, therefore, constitutes probably the primary source of *rational morality.*

These two fundamental social attitudes supplement each other, in normal conditions, in producing the general basis for a unified character, such as is needed in and demanded by the primary group. If they sometimes conflict—as when the desire for recognition impels the individual to ignore the attitudes of his family when its standing in the community is low—the existence of a conflict usually shows a certain disorganization of the primary group itself; as long as the latter is consistent and strong the two fundamental social attitudes are more apt to strengthen each other than to conflict; for instance, family solidarity in the peasant community is one of the grounds of recognition, and a high recognition shown to a member by the community may produce in the relatives of this member a readiness to respond to him proportionate to the degree in which they are influenced by social opinion.

It is clear that an individual dominated by these attitudes, if he stays permanently within a primary group, can develop the very kind of character which society requires. His personality will be relatively stabilized at an early period—a good example is the precocious maturity of young people of the peasant class—his character will be relatively simple, because primarily constituted by attitudes on the ground of which he can get response and recognition of many members of the group; *i.e.,* by the most average and commonplace attitudes; it will present few, if any, important conflicts, for conflicts appear when the individual has many incompatible interests, whereas here all interests are subordinated to the social interest; finally, it will be positively appreciated by the whole group, since all the members of the latter possess and want to possess in a large measure similar tendencies.

But such a stabilization and unification of character on the ground of the desires for response and recognition becomes more and more rare with the progress of civilization. Even in the still existing primary groups it tends to diminish as members of these groups get in contact with the external world. Every attempt of a member of such a group to define his situations from the standpoint of his hedonistic, economic, religious, intellectual, instead of his social attitudes, is in fact a break in his character, and such attempts become more and more frequent as, through extra-communal experiences, the individual finds before him situations that are not connected with the primary group—for example, when in the city he has the opportunity of drinking without any ceremonial occasion, when he earns money by hired labor instead of working on the family farm, when he can have a sexual experience without passing through the system of familial courtship, when he learns anything alone by reading and not in common with the whole village from a news-bearer, etc. But since the educational factors of his new environment which might replace those of the old are not at first given him, and he is unable to develop a character by his own efforts, such new experiences destroy the old unity of character without constructing a new one, and we witness partial disorganization from which only gradually new types emerge —the economic climber, the student, etc. And then the problem assumes a new form.

A complex modern society is no longer in all its parts in immediate touch with its members. It is composed, indeed, of small groups whose members are in personal interrelations; but none of these groups can enclose all the interests of the individual, because each one has only a limited and specialized field. Therefore individual character can be no longer unified upon the basis of the general desires for response and recognition, for even if these desires always remain fundamental for social relations, they must be differently qualified in different groups. The kind of response and recognition the individual gets in his family, in his church, in his professional group, in his political party, among his companions in pleasure, varies within very wide limits. It is based now upon the special activities which constitute the object of interest of every special group. Therefore the ground of the unity of character must now be sought in attitudes corresponding to these activities; the character of the social personality can no longer be unified by a reduction of all special attitudes to a general social basis but by an organization of these attitudes themselves.

But the difficulty is that each limited and specialized social group tends to impose upon every member a specific character corresponding to its particular line of common interests, wants him to be mainly, if not exclusively, a family member, a religious person, a professional, a political party member, a sportsman, a drunkard, etc., and expects his other attitudes to be subordinated to one particular kind of attitude. The individual cannot satisfy completely the claims of any of these groups, and he may either yield to the old social claim that he should possess an early, fixed, stable and simple character upon which society can count, and satisfy completely the claims of a specialized group, or he may reject all claims together. In the first case he can attain a unity of character only at the cost of a narrowness of interests such as no member of a primary group, peasant or savage, ever knows. Examples of this are found among the professional types. Certain occupations, such as military service, school-teaching, the ministry, administrative service in a strongly developed bureaucracy, small shopkeeping, farming, housekeeping, tend to influence character in a measure sufficiently strong to produce types which in their fundamental features are similar in all societies. Occupational groups tend more and more to exclude from the sphere of their interests anything that is not directly connected with their "business," and an individual whose character is formed by a modern professional group is the narrowest type of Philistine the world has ever seen, particularly if the profession itself does not afford much opportunity for development.[1]

But even so, the narrowness of the occupational type has probably not yet attained the extreme limit it is able to reach—and would reach if evolution went on undisturbed in the same direction as in the last two centuries—because social tradition still preserves some of the remnants of the old primary group conditions, in which the individual is supposed to share all the interests of his social group, and the latter includes a large variety of interests. An occupational group of the type of a mediæval guild, though not satisfying all individual interests as completely as a peasant community, appealed nevertheless to many interests besides the professional ones; it controlled individual character rather tyrannically, imposed a very definite complex of attitudes, but the complex was much less narrow than, for instance, the one which in recent times was imposed upon a Prussian army officer. In the past the occupational group put both negative and positive demands as to what character and interests its members should possess so as to uphold the standing of the group within the larger society of which it was a part by taking a definite standpoint toward the most important social problems, even those which did not belong in the special domain of the group's profession. But this type of occupational group, which seemed to be intermediary between the old primary group and the modern forms of social organization, is clearly decaying everywhere, in spite of the occasional efforts to revive it.

But precisely because of the growing specialization of occupational groups, cases of character formed exclusively by adaptation to one occupational group are becoming less and less frequent. The modern individual usually belongs to different groups, each of which undertakes to organize a certain kind of his attitudes. But it remains true that the way

[1] The exclusive pursuit of certain hedonistic (as distinguished from æsthetic) interests, represented by the gastronomer and seducer, tends, indeed, to produce narrow characters, and men of this type are, in point of fact, often Philistine in their general dispositions, but because of the difficulty of finding groups in which these interests are exclusively pursued, and because of the social condemnation attached to them, they are usually pushed into Bohemianism.

in which these various complexes of attitudes are combined usually shows a complete lack of organization. An individual of this type is a completely different man in his shop, in his family, with his boon companions, preserving his balance by distributing his interests between different social groups, until it is impossible to understand how such a multiplicity of disconnected, often radically conflicting characters, can co-exist in what seems to be one personality. This is a new style Philistinism—the Philistinism of the dissociated personality, amounting to a sort of stabilized Bohemianism. And a striking feature of modern society, showing how little reflective attention is paid to the problem of developing organized and rich human personalities, is the fact that society does not notice this chaotic and mechanical stabilization of the character of its member, provided he shows himself properly adapted to the minimum demands of each of the special groups to which he belongs, and does not give an undue prevalence to one of his particular characters at the expense of others. The weakness of this Philistinism, in spite of the seeming broadness of interests which the Philistine exhibits, shows itself at periods of social crisis when old special groups break down. Each such breakdown brings a complete disorganization of the corresponding attitudes. A striking recent example is the sudden decay of intellectual life in American colleges and universities during the present war; all those members whose intellectual attitudes were organized in an exclusive adaptation to the routine of the institution and to the common educational pursuits of their limited intellectual milieu lost temporarily all ability to do productive work as soon as this routine was interrupted and the common pursuits dropped or diminished in vitality—unless they found in war work a milieu with intense common interests of another kind to which they were forced to adapt themselves. A wider and more complex example of a disorganization of individual characters resulting from a dissolution of common standards and pursuits in special groups is the often described and emphasized "lack of character" of the Russian middle and higher classes since the old social interests lost their influence on individuals. We may even make a more general supposition: The "moral unrest" so deeply penetrating all western societies, the growing vagueness and indecision of personalities, the almost complete disappearance of the "strong and steady character" of old times, in sort, the rapid and general increase of Bohemianism and Bolshevism in all societies, is an effect of the fact that not only the early primary group controlling all interests of its members on the general social basis, not only the occupational group of the mediæval type controlling most of the interests of its members on a professional basis, but even the special modern group dividing with many others the task of organizing permanently the attitudes of each of its members, is more and more losing ground. The pace of social evolution has become so rapid that special groups are ceasing to be permanent and stable enough to organize and maintain organized complexes of attitudes of their members which correspond to their common pursuits. In other words, society is gradually losing all its old machinery for the determination and stabilization of individual characters.

But under these conditions it is both illogical and impractical to continue to treat the formation of stable characters as the chief aim of social education. Our pedagogical and ethical concepts and methods correspond to a stage of civilization when individual attitudes were sufficiently stabilized at an age between sixteen and twenty-five to permit practical reflection and social control to ignore their subsequent evolution as insignificant. It was then all right to identify social maturity and stabilization of character, to assign to both a term approximately coincident with physical maturity, and to consider the period of change preceding stabilization as a mere preparation for the latter. But when the limit of an even approximate fixation of attitudes is pushed further and further, when the individual continues to evolve psychologically long after having reached biological maturity and social productivity, the social importance of the period during which he is changing increases at the expense of the period during which he remains approximately stable. For a modern civilized personality the fixation of character begins to identify itself more and more not with the attainment of maturity, but with old age; it no longer expresses the establishment of full civilized life but corresponds with retirement from active civilized life, to a growing passivity and limitation of social interests. The center of pedagogical and ethical attention must, therefore, be entirely shifted; not attainment of stability, but organization of the very process of personal evolution for its own sake should be the conscious task of social control. At the present moment society not only lacks any methods by which it could actually and continuously organize the change of attitudes of its members, but it is only beginning (in our experimental schools) to search consistently for methods of education by which the individual can be trained in his youth to organize his later evolution spontaneously and without social help. At present the individual who succeeds in producing for himself such a dynamic organization has to do it by his own devices, is forced to invent for himself all the methods of self-education which he needs without profiting by the past experiences of others, and must consider himself lucky if his environment does not interfere with him too efficiently by trying to impose upon him a stable character.

4. The chief social problem arising with reference to the relation between individual life-organization and social organization is the reconciliation of the stability of social systems with the efficiency of individual activities, and the most significant feature of social evolution in this line is the growing difficulty of maintaining a stable social organization in the face of the increasing importance which individual efficiency assumes in all domains of cultural life.

In early societies we find individual efficiency entirely subordinated to the demand for social stability. All the social schemes of the group are connected, are parts of one whole, one large complex of social tradition, and any innovation is considered a break not only of the one particular scheme which it modifies, but of this entire complex. There is, of course, no objective rational ground whatever for taking the traditional schemes *en bloc*, no finalistic connection between the corresponding activities; the real results of a change of practical methods in a certain line may have little or no bearing on the results of other traditional forms of behavior. Thus, a modification introduced into some social ceremony has nothing to do objectively with the technique of hunting or warfare, a new technical device in constructing houses has no direct effect upon the political organization of the group, etc. But the common bond between all these schemes lies in the character of sacredness which all of them possess in the eyes of the group as parts of the same traditional stock whose unity is ultimately founded on the unity and continuity of the group itself. The individual must make each and all of these schemes his own in order to be a full member of the group. If for the formation of his character the important point is that all his interests are satisfied within the group and therefore are supposed to be founded on his social interest, the essential thing about his life-organization is that he is supposed to share in all the interests of his group and to adopt all social schemes as schemes of his personal behavior. There may be some differentiation between individuals as to the relative importance which certain particular interests assume in their lives, but no specialization in the sense of an absorption by some particular interests to the exclusion of others. Each member of a primary group is by a gradual initiation introduced into all the domains which compose the civilization of the group and is as all-sided in his activities as the stage of civilization which his group has reached permits him to be.

But this all-sidedness is attained at the cost of efficiency. There is a maximum of efficiency in each line which no member of the group can transgress, not because—as is the case on a higher level of culture—a higher efficiency in one particular line would impair his activities in other lines in which he is also expected to be active, but because in each particular line the domination of traditional schemes excludes not only the creation of new and better working schemes, but limits even the possibility of extending old methods to new classes of problems. The only increase of efficiency which is allowed and encouraged is the more and more perfect solution of traditional problems—an increase whose results are well exemplified in the perfection of primitive art and technique, in elaborate religious rituals, in the reliability of information which much of primitive knowledge shows, in the perfect rational order presented by many complex early systems of social and political organization, etc. Under these conditions, spontaneous social evolution is possible only by an agglomeration of small changes which are not noticed at once but modify from generation to generation the stock of traditions while leaving the illusion of its identity. When, on the contrary, the primary group is brought rapidly into contact with the outside world with its new and rival schemes, the entire old organization is apt to break down at once, precisely because all the old schemes were interconnected in social consciousness; and the individual whose life-organization was based on the organization of his primary group is apt also to become completely disorganized in the new conditions, for the rejection of a few traditional schemes brings with it a general negative attitude toward the entire stock of traditions which he has been used to revere, whereas he is not prepared for the task of reorganizing his life on a new basis. This occurs very frequently with the European peasant who emigrates and we have given in our first two volumes examples showing that the peasants themselves realize the effect which the rejection of certain elements of this stock has on the total personal complex of schemes.

But with the growing social differentiation and the increasing wealth and rationality of social values, the complex of traditional schemes constituting the civilization of a group becomes subdivided into several more or less independent complexes. The individual can no longer be expected to make all these complexes his own; he must specialize. There arises also between the more or less specialized groups representing different more or less systematic complexes of schemes a conscious or half-conscious struggle for the supremacy of the respective complexes or systems in social life, and it happens that a certain system succeeds in gaining a limited and temporary supremacy. Thus, among the ancient Hebrews, in some European countries during and after the Reformation, and in the early American colonies, certain religious systems predominated over all other cultural complexes; in Russia and Prussia, up to the present war, a similarly dominant role was assumed by the state; in Poland and Bohemia during the nineteenth century the concept of nationality, determined mainly by language, historial tradition and the feeling of solidarity, constituted the chief ground of social organization and was supposed to dominate individual life-organization; in societies with a powerful economic development like modern England and America the leading part is played by industrial and commercial schemes. The family system was until lately supposed to be the exclusive foundation of individual life-organization for women. During the present war, military interests have almost everywhere taken the center of attention and imposed far-reaching modifications of the life-organization on all the members of western societies.

But it is clear from the above examples that no special social complex, however wide, rich and consistent, can regulate all the activities which are going on in the group; the predominance of a complex is not only limited in time and space, but always incomplete and relative. Moreover each of the broad complexes which we designate by the terms "religion," "state," "nationality," "industry," "science," "art," etc., splits into many smaller ones and specialization and struggle continue between these. The prevalent condition of our civilization in the past and perhaps in the present can thus be characterized as that of a plurality of rival complexes of schemes each regulating in a definite traditional way certain activities and each contending with others for supremacy within a given group. The antagonism between social stability and individual efficiency is under these circumstances further complicated by the conflicting demands put upon the individual by these different complexes, each of which tends to organize personal life exclusively in view of its own purposes.

Whenever there are many rival complexes claiming individual attention the group representing each complex not only allows for but even encourages a certain amount of creation, of new developments, within the limits of the traditional schemes, for a complex of schemes which excluded new experiences as it does in the primary group would be unable to maintain itself in its implicit or explicit contest with other complexes. Therefore the conservative groups which support any existing schematism want it to be alive, to be as adaptable to the changing conditions of life as is compatible with the existence of the traditional schemes. The amount of efficiency which a scheme makes possible varies, of course, with the nature of the scheme itself, with the rigidity with which the group keeps the mere form, with the rapidity of the social process. And thus society demands from the individual productivity in the line of his career; in morality it is seldom satisfied with passive acceptance of the norms, with their limitation to old and known actions, but usually wants their application to new facts coming under their definition; in custom it is glad to see every extension of tradition; in science or art it greets with satisfaction every new work done in accordance with the traditional system; in religion it meets with joy every revival which proves that the old emotions can stir some modern souls, every theoretic application of dogma which proves that the old conceptions can satisfy some modern intellects; in family life everything is welcome that can enliven the content without changing the form of relation between husband and wife, parents and children; in politics, in law, in economic organization, every reform increasing the efficiency of the existing system without modifying it in the slightest is highly appreciated.

The fact that most if not all social schemes are incorporated in more or less comprehensive and systematic complexes helps to maintain the feeling of their immutability. The unity of many special traditional complexes is still almost as firmly established in modern civilized society as is the unity of its total stock of traditions in a savage primary group. The breakdown of any scheme belonging to a traditional complex seems to imperil the complex itself. And the individual who might easily reject a single scheme will hesitate before rejecting the whole complex. How consciously and masterfully incorporation of the most insignificant schemes into a great system is often made is manifested by such examples as religion and legal state-control. In the Roman Catholic Church disaccordance with the apparently most insignificant detail of the system of beliefs or an infraction of any rule of behavior is supposed to produce estrangement from the congregation, because it involves in social consciousness a break with the whole system; the individual must either admit that he is in error, recant and recognize the scheme—at least in the form of a confession and penance—or consider himself outside the church. In the same way, by breaking any law or ordinance of the state the individual is considered a rebel against the whole system of legal state-control and loses in fact his rights as member of the group, since he may become the object of any violence decreed as punishment for this break; the punishment becomes thus a forcible recognition of the broken scheme. The same method, with only less consistency and less power to enforce obedience, is followed in morality, in class-organization, even in customs, as when one break of social etiquette is sufficient to disqualify a person as member of polite society, or one act opposed to traditional morals sufficient to make all "well-behaved" members of a group disclaim every connection with the offending member.

But such a traditional fixation of special complexes of schemes within which efficiency is required with the condition that all schemes remain recognized does not correspond at all with the spontaneous tendencies of individuals. First of all, the scheme represents for the evolving individual either the minimum of stability which he reaches after a period of changing active experiences, or the minimum of new active experiences which he reaches after a period of passive security. In other words, as long as the individual evolves, an activity regulated by the scheme and efficient within the limits of this regulation does not represent a definite level; it corresponds always only to an intermediary stage, either of progression from the passive acceptance of socially imposed situations toward a creative activity free from all subordination to schemes, or of regression in the opposite direction. The individual may indeed oscillate, so to speak, from relative passivity to relative creativeness without going far enough in the first direction to become entirely inefficient, and without becoming so efficient as to have to reject the scheme; the less radical these oscillations, the more the individual's conduct approaches the average prescribed by the scheme. Such an individual represents then a social model of behavior in the given sphere; he is the moderately productive conservative, the famous *juste milieu* type. Frequently, however, the individual goes on with a progressively intense and efficient activity, tries continually to find and to define new situations; his efficiency becomes then increasingly dangerous to the scheme, because even if activity begins in perfect conformity with the scheme, the accumulating novelty of experience sooner or later makes the scheme appear insufficient. There are innumerable examples of individuals who began creative activity with the firm intention of keeping within the limits of the traditional schematism and ended by rejecting it altogether. The history of morality, of science, of political and social reform, and particularly of religious heresies is full of such biographies. And therefore the social group which is the bearer of a traditional complex is mistrustful of the individual who is too creative, particularly as the majority is usually composed of personalities whose evolution tends to the opposite limit—to the purely passive acceptance of the formal elements of tradition and the repetition of old activities bordering on habit. In normal times this passivity may be scorned by the active part of the group, but at moments of crisis we find the group condemning all "imprudent" innovations and falling back upon the most abject Philistinism as upon the only absolutely unshakable basis of security.

The second difficulty concerning the adaptation of individual life-organization to the social complexes is the fact that while a complex has to be accepted or rejected in its entirety, since the group does not permit the individual to accept some schemes and to reject others, the individual in his spontaneous development tends to make a selection of schemes from various complexes, thus cutting across social classifications of schemes, and often including in his dynamic life-organization successively, or even simultaneously, elements which from the traditional standpoint may seem contradictory. This difficulty is increased by the fact that many—perhaps most—social complexes are not freely chosen by the individual, but their acceptance is either expected to follow from a position that the individual occupies in the group from birth—as member of a certain class, a certain race, as male or female, handsome or homely, etc.—or from a position which is imposed on him in his early youth through a certain moral code, religion or form of education, or, finally, from a position which he is forced to take in order to satisfy his elementary needs—for example, marriage or choice of a profession. There are complexes prescribed for the son and the daughter, for the bachelor and the married man, for the girl, the wife and the mother, for the society person and the member of a lower class, for the adherent of a religious creed and the atheist, for the professional in any line, for the city and the country inhabitant, for the householder, the tenant of an apartment and the roomer, for the person who eats at home, in a boarding house or in a restaurant, for the pedestrian, the car-passenger and the owner of an automobile, etc. The individual who has a complex imposed upon him or accepts it voluntarily is expected to show the prescribed amount of efficiency—neither more nor less—in all the activities regulated by the schemes belonging to the complex, and is not expected to perform any activities demanded by a rival complex, or to invent any new schemes which may seem to disagree with the accepted ones. More than this, he is often required to abstain from activities which, even if they do not contradict directly the existing schematism, may take his time and energy from the performance of the prescribed activities.

It is obvious that this type of social organization disregards entirely the personal conditions of efficiency. The organization of schemes in a traditionally fixed complex represents usually a degree of methodical perfection sufficient to obtain from individuals an average amount of efficiency, making each individual contribute in some measure to the maintenance of the existing social status, so that an activity organized in accordance with the complex is indubitably more productive socially than an unorganized one. But no socially fixed complex of schemes in whatever line—economic, political, moral, scientific, æsthetic, religious— can obtain from any individual the highest amount of efficiency of which he is capable, not only because it prohibits creation beyond the limits traced by the schemes, but also because it ignores both the differences of personal endowment which make one individual more capable of performing certain activities than others and the variations of personal evolution which make the individual more efficient in a certain line at one period of his life than at another. The organization of activities demanded by a social complex is both impersonal and changeless, whereas an organization which would fulfill the conditions of the highest individual efficiency would have to be personal and changing.

An unavoidable consequence of the now prevalent social organization is that the immense majority of individuals is forced either into Philistinism or Bohemianism. An individual who accepts any social system in its completeness, with all the schemes involved, is necessarily drifting toward routine and hypocrisy. A part of the system may satisfy his personal needs for a time, particularly as long as he is gradually assimilating and applying certain of its schemes, but the rest of the system will not correspond to his predominant aspirations and may be even opposed to them. If the development of life-organization goes on spontaneously, the individual is gradually led to realize the importance for his chief aims of even activities which originally did not appeal to him—his efficiency in the line of his main interest gradually spreads to many side lines— whereas if a life-organization is socially imposed, the personally uninteresting elements of the social complex cannot become personally attractive by being gradually connected with the interesting ones in the course of personal evolution, since this evolution is limited. As a consequence we find the original inefficiency along uninteresting side lines influencing even those activities in which the individual was actually interested at some period of his life, and the whole productivity in the given field drops below the minimum required by the group. In order to remain socially adapted, to avoid active criticism of the group, the individual has then to display in words interests which he does not possess and to invent all kinds of devices in order to conceal his lack of efficiency. This tendency to hypocrisy and pretense is greatly facilitated in such cases by the fact that the majority of the group is in a similar situation and is not only willing to accept any plausible pretension designed to cover individual inefficiency but even often develops a standardized set of "conventional lies" to be used for this purpose, which every one knows to be lies but tacitly agrees to treat as true.

If, on the contrary, the individual either refuses to accept certain of the schemes included in a social complex or develops some positive form of behavior contradicting in the eyes of society some of the schemes of the complex, he is forced to reject the complex in its entirety, and becomes thus, voluntarily or not, a rebel. His situation is then rather difficult, for society has not trained him to develop a life-organization spontaneously and the social organization of the type outlined above opposes innumerable obstacles to such a development. With rare exceptions, he can do nothing but adopt some other ready system instead of the rejected one. But then the same problem repeats itself, and every successive attempt at complete adaptation to a new system after rebellion is usually more difficult than the preceding ones, both because the personal demands of the individual become better and better defined in opposition to social regulation and because each particular rebellion undermines the prestige of social systems in general. The usual consequence of rebellion is thus Bohemianism, a permanent tendency to pass from one system to another, attracted at first by the personally interesting sides of a system and soon repelled by the personally uninteresting ones. The result is again unproductivity.

Under such conditions the appearance of a really efficient, creative personality is actually a very exceptional social happening, for it needs a very high personal ability and persistence to develop a dynamic individual organization for efficiency instead of adopting a static social organization for stability when social education has exclusively the second purpose in view, and only by a rare concurrence of circumstances individuals who have this high ability of developing without proper educational help happen to be left in peace to pursue their own self-made lines. And it is no wonder that the scarcity of creative individuals has led to the concept of the genius, and high efficiency is still treated as a prodigy.

15. Georg Simmel

The Metropolis and Mental Life

The deepest problems of modern life derive from the claim of the individual to preserve the autonomy and individuality of his existence in the face of overwhelming social forces, of historical heritage, of external culture, and of the technique of life. The fight with nature which primitive man has to wage for his *bodily* existence attains in this modern form its latest transformation. The eighteenth century called upon man to free himself of all the historical bonds in the state and in religion, in morals and in economics. Man's nature, originally good and common to all, should develop unhampered. In addition to mere liberty the nineteenth century demanded the functional specialization of man and his work; this specialization makes one individual incomparable to another and each of them indispensable to the highest possible extent. However, this specialization makes each man the more directly dependent upon the supplementary activities of all others. Nietzsche sees the full development of the individual conditioned by the most ruthless struggle of individuals; Socialism believes in the suppression of all competition for the same reason. Be that as it may, in all these positions the same basic motive is at work: the person resists to being levelled down and worn out by a technological mechanism. An inquiry into the inner meaning of specifically modern life and its products, into the soul of the cultural body, so to speak, must seek to solve the equation which structures like the metropolis set up between the individual and the supra-individual contents of life. Such an inquiry must answer the question of how the personality accomodates itself in the adjustments to external forces. This will be my task today.

The psychological basis of the metropolitan type of individuality consists in the *intensification of neurotic agitation* which results from the swift and uninterrupted change of outer and inner stimuli. Man is a dis-

From Simmel, *Sociology of Georg Simmel*, "The Metropolis and Mental Life" (Glencoe, Illinois: The Free Press, 1950), pp. 409-424. Translated by H. H. Gerth with the assistance of C. Wright Mills from "Die Grosstaedte und das Geitesleben," *Jahrbuch der Gehe—Stiftung zu Dresden*, vol. 9. Reprinted with the permission of The Free Press of Glencoe, Illinois.

tinguishing creature. His mind is stimulated by the difference between a momentary impression and the one which preceded it. Lasting impressions, impressions which differ only slightly from one another, impressions which take a regular and habituated course—all these use up, so to speak, less conscious energy than does the rapid crowding of changing images, the sharp discontinuity in the grasp of a single glance, and the unexpectedness of onrushing impressions. These are the psychological conditions which the metropolis creates. With each crossing of the street, with the tempo and multiplicity of economic, occupational and social life the city sets up a deep contrast with small town and rural life with reference to the sensory foundations of psychic life. The metropolis exacts from man as a discriminating creature a different amount of consciousness than does rural life. Here the rhythm of life and of sensory mental imagery flows more slowly, more habitually, and more evenly. Precisely in this connection the sophisticated character of metropolitan psychic life becomes understandable—as over against small town life which rests more upon deeply felt and emotional relationships. These latter are rooted in the more unconscious layers of the psyche and grow most readily in the steady rythym of uninterrupted habituations. The intellect, however, has its locus in the transparent, conscious, higher layers of the soul, it is the most adaptable of our inner forces. In order to accomodate to change and to the contrast of phenomena, the intellect does not require any shocks and inner upheavals; it is only through such upheavals that the more conservative mind could accomodate to the metropolitan rhythm of events. Thus the metropolitan type of man—which, of course, exists in a thousand individual varients—develops an organ protecting him against the threatening currents and discrepancies of his external environment which would uproot him. He reacts with his head instead of his heart. In this an increased awareness assumes the psychic prerogative. Metropolitan life, thus, underlies an heightened awareness and a predominance of intelligence in metropolitan man. The reaction to metropolitan phenomena is shifted to that organ which is least sensitive and quite remote from the depth of the personality. Intellectuality is thus seen to preserve subjective life against the overwhelming power of metropolitan life, and intellectuality branches out in many directions and is integrated with numerous discrete phenomena.

The metropolis has always been the seat of the money economy. Here the multiplicity and concentration of economic exchange gives an importance to the means of exchange which the scantiness of rural commerce would not have allowed. Money economy and the dominance of the intellect are intrinsically connected. They share a matter-of-fact attitude in dealing with men and with things; and, in this attitude, a formal justice is often coupled with an inconsiderate hardness. The intellectually sophisticated person is indifferent to all genuine individuality, because relationships and reactions result from it which cannot be exhausted with logical operations. In the same manner the individuality of phenomena is not commensurate with the pecuniary principle. Money is concerned only with what is common to all: it asks for the exchange value, it reduces all quality and individuality to the question: How Much? All intimate emotional relations between persons are founded in their individuality, whereas in rational relations man is reckoned with like a number, like an element which is in itself indifferent. Only the objective measurable achievement is of interest. Thus metropolitan man reckons with his merchants and customers, his domestic servants and often even with persons with whom he is obliged to have social intercourse. These features of intellectuality contrast with the nature of the small circle in which the unavoidable knowledge of individuality inevitably produces a warmer tone of behavior, a behavior which is beyond a mere objective balancing of service and return. In the sphere of the economic psychology of the small group it is of importance that under primitive conditions production serves the customer who orders the good, so that the producer and the consumer are acquainted. The modern metropolis, however, is supplied almost entirely by production for the market, that is for entirely unknown purchasers who never personally enter the producer's actual field of vision. Through this anonymity the interests of each party acquire an unmerciful matter-of-factness; and the intellectually calculating economic egoisms of both parties need not fear any deflection because of the imponderables of personal relationships. The money economy dominates the metropolis; it has displaced the last survivals of domestic production (Eigenproduktion) and the direct barter of goods; it minimizes, from day to day, the amount of work ordered by customers (Kundenarbeit). The matter-of-fact attitude is obviously so intimately interrelated with the money economy which is dominant in the metropolis that nobody can say whether the intellectualist mentality first promoted the money economy or whether the latter has been the determining factor of the former. What is certain is that the form of metropolitan life is the most fertile soil for this reciprocity, a point which I shall document merely by citing the dictum of the most eminent English constitutional historian: throughout the whole course of English History, London has never acted as England's heart but often as England's intellect and always as her money bag!

In certain seemingly insignificant traits which lie upon the surface of life the same psychic currents characteristically unite. Modern mind has become more and more calculative. The calculative exactness of practical life which the money economy has brought about corresponds to the ideal of natural science: to transform the world into an arithmetic problem, to fix every part of the world by mathematical formulae. Only money economy has filled the days of so many people with weighing, calculating, with numerical determinations, with a reduction of qualitative values to quantitative ones. Through the calculative nature of money a new precision, a certainty in the definition of identities and differences, an unambiguity in agreements and resolutions has been brought about in the relations of life elements—just as externally this precision has been effected by the universal diffusion of pocket watches. However, the conditions of metropolitan life are at once cause and effect of this trait. The relationships and affairs of the typical metropolitan man are so varied and complex that without the strictest punctuality in agreements and services the whole structure would break down into an inextricable chaos. Above all, this necessity is brought about by the agregation of so many people with such differentiated interests who must integrate their relations and activities into a many-membered organism. If all clocks and watches in Berlin would suddenly go wrong in different directions, even if only by one hour, all economic life and communication of the city would be disrupted for quite some time. In addition an apparently mere external factor: long distances, would make all waiting and broken appointments result in an ill-afforded waste of time. Thus, the technique of metropolitan life is unimaginable without the most punctual integration of all activities and mutual relations into a stable and trans-personal time schedule. Here again the general conclusions of this entire task of reflection become obvious, namely, that from each point on the surface of existence—however closely attached to the surface alone—one may drop a sounding into the depths of the psyche so that all the most banal externalities of life finally are connected with the ultimate decisions concerning the meaning and style of life. Punctuality, calculability, exactness are forced upon life by the complexity and extension of metropolitan existence and are not only most intimately connected with its money economy and intellectualist character. These traits must also color the contents of life and favor the exclusion of those irrational, instinctive, sovereign traits and impulses which aim at determining the mode of life from within instead of receiving the general and precisely schematized form of life from without. Even though sovereign types of personality, characterized by irrational impulses, are by no means impossible in the city, they are, nevertheless, opposed to typical city life. The passionate hatred of men like Ruskin and Nietzsche for the metropolis is understandable in these terms. Their natures discovered the value of life alone in the unschematized existence which cannot be defined with precision for all alike. From the same source of this hatred of the metropolis surged their hatred of money economy and of the intellectualism of modern existence.

The same factors which have thus coalesced into the exactness and minute precision of the form of life have coalesced into a structure of the highest impersonality; on the other hand they have promoted a highly personal subjectivity. There is perhaps no psychic phenomenon which has been so unconditionally reserved to the metropolis as has the blasé attitude. The blasé attitude results first from the rapidly changing and closely compressed contrasting stimulations of the nerves. From this, the enhancement of metropolitan intellectuality, also, seems originally to stem. Therefore, stupid people who are not intellectually alive in the first place usually are not exactly blasé. A life in boundless pursuit of pleasure makes one blasé because it agitates the nerves to their strongest reactivity for such a long time that they finally cease to react at all. In the same way, through the rapidity and contradictoriness of their changes, more harmless impressions force such violent responses, tearing the nerves so brutally hither and thither that their last reserves of strength are spent, and if one remains in the same milieu they have no time to gather new strength. An incapacity thus emerges to react to new sensations with the appropriate energy. This constitutes that blasé attitude which, in fact, every metropolitan child shows when compared with children of a quieter and less changeable milieu.

This physiological source of the metropolitan blasé attitude is joined by another source which flows from the money economy. The essence of the blasé attitude consists in the blunting of discrimination. This does not mean that the objects are not perceived, as is the case with the halfwit, but rather that the meaning and differing values of things, and thereby the things themselves, are experienced as insubstantial. They appear to the blasé person in an evenly flat and grey tone; no one object deserves preference over any other. This mood is the faithful reflection of the completely internalized money economy. By being the equivalent to all the manifold things in one and the same way money becomes the most frightful leveler. For money expresses all qualitative differences of things in terms of "how much?" Money with all its colorlessness and indifference becomes the common denominator of all values; irreparably it hollows out the core of things, their individuality, their specific value and their incomparability. All things float with equal specific gravity in the constantly moving stream of money. All things lie on the same level and differ from one another only in the size of the area which they cover. In the individual case this coloration, or rather decoloration of things through their money equivalents may be unnoticeably minute. However, through the relations of the rich to the objects to be had for money, perhaps even through the total character which the mentality of the contemporary public everywhere imparts to these objects, the exclusively pecuniary evaluation of objects has become quite considerable. The large cities, the main seats of the money exchange, bring the purchasability of things to the fore much more impressively than do smaller localities. That is why cities are also the genuine locale of the blasé attitude. In the blasé attitude the concentration of men and things stimulate the nervous system of the individual to its highest achievement so that it attains its peak. Through the mere quantitative intensification of the same conditioning factors this achievement is transformed into its opposite and appears in the peculiar adjustment of the blasé attitude. In this phenomenon the nerves find in the refusal to react to their stimulation the last possibility of accomodating to the contents and forms of metropolitan life. The self-preservation of certain personalities is bought at the price of devaluating the whole objective world, a devaluation which in the end unavoidably drags one's own personality down into a feeling of the same worthlessness.

Whereas the subject of this form of existence has to come to terms with it entirely for himself, his self-preservation in the face of the large city demands from him a no less negative behavior of a social nature. This mental attitude of metropolitan men we may designate, from a formal point of view, as reserve. If so many inner reactions were responses to the continuous external contacts with innumerable people as are those in the small town where one knows almost everybody one meets and where one has a positive relation to almost everyone, one would be completely atomized internally and come to an unimaginable psychic state. Partly this psychological fact, partly the right to distrust which men have in the face of the touch and go elements of metropolitan life, necessitate our reserve. As a result of this reserve we frequently do not even know by sight those who have been our neighbors for years. And it is this reserve which in the eyes of small town people makes us appear to be cold and heartless. Indeed, if I do not deceive myself, the inner aspect of this outer reserve is not only indifference but, more often than we are aware, it is a slight aversion, a mutual strangeness and repulsion which will break into hatred and fight at the moment of a closer contact however caused. The whole inner organization of such an extensive communicative life rests upon an extremely varied hierarchy of sympathies, indifferences, and aversions of the briefest as well as of the most permanent nature. The sphere of indifference in this hierarchy is not as large as might appear on the surface. Our psychic activity still responds to almost every impression of somebody else with a somewhat distinct feeling. The unconscious, fluid and changing character of this impression seems to result in a state of indifference. Actually this indifference would be just as unnatural as the diffusion of indiscriminate mutual suggestion would be unbearable. From both these typical dangers of the metropolis, indifference and indiscriminate suggestability, antipathy protects us. A latent antipathy and the preparatory stage of practical antagonism effect the distances and aversions without which this mode of life could not at all be led. The extent and the mixture of this style of life, the rhythm of its emerging and disappearing elements, the forms in which it is satisfied—all these with the unifying motives in the narrower sense, form the inseparable whole of the metropolitan style of life. What appears in the metropolitan style of life directly as dissociation is in reality only one of its elemental forms of socialization.

This reserve with its overtones of hidden aversion appears in turn as the form or the cloak of a more general mental phenomenon of the metropolis: it grants to the individual a kind and an amount of personal freedom which has no analogy whatsover under other conditions. The metropolis goes back to one of the large developmental tendencies of social life as such, to one of the few tendencies for which an approximately universal formula can be discovered. The earliest phase of social formations found in historical as well as in contempory social structures is this: a relatively small circle firmly closed against neighboring, strange, or in some way antagonistic circles. However, this circle is closely coherent and allows its individual members only a narrow field for the development of unique qualities and free, self-responsible movements. Political and kinship groups, parties and religious associations begin in this way. The self-preservation of very young associations requires the establishment of strict boundaries and a centripetal unity. Therefore they cannot allow the individual freedom and unique inner and outer development. From this stage social development proceeds at once in two different, yet corresponding, directions. To the extent to which the group grows—numerically, spatially, in significance and in content of life—to the same degree the group's direct, inner unity loosens, and the rigidity of the original demarcation against others is softened through mutual relations and connections. At the same time, the individual gains freedom of movement, far beyond the first jealous delimitation. The individual also gains a specific individuality to which the division of labor in the enlarged group gives both occasion and necessity. The state and Christianity, guilds and political parties, and innumerable other groups have developed according to this formula, however much, of course, the special conditions and forces of the respective groups have modified the general scheme. This scheme seems to me distinctly recognizable also in the evolution of individuality within urban life. The small town life in Antiquity and in the Middle Ages set barriers against movement and relations of the individual toward the outside, and it set up barriers against individual independence and differentiation within the individual self. These barriers were such that under them modern man could not have breathed. Even today a metropolitan man who is placed in a small town feels a restriction about similar in kind. The smaller the circle which forms our milieu is and the more restricted those relations to others which dissolve the boundaries of the individual are, the more anxiously the circle guards the achievements, the comportment of life and the outlook of the individual, and the more readily a quantitative and qualitative specialization would break up the framework of the whole little circle.

The ancient *polis* in this respect seems to have had the very character of a small town. The constant threat to its existence at the hands of enemies from near and afar effected that strict coherence in political and military respects, that supervision of the citizen by the citizen, that jealousy of the whole against the individual whose particular life was suppressed to such a degree that he could compensate himself only by acting as a despot in his own household. The tremendous agitation and excitement, the unique colorfulness of Athenian life can perhaps be understood in terms of the fact that a people of incomparably individualized personalities struggled against the constant inner and outer pressure of a de-individualizing small town. This produced a tense atmosphere in which the weaker individuals were suppressed and those of stronger natures were incited to prove themselves in the most passionate manner. This is precisely why it was that there blossomed in Athens what must be called, without defining it exactly, "the general human character" in the intellectual development of our species. For we maintain factual as well as historical validity for the following connection: the most extensive and the most general contents and forms of life are most intimately connected with the most individual ones. They have a preparatory stage in common, that is, they find their enemy in narrow formations and groupings the maintenance of which place both of them into a state of defense against expanse and generality lying without and the freely moving individuality within. Just as in the Feudal age, the "free" man was the one who stood under the law of the land, that is under the law of the largest social orbit and the unfree man was the one who derived his right merely from the narrow circle of a Feudal association and was excluded from the larger social orbits—so today metropolitan man is "free" in a spiritualized and refined sense, in contrast to the pettiness and prejudices which hem in the small town man. For the reciprocal reserve and indifference, the intellectual life conditions of large circles are never felt more strongly by the individual in their impact upon his independence than in the thickest crowd of the big city. This is because the bodily proximity and narrowness of space makes the mental distance only the more visible. It is obviously only the obverse of this freedom if, under certain circumstances, one nowhere feels as lonely and lost as in the metropolitan crowd. For here as elsewhere it is by no means necessary that the freedom of man be reflected in his emotional life as comfort.

It is not only the immediate size of the area and the number of persons which, because of the universal historical correlation between the enlargement of the circle and the personal inner and outer freedom, has made the metropolis the locale of freedom. It is rather in transcending this visible expanse that any given city becomes the seat of cosmopolitanism. The horizon of the city expands in a manner comparable to the way in which wealth develops; a certain amount of property increases in a quasi automatical way in ever more rapid progression. As soon as a certain limit has been passed, the economic, personal, and intellectual relations of the citizenry, the sphere of intellectual predominance of the city over its hinterland, grow as in geometrical progression. Every gain in dynamic extension becomes a step not for an equal but for a new and larger extension. From every thread spinning out of the city, ever new threads grow by themselves, just as within the city the unearned increment of ground rent, through the mere increase in communication, brings the owner automatically increasing profits. At this point, the quantitative aspect of life is transformed directly into qualitative traits of character. The sphere of life of the small town is, in the main, self-contained and autarkic. For it is the decisive nature of the metropolis that its inner life overflows by waves into a far flung national or international area. Weimar is not an example to the contrary, precisely because its significance was hinged upon individual personalities and died with them; whereas the metropolis is indeed characterized by its essential independence even from the most eminent individual personalities. This is the counterpart to the independence and it is the price the individual pays for the independence which he enjoys in the metropolis. The most significant characteristic of the metropolis is this functional extension beyond its physical boundaries. And this efficacy reacts in turn and gives weight, importance, and responsibility to metropolitan life. Man does not end with the limits of his body or the area comprising his immediate activity. Rather is the range of the person constituted by the sum of effects emanating from him temporally and spatially. In the same way, a city consists of its total effects which extend beyond its immediate confines. Only this range is the city's actual extent in which its existence is expressed. This fact makes it obvious that individual freedom, the logical and historical complement of such extension, is not to be understood only in the negative sense of mere freedom of mobility and elimination of prejudices and petty philistinism. The essential point is that the particularity and incomparability, which ultimately every human being possesses, be somehow expressed in the working out of a way of life. That we follow the laws of our own nature, and this after all is freedom, becomes obvious and convincing to others and to ourselves if the expressions of this nature differ from the expressions of others. Only our unmistakability proves that our way of life has not been superimposed by others.

Cities are, first of all, seats of the highest economic division of labor. They produce, thereby, such extreme phenomena as in Paris the renumerative occupation of the *quatorzième*. They are persons who identify themselves by signs on their residences and who are ready at the dinner hour in correct attire, so that they can be quickly called upon if a dinner party should consist of thirteen persons. In the measure of its expansion, the city offers more and more the decisive conditions of the division of labor. It offers a circle which through its size can absorb a highly diverse variety of services. At the same time, the concentration of individuals and their struggle for customers compels the individual to specialize himself into a function from which he cannot be readily displaced by another. It is

decisive that city life has transformed the struggle with nature for livelihood into an inter-human struggle for gain which here is not granted by
nature but by other men. For specialization does not flow only from the
competition for gain but also from the underlying fact that the seller
must always seek to call forth new and differentiated needs of the lured
customer. In order to find a source of income which is not yet exhausted
and to find a function which cannot readily be displaced it is necessary to
specialize one's services. This process promotes differentiation, refinement
and the enrichment of the public's needs, which obviously must lead to
growing personal differences within this public.

All this forms the transition to the individualization of mental and
psychic traits which the city occasions in proportion to its size. There is a
whole series of obvious causes underlying this process. First, one must
meet the difficulty of asserting his own personality within the dimensions
of metropolitan life. Where the quantitative increase in importance and
the expense of energy reach their limits, one seizes upon qualitative
differentiation in order somehow to attract the attention of the social
circle by playing upon its sensitivity for distinction. Finally, man is
tempted to adopt the most tendencious peculiarities that is the specifically
metropolitan extravagances of aloofness, caprice, and preciousness. Now,
the meanings of those extravagances do not at all lie in the content of
such comportment, but rather in its form of "being different," of standing
out in a striking manner and thereby attracting attention. For many
character types ultimately the only means of saving for themselves some
modicum of self esteem and the sense of filling a position is indirectly,
through the awareness of others. In the same sense, a seemingly insignificant factor is operating, the cumulative effects of which are, however,
still noticeable. I refer to the brevity and scarcity of the inter-human contacts granted to the metropolitan man, as compared with social intercourse in the small town. The temptation to appear "to the point," to
appear concentrated and strikingly characteristic lies much closer to the
individual in brief metropolitan contacts than in an atmosphere in which
frequent and prolonged association assure the personality of an unambiguous image of himself in the eyes of the other.

The most profound reason, however, why the metropolis conduces to
the urge for the most individual personal existence—no matter whether
justified and successful—appears to me to be the following: the development of modern culture is characterized by the preponderance of what
one may call the "objective spirit" over the "subjective spirit." This is to
say in language as well as in law, in the technique of production as well as
in art, in science as well as in the objects of the domestic environment
there is embodied a sum of spirit. The individual in his intellectual development follows this growth very imperfectly and at an ever increasing
distance behind it. If, for instance, we view the immense culture which

for the last hundred years has been embodied in things and in knowledge, in institutions and in comforts, and if we compare all this with the cultural progress of the individual of the same period—at least in high status groups—a frightful disproportion in growth between the two becomes evident. Indeed, at some points we notice a retrogression in the culture of the individual with reference to spirituality, delicacy, and idealism. This discrepancy results essentially from the successful growth in the division of labor. For the division of labor demands from the individual an ever more one-sided accomplishment, and the greatest advance in a one-sided pursuit only too frequently means dearth to the personality of the individual. In any case he can cope less and less with the overgrowth of objective culture. The individual is pressured into a negligible quantity. Perhaps this lies less in his consciousness than in his practice and in his totality of obscure emotional states derived from this practice. The individual has become a mere cog in an enormous organization of things and powers which tease from his hands all progress, spirituality and value in order to transform them from their subjective form into the form of a purely objective life. It needs merely to be pointed out that the metropolis is the genuine arena of this culture which outgrows all personal life. Here in buildings and educational institutions, in the wonders and comforts of space-conquering techniques, in the formations of community life, and in the visible institutions of the state is offered such an overwhelming fullness of crystallized and impersonalized spirit that the personality, so to speak, cannot maintain itself under their impact. On the one hand, life is made infinitely easy for the personality in that stimulations, interests, contents of time and consciousness are offered to it from all sides. They carry the person as if in a stream and one needs hardly to swim for oneself. On the other hand, however, life is composed more and more of these impersonal contents and presentations, they aim at displacing the genuine personal colorations and incomparabilities. This results in the individuals summoning the utmost in uniqueness and particularization, in order to preserve his most personal care. He has to exaggerate this personal element in order to remain audible even to himself. The atrophy of individual culture through the hypertrophy of objective culture is one reason for the bitter hatred which the preachers of the most extreme individualism, above all Nietzsche, harbor against the metropolis. But it is, indeed, also a reason why these preachers are so passionately loved in the metropolis and why they appear to the metropolitan man as the prophets and saviors of his most unsatisfied yearnings.

If one asks for the historical position of these two forms of individualism which are nourished by the quantitative relations of the metropolis, namely, individual independence and the elaboration of individuality itself, then the metropolis assumes an entirely new rank order in the world history of the spirit. The 18th century found the individual in oppressive bonds which had become meaningless—bonds of a political, agrarian, guild, and religious character. They were restraints which, so to speak, forced upon man an unnatural form and outmoded, unjust inequalities. In this situation the cry for liberty and equality, the belief in the individual's full freedom of movement in all social and intellectual relationships arose. Freedom would at once permit the noble substance common to all to come to the fore, a substance which nature had deposited in every man and which society and history had only deformed. Besides this 18th century ideal of liberalism in the 19th century through Goethe and Romanticism, on the one hand, and through the economic division of labor on the other hand, another ideal arose: individuals liberated from historical bonds now wished to distinguish themselves from one another. The carrier of man's values is no longer the "general human being" in every individual but rather man's qualitative uniqueness and irreplacability. The external and internal history of our time takes its course within the struggle and in the changing entanglements of these two ways of defining the individual's role in the whole of society. It is the function of the metropolis to provide the arena for this struggle and its reconciliation. For the metropolis presents the peculiar conditions which are revealed to us as the opportunities and the stimuli for the development of both these ways of allocating roles to men. Therewith these conditions gain quite a unique place, pregnant within estimable meanings for the development of psychic existence. The metropolis reveals itself as one of those great historical formations in which opposing streams which engulf life join one another with equal rights. At the same time, they branch again into their separate courses. However, in this process the currents of life, whether their individual phenomena touch us sympathetically or antipathetically, entirely transcend the sphere for which the judge's attitude is appropriate. Since such forces of life have grown into the roots and into the crown of the whole of the historical life in which we, in our fleeting existence, as a cell, belong only as a part, it is not our task either to accuse or to pardon but only to understand.[1]

[1] The context of this lecture by its very nature does not derive from a citable literature. The argument and its elaboration, the major cultural-historical ideas are contained in my *"Philosophie des Geldes,"* (The philosophy of money), Muenchen & Leipzig: Verlag Duncker & Humblot, 1922.

16. Emile Durkheim

On Anomie

I. Social Order and Anomie

No living thing can be contented, or even go on living, unless its wants are sufficiently harmonized with the means at its disposal. If these wants require more or something different than is available, they will constantly be thwarted and will be unable to function without pain. Now, a movement which cannot occur without pain tends not to be repeated. Tendencies which fail of fulfilment atrophy, and, since the urge to live is merely the resultant of all other tendencies, it cannot but weaken if these other tendencies lose their force.

In the case of an animal, at least under normal circumstances, this equilibrium between wants and resources is established automatically and spontaneously because it depends upon purely material conditions. The organism requires only that the quantities of matter and energy which are endlessly consumed in the mainteneance of life be periodically replaced by equivalent amounts, i.e., that replacement be equal to wear and tear. When the hole which living digs in its own resources has been filled up again, the animal is satisfied and asks for nothing more. Its reflective powers are not sufficiently well developed to conceive of aims other than those implicit in its physical structure. On the other hand, as the work required of each organ itself depends on the general condition of the life processes and on the necessities of organic equilibrium, the wear and tear involved in the use of the organ is regulated by its replacement and thus a balance is struck automatically. The limits of the one are the limits of the other; they are both alike registered in the very constitution of the living organism, which has no way of going beyond them.

The situation of man is different, however, for most of his wants are not at all, or at least not to the same degree, dependent upon his body. At the most, one can conceive as determinable the physical quantity of ma-

Sections I and II are translated by W. C. Bradbury, Jr. from Durkheim's *Le Suicide, Etude de Sociologie* (Paris: Felix Alcan, 1897). Reprinted by permission of the *University Observer* in which the translation first appeared, Winter, 1947. Sections III and IV have been taken from Durkheim's *The Division of Labor in Society*, translated by George Simpson (Glencoe, Illinois: The Free Press, 1947), pp. 353-373, 396-409. Reprinted by permission of The Free Press of Glencoe, Illinois.

terial nourishment that is essential for the maintenance of a human life. However, even this determination would be less precise and the scope for variable combinations of desires greater than in the preceding case of lower animals. For, beyond the indispensable minimum with which nature is willing to content herself when she functions instinctively, reflective thought, being more vigorous in man than in animals, leads man to imagine better conditions which then appear as desirable goals and incite his activity. However, we may admit that desires of this kind [bodily desires]¹ sooner or later reach a limit beyond which they cannot pass. Yet how is one to determine exactly the amount of well-being, of comfort, of luxury, to which a human being can legitimately aspire? In neither the organic nor the psychological constitution of man is anything to be found which sets a boundary to such propensities. The operation of the individual's life process does not require that those wants stop at one point rather than at another. This is proved by the fact that they have grown periodically since the beginning of history, that progressively fuller satisfaction has been given to them, and that, in spite of these changes, the average level of health has not declined. Above all, how is one to determine the manner in which these wants should vary according to social conditions, occupation, relative importance of services, etc.? There is no society in which they are satisfied equally at the different levels of the social hierarchy. And yet, in its essential characteristics, human nature obviously is the same for all members of society. Thus, it is not human nature which would be capable of setting such a variable limit to human desires [for well-being, comfort and luxury] as they require. Therefore, insofar as they depend upon the individual alone, these desires are boundless. In itself, disregarding all external forces which control it, our capacity for feeling (sensibilité) is a bottomless abyss which nothing could fill.

But then, if no external force limits our feeling, it can be by itself nothing but a source of pain. For unlimited desires are insatiable by definition, and it is not without reason that insatiability is regarded as a sign of morbidity. Since nothing restricts them, such wants are forever and infinitely outdistancing the means available for their satisfaction; hence nothing can appease them. An unquenchable thirst is a perpetually renewed agony. To be sure, the saying goes that it is characteristic of human activity to unfold without assignable end and to set up for itself aims which it cannot realize. But it is impossible to see how such a state of indeterminateness can be reconciled any more readily with the conditions of mental life than with the exigencies of physical life. Whatever pleasure man may experience in acting, moving, exerting effort, he still needs to feel that his efforts are not futile and that as he travels he

---

¹ Brackets are used throughout where the translator has added a word or phrase to the text in the interests of clarity.

gets somewhere. But one does not progress when one is moving toward no goal, or, what comes to the same thing, when the goal toward which one is moving is infinitely far away. If one's distance from the goal remains always the same, however far one has gone, the result is the same as if one were running on a treadmill. Even backward glances, and the feeling of pride which one may have as one looks over the ground already covered, can bring only an illusory satisfaction, since the distance still to be covered has not been reduced correspondingly. To pursue a goal that is by hypothesis unattainable is thus to condemn oneself to a perpetual state of discontent. No doubt man does hope against all reason; and, even when it is irrational, hope has its joys. Hence, it may sustain him for a while; but it cannot indefinitely survive the repeated disillusionments of experience. Now, what more can the future possibly offer than the past, since it is forever impossible to reach a place where a stand can be made, and since one cannot even approach the ideal at which one aims? Thus, the more one has and the more one wants, the more the satisfactions already attained have the effect only of stimulating, never of appeasing, one's wants. But in the first place, that is true only if one closes one's eyes sufficiently to remain unaware of the action's futility. Then, too, if this pleasure is to be felt and if it is even partly to assuage and disguise the painful anxiety by which it is accompanied, this endless striving must at least go on easily and without any obstacles. Let it be thwarted, and only the anxiety is left, together with the discomfort which it induces. Now, it would be miraculous if no insurmountable obstacle ever arose. Under these circumstances, one holds onto life only by an extremely slender thread, which may snap at any moment.

If the outcome is to be different, the first requisite is that bounds be set to the passions. Only then can they be harmonized with one's powers and consequently gratified. But since there is nothing within the individual which can set a limit to his propensities, any such limitation must come from a source outside himself. Some regulating power must play the same role with reference to the social wants that the physical organism plays with reference to the biological wants. In other words, this power must itself be a moral [social] force. For it was the awakening of the mind which began to upset the equilibrium in which the animal lay sleeping; thus mind alone can provide the means for restoring it. Physical checks would be useless here; human passions cannot be changed by physico-chemical forces. To the extent that appetites are not curbed automatically by physiological mechanisms, they cannot be halted except by a limitation which they themselves recognize as just. Men would not consent to limit their desires if they believed themselves justified in overriding the assigned boundaries. Yet they cannot prescribe this rule of justice to themselves, for the reasons we have indicated. They must receive it from an authority which they respect and before which they bow

spontaneously. Only society, whether directly and as a whole, or indirectly through one of its agencies, is in a position to play this restraining role; for it is the only moral power which is superior to the individual
and which he acknowledges as superior. Society alone has the authority
necessary to say what is right, and set for the passions the point beyond
which they are not to go. Furthermore, society alone can act as judge
to determine what reward should be offered to each group for the
performance of its particular social function, for the sake of the common interest.

And in fact, at every moment in history there exists in the mores
(*conscience des sociétés*) a vague notion of what the various social functions are worth, of the relative remuneration due each of them, and,
consequently, of the degree of comfort appropriate to the average worker
in each occupation. The various functions are ranked by public opinion
into a sort of hierarchy, and a certain coefficient of welfare is assigned to
each according to the place it occupies in the hierarchy. Traditionally,
for example, there is a certain mode of life which is regarded as the upper
limit to which the manual worker may aspire in his efforts to improve his
lot, and a lower limit below which we can hardly bear to see him fall
unless he has forfeited our respect. Both these limits differ as between
the urban and the rural worker, the domestic servant and the journeyman,
the commercial employee and the public official, etc., etc. Similarly, again,
people find fault with the rich man who lives as if he were poor, but
they condemn him also if he tries to acquire too many of the refinements
of luxury. In vain do the economists protest; it will always offend public
sentiment that any single person may consume in utterly needless waste an
over-large amount of wealth, and in fact it seems that this intolerance is
relaxed only in periods of moral confusion.[1]

There is, consequently, a very real set of rules which, though it does
not always have a legal form, nonetheless sets more or less precisely the
maximum standard of living which each class may legitimately seek to
attain. Yet the scale thus set up is by no means unalterable. It changes as
the total social income grows or diminishes, and in accordance with the
changes which occur in the mores of the society. So it happens that things
which look like luxury to one age no longer look so to another; that a level
of comfort which for a long time was granted to a particular class only as
an exceptional and superfluous right, now is regarded as absolutely necessary and a matter of strict equity.

Under this pressure, each person in his own orbit takes account in a
general way of the extreme point to which his ambitions may go, and
aspires to nothing beyond it. At least, if he respects the rule and submits to

---

[1] This condemnation nowadays is entirely of an informal moral character, and
seems to be scarcely capable of legal enforcement. We do not believe that any re-
introduction of sumptuary laws would be desirable or even possible.

group authority—that is, if he is of sound moral make-up—he feels that it is not right to demand more. An objective and a limit are thus marked out for human passions. To be sure, this determination has nothing either rigid or absolute about it. The economic ideal assigned to each category of citizens is defined by certain upper or lower limits between which there is a large area within which their desires may move about freely. But this area is not unlimited. It is just this relative limitation and the resulting moderation which make men content with their lot and at the same time spur them on moderately to improve it; and it is this contentment which gives birth to that feeling of serene yet active delight, to that enjoyment of being and living which, in societies as well as in individuals, is the sign of health. Generally speaking, everyone is then well adjusted to his station in life and desires only those things for which he can legitimately hope as the normal reward for his efforts. Moreover, a man is not thereby condemned to immobility. He can try to embellish or improve his life; but such attempts may fail without leaving him despondent. For, as he enjoys what he has, and does not put his whole soul into seeking what he has not, he may not succeed in getting all the new things he desired and hoped to acquire, without feeling that he has lost everything at the same time. The essentials he still has. The equilibrium of his happiness is stable because it is determinate and a few disappointments are not enough to upset it.

However, it would not be sufficient that everyone accept as equitable the hierarchy of functions as it is set up by the mores, if he did not also consider equally equitable the manner in which the individuals who are to perform these social functions are recruited. The worker is not adjusted to his social position if he is not convinced that he really has the position he deserves. If he believes he should in justice hold some other rank, the one he occupies cannot satisfy him. Thus it is not enough that the general level of wants for each social rank should be regulated by public sentiment; there must exist along with this another, more precise system of regulation which determines the manner in which the various ranks are to be opened up to individuals. And as a matter of fact, there is no society in which such regulation does not exist. It varies with time and place. Formerly it made birth the almost exclusive principle of social stratification; today it recognizes no native inequalities but those which stem from inherited wealth or personal worth. Yet beneath these widely varying forms this type of regulation has the same purport everywhere. Everywhere, too, it is effective only if imposed upon individuals by an authority which is superior to them—that is, by collective authority. For this control cannot operate without requiring sacrifices and concessions from one group or another—or more generally from all groups—in the name of public interest.

Certain writers, to be sure, have argued that this social pressure would become useless as soon as economic position ceased to be transmitted by inheritance. If, they have said, the inheritance system has been abolished and each person begins life with the same resources, if, therefore, the competitive struggle is joined under conditions of perfect equality, no one could consider the results of this struggle unjust. Everyone would recognize spontaneously that things are as they ought to be.

As a matter of fact, there is no doubt that, the closer we approach to that ideal equality, the less necessary social control will be. But this is only a question of degree. For one kind of heritage will always remain, namely that of natural endowments. Intelligence, taste, scientific or artistic or literary or industrial ability, courage, manual dexterity are powers which each of us receives at birth, just as the property-owner by inheritance receives his capital, or as the noble used to receive his title and feudal office. A moral discipline will still be needed to induce those least favored by nature to accept the inferior station in life which they owe to the accidents of birth. Some will go so far as to insist that everyone's share should be identical, that no advantage should be given to the more productive and deserving. But if that is to be the case, a very different yet equally vigorous discipline will be required to get these latter to accept treatment no better than that accorded to the mediocre and inefficient.

However, this discipline, like the type mentioned earlier, can be socially useful only if the people subjected to it believe it to be fair. When it is maintained only by habit and force, peace and harmony continue to exist only outwardly; the spirit of restlessness and discontent are latent; appetites, only superficially held in check, will soon break loose. This is what happened in Rome and in Greece when the beliefs on which rested the ancient organization of patriciate and plebs were shaken, and in our modern societies when the traditional aristocratic principles began to lose their former ascendancy. But this state of disturbance is unusual; it occurs only when society is passing through some abnormally disturbed period of transition (*crise maladive*). Normally, the social order is acknowledged as equitable by the vast majority of its subjects. Thus, when we say that an authority is required to impose this order upon the individuals, we do not imply at all that violence is the only means by which it can be imposed. Because this control is to restrain the passions of individuals, it must emanate from a power which can master these individuals; but it is equally true that this power must be obeyed from respect and not from fear.

Accordingly, it is not true that human activity can be freed of every restraint. Nothing in this world can enjoy such a privilege. For every being, since it is part of the universe, is relative to the rest of the universe; its nature and the way in which it manifests that nature depend not only upon itself, but also upon the other beings, which as a natural consequence, restrain and control it. In this respect, the only differences between inorganic matter and thinking beings are differences of degree and form. The unique characteristic of man is the fact that the check to which he is subjected is not physical but moral, that is, social. He receives his law not from a material environment which imposes itself upon him by brute force, but from a mind that is superior to his own, and whose superiority he realizes. Because the greater and better part of his life transcends the life of the body, he escapes the yoke of the body but becomes subject to that of society.

However, when society is disturbed or disorganized, whether by a painful crisis or by a fortunate but too sudden turn of events, it is temporarily incapable of exercising this influence upon the individual; and such conditions lead to those abrupt rises in the suicide curve which we have proved in a preceding section of this book.

As a matter of fact, in severe economic depressions there occurs, so to speak, a lowering in the social scale (*déclassement*), a process that flings certain individuals suddenly into a social position lower than that which they had previously occupied. They must reduce their demands, restrain their wants, learn to control themselves even more than before. All the fruits of society's "moral" influence upon them are lost as far as they are concerned; their moral education has to be started all over again. But this social process of remolding them to fit into the conditions of their new life and of teaching them to exercise this unwonted additional self-restraint cannot be completed overnight. Consequently, they are not adjusted to the situation which is thrust upon them. Even the thought of it they find unbearable; and this is the source of sufferings which lead them to abandon an impaired life even before they have had much actual experience with it.

The results are not different if the disturbance originates in an abrupt increase in power and wealth. Then, indeed, as the conditions of life are changed, the scale in accordance with which people's wants were controlled cannot remain unchanged; for it varies with the resources of society, since it determines roughly the share which is to go to each class of producers. Its gradations are overthrown; yet on the other hand, no new pattern can be quickly improvised. It takes time for public sentiment to develop a new social classification of people and goods. As long as the social forces thus let loose have not attained a new equilibrium, their relative social values remain indeterminate, and consequently all coordination is lacking for a while. People no longer feel sure about what is possible and what is not, what is just and what is unjust, which claims or aspirations are legitimate and which go beyond the bounds of propriety. As a result, there is nothing to which men do not lay claim. If the disturbance is at all profound, it affects even the principles which govern the distribution of individuals among the various occupations. For as the relations among the different parts of society are necessarily modified, the ideas which express these relationships cannot remain the same. Whatever class has been especially favored by the disturbance is no longer disposed to its former self-restraint, and, as a repercussion, the sight of its enhanced fortune awakens in the groups around and below it every manner of covetousness. Thus the appetites of men, unrestrained now by a public opinion which has become bewildered and disoriented, no longer know where the bounds are before which they ought to come to a halt. Furthermore, at just this moment they are in a state of abnormal excitement simply by virtue of the fact that general vitality is more intense. Because prosperity has increased, desires are inflamed. The richer prize offered to them stimulates them, makes them more exacting, more impatient of every rule, just at the time when the traditional rules have lost their authority. The state of rulelessness (*dérèglement*) or *anomie* is further heightened by the fact that human desires are less disciplined at the very moment when they would need a stronger discipline.

But under such circumstances their very unreasonableness renders it impossible to satisfy them. Overexcited ambitions always go on beyond the results achieved, whatever these may be, for they are not warned to go no further. Thus far nothing can appease them and all this excitement sustains itself perpetually without leading to any satiation. Above all, since this race toward an unattainable end can produce no pleasure but that of activity itself, if indeed there is any such pleasure at all, let it be blocked by an obstacle and one is left completely empty-handed. Now, it happens that at the same time the struggle becomes more violent and more painful, both because it is less regulated and because the competition is more intense. All classes are at grips with each other because there is no longer any established system of social stratification. Thus effort increases just when it becomes less productive of results. How, under these conditions, could the will to live do other than languish?

This explanation [of suicide] is confirmed by the singular immunity enjoyed by poor countries. If poverty protects people against suicide, it is because by its very nature it acts as a restraint. Whatever one may do, one's desires are obliged, in some measure, to reckon with the available resources; what one has acts in part as a guide in determining what one would like to have. Consequently, the less one possesses, the less he is inclined to extend endlessly the range of his wants. By subjecting us forcibly to moderation, poverty habituates us to it, and, besides, where mediocrity is a general condition, nothing occurs to excite envy. Wealth, on the other hand, by virtue of the power which it confers upon its possessor, creates the illusion that we can rise simply by our own efforts. By reducing the obstacles which are placed in our way, riches lead us to believe that such obstacles can be mastered indefinitely. Now the less a man feels himself restrained, the more intolerable any actual restraint seems to him. It is not without reason, then, that so many religions have glorified the benefits and the moral worth of poverty. Poverty is, indeed, the best school for teaching a man self-restraint. By obliging us to exercise constant discipline over our selves, it prepares us docilely to accept social discipline, while opulence, by overexciting the individual, always runs the risk of awakening that spirit of rebellion which is the very well-spring of immorality. To be sure, that is no reason for preventing humanity from improving its material condition. But if the moral danger entailed in every increase in comfort is not without remedy, it is still necessary not to lose sight of its existence.

II. Anomie in the Economic Sphere

If anomie only occurred in the forms indicated above, that is, in intermittent attacks and in the form of sharp disturbances [i.e., in depressions or sudden abnormal prosperity], anomie itself would not be a regular and constant factor in determining suicide rates, though it might well account for variations from time to time. However, there is one area of social life in which it is chronic, namely in the world of commerce and industry.

For a century, economic progress has consisted principally in liberating industrial relationships from all regulation. Until modern times, it was the function of a whole system of moral powers to control such relationships. In the first place, religion exerted an influence which was felt equally by workers and masters, poor and rich. It consoled the first, and taught them to rest content with their lot by teaching them that the social order is designed by Providence, that God Himself has determined the share each class receives, and inducing them to hope for a future world in which just compensation will be made for the inequalities of this life. Religion restrained the rich and powerful by reminding them that worldly interests are not man's all but should be subordinated to other, higher interests, and therefore do not deserve to be pursued without rule or moderation. Secondly, the state, by virtue of the control it exercised over economic processes and the subordinate role it assigned to them, restricted the impetus of economic interests. Finally, at the very core of the economic world itself, the craft guilds, by regulating wages, prices of products, and production itself, indirectly established the average level of incomes through which wants are, in the nature of the case, in part determined. In describing this system of economic order we do not wish to suggest it as a model to be followed. Clearly, without profound changes it could not fit present-day societies. We assert merely that it did exist, that it had useful results, and that there is nothing taking its place today.

In fact, religion has lost the greater part of its power over men. Governmental authority, once the regulator of economic life, has become its instrument and servant. The most contradictory schools of thought, orthodox economists and extreme socialists, are agreed upon reducing the state to the role of a more or less passive intermediary among the various groups in society. The former want to make it simply a guardian of private contracts; the latter leave to the government only the task of doing society's bookkeeping, that is, of recording the demands of consumers, passing them on to the producers, tallying the total income and distributing it according to a set formula. But both deny that it has any right to subordinate the other organs of society to itself and to co-ordinate all their activities for the attainment of any one dominant aim. On both sides it is asserted that the only, or at any rate the main, objective of nations should be industrial prosperity; this is implied in the dogma of economic materialism, which forms the basis of both these systems, ostensibly opposed though they are. And, as these theories merely reflect the state of public sentiment, industry, which was formerly regarded as one means toward a higher end, has become the supreme end for individuals as well as for whole societies. But then it came to pass that the appetites which [modern capitalistic] industry brings into play find themselves freed of all constraining authority. This apotheosis of material well-being, by so to speak sanctifying them, has placed economic appetites above every human law. People view any attempt to dam up the flood of their desires as a sort of sacrilege. Consequently, even that purely expediential control which the business world itself used to exert over them through the medium of guilds no longer remains in force. Finally, this unleashing of desires has been still further aggravated by the sheer development of industry and the virtually infinite expansion of the market area. As long as the producer could dispose of his output only in his own immediate neighborhood, the rather modest profit to be expected could not inflame any great surge of ambition. But now that he can almost claim the whole world as his customer, how can we expect that in the face of these limitless opportunities men will submit to such regulations of their wants as prevailed in an earlier day?

Thus arises the instability which is especially prevalent in this segment of society, but which has spread from there through all activities and groups. The fact is that there [in the world of commerce and industry] a state of disturbance and of anomie is constant, and, so to speak, normal. From top to bottom of the social scale, violent but indefinite and unfocused desires are aroused. Nothing could possibly appease them, since the goal they seek is infinitely far beyond anything they can attain. Reality seems worthless compared with what these fevered imaginations conceive to be possible; thus people abandon reality, only to abandon the possible when it in turn becomes real. They thirst for novelty, for unknown delights, for nameless sensations, which nevertheless lose all their zest as soon as they are experienced. Then, let the slightest reverse occur and men are powerless to bear it. The whole fever drops and people discover how futile the whole uproar was, and realize that any number of these novel experiences piled up indefinitely has not succeeded in accumulating a solid capital of happiness on which they might live in times of trial. The wise man, who knows how to enjoy the results he has attained without constantly feeling a need to replace them with others, finds in this mode of life something that helps him to hold onto life when the hour of adversity has sounded. But the man who always expected everything from the future, who has lived with his eyes riveted on what is to come, has nothing in his past to fortify him against the tribulations of the present; for the past has been to him but a series of way-stations which he passed through impatiently. He was able to blind himself about his own condition precisely because he continually counted on finding around the next corner that happiness which he had not yet encountered. But now his progress is halted; from this time on, he has nothing either behind or before him on which he can rest his gaze. Besides, sheer fatigue is enough to produce disillusionment, for it is difficult in the long run to avoid feeling the futility of an endless chase.

One might even ask whether it is not primarily this social-psychological condition (*état moral*) which makes economic crises so prolific of suicides. In societies where he is subjected to a healthy discipline, man resigns himself more readily to strokes of bad luck. Since he is already used to self-restraint and self-control, the effort required to impose on himself a little more forbearance costs him relatively little. But when every limitation is in itself odious, how can we expect that a more rigorous limitation should seem other than unbearable? The feverish impatience in which men live scarcely disposes them to resignation. When a man has no goal but that of driving continually past the point he has just reached, how grievous it is to be thrown back! Yet the very lack of organization [lack of social-moral control] which characterizes our economic system opens the door to all kinds of risks. As imaginations are avid for novelty and know no rule, they grope their way forward at random. Necessarily, the losses grow with the risks taken, and thus crises multiply at the very time when they are becoming more destructive.

And meanwhile, these tendencies have become so chronic that society has got itself used to regarding them as normal. People repeat endlessly that it is in the nature of man to be eternally discontented, to move ever forward without truce or rest toward an unknown destination. The passion for the infinite is presented every day as a mark of moral distinction, when in fact it can come into existence only in ruleless minds which elevate to the dignity of a rule the very rulelessness of which they are the victims. The doctrine of progress at any cost and as rapidly as possible has become an article of faith. But also, paralleling the theories which glorify the blessings of instability, there appear others which generalize the situation out of which they arise, declare that life is evil, and accuse it of producing more pain than pleasure and of seducing man with wholly delusive charms. And since it is in the economic world that this confusion is at its height, it is there also that it finds most of its victims.

The industrial and commercial occupations are, as a matter of fact, among those which produce the highest suicide rates. . . . Their rate is almost as high as that of the liberal professions, sometimes even exceeding it; above all, they are noticeably more afflicted than is agriculture. For farming is the occupation in which the oldtime regulative forces still make themselves felt most powerfully and into which the feverish excitement of business has penetrated least. It is agriculture which best recalls the former structure of the economic order. And the difference would be still more marked if, among the suicides in industry, the employers were distinguished from the workers, for the former probably are the principal group very strongly affected by anomie. The enormous rate in the rentier class (720 per million) shows clearly enough that it is the most fortunate who suffer most from anomie. Whatever compels subordination mitigates the effects of that condition. The lower classes at least have their horizon limited by those who stand above them, and by virtue of that very fact their desires are more determinate. But those who have only the void above them are almost bound to lose themselves in it, if there is no force to hold them back.

Anomie in our modern societies is, then, a steady and specific factor in suicide; it is one of the sources from which the annual quota is fed. Consequently, we are faced with a new type of suicide, which must be distinguished from the others. It differs from them in that it depends not on the manner in which individuals are attached to society, but on the way in which society controls them. Egoistic suicide arises from the fact that men no longer see any reason for staying alive; altruistic suicide from the fact that this reason seems to them to lie outside life itself; the third type of suicide, the existence of which we have just established, arises from the fact that their actions become ruleless and that they suffer from this condition. Because of its origin, we shall give to this last species the name anomic suicide.

Assuredly, anomic and egoistic suicide are not without kinship resemblance. Both result from the fact that society is not sufficiently strongly present to the individuals concerned. But the sphere from which it is absent is not the same in both. In egoistic suicide, it is from specifically collective activity that [the claims of and regard for] society are absent, thus leaving such activity destitute of both object and meaning. In anomic suicide, [the claims of and regard for] society is [are] missing from specifically private activities, thus leaving them without a restraining harness. Consequently, despite their similarity, these two types of suicide remain distinct from one another. We can render unto society all that is social in us, and still be unable to limit our desires; without being an egoist, one can live in a state of anomie, and vice versa. Furthermore, these two types of suicide do not recruit their main clientele from the same social milieus: the one is found primarily in the intellectual occupations, the world of thought, the other in the world of industry and commerce.

III. The Anomic Division of Labor

Up to now, we have studied the division of labor only as a normal phenomenon, but, like all social facts, and, more generally, all biological facts, it presents pathological forms which must be analyzed. Though normally the division of labor produces social solidarity, it sometimes happens that it has different, and even contrary results. Now, it is important to find out what makes it deviate from its natural course, for if we do not prove that these cases are exceptional, the division of labor might be accused of logically implying them. Moreover, the study of these devious forms will permit us to determine the conditions of existence of the normal state better. When we know the crcumstances in which the division of labor ceases to bring forth solidarity, we shall better understand what is necessary for it to have that effect. Pathology, here as elsewhere, is a valuable aid of physiology.

One might be tempted to reckon as irregular forms of the division of labor criminal occupations and other harmful activities. They are the very negation of solidarity, and yet they take the form of special activities. But to speak with exactitude, there is no division of labor here, but differentiation pure and simple. The two terms must not be confused. Thus, cancer and tuberculosis increase the diversity of organic tissues without bringing forth a new specialization of biologic functions.[1] In all these cases, there is no partition of a common function, but, in the midst of the organism, whether individual or social, another is formed which seeks to live at the expense of the first. In reality, there is not even a function, for a way of acting merits this name only if it joins with others in maintaining general life. This question, then, does not enter into the body of our investigation.

We shall reduce to three types the exceptional forms of the phenomenon that we are studying. This is not because there can be no others, but rather because those of which we are going to speak are the most general and the most serious.

The first case of this kind is furnished us by industrial or commercial crises, by failures, which are so many partial breaks in organic solidarity.

[1] This is a distinction that Spencer does not make. It seems that, for him, the two terms are synonymous. The differentiation, however, which disintegrates (cancerous, microbic, criminal) is very different from that which brings vital forces together (division of labor).

They evince, in effect, that at certain points in the organism certain social functions are not adjusted to one another. But, in so far as labor is divided more, these phenomena seem to become more frequent, at least in certain cases. From 1845 to 1869, failures increased 70%.[1] We cannot, however, attribute this fact to the growth in economic life, since enterprises have become a great deal more concentrated than numerous.

The conflict between capital and labor is another example, more striking, of the same phenomenon. In so far as industrial functions become more specialized, the conflict becomes more lively, instead of solidarity increasing. In the middle ages, the worker everywhere lived at the side of his master, pursuing his tasks "in the same shop, in the same establishment."[2] Both were part of the same corporation and led the same existence. "They were on an almost equal footing; whoever had served his apprenticeship could, at least in many of the occupations, set himself up independently if he had the means."[3] Hence, conflicts were wholly unusual. Beginning with the fifteenth century things began to change. "The occupational circle is no longer a common organization; it is an exclusive possession of the masters, who alone decided all matters. . . . From that time, a sharp line is drawn between masters and workers. The latter formed, so to speak, an order apart; they had their customs, their rules, their independent associations."[4] Once this separation was effected, quarrels became numerous. "When the workers thought they had a just complaint, they struck or boycotted a village, an employer, and all of them were compelled to obey the letter of the order. . . . The power of association gave the workers the means of combating their employers with equal force."[5] But things were then far from reaching "the point at which we now see them. Workers rebelled in order to secure higher wages or some other change in the condition of labor, but they did not consider the employer as a permanent enemy whom one obeyed because of his force. They wished to make him concede a point, and they worked energetically towards that end, but the conflict was not everlasting. The workshops did not contain two opposing classes. Our socialist doctrines were unknown."[6] Finally, in the seventeenth century, the third phase of this history of the working classes begins: the birth of large-scale industry. The worker is more completely separated from the employer. "He becomes somewhat regimented. Each has his function, and the system of the division of labor makes some progress. In the factory of Van-Robais, which employed 1692 workers, there were particular shops for wheelwrighting, for cutlery, for washing, for dyeing, for warping, and the shops for weaving them-

[1] Block, *Statistique de la France.*
[2] Levasseur, *Les classes ouvrières en France jusqu'à la Révolution,* II, p. 315.
[3] *Ibid.,* I, p. 496.
[4] Levasseur, I, p. 496.
[5] *Ibid.,* I, p. 504.
[6] Hubert Valleroux, *Les Corporations d'arts et de métiers,* p. 49.

selves contained several types of workers whose labor was entirely distinct."[1] At the same time that specialization becomes greater, revolts become more frequent. "The smallest cause for discontent was enough to upset an establishment, and cause a worker unhappiness who did not respect the decision of the community."[2] We well know that, since then, the warfare has become ever more violent.

To be sure, we shall see in the following chapter that this tension in social relations is due, in part, to the fact that the working classes are not really satisfied with the conditions under which they live, but very often accept them only as constrained and forced, since they have not the means to change them. This constraint alone, however, would not account for the phenomenon. In effect, it does not weigh less heavily upon all those generally bereft of fortune, and yet this state of permanent hostility is wholly special to the industrial world. Then, in the interior of this world, it is the same for all workers indiscriminately. But, small-scale industry, where work is less divided, displays a relative harmony between worker and employer.[3] It is only in large-scale industry that these relations are in a sickly state. That is because they depend in part upon a different cause.

Another illustration of the same phenomenon has often been observed in the history of sciences. Until very recent times, science, not being very divided, could be cultivated almost entirely by one and the same person. Thus was had a very lively sense of its unity. The particular truths which composed it were neither so numerous nor so heterogeneous that one could not easily see the tie which bound them in one and the same system. Methods, being themselves very general, were little different from one another, and one could perceive the common trunk from which they imperceptibly diverged. But, as specialization is introduced into scientific work, each scholar becomes more and more enclosed, not only in a particular science, but in a special order of problems. Auguste Comte had already complained that, in his time, there were in the scientific world "very few minds embracing in their conception the total scope of even a single science, which is, however, in turn, only a part of a greater whole. The greater part were already occupied with some isolated consideration of a more or less extensive section of one certain science, without being very much concerned with the relation of the particular labors to the general system of positive knowledge."[4] But then, science, parcelled out into a multitude of detailed studies which are not joined together, no longer forms a solidary whole. What best manifests, perhaps, this absence of concert and unity is the theory, so prevalent, that each particular

---

[1] Levasseur, II, p. 315.
[2] *Ibid.*, p. 319.
[3] See Cauwes, *Précis d'économie politique*, II, p. 39.
[4] *Cours de philosophie positive*, I, p. 27.

science has an absolute value, and that the scholar ought to devote himself to his special researches without bothering to inquire whether they serve some purpose and lead anywhere. "This division of intellectual labor," says Schaeffle, "offers good reason for fearing that this return to a new Alexandrianism will lead once again to the ruin of all science."[1]

What makes these facts serious is that they have sometimes been considered a necessary effect of the division of labor after it has passed beyond a certain stage of development. In this case, it is said, the individual, hemmed in by his task, becomes isolated in a special activity. He no longer feels the idea of a common work being done by those who work side by side with him. Thus, the division of labor could not be pushed farther without becoming a source of disintegration. "Since all such decomposition," says Auguste Comte, "necessarily has the tendency to determine a corresponding dispersion, the fundamental partition of human labors cannot avoid evoking, in a proportionate degree, individual divergences, both intellectual and moral, whose combined influence must, in the same measure, demand a permanent discipline able to prevent or unceasingly contain their discordant flight. If, on the one hand, indeed, the separation of social functions permits a felicitous development of the spirit of detail otherwise impossible, it spontaneously tends, on the other hand, to snuff out the spirit of togetherness or, at least, to undermine it profoundly. Likewise, from the moral point of view, at the same time that each is thus placed in strict dependence upon the mass, he is naturally deterred by the peculiar scope of his special activity which constantly links him to his own private interest whose true relation with the public interest he perceives but very vaguely. . . . Thus it is that the same principle which has alone permitted the development and the extension of general society threatens, in a different aspect, to decompose it into a multitude of incoherent corporations which almost seem not to be of the same species."[2] Espinas has expressed himself almost in the same terms: "Division," he says, "is dispersion."[3]

The division of labor would thus exercise, because of its very nature, a dissolving influence which would be particularly obvious where functions are very specialized. Comte, however, does not conclude from his principle that societies must be led to what he himself calls the age of generality, that is, to that state of indistinctness and homogeneity which was their point of departure. The diversity of functions is useful and necessary, but as unity, which is no less indispensable, does not spontaneously spring up, the care of realizing it and of maintaining it would con-

[1] *Bau und Leben des sozialen Korpers,* IV, p. 113.
[2] *Cours,* IV, p. 429.
[3] *Sociétés animales,* conclusion, IV.

stitute a special function in the social organism, represented by an independent organ. This organ is the State or government. "The social destiny of government," says Comte, "appears to me to consist particularly in sufficiently containing, and preventing, as far as possible, this fatal disposition towards a fundamental dispersion of ideas, sentiments, and interests, the inevitable result of the very principle of human development, and which, if it could follow its natural course without interruption, would inevitably end by arresting social progress in all important respects. This conception, in my eyes, constitutes the first positive and rational basis of an elementary and abstract theory of government properly so called, seen in its noblest and greatest scientific extension, as characterized in general by a universal and necessary reaction, at first spontaneous and then regulated, of the totality of the parts that go to make it up. It is clear, in effect, that the only real means of preventing such a dispersion consists in this indispensable reaction in a new and special function, susceptible of fittingly intervening in the habitual accomplishment of all the diverse functions of social economy, so as to recall to them unceasingly the feeling of unity and the sentiment of common solidarity."[1]

What government is to society in its totality philosophy ought to be to the sciences. Since the diversity of science tends to disrupt the unity of science, a new science must be set up to re-establish it. Since detailed studies make us lose sight of the whole vista of human knowledge, we must institute a particular system of researches to retrieve it and set it off. In other words, "we must make an even greater specialty of the study of scientific generalities. A new class of scholars, prepared by suitable education, without devoting themselves to a special culture of any particular branch of natural philosophy, will busy themselves with considering the various positive sciences in their present state, with exactly determining the spirit of each of them, with discovering their relations and their continuity, with summing up, if possible, all their principles in a very small number of principles common to all, and the division of labor in the sciences will be pushed, without any danger, as far as the development of the various orders of knowledge demand."[2]

Of course, we have ourselves shown[3] that the governmental organ develops with the division of labor, not as a repercussion of it, but because of mechanical necessity. As organs are rigorously solidary where functions are very divided, what affects one affects the others, and social events take on a more general interest. At the same time, with the

---

[1] *Cours de Philosophie positive,* IV, pp. 430-431.

[2] This bringing together of government and philosophy ought not to surprise us, for, in Comte's eyes, the two institutions are inseparable. Government, as he conceives it, is possible only upon the institution of the positive philosophy.

[3] See above, Book I, ch. vii, §3.

effacement of the segmental type, they penetrate more easily throughout the extent of the same tissue or the same system. For these two reasons, there are more of them which are retained in the directive organ
whose functional activity, more often exercised, grows with the volume.
But its sphere of action does not extend further.

But beneath this general, superficial life there is an intestine, a world
of organs which, without being completely independent of the first,
nevertheless function without its intervention, without its even being
conscious of them, at least normally. They are freed from its action because it is too remote for them. The government cannot, at every instant,
regulate the conditions of the different economic markets, fixing the
prices of their commodities and services, or keeping production within the
bounds of consumptionary needs, etc. All these practical problems arise
from a multitude of detail, coming from thousands of particular circumstances which only those very close to the problems know about.
Thus, we cannot adjust these functions to one another and make them
concur harmoniously if they do not concur of themselves. If, then, the
division of labor has the dispersive effects that are attributed to it, they
ought to develop without resistance in this region of society, since there
is nothing to hold them together. What gives unity to organized societies,
however, as to all organisms, is the spontaneous consensus of parts. Such
is the internal solidarity which not only is as indispensable as the regulative action of higher centres, but which also is their necessary condition,
for they do no more than translate it into another language and, so to
speak, consecrate it. Thus, the brain does not make the unity of the
organism, but expresses and completes it. Some speak of the necessity of
a reaction of the totality of parts, but it still is necessary for this totality
to exist; that is to say, the parts must be already solidary with one
another for the whole to take conscience of itself and react in this way.
Else, as work is divided, one would see a sort of progressive decomposition produced, not only at certain points, but throughout society, instead
of the ever stronger concentration that we really observe.

But, it is said, there is no need for going into detail. It is sufficient to
call to mind whenever necessary "the spirit of the whole and the sentiment of common solidarity," and this action the government alone can
execute. This is true, but it is much too general to assure the concourse of
social functions, if that has not been realized by itself. In effect, what is
the point at issue? Is it to make each individual feel that he is not self-
sufficient, but is a part of a whole on which he depends? But such an
abstract, vague, and, withal, intermittent representation, just as all complex representations, can avail nothing against lively, concrete impressions
which occupational activity at every instant evokes in each one of us. If,
then, occupational activity has the effects that are adduced, if the occupations which fill our daily life tend to detach us from the social group

to which we belong, such a conception, which is quite dormant and never occupies more than a small part of the field of conscience, will not be sufficient to hold us to it. In order that the sentiment of our state of dependence be effective, it would be necessary for it also to be continuous, and it can be that only if it is linked to the very practice of each special function. But then specialization would no longer have the consequences which it is said to produce. Or else governmental action would have as its object the maintenance of a certain moral uniformity among occupations, the preventing of "social affections gradually concentrated in individuals of the same occupation from becoming more and more foreign to other classes, for want of sufficient likeness in customs and thoughts."[1] But this uniformity cannot be maintained by force and against the nature of things. Functional diversity induces a moral diversity that nothing can prevent, and it is inevitable that one should grow as the other does. We know, moreover, why these two phenomena develop in parallel fashion. Collective sentiments become more and more impotent in holding together the centrifugal tendencies that the division of labor is said to engender, for these tendencies increase as labor is more divided, and, at the same time, collective sentiments are weakened.

For the same reason, philosophy becomes more and more incapable of assuring the unity of science. As long as the same mind could, at once, cultivate different sciences, it was possible to acquire the competency necessary for their unification. But, as they become specialized, these grand syntheses can no longer be anything more than premature generalizations, for it becomes more and more impossible for one human intelligence to gain a sufficiently exact knowledge of this great multitude of phenomena, of laws, of hypotheses which must be summed up. "It would be interesting to speculate," Ribot justly says, "what philosophy, as the general conception of the universe, will be when particular sciences, because of their growing complexity, become overwhelming in their detail and philosophers are reduced to knowledge of the most general results, which are necessarily superficial."[2]

To be sure, there is some reason for judging as excessive this pride of the scholar, who, hemmed in by his special researches, refuses to recognize any other control. It is certain, however, that to gain an exact idea of a science one must practice it, and, so to speak, live with it. That is because it does not entirely consist of some propositions which have been definitively proved. Along side of this actual, realized science, there is another, concrete and living, which is in part ignorant of itself, and yet seeks itself; besides acquired results, there are hopes, habits, instincts, needs, presentiments so obscure that they cannot be expressed in words, yet so powerful that they sometimes dominate the whole life of the

[1] *Cours de philosophie positive*, IV, p. 42.
[2] *Psychologie allemande*, Introduction, p. xxvii.

scholar. All this is still science; it is even its best and largest part, for the discovered truths are a little thing in comparison with those which remain to be discovered. Moreover, in order to possess a good idea of the first and understand what is found condensed therein, one must have been close to scientific life while it was still in a free state; that is to say, before it became fixed in the form of definite propositions. Otherwise, one will have the letter, but not the spirit. Each science has, so to speak, a soul which lives in the conscience of scholars. Only a part of this soul assumes sensible bodily form. The formulas which express it, being general, are easily transmitted. But such is not the case with this other part of science which no symbol translates without. Here, all is personal and must be acquired through personal experience. To take part in it, one must put oneself to work and place oneself before the facts. According to Comte, to assure the unity of science, it would be enough to have methods reduced to unity;[1] but it is just the methods which are most difficult to unify, for, as they are immanent in the very sciences, as it is impossible to disengage them completely from the body of established truths in order to codify them separately, we can know them only if we have ourselves practiced them. But it is now impossible for the same man to practice a large number of sciences. These grand generalizations can rest only on a very summary view of things. If, moreover, we remember how slowly and with what patient precautions scholars ordinarily proceed in the discovery of even their most particular truths, we see that improvised disciplines no longer have anything more than a very feeble authority over them.

But, whatever may be the value of these philosophic generalities, science would not find therein the unity it needs. They well express what there is in common among the sciences,—laws, specific method,—but, besides these resemblances, there are differences which have to be integrated. We often say that the general holds in its power particulars that it sums up, but the expression is not exact. It contains only what is common to them. Now, there are no two phenomena in the world which resemble each other, simple as they may be. That is why every general proposition lets a part of the material it tries to master escape. It is impossible to establish the concrete characters and distinctive properties of things in the same impersonal and homogeneous formula. But, as long as resemblances exceed differences, they are sufficient to integrate the representations thus brought together. The dissonances of detail disappear in the total harmony. On the contrary, as the differences become more numerous, cohesion becomes more unstable and must be consolidated by other means. If we picture the growing multiplicity of special sciences, with their theorems, their laws, their axioms, their conjectures,

[1] *Op. cit.*, I, p. 45.

their methods of procedure, we shall see that a short and simple formula, as the principle of evolution, for example, is not enough to integrate such a prodigious complexity of phenomena. Even when these total views exactly correspond to reality, the part they explain is too small a thing beside what they leave unexplained. It is not, then, by this means that we shall ever be able to take the positive sciences out of their isolation. There is too great a chasm between detailed researches which are their backbone and such syntheses. The tie which binds these two orders of knowledge together is too slight and too loose, and, consequently, if particular sciences can take cognizance of their mutual dependence only through a philosophy which embraces all of them, the sentiment of unity they will have will always be too vague to be efficacious.

Philosophy is the collective conscience of science, and, here as elsewhere, the role of the collective conscience becomes smaller as labor is divided.

Although Comte recognized that the division of labor is a source of solidarity, it seems that he did not perceive that this solidarity is *sui generis* and is little by little substituted for that which social likenesses give rise to. That is why, in remarking that the latter were very much obliterated where functions are very specialized, he considered this obliteration a morbid phenomenon, a menace to social cohesion due to the excess of specialization, and by that he explained the facts of lack of coordination which sometimes accompany the development of the division of labor. But since we have shown that the enfeeblement of the collective conscience is a normal phenomenon, we cannot consider it as the cause of the abnormal phenomena that we are studying. If, in certain cases, organic solidarity is not all it should be, it is certainly not because mechanical solidarity has lost ground, but because all the conditions for the existence of organic solidarity have not been realized.

We know, in effect, that, wherever organic solidarity is found, we come upon an adequately developed regulation determining the mutual relations of functions.[1] For organic solidarity to exist, it is not enough that there be a system of organs necessary to one another, which in a general way feel solidary, but it is also necessary that the way in which they should come together, if not in every kind of meeting, at least in circumstances which most frequently occur, be predetermined. Otherwise, at every moment new conflicts would have to be equilibrated, for the conditions of equilibrium can be discovered only through gropings in the course of which one part treats the other as an adversary as much as an auxiliary. These conflicts would incessantly crop out anew, and, con-

[1] See Book I, ch. vii.

sequently, solidarity would be scarcely more than potential, if mutual obligations had to be fought over entirely anew in each particular instance. It will be said that there are contracts. But, first of all, all social relations are not capable of assuming this juridical form. We know, moreover, that a contract is not self-sufficient, but supposes a regulation which is as extensive and complicated as contractual life itself. Besides, the links which have this origin are always of short duration. A contract is only a truce, and very precarious; it suspends hostilities only for a time. Of course, as precise as this regulation may be, it will always leave a place for many disturbances. But it is neither necessary nor even possible for social life to be without conflicts. The role of solidarity is not to suppress competition, but to moderate it.

Moreover, in the normal state, these rules disengage themselves from the division of labor. They are a prolongation of it. Assuredly, if it only brought together individuals who united for some few moments to exchange personal services, it could not give rise to any regulative action. But what it brings face to face are functions, that is to say, ways of definite action, which are identically repeated in given circumstances, since they cling to general, constant conditions of social life. The relations which are formed among these functions cannot fail to partake of the same degree of fixity and regularity. There are certain ways of mutual reaction which, finding themselves very conformable to the nature of things, are repeated very often and become habits. Then these habits, becoming forceful, are transformed into rules of conduct. The past determines the future. In other words, there is a certain sorting of rights and duties which is established by usage and becomes obligatory. The rule does not, then, create the state of mutual dependence in which solidary organs find themselves, but only expresses in clear-cut fashion the result of a given situation. In the same way, the nervous system, far from dominating the evolution of the organism, as we have already said, results from it.[1] The nerve-cords are probably only the lines of passage which the streams of movements and excitations exchanged between different organs have followed. They are the canals which life has hewed for itself while steadily flowing in the same direction, and the ganglia would only be the place of intersection of several of these lines.[2] Because they misunderstood this aspect of the phenomena, certain moralists have claimed that the division of labor does not produce true solidarity. They have seen in it only particular exchanges, ephemeral combinations, without past or future, in which the individual is thrown on his own resources. They have not perceived the slow work of consolidation, the network of links which little by little have been woven and which makes something permanent of organic solidarity.

But, in all the cases that we have described above, this regulation

[1] Perrier, *Colonies animales*, p. 746.
[2] See Spencer, *Principles of Biology*, II, pp. 438ff.

either does not exist, or is not in accord with the degree of development of the division of labor. Today, there are no longer any rules which fix the number of economic enterprises, and, in each branch of industry, production is not exactly regulated on a level with consumption. We do not wish to draw any practical conclusion from this fact; we are not contending that restrictive legislation is necessary; we do not here have to weigh its advantages and disadvantages. What is certain is that this lack of regulation does not permit a regular harmony of functions. The economists claim, it is true, that this harmony is self-established when necessary, thanks to rises or declines in prices which, according to needs, stimulate or slacken production. But, in every case, this is established only after ruptures of equilibrium and more or less prolonged disturbances. Moreover, these disturbances are naturally as much more frequent as functions are more specialized, for the more complex an organization is, the more is the need of extensive regulation felt.

The relations of capital and labor have, up to the present, remained in the same state of juridical indetermination. A contract for the hire of services occupies a very small place in our Codes, particularly when one thinks of the diversity and complexity of the relations which it is called upon to regulate. But it is not necessary to insist upon a gap whose presence is keenly felt by all, and which everybody seeks to fill.[1]

Methodological rules are for science what rules of law and custom are for conduct; they direct the thought of the scholar just as the others govern the actions of men. But if each science has its method, the order that it realizes is wholly internal. It co-ordinates the findings of scholars who cultivate the same science, not their relations with the outside world. There are hardly any disciplines which bring together the work of the different sciences in the light of a common end. This is particularly true of the moral and social sciences, for the sciences of mathematics, physics, chemistry, and even biology, do not seem to be strangers to one another in this respect. But the jurist, the psychologist, the anthropologist, the economist, the statistician, the linguist, the historian, proceed with their investigations as if the different orders of fact they study constituted so many independent worlds. In reality, however, they penetrate one another from all sides; consequently, the case must be the same with their corresponding sciences. This is where the anarchical state of science in general comes from, a state that has been noted not without exaggeration, but which is particularly true of these specific sciences. They offer the spectacle of an aggregate of disjointed parts which do not concur. If they form a whole without unity, this is not because they do not have a sentiment of their likenesses; it is because they are not organized.

These different examples are, then, varieties of the same species. If the

---

[1] This was written in 1893. Since then, industrial legislation has taken a more important place in our law. This is proof of how serious the gap was, and that there was need of its being filled.

division of labor does not produce solidarity in all these cases, it is because the relations of the organs are not regulated, because they are in
a state of *anomie.*

But whence comes this state?

Since a body of rules is the definite form which spontaneously established relations between social functions take in the course of time, we
can say, *a priori,* that the state of *anomie* is impossible wherever solidary
organs are sufficiently in contact or sufficiently prolonged. In effect, being
contiguous, they are quickly warned, in each circumstance, of the need
which they have of one another, and, consequently, they have a lively
and continuous sentiment of their mutual dependence. For the same
reason that exchanges take place among them easily, they take place
frequently; being regular, they regularize themselves accordingly, and in
time the work of consolidation is achieved. Finally, because the smallest
reaction can be felt from one part to another, the rules which are thus
formulated carry this imprint; that is to say, they foresee and fix, in detail,
the conditions of equilibrium. But, on the contrary, if some opaque environment is interposed, then only stimuli of a certain intensity can be
communicated from one organ to another. Relations, being rare, are not
repeated enough to be determined; each time there ensues new groping.
The lines of passage taken by the streams of movement cannot deepen
because the streams themselves are too intermittent. If some rules do
come to constitute them, they are, however, general and vague, for under
these conditions it is only the most general contours of phenomena that
can be fixed. The case will be the same if the contiguity, though sufficient,
is too recent or has not endured long enough.[1]

Generally, this condition is found to be realized in the nature of things.
A function can be apportioned between two or several parts of an organism only if these parts are more or less contiguous. Moreover, once
labor is divided, since they need one another, they naturally tend to
lessen the distance separating them. That is why as one goes up in the
animal scale, one sees organs coming together, and, as Spencer says,
being introduced in the interstices of one another. But a set of exceptional
circumstances can bring this about differently.

This is what happens in the cases we are discussing. In so far as the
segmental type is strongly marked, there are nearly as many economic
markets as there are different segments. Consequently, each of them is
very limited. Producers, being near consumers, can easily reckon the
extent of the needs to be satisfied. Equilibrium is established without any

---

[1] There is, however, a case where *anomie* can be produced, although the contiguity is sufficient. This occurs when the necessary regulation can be established only
by submitting to transformations of which the social structure is incapable. The
plasticity of societies is not indefinite. When it reaches its limit, even necessary
changes are impossible.

trouble and production regulates itself. On the contrary, as the organized type develops, the fusion of different segments draws the markets together into one which embraces almost all society. This even extends beyond, and tends to become universal, for the frontiers which separate peoples break down at the same time as those which separate the segments of each of them. The result is that each industry produces for consumers spread over the whole surface of the country or even of the entire world. Contact is then no longer sufficient. The producer can no longer embrace the market in a glance, nor even in thought. He can no longer see its limits, since it is, so to speak, limitless. Accordingly, production becomes unbridled and unregulated. It can only trust to chance, and in the course of these gropings, it is inevitable that proportions will be abused, as much in one direction as in another. From this come the crises which periodically disturb economic functions. The growth of local, restricted crises which result in failures is in all likelihood an effect of the same cause.

As the market extends, great industry appears. But it results in changing the relations of employers and employees. The great strain upon the nervous system and the contagious influence of great agglomerations increase the needs of the latter. Machines replace men; manufacturing replaces hand-work. The worker is regimented, separated from his family throughout the day. He always lives apart from his employer, etc. These new conditions of industrial life naturally demand a new organization, but as these changes have been accomplished with extreme rapidity, the interests in conflict have not yet had the time to be equilibrated.[1]

Finally, the explanation of the fact that the moral and social sciences are in the state we have suggested is that they were the last to come into the circle of positive sciences. It is hardly a century since this new field of phenomena has been opened to scientific investigation. Scholars have installed themselves in them, some here, some there, according to their tastes. Scattered over this wide surface, they have remained until the present too remote from one another to feel all the ties which unite them. But, solely because they will push their researches farther from their points of departure, they will necessarily end by reaching and, consequently, taking conscience of their solidarity. The unity of science will thus form of itself, not through the abstract unity of a formula, far too scanty for the multitude of things that it must embrace, but through the living unity of an organic whole. For science to be unitary, it is not necessary for it to be contained within the field of one and the same conscience

[1] Let us remember, however, that, as we shall see in the following chapter, this antagonism is not entirely due to the rapidity of these changes, but, in good part, to the still very great inequality of the external conditions of the struggle. On this factor, time has no influence.

—an impossible feat anyhow—but it is sufficient that all those who cultivate it feel that they are collaborating in the same work.

The preceding has removed one of the most serious charges brought against the division of labor.

It has often been accused of degrading the individual by making him a machine. And truly, if he does not know whither the operations he performs are tending, if he relates them to no end, he can only continue to work through routine. Every day he repeats the same movements with monotonous regularity, but without being interested in them, and without understanding them. He is no longer a living cell of a living organism which unceasingly vibrates with neighboring cells, which acts upon them, and to whose action it responds and with whose needs and circumstances it changes. He is no longer anything but an inert piece of machinery, only an external force set going which always moves in the same direction and in the same way. Surely, no matter how one may represent the moral ideal, one cannot remain indifferent to such debasement of human nature. If morality has individual perfection as its goal, it cannot thus permit the ruin of the individual, and if it has society as its goal, it cannot let the very source of social life be drained, for the peril does not threaten only economic functions, but all social functions, as elevated as they may be. "If," says Comte, "we have often justly deplored, in the material world, the workman being exclusively occupied during his whole life with the manufacture of knife-handles or pin-heads, healthy philosophy ought not less bemoan, in the intellectual order, the exclusive and continuous employment of the human brain in the resolution of some equations or in the classification of some insects. The moral effect, in one case, as in the other, is unfortunately very much the same."[1]

As a remedy, it has sometimes been proposed that, in addition to their technical and special instruction, workers be given a general education. But, suppose that we can thus relieve some of the bad effects attributed to the division of labor; that is not a means of preventing them. The division does not change its nature because it has been preceded by general culture. No doubt, it is good for the worker to be interested in art, literature, etc., but it is none the less bad that he should be treated as a machine all day long. Who cannot see, moreover, that two such existences are too opposed to be reconciled, and cannot be led by the same man! If a person has grown accustomed to vast horizons, total views, broad generalities, he cannot be confined, without impatience, within the strict limits of a special task. Such a remedy would make specialization inoffensive by making it intolerable, and, consequently, more or less impossible.

What solves the contradiction is that, contrary to what has been said,

[1] *Cours*, IV, p. 430.

the division of labor does not produce these consequences because of a necessity of its own nature, but only in exceptional and abnormal circumstances. In order for it to develop without having such a disastrous influence on the human conscience, it is not necessary to temper it with its opposite. It is necessary and it is sufficient for it to be itself, for nothing to come from without to denature it. For, normally, the role of each special function does not require that the individual close himself in, but that he keep himself in constant relations with neighboring functions, take conscience of their needs, of the changes which they undergo, etc. The division of labor presumes that the worker, far from being hemmed in by his task, does not lose sight of his collaborators, that he acts upon them, and reacts to them. He is, then, not a machine who repeats his movements without knowing their meaning, but he knows that they tend, in some way, towards an end that he conceives more or less distinctly. He feels that he is serving something. For that, he need not embrace vast portions of the social horizon; it is sufficient that he perceive enough of it to understand that his actions have an aim beyond themselves. From that time, as special and uniform as his activity may be, it is that of an intelligent being, for it has direction, and he knows it. The economists would not have left this essential character of the division of labor in the shade and, accordingly, would not have exposed it to this unmerited reproach, if they had not reduced it to being merely a means of increasing the produce of social forces, if they had seen that it is above all a source of solidarity.

IV. Conclusion

We are now in a position to solve the practical problem that we posed for ourselves at the beginning of this work.

If there is one rule of conduct which is incontestable, it is that which orders us to realize in ourselves the essential traits of the collective type. Among lower peoples, this reaches its greatest rigor. There, one's first duty is to resemble everybody else, not to have anything personal about one's beliefs or actions. In more advanced societies, required likenesses are less numerous; the absences of some likenesses, however, is still a sign of moral failure. Of course, crime falls into fewer different categories; but today, as heretofore, if a criminal is the object of reprobation, it is because he is unlike us. Likewise, in lesser degree, acts simply immoral and prohibited as such are those which evince dissemblances less profound but nevertheless considered serious. Is this not the case with the rule which common morality expresses when it orders a man to be a man in every sense of the word, which is to say, to have all the ideas and sentiments which go to make up a human conscience? No doubt, if this formula is taken literally, the man prescribed would be man in general and not one of some particular social species. But, in reality, this human conscience that we must integrally realize is nothing else than the collective conscience of the group of which we are a part. For what can it be composed of, if not the ideas and sentiments to which we are most attached? Where can we find the traits of our model, if not within us and around us? If we believe that this collective ideal is that of all humanity, that is because it has become so abstract and general that it appears fitting for all men indiscriminately. But, really, every people makes for itself some particular conception of this type which pertains to its personal temperament. Each represents it in its own image. Even the moralist who thinks he can, through thought, overcome the influence of transient ideas, cannot do so, for he is impregnated with them, and no matter what he does, he finds these precepts in the body of his deductions. That is why each nation has its own school of moral philosophy conforming to its character.

On the other hand, we have shown that this rule had as its function the prevention of all agitation of the common conscience, and, consequently, of social solidarity, and that it could accomplish this role only by having a moral character. It is impossible for offenses against the most fundamental collective sentiments to be tolerated without the disintegration of society, and it is necessary to combat them with the aid of the particularly energetic reaction which attaches to moral rules.

But the contrary rule, which orders us to specialize, has exactly the same function. It also is necessary for the cohesion of societies, at least at a certain period in their evolution. Of course, its solidarity is different from the preceding, but though it is different, it is no less indispensable. Higher societies can maintain themselves in equilibrium only if labor is divided; the attraction of like for like less and less suffices to produce this result. If, then, the moral character of the first of these rules is necessary to the playing of its role, it is no less necessary to the second. They both correspond to the same social need, but satisfy the need differently, because the conditions of existence in the societies themselves differ. Consequently, without speculating concerning the first principle of ethics, we can induce the moral value of one from the moral value of the other. If, from certain points of view, there is a real antagonism between them, that is not because they serve different ends. On the contrary, it is because they lead to the same end, but through opposed means. Accordingly, there is no necessity for choosing between them once for all nor of condemning one in the name of the other. What is necessary is to give each, at each moment in history, the place that is fitting to it.

Perhaps we can even generalize further in this matter.

The requirements of our subject have obliged us to classify moral rules and to review the principal types. We are thus in a better position than we were in the beginning to see, or at least to conjecture, not only upon the external sign, but also upon the internal character which is common to all of them and which can serve to define them. We have put them into two groups: rules with repressive sanctions, which may be diffuse or organized, and rules with restitutive sanctions. We have seen that the first of these express the conditions of the solidarity, *sui generis*, which comes from resemblances, and to which we have given the name mechanical; the second, the conditions of negative solidarity[1] and organic solidarity. We can thus say that, in general, the characteristic of moral rules is that they enunciate the fundamental conditions of social solidarity. Law and morality are the totality of ties which bind each of us to society, which make a unitary, coherent aggregate of the mass of individuals. Everything which is a source of solidarity is moral, everything which forces man to take account of other men is moral, everything which forces him to regulate his conduct through something other than the striving of his ego is moral, and morality is as solid as these ties are numerous and strong. We can see how inexact it is to define it, as is often done, through liberty. It rather consists in a state of dependence. Far from serving to emancipate the individual, or disengaging him from the environment which surrounds him, it has, on the contrary, the function of making him an integral part of a whole, and, consequently, of depriving him of some liberty of movement. We sometimes, it is true, come across people not without nobility who find the idea of such dependence intolerable. But that is because they do not perceive the source from which their own morality flows, since these sources are very deep. Conscience is a bad judge of what goes on in the depths of a person, because it does not penetrate to them.

Society is not, then, as has often been thought, a stranger to the moral world, or something which has only secondary repercussions upon it. It is, on the contrary, the necessary condition of its existence. It is not a simple juxtaposition of individuals who bring an intrinsic morality with them, but rather man is a moral being only because he lives in society, since morality consists in being solidary with a group and varying with this solidarity. Let all social life disappear, and moral life will disappear with it, since it would no longer have any objective. The state of nature of the philosophers of the eighteenth century, if not immoral, is, at least, *amoral*. Rousseau himself recognized this. Through this, however, we do not come upon the formula which expresses morality as a function of social interest. To be sure, society cannot exist if its parts are not solidary, but solidarity is only one of its conditions of existence. There are many others which are no less necessary and which are not moral. Moreover, it can happen that, in the system of ties which make up morality, there are some which are not useful in themselves or which have power with-

[1] See Book I, ch. iii, §2.

out any relation to their degree of utility. The idea of utility does not enter as an essential element in our definition.

As for what is called individual morality, if we understand by that a totality of duties of which the individual would, at the same time, be subject and object, and which would link him only to himself, and which would, consequently, exist even if he were solitary,—that is an abstract conception which has no relation to reality. Morality, in all its forms, is never met with except in society. It never varies except in relation to social conditions. To ask what it would be if societies did not exist is thus to depart from facts and enter the domain of gratuitous hypotheses and unverifiable flights of the imagination. The duties of the individual towards himself are, in reality, duties towards society. They correspond to certain collective sentiments which he cannot offend, whether the offended and the offender are one and the same person, or whether they are distinct. Today, for example, there is in all healthy consciences a very lively sense of respect for human dignity, to which we are supposed to conform as much in our relations with ourselves as in our relations with others, and this constitutes the essential quality of what is called individual morality. Every act which contravenes this is censured, even when the agent and the sufferer are the same person. That is why, according to the Kantian formula, we ought to respect human personality wherever we find it, which is to say, in ourselves as in those like us. The sentiment of which it is the object is not less offended in one case than in the other.

But not only does the division of labor present the character by which we have defined morality; it more and more tends to become the essential condition of social solidarity. As we advance in the evolutionary scale, the ties which bind the individual to his family, to his native soil, to traditions which the past has given to him, to collective group usages, become loose. More mobile, he changes his environment more easily, leaves his people to go elsewhere to live a more autonomous existence, to a greater extent forms his own ideas and sentiments. Of course, the whole common conscience does not, on this account, pass out of existence. At least there will always remain this cult of personality, of individual dignity of which we have just been speaking, and which, today, is the rallying-point of so many people. But how little a thing it is when one contemplates the ever increasing extent of social life, and, consequently, of individual consciences! For, as they become more voluminous, as intelligence becomes richer, activity more varied, in order for morality to remain constant, that is to say, in order for the individual to remain attached to the group with a force equal to that of yesterday, the ties which bind him to it must become stronger and more numerous. If, then, he formed no others than those which come from resemblances, the effacement of the segmental type would be accompanied by a systematic debasement of morality. Man would no longer be sufficiently obligated; he would no longer feel about and above him this salutary pressure of society which moderates his egoism and makes him a moral being. This is what gives moral value to the division of labor. Through it, the individual becomes cognizant of his dependence upon society; from it come the forces which keep him in check and restrain him. In short, since the division of labor becomes the chief source of social solidarity, it becomes, at the same time, the foundation of the moral order.

We can then say that, in higher societies, our duty is not to spread our activity over a large surface, but to concentrate and specialize it. We must contract our horizon, choose a definite task and immerse ourselves in it completely, instead of trying to make ourselves a sort of creative masterpiece, quite complete, which contains its worth in itself and not in the services that it renders. Finally, this specialization ought to be pushed as far as the elevation of the social type, without assigning any other limit to it.[1] No doubt, we ought so to work as to realize in ourselves the collective type as it exists. There are common sentiments, common ideas, without which, as has been said, one is not a man. The rule which orders us to specialize remains limited by the contrary rule. Our conclusion is not that it is good to press specialization as far as possible, but as far as necessary. As for the part that is to be played by these two opposing necessities, that is determined by experience and cannot be calculated *a priori*. It is enough for us to have shown that the second is not of a different nature from the first, but that it also is moral, and that, moreover, this duty becomes ever more important and pressing, because the general qualities which are in question suffice less and less to socialize the individual.

It is not without reason that public sentiment reproves an ever more pronounced tendency on the part of dilettantes and even others to be taken up with an exclusively general culture and refuse to take any part in occupational organization. That is because they are not sufficiently attached to society, or, if one wishes, society is not sufficiently attached to them, and they escape it. Precisely because they feel its effect neither with vivacity nor with the continuity that is necessary, they have no cognizance of all the obligations their positions as social beings demand

[1] There is, however, probably another limit which we do not have to speak of since it concerns individual hygiene. It may be held that, in the light of our organico-psychic constitution, the division of labor cannot go beyond a certain limit without disorders resulting. Without entering upon the question, let us straightaway say that the extreme specialization at which biological functions have arrived does not seem favorable to this hypothesis. Moreover, in the very order of psychic and social functions, has not the division of labor, in its historical development, been carried to the last stage in the relations of men and women? Have not there been faculties completely lost by both? Why cannot the same phenomenon occur between individuals of the same sex? Of course, it takes time for the organism to adapt itself to these changes, but we do not see why a day should come when this adaptation would become impossible.

of them. The general ideal to which they are attached being, for the reasons we have spoken of, formal and shifting, it cannot take them out of themselves. We do not cling to very much when we have no very determined objective, and, consequently, we cannot very well elevate ourselves beyond a more or less refined egotism. On the contrary, he who gives himself over to a definite task is, at every moment, struck by the sentiment of common solidarity in the thousand duties of occupational morality.[1]

But does not the division of labor by making each of us an incomplete being bring on a diminution of individual personality? That is a reproach which has often been levelled at it.

Let us first of all remark that it is difficult to see why it would be more in keeping with the logic of human nature to develop superficially rather than profoundly. Why would a more extensive activity, but more dispersed, be superior to a more concentrated, but circumscribed, activity? Why would there be more dignity in being complete and mediocre, rather than in living a more specialized, but more intense life, particularly if it is thus possible for us to find what we have lost in this specialization, through our association with other beings who have what we lack and who complete us? We take off from the principle that man ought to realize his nature as man, to accomplish his ὀικεῖον ἔργον, as Aristotle said. But this nature does not remain constant throughout history; it is modified with societies. Among lower peoples, the proper duty of man is to resemble his companions, to realize in himself all the traits of the collective type which are then confounded, much more than today, with the human type. But, in more advanced societies, his nature is, in large part, to be an organ of society, and his proper duty, consequently, is to play his role as an organ.

Moreover, far from being trammelled by the progress of specialization, individual personality develops with the division of labor.

To be a person is to be an autonomous source of action. Man acquires this quality only in so far as there is something in him which is his alone and which individualizes him, as he is something more than a simple incarnation of the generic type of his race and his group. It will be said

---

[1] Among the practical consequences that might be deduced from the proposition that we have just established there is one of interest to education. We always reason, in educational affairs, as if the moral basis of man was made up of generalities. We have just seen that such is not the case at all. Man is destined to fill a special function in the social organism, and, consequently, he must learn, in advance, how to play this role. For that an education is necessary, quite as much as that he should learn his role as a man. We do not, however, wish to imply, that it is necessary to rear a child prematurely for some certain profession, but that it is necessary to get him to like the idea of circumscribed tasks and limited horizons. But this taste is quite different from that for general things, and cannot be aroused by the same means.

that he is endowed with free will and that is enough to establish his personality. But although there may be some of this liberty in him, an object of so many discussions, it is not this metaphysical, impersonal, invariable attribute which can serve as the unique basis for concrete personality, which is empirical and variable with individuals. That could not be constituted by the wholly abstract power of choice between two opposites, but it is still necessary for this faculty to be exercised towards ends and aims which are proper to the agent. In other words, the very materials of conscience must have a personal character. But we have seen in the second book of this work that this result is progressively produced as the division of labor progresses. The effacement of the segmental type, at the same time that it necessitates a very great specialization, partially lifts the individual conscience from the organic environment which supports it, as from the social environment which envelops it, and, accordingly, because of this double emancipation, the individual becomes more of an independent factor in his own conduct. The division of labor itself contributes to this enfranchisement, for individual natures, while specializing, become more complex, and by that are in part freed from collective action and hereditary influences which can only enforce themselves upon simple, general things.

It is, accordingly, a real illusion which makes us believe that personality was so much more complete when the division of labor had penetrated less. No doubt, in looking from without at the diversity of occupations which the individual then embraces, it may seem that he is developing in a very free and complete manner. But, in reality, this activity which he manifests is not really his. It is society, it is the race acting in and through him; he is only the intermediary through which they realize themselves. His liberty is only apparent and his personality borrowed. Because the life of these societies is, in certain respects, less regular, we imagine that original talents have more opportunity for free play, that it is easier for each one to pursue his own tastes, that a very large place is left to free fantasy. But this is to forget that personal sentiments are then very rare. If the motives which govern conduct do not appear as periodically as they do today, they do not leave off being collective, and, consequently, impersonal, and it is the same with the actions that they inspire. Moreover, we have shown above how activity becomes richer and more intense as it becomes more specialized.[1]

Thus, the progress of individual personality and that of the division of labor depend upon one and the same cause. It is thus impossible to desire one without desiring the other. But no one today contests the obligatory character of the rule which orders us to be more and more of a person.

One last consideration will make us see to what extent the division of labor is linked with our whole moral life.

[1] See above, pp. 272 ff. and p. 318.

Men have long dreamt of finally realizing in fact the ideal of human fraternity. People pray for a state where war will no longer be the law of international relations, where relations between societies will be pacifically regulated, as those between individuals already are, where all men will collaborate in the same work and live the same life. Although these aspirations are in part neutralized by those which have as their object the particular society of which we are a part, they have not left off being active and are even gaining in force. But they can be satisfied only if all men form one society, subject to the same laws. For, just as private conflicts can be regulated only by the action of the society in which the individuals live, so intersocial conflicts can be regulated only by a society which comprises in its scope all others. The only power which can serve to moderate individual egotism is the power of the group; the only power which can serve to moderate the egotism of groups is that of some other group which embraces them.

Truly, when the problem has been posed in these terms, we must recognize that this ideal is not on the verge of being integrally realized, for there are too many intellectual and moral diversities between different social types existing together on the earth to admit of fraternalization in the same society. But what is possible is that societies of the same type may come together, and it is, indeed, in this direction that evolution appears to move. We have already seen that among European peoples there is a tendency to form, by spontaneous movement, a European society which has, at present, some idea of itself and the beginning of organization.[1] If the formation of a single human society is forever impossible, a fact which has not been proved,[2] at least the formation of continually larger societies brings us vaguely near the goal. These facts, moreover, in no wise contradict the definition of morality that we have given, for if we cling to humanity and if we ought to cling to it, it is because it is a society which is in process of realizing itself in this way, and with which we are solidary.[3]

But we know that greater societies cannot be formed except through the development of the division of labor, for not only could they not maintain themselves in equilibrium without a greater specialization of functions, but even the increase in the number of those competing would suffice to produce this result mechanically; and that, so much the more, since the growth of volume is generally accompanied by a growth in

[1] See pp. 280-282.

[2] There is nothing that forces the intellectual and moral diversity of societies to be maintained. The ever greater expansion of higher societies, from which there results the absorbtion or elimination of less advanced societies, tends, in any case, to diminish such diversity.

[3] Thus, the duties that we have toward it do not oppress those which link us to our country. For the latter is the only actually realized society of which we are members; the other is only a desideratum whose realization is not even assured.

density. We can then formulate the following proposition: the ideal of human fraternity can be realized only in proportion to the progress of the division of labor. We must choose: either to renounce our dream, if we refuse further to circumscribe our activity, or else to push forward its accomplishment under the condition we have just set forth.

But if the division of labor produces solidarity, it is not only because it makes each individual an *exchangist*, as the economists say;[1] it is because it creates among men an entire system of rights and duties which link them together in a durable way. Just as social similitudes give rise to a law and a morality which protect them, so the division of labor gives rise to rules which assure pacific and regular concourse of divided functions. If economists have believed that it would bring forth an abiding solidarity, in some manner of its own making, and if, accordingly, they have held that human societies could and would resolve themselves into purely economic associations, that is because they believed that it affected only individual, temporary interests. Consequently, to estimate the interests in conflict and the way in which they ought to equilibrate, that is to say, to determine the conditions under which exchange ought to take place, is solely a matter of individual competence; and, since these interests are in a perpetual state of becoming, there is no place for any permanent regulation. But such a conception is, in all ways, inadequate for the facts. The division of labor does not present individuals to one another, but social functions. And society is interested in the play of the latter; in so far as they regularly concur, or do not concur, it will be healthy or ill. Its existence thus depends upon them, and the more they are divided the greater its dependence. That is why it cannot leave them in a state of indetermination. In addition to this, they are determined by themselves. Thus are formed those rules whose number grows as labor is divided, and whose absence makes organic solidarity either impossible or imperfect.

But it is not enough that there be rules; they must be just, and for that it is necessary for the external conditions of competition to be equal. If, moreover, we remember that the collective conscience is becoming more and more a cult of the individual, we shall see that what characterizes the morality of organized societies, compared to that of segmental societies, is that there is something more human, therefore more rational, about them. It does not direct our activities to ends which do not immediately concern us; it does not make us servants of ideal powers of a nature other than our own, which follow their directions without occupying themselves with the interests of men. It only asks that we be

---

[1] The word is de Molinari's, *La morale économique*, p. 248.

thoughtful of our fellows and that we be just, that we fulfill our duty, that we work at the function we can best execute, and receive the just reward for our services. The rules which constitute it do not have a constraining force which snuffs out free thought; but, because they are rather made for us and, in a certain sense, by us, we are free. We wish to understand them; we do not fear to change them. We must, however, guard against finding such an ideal inadequate on the pretext that it is too earthly and too much to our liking. An ideal is not more elevated because more transcendent, but because it leads us to vaster perspectives. What is important is not that it tower high above us, until it becomes a stranger to our lives, but that it open to our activity a large enough field. This is far from being on the verge of realization. We know only too well what a laborious work it is to erect this society where each individual will have the place he merits, will be rewarded as he deserves, where everybody, accordingly, will spontaneously work for the good of all and of each. Indeed, a moral code is not above another because it commands in a drier and more authoritarian manner, or because it is more sheltered from reflection. Of course, it must attach us to something besides ourselves but it is not necessary for it to chain us to it with impregnable bonds.

It has been said[1] with justice that morality—and by that must be understood, not only moral doctrines, but customs—is going through a real crisis. What precedes can help us to understand the nature and causes of this sick condition. Profound changes have been produced in the structure of our societies in a very short time; they have been freed from the segmental type with a rapidity and in proportions such as have never before been seen in history. Accordingly, the morality which corresponds to this social type has regressed, but without another developing quickly enough to fill the ground that the first left vacant in our consciences. Our faith has been troubled; tradition has lost its sway; individual judgment has been freed from collective judgment. But, on the other hand, the functions which have been disrupted in the course of the upheaval have not had the time to adjust themselves to one another; the new life which has emerged so suddenly has not been able to be completely organized, and above all, it has not been organized in a way to satisfy the need for justice which has grown more ardent in our hearts. If this be so, the remedy for the evil is not to seek to resuscitate traditions and practices which, no longer responding to present conditions of society, can only live an artificial, false existence. What we must do to relieve this anomie is to discover the means for making the organs which are still wasting themselves in discordant movements harmoniously concur by introducing into their relations more justice by more and more extenuating the external inequalities which are the source of the evil. Our

---

[1] Beaussire, *Les principes de la morale*, Introduction.

illness is not, then, as has often been believed, of an intellectual sort; it has more profound causes. We shall not suffer because we no longer know on what theoretical notion to base the morality we have been practicing, but because, in certain of its parts, this morality is irremediably shattered, and that which is necessary to us is only in process of formation. Our anxiety does not arise because the criticism of scholars has broken down the traditional explanation we use to give to our duties; consequently, it is not a new philosophical system which will relieve the situation. Because certain of our duties are no longer founded in the reality of things, a breakdown has resulted which will be repaired only in so far as a new discipline is established and consolidated. In short, our first duty is to make a moral code for ourselves. Such a work cannot be improvised in the silence of the study; it can arise only through itself, little by little, under the pressure of internal causes which make it necessary. But the service that thought can and must render is in fixing the goal that we must attain. That is what we have tried to do.

17. Karl Marx and Friedrich Engels

On Alienation

I. Concerning the Production of Consciousness

In history up to the present it is certainly an empirical fact that separate individuals have, with the broadening of their activity into world-historical activity, become more and more enslaved under a power alien to them (a pressure which they have conceived of as a dirty trick on the part of the so-called universal spirit), a power which has become more and more enormous and, in the last instance, turns out to be the *world-market*. But it is just as empirically established that, by the overthrow of the existing state of society by the communist revolution (of which more below) and the abolition of private property which is identical with it, this power, which so baffles the German theoreticians, will be dissolved; and that then the liberation of each single individual will be accomplished in the measure in which history becomes transformed into world-history. From the above it is clear that the real intellectual wealth of the individual depends entirely on the wealth of his real connections. Only then will the separate individuals be liberated from the various national and local barriers, be brought into practical connection with the material and intellectual production of the whole world and be put in a position to acquire the capacity to enjoy this all-sided production of the whole earth (the creations of man). Universal dependence, this natural form of the world-historical co-operation of individuals, will be transformed by this communist revolution into the control and conscious mastery of these powers, which, born of the action of men on one another, have till now overawed and governed men as powers completely alien to them. Now this view can be expressed again in speculative-idealistic, i.e. fantastic, terms as "spontaneous generation of the species," ("society as the subject"), and thereby the series of inter-related individuals can be conceived as a single individual, which accomplishes the mystery of generating itself. It is clear here that individuals certainly

Section I is from Marx and Engels, *The German Ideology* (New York: International Publishers, 1939), pp. 27-43. Section II is from Karl Marx, *Economic and Philosophic Manuscripts of 1844.* (London: Lawrence and Wishart, 1959), pp. 67-84. Footnotes in Section I have been omitted. The title and editorial footnotes in Sec. II have been supplied by the editor of "the manuscripts."

make one another, physically and mentally, but do not make themselves either in the non-sense of Saint Bruno, nor in the sense of the "unique," of the "made" man.

Our conception of history depends on our ability to expound the real process of production, starting out from the simple material production of life, and to comprehend the form of intercourse connected with this and created by this (i.e. civil society in its various stages), as the basis of all history; further, to show it in its action as State; and so, from this starting-point, to explain the whole mass of different theoretical products and forms of consciousness, religion, philosophy, ethics etc., etc., and trace their origins and growth, by which means, of course, the whole thing can be shown in its totality (and therefore, too, the reciprocal action of these various sides on one another). It has not, like the idealistic view of history, in every period to look for a category, but remains constantly on the real ground of history; it does not explain practice from the idea but explains the formation of ideas from material practice; and accordingly it comes to the conclusion that all forms and products of consciousness cannot be dissolved by mental criticism, by resolution into "self-consciousness" or transformation into "apparitions," "spectres," "fancies," etc., but only by the practical overthrow of the actual social relations which gave rise to this idealistic humbug; that not criticism but revolution is the driving force of history, also of religion, of philosophy and all other types of theory. It shows that history does not end by being resolved into "self-consciousness" as "spirit of the spirit," but that in it at each stage there is found a material result: a sum of productive forces, a historically created relation of individuals to nature and to one another, which is handed down to each generation from its predecessor; a mass of productive forces, different forms of capital, and conditions, which, indeed, is modified by the new generation on the one hand, but also on the other prescribes for it its conditions of life and gives it a definite development, a special character. It shows that circumstances make men just as much as men make circumstances.

This sum of productive forces, forms of capital and social forms of intercourse, which every individual and generation finds in existence as something given, is the real basis of what the philosophers have conceived as "substance" and "essence of man", and what they have deified and attacked: a real basis which is not in the least disturbed, in its effect and influence on the development of men, by the fact that these philosophers revolt against it as "self-consciousness" and "the unique." These conditions of life, which different generations find in existence, decide also whether or not the periodically recurring revolutionary convulsion will be strong enough to overthrow the basis of all existing forms. And if these material elements of a complete revolution are not present (namely, on the one hand the existence of productive forces, on the other the formation of a revolutionary mass, which revolts not only against separate conditions of society up till then, but against the very "production of life" till then, the "total activity" on which it was based), then, as far as practical development is concerned, it is absolutely immaterial whether the "idea" of this revolution has been expressed a hundred times already; as the history of communism proves.

In the whole conception of history up to the present this real basis of history has either been totally neglected or else considered as a minor matter quite irrelevant to the course of history. History must therefore always be written according to an extraneous standard; the real production of life seems to be beyond history, while the truly historical appears to be separated from ordinary life, something extra-superterrestrial. With this the relation of man to nature is excluded from history and hence the antithesis of nature and history is created. The exponents of this conception of history have consequently only been able to see in history the political actions of princes and States, religious and all sorts of theoretical struggles, and in particular in each historical epoch have had to share the *illusion of that epoch*. For instance, if an epoch imagines itself to be actuated by purely "political" or "religious" motives, although "religion" and "politics" are only forms of its true motives, the historian accepts this opinion. The "idea," the "conception" of these conditioned men about their real practice, is transformed into the sole determining, active force, which controls and determines their practice. When the crude form in which the division of labour appears with the Indians and Egyptians calls forth the caste-system in their State and religion, the historian believes that the caste-system is the power which has produced this crude social form. While the French and the English at least hold by the political illusion, which is moderately close to reality, the Germans move in the realm of the "pure spirit", and make religious illusion the driving force of history.

The Hegelian philosophy of history is the last consequence, reduced to its "finest expression," of all this German historiography, for which it is not a question of real, nor even of political, interests, but of pure thoughts, which inevitably appear, even to Saint Bruno, as a series of "thoughts" that devour one another and are finally swallowed up in "self-consciousness." And equally inevitably, and more logically, the course of history appears to the Blessed Max Stirner, who knows not a thing about real history, as a mere tale of "knights," robbers and ghosts, from whose visions he can, of course, only save himself by "unholiness." This conception is truly religious: it postulates religious man as the primitive man, and in its imagination puts the religious production of fancies in the place of the real production of the means of subsistence and of life itself. This whole conception of history, together with its dissolution and the scruples and qualms resulting from it, is a purely *national* affair of the Germans and has only *local* interest for the Germans, as for instance the important question treated several times of late: how really we "pass from the realm of God to the realm of man"—as if this "realm of God" had ever existed anywhere save in the imagination, and the learned gentlemen, without being aware of it, were not constantly living in the "realm of man" to which they are now seeking the way; and as if the learned pastime (for it is nothing more) of explaining the mystery of this theoretical bubble-blowing did not on the contrary lie in demonstrating its origin in actual earthly conditions.

Always, for these Germans, it is simply a matter of resolving the nonsense of earlier writers into some other freak, i.e. of presupposing that all this nonsense has a special meaning which can be discovered; while really it is only a question of explaining this theoretical talk from the actual existing conditions. The real, practical dissolution of these phrases, the removal of these notions from the consciousness of men, will, as we have already said, be effected by altered circumstances, not by theoretical deductions. For the mass of men, i.e. the proletariat, these theoretical notions do not exist and hence do not require to be dissolved, and if this mass ever had any theoretical notions, e.g. religion, etc., these have now long been dissolved by circumstances. The purely national character of these questions and solutions is shown again in the way these theorists believe in all seriousness that chimeras like "the God-Man," "Man," etc., have presided over individual epochs of history (Saint Bruno even goes so far as to assert that "only criticism and critics have made history") and when they themselves construct historical systems, they skip over all earlier periods in the greatest haste and pass immediately from Mongolism to history "with meaningful content," that is to say, to the history of the Halle and German Annals and the dissolution of the Young-Hegelian school into a general squabble. They forget all other nations, all real events, and the *threatrum mundi* is confined to the Leipzig Book Fair and the mutual quarrels of "Criticism," "Man," and "the Unique."

If these theorists treat really historical subjects, as for instance the eighteenth century, they merely give a history of the ideas of the times, torn away from the facts and the practical development fundamental to them; and even then they only give these ideas in order to represent them as an imperfect preliminary stage, the as yet limited predecessor of the real historical age, i.e. the period of the German philosophic struggle from 1840 to 1844. As might be expected when the history of an earlier period is written with the aim of accentuating the brilliance of an unhistoric person and his fantasies, all the really historic events, even the really historic invasions of politics into history, receive no mention. Instead we get a narrative based on systematic constructions and literary gossip, such as Saint Bruno provided in his now forgotten history of the eighteenth century. These high-falutin, bombastic hucksters of ideas, who imagine themselves infinitely exalted above all national prejudices, are thus in practice far more national than the beer-quaffing German philistines who dream of a united Germany. They do not recognize the deeds of other nations as historical: they live in Germany, to Germany, and for Germany; they turn the Rhine-song into a religious hymn and conquer Alsace-Lorraine by robbing French philosophy instead of the French State, by Germanizing French ideas instead of French provinces. Herr Venedey is a cosmopolitan compared with the Saints Bruno and Max, who, in the universal dominance of theory, proclaim the universal dominance of Germany.

It is also clear from these arguments how grossly Feuerbach is deceiving himself, when (*Wigand's Quarterly* 1845, Vol. 2) by virtue of the qualification "common man" he declares himself a communist, transforms the latter into a predicate of *"man,"* and thereby thinks it possible to change the word "communist," which in the real world means the follower of a definite revolutionary party, into a mere category. Feuerbach's whole deduction with regard to the relation of men to one another goes only so far as to prove that men need and always have needed each other. He wants to establish consciousness of this fact, that is to say, like the other theorists, merely to produce a correct consciousness about an existing fact; whereas for the real communist it is a question of overthrowing the existing state of things. We thoroughly appreciate, moreover, that Feuerbach, in endeavouring to produce consciousness of just *this* fact, is going as far as a theorist possibly can, without ceasing to be a theorist and philosopher. It is characteristic, however, that Saint Bruno and Saint Max seize on Feuerbach's conception of the communist and put it in place of the real communist—which occurs, partly, merely in order that they can combat communism too as "spirit of the spirit," as a philosophical category, as an equal opponent and, in the case of Saint Bruno, partly also for pragmatic reasons.

Like our opponents, Feuerbach still accepts and at the same time misunderstands existing reality. We recall the passage in the *Philosophy of the Future*, where he develops the view that the existence of a thing or a man is at the same time its or his essence, that the conditions of existence, the mode of life and particular activity of an animal or human individual are those, in which its "essence" feels itself satisfied. Here every exception is expressly conceived as an unhappy chance, as an abnormality which cannot be altered. Thus if millions of proletarians feel themselves by no means contented in their conditions of life, if their existence [is in contradiction with their "essence," then it is certainly an abnormality, but not an unhappy chance; an historical fact based on quite definite social relationships. Feuerbach is content to affirm this fact; he only interprets the existing sensuous world, has only the relation of a theorist to it], while in reality for the practical materialist, i.e. the communist, it is a question of revolutionizing the existing world, of practically attacking and changing existing things. When occasionally we find such views with Feuerbach, they are never more than isolated surmises and have much too little influence on his general outlook to be considered here as anything else than embryos capable of development.

Feuerbach's "interpretation" of the sensuous world is confined on the one hand to mere contemplation of it, and on the other to mere feeling; he says "man" instead of "real, historical men." "Man" is really "the German." In the first case, the contemplation of the sensuous world, he necessarily lights on things which contradict his consciousness and feeling, which upset the harmony of all parts of the sensuous world and especially of man and nature, a harmony he presupposes.* To push these on one side, he must take refuge in a double perception, a profane one which only perceives the "flatly obvious" and a higher more philosophical one which perceives the "true essence" of things. He does not see how the sensuous world around him is, not a thing given direct from all eternity, ever the same, but the product of industry and of the state of society; and, indeed, in the sense that it is an historical product, the result of the activity of a whole succession of generations, each standing on the shoulders of the preceding one, developing its industry and its intercourse, modifying its social organization according to the changed needs. Even the objects of the simplest "sensuous certainty" are only given him through social development, industry and commercial intercourse. The cherry-tree, like almost all fruit-trees, was, as is well known, only a few centuries ago transplanted by commerce into our zone, and therefore only by this action of a definite society in a definite age provided for the evidence of Feuerbach's "senses." Actually, when we conceive things thus, as they really are and happened, every profound philosophical problem is resolved, as will be seen even more clearly later, quite simply into an empirical fact.

For instance, the important question of the relation of man to nature (Bruno goes so far as to speak of "the antitheses in nature and history", as though these were two separate "things" and man did not always have before him an historical nature and a natural history) out of which all the "unfathomably lofty works" on "substance" and "self-consciousness" were born, crumbles of itself when we understand that the celebrated "unity of man with nature" has always existed in industry and has existed in varying forms in every epoch according to the lesser or greater development of industry, just like the "struggle" of man with nature, right up to the development of his productive powers on a corresponding basis.

---

* Feuerbach's failing is not that he subordinates the flatly obvious, the sensuous appearance, to the sensuous reality established by more accurate investigation of the sensuous facts, but that he cannot in the last resort cope with the sensuous world except by looking at it with the "eyes" i.e. through the "spectacles" of the *philosopher*.

Industry and commerce, production and the exchange of the necessities of life, themselves determine distribution, the structure of the different social classes and are, in turn, determined by these as to the mode in which they are carried on; and so it happens that in Manchester, for instance, Feuerbach sees only factories and machines where a hundred years ago only spinning-wheels and weaving-looms were to be seen, or in the Campagna of Rome he finds only pasture lands and swamps, where in the time of Augustus he would have found nothing but the vineyards and villas of Roman capitalists. Feuerbach speaks in particular of the perception of natural science; he mentions secrets which are disclosed only to the eye of the physicist and chemist: but where would natural science be without industry and commerce? Even this "pure" natural science is provided with an aim, as with its material, only through trade and industry, through the sensuous activity of men. So much is this activity, this unceasing sensuous labour and creation, this production, the basis of the whole sensuous world as it now exists, that, were it interrupted only for a year, Feuerbach would not only find an enormous change in the natural world, but would very soon find that the whole world of men and his own perceptive faculty, nay his own existence, were missing.

Of course, in all this the priority of external nature remains unassailed, and all this has no application to the original men produced by "generatio æquivoca" (spontaneous generation); but this differentiation has meaning only in so far as man is considered to be distinct from nature. For that matter, nature, the nature that preceded human history, is not by any means the nature in which Feuerbach lives, nor the nature which to-day no longer exists anywhere (except perhaps on a few Australian coral-islands of recent origin) and which, therefore, does not exist for Feuerbach. . . .

Certainly Feuerbach has a great advantage over the "pure" materialists in that he realizes how man too is an "object of the senses." But apart from the fact that he only conceives him as a "sensuous object," not as "sensuous activity," because he still remains in the realm of theory and conceives of men not in their given social connection, not under their existing conditions of life, which have made them what they are, he never arrives at the really existing active men, but stops at the abstraction "man", and gets no further than recognizing "the true, individual, corporeal man" emotionally, i.e. he knows no other "human relationships" "of man to man" than love and friendship, and even then idealized. He gives no criticism of the present conditions of life. Thus he never manages to conceive the sensuous world as the total living sensuous activity of the individuals composing it; and therefore when, for example, he sees instead of healthy men a crowd of scrofulous, over-worked and consumptive starvelings, he is compelled to take refuge in the "higher perception" and in the ideal "compensation in the species," and thus to relapse into idealism at the very point where the communist materialist sees the necessity, and at the same time the condition, of a transformation both of industry and of the social structure.

As far as Feuerbach is a materialist he does not deal with history, and as far as he considers history he is not a materialist. With him materialism and history diverge completely, a fact which explains itself from what has been said.

History is nothing but the succession of the separate generations, each of which exploits the materials, the forms of capital, the productive forces handed down to it by all preceding ones, and thus on the one hand continues the traditional activity in completely changed circumstances and, on the other, modifies the old circumstances with a completely changed activity. This can be speculatively distorted so that later history is made the goal of earlier history, e.g. the goal ascribed to the discovery of America is to further the eruption of the French Revolution. Thereby history receives its own special aims and becomes "a person ranking with other persons" (to wit: "self-consciousness, criticism, the Unique," etc.), while what is designated with the words "destiny," "goal," "germ," or "idea" of earlier history is nothing more than an abstraction formed from later history, from the active influence which earlier history exercises on later history. The further the separate spheres, which interact on one another, extend in the course of this development, the more the original isolation of the separate nationalities is destroyed by the developed mode of production and intercourse and the division of labour naturally brought forth by these, the more history becomes world-history. Thus, for instance, if in England a machine is invented, which in India or China deprives countless workers of bread, and overturns the whole form of existence of these empires, this invention becomes a world-historical fact. Or again, take the case of sugar and coffee which have proved their world-historical importance in the nineteenth century by the fact that the lack of these products, occasioned by the Napoleonic Continental system, caused the Germans to rise against Napoleon, and thus became the real basis of the glorious Wars of Liberation of 1813. From this it follows that this transformation of history into world-history is not indeed a mere abstract act on the part of the "self-consciousness," the world-spirit, or of any other metaphysical spectre, but a quite material, empirically verifiable act, an act the proof of which every individual furnishes as he comes and goes, eats, drinks and clothes himself.

The ideas of the ruling class are in every epoch the ruling ideas: i.e. the class, which is the ruling material force of society, is at the same time its ruling intellectual force. The class which has the means of material production at its disposal, has control at the same time over the means of mental production, so that thereby, generally speaking, the ideas of those who lack the means of mental production are subject to it. The ruling ideas are nothing more than the ideal expression of the dominant material relationships, the dominant material relationships grasped as ideas; hence of the relationships which make the one class the ruling one, therefore the ideas of its dominance. The individuals composing the ruling class possess among other things consciousness, and therefore think. In so far, therefore, as they rule as a class and determine the extent and compass of an epoch, it is self-evident that they do this in their whole range, hence among other things rule also as thinkers, as producers of ideas, and regulate the production and distribution of the ideas of their age: thus their ideas are the ruling ideas of the epoch. For instance, in an age and in a country where royal power, aristocracy and bourgeoisie are contending for mastery and where, therefore, mastery is shared, the doctrine of the separation of powers proves to be the dominant idea and is expressed as an "eternal law." The division of labour, which we saw above as one of the chief forces of history up till now, manifests itself also in the ruling class as the division of mental and material labour, so that inside this class one part appears as the thinkers of the class (its active, conceptive ideologists, who make the perfecting of the illusion of the class about itself their chief source of livelihood), while the others' attitude to these ideas and illusions is more passive and receptive, because they are in reality the active members of this class and have less time to make up illusions and ideas about themselves. Within this class this cleavage can even develop into a certain opposition and hostility between the two parts, which, however, in the case of a practical collision, in which the class itself is endangered, automatically comes to nothing, in which case there also vanishes the semblance that the ruling ideas were not the ideas of the ruling class and had a power distinct from the power of this class. The existence of revolutionary ideas in a particular period presupposes the existence of a revolutionary class; about the premises for the latter sufficient has already been said above.

If now in considering the course of history we detach the ideas of the ruling class from the ruling class itself and attribute to them an independent existence, if we confine ourselves to saying that these or those ideas were dominant, without bothering ourselves about the conditions of production and the producers of these ideas, if we then ignore the individuals and world conditions which are the source of the ideas, we can say, for instance, that during the time that the aristocracy was dominant, the concepts honour, loyalty, etc., were dominant, during the dominance of the bourgeoisie the concepts freedom, equality, etc. The ruling class itself on the whole imagines this to be so. This conception of history, which is common to all historians, particularly since the eighteenth century, will necessarily come up against the phenomenon that increasingly abstract ideas hold sway, i.e. ideas which increasingly take on the form of universality. For each new class which puts itself in the place of one ruling before it, is compelled, merely in order to carry through its aim, to represent its interest as the common interest of all the members of society, put in an ideal form; it will give its ideas the form of universality, and represent them as the only rational, universally valid ones. The class making a revolution appears from the very start, merely because it is opposed to a *class,* not as a class but as the representative of the whole of society; it appears as the whole mass of society confronting the one ruling class. It can do this because, to start with, its interest really is more connected with the common interest of all other non-ruling classes, because under the pressure of conditions its interest has not yet been able to develop as the particular interest of a particular class. Its victory, therefore, benefits also many individuals of the other classes which are not winning a dominant position, but only in so far as it now puts these individuals in a position to raise themselves into the ruling class. When the French bourgeoisie overthrew the power of the aristocracy, it thereby made it possible for many proletarians to raise themselves above the proletariat, but only in so far as they became bourgeois. Every new class, therefore, achieves its hegemony only on a broader basis than that of the class ruling previously, in return for which the opposition of the non-ruling class against the new ruling class later develops all the more sharply and profoundly. Both these things determine the fact that the struggle to be waged against this new ruling class, in its turn, aims at a more decided and radical negation of the previous conditions of society than could all previous classes which sought to rule.

This whole semblance, that the rule of a certain class is only the rule of certain ideas, comes to a natural end, of course, as soon as society ceases at last to be organized in the form of class-rule, that is to say as soon as it is no longer necessary to represent a particular interest as general or "the general interest" as ruling.

Once the ruling ideas have been separated from the ruling individuals and, above all, from the relationships which result from a given stage of the mode of production, and in this way the conclusion has been reached that history is always under the sway of ideas, it is very easy to abstract from these various ideas "the idea," "die Idee," etc., as the dominant force in history, and thus to understand all these separate ideas and concepts as "forms of self-determination" on the part of *the* concept developing in history. It follows then naturally, too, that all the relationships of men can be derived from the concept of man, man as conceived, the essence of man, *man.* This has been done by the speculative philosophers. Hegel himself confesses at the end of *The Philosophy of History* that he "has considered the progress of *the concept* only" and has represented in history "the true theodicy." Now one can go back again to the "producers of the concept," to the theoreticians, ideologists and philosophers, and one comes then to the conclusion that the philosophers, the thinkers as such, have at all times been dominant in history: a conclusion, as we see, already expressed by Hegel. The whole trick of proving the hegemony of the spirit in history (hierarchy Stirner calls it) is thus confined to the following three tricks.

1. One must separate the ideas of those ruling for empirical reasons, under empirical conditions and as empirical individuals, from these actual rulers, and thus recognize the rule of ideas or illusions in history.

2. One must bring an order into this rule of ideas, prove a mystical connection among the successive ruling ideas, which is managed by understanding them as "acts of self-determination on the part of the concept" (this is possible because by virtue of their empirical basis these ideas are really connected with one another and because, conceived as *mere* ideas, they become self-distinctions, distinctions made by thought).

3. To remove the mystical appearance of this "self-determining concept" it is changed into a person—"self-consciousness"—or, to appear thoroughly materialistic, into a series of persons, who represent the "concept" in history, into the "thinkers," the "philosophers," the ideologists, who again are understood as the manufacturers of history, as "the council of guardians," as the rulers. Thus the whole body of materialistic elements has been removed from history and now full rein can be given to the speculative steed.

Whilst in ordinary life every shopkeeper is very well able to distinguish between what somebody professes to be and what he really is, our historians have not yet won even this trivial insight. They take every epoch at its word and believe that everything it says and imagines about itself is true.

This historical method which reigned in Germany, (and especially the reason why), must be understood from its connection with the illusion of ideologists in general, e.g. the illusions of the jurists, politicians (of the practical statesmen among them, too), from the dogmatic dreamings and distortions of these fellows; this illusion is explained perfectly easily from their practical position in life, their job, and the division of labour.

II. Estranged Labour[1]

We have proceeded from the premises of political economy. We have accepted its language and its laws. We presupposed private property, the separation of labour, capital and land, and of wages, profit of capital and rent of land—likewise division of labour, competition, the concept of exchange-value, etc. On the basis of political economy itself, in its own words, we have shown that the worker sinks to the level of a commodity and becomes indeed the most wretched of commodities; that the wretchedness of the worker is in inverse proportion to the power and

[1] Estranged Labour—*Die Entfremdete Arbeit*

magnitude of his production; that the necessary result of competition is the accumulation of capital in a few hands, and thus the restoration of monopoly in a more terrible form; that finally the distinction between capitalist and land-rentier, like that between the tiller of the soil and the factory-worker, disappears and that the whole of society must fall apart into the two classes—the property-*owners* and the propertyless *workers*.

Political economy proceeds from the fact of private property, but it does not explain it to us. It expresses in general, abstract formulae the *material* process through which private property actually passes, and these formulae it then takes for *laws*. It does not *comprehend* these laws —i.e., it does not demonstrate how they arise from the very nature of private property. Political economy does not disclose the source of the division between labour and capital, and between capital and land. When, for example, it defines the relationship of wages to profit, it takes the interest of the capitalists to be the ultimate cause; i.e., it takes for granted what it is supposed to evolve. Similarly, competition comes in everywhere. It is explained from external circumstances. As to how far these external and apparently fortuitous circumstances are but the expression of a necessary course of development, political economy teaches us nothing. We have seen how, to it, exchange itself appears to be a fortuitous fact. The only wheels which political economy sets in motion are *avarice* and the *war amongst the avaricious—competition*.

Precisely because political economy does not grasp the connections within the movement, it was possible to counterpose, for instance, the doctrine of competition to the doctrine of monopoly, the doctrine of craft-liberty to the doctrine of the corporation, the doctrine of the division of landed property to the doctrine of the big estate—for competition, craft-liberty and the division of landed property were explained and comprehended only as fortuitous, premeditated and violent consequences of monopoly, the corporation, and feudal property, not as their necessary, inevitable and natural consequences.

Now, therefore, we have to grasp the essential connection between private property, avarice, and the separation of labour, capital and landed property; between exchange and competition, value and the devaluation of men, monopoly and competition, etc.; the connection between this whole estrangement and the *money*-system.

Do not let us go back to a fictitious primordial condition as the political economist does, when he tries to explain. Such a primordial condition explains nothing. He merely pushes the question away into a grey nebulous distance. He assumes in the form of fact, of an event, what he is supposed to deduce—namely, the necessary relationship between two things—between, for example, division of labour and exchange. Theology in the same way explains the origin of evil by the fall of man: that is, it assumes as a fact, in historical form, what has to be explained.

We proceed from an *actual* economic fact.

The worker becomes all the poorer the more wealth he produces, the more his production increases in power and range. The worker becomes an ever cheaper commodity the more commodities he creates. With the *increasing value* of the world of things proceeds in direct proportion the *devaluation* of the world of men. Labour produces not only commodities: it produces itself and the worker as a *commodity*—and does so in the proportion in which it produces commodities generally.

This fact expresses merely that the object which labour produces—labour's product—confronts it as *something alien*, as a *power independent* of the producer. The product of labour is labour which has been congealed in an object, which has become material: it is the *objectification* of labour. Labour's realization is its objectification. In the conditions dealt with by political economy this realization of labour appears as *loss of reality* for the workers; objectification as *loss of the object* and *object-bondage;* appropriation as *estrangement*, as *alienation.*[1]

So much does labour's realization appear as loss of reality that the worker loses reality to the point of starving to death. So much does objectification appear as loss of the object that the worker is robbed of the objects most necessary not only for his life but for his work. Indeed, labour itself becomes an object which he can get hold of only with the greatest effort and with the most irregular interruptions. So much does the appropriation of the object appear as estrangement that the more objects the worker produces the fewer can he possess and the more he falls under the dominion of his product, capital.

All these consequences are contained in the definition that the worker is related to the *product of his labour* as to an *alien* object. For on this premise it is clear that the more the worker spends himself, the more powerful the alien objective world becomes which he creates over-against himself, the poorer he himself—his inner world—becomes, the less belongs to him as his own. It is the same in religion. The more man puts into God, the less he retains in himself. The worker puts his life into the object; but now his life no longer belongs to him but to the object. Hence, the greater this activity, the greater is the worker's lack of objects. Whatever the product of his labour is, he is not. Therefore the greater this product, the less is he himself. The *alienation* of the worker in his product means not only that his labour becomes an object, an *external* existence, but that it exists *outside him*, independently, as something alien to him, and that it becomes a power on its own confronting him; it means that the life which he has conferred on the object confronts him as something hostile and alien.

Let us now look more closely at the *objectification,* at the production of the worker; and therein at the *estrangement,* the *loss* of the object, his product.

[1] Alienation—*Entäusserung*

The worker can create nothing without *nature,* without the *sensuous external world.* It is the material on which his labour is manifested, in which it is active, from which and by means of which it produces.

But just as nature provides labour with the *means of life* in the sense that labour cannot *live* without objects on which to operate, on the other hand, it also provides the *means of life* in the more restricted sense—i.e., the means for the physical subsistence of the *worker* himself.

Thus the more the worker by his labour *appropriates* the external world, sensuous nature, the more he deprives himself of *means of life* in the double respect: first, that the sensuous external world more and more ceases to be an object belonging to his labour—to be his labour's *means of life;* and secondly, that it more and more ceases to be *means of life* in the immediate sense, means for the physical subsistence of the worker.

Thus in this double respect the worker becomes a slave of his object, first, in that he receives an *object of labour,* i.e., in that he receives *work;* and secondly, in that he receives *means of subsistence.* Therefore, it enables him to exist, first, as a *worker;* and, second, as a *physical subject.* The extremity of this bondage is that it is only as a *worker* that he continues to maintain himself as a *physical subject,* and that it is only as a *physical subject* that he is a *worker.*

(The laws of political economy express the estrangement of the worker in his object thus: the more the worker produces, the less he has to consume; the more values he creates, the more valueless, the more unworthy he becomes; the better formed his product, the more deformed becomes the worker; the more civilized his object, the more barbarous becomes the worker; the mightier labour becomes, the more powerless becomes the worker; the more ingenious labour becomes, the duller becomes the worker and the more he becomes nature's bondsman.)

Political economy conceals the estrangement inherent in the nature of labour by not considering the direct relationship between the worker (labour) *and production.* It is true that labour produces for the rich wonderful things—but for the worker it produces privation. It produces palaces—but for the worker, hovels. It produces beauty—but for the worker, deformity. It replaces labour by machines—but some of the workers it throws back to a barbarous type of labour, and the other workers it turns into machines. It produces intelligence—but for the worker idiocy, cretinism.

The direct relationship of labour to its produce is the relationship of the worker to the objects of his production. The relationship of the man of means to the objects of production and to production itself is only a *consequence* of this first relationship—and confirms it. We shall consider this other aspect later.

When we ask, then, what is the essential relationship of labour we are asking about the relationship of the *worker* to production.

Till now we have been considering the estrangement, the alienation of the worker only in one of its aspects, i.e., the worker's *relationship to the products of his labour.* But the estrangement is manifested not only in the result but in the *act of production*—within the *producing activity* itself. How would the worker come to face the product of his activity as a stranger, were it not that in the very act of production he was estranging himself from himself? The product is after all but the summary of the activity, of production. If then the product of labour is alienation, production itself must be active alienation, the alienation of activity, the activity of alienation. In the estrangement of the object of labour is merely summarized the estrangement, the alienation, in the activity of labour itself.

What, then, constitutes the alienation of labour?

First, the fact that labour is *external* to the worker, i.e., it does not belong to his essential being; that in his work, therefore, he does not affirm himself but denies himself, does not feel content but unhappy, does not develop freely his physical and mental energy but mortifies his body and ruins his mind. The worker therefore only feels himself outside his work, and in his work feels outside himself. He is at home when he is not working, and when he is working he is not at home. His labour is therefore not voluntary, but coerced; it is *forced labour.* It is therefore not the satisfaction of a need; it is merely a *means* to satisfy needs external to it. Its alien character emerges clearly in the fact that as soon as no physical or other compulsion exists, labour is shunned like the plague. External labour, labour in which man alienates himself, is a labour of self-sacrifice, of mortification. Lastly, the external character of labour for the worker appears in the fact that it is not his own, but someone else's, that it does not belong to him, that in it he belongs, not to himself, but to another. Just as in religion the spontaneous activity of the human imagination, of the human brain and the human heart, operates independently of the individual—that is, operates on him as an alien, divine or diabolical activity—in the same way the worker's activity is not his spontaneous activity. It belongs to another; it is the loss of his self.

As a result, therefore, man (the worker) no longer feels himself to be freely active in any but his animal functions—eating, drinking, procreating, or at most in his dwelling and in dressing-up, etc.; and in his human functions he no longer feels himself to be anything but an animal. What is animal becomes human and what is human becomes animal.

Certainly eating, drinking, procreating, etc., are also genuinely human functions. But in the abstraction which separates them from the sphere of all other human activity and turns them into sole and ultimate ends, they are animal.

We have considered the act of estranging practical human activity, labour, in two of its aspects. (1) The relation of the worker to the *product of labour* as an alien object exercising power over him. This relation is at the same time the relation to the sensuous external world, to the objects of nature as an alien world antagonistically opposed to him. (2) The relation of labour to the *act of production* within the *labour* process. This relation is the relation of the worker to his own activity as an alien activity not belonging to him; it is activity as suffering, strength as weakness, begetting as emasculating, the worker's *own* physical and mental energy, his personal life or what is life other than activity—as an activity which is turned against him, neither depends on nor belongs to him. Here we have *self-estrangement,* as we had previously the estrangement of the *thing*.

We have yet a third aspect of *estranged labour* to deduce from the two already considered.

Man is a species being, not only because in practice and in theory he adopts the species as his object (his own as well as those of other things), but—and this is only another way of expressing it—but also because he treats himself as the actual, living species; because he treats himself as a *universal* and therefore a free being.

The life of the species, both in man and in animals, consists physically in the fact that man (like the animal) lives on inorganic nature; and the more universal man is compared with an animal, the more universal is the sphere of inorganic nature on which he lives. Just as plants, animals, stones, the air, light, etc., constitute a part of human consciousness in the realm of theory, partly as objects of natural science, partly as objects of art—his spiritual inorganic nature, spiritual nourishment which he must first prepare to make it palatable and digestable—so too in the realm of practice they constitute a part of human life and human activity. Physically man lives only on these products of nature, whether they appear in the form of food, heating, clothes, a dwelling, or whatever it may be. The universality of man is in practice manifested precisely in the universality which makes all nature his *inorganic* body—both inasmuch as nature is (1) his direct means of life, and (2) the material, the object, and the instrument of his life-activity. Nature is man's *inorganic body*—nature, that is, in so far as it is not itself the human body. Man *lives* on nature—means that nature is his *body*, with which he must remain in continuous intercourse if he is not to die. That man's physical and spiritual life is linked to nature means simply that nature is linked to itself, for man is a part of nature.

In estranging from man (1) nature, and (2) himself, his own active functions, his life-activity, estranged labour estranges the *species* from man. It turns for him the *life of the species* into a means of individual life. First it estranges the life of the species and individual life, and secondly it makes individual life in its abstract form the purpose of the life of the species, likewise in its abstract and estranged form.

For in the first place labour, *life-activity, productive life* itself, appears to man merely as a *means* of satisfying a need—the need to maintain the physical existence. Yet the productive life is the life of the species. It is life-engendering life. The whole character of a species—its species character—is contained in the character of its life-activity; and free, conscious activity is man's species character. Life itself appears only as a *means to life.*

The animal is immediately identical with its life-activity. It does not distinguish itself from it. It is *its life-activity.* Man makes his life-activity itself the object of his will and of his consciousness. He has conscious life-activity. It is not a determination with which he directly merges. Conscious life-activity directly distinguishes man from animal life-activity. It is just because of this that he is a species being. Or it is only because he is a species being that he is a Conscious Being, i.e., that his own life is an object for him. Only because of that is his activity free activity. Estranged labour reverses this relationship, so that it is just because man is a conscious being that he makes his life-activity, his *essential* being, a mere means to his *existence.*

In creating an *objective world* by his practical activity, in *working-up* inorganic nature, man proves himself a conscious species being, i.e., as a being that treats the species as its own essential being, or that treats itself as a species being. Admittedly animals also produce. They build themselves nests, dwellings, like the bees, beavers, ants, etc. But an animal only produces what it immediately needs for itself or its young. It produces one-sidedly, whilst man produces universally. It produces only under the dominion of immediate physical need, whilst man produces even when he is free from physical need and only truly produces in freedom therefrom. An animal produces only itself, whilst man reproduces the whole of nature. An animal's product belongs immediately to its physical body, whilst man freely confronts his product. An animal forms things in accordance with the standard and the need of the species to which it belongs, whilst man knows how to produce in accordance with the standard of every species, and knows how to apply everywhere the inherent standard to the object. Man therefore also forms things in accordance with the laws of beauty.

It is just in the working-up of the objective world, therefore, that man first really proves himself to be a *species being.* This production is his active species life. Through and because of this production, nature appears as *his* work and his reality. The object of labour is, therefore, the *objectification of man's species life*: for he duplicates himself not only, as in consciousness, intellectually, but also actively, in reality, and therefore he contemplates himself in a world that he has created. In tearing away from man the object of his production, therefore, estranged labour tears from him his *species life*, his real species objectivity, and transforms his advantage over animals into the disadvantage that his inorganic body, nature, is taken from him.

Similarly, in degrading spontaneous activity, free activity, to a means, estranged labour makes man's species life a means to his physical existence.

The consciousness which man has of his species is thus transformed by estrangement in such a way that the species life becomes for him a means.

Estranged labour turns thus:

(3) *Man's species being,* both nature and his spiritual species property, into a being *alien* to him, into a *means* to his *individual existence.* It estranges man's own body from him, as it does external nature and his spiritual essence, his *human* being.

(4) An immediate consequence of the fact that man is estranged from the product of his labour, from his life-activity, from his species being is the *estrangement of man* from *man.* If a man is confronted by himself, he is confronted by the *other* man. What applies to a man's relation to his work, to the product of his labour and to himself, also holds of a man's relation to the other man, and to the other man's labour and object of labour.

In fact, the proposition that man's species nature is estranged from him means that one man is estranged from the other, as each of them is from man's essential nature.[1]

---

[1] Species nature (and earlier species being)—*Gattungswesen*: man's essential nature—*menschlichen Wesen*: see *Wesen* in "Translator's Note on Terminology."

The following short passages from Feuerbach's *Essence of Christianity* may help readers to understand the ideological background to this part of Marx's thought, and, incidentally, to see how Marx accepted but infused with new content concepts made current by Feuerbach as well as Hegel and the political economists:

"What is this essential difference between man and the brute? . . . Consciousness— but consciousness in the strict sense; for the consciousness implied in the feeling of self as an individual, in discrimination by the senses, in the perception and even judgment of outward things according to definite sensible signs, cannot be denied to the brutes. Consciousness in the strictest sense is present only in a being to whom his species, his essential nature, is an object of thought. The brute is indeed conscious of himself as an individual—and he has accordingly the feeling of self as the common centre of successive sensations—but not as a species. . . . In practical life we have to do with individuals; in science, with species. . . . But only a being to whom his own species, his own nature, is an object of thought, can make the essential nature of other things or beings an object of thought. . . . The brute has only a simple, man a twofold life; in the brute, the inner life is one with the outer. Man has both an inner and an outer life. The inner life of man is the life which has relation to his species—to his general, as distinguished from his individual nature. . . . The brute can exercise no function which has relation to its species without another individual external to itself; but man can perform the functions of thought and speech, which strictly imply such a relation, apart from another individual. . . . Man is in fact at once I and Thou; he can put himself in the place of another, for this reason, that to him his species, his essential nature, and not merely his individuality, is an object of thought. . . . An object to which a subject essentially, necessarily relates, is nothing else than this subject's own, but objective nature. . . .

"The relation of the sun to the earth is, therefore, at the same time a relation of the earth to itself, or to its own nature, for the measure of the size and of the intensity of

The estrangement of man, and in fact every relationship in which man stands to himself, is first realized and expressed in the relationship in which a man stands to other men.

Hence within the relationship of estranged labour each man views the other in accordance with the standard and the position in which he finds himself as a worker.

We took our departure from a fact of political economy—the estrangement of the worker and his production. We have formulated the concept of this fact—*estranged, alienated* labour. We have analysed this concept—hence analysing merely a fact of political economy.

Let us now see, further, how in real life the concept of estranged, alienated labour must express and present itself.

If the product of labour is alien to me, if it confronts me as an alien power, to whom, then, does it belong?

If my own activity does not belong to me, if it is an alien, a coerced activity, to whom, then, does it belong?

To a being *other* than me.

Who is this being?

The *gods*? To be sure, in the earliest times the principal production (for example, the building of temples, etc., in Egypt, India and Mexico) appears to be in the service of the gods, and the product belongs to the gods. However, the gods on their own were never the lords of labour. No more was *nature*. And what a contradiction it would be if, the more man subjugated nature by his labour and the more the miracles of the gods were rendered superfluous by the miracles of industry, the more man were to renounce the joy of production and the enjoyment of the produce in favour of these powers.

The *alien* being, to whom labour and the produce of labour belongs, in whose service labour is done and for whose benefit the produce of labour is provided, can only be *man* himself.

If the product of labour does not belong to the worker, if it confronts him as an alien power, this can only be because it belongs to some *other man than the worker*. If the worker's activity is a torment to him, to another it must be *delight* and his life's joy. Not the gods, not nature, but only man himself can be this alien power over man.

We must bear in mind the above-stated proposition that man's relation to himself only becomes *objective* and *real* for him through his relation to the other man. Thus, if the product of his labour, his labour *objectified*, is for him an *alien,* hostile, powerful object independent of him, then his

---

light which the sun possesses as the object of the earth, is the measure of the distance, which determines the peculiar nature of the earth. . . . In the object which he contemplates, therefore, man becomes acquainted with himself. . . . The power of the object over him is therefore the power of his own nature."

(*The Essence of Christianity*, by Ludwig Feuerbach, translated from the second German edition by Marian Evans, London, 1854, pp. 1-5.)—*Ed.*

position towards it is such that someone else is master of this object, someone who is alien, hostile, powerful, and independent of him. If his own activity is to him an unfree activity, then he is treating it as activity performed in the service, under the dominion, the coercion and the yoke of another man.

Every self-estrangement of man from himself and from nature appears in the relation in which he places himself and nature to men other than and differentiated from himself. For this reason religious self-estrangement necessarily appears in the relationship of the layman to the priest, or again to a mediator, etc., since we are here dealing with the intelletual world. In the real practical world self-estrangement can only become manifest through the real practical relationship to other men. The medium through which estrangement takes place is itself *practical*. Thus through estranged labour man not only engenders his relationship to the object and to the act of production as to powers that are alien and hostile to him; he also engenders the relationship in which other men stand to his production and to his product, and the relationship in which he stands to these other men. Just as he begets his own production as the loss of his reality, as his punishment; just as he begets his own product as a loss, as a product not belonging to him; so he begets the dominion of the one who does not produce over production and over the product. Just as he estranges from himself his own activity, so he confers to the stranger activity which is not his own.

Till now we have only considered this relationship from the standpoint of the worker and later we shall be considering it also from the standpoint of the non-worker.

Through *estranged, alienated labour,* then, the worker produces the relationship to this labour of a man alien to labour and standing outside it. The relationship of the worker to labour engenders the relation to it of the capitalist, or whatever one chooses to call the master of labour. *Private property* is thus the product, the result, the necessary consequence, of alienated labour, of the external relation of the worker to nature and to himself.

Private property thus results by analysis from the concept of *alienated labour*—i.e., of *alienated man,* of estranged labour, of estranged life, of *estranged* man.

True, it is as a result of the *movement of private property* that we have obtained the concept of *alienated labour* (*of alienated life*) from political economy. But on analysis of this concept it becomes clear that though private property appears to be the source, the cause of alienated labour, it is really its consequence, just as the gods *in the beginning* are not the cause but the effect of man's intellectual confusion. Later this relationship becomes reciprocal.

Only at the very culmination of the development of private property does this, its secret, re-emerge, namely, that on the one hand it is the *product* of alienated labour, and that secondly it is the *means* by which labour alienates itself, the *realization of this alienation*.

This exposition immediately sheds light on various hitherto unsolved conflicts.

(1) Political economy starts from labour as the real soul of production; yet to labour it gives nothing, and to private property everything. From this contradiction Proudhon has concluded in favour of labour and against private property. We understand, however, that this apparent contradiction is the contradiction of *estranged labour* with itself, and that political economy has merely formulated the laws of estranged labour.

We also understand, therefore, that *wages* and *private property* are identical: where the product, the object of labour pays for labour itself, the wage is but a necessary consequence of labour's estrangement, for after all in the wage of labour, labour does not appear as an end in itself but as the servant of the wage. We shall develop this point later, and meanwhile will only deduce some conclusions.

A *forcing-up of wages* (disregarding all other difficulties, including the fact that it would only be by force, too, that the higher wages, being an anomaly, could be maintained) would therefore be nothing but *better payment for the slave*, and would not conquer either for the worker or for labour their human status and dignity.

Indeed, even the *equality of wages* demanded by Proudhon only transforms the relationship of the present-day worker to his labour into the relationship of all men to labour. Society is then conceived as an abstract capitalist.

Wages are in direct consequence of estranged labour, and estranged labour is the direct cause of private property. The downfall of the one aspect must therefore mean the downfall of the other.

(2) From the relationship of estranged labour to private property it further follows that the emancipation of society from private property, etc., from servitude, is expressed in the *political* form of the *emancipation of the workers;* not that *their* emancipation alone was at stake but because the emancipation of the workers contains universal human emancipation— and it contains this, because the whole of human servitude is involved in the relation of the worker to production, and every relation of servitude is but a modification and consequence of this relation.

Just as we have found the concept of *private property* from the concept of *estranged, alienated labour by analysts,* in the same way every *category* of political economy can be evolved with the help of these two factors; and we shall find again in each category, e.g., trade, competition, capital, money, only a *definite* and *developed expression* of the first foundations.

Before considering this configuration, however, let us try to solve two problems.

(1) To define the general *nature of private property*, as it has arisen

as a result of estranged labour, in its relation to *truly human, social property*.

(2) We have accepted the *estrangement of labour*, its *alienation*, as a fact, and we have analysed this fact. How, we now ask, does *man* come to *alienate*, to estrange, *his labour*? How is this estrangement rooted in the nature of human development? We have already gone a long way to the solution of this problem by *transforming* the question as to the *origin of private property* into the question as to the relation of *alienated labour* to the course of humanity's development. For when one speaks of *private property*, one thinks of being concerned with something external to man. When one speaks of labour, one is directly concerned with man himself. This new formulation of the question already contains its solution.

As to (1): The general nature of private property and its relation to truly human property.

Alienated labour has resolved itself for us into two elements which mutually condition one another, or which are but different expressions of one and the same relationship. *Appropriation* appears as *estrangement*, as *alienation*; and *alienation* appears as *appropriation, estrangement* as true *enfranchisement*.

We have considered the one side—*alienated* labour in relation to the *worker* himself, i.e., the *relation of alienated labour to itself*. The *property-relation of the non-worker to the worker and to labour* we have found as the product, the necessary outcome of this relation of alienated labour. *Private property*, as the material, summary expression of alienated labour, embraces both relations—the *relation of the worker to work, to the product of his labour and to the non-worker*, and the relation of the *non-worker to the worker and to the product of his labour*.

Having seen that in relation to the worker who *appropriates* nature by means of his labour, this appropriation appears as estrangement, his own spontaneous activity as activity for another and as activity of another, vitality as a sacrifice of life, production of the object as loss of the object to an alien power, to an *alien* person—we shall now consider the relation to the worker, to labour and its object of this person who is *alien* to labour and the worker.

First it has to be noticed, that everything which appears in the worker as an *activity of alienation, of estrangement*, appears in the non-worker as a *state of alienation, of estrangement*.

Secondly, that the worker's *real, practical attitude* in production and to the product (as a state of mind) appears in the non-worker confronting him as a *theoretical* attitude.

Thirdly, the non-worker does everything against the worker which the worker does against himself; but he does not do against himself what he does against the worker.

Let us look more closely at these three relations.[1]

[1] At this point the first manuscript breaks off unfinished—*Ed.*

18. Karl Mannheim

Types of Rationality and
Organized Insecurity

I. Clarification of the Various Meanings of the Word "Rationality"

Before turning to the central question concerning the typical situations in industrial society from which certain forms of rationality or irrationality arise, we must first make certain observations about the general nature and species of rationality and irrationality. Few words are used in so many contradictory ways. For this very reason we will have to limit ourselves to explaining two of the most important uses of the words "rational" and "irrational", which, in our opinion, are indispensable in sociological analysis.

Sociologists use the words "rational" and "irrational" in two senses, which we will call "substantial" and "functional" rationality or irrationality.

It is not very difficult to explain the nature of "substantial" rationality. We understand as substantially rational an act of thought which reveals intelligent insight into the inter-relations of events in a given situation. Thus the intelligent act of thought itself will be described as "substantially rational", whereas everything else which either is false or not an act of thought at all (as for example drives, impulses, wishes, and feelings, both conscious and unconscious) will be called "substantially irrational".

But in sociology as well as in everyday language, we also use the word "rational" in still another sense when we say, for instance, that this or that industry or administration staff has been "rationalized". In such cases we do not at all understand by the term "rational" the fact that a person carries out acts of thinking and knowing, but rather that a series of actions is organized in such a way that it leads to a previously defined goal, every element in this series of actions receiving a functional position and rôle. Such a functional organization of a series of actions will,

From Mannheim, *Man and Society in an Age of Reconstruction*. (New York: Harcourt, Brace and Co., 1940), pp. 51-60, 117-120, 124-126, 128-143. Translated by Edward Shils. Reprinted by permission of Harcourt, Brace and Company, Inc. Bibliographic footnotes have been omitted.

moreover, be at its best when, in order to attain the given goal, it co-ordinates the means most efficiently.[1] It is by no means characteristic, however, of functional organization in our sense that this optimum be attained or even that the goal itself be considered rational as measured by a certain standard. One may strive to attain an irrational eschatological goal, such as salvation, by so organizing one's ascetic behaviour that it will lead to this goal or, at any rate, to a state of irrational ecstasy. Nevertheless, we should call this behaviour rational because it is organized, since every action has a functional rôle to play in achieving the ultimate aim. Whether a series of actions is functionally rational or not is determined by two criteria: (a) Functional organization with reference to a definite goal; and (b) a consequent calculability when viewed from the standpoint of an observer or a third person seeking to adjust himself to it.

At first sight the distinction between substantial and functional rationality does not seem to be so important. One may object that a functionally rational series of actions must in imagination be planned out by somebody and during its execution it must be also thought out by the person executing it, consequently both forms are only different aspects of the same type of rationality. This, however, is by no means, or at least not always, true. And in order to recognize this one need only think of an army. The common soldier, for example, carries out an entire series of functionally rational actions accurately without having any idea as to the ultimate end of his actions or the functional rôle of each individual act within the framework of the whole. Nevertheless each act is functionally rational since both criteria apply to it, (a) it is organized with reference to a definite goal, and (b) one can adjust oneself to it in calculating one's own actions. We shall, however, speak of the functional rationality of conduct not only when the organization, as in an army, depends in the last analysis on the plans of certain authorities far removed from the actors, but also when this organization and calculability can be traced back to traditionally inherited regulations. Even societies which are held together by tradition are rational in the functional sense since their activities are definitely calculable and individual actions derive their meaning from the part they play in achieving the goal of the whole course of actions. The most that one can say about them is that very often they are as yet not perfectly organized.

If, therefore, in the definition of functional rationality, emphasis is laid on the co-ordination of action with reference to a definite goal, everything which breaks through and disrupts this functional ordering is functionally irrational. Such disruption can be brought about not only through substantial irrationalities such as daydreams and the violent

---

[1] In the following we are not concerned with *optimal* functional rationality because it is not of particular importance for the central theme of this investigation.

outbursts of unruly individuals, to mention the most extreme cases, but also through completely intellectual actions which do not harmonize with the series of actions on which attention is focused. An illuminating example of the disturbance which can arise from substantial irrationality may be seen, where, for example, the diplomatic staff of a state has carefully thought out a series of actions and has agreed on certain steps, when suddenly one of its members falls prey to a nervous collapse and then acts contrary to the plan, thereby destroying it. The functional rationality of the conduct of the diplomatic corps can also be disturbed, however, when it is opposed and rendered impotent by certain actions of the war ministry which have also been organized with the same amount of care and thoroughness. In this case the rationalization of the war ministry can be described as functionally irrational from the standpoint of the diplomatic staff. It therefore becomes clear that the term "functional irrationality" never characterizes an act in itself but only with reference to its position in the entire complex of conduct of which it is a part.

Now that we have made these distinctions, we can safely make the following statement. The more industrialized a society is and the more advanced its division of labour and organization, the greater will be the number of spheres of human activity which will be functionally rational and hence also calculable in advance. Whereas the individual in earlier societies acted only occasionally and in limited spheres in a functionally rational manner, in contemporary society he is compelled to act in this way in more and more spheres of life. This leads us directly to the description of a particular type of rationalization which is most intimately connected with the functional rationalization of conduct, namely the phenomenon of self-rationalization.

By self-rationalization we understand the individual's systematic control of his impulses—a control which is always the first step to be taken, if an individual wants to plan his life so that every action is guided by principle and is directed towards the goal he has in mind. My mode of conduct, my control over and my regulation of my impulses will obviously be quite different when I am a member of a far-reaching organization, in which every action must be carefully adjusted to all the others, from what it is when I am more or less isolated and independent and can do whatever I think right. As a factory worker, I should have to control my impulses and wishes far more completely than as an independent craftsman, where my professional activities would be so loosely organized that I could from time to time satisfy wishes which were not always immediately connected with the work in hand. Modern society attains perhaps its highest stage of functional rationalization in its administrative staff, in which the individuals who take part not only have their specific actions prescribed—this sort of rationalization of tasks may possibly be more advanced in the Taylorization of workers in an industrial plant—but in addition have their life-plan to a large extent imposed in the form of a "career", in which the individual stages are specified in advance. Concern with a career requires a maximum of self-mastery since it involves not only the actual processes of work but also the prescriptive regulation both of the ideas and feelings that one is permitted to have and of one's leisure time.

Thus we see that the different forms of functional rationalization are closely linked up with each other: the functional rationalization of objective activities ultimately evokes self-rationalization. But self-rationalization as we have met it so far does not represent the most radical form of the rationalization of the acting subject. Reflection and self-observation, as distinguished from sheer self-rationalization, are an even more radical form of it.

It is an example of self-rationalization if I adjust my spontaneous wishes or sudden impulses so as to attain a given end: thus if I obey the laws of a technique of thought or keep to the motions prescribed by the technique of a particular type of manual work, I am, by a process of mental training, subordinating my inner motives to an external aim. Self-observation, on the other hand, is more than such a form of mental training. Self-observation aims primarily at an inner self-transformation. Man reflects about himself and his actions mostly for the sake of re-moulding or transforming himself more radically. Normally man's attention is directed not towards himself but towards things which he wishes to manipulate, to change, and to form. He usually does not observe how he himself functions. He lives in immediate acts of experience; he is absorbed in them without ordinarily comprehending them. He reflects, and sees himself for the first time when he fails to carry through some projected action and, as a result of this failure, is thrown, so to speak, back upon himself. "Reflection," "self-observation," "taking account of one's own situation" assume, in such moments, the functions of self-reorganization. It is clear that persons who are confronted more frequently with situations in which they cannot act habitually and without thinking and in which they must always organize themselves anew will have more occasion to reflect on themselves and on situations than persons who have adapted themselves once and for all. The impulses and drives of the latter have been organized as far as a few situations which are important for them are concerned, they function, so to speak, without friction.[1] On that account mobile types of persons—among them the Jews—tend more frequently to be abstract and reflective than the so-

[1] W. I. Thomas's distinction between the Creative, Philistine, and Bohemian types represents a recognition of this phenomenon from a different point of view. Thomas studies the differential reactions to change of three personality types, while we are interested in the types of personalities created by changing or relatively static conditions. Cf. Thomas, W. I., and Znaniecki, F., *The Polish Peasant in Europe and America*, New York, 1927, vol. ii, pp. 1853 seqq.

called "stable" and deeply rooted types. At the same time it becomes apparent that a society which must carry out more complicated processes based upon thinking and acting with a purpose in view, will, in certain situations, necessarily tend to produce the reflective type of person. From this point of view it is clearly fallacious to regard reflectiveness—as many romantic thinkers do—as being under all circumstances a life-extinguishing force. On the contrary, in most cases, reflectiveness preserves life by helping us to adjust ourselves to new situations so complex that in them the naïve and unreflective man would be utterly at a loss.

II. Functional Rationalization by no means Increases Substantial Rationality

Thus here, too, we see that the social source of rationalization can be clearly determined and that indeed the force which creates in our society the various forms of rationality springs from industrialization as a specific form of social organization. Increasing industrialization, to be sure, implies functional rationality, i.e. the organization of the activity of the members of society with reference to objective ends. It does not to the same extent promote "substantial rationality", i.e. the capacity to act intelligently in a given situation on the basis of one's own insight into the interrelations of events. Whoever predicted that the further industrialization of society would raise the average capacity for independent judgment must have learned his mistake from the events of the past few years. The violent shocks of crises and revolutions have uncovered a tendency which has hitherto been working under the surface, namely the paralysing effect of functional rationalization on the capacity for rational judgment.[1]

If, in analysing the changes of recent years, people had kept in mind the distinction between various types of rationality, they would have seen clearly that industrial rationalization served to increase functional rationality but that it offered far less scope for the development of substantial rationality in the sense of the capacity for independent judgment. Moreover, if the distinction between the two types of rationality which emerges from this explanation had been thought out, people would have been forced to the conclusion that functional rationalization is, in its very nature, bound to deprive the average individual of thought, insight, and responsibility and to transfer these capacities to the individuals who direct the process of rationalization.

The fact that in a functionally rationalized society the thinking out of a complex series of actions is confined to a few organizers, assures these men of a key position in society. A few people can see things more and

---

[1] Cf. Veblen, Th. B., *The Vested Interests and the Common Man* (New York, 1920), for an exposition of a divergent interpretation of the influence of industrialization on the possibilities of substantial rationality.

more clearly over an ever-widening field, while the average man's capacity for rational judgment steadily declines once he has turned over to the organizer the responsibility for making decisions. In modern society not only is the ownership of the means of production concentrated in fewer hands, but as we have just shown, there are far fewer positions from which the major structural connections between different activities can be perceived, and fewer men can reach these vantage points.

This is the state of affairs which has led to the growing distance between the élite and the masses, and to the "appeal to the leader" which has recently become so widespread. The average person surrenders part of his own cultural individuality with every new act of integration into a functionally rationalized complex of activities. He becomes increasingly accustomed to being led by others and gradually gives up his own interpretation of events for those which others give him. When the rationalized mechanism of social life collapses in times of crisis, the individual cannot repair it by his own insight. Instead his own impotence reduces him to a state of terrified helplessness. In the social crisis he allows the exertion and the energy needed for intelligent decision to run to waste. Just as nature was unintelligible to primitive man, and his deepest feelings of anxiety arose from the incalculability of the forces of nature, so for modern industrialized man the incalculability of the forces at work in the social system under which he lives, with its economic crisis, inflation, and so on, has become a source of equally pervading fears.

The liberal social order offered a much better chance of psychological preparation for the growth of substantial rationality. Based on relatively small economic units and on moderate individual property holdings, this first stage in the epoch of industrialization produced a relatively larger élite whose members were rather independent in their judgments and who had to direct and organize economic units according to their own more or less rational interpretation of the course of events. Side by side with these independent entrepreneurs with their intelligent self-interest, a relatively independent intelligentsia grew up. Together they guaranteed the existence of substantial rationality.

III. Correlation between the Disorganization of Society and the Disorganization of Personality

In the first part [of this book] we observed the factors which create crowd behaviour and irrationality in our society. In the second we watched the less eruptive, more slowly working social mechanisms which have a detrimental effect upon culture. The enumeration of these negative effects upon social life would not be complete were we not to study the causes of disorganization in their most disastrous forms as they make for crisis, dictatorship, and war. This rhythm of events is in everybody's mind;

but in spite of it the interconnection and necessity of this sequence have not yet been sufficiently thought out. The tangle of economic, social, and psychological factors which brings about the general drift into war in our age has not yet been clearly enough analysed.

Recent experiences have shown us the starting point for our investigations by teaching us that there must definitely be a deeper correlation between the disorganization of society and the disorganization of individual behaviour, and even of certain levels of the human mind, and vice versa that the more strongly a society is organized, the more strongly forms of behaviour and the corresponding attitudes of the mind seem to be integrated. One has only to look at pictures like those of Bosch and Grünewald in order to see that the disorganization of the Medieval order expressed itself in a general fear and anxiety, the symbolic expression of which was the attention given to the underworld with its demons, and the widespread fear of the devil. In the Medieval order the luciferic element was present but had its place in the plan of the universe. When the social order goes wrong psychosis spreads, the diabolic forces are no longer integrated into the Cosmos. In an "adequately" functioning society the neurotic is only the borderline case. In a state of "general disorganization" it is he who sets the pattern. But this correlation between social disorganization and mental disorganization seems to be much stricter than this general statement would lead one to believe. A careful observer, even on the basis of a preliminary contact with the relevant phenomena, would see that the predominant associations, for instance, of a man brought up in a well-integrated traditional society are more conventionalized than those of the average man in a society in the making, or in course of transformation. What we frequently call imagination is perhaps essentially characterized by unexpected mental associations and connections which do not form part of the usual chain of ideas. Also the increased awareness of the new and the sensational which is widespread in America seems to correspond to a society in the making where it was very difficult to stabilize social groups, develop folkways, and thus to determine the flow of mental associations. The lesser premium put on imagination in England, both in science and in life, in spite of its poets and social outsiders, perhaps also falls under that heading. As imagination and free association are mainly dissociated elements springing from the unconscious, their overflow or repression in the individual somewhere corresponds to the general pressure existing in society. The individual organism, according to its hereditary equipment and to its early life history, may put up with these pressures in different ways, but in the long run and in dealing with great numbers of people general causes will serve to create a single dominant pattern. But there are other indications, too. The study of disorganized behaviour as it prevails among delinquents, hobos, and primitives displaced from their community and brought into contact with industrial and urban civilization, shows that it is the disorganized part of a social structure in which disorganized behaviour and personality most frequently occurs. Another instance pointing in the same direction is that the individual by means of self-observation may realize that his psychological adjustment relaxes continuously according to the repressive power of the different social groups in which he lives. Thus the most conventional and most orderly people when they travel in foreign countries very easily drop out of their fixed mental associations and habits. All these are merely different forms of social and mental disintegration which naturally ought to be studied more carefully, but which reveal the meaning of general social tendencies only if they are watched from the point of view of a comprehensive theory. The corresponding phenomenon on a larger scale is presented to us if we watch the suddenly changing behaviour of people living in the socially disintegrated parts of the European continent. History is producing a sad experiment before our eyes, and shows what happens to the individual when the basic integrating factors are put out of action. This is the best place to study the continuous interrelatedness of sociological and psychological mechanisms. These transformations in the characters of individuals should be investigated in concrete field work by trained observers in connection with the transformation of social mechanisms. But such studies would not furnish us with the necessary answers unless two pre-conditions were fulfilled: first, we must have a wider hypothesis concerning the major trends of development in order to be able to allocate carefully the more detailed observations in the different parts of the social field, and secondly some widespread misrepresentations concerning human psychology and its relatedness to the social texture must be set right. As to the main trends in the events of the last decades, the facts are sufficiently well known to be able to reconstruct "their inner sequence." It is possible to describe the great phases in the fundamental, social, and psychological transformation through which the Fascist states are passing. As to the latter, namely the false psychological presumptions with which we used to work, recent developments in psychology and sociology have done their best to revise some of our obsolete hypotheses so that we may be able to characterize these changes. The trouble is that in thinking about these great issues, we have never brought these two different pieces of knowledge together. This is the reason why in the present chapter I shall take at random some of the fundamental questions which invariably occur in discussions on these issues. Let us start with the more general question which is often put first in this context: "What is the contribution psychology can make to the solution of the problem of war or peaceful change? Is there anything in human nature which necessarily makes for war? If not, what is the process whereby a highly industrialized society becomes a martial state with a wholly different psychology?"

In this connection there is another question which presents itself: "Under what circumstances do people who were formerly striving for economic gains, for the raising of their standard of life, invert their scale of values in a relatively short time, and now seem to rank the honour, prestige, and glory of their country far higher than before? In short, why do people sometimes prefer guns and sometimes butter? And, finally, if such fundamental psychological changes do occur are they the ultimate causes of war or are they rather the effect of institutional maladjustments in society?"

A sociology of war and peace aiming at completeness should therefore answer the following two questions: (a) Have there been any societies in history which, on the whole, have made for peaceful attitudes? (b) For what reasons and by what mechanism do peaceful modern societies turn into bellicose ones?

The first question I shall not discuss in detail. It is sufficient to state that nations once bellicose have lived for hundreds of years without war, and this in itself is answer enough to those who assert that war is the necessary consequence of the instinctive equipment of man. First of all we find among the so-called primitive tribes some who do without war, or at least show only mildly bellicose attitudes. These attitudes, however, are less a moral achievement than the outcome of narrow conditions of life. Mostly, as with the Eskimos, it is the hardness of the immediate struggle with nature and the absence of crowding that account for their freedom from aggressiveness. Generally it is the food-gatherers and the agriculturists who are known to be peaceful. Furthermore, trade and commerce very often make for peace; it is dangerous to generalize, however, for under certain conditions the same factors might foster war.

Of the fact that, in our modern civilization, peoples can live for many hundreds of years without war, the Dutch are an example. Although the bellicose peoples by far outnumber the peaceful ones, the mere existence of the latter, as I mentioned, is a sufficient indication that human nature can very well do without war. The main problem, therefore, is to identify those mechanisms, those social processes, which tend to turn peaceful attitudes into pugnacity.

Once peaceful attitudes have been established in a given society the spontaneous growth of warlike attitudes en masse will represent a case of collective "regression." Our next problem, therefore, is: What brings about such a social regression, such a dissolution of all those smoothly working tendencies which are needed by a society based upon work as opposed to conflict?

I think that one of the main causes of a sudden disintegration of socially established attitudes is any kind of collective insecurity such as leads to a partial or total dissolution of society. The present crisis especially has been making us realize that "collective insecurity" has been throughout history the great factor in the rapid dissolution of old attitudes and the creation of new ones.

IV. Different Forms of Insecurity and their Impact upon Behaviour. Disintegration in Animal and Human Societies

But it is not enough to make the general statment that collective insecurity may suddenly change human nature: one must define the "historically specific forms of insecurity," and the ways in which they react upon the psychology of the individual.

The insecurity of nomadic peoples forced by drought, or animal epidemics, to migrate or to plunder their neighbours, differs in many ways from the insecurity from which nations suffer in the modern world. But even in modern societies we have to distinguish between several different causes to which a general feeling of insecurity may be due. In the first stage of capitalism, the maladjustment between absolutism and a growing industrialism led to dissatisfaction and to acute tension between the rising bourgeoisie, on the one hand, and the landed aristocracy and the army on the other. It was this "tension" which sought an outlet in war. In the monopolistic stage of capitalism, the underlying "tension" between capital and labour grows acute when structural unemployment of large masses transforms their latent hostility into despair. This leads to disturbances and even to that state of partial social dissolution in which war appears to be the simplest means of diverting attention from internal difficulties. Thus we must begin by clearly understanding the meaning of this partial dissolution of society and its reaction upon the attitudes and mentality of its members . . .

Even in the details of the transformation of attitudes connected with this dissolution of society, there is an analogy with animal life. In the case of the bee, for example, anxiety and regression begin with a dissolution of the social order which deprives the instinct of the objects towards which it has normally been directed. When the normal co-ordination of tasks characteristic of life in the hive is disturbed, the working drives of the bees are left with no means of gratification.

Is not such a partial dissolution of the social order the outstanding feature of that social insecurity of which unemployment has become a general symptom? For man, however, the catastrophe lies not merely in the disappearance of external opportunities for work but also in the fact that his elaborate emotional system, intricately connected as it is with the smooth working of social institutions, now loses its object-fixation. The petty aims towards which almost all his strivings are directed suddenly disappear, and, not merely does he now lack a place of work, a daily task, and an opportunity for using the integrated labour attitudes formed through long training, but his habitual desires and impulses remain ungratified. Even if the immediate needs of life are satisfied, by means of unemployment relief, the whole life-organization and the family hopes and expectations are annihilated. One has only to remember how much libidinous energy is normally invested, in a capitalistic society, in social ambitions to realize what this means.

The frustration of the desire to rise in the social scale means not only that hopes of raising the standard of life must be abandoned, but also that social esteem is shattered and with it self-respect. The symptoms of such general insecurity may differ in different strata: the petty rentier, the black-coated worker, the skilled artisan and the unskilled labourer, the intelligentsia and the student. But, despite their social differences, shattered self-respect is at work in all of them. Lasswell has shown that, when the former ideal of the "successful self" is once disturbed and former attitudes are left objectless, the old impulses turn inward and take the form of self-punishment, which degenerates into masochistic or psychologically self-mutilating orgies. In this situation the scapegoat, such as the Jew, affords a real relief by providing an opportunity for once more externalizing the aggressive tendencies, an opportunity that is equally welcome to the frustrated in every class.

V. From Unorganized Insecurity to Organized Insecurity

This is the stage of unorganized insecurity, which is fraught with incalculable possibilities. It is the stage of general psychological and emotional experimentation; and of the decay of our belief in institutions, mores, traditions, and historically established prestige. These are the sociological conditions in which ideologies are unmasked and the validity of established principles and values comes to be doubted. This is the moment of scepticism, hard for the individual yet productive for science, as it destroys the petrified habits of thought of the past. In this general experimentation, the individual who cannot reorganize himself may perish, but for the social body it means the possibility of a selection of new models of behaviour and of new representative dominant types. That is why Fascism and Communism, and any other new social fixation, seem at certain moments to have equal chances as far as psychology is concerned. And, indeed, Michels does observe that, in the rise of Italian Fascism, men who had once been Socialists often joined the Fascists.

Finally long-term calculation also ceases, at least among those social groups most strongly affected by the partial dissolution of society. The panic reaches its height when the individual comes to realize that his insecurity is not simply a personal one, but is common to masses of his fellows, and when it becomes clear to him that there is no longer any social authority to set unquestioned standards and determine his behaviour. Herein lies the difference between individual unemployment and general insecurity. If in normal times an individual loses his job, he may indeed despair, but his reactions are more or less prescribed and he follows a general pattern in his distress. Even if he rebels against society by stealing, his activities will fall into some mould not created by him.

The distress of man in a situation of insecurity is worse than that of social animals, such as Hodgson's "old unhappy bull"

> Sick in mind and body both,
> Outcast from the herd he led,
> Bulls and cows a hundred head . . .

because the bull may still rely on the prompting of instincts that are uncorrupted by membership of a society based on an all-pervading division of labour. Such a society destroys the spontaneity of responses; and man, if the usual objects of his strivings are withdrawn, is lost and without orientation. His socially moulded instincts are useless when conditions alter, his old emotional strivings are homeless in a situation of unorganized insecurity, and his common sense is too narrow in outlook to understand what is happening around him in this invisible society with its unintelligible structure.

Here lies another difference between animals and men, for, whereas after the loss of the object the bee falls back on an earlier biological stage of instinctive reaction, man, deprived of his original goal, finds relief in the creation of symbolic goals and symbolic activities. For man is a being living in a community whose reaction is not based simply on instinct but on symbols of his own creation, such as words, images, and ideas, which serve as a fundamental means of communication.

Some of these symbols, words for instance, stand for things that really exist, others are symbols or symbolic activities that serve as substitutes for real activities. When desired objects are withdrawn from our reach, when we find it impossible to get full and immediate gratification in real things, then we use these symbols as substitutes. Experimental psychology provides us with information showing how substitute activities function in simpler situations. I refer to experiments and investigations carried out by Lewin, Ovsiankina, Mahler, Lissner, Hoppe, and others. An instructive case is quoted by Lewin. A young feeble-minded child wants to throw a ball a long way, and although he fails, is happy because he finds a substitute in the vigorous movement he has made. Lazar calls this type of child a "gesture-child," because he is satisfied with gestures when others are striving for concrete goals.

During a period of unorganized insecurity, the normal person, owing to the lack of an immediate and real gratification for his strivings in the field of work and social acknowledgment, tends to become a "gesture-adult", existing on substitute goals and being satisfied with gestures and symbols.

As Lewin realized, the term substitute goal, or substitute activity, has no meaning in itself, but only when measured against the original intention, or original tension-system, of the individual. Since in capitalist society the normal working incentive is acquisition, a desire to raise the income-level, any goal will be regarded as substitute which compensates for some failure in this field. The symbolic substitute is felt as being unreal only as long as the original tension-system, the striving for money, persists.

As soon as it is possible to change the original level of aspiration and to induce people to strive for symbolic goals as if they were primary goals, so that instead of butter they desire national prestige, they will cease to feel the latter as symbols and consider them rather as real gratifications.

According to the observations of individual psychology, once the individual tension-system is built up it is not very easy to alter, except in the case of children. But in my view the characteristic feature of any revolutionary period is that failure of original expectations occurs to hundreds of thousands at the same time, the search for substitutes follows the same rhythm, and the meaning of what is real or unreal is established in common. If there are many who think it is better to have guns than butter it will be easier for the single individual to change over from one tension-system to the other than it would be if he had to reorganize the system for himself.

The collective transformation of the system of symbols into new realities occurs in three stages. The symbol may remain unchanged externally while the real dynamic transformation which changes its function and meaning takes place behind this façade. The three stages of this transformation are:—

(a) The symbol is a pure substitute goal;
(b) The symbol becomes the new driving force for new forms of spontaneous group-integration (this we may call the utopian stage of the symbol);
(c) The symbol becomes the rigid emblem of an organized group.

In the first stage men flee to symbols and cling to them mainly because they want to avoid that anxiety which, according to Freud, overwhelms us whenever the libidinous energy remains for long without an object. Hammer and sickle, swastika, brown and black shirts, red and black flags, outstretched arms, clenched fists, phrases like "freedom and glory of the nation"—are fictions providing an outlet and goal for displaced energy.

But as soon as people by these very gestures and substitute goals become integrated into spontaneously growing groups, they reach the utopian stage in the development of the symbol. The utopian symbol makes people act; it makes them act against the system of established relationships, and in acting against it they not only try to wreck this network of relationships, but seek to call in question the former definition of the situation, devaluating the meaning and significance of the original level of aspirations.

Thus not only does the new symbol gain in significance but its reality-prestige is raised; striving for the honour and glory of the nation seems to be every bit as real a business as striving for economic gain. Another reason why the new symbol seems to become more than a substitute, and indeed becomes a new social reality, is that it in its turn likewise generates its own network of inter-related activities. Although these activities may for some time remain sterile and may consist mainly of endless discussions without rhyme or reason, or of loitering in groups and marching about, later they will lead to quasi-military exercises and to the forming of "pressure-groups" which will from time to time press upon that social system which is still the acknowledged order.

During the utopian phase, important changes take place in the individuals themselves. Whereas in the first stage the symbol was merely an occasional substitute in their lives, it now becomes both a factor in the reorganization of their whole personality and the ferment which brings them to a new kind of group-cohesion. In such a situation it is obvious that radical changes in the individual only take place where some sudden shock has destroyed the network of his established habits and expectations, and that the stabilization of his new hopes and values is intimately linked up with the integration of new groups. Old traditions fall to bits, new forms of social adjustment occur, and we speak of a re-birth of men and society. It was perhaps this same psychological mechanism which in the ancient world produced the new spirit of Christianity, or which in the sects of the later Middle Ages gave rise to the modern forms of utopian spirit.

In the utopian stage of symbolic integration a certain social differentiation becomes perceptible. Not all the symbols appeal to everyone equally. Their growth is intimately connected with that of the particular groups to which they belong. Even if different groups have the same symbols, they stress different aspects of them, because memories of the pre-insecurity phase of society are, unconsciously, still active in their mind. Thus to one man perhaps the symbol of security and order has an appeal, because the group to which he belongs is a petty bourgeois one now threatened in its slumber; or else, since the man is a member of a group such as the army or the bureaucracy whose prestige is bound up with the growth of the State, what he values is glory. There are still others, for whom local independence or folkways constitute the lost paradise, and those to whom it is equality that represents the supreme value, because even in the former stable society they had been outcasts. The

several symbols correspond immediately to the characteristic wishes of
the several social strata.

But this stage of spontaneity in the recreation of man and of groups
does not last very long, as in mass society it has to be succeeded by a
stage of strict organization; for, of the achievements of modern mass
society, only those can endure which are sponsored by definite organizations or are continuously reproduced through the very working of the
social structure. Thus spontaneous activity on the basis of enthusiasm gives
place to rigid organization, for which the symbol has become nothing
more than a lifeless emblem. Just as, in an earlier example, hatred, in order
to become socially effective, had to be turned into trained hatred, so
the new emotional attitudes and working incentives now tend to be in-
culcated and enforced by the group.[1]

Through this petrifying of human relations, which in modern nations
tend to crystallize into the militarist pattern,[2] society passes from the
stage of unorganized insecurity into that of "organized insecurity." Society
as a whole is still insecure, for the causes of the disorder in its functioning
are not removed and the economic disequilibrium which brought about
structural unemployment is still present, and is perhaps even increased
by tendencies towards self-sufficiency. But, though the nation be insecure,
new social formations are being built up which, while providing psychological substitutes to some extent for the lost honeycomb of work (e.g.
unnecessary roads, labour-camps, and rearmament), at the same time help
to run the national economy at less expense. It is now possible gradually
to lower the standard of living, without resistance, by balancing every
dose of deprivation with some psychological substitute, by finding scape-
goats and creating occasions for collectively guided enthusiasm. The
less bread, the more circuses!

The essential feature of this new type of society is that it affords
channels not only for economic and administrative activities, but also for
new psychological adjustments. Not only government and industry are
planned, but the psychic disturbances and the general breakdown are

[1] This passing from the purely emotional, through the utopian, to the organized
stage, may have been the typical process of genesis of institutions in the past. Only
to-day, when we are witnessing the sudden growth of new institutions in our midst,
do we realize the importance of the symbolic element in primitive institutions. Most
of our institutions have long since solidified into relations and functions with no
symbolic aura (take, for instance, our business relations or, say, a post-office). In
primitive communities the symbolic glorification of the institution still prevails and
there is an appeal, through magic or mere customary rites, to the original emotions.

[2] There are special reasons for the choice in this case of the militarist model. We
have seen how in the first stage of unorganized insecurity, when the old order of
society is vanishing, a regression to earlier social patterns is to be expected. In inland
states the old army pattern naturally had great strength. The officials dismissed from
the old army were busy after the war in reorganizing the dissolved cadres of bourgeois
society into quasi-military formations. The military mind had no other conception of
organized security but that characteristic of a state of war.

deliberately guided for the benefit of those who still maintain their rational calculation and, because they stand more or less outside the focal points of the general collapse, are able to remain sober. They may consciously desire even war or autarchy, for what is economically irrational for a whole nation may still be profitable to particular groups—of industrialists, army leaders, and officials. Their psychology is mainly to be explained in terms of a gamble in which, though the nation lose, they should still get rich. Just as the military caste re-establishes itself by using in its own country the same methods as during the war it used in occupied territory, the industrial and commercial bosses consider their country, once the stage of organized insecurity is reached, as a field for exploitation almost equivalent to a colony. And they use the new situation for the preparing of an imperialist expansion, because for their enormous monopolies the closed territory of their own country is too small.

Within the network of new pseudo-activities a psychological readjustment seems to take place. Through the instituting of inexpensive new systems of honours and distinctions, social ambitions are once more given satisfaction and the man who, following the loss of his job, had lost his self-respect finds it again through a position in some organization which puts others under his control. In the party there is no one at the bottom, for below the lowest is the outcast, the Jew. Foresight and calculation are restored, too, as tasks have some sort of pattern again, and festivities and manœuvres have to be prepared a long way ahead. There is no longer reason to resort to the diverse forms of self-mutilation; the continuous exhibition of the organized power of the state does away with that.

The organization of insecurity has above all the advantage that there is no longer a feeling of object-loss and as long as the system functions and an emotional and symbolic atmosphere overlies its rigid military order people will willingly obey and subordinate their individual preferences to the dictates of the central machinery. Those who formerly lacked direction enjoy the inescapable automatism of the machine. To them it does not matter that in certain fields freedom has gone; only social types who, like the intelligentsia and some of the entrepreneurs, have previously learned to use and value freedom of thought, lament its loss. Most men have their roots in the older types of traditional society and lack the habit of personal initiative and the capacity to enjoy responsibility. They crave rather for subjection to a rule and are glad when they can glide on from one well-defined situation to another.

In such a society those who are leaders enjoy the possibility of raising hatred on one day and appeasing it on the next. Society becomes a structure where one presses a button and the expected reaction occurs. One day the detestation of a neighbouring country may be preached, on the next you decide to live in friendship with it for ten years. In the phase of unorganized, as compared with that of organized insecurity, quite a different psychology characterizes the individual. In the former phase the psychological reaction of the people was important, the psychology of the masses governed everything. In the latter it seems as if the masses have abandoned their individual psychic life, at least as far as public affairs are concerned, and are ready to turn into robots. It is as if the sociologist had only to deal with the peculiar psychology of the leaders.

In the first stage of unorganized insecurity these leaders play no very important rôle. So long as everything is fluid numerous petty leaders arise —in place of the notabilities of the vanishing order—but theirs is only a transitory influence. After the first fermentation, however, a new differentiation into guiding, and guided, groups occurs. Spontaneous symbol-integration can take place only in a small community; in mass societies after the first spontaneous reactions a more or less conscious control of these symbols and of the emotions connected with them is needed. This manipulation is performed by people whose personal psychological constitution and aptitudes especially enable them to take the lead.

Max Weber observed that even in primitive communities the psycho-pathological types usually become the prophets, saviours, and reformers, changing the old ways of life and breaking down the old magical attitudes. In his view this is because in societies whose customs are sanctioned mainly by magic it is the psychopath who is unadjusted and who therefore dares to break these old habits, which are no longer fitted to the changed situations, and is able to discover new and better adjusted attitudes. Thus it was the Jewish ecstatic prophets who destroyed those established traditional attitudes personified in the official priesthood.

It is not to be expected that the old bureaucracy of the country or the former commercial and industrial leaders trained in the ways of rational calculation will find the secret of symbol-manipulation. They need an alliance with a new kind of leader, and this leader, and the petty leaders, must come chiefly from those holes and corners of society where even in normal times irrational attitudes prevailed and where the catastrophe of unorganized insecurity was most severe and prolonged. Thus the leader must himself have experienced that emotional rhythm which is common to those who have been most exposed to the shocks of a partial dissolution of society. But, by itself, mere emotional irrationality is not enough, and the leader and most of the petty leaders must also have a sense of calculation which will grow more acute as unorganized gives way to organized insecurity.

The calculation connected with symbol-manipulation is not the same as, for example, commercial calculation, and, as a woman may be of little use in business yet skilful in judging the moods of her husband, so an individual, hopeless as a bureaucrat, may be expert in calculating and expressing the changing shifts or emotions in others. In modern mass society these leaders purposefully transform the spontaneous symbolic attitudes into manipulated patterns of thought, sentiment, and action.

It is not very easy to distinguish, in the first stage, between rational interest and wish-fulfilling dreams and gestures. The interconnectedness between interest and irrational symbolic striving is far deeper than some abstract thinkers would imagine. Marxism, as the product of a highly rational and intellectualized age and group, not only over estimates the driving power of explicit economic interests, but puts alternatives in too sharp a contrast, as also did the commercial and liberal mentality of the eighteenth- and nineteenth-century philosophers and economists.

Even in rational strivings irrational tendencies are latent, and Glover is not wrong when he says that, very often, "conscious preoccupation with reality and mainly self-preservative situations" covers unconscious motivations.[1] It frequently occurs that through unconscious urges, such as transformed or displaced sadistic attitudes, or for the sake of glory, we indulge in rational calculation, in money making, and in ruthless pursuit of personal advantage. On the other hand the American sociologist Wirth hit the nail on the head when he wrote that "interests slumber below the surface of any kind of activity and it is only in certain spheres of life, in economics, and to a lesser degree in politics, that they have been made explicit and articulate."[2] Therefore, in my view, the crucial problem is not whether irrational motives disguise themselves under rational attitudes, or whether behind rational behaviour some unconscious interest is at work. Taking it for granted that the rational and irrational are interwoven, we must discover in what circumstances the various forms of rational interests, slumbering under the surface, become explicit.

It remains, therefore, for us to ask what those social factors are which help to bring to consciousness the so-called rational interest and thus may possibly lead to the breakdown of the sort of society we have been considering.

The system has, as we have seen, a relatively great elasticity for not only does it manage production and consumption, the defence services and administration, but by means of regulation it assists in the adjustment of men's wishes to changing situations. It is capable of postponing the breakdown in that it controls the subjective side of the process, and is able to compensate if not for the economic dis-equilibrium at least for the psychological maladjustment.

There is, nevertheless, a fundamental contradiction which makes for its possible collapse. And this contradiction is to be found in the mutually antagonistic working of mechanisms within it which foster the growth of conflicting impulses. Everything depends on whether the new organiza-

[1] Glover, E., *War, Sadism, and Pacifism,* London, 1933, p. 133.
[2] Wirth, L., in his Preface to Mannheim, K., *Ideology and Utopia,* op. cit., p. xxiv.

tions which have been superimposed upon society during the period of organized insecurity are strong enough to establish the new set of values and symbolic strivings as having more reality than the older motivations, the desire for economic gain and for a higher standard of life. This does not mean that I am assuming that man's wishes in themselves are only real when conforming to the concept of the *homo economicus*. We all know how very difficult it was for the absolutist mercantilist system in Prussia for instance to train people to strive for profits instead of keeping to their former humble standards. But I am convinced that any new system which departs from capitalism has to reckon with the possibility that the masses may rapidly identify themselves once more with the older tension-system, the original aim of which is economic gain. If this happens, the new standards of honour and prestige will be felt once more as mere substitutes. Thus the problem of the new élites who control the symbols is to suppress the older mechanism of capitalist society by means of the superimposed institutions of the new social technique. If there are factors in the industrial system and in the remnants of the property system which keep alive the old set of acquisitive wishes, then they may easily fail.

The underlying crisis produced by unemployment, even in the stage of organized insecurity, will make itself felt as soon as the new form of psychological adjustment, with its motivations of honour and prestige, ceases to function. The whole propaganda machinery becomes vain and meaningless as soon as the capitalistic aspirations break through and the new symbols are felt as being mere symbols and people cease to have faith in the corresponding activities. Once this happens on a large enough scale and penetrates even to the ranks of the armed forces, the crisis becomes apparent and panic breaks through once more. But at this stage the psychological breakdown, the panic, is much more dangerous than it was in the phase of unorganized insecurity.

It is not so much an object-withdrawal which brings about the general tension, but what I would call a "motive-withdrawal". The institutions, the reified relations, are still present, but dissociated from those motivations which originally worked through them. Such an estrangement from the goods of the world, and its powers, occurred among the early Christians. Such an alienation or motive-withdrawal may occur as soon as the more fundamental mechanisms of industrial society assert themselves against the totalitarian superstructure. As is well known, the greatest danger of war lies in the situation just described. In capitalist surroundings, in a society which is still based on private property, it is very likely that sooner or later the symbols of prestige and honour will lose their character of reality in the estimation of the masses and loyalty to the social machine will thus become problematic.

In the stage of unorganized insecurity, the object-withdrawal had not led to war because the psychological breakdown was not canalized. The confusion was intense enough to destroy a part of the former élite, but could not be drawn upon for purposes of outward aggression. It may be simpler for the élites, now that the emotional channels have been established and the war machine is ready, to divert the mind of the masses from the growing social tension by taking refuge in war and so obviating the alienation of the population.

To sum up, this brief study has not attempted to give a complete analysis of the causes of war. My examples are not even meant as an exhaustive study of the evolution of unemployment, insecurity, and Fascism as factors making for war in our age, but merely to show more concretely the kind of help psychology can give if it is integrated into the economic analysis of capitalistic development in its present stage. The meaning of these considerations is not that psychological processes are independent and therefore ultimately responsible for what has happened and what is going to happen, but that the economic maladjustment cannot be fully understood unless its psychological implications and consequences are put into their proper place. It is the concrete sequence, the real concatenation of structural changes, which must be reconstructed in its main phases if a real control is to be achieved.

War itself is the outcome not of some invariable instinct like aggressiveness, but partly of the faulty elaboration of psychological tendencies through institutions, and partly of the desperate flight of people into collective aggression when unco-ordinated institutions clash and bring about the feeling of general insecurity.

Hardly anyone wants war. The new ways of drifting into a world catastrophe which neither the leaders nor their peoples really desire is the most tragic example of what one can call "objective dynamics in history." Through the accumulation of effects, economic, social, and psychological, which are not intended by those who initiate them, things happen which are definitely repulsive to the people who are acting. It is a veritable nightmare that we should arm and drill men for ends which very few, if any of them, in their hearts really want. We are liars caught in our lies. Public utterances were never less believed. Most of our great ideals are being more discredited than ever by their wholesale use in the market-place, and still we march whenever the command comes. In our solitary hours our most horrible vision is the collapse of civilization by the explosion of the bombs we store, but we blackmail each other with the fear of war until the blackmail catches up with the blackmailers. We anticipate that there will be war. People predict dates for its beginning. Only who fights whom and why is still unknown. Nationalist slogans call little people who love their homes and gardens to become heroes by killing other little people who love their homes and gardens. There has seldom been a generation which was less willing for petty sacrifice and more likely to pay the supreme one without even understanding why.

Hardly anyone wants war. It is in the main a calamity which occurs because men in their activities have not learned to take a long range view, to adjust one institution to another, and to think in terms of a real psychology. But how can they learn to act on the basis of a broader insight if not even the social scientists aim at correlating the results of partial observations in order to detect the reason for the maladjustment in the structure of society as a whole, if they, too, do not aim at real knowledge, but divide their investigations into watertight compartments in order to escape responsibility, and work with a fictitious *ad hoc* instinct-philosophy of some kind or other which itself is part of a mentality that is unconsciously making for war?

The disentanglement of this network that is strangling us can only come about through action. But it is untrue, despite the scepticism so frequently put forward to the contrary, that we can know little or nothing about the working of our society and about the forms that action can take. We could know enough to understand the main direction of events if we only had the will to control the situation which will otherwise enslave us, and the courage for the kind of thought necessary in our age.

Index

Absenteee ownership, 336-69, 345n., 346n., 353n., 355n.
Absolute monarchy, 182, 376
Adaptation of the individual, 405-36
Administration, bureaucratic, 149-91
Adoratsky, V., 101n.
Alexander the Great, 211
Amari, Michele, 214n.
American Federation of Labor, 343n., 362n.
Americanization, 40
Anomic suicide, 460-61
Anomie, 449-85, 472n.
Antipodes, problem of, 22-23
Aretino, Pietro, 387, 387n.
Aristocracies, 200-02, 268
Aristotle, 46, 194, 228, 480
Athens, 176, 185, 210, 444
Augustus, 275, 275n.
Ayres, Clarence, 336n.

Bagehot, Walter, 15, 324
Bakuninism, 178
Barter, origin of, 314
Barthou, Jean Louis, 288n.
Beaussire, 484n.
Bebel, August, 250
Beckerath, E. von, 84n., 88n.
Behavior, disorganized, 513-18
Bekker, 72n.
Berenson, Bernard, 39-40, 39n.
Bergson, Henri, 83, 84n.
Bierstadt, Edward Hale, 40n.
Bismarck-Schönhausen, Prince Otto Eduard Leopold von, 178, 182, 186, 303
Blanc, Louis, 233
Block, Maurice, 462n.
Bohemianism, 408, 418, 423, 427n., 428, 435, 436, 511n.
Bolshevism, 423, 428
Boris Godunov, 196
Borkenau, Franz, 272n.
Bosses, political, 153
Bourgeoisie: and capitalism, 370-401; and intellectualism, 74-76, 95; and proletariat, 103-20, 103n.
Bousquet, 86n.

Boycotts, 348, 362
Briand, Aristide, 288n.
Bribery of officials, 290
Brodrero, 84n., 85
Bruno, 487, 488, 489, 490, 491
Buddhism, 130, 205, 211, 214
Buonarroti, Filippo, 249
Burckhardt, Jacob, 14, 14n.
Bureaucracy, 71-76, 149-91, 217-21, 394
Burke, Edmund, 73, 73n.
Business: and absentee ownership, 336-339; failures, 461-62; interests, 341-342, 347n., 367, 368; see also Capitalism; Industry

Caesar, Gaius Julius, 197, 223-24
Caesarism, 154
Caillaux, Joseph, 288, 288n.
Capital, 114-15; and labor, 462-63, 471
Capitalism, 8n., 92n., 370-401; and bureaucracy, 165-66; growth of, 104-108; and Marxism, 248-49; see also Bourgeoisie; Industry
Capitalistic enterprise, 125, 374
Capponi, Gino, 217n.
Casimir III the Great, King of Poland, 196
Caste system, 129-30, 200-05, 266-67
Chamber of Deputies (France), 279
Chamber of Deputies (Italy), 279
Charles V, Holy Roman Emperor, 387
Chesterton, Gilbert Keith, 31-32, 32n.
China, 63, 156-219 passim, 274-75, 331
Christianity, 118, 211, 214-15, 521
Civil-service reform, 188
Class: action, 124, 125, 126; antagonism, 126; bias, 48-64; circulation, 262-68; 264n.; formation, 132; interests, 124-125, 316, 338; ruling, 59-64, 192-232, 253, 262-91, 493-96; situation, 122-23, 124, 125, 126, 127, 130, 133, 134, 166; struggle, 78n., 103, 110, 113, 123, 125-127, 244n., 254; subordination, 60, 61; see also Status
Clemenceau, Georges, 38
Combination-instincts, 272, 273, 274
Commodities market, 125, 126

Communal action, 122, 124-25, 129, 133, 134, 177
Commune of Paris, 119n.
Communism, 8n., 76-83, 102, 113-20, 490, 518
Communist Manifesto, 102-20
Competition, 126, 145-47, 352
Compulsory cooperation, 296-97, 298, 304, 313, 321
Comte, Auguste, 15, 87, 221-28, 222n., 463, 464-65, 465n., 468, 469, 474
Conduct, 69
Confucius, 214, 225
Congress (U.S.), 279
Conscience, 475-76, 478, 483
Conservatism, 73-74, 78-80, 95
Considérant, Victor, 259
Constitutional government, 146-47, 182-183
Consumption credit, 126
Contract, system of, 144-48, 312, 317-18, 319, 321, 330, 334, 470
Corporate action, 137, 293, 295, 297, 311, 314-15, 317, 319, 334
Corporations, 347, 381
Cosmas (monk), 22-23
Craft unions, 343, 348
Creative types, 408, 409, 417-18, 511n.
Credit, control of, 341
Credit market, 123
Credit system, 344
Crimes: in England, 326-27, 333; in France, 324-25; private and political, 271
Crispi, Francesco, 285, 286
Crusades, 105n., 161
Curiosity, tendency of, 411

Dahomey, 306, 307, 308, 311
Dante, 40n.
Debt bondage, 126
Déclaration des Droits de l'Homme, 234, 248
Democracy, 127, 194, 238-41, 258-61; and bureaucracy, 173-77, 180, 188, 189; evolution toward, 290
Democratic parties, 242-43
Demonolatry, 227
Demos, 175
Depretis, Agostino, 285
Dewey, John, 37-38, 37n.
Dialectical thinking, 82-83
Dictatorship, 250; of proletariat, 119n.
Distribution, 122-23
Divine right, 208, 278
Division of labor, 48, 104, 108, 445-46, 447, 461-85, 461n., 479n., 494
Druids, 199

Duma (Russia), 279
Durkheim, Émile, 11, 12, 15, 449n.

Economic determinism, theory of, 277
Economic emulation, 141-43
Economic order, 122, 131-33, 457-61
Education, 391n., 480n.; and capitalism, 391; and communism, 117; and life-organization, 418-19; party schools, 93-94, 236-37; political, 93-94; and priestly aristocracy, 199-200; rationalization of, 187-91; social, 429
Egypt, ancient, 156-221 *passim*, 308-14 *passim*, 331
Election: democratic, 201; of officials, 153-54, 235
Élites, 84, 88, 90, 91, 262-68, 264n., 266n., 513, 526, 527; circulation of, 264n., 266
Ends, theory of, 75
Engels, Friedrich, 12, 78n., 103n., 104n., 105n., 108n., 119n., 245n., 246n., 486n.
England, 73, 110, 111, 158-202 *passim*, 235-88 *passim*, 311, 322-35 *passim*, 388-89, 431, 439, 514
Entrepreneurial function, 122-23, 371-74
Equality before the law, 170-71, 174, 175
Espinas, 464

Failures, business, 461-62
Family, bourgeois, 395-98, 401; Marx on, 116-17
Fascism, 71, 83-92, 84n., 96, 515, 518
Fear, tendency of, 411
Feudalism, 60-61, 103-04, 105n., 216-17, 225-27, 321-23, 375, 385n., 444
Feuerbach, Ludwig Andreas, 490-93, 491n., 503n., 504
Fiji, 63, 305-06, 306-07, 308
Force, use of, 269-77, 279-80, 281
Fourier, François Marie Charles, 254
France, 111, 114, 114n., 158, 174-201 *passim*, 221, 230, 269-98 *passim*, 306, 322, 323-25, 389
Frederick II the Great, King of Prussia, 172, 182
Frederick William I, King of Prussia, 184
French Revolution, 114, 175, 274, 389
Freudianism, 34
Friedeberg, Raphael, 244n.

Gebhart, Émile, 226n.
Gennep, A. von, 38n.
Germany, 71, 73, 112, 128, 154-202 *passim*, 234-51 *passim*, 274, 288, 302-303, 311, 380n., 489-90
Gerth, H. H., 121n., 149n.
Giolitti, Giovanni, 285, 286, 287
Glaber, Raoul (Radulfus), 226
Glover, E., 525, 525n.

Gods and government, 210-11
Goldscheid, Rudolf, 250-51
Government: bureaucratic, 149-91, 217-221; business men in, 344-45, 345n., 347; and capitalism, 375-79; constitutional, 146-47, 182-83; and division of labor, 465-67; force, use of, 269-77, 279-80, 281; forms of, 193-94, 277-91; governing *élite*, 264-69; and intellectuals, 389-90; militant form of, 296; national establishment, 341, 344-45, 357, 367; oligarchic, 233-61; ruling classes, 59-64, 192-232, 253, 262-91, 493-96; social destiny of, 465; *see also* Political organization
Greece, ancient, 116n., 132, 135, 158-229 *passim*, 281, 300-01, 310, 311, 454
Guesde, Jules, 257
Gumplowicz, Ludwig, 201-02, 202n., 203, 209, 209n.

Harden, Maximilian, 246n.
Haxthausen, August von, 103n.
Hegel, Georg Wilhelm Friedrich, 96, 97, 488, 495-96, 503n.
Herkner, Heinrich, 235
Hervé, Gustave, 244n.
Herzen, Alexandre, 254
History, philosophy of, 486-96
Hodgson, 328, 329, 519
Holy Roman Empire, 160-61
Humanism, 387

Ideal state, theory of, 75
Ideology, 76-77, 76n., 87, 95
Imperialism, 367
India, 52, 133, 195, 197, 199, 200, 205, 212, 216
Individualism: and division of labor, 474-475, 480-85; efficiency of, 429-31; and industrialism, 315-16, 322, 331-35; and metropolitan life, 437-48; and militarism, 294-95, 322, 331-35; in primitive societies, 327-30; *see also* Personality
Individuals, capacity indices of, 263
Industrialism, 227-32, 312-35; and rationality, 510, 512; and suicide, 460
Industry: and absentee ownership, 336-339; bourgeois and proletarian, 102-20 *passim;* and market, 473; nationalization of, 136-37, 143-44, 147-48; *see also* Capitalism
Inheritance, 296-97, 319, 454
Injunction, uses of, 345n., 349
Insecurity, forms of, 517-28
Intellectualism, 78; bourgeois, 74-76; metropolitan, 437-48; modern, 75-76; sociology of, 385-94
Intelligence Service of the Army, 362n.

Interchurch Movement, 349n.
Interests, business, 341-42, 367, 368
Iran, *see* Persia
Irrationalism, 70, 74-76, 78, 82-83
Irrationality, 508-10
Israel, ancient, 210, 211
Italy, 193, 201, 217-37 *passim*, 249, 279, 285-88, 289
Ivan IV the Terrible, 197

James, William, 28, 28n., 37n.
Jannet, 198n.
Japan, 200, 214, 216, 274-75, 279, 306, 307
Jehovah, 210-11
Jewish religion, 211n.
Jews, 129, 210, 431, 511
Joffre, Joseph Jacques Césaire, 24-25, 26
Justice, administration of, 167-71, 316-317, 334

Kadi-justice, 167, 169, 171
Kalabinska, 264n., 266n.
Kautsky, Karl Johann, 245n.
Kempf, Edward J., 34n.
Knowledge, political and social determinants of, 71-92
Kulturkampf, 303

Labor: and absentee ownership, 336-69; alienation of, 496-507; and anomie, 461-75; and capital, 462-63, 471; and class bias, 53-64; division of, 48, 104, 108, 445-46, 447, 461-85, 461n., 479n., 494; and intellectuals, 391-94; and militarism, 313; party schools, 236-37; price of, 126; troubles, 346-53; unemployment, 344, 346, 346n., 351-53, 391, 517-18, 526
Labor market, 125, 126
Labor movement, 79n., 392-93
Labor unions, 235-37, 237n., 241, 343, 348, 355n.
Labriola, Arturo, 246n.
La Marck, Comte de, 203n.
Langenhove, F. van, 38n.
Law and bureaucracy, 167-71, 187
Leaders, 88, 90, 239-41, 252, 255-57, 513, 523-25
League of Nations, 29-30, 75
Legal order, 121-22, 125, 253
Lenin, Nikolai, 79n., 80n., 81n., 82n., 119
Leninism, 83, 92
Lenormant, 205n., 210n., 219n., 221
Leroy-Beaulieu, Anatole, 182, 197n., 213n.
Levasseur, Pierre Émile, 462n.
Lewis, Sinclair, 26n.
Lex talionis, 305-06, 328, 333

Lincoln, Abraham, 23-24
Lippmann, Walter, 11, 21n.
Locard, Edmond, 37n.
Lockouts, 348
Louis XIV, King of France, 375
Louis XVI, King of France, 269, 275
Löwith, Karl, 14n.
Loyalty, 308-09, 330-32
Lukács, Georg, 78n., 79n.
Luxemburg, Rosa, 238n.
Luzzatti, Luigi, 287

Machiavelli, Niccolò, 88, 232
Maine, Sir Henry, 144, 145
Malaterra, Goffredo, 226, 227
Man power, industrial, 342-43, 347n.
Mannheim, Karl, 10, 11, 12, 65n., 508n.
Marginal utility, 122-23
Market situation, 122-23
Marquardt, Joachim, 205n., 221n.
Marx, Karl, 9, 10, 12, 13, 14, 76, 77, 77n.,
    78n., 80n., 82n., 97, 101n., 108n., 113n.,
    119, 245n., 248, 249, 380, 389, 400,
    401, 486n., 503n.
Marxism, 7, 8, 76-83, 87-88, 95, 240,
    244n., 248-55, 371, 525
Mas y Sans, 199n.
Maspero, Sir Gaston Camille Charles,
    205n., 219n., 221
Mass actions, 124, 177
Mass democracy, 173-77
Mass mind, 88
Masses: immaturity of, 258-59; sover-
    eignty of, 233-42
Materialism, historical, 244n.
Maurer, Georg Ludwig von, 103n.
Mazzini, Giuseppe, 249
Meisel, James H., 15n.
Metaphysical period, 221, 225-27
Metropolitan type of man, 437-48
Mexico, 195, 200, 289
Meyers, Gustavus, 10
Michels, Robert, 12, 14-15, 233n., 518
Mickiewicz, 196n.
Middle Ages, 103-04, 105, 110, 125, 126,
    132, 135, 150-200 passim, 214-26 pas-
    sim, 373, 443, 462, 514
Militarism, 224-25, 228-32, 292-312, 312-
    335 passim, 522-23, 522n.; bureaucratic,
    171-73; and social classes, 203-04; war-
    rior class, 195-97, 293-94; see also War
Mill, John Stuart, 200
Mills, C. Wright, 9n., 101n., 121n., 149n.
Minority rule, 194-95, 253
Mirabeau, Comte de, 203, 203n.
Mohammedan societies, 207, 213-14
Mohammedanism, 211, 212-14
Molinari, Gustave de, 483n.

Money economy, 156, 160, 438-40
Monopolization, 130-31, 132, 145, 380
Monotheism, 225
Montesquieu, Baron de La Brède et de,
    194
Morality in society, 424-25, 478-80, 483-
    485
Morgan, Lewis Henry, 103n.
Mosca, Gaetano, 12, 15, 15n., 192n.,
    207n., 209n., 248, 253, 255
Motive withdrawal, 526
Municipal Reform Bill (England), 327
Münsterberg, Hugo, 37n.
Mussolini, Benito, 84n., 85n., 86n., 87n.,
    89, 89n., 92n.

Napoleon I (Napoleon Bonaparte), 79,
    91, 220, 263, 373
Napoleon III, 276, 277, 278, 289
National establishment, 341, 344-45, 357,
    367; see also Government
Nationality, abolition of, 117-18
Nationalization of industry, 136-37, 143-
    144, 147-48
Newspapers, 390, 390n.
Nietzsche, Friedrich, 130, 437, 440, 447
Nineveh, 210
North German Confederation, 302

Object withdrawal, 526-27
Occupational groups, 133
Office, purchase of, 158
Office-holding, 151-56
Office management, 150-51
Officialdom, modern, 149-56, 178
Oligarchy, 233-61
Open shop, 344n.
Overproduction, 107-08
Ownership, absentee, 336-69, 345n.,
    346n., 353n., 355n.

Pareto, Vilfredo, 12, 14, 83, 84n., 86, 86n.,
    87, 262n., 272n.
Parliament (Great Britain), 186, 269, 279,
    324, 325, 327
Parliamentarism, 75, 76, 182, 227-28, 243
Parties, see Political organization
Party schools, 93-94, 236-37
Patriotism, 308, 332
Perrier, Edmond, 470n.
Persia, 164, 181, 308
Personality: disorganization of, 513-17;
    fictitious, 23-28; types of, 405-36
Peru, ancient, 145, 216, 230, 299-300,
    309, 311
Peter I the Great, 197, 301
Philistinism, 408, 418, 423, 427, 427n.,
    428, 434, 435, 511n.

Philosophy and science, 467-69
Pierrefeu, Jean de, 24, 24n., 26
Pike, 326, 333
Pirou, Gaëtan, 85n.
Plato, 22, 267
Poland, 195-96, 197, 422, 431
Political class, 192-232, 253, 254-55
Political economy, 496-506
Political formula, 207-10
Political machines, 289-90
Political organization, 238-48; parties, 133-35, 174-75, 242-48, 251-53, 256; types of, 215-16, 221-32, 292-335; see also Government; Social organization
Political sociology, 93-97
Politics, scientific, 65-97
Positive period, 221, 227-28
Positive state, theory of, 75
Positivism, 87
Posse, Ernst, 85n.
Potter, George, 55, 59
Power, 121-22
Price system, 341, 343-44, 345n.
Price wars, 126-27
Priestly classes, 199, 225
Primitive societies, 327-30, 524
Private property, 142, 497, 505-07; abolition of, 114, 115-16, 120, 143, 486
Profits, source of, 342
Proletariat, 78n., 125, 251-52; dictatorship of, 119n., 249; Marx and Engels on, 103-20, 103n.
Prostitution, 117
Protectionist policy, 298
Proudhon, Pierre Joseph, 89, 233, 258, 506
Prussia, 73, 165, 172, 174, 181, 183, 184, 302, 431, 526
Psychism, historical, 244n.
Public opinion, 35, 175; symbols of, 25-26
Pueblo Indians, 229
Putschist tactics, 89, 89n.

Racial differences, 130
Railways, assets of, 351n.
Rameses II, 220-21
Ranke, Leopold von, 74, 74n.
Rathenau, Walther, 340n.
Rationalism, 83, 187
Rationality, types of, 508-28
Recognition, desire for, 424-26
Reichstag (Germany), 186, 279
Religion, 211-15, 457
Residues, societal, 272, 272n., 280-87
Response, desire for, 424-26
Revolution, 72, 79n., 82-83, 178, 245, 245n., 268-69, 273, 276, 487-88, 495; Communist, 119-20, 249, 254, 486

Revolution of 1848, 119
Ribot, Théodule Armand, 467
Rickert, Heinrich, 75, 75n.
Rodbertus, Johann Karl, 251
Roger I, Count of Sicily, 226
Roman Catholic Church, 156, 175-76, 214-15, 227, 433
Roman law, 167-69
Rome, ancient, 103, 116n., 132, 156-207 passim, 218-29 passim, 265-311 passim, 454, 492
Rousseau, Jean Jacques, 194, 248, 255, 388, 477
Rousset, 198n., 213n., 218n.
Rouvier, Pierre Maurice, 288
Ruling class, see Class; Government
Ruskin, John, 440
Russia, 175-279 passim, 301-02, 311, 431
Russian Revolution, 152
Ryazanov, D., 78n.

Sabotage, 346, 362
St. Ambrose, 22
Saint-Simon, Comte de, 14, 15
Salaries of officials, 155, 367
Satan, role of, 226
Savigny, Friedrich Karl von, 90n.
Savorgnan, Franco, 242n.
Schäffle, Albert, 67, 67n., 68, 244n., 464
Schmitt, Carl, 70n., 76, 76n., 87n., 89n.
Schumpeter, Joseph A., 12, 370n.
Science: method in, 471; scepticism toward, 86-87; specialization in, 463-464; unity of, 465, 467-69, 473-74
Scientific politics, 65-96
Segregation, ethnic, 129-30
Self-determination of nations, 365n.
Self-rationalization, 510-12
Senate: ancient Rome, 162, 185, 186, 200; France, 279; Italy, 279; U.S., 28-30
Shakespeare, William, 132
Shaw, George Bernard, 34, 386
Sherrington, Sir Charles Scott, 37n.
Shinto, 214
Simmel, Georg, 12, 437n.
Slave labor, 180-81
Slavery, 46-47
Social Democratic party (Germany), 174, 237n.
Social differences, leveling of, 173-77
Social groups, 208-09; see also Social organization
Social honor, 121-22, 133
Social organization: and anomie, 449-85; bureaucracy, 71-76, 149-91, 217-21, 394; groups, 208-09; and individualism, 405-36, 512-18; and insecurity, 517-28; metropolitan, 437-48; oligarchy, 233-61;

and power, 121-22; rationality, 508-12; and symbolism, 519-22; types of, 221-232, 292-335; *see also* Class; Capitalism; Political organization
Social psychology, 87
Social science, 1-17, 64, 66
Social stability, 276-77, 429-30
Socialism, 76-83, 240, 244n., 248-55, 257-260, 401, 437
Socialist party, 243-48, 244n., 246n., 251-252, 257
Societal action, 124, 177
Society, *see* Social organization
Sociology, 1-17, 49, 64, 65
Sombart, Werner, 246n., 257
Sonnino, Baron Sidney, 287-88
Sorel, Georges, 83, 84n., 85, 85n., 86, 86n., 89, 91, 92n., 275
Sovereign masses, 233-42
Sovereignty, principle of, 207
Soviet Union, 8n.
Sparta, 210, 300-01, 307, 308, 310, 311
Specialization, *see* Division of labor
Speculators, role of, 283-85
Spencer, Herbert, 3, 11, 12, 13-14, 15, 27-28, 48n., 136, 137, 144, 147, 208, 221, 228-32, 292n., 461, 470n., 472
Stahl, Friedrich Julius, 88, 88n., 97
Stalin, Joseph, 79n., 119n.
Standard of living, 140-41
States' Council (Germany), 279
States General (France), 324
Status: and discontent, 136-48; disqualification of, 131; groups, 123, 126-34; honor, 127-33, 166; order, 132, 133; privileges, 130-31; segregation, 129-130; situation, 127, 134; stratification, 128, 130, 131-33; system of, 144-48, 295, 312, 317-18, 321, 334; *see also* Class
Stein, Ludwig, 246n.
Stereotypes, 38-47, 69n.
Stirner, Max, 488, 496
Strachey, Lytton, 24, 24n.
Strikes, labor, 343, 348
Sublimation, 416-17
Suicide, 455, 456, 457, 459-60
Sullivan Law, 349
Supernaturalism, 310
Suppression, mechanism of, 414-15
Surplus value, theory of, 108n.
Switzerland, 278, 278n.
Symbolic substitutes, 519-22, 522n.
Syndicalism, 84n., 89

Talmud, 169
Taxation, 157-58, 160
Tax-farming system, 157-58
Taylor, Henry Osborn, 22n.
Theological period, 221-25
Theories, sociological, 3
Theory and practice, 77-92
Third Estate, 104, 104n., 105n.
Thomas, William I., 12, 405n., 511n.
Tönnies, Ferdinand, 235
Trade unions, 235-37, 237n., 241, 343, 348, 355n.
Turkey, 193, 229

Umanitaria, L', 236-37
Unemployment, 344, 346, 346n., 351-53, 391, 517-18, 526
Unions, *see* Trade unions
United States, 8n., 9, 111, 128-289 *passim,* 327, 332, 355n., 431
Universal suffrage, 276-77

Valleroux, Hubert, 462n.
Veblen, Thorstein, 10, 12, 13, 14, 336n., 512n.
Vendetta, 230, 274
Venice, 185, 186, 200, 204
Victoria, Queen, 24
Villeinage, 323
Voltaire, 388
Voluntary cooperation, 297-98, 304, 318, 319, 321, 334

Wage disputes, 126
Wage labor, 113, 114-15
Wage struggle, 238n.
Wages, 114-15, 506
Wallas, Graham, 32n., 44, 44n.
War, 272, 373, 515-16, 527-28; bureaucracy in, 171-72; Spencer on, 231-32
Warrior class, 195-97, 293-94
Wars of the Roses, 324
Weber, Max, 7, 9, 11, 11n., 12, 13, 68n., 69n., 121n., 149n., 524
Wellington, Duke of, 386, 386n.
Wilhelm II, Kaiser of Germany, 182
Wilkes, John, 388-89, 388n.
Wirth, L., 525, 525n.
Women, status of, 117
World War I, 336
Wundt, Wilhelm, 371n.

Xenophon, 223

Ziegler, H. O., 86n.
Zimmern, Sir Alfred, 46, 46n.
Znaniecki, Florian, 12, 405n., 511n.